# ROLLS AND LISTS

OF

# CONNECTICUT MEN

IN THE

# REVOLUTION.

1775-1783.

HARTFORD:
CONNECTICUT HISTORICAL SOCIETY.
1901.

## Notice

In many older books, foxing (or discoloration) occurs and, in some instances, print lightens with wear and age. Reprinted books, such as this, often duplicate these flaws, notwithstanding efforts to reduce or eliminate them. The pages of this reprint have been digitally enhanced and, where possible, the flaws eliminated in order to provide clarity of content and a pleasant reading experience.

*Rolls and Lists of Connecticut Men in the Revolution 1775-1783*

Originally published
Hartford, Connecticut
1901

Reprinted by:

Janaway Publishing, Inc.
732 Kelsey Ct.
Santa Maria, California 93454
(805) 925-1038
www.janawaygenealogy.com

2014

ISBN: 978-1-59641-337-5

*Made in the United States of America*

# CONTENTS.

|  | PAGE. |
|---|---|
| INTRODUCTION, | ix |
| LEXINGTON ALARM LIST, | 1 |
| CONTINENTAL REGIMENTS, 1775, | 9 |
| CONTINENTAL REGIMENTS, 1776, | 27 |
| CONNECTICUT LINE, 1777–1781, | 45 |
| CONNECTICUT LINE, 1781–1783, | 93 |
| CONNECTICUT LINE, 1783, | 129 |
| STATE TROOPS, 1775, | 132 |
| STATE TROOPS, 1776, | 133 |
| STATE TROOPS, 1777, | 145 |
| MILITIA REGIMENTS, 1776, | 149 |
| MILITIA REGIMENTS, 1777, | 177 |
| MILITIA REGIMENTS, 1778, | 183 |
| MILITIA REGIMENTS, 1779, | 189 |
| MILITIA REGIMENTS, 1780, | 213 |
| MILITIA REGIMENTS, 1781, | 215 |
| MILITIA REGIMENTS, 1782, | 217 |
| MILITIA REGIMENTS, | 219 |
| NAVAL RECORD, | 229 |
| PENSIONERS, | 265 |
| APPENDIX, | 273 |
| INDEX, | 281 |

# INTRODUCTION.

The State of Connecticut issued in 1889 through the Adjutant-General's office the splendid volume edited by Prof. Henry P. Johnston, entitled "Record of Service of Connecticut Men in the War of the Revolution." Later investigations have brought to light new rolls and additional information not contained in that volume. It is these new rolls which are here printed to serve as a supplement to the volume issued by the State.

This volume of Rolls and Lists is published under the provisions of a recent special Act of the General Assembly making an annual appropriation of one thousand dollars to the Connecticut Historical Society; one of the purposes specifically named in this act being "to publish its rolls of soldiers in the revolutionary and colonial wars, not heretofore printed." Another provision is that the Society "shall deposit in the State Library three hundred copies of each catalogue, report, or other work published" under this act, to be disposed of by the State Librarian. This is the third publication issued under the provisions of this act, and the first important work so issued.

The late Judge Sherman W. Adams, while chairman of the Society's publication committee, undertook the task of preparing the manuscript copy for this volume for the printer. He placed the Society's unpublished rolls in his office-safe where they would be conveniently at hand for the work, examined and compared them with those already in print, and began the labor of copying. But poor health soon caused him to lay aside the work for many months, only to take it up a second time and be again forced by illness to drop it, this time permanently, and he sadly returned the manuscript to the Society's vault.

Meanwhile work was progressing, with considerable delays and occasional cessations, upon two other volumes of Collections, the fifth and seventh, which the Society already had in press; and between the issuing of these two another, the sixth volume, was published, the gift of our first Vice-President.

While the last of these three volumes was yet in press another effort was made to prepare the volume of Revolutionary War Rolls for the printer, the Corresponding Secretary and the Librarian of the Society undertaking the work as a special volunteer committee. But the task was greater than either had, perhaps, anticipated, and after a spasmodic effort and the preparation of about one hundred pages of copy the work again came to a standstill.

At the annual meeting last May the Standing Committee of the Society took the matter in hand and instructed the publication committee to take up and carry to completion the publication of the Revolutionary Rolls belonging to the Society, and such others remaining unpublished as could be found. From that time to the present the work has been constantly in progress, the labor falling naturally upon the chairman of the publication committee. He has been fortunate in having the assistance of Edmund C. Thomas of Trinity College, Hartford, in making the copy, and of Miss Alice M. Gay, also of Hartford, in writing the cards for the index. All of the proofs, however, have been read by him, and with a half-dozen exceptions the proof of every roll or list has been read with the original manuscript. The index cards also were all compared by him with the printed sheets before they were printed.

The fact of this volume being in the nature of a supplement to one already in print made its preparation more difficult in some ways than it would otherwise have been; for it became necessary to examine each manuscript roll in order to determine whether it had been printed in the volume already issued by the State, or whether it should be copied for the Society's volume. A further complication was the frequent finding of rolls the names on which appeared to have been already printed though in a different arrangement. Often a part or all of the names appearing on a manuscript company roll would be found scattered through an alphabetically arranged regimental roll in the printed Record of Connecticut Men in the Revolution. In many such cases it was only after the most careful comparison that a decision as to printing the manuscript could be reached.

Every roll and list here printed is either entirely new, or contains sufficient that is new in the way of new names, additional service, or names of the towns from which the men came to justify its printing. In a work of this character it is difficult to avoid duplicating some of the matter already printed, but it is believed that there is very little of such duplication. It has been thought better to print, with a few exceptions, the whole of each roll or list, even at the risk of occasional duplication, than to attempt to extract and print new names from lists already partially in print. In a few cases a roll has been reprinted entire from another source than the State's publication, to show variations in spelling. The name of a town from which a man came has in many instances proved an important means of identification, and special attention has been paid to giving the towns wherever they appear on the rolls.

The arrangement of the material in this volume follows closely the arrangement adopted in the Record of the Service of Connecticut Men in the War of the Revolution, and a reference to that work accompanies many of the rolls here printed, showing where the roll would have appeared had it been printed in that volume. In many instances it is difficult to decide whether an organization served as State Troops or as Militia, and later investigation may change the present arrangement of many companies in this respect. It seems probable that some companies now credited to the Militia will prove to have served as State Troops.

This work does not profess to be more than a list of men who served as soldiers, with an account of their service and such further records as will aid in identifying them. Consequently much has been omitted in the printing of these rolls which has appeared irrelevant to the object in view. It has seemed outside the scope of the work to give the amount with which a soldier was charged for his gun, cartouch-box, or blanket, the number of months and days in service when dates of both his enlistment and discharge are given, the total amount disbursed by a captain for the wages and expenses of the men in his company, and numerous similar items. As the location of the manuscript of each roll is given, the curious can find such items as occur by reference to the originals.

In indexing all names have been spelled exactly as they appear in the text, with the following exceptions. Where an abbreviation appeared and there was no reasonable doubt as to the name for which the abbreviation stood, the name has been given in full in the index. The names of a few prominent officers have been indexed under one uniform and recognized spelling rather than to follow the various misspellings found in the text. All place names have been properly spelled in the index regardless of their spelling in the text.

The rolls here printed from the Society's archives have been presented to the Society at various times by sundry persons; many of them are from the collection of Trumbull papers received in 1845 from the executor of the estate of William T. Williams, a grandson of the elder Governor Trumbull. The Revolutionary War manuscripts in the State Library which have been examined for this work comprise thirty-seven folio volumes consisting of every description of document relating to the subject mounted upon or between the leaves of the volumes; also documents mounted in one large folio volume which were presented in 1877 by Charles Hebard of Lebanon, great-grandson of Hon. William Williams; also a package of documents purchased in 1893 from Samuel A. Drake of Boston. The manuscripts in the Comptroller's office include several small unbound or paper-covered books of accounts; the thick folio volume of Haskell's Receipts; and a large, square, thin volume referred to as "Copy in Comptroller's Office." This last mentioned volume was evidently made in recent years and consists of copies of rolls, probably made from original manuscripts. Originals of some of these are found in the State Library, many are already in print in the Record of Connecticut Men in the Revolution, though probably taken from another source, while the others are new material and the location of the originals from which they were copied is unknown. The volume of Haskell's Receipts is of much interest. It consists of records of accounts preferred by the State of Connecticut against the United States for payments made by the State for the wages and expenses of State Troops and Militia, each of which is certified as correct by "E. Haskell Com' Eastern States."

A complete roster of Col. David Waterbury Jr.'s regiment of Connecticut volunteers, 1776, was published in 1897. As the original rolls are in private hands and the pamphlet was issued under the United States copyright law, the material is not included in this volume.

Sufficient material is at hand to form another volume of the size of the present one. This material consists not of rolls but of returns forwarded from the different towns to the Colony and State authorities, giving the names of soldiers serving from each town, and of lists of soldiers prepared by their commanding officers, giving the town from which each soldier came. The Society hopes to publish this material soon and would welcome the knowledge of any other unpublished rolls or lists which might add to the interest of the volumes.

ALBERT C. BATES,
*Chairman of the Publication Committee,*
*and Editor of this Volume.*

THE SOCIETY'S LIBRARY, DECEMBER 26, 1901.

# LEXINGTON ALARM LIST.

## EAST WINDSOR.

[*See Record of Connecticut Men in the Revolution, page 9.*]

| | |
|---|---|
| Samuel King | 11 ⎫ |
| Ichabod Wadsworth | 11 ⎬ Sarj |
| John Hall | 9 ⎪ |
| Daniel Warner | 11 ⎭ |
| James McKenney Jr | 2 ⎫ |
| John Craw Jr | 8 ⎬ Corp |
| Jacob Bottom | 10 ⎪ |
| Isaac Mason | 11 ⎭ |
| Stephen Warner | 11 ⎫ Drumr |
| Stephen Russell | 11 ⎭ |
| Oliver Chapman | 11 ⎫ |
| Lemuel Pinney | 11 ⎬ fifer |
| Chauncey Foster | 10 ⎭ |

| | | | |
|---|---|---|---|
| John Aldich Jr | 11 | Aaron Damon | 10 |
| Samuel Andress | 11 | Charles Day | 11 |
| Christopher Allien | 8 | David Davis | 11 |
| Benjamin Allien | 10 | Joseph Durfy Jr | 10 |
| Eliphas Bartlet | 8 | Jedediah Durfy | 11 |
| Alexander Buckland | 11 | Adonijah Day Jr | 6 |
| Edmond Bragg | 11 | Hezekiah Elsworth | 11 |
| Stephen Burroughs | 8 | Daniel Elsworth 3rd | 10 |
| Abner Burroughs Jr | 11 | Jesse Fitch | 2 |
| Francis Belknap | 9 | Wareham Foster | 11 |
| Edmond Bartlet Jr | 11 | Josiah Frost Jr | 10 |
| Samuel Bartlet | 8 | Noah Frost | 6 |
| Stephen Bradley | 11 | Ephrim Frost | 10 |
| Zebulon Burroughs | 10 | Daniel Green | 11 |
| Josiah Bradley Jr | 11 | Seth Gibbs | 10 |
| Reuben Bradley | 10 | Levy Gibbs | 10 |
| Jonathan Brown | 4 | Oliver Gibbs | 2 |
| Stephen Bartlet | 10 | Nathan Hall | 10 |
| Mathew Campbell | 11 | Amos Huntley | 3 |
| Thomas Cook | 9 | Thomas Kennedy | 10 |
| George Charter | 10 | Andrew Kenedy | 11 |
| John Charter Jr | 11 | Elijah H. Kingsbery | 3 |
| Eli Carpenter | 9 | Joseph Kingsbery | 10 |
| Timothy Cook | 11 | Joseph Kneeland | 9 |
| Hoseah Chapman | 2 | Simon Kingsbery Jr | 2 |
| Zenus Cleavland | 1 | Jesse Ladd | 11 |
| Rufus Cleavland | 6 | Elijah Lee | 7 |
| Caleb Downer | 6 | Eliphalet Lord | 8 |
| Jonathan Damon Jr | 11 | David Lovet | 8 |

REVOLUTION ROLLS AND LISTS.

|  | | | | |  | | | | |
|---|---|---|---|---|---|---|---|---|---|
| John Lovet | . | . | . | 10 | Ephrim Parker Jr | . | . | . | 11 |
| Samuel Lovet | . | . | . | 11 | Thomas Pember | . | . | . | 11 |
| James Lovet | . | . | . | 10 | Samuel Peak | . | . | . | 11 |
| Benjamin Lewis | . | . | . | 11 | John Pease | . | . | . | 8 |
| Wiham McKenney | . | . | . | 11 | Edward Pain | . | . | . | [ ] |
| Andrew McKenney | . | . | . | 11 | Seth Parker | . | . | . | 6 |
| Peter Mills | . | . | . | 7 | Hezekiah Russell | . | . | . | 11 |
| Ezekiel McKenstry | . | . | . | 10 | Silas Read | . | . | . | 9 |
| Wiliam McCray Jr | . | . | . | 11 | Philip Read | . | . | . | 3 |
| Reuben McCray | . | . | . | 11 | Nathan Russell Jr | . | . | . | 11 |
| David McCray | . | . | . | 11 | Wm Shurtliff | . | . | . | 1 |
| James McKenney 3rd | . | . | . | 11 | Lothrup Shurtliff | . | . | . | 10 |
| Nathan McWavy | . | . | . | 9 | Wm Spear Jr | . | . | . | 10 |
| Thomas McKnight | . | . | . | 11 | Moses Smith Jr | . | . | . | 11 |
| Caleb More | . | . | . | 7 | John Stiles | . | . | . | 10 |
| Ephrim McWavy | . | . | . | 3 | Aaron Slade | . | . | . | 11 |
| Isaac Newton | . | . | . | 11 | Abner Slade | . | . | . | 11 |
| Daniel Newhall | . | . | . | 11 | John Shurtliff | . | . | . | 5 |
| John Newhall | . | . | . | 11 | Assel Shurtliff | . | . | . | 10 |
| Jacob Newhall | . | . | . | 11 | Graves Smith | . | . | . | 8 |
| Andrew Pember | . | . | . | 11 | Daniel Slade | . | . | . | 1 |
| John Porter | . | . | . | 11 | Jonathan Sexton | . | . | . | 11 |
| Joseph Pinney Jr | . | . | . | 7 | Moses Slafter | . | . | . | 2 |
| John Pinney | . | . | . | 6 | James Thompson | . | . | . | 9 |
| Samuel Pember | . | . | . | 11 | John Taylor | . | . | . | 8 |
| James Parsivel | . | . | . | 6 | John Taylor Jr | . | . | . | 8 |
| Jonathan Porter Jr | . | . | . | 11 | James Wallace | . | . | . | 10 |
| Daniel Porter | . | . | . | 5 | John Wallace | . | . | . | 11 |
| Joseph Parkhurst | . | . | . | 10 | Benjamin Woodward | . | . | . | 9 |
| Elezer Pinney | . | . | . | 8 | Abram Walace Jr | . | . | . | 1 |
| Daniel Pearson | . | . | . | 11 | William Wallace | . | . | . | 11 |
| Samuel Pearson Jr | . | . | . | 9 | Alexander Young | . | . | . | 6 |
| Ephrim Pearson Jr | . | . | . | 2 | | | | | |

[                    ]ue Coppy from [          ] Rooles Errors Excepted
[                    ] those th[          ]ent in the Alarrum
                    [                                                    ]

[*Connecticut Historical Society.*]

## LEBANON.

[*See Record of Connecticut Men in the Revolution, page 15.*]

The following is the Names of those that inlisted under my Command in the time of the Alarm with the Money they Spent & the time when they left the Service. Marched from home Sat. 22 Apl 1775

|  |  | Capt Daniel Tilden | | | | | |
|---|---|---|---|---|---|---|---|
|  |  | Lieut Thos Tirrel | } Com | . | . | . | |
|  |  | Ensign Thos Bill |  | . | . | . | |
|  |  | Jeddiah Phelps | } Left Service | . | . | | |
| May | 1 | John H. Buell | } Sargt | . | . | . | 12/ |
| Apl | 26 | Nathan Lee | | . | . | . | 9/ |
| May | 7 | Peletiah Holebrook | } | . | . | . | 10/ |
|  | 10 | Jos Howes | } Corpl | . | . | . | 20/ |
|  | 11 | Simon House | } | | | | |
|  | 1 | Ephram Bemiss | . | . | . | . | 12/ 8 |
|  | 11 | Adonijah White | . | . | . | . | 15/ |
|  | 11 | Ebenr Gillit Jur | . | . | . | . | 12/ |
|  | 3 | Andrew Dewey | . | . | . | . | |
|  | 8 | Simon Jones | . | . | . | . | |

## LEXINGTON ALARM, 1775.

|  |  |  |  |  |
|---|---|---|---|---|
| Listed | 7 M | Beriah Sprague | 6/ | 8 |
|  | 28 | Andrew Richardson |  |  |
|  | 1 | Dan'l Badcock |  |  |
|  | 11 | Eben'r Bailey | 12/ |  |
|  |  | Jabez Foster inlisted 8 May |  |  |
| Ap'l | 25 | Jonah Gross | 2/ |  |
|  |  | Asahel Williams | 13/ |  |
| May | 8 | Edmund Daman | 6/ |  |
|  | 1 | James Barnaba | 12/ | 8 |
| Ap'l | 26 | Rufus Rude Ju'r |  |  |
| May | 15 | Sam'l Beamont |  |  |
|  |  | Tho' Brooks |  |  |
|  | 7 | Michael Bestow | 6/ | 6 |
| Ap'l | 26 | Jonathan Bliss |  |  |
|  |  | Abner Doubleday | 6/ |  |
|  |  | Oliver Hyde | 12/ |  |
|  | 26 | Adonijah Crocker |  |  |
|  | 7 | Jerom Clark | 15/ |  |
| May | 1 | Joseph Severoy |  |  |
|  | 7 | Garshom Gillet | 4/ |  |
| Ap'l | 26 | Sam'l Davis |  |  |
| May | 1 | Zebedee Goodwine |  |  |
|  |  | Asa Loomise | 12/ |  |
|  |  | provision found for him by Cap Tisdale to amt of 0 4 0 |  |  |
|  | 2 | Jacob Loomise | 8/ | 6 |
|  | 15 | Asel Gay |  |  |
|  |  | Amos Miner  Cap. C. says listed ye 8 May | 7/ |  |
|  | 1 | Tho' Saveroy |  |  |
|  | 11 | Lem'l Clark | 12/ |  |
|  | 11 | Benjamin Woodwarth |  |  |
| Ap'l | 25 | Jacob Gillet. Returned with horses: sit out for boston 21 of April | 6/ |  |

[*Connecticut Historical Society*.]

D'r Colony, To Wages & Billeting, of sundry Officers & Soldiers who marched, from Lebanon, to the Relief of y'e Country in the late Alarm at Lexington & Concord &c under Dan'l Tilden as Capt 1775
  N B the Soldiers 1d P Day too High

|  | Days in ye Service | Wages | | |
|---|---|---|---|---|
| Dan'l Tilden Cap'a | 9 | 1 | 18 | 8 |
| Tho' Tyrrel L't | 19 | 2 | 14 | 3 |
| Tho' Bill Ens'n | 9 | 0 | 19 | 4 |
| Jed'h: Phelps Serj't | 8 | 0 | 5 | 1½ |
| Jn'o H. Buell Serj't | 13 | 1 | 2 | 2½ |
| Nath'n Lee Serj't | 5 | 0 | 8 | 6½ |
| Pel'e Holbrook Serj't | 18 | 1 | 10 | 9 |
| Jos. Howes Corp'o | 22 | 1 | 13 | 11 |
| Simon House Corp'o | 21 | 1 | 12 | 4½ |
| Sam'l Bemont Cor | 24 | 1 | 17 | 0 |
| Ep'm Bemus | 13 | 0 | 18 | 5 |
| Adonij: White | 23 | 1 | 12 | 7 |
| Eb'r Gillet Ju'r | 23 | 1 | 12 | 7 |
| And: Dewey | 11 | 0 | 15 | 7 |
| Simon Jones | 21 | 1 | 9 | 9 |
| Beri: Sprague | 15 | 1 | 1 | 3 |
| And: Richardson | 35 | 2 | 9 | 7 |

|  | Days in ye Service | Wages |  |  |
|---|---|---|---|---|
| Danll Badcock | 13 | 0 | 18 | 5 |
| Eb{r} Bailey | 22 | 1 | 11 | 2 |
| Jabez Foster | 16 | 1 | 2 | 8 |
| Elisha Hutchin{n} | 8 | 0 | 4 | 3 |
| Jonah Gross | 4 | 0 | 5 | 8 |
| Asa{l} Williams | 19 | 1 | 6 | 11 |
| Edm{d} Daman | 19 | 1 | 6 | 11 |
| Ja{s} Barnabee | 12 | 0 | 17 | 0 |
| Rufus Rude Ju{r} | 07 | 0 | 9 | 11 |
| Samll Bemont | 27 | 1 | 18 | 3 |
| Thos Brooks | 27 | 1 | 18 | 3 |
| Micha{l} Barstow | 18 | 1 | 5 | 6 |
| Jon{a} Bliss | 7 | 0 | 9 | 11 |
| Abner Doubleday | 7 | 0 | 9 | 11 |
| Oliv{r} Hyde | 7 | 0 | 9 | 11 |
| Zenas Howis | 2 | 0 | 2 | 10 |
| Adonij: Crocker | 7 | 0 | 9 | 11 |
| Jerom Clark Cap Wrights Lad | 16 | 1 | 2 | 8 |
| Jos. Savory | 12 | 0 | 17 | 0 |
| Ger. Gillet | 16 | 1 | 2 | 8 |
| Samll Davis | 7 | 0 | 9 | 11 |
| Zebedee Goodwin | 12 | 0 | 17 | 0 |
| Asa Loomis | 12 | 0 | 17 | 0 |
| Jacob Loomis | 14 | 0 | 19 | 10 |
| Asael Gay | 27 | 1 | 18 | 6 |
| Amos Miner | 16 | 1 | 2 | 8 |
| Thos Savory | 12 | 0 | 17 | 0 |
| Lem{ll} Clark | 22 | 1 | 11 | 2 |
| Benja Woodworth | 22 | 1 | 11 | 2 |
| Jacob Gillet returnd w{h} horses | 5 | 0 | 7 | 1 |
| Elijah House | 2 | 0 | 2 | 10 |
| John Sprague |  |  |  |  |
| Sol{o} Parker Case | 3 | 0 | 4 | 3 |
| Jno Doggett |  |  |  |  |

The following Persons set out on the March & did not go thro:

|  | Days gone | Wages |  |  |
|---|---|---|---|---|
| Capt Danll Dewey | 3 | 0 | 12 | 11 |
| Lieut James Pinneo as a Lt is so at home | 3 | 0 | 8 | 7 |
| Serj{t} Danll Dunham | 3 | 0 | 5 | 0 |
| Cler Samll West | 3 | 0 | 4 | 9 |
| Corp{o} Henry Bliss | 3 | 0 | 4 | 9 |
| Corp{o} Ab{m} Bliss | 2 | 0 | 3 | 2 |
| John Henry | 3 | 0 | 4 | 3 |
| John Joy | 3 | 0 | 4 | 3 |
| Azariah Brown | 3 | 0 | 4 | 3 |
| Dav{d} Treadway | 3 | 0 | 4 | 3 |
| Josiah Fitch | 3 | 0 | 4 | 3 |
| Thos Clark | 3 | 0 | 4 | 3 |
| Reuben Woodworth | 3 | 0 | 4 | 3 |
| Benja Gary sick on ye road & returned | 11 | 0 | 15 | 7 |
| Wm Swift 3d | 5 | 0 | 7 | 1 |
| Jos. Doubleday, & was sent Post to N London from Cambridge | 9 | 0 | 12 | 9 |

The foregoing is a just & true Acc{o} & Roll of the 2d Comp{a} in Lebanon who marchd under the Command of Danll Tilden as Captain, in the late

## LEXINGTON ALARM, 1775.

Alarm occasioned by the Ministerial Troops, firing on the Inhabitans of Lexington &c in April 1775 & of their Expences Provisions &c in the most exact & perfect manner We have been able to come at it

Aug' 30 1775

Test

W<sup>m</sup> Williams  
Vetch Williams  
Elijah Hyde Jun'  
Jeams Pineo Jun'  
Pelatiah Marsh

} Select Men of Lebanon

[*Connecticut Historical Society.*]

D' Colony Connecticut, To Wages, Billiting, Horse Hire &c for sund: Officers & Soldiers, who marchd from Lebanon, to relief of y° Country &c in the late Lexington Alarm &c marched 22 April 1775 under Cap James Clark

N B ye Soldiers 1<sup>d</sup> P D . too high

|  | Days | Wages |  |  |
|---|---|---|---|---|
| James Clark Cap | 9 | 1 | 18 | 8 |
| And<sup>w</sup> Waterman Lieu' | 19 | 2 | 14 | 3 |
| Dan Throop L' | 19 | 2 | 14 | 3 |
| Joel Chamberlin Ens | 19 | 2 | 0 | 9 |
| Jos. Abel Serj' | 16 | 1 | 7 | 4 |
| Malachi Thomas Ser | 19 | 1 | 12 | 5½ |
| Ich<sup>a</sup> Bosworth Serj' | 16 | 1 | 7 | 4 |
| Jos. Loomis Serj' | 6 | 0 | 10 | 3 |
| And<sup>w</sup> Fitch Cler | 9 | 0 | 14 | 3 |
| Josh<sup>a</sup> Chappel Ju' Cor' | 16 | 1 | 5 | 4 |
| Cha' Williams Cor' | 19 | 1 | 10 | 1 |
| Jehiel Williams Cor' | 23 | 1 | 16 | 5 |
| Elip' Hyde Cor' | 18 | 1 | 8 | 6 |
| Rog' Strong Fifer | 23 | 1 | 16 | 5 |
| Dav<sup>d</sup> Barber | 15 | 1 | 1 | 3 |
| Cary Prat | 15 | 1 | 1 | 3 |
| Abel Hackly | 15 | 1 | 1 | 3 |
| Asa Loomis in T. |  |  |  |  |
| Oliver Hide in T. |  |  |  |  |
| Sam<sup>ll</sup> Lothrop | 15 | 1 | 1 | 3 |
| James Law | 15 | 1 | 1 | 3 |
| Beri: Sprague in T. |  |  |  |  |
| Zera Page | 16 | 1 | 2 | 8 |
| Abner Doubleday in T. |  |  |  |  |
| Tim° Peepoon | 15 | 1 | 1 | 3 |
| Jn° Fowler | 16 | 1 | 2 | 8 |
| Jon<sup>a</sup> Blackman | 15 | 1 | 1 | 3 |
| Amos Miner in T. |  |  |  |  |
| Ich<sup>a</sup> Fitch Ju' | 16 | 1 | 2 | 8 |
| And<sup>w</sup> Chapman | 15 | 1 | 1 | 3 |
| Benj<sup>a</sup> Keeney | 16 | 1 | 2 | 8 |
| And<sup>w</sup> Williams | 16 | 1 | 2 | 8 |
| Sam<sup>ll</sup> Wattles Ju' | 16 | 1 | 2 | 8 |
| Tho<sup>s</sup> Loomis | 16 | 1 | 2 | 8 |
| Billy Williams | 16 | 1 | 2 | 8 |
| Beri<sup>h</sup> Badcock | 23 | 1 | 12 | 7 |
| Squire Lee | 26 | 1 | 16 | 10 |
| Rich<sup>d</sup> Lyman | 27 | 1 | 18 | 3 |
| Sam<sup>ll</sup> Goodwin | 20 | 1 | 8 | 4 |
| Dan<sup>ll</sup> Rockwell | 24 | 1 | 14 | 0 |

|  | Days | Wages |
|---|---|---|
| Sol° Tracy | 26 | 1 16 10 |
| Jacob Baldwin | 87 | 2 12 5 |
| Vetch Williams J<sup>r</sup> in y<sup>e</sup> Cap<sup>s</sup> return | 29 | 2 1 5 |
| Benj<sup>a</sup> Payn Ju<sup>r</sup> | 18 | 1 5 6 |
| Jon<sup>a</sup> Wills | 18 | 1 5 6 |
| Nath<sup>l</sup> Porter | 18 | 1 5 6 |
| Cap Wright, says is pay<sup>d</sup> ⎱ | | |
| Jerom Clark marchd 22 ⎰ in T | | |
| Ap<sup>l</sup> & listed 8 June | | |
| Benj: Seabury Ju<sup>r</sup> | 18 | 1 5 6 |
| Stephen Payn | 15 | 1 1 3 |
| Neh<sup>h</sup> Payn | 14 | 0 19 10 |
| Stephen Payn J<sup>r</sup> | 5 | 0 7 1 |
| Jon<sup>a</sup> Webster Ju<sup>r</sup> | 15 | 1 1 3 |
| Guida Webster | 13 | 0 18 5 |
| James Webster | 15 | 1 1 3 |
| Jn° P. Bissell | 18 | 1 5 6 |
| And<sup>w</sup> Clark | 18 | 1 5 6 |
| And Clark is not twice enterd see below | | |
| Dan<sup>ll</sup> Wilcox | 19 | 1 6 11 |
| Theodore Metcalf | 19 | 1 6 11 |
| Jn° Williams returd for Killingley | 6 | 0 8 6 |
| Tho<sup>s</sup> Wattles Do | 6 | 0 8 6 |
| Dan Payn Do | 6 | 0 8 6 |
| Geo. Webster Do | 6 | 0 8 6 |
| Jos. Barstow Do | 6 | 0 8 6 |
| Dav<sup>d</sup> Webster | 4 | 0 5 8 |
| Jude West | 16 | 1 2 8 |
| And<sup>w</sup> Clark | 18 | 1 5 6 |
| A B | 20 | 1 8 4 |
| Jon<sup>a</sup> Brewster | 5 | 0 7 1 |
| David Stoddard | 6 | 0 8 6 |
| W<sup>m</sup> Torrey Ju<sup>r</sup> | 7 | 0 9 11 |

The foregoing is a just & true Acc° & Roll of the Company who marchd under the Command of Cap James Clark of Lebanon, in the late Alarm occasioned by the Ministerial Troops, firing on the Inhabitants of Lexington &c in April 1775 & of their Expence Provisions &c in ye most exact and perfect manner, We are able to get at it

Test      W<sup>m</sup> Williams ⎫
               Vetch Williams ⎪ Select Men
               Elijah Hyde Jun<sup>r</sup> ⎬ of Lebanon
               Jeams Pinneo Ju<sup>r</sup> ⎪
30 Aug<sup>t</sup> 1775    Pelatiah Marsh ⎭

[*Connecticut Historical Society.*]

## SIMSBURY.

[*See Record of Connecticut Men in the Revolution, page 21.*]

Wee the Subscribers Hearing of the Distressing Situasion our Breatheren are in at Boston by the mourders and Barbcraties Committed on them By the King Troop: wee Do volontarely Enlist our Selves to Go to Boston to assist our Brothering and to Defend our Just Rights and Prevledges under the Command of Elisha Phelps & Job Case or any other man wee

Shall Chuse to be our Commander as witness our hand this 21ˢᵗ Day of pril 1775

Jacob Pettibone
Loam Nearen
Benjᵃ Bodwell
Theoˢ Woodbridge
William Andrews
Thoˢ Phelps Jʳ
Martain Case
Seth Higley
Parmeno Adams

Joshua Egeton
Jacob Davis Jur
Joseph Grimes Jur
Joseph Humphry
John Case Jur
Daniel Barber Jur
Elisha Phelps
Job Case

[*Connecticut Historical Society.*]

# CONTINENTAL REGIMENTS—1775.

## FIRST REGIMENT—GEN. WOOSTER.

### SIXTH COMPANY—CAPT. DOUGLAS.

[See *Record of Connecticut Men in the Revolution*, page 41.]

[Extract from Capt. William Douglas' account book, giving names of soldiers in his Company in 1775, and the time for which they received wages. The privates each received 52 shillings bounty money, and the majority of them are credited with mileage for 258 miles.]

|  | Time of service | |
|---|---|---|
|  | Months | Days |
| Lieut. Sam¹ Barker |  |  |
| Lieut. Jared Robinson | 7 | 14 |
| Ens. Ebenezer Trusdell | 7 | 14 |
| Serj. Levi Munson | 4 | 17 |
| Serj. Benj ͣ Bartholomew | 7 | 7 |
| Serj. Thomas Smith | 6 |  |
| Serj. Asahel Harrison | 5 | 24 |
| Sam¹ August ͣ Barker | 7 | 9 |
| Qr. Master Serj. Mark Mazuzen | 6 | 12 |
| Corpl. Benj ͣ Henshaw Jr. | 6 | 18 |
| Corpl. Josiah Fowler Jr. | 8 | 7 |
| Corpl. Abijah Bradly | 5 | 29 |
| Corpl. John Aberhart | 5 | 8 |
| Samuel Whedon | 7 | 8 |
| Drummer John Bunnel | 5 | 1 |
| Fifer Asahel Strong | 5 | 27 |
| Timothy Andrus | 7 |  |
| Philemon Augur | 6 | 28 |
| Levi Baldwin | 7 | 7 |
| Aaron Baldwin | 4 | 20 |
| Timothy Barker | 7 | 5 |
| Isaac Barns | 7 | 9 |
| Solomon Barns | 7 | 7 |
| Eliphalet Barns | 5 | 28 |
| Gideon Bartholomew | 7 | 7 |

| Name | Time of service | |
|---|---|---|
| | Months | Days |
| Zealous Blaksley | 6 | 9 |
| Samuel Britain | 7 | 9 |
| Zebulon Bradly | 7 | 6 |
| Joseph Brown | 7 | |
| Samuel Brown | 7 | |
| Abraham Bunnel | 7 | |
| Matthew Butler | 5 | 29 |
| Titus Butler | 6 | 23 |
| Walter Butler | 6 | 10 |
| Ebenezer Byintun | 5 | 1 |
| Joseph Cheney | 6 | 3 |
| Ephraim Chidsey | 4 | 10 |
| Street Chidsey | 6 | 3 |
| Samuel Cook | 5 | 9 |
| Caleb Cook | 4 | 18 |
| Abraham Cook | 5 | 2 |
| Eliakim Culver | 7 | 7 |
| William Evertun | 5 | 20 |
| Zebulon Farrin | 5 | |
| Ebenezer Foot | 5 | 20 |
| Heli Foot | 7 | 23 |
| Elias Forbs | 4 | 24 |
| Caleb Frisbie | 7 | 23 |
| Titus Frisbie | 5 | 7 |
| Samuel Goodsell | 5 | |
| Henry Gilner | 6 | 5 |
| Isaac Grannis | 7 | 9 |
| Amos Green | 4 | 24 |
| John Guy | 6 | 27 |
| Wooster Harrison | 7 | |
| Jarius Harrison | 7 | 2 |
| David Hill | 7 | 7 |
| Sam¹ Hoadly | 4 | 29 |
| Jared Heminway | 5 | 4 |
| Moses Heminway | 6 | 1 |
| Enos Heminway | 7 | 5 |
| Mason Hobart | 7 | 5 |
| Joel Howd | 5 | 1 |
| Zebulon Jacobs | 7 | 7 |
| Artemas Johnson | 7 | |
| Joseph Jones | 6 | 10 |
| Samuel Ludonton | 7 | 5 |
| Eliphalet Ludinton | 5 | 25 |
| David Mallery | 5 | 21 |
| John Mallery | 4 | 29 |
| Zaccheus Maltbie | 6 | 26 |
| Joseph Moltroup | 4 | 26 |
| Elihu Moltroup | 4 | 11 |
| Eli Moltroup | 7 | 2 |
| John Negus | 7 | 7 |
| Benjamin Norton | 7 | 7 |
| Jacob Page | 7 | |
| Luther Page | 7 | 25 |
| John Palmer | 6 | 12 |
| Barnabas Palmer | 7 | 5 |
| Jacob Pardee | 7 | |
| Isaac Pardee | 7 | 7 |
| Ephraim Rogers | 6 | 29 |

## CONTINENTAL REGIMENTS, 1775.

|  | Time of service | |
|---|---|---|
|  | Months | Days |
| Thomas Pierpoint | 5 | 2 |
| Levi Potter | 7 | 6 |
| Jacob Rogers | 7 | 7 |
| Rufus Rogers | 7 | 5 |
| Levi Rogers | 5 | 20 |
| Philemon Rogers | 4 | 20 |
| Chandler Robinson | 8 | 16 |
| Levi Rose | 7 | 7 |
| John Shepard | 5 | 4 |
| Caleb Smith | 7 | 20 |
| Robert Stewart | 5 | 7 |
| Solomon Talmage | 7 | 7 |
| Abner Tharp | 7 |  |
| John Thomas | 4 | 21 |
| Benjamin Pratt | 7 | 1 |

[*Comptroller's Office.*]

## PROVISIONAL REGIMENT—GEN. WOOSTER.

[*See Record of Connecticut Men in the Revolution, page 44.*]

### CAPT. WOODBRIDGE'S COMPANY.

A Pay Roll of Cap$^t$ Theodore Woodbridge's Company in Gen$^l$ Woosters Reg$^t$ in the Service of the United Colonies from Nov$^r$ 10$^{th}$ 1775 to Feb$^y$ 29$^{th}$ 1776 both Days included.— Copy

| Officers & Soldiers Names Officers Non Commisioned | which the Man Inlisted last Campain Companies and Colonies in | | Time of entry Company into this inlistment | No. of Days in the Service between the time of to 29 Feb$^y$ inlistment |
|---|---|---|---|---|
| Theodore Woodbridge Cap$^t$ | | | 18 Nov | 104 |
| Uriah Church 1 Lieu$^t$ | Cap$^t$ Woodbridge | Connecticut | " | 104 |
| Daniel Barns 2 Lieu$^t$ | " | " | " | 104 |
| Trial Tanner Serj$^t$ | " | " | " | 104 |
| William Hart Serj$^t$ | " | " | " | 104 |
| James Doal Serj$^t$ | Cap$^t$ M$^c$Cracken | New York | " | 104 |
| Abraham M$^c$Killiss Serj$^t$ | Cap$^t$ Noble | Massachusetts | 23 Nov | 99 |
| Silas Sperry Corp$^l$ | Cap$^t$ Stanton | N. Hampshire | 18 Nov | 104 |
| John Henderson Corp$^l$ | Cap$^t$ M$^c$Cracken | N. York | " | 104 |
| Ezekiel Cook Corp$^l$ | Col$^n$ Hinman | Connecticut | " | 104 |
| Asa Darga Corp$^l$ | " | " | " | 104 |
| John Datton | " | " | " | 104 |
| James Ledley | " | Cap$^t$ Noble | Massachu$^s$ | 23 Nov | 99 |
| Thom$^s$ Kane | " | | New York | 18 Nov | 104 |
| Richard Hodnett | " | | " | " | 104 |
| Joseph Kitchel | " | Cap$^t$ Noble | Massa$^s$ | 23 Nov | 99 |
| David Kitchel | " | " | " | " | 99 |
| Samuel Brown | " | | Cannada | 18 Nov | 104 |
| Stephen Hadlock | " | Cap$^t$ Badcock | Massac$^s$ | 1 Jan. | 60 |
| Isaac Moon | " | | Cannada | 18 Nov | 104 |
| Richard Northover | " | | Connecticut | " | 104 |
| James Steward | " | | " | " | 104 |
| Peter Ferris | " | Cap$^t$ Noble | Massachu$^s$ | 23 Nov | 99 |
| Aaron Bond | | Cap$^t$ Stanton | N. Hampshire | 18 Nov | 99 |
| Jairus Bonny | " | | Connecticut | " | 104 |
| Lemuel Baker | " | Capt Stanton | N. Hamp$^s$ | " | 104 |
| Daniel Benjamin | " | | Connect$^t$ | " | 104 |
| James Call | " | Cap$^t$ Grant | N. Hamp$^s$ | " | 104 |
| James Call Jun$^r$ | " | " | " | " | 104 |
| John Call | " | " | " | " | 104 |
| Joseph Chandler | " | | Connecticut | " | 104 |
| Eliphalet Everit | " | | " | " | 104 |
| Edward Fox | " | | Cannada | " | 104 |
| Nath$^{nl}$ Spears | " | | Connecticut | " | 104 |
| Samuel Cook | " | Cap$^t$ Hanchet | Massachu$^s$ | 1 Jan. | 60 |
| John Doal | " | Cap$^t$ M$^c$Cracken | N. York | 18 Nov. | 104 |
| William Galaspy | " | " | " | " | 104 |

## CONTINENTAL REGIMENTS, 1775.

| Officers & Soldiers Names Officers Non Commisoned | which the Man Inlisted last Campain Companies and Colonies in | | Time of entry into this Company inlistment | No. of Days in the Service between the time of to 29 Feby |
|---|---|---|---|---|
| John Green | — | Capt McCracken | N. York | 18 Nov. | 104 |
| Saml Hall | " | | Connecticut | " | 104 |
| John Harrison | " | | Cannada | " | 104 |
| Ebenezer Hastings | " | Capt Stanton | N. Hamp | " | 104 |
| Gilbert Hall | " | | " | " | 104 |
| Ebenezer Leech | " | | Connecticut | " | 104 |
| Abel Moses | " | " | " | " | 104 |
| Robert McCauley | " | Capt McCracken | N. York | " | 104 |
| Neil McNeil | " | | Connecticut | " | 104 |
| William Pierce | " | Capt Hanchin | Massachus | 1 Jan | 60 |
| William Patterson | " | Col. Warner | N. Hamps | 18 Nov | 104 |
| Daniel Russ | " | " | " | " | 104 |
| Charles Robinson | " | | Connecticut | " | 104 |
| Solomon Tuttle | " | Capt Stanton | N. Hamp | " | 104 |
| Samuel Wiry | " | Capt McCra | 2d Battn N. York | " | 104 |
| Caleb Waddams | " | | Connecticut | " | 104 |
| John Welch | " | " | " | " | 104 |
| Charles Tilden | " | Capt Stanton | New Hamps | " | 104 |
| Thomas Watkins | " | " | " | " | 104 |
| Jacob Norton* | " | | Connecticut | " | 39 |
| Thomas Tibbals Drumr | | | " | " | 104 |
| Mathew St John | | Capt Stanton | N. Hampshire | " | 104 |
| Giles Gaylord | | | Connecticut | " | 104 |

[*Connecticut Historical Society.*]

* Discharged 26 December

## THIRD REGIMENT—GEN. PUTNAM.

### FIFTH COMPANY—CAPT. KNOWLTON.

[*See Record of Connecticut Men in the Revolution, page 55.*]

[From roll and individual accounts entered by Thomas Knowlton in his account book.]

Cap$^t$ Thom$^s$ Knowlton
Lieu$^t$ John Kyes
Lieu$^t$ Daniel Allen Signs his name Daniel Allen Jr.
Ensign Squire Hill Signs his name Squier Hill
Serj$^t$ Daniel Eldridge
Serj$^t$ Obadiah Perry
Serj$^t$ Tymothy Dimmick
Serj$^t$ Amos Woodward Signs his name Amos Woodard
Clark Sam$^{ll}$ Moseley Served from May 6 to Dec. 10, 1775
Serj$^t$ Joseph Snow Signs his name Joseph Snow Jr
Drum$^r$ Nath$^l$ Hayward
Corp$^l$ David Allen
Corp$^l$ Daniel Squire Signs his name Daniel Squier
Corp$^l$ Christo$^r$ Boing Signs his name Christopher Bowen
Corp$^l$ Jeddi$^h$ Ammidown Signs his name Jedidiah Amidown
Fifer Benj$^a$ Russel Signs his name Benjamin Russell Jr
Fifer Isack Abbe Signs his name Isaac Abbe
      Phillip Abbot
      Jonathan Avery
      William Allen Signs his name W$^m$ Allin
      George Anderson
      Thom$^s$ Anderson
      Steven Anderson Signs his name Stephen Anderson
      Amos Bugbe
      Joseph Berney Signs his name Joseph Barney Jr
      Thom$^s$ Bragg
      Abihel Bugbe
      John Braughton
      Aseph Burley
      Thaddeus Brown
      Jacob Burley
      Jonath$^n$ Badger
      Daniel Bozwarth
      John Bowing Signs his name John Boen
      Joseph Bowing Signs his name Joseph Boen
      Lemuel Boles
      Jonathan Chase Signs his name Jonathan Chaffe
      Jerimiah Cinnel
      Jonathan Crane
      William Cheney Kild June y$^e$ 17$^{th}$
      Christ$^r$ Chapman
      Thom$^s$ Chapman
      William Curtis
      Benj$^a$ Dimmick

# CONTINENTAL REGIMENTS, 1775.

Thom⁸ Davison
Asa Davison
Amos Dowset Signs his name Amas Douset
Isack Dimmick Signs his name Isaac Dimmuck
Jonath$^n$ Dowset
Timothy Eastman
Josiah Eaton
Daniel Fitts
Steven Foster Signs his name Stephen Foster
James Grant
Hamilton Grant
Sam$^{ll}$ Hale
Robert Hale
Caleb Hande Signs his name Caleb Hendee
Benj$^a$ Henfield Signs his name Benja Hanfield
John Holmes Signs his name John Holmes y$^e$ 3$^d$
Silas Holt
Josiah Holt Discharged August y$^e$ 26
Charles Kimbal
Steven Knowlton Signs his name Stephen Knowlton
Edward Kyes
Fred$^k$ Knowlton
Asahel Lyon Kild June y$^e$ 17
Abraham Laflin
Alexand$^r$ Macknel
William Morce Written on another page William More
Adin Marcy
Daniel Owens
John Potter
Robert Patterson
Benj$^a$ Pitts
Zera Preston
Benj$^a$ Rus Kild June y$^e$ 17
Eprai$^m$ Squire
Ruben Simmonds Signs his name Reuben Simmons
James Shepard
Daniel Smith
Richard Smith
Salvanus Snow Discharg$^d$ Sep$^t$ 11$^{th}$ 1775
Abijah Smith
Josiah Smith
Steven Scrborough Signs his name Stephen Scarbrough
Thom⁸ Southward Signs his name Tho$^s$ Southworth
William Watrous
William Watkins
Aron Wales
Nathan Ward
Nathan Watkins
Sam$^{ll}$ Walker
Elieazr Wales Signs his name Eben$^r$ Wales
James Walker
Daniel Ward
John Woodward Signs his name John Woodard
Zachariah Kyes
Amariah Lyons
John Laflen
Robert Hosmer signs receipt for service in the company "in the Room of Abijah Smith" from Oct. 18 to Nov. 10.
William Williams

[*Connecticut Historical Society.*]

## SICK BILLS.

[See *Record of Connecticut Men in the Revolution*, pages 37–90.]

[Names of soldiers extracted from a volume of "Sick Bills", 1775, being itemized accounts of the expenses of individual soldiers during sickness.]

| Name of soldier | His Company | His Regiment | Remarks |
|---|---|---|---|
| William Whiting | Capt. Sedgwick | Hinman | Of Hartford Died |
| Silvanus Snow |  | Putnam |  |
| Benajah Geer |  | " |  |
| Capt. Abraham Tyler |  | Huntington | In Rhode Island |
| Daniel Brown | Capt. Putnam | Putnam | Of Coventry |
| Benjamin Babcock | " | " | " |
| Benjamin Hoskins | Capt. W<sup>m</sup> Gaylor Hubble | Charles Webb |  |
| William Raymont | Capt. Doolittle |  |  |
| Chauncey Smith |  | Wooster |  |
| Thomas Pierpont |  | " |  |
| Ebenezer Hall |  | " |  |
| Serj. Cochram | Capt. Mott's guard |  |  |
| Jude Bill | Maj. Elmore |  |  |
| Daniel Bill | Capt. Watson |  |  |
| Samuel Hough | Capt. Cook | Wooster |  |
| John Pearce | " | " |  |
| Phineas Lyman | " | " |  |
| Gideon Bill | " | " |  |
| Jarius Harrison | Capt. Douglas |  |  |
| Jacob Page | " |  |  |
| Eli Moulton | " |  |  |
| Samuel Orsborn | Capt. Cook |  |  |
| Amos Austin | " |  |  |
| Ichabod Merriam | " |  |  |
| Reuben Rowleson | Col. Ward |  |  |
| Abraham Bunnell | Capt. Douglas |  |  |
| Titus Butler | " |  |  |
| Clement Tuttle | " |  |  |
| Ezra Prindle | Capt. Peck |  |  |
| Samuel Donaldson |  |  |  |
| Nathaniel Taylor | Maj. Dimon |  |  |
| David Annibal | " |  |  |
| Levi Mallery | " |  |  |
| Lyman Jennings | " |  |  |
| David Sturgis |  |  |  |
| Chauncey Dowens |  |  |  |
| Isaac Squires |  |  |  |
| Nehemiah Thorp |  |  |  |
| Nath<sup>l</sup> Whitehead |  |  |  |
| John Knapp |  |  |  |
| David Dickson | Maj. Elmor |  |  |
| John Comstock | " |  |  |
| Asa Cole | " |  |  |

## CONTINENTAL REGIMENTS, 1775.

| Name of soldier | His Company | His Regiment | Remarks |
|---|---|---|---|
| Billy Hatch | Capt. Watson | | |
| Thaddeus Betts | Col. Waterbury | | |
| Timothy Scott | " | | |
| Henry Scofield | " | | |
| Aaron Peck | " | | |
| Joseph Beebe | Capt. Peck | | |
| Reuben Beebe | " | | |
| Thomas Wedge | Maj. Elmore | | |
| Elias Chapman | " | | |
| Joseph Jones | Capt. Watson | | |
| John Trowbridge | " | | |
| Joseph Thomson | " | | |
| Nathaniel Marvin | " | | |
| Jason Perkins | " | | |
| Jared Benham | Capt. Cook | | |
| Amos Austin | " | | |
| James Olcott | Capt. William G. Hubble | Webb | Went on to Cambridge in Sept. 1775. |
| John Camp | " | " | Went on to Cambridge in Oct. 1775. |
| Eli Tuttle | " | " | |
| Thomas Merchant | Capt. Caleb Trowbridge | Wooster | Of Waterbury |
| Benj. Freeman | Capt. Mott | Parsons | |
| Zebulon Butten | " | " | |
| Roger Billings | " | " | |
| Peter Quecheats | " | " | |
| Jabez Avery | " | " | |
| Isaac Teacomwaus | " | " | |
| Jonathan Cartwright | Maj. Thomson | Wooster | Died |
| Aaron Camp | Capt. James Arnold | " | Returned from St Johns |
| John Higbee | Capt. Meigs | Spencer | |
| Nathaniel Miller | " | " | |
| Dan¹ Churchill | " | " | |
| Samuel Markham | " | " | |
| William Lucas | " | " | |
| Wickham Brooks | " | " | |
| Amos Roberts | " | " | |
| Frederick Winthrop | " | " | |
| Benj. Pearce | Maj. Meigs | " | Dislocated shoulder |
| David Mallery | Capt. Douglas | Wooster | |
| Joseph Hotchkiss | Capt. Caleb Trowbridge | " | |
| Charles Parmerle | Capt. James Arnold | " | |
| David Hyllyard | Maj. Prentis | Parsons | Wounded with a bayonet |
| —— Tyler | Col. Street Hall | Webb | |
| Jonah Hall | Capt. Porter | " | From Stillwater |
| David Pease | Maj. Clark | Huntington | Of Somers |
| John Willson | Col. Store | Putnam | |
| Benajah Geer | | " | Wounded at the Battle of Bunker's Hill |
| Capt. Joseph Eliot | | " | Of the army at Cambridge. In his last sickness |

| Name of soldier | His Company | His Regiment | Remarks |
|---|---|---|---|
| Reuben Judd | Capt. John Sedgwick | Hinman | |
| James FitzGerald | | Parsons | |
| Nathaniel Watson | Capt. Shubael Griswold | Hinman | Died Dec. 1775. |
| Samuel Benham | Capt. Isaac Cook | Wooster | Northern army |
| Titus Negro | Capt. Hanchet | Spencer | |
| John Hatchway | " | " | |
| Thomas McKnight | | Huntington | At Roxbury |
| Jacob Tocomuaus | Capt. Mott | Parsons | |
| Peter Cochecks or Quochecks | " | " | |
| Beriah Brunson | Col. Pitkin | Hinman | Wounded |
| Samuel Dealing | Capt. Chester | " | |
| Thomas Brooks | Capt. Parsons | " | |
| Sim. Wright | " | " | |
| Enos Skinner | Capt. Putnam (?) | " | |
| James Converse | Capt. Levi Wells | Spencer | |
| Ens. James Peck | Capt. Cook | Wooster | Of Wallingford |
| Lieut. John Hough | " | " | Not sick |
| Judah Leaming | Maj. Welch | Wooster | From Ticonderoga |
| Bethuel Norton | | Spencer | Of Farmington |
| —— Benham | Maj. Welch | Wooster | From Lake Champlain |
| Joseph C. Hawley | Capt. Starr | Hinman | Of Harrington From Northern Army |
| David Smith | Maj. Welch | Wooster | From Ticonderoga |
| Capt. Noadiah Hooker | | Spencer | |
| Jabez West | Capt. Solomon Willes | " | Of Tolland |
| Sam¹ Savage | Capt. James Arnold | Wooster | Of Middletown |
| Silas Gaylord | Capt. Arnold | " | |
| Nathaniel Averill | Capt. Eleazer Curtiss | Hinman | |
| William Crane | Capt. Hezekiah Parsons | " | |
| Charles Hall | Capt. Cook | Wooster | Of Wallingford |
| Lieut. Jonathan Parker | Capt. Willes | Spencer | |
| Lieut. Moses Hall | Maj. Eno | " | |
| Jesse Converse | " | " | |
| David Rice | " | " | |
| Caleb Orcutt | Capt. Solomon Willes | " | |
| Jabez West | " | " | |
| Nathan Carpenter | " | " | |
| Justus Thomson | " | " | |
| Nathan Jennings Jr. | " | " | |
| Daniel Johnson | " | " | |
| Jacob Green | Capt. Robinson | " | |
| Daniel Colburn Jr. | " | " | |
| Stephen Cross | | " | |
| Gideon Noble Jr. | Capt. Shipman | " | |
| Aaron Cadwell | Capt. John Sedgwick | Hinman | Of Hartford |
| William Russell | Col. Whiting | Waterbury | |
| Silas Gaylord | Capt. James Arnold | Wooster | Died. Probably Of Wallingford |
| —— Fowler | | " | Died Sep. 5, 1775. Of Guilford |
| Jacob Averill | | | At Stillwater |
| Silas Brewster | | | " |

## CONTINENTAL REGIMENTS, 1775.

| Name of soldier | His Company | His Regiment | Remarks |
|---|---|---|---|
| Phicol Moody | | | At Stillwater |
| Samson Obey | | | " |
| Thomas Averill | | | " |
| —— Smith | | | " |
| Solomon Martin | | Hinman | " |
| —— Way | | " | " |
| Peter Jermain or German | | | " |
| Charles Jermain or German | | | " |
| Rev. William Seward | | Waterbury | "Chaplain |
| Nathan Hicock | | | " |
| Thomas Andrus | | | " |
| Ezekiel Trumbull | Maj. Welch | Hinman | " |
| Friend Dickinson | " | " | " |
| David Morris | | | " |
| Elishia Burret | | | " |
| Elihu Burret | | | " |
| Nathan Newell | Capt. Watson | Hinman | " |
| Jesse Foster | Capt. Doolittle | Waterbury | " |
| Salmond Taylor | " | " | " |
| Joseph Thorp | Capt. Buel | Hinman | " |
| Phineas Allen | Gen. Wooster | | " |
| Abraham Chittenton | " | | " |
| Jasphat Tuttle | Capt. Porter | | " |
| Isaac Camp | | | " |
| Jonah Hall | " | Wooster | " |
| Ashbel Beecher | Gen. Wooster | | " |
| Jonathan Beecher | Capt. Peck | | " |
| Daniel Gates | Capt. Doolittle | | " Died |
| Job Marshall | Capt. Griswold | | " |
| Stephen Marsh | Gen. Wooster | | " |
| Phineas Squire | Capt. Reed | | " |
| Samuel Gilbert | " | | " |
| Daniel Silliman | Maj. Demon | | " |
| Isaac Silliman | Capt. Reed | | " |

The above men noted as at Stillwater belonged to Wooster's, Waterbury's and Hinman's regiments.

| | | | |
|---|---|---|---|
| Ezra Ramsdale | | Spencer | |
| Bethuel Fuller | | " | |
| Lieut. Daniel Cone | Gen. Spencer | " | At Brookline |
| Corpl. Phineas Cone | | " | |
| William Smith | Capt. Mott | Parsons | At Hartford |
| Charles Hall | Capt. Isaac Cook | Wooster | |
| Ephraim Chamberlain | " | " | |
| Dan Smith | " | " | |
| Levy Ives | " | " | |
| James Corbett Jr. | " | " | |
| Ens. James Peck | " | " | Of Wallingford |
| Thomas Brooks Jr. | Capt. Chester | Huntington | |
| Joseph Lamb | Capt. Hanchet | " | |
| Elizur Brooks | Col. Douglas | Huntington | |
| Jonathan Riley | " | " | |
| Joel Buck | Capt. Smith | Waterbury | |
| Silas Gaylord | Capt. James Arnold | Wooster | |
| Andrew Hull | " | " | |
| Nathaniel Bull | " | " | |
| Asa Blakesley | " | " | |
| William Perkins | " | " | |
| Archibald Rice | " | " | |

| Name of soldier | His Company | His Regiment | Remarks |
|---|---|---|---|
| Oliver Bradley | Capt. James Arnold | Wooster | |
| Stephen Brooks | Lieut-Col. Street-Hall | Webb | |
| Josiah Smith | " | " | |
| Ebenezer Thomson | | Wooster | |
| Cyperan Merrell | Capt. Griswold | Hinman | Dislocated Knee |
| Noadiah Emmons | Capt. John Willes | Spencer | |
| Timothy Tiffany | Capt. John Watson | Hinman | |
| Ashbel Beach | " | " | |
| Gibbon Wentworth | " | " | Of Canaan |
| Elias Lee | " | " | |
| Amos Phelps | " | " | |
| Reuben Rowlison | " | " | |
| Hiland Hall | " | " | At Fort Edward |
| Samuel Borden | " | " | |
| Nathaniel Clark | " | " | |
| Billy Hatch | " | " | |
| Samuel Hotchkiss | " | " | |
| Ens. Jehiel Hull | " | " | |
| Nathan Newell | " | " | |
| Samuel Fellows | ." | " | |
| Asa Andruss | " | " | |
| Benjamin Austin | Capt. Isaac Cook | Wooster | |
| Jared Benham | " | " | |
| Salmon Stanly | " | " | At Fort George |
| Serj. Joseph Shaylor | " | " | |
| Lieut. Morgan Noble | | Hinman | |
| Reuben Clark | Capt. Hanchet | Spencer | |
| Ichabod Fitch Jr. | Capt. James Clarke | Putnam | |
| Nathan Linkhorn | Capt. Ripley | " | |
| Jabez Frisbee | | Hinman | { Discharged Aug. 75 |
| Ashbel Porter | Capt. Starr | " | " |
| Dan¹ Cook | " | " | " |
| Nathaniel Catlin | Capt. James Arnold | Wooster | |
| Dr. Francis Percival | | Spencer | |
| Corpl. Abner Cole | Capt. Scott | " | |
| Samuel Savage | Capt. Arnold | Wooster | |
| Amaziah Barber | Capt. Pettibone | Spencer | Lame |
| Abiel Willson | Capt. Humphries | " | Wounded |
| Othniel Gillet Jr. | Capt. Pettibone | " | |
| Lieut. James Thomson | Capt. Sedgwick | Hinman | |
| Hezekiah Clark | " | " | |
| Jeremiah Hurlburt | " | " | |
| Serg. Abner Willson | Capt. Starr | " | |
| Benjamin Barber | " | " | Of Torrington |
| Simeon Barber | " | " | " |
| Oliver Phelps | " | " | Of Harwinton |
| Enos Scott | " | " | " |
| Adj. Jonas Prentice | | Wooster | |
| Thomas Catlin | Capt. Samuel Willmot | " | Not sick |
| Benjamin Smith | " | " | |
| Joshua Morse Jr. | Parsons | Parsons | |
| Eli Tuttle | Capt. Wm Gaylord Hubble | Webb | |
| David White | Capt. Nathaniel Buell | Hinman | |
| Judah Lewis | Capt. Nathaniel Tuttle | Webb | Of Woodbury |
| Daniel Brown | Capt. Putnam | Putnam | |
| Joshua Leach | Capt. Shubael Griswold | Hinman | |
| Caleb Leach | " | " | |

## CONTINENTAL REGIMENTS, 1775.

| Name of soldier | His Company | His Regiment | Remarks |
|---|---|---|---|
| James Benham | Capt. Shubael Griswold | Hinman | |
| Job Marshall | " | " | |
| Serg: Charles Wright | Capt. John Sedgwick | " | |
| David Wright | " | " | |
| Tryal Tanner | " | " | |
| Lemuel Gillet | " | " | |
| Ezekiel Perry | " | " | |
| Ebenezer Shepard | " | " | |
| Kirtland Griffing | Capt. Nathaniel Buell | " | |
| Nathaniel Douglass | " | " | |
| Caleb Chatfield | " | " | |
| Samuel Kelcey | " | " | Of Salisbury |
| Eber Everts | " | " | |
| Aaron Mills | " | " | |
| Daniel Burton | " | " | |
| Samuel Williams | " | " | Of Canaan |
| Josiah Whitney | " | " | " |
| John McLean | " | " | |
| Joseph Plumley | " | " | |
| Henry Hull | " | " | |
| Reuben Smith | " | " | |
| James Russ | " | " | |
| Jonathan Russ | " | " | |
| Gideon Dunning | Capt. Joseph Smith | Waterbury | |
| Levi Bostwick | " | " | |
| James Fairchild | " | " | |
| Charles McDaniel | " | " | |
| Serg. Timothy Munson | " | " | Of New Milford |
| William Hamlin | " | " | Died |
| Serg. Jonas Brush | Capt. Nehemiah Beardsley | " | |
| Joseph Bearse | " | " | |
| Job Scribner | " | " | |
| Titus Brockett | Capt. Isaac Cook | Wooster | |
| Daniel Gates | Capt. Doolittle | Waterbury | |
| Caleb Hurlburt | Capt. Griswold | Hinman | |
| Eber Beach | " | " | |
| Obed Crosbey | " | " | |
| Amariah Clumb | Capt. Watson | " | |
| Dick Gudeahn | Col. Ward | " | |
| David Moretrup | Capt. Willmot | " | |
| Benj. Gaylord | Capt. Griswold | " | |
| Elihu Thomson | Capt. Cook | " | |
| Thomas Marsh | Col. Wooster | " | |
| Lieut. Jesse Cook | Capt. Hubble | Webb | |
| Abraham Catlin | Maj. Welch | Wooster | |
| Samuel Wesson | " | " | |
| George Jones | " | | |
| Amos Gilbert | " | " | |
| Moses Steel | Capt. Sedgwick | Hinman | Of Hartford |
| William Whiting | " | " | |
| Martin Woodruff | Capt. Hanchet | Spencer | |
| Lieut. Timothy Holcomb | Capt. Buell | Hinman | Died at Shaftsbury |
| Jacob Sayer | | Parsons | |
| Jonathan Reynolds | Lieut-Col. Hobby | Waterbury | Wounded |
| Sam¹ Whitman | Capt. Noadiah Hooker | Spencer | |
| Sam¹ Coe | " | " | |
| Jonathan Reynolds | Maj. Hobby | Waterbury | Wounded |

| Name of soldier | His Company | His Regiment | Remarks |
|---|---|---|---|
| Wm. Manning | Capt. Mott | Huntington | |
| Serg. Timothy Munson | Capt. Starr | Hinman | |
| Jeremiah Smith | Capt. Sedgwick | " | |
| Jabez Avery | Capt. Edward Mott | Parsons | Of Preston |
| William Hamlin | Capt. Joseph Smith | Waterbury | |
| Augustus Lewis | Capt. Gale | Parsons | |
| Reuben Bates | " | | |
| Sam¹ Bone | | Spencer | |
| Josiah Arnold | | Parsons | |
| George Dear Jr. | Capt. John Sedgwick | Hinman | Of Goshen |
| William Beech | " | " | |
| Heman Smith | Capt. Starr | " | |
| Samuel Kellogg | Capt. Sedgwick | " | A minor |
| Joseph Brooks | Capt. Starr | " | Of Goshen |
| Charles Miles | Capt. Sedgwick | " | " |
| Abel Butler Jr. | " | " | " |
| Samuel Hayden | " | " | " |
| William Matson | Capt. Willmot | " | Died |
| Salmon Stanley | Capt. Cook | Wooster | Of Wallingford |
| Amos Austin | Capt. Cook | Wooster | |
| Jesse Fairchild | Capt. Smith | Waterbury | Of Newtown |
| John Willson | | Storrs | |
| Lieut. Trowbridge | | Webb | |
| Duke Hamlinton | | " | |
| —— Cook | | " | |
| Daniel Winchel | | " | |
| Roger Umsted | | " | Died |
| —— Filow | | " | |
| Daniel Smith | | " | |
| Benjamin Bennet | | " | |
| —— Olcott | | " | |
| Serg. Taylor | | " | |
| Serg. Phelps | | " | |
| William Hamlin | | Waterbury | |
| Serg. Josiah Fowler | Capt. Douglas | Wooster | |
| Lieut. Elizur Hubbard | Col. Douglass | Huntington | Of Glastenbury |
| Levi Deans | | Parsons | |
| Richard Olmsted | | Waterbury | |
| Nathan Carpenter | | Spencer | |
| John Fairchild | Col. Samuel Whiting | Waterbury | |
| Serg. John Jones | Capt. James Arnold | Wooster | Of Durham |
| Thomas Cheesborough | Capt. Jewett | Waterbury | |
| John Willson | Col. Storrs | Putnam | Of Yorkshire Eng. |
| Ebenezer Pitcher Jr. or Ebenezer Pritchard Jr. | Col. Hinman | Hinman | Of Woodbury |
| Jabez Syzer | Col. John Douglas | Huntington | |
| Aaron Minor | Capt. Phineas Porter | Hinman | |
| Timothy Pond | | Spencer | |
| Fifer James Wells | Capt. Mott | Parsons | |
| Gilbert Crittenden | Col. Ward | Wooster | |
| Angus McFee | Capt. Peck | " | |
| James Fairchild | Capt. Smith | " | |
| Jedediah French Wells | Capt. Reed | " | |
| Capt. John Watson | | Hinman | Of Canaan, Wounded at St. Johns Sept. 18, 1775. |

## CONTINENTAL REGIMENTS, 1775.

| Name of soldier | His Company | His Regiment | Remarks |
|---|---|---|---|
| Henry Norton | Col. Andrew Ward | Wooster | Of Guilford |
| John Scovill Jr. | " | " | |
| Eber Hall | " | " | Of Guilford |
| Zebulon Benton | " | " | |
| Thomas Cheeseborough | Capt. Jewet | Huntington | |
| Pettet Scofield | Col. Waterbury | Waterbury | |
| Jacob Scofield | Capt. Hait | " | |
| David Selleck | Col. Waterbury | " | |
| Isaac Brown | | " | |
| Andrew Bennet | Capt. Bardsley | " | |
| Nathaniel Scribner | Capt. Mead | | |
| Nathaniel Little | Capt. Joseph Smith | Wooster | |
| John Clemons | Maj. David Welch | " | |
| Smith Clark | " | " | |
| David Smith | " | " | |
| Beriah Birge | | | |
| William Russel Jr. | Col. Whiting | Waterbury | |
| Isaac Miles | Capt. Sedgwick | Hinman | Of Goshen |
| David Mitchell | Col. Hinman | " | Of Woodbury |
| William Hamblin Jr. | Capt. Joseph Smith | Waterbury | Died Sept. 30, 1775 Of New Milford |
| Thomas Olmsted | Capt. Doolittle | " | Died Oct. 26, 1775 |
| Samuel Stubbs | Capt. Ebenezer Mosely | Putnam | Of Windham |
| Amos Ormsby | Capt. John Watson | Hinman | |
| John Curtiss | " | " | Of Canaan |
| Nathan Jennings | | Spencer | |
| Jeremiah Chase | Capt. Mead | Waterbury | |
| Lieut. Morgan Noble | Capt. Eleazer Curtiss | Hinman | |
| Charles Kilborn | Maj. Welch | Wooster | Of Litchfield |
| Solomon Goodwin | " | " | |
| Josiah Remington | | Spencer | With Col. Arnold in Canada. |
| Thomas Averill | Capt. Edward Mott | Parsons | |
| Torrey Scranton | Col. Andrew Ward | Wooster | |
| Corp. Prentice Hosmer | Capt. Sedgwick | Hinman | Of Hartford |
| Isaac Willcox | Maj. Joel Clark | Huntington | His last sickness |
| Caleb Orcutt | Capt. Wells | Spencer | Of Willington |
| Luther Page | Capt. William Douglas | Wooster | |
| Daniel Johnson | Capt. Solomon Wells | Spencer | |
| William Bearce | Capt. John Sedgwick | Hinman | Of Cornwall |
| Justus Thomson | Lieut. Jonathan Parker | Spencer | Of Willington |
| Amos Mix | Col. Street Hall | Webb | |
| Moses Warner | Capt. Ellsworth | Huntington | |
| Eli Pease | " | " | |
| Roswell Blotchet | | " | |
| David Shaw | Capt. Parsons | " | |
| Ebenezer Prior | Capt. Ellsworth | " | |
| Chester Allyn | Capt. Hanchet | " | |
| Samuel Barlow | Capt. Zalmon Read | Waterbury | Died at Poughkeepsie |
| John Patterson | Capt. Dimon | Wooster | |
| Ichabod Canfield | " | " | |
| Timothy Stevens | Capt. Rowley | Huntington | |
| Obediah Fox | Col. Douglas | " | |
| Elijah Hollister | Capt. Chester | Spencer | |
| Robert Harvey Jr. | Capt. John Willis | Wyllys | Of East Haddam |

| Name of soldier | His Company | His Regiment | Remarks |
|---|---|---|---|
| Mason Hobart | Capt. Douglas | Wooster | |
| Ebenezer Judd | Capt. Porter | " | |
| Daniel Williams | Capt. Peck | " | |
| Artemas Johnson | Capt. Douglas | " | |
| Isaac Camp | Capt. Porter | " | Of Farmington |
| Edmund Clarke | Capt. John Ripley | Huntington | |
| Ens. David Hitchcock | Capt. Peck | Wooster | Of Wallingford |
| Solomon Martin | Col. Hinman | Hinman | Of Woodbury |
| Lemuel Herrick | Capt. Mott | Parsons | Of Preston |
| Elijah Crane | Capt. Beardsley | Waterbury | |
| Benjamin Mack | | Parsons | |
| John Willson | Col. Storrs | Putnam | Of Windham |
| Moses Warner | Capt. Cook | Wooster | |
| Samuel Hall | " | " | |
| Peter Van Dyke | Capt. Eleazer Curtis | Hinman | |
| Phinehas Sherwood | " | " | |
| Daniel Seward | Capt. Peck | Wooster | |
| Joel Buck | Capt. Smith | Waterbury | |
| Benajah Gears | Col. Storrs | Putnam | Wounded in Bunker Hill fight. |
| Samuel Stubbs | Capt. Moseley | " | Of Windham |
| Nathaniel Watson | Capt. Griswold | Hinman | Died |
| Silvanus Snow | Capt. Knowlton | Putnam | Wounded in the battle at Bunker Hill |
| Samuel Barlow | Capt. Zalmon Read | Waterbury | Died |
| Eleazer Fenton Jr. | Maj. Enos | Spencer | |
| Ebenezer Drinkwater | Capt. Starr | Hinman | |
| Serg. John Stevens | " | " | |
| Oliver Bostwick | " | " | |
| Thomas Perry | Capt. Ichabod Doolittle | Waterbury | |
| Andrew Minor | Capt. Solomon Willes | Spencer | Died |
| Asa Brownson | Capt. Starr | Hinman | |
| Elnathan Filley | Maj. Enos | Spencer | |
| Richard Gay Jr. | Capt. Elihu Humphry | Huntington | |
| Charles Tuttle | Capt. Isaac Cook | Wooster | Of Wallingford |
| Joseph Ruggles | Capt. Joseph Smith | Waterbury | Of New Milford |
| Edward Barnerd Jr. | | Spencer | Of Windsor. Died. |
| Japhat Tuttle | Capt. Phineas Porter | Wooster | |
| Paul Wellman | " | " | |
| Serg. Amos Dutton | | | |
| Peter Bradley | Capt. David Dimon | Waterbury | |
| John Slater | Col. Whiting | " | |
| Samuel Perritt | Capt. Peck | Wooster | |
| Henry Bull | " | " | |
| Jeremiah Bull | " | " | |
| Reubin Rowlinson | Col. Ward | " | Of Guilford |
| William Morce | " | " | " |
| David Lewis | Capt. Hooker | Wyllys | |
| Titus Fulford | Capt. Trowbridge | Wooster | Of Waterbury |
| Ens. Ebenezer Banks Jr. | Capt. Ichabod Doolittle | Waterbury | |
| Serg. William Fowler | Col. Ward | Wooster | Of Guilford |
| Joel Norton | " | " | " |
| James Needham Griffin | " | " | " |
| Richard Dick | " | " | " |

## CONTINENTAL REGIMENTS, 1775.

| Name of soldier | His Company | His Regiment | Remarks |
|---|---|---|---|
| Joseph Barney Sr. | Capt. Knowlton | Putnam | Of Ashford |
| Eli Stevens | Capt. Noble Benedict | Waterbury | |
| Daniel Eldredge | Capt. Knowlton | Putnam | Of Ashford |
| William Williams | " | " | " |
| Caleb Smith | Capt. William Douglas | Wooster | Of East Haven |
| John Hills | Col. Ward | " | Of Guilford |
| Angus McFee | Capt. Samuel Peck | " | |
| George Clark Smith | Capt. Starr | Hinman | |
| Lieut. Ezekiel Sanford | Capt. Zalmon Read | Waterbury | |
| Talmage Hall | Capt. Nehemiah Beardsley | " | |
| Samuel Baldwin | Capt. Porter | Wooster | |
| John Bunnel | Capt. William Douglas | " | Of Branford |
| Allyn Steel | Capt. John Sedgwick | Hinman | |
| Edward Dimock | Capt. Solomon Willes | Spencer | |
| John Charter Jr. | " | " | |
| Amasa Allen | " | " | |
| Samuel Wright | " | " | |
| Samuel Perkins | Capt. John Ripley | Huntington | |
| John Babcock | | | Of Lebanon |
| Ichabod Hawley | Capt. Hooker | Wyllys | |
| Eli Wood | Capt. Nathaniel Buel | Hinman | |
| Isaac Perry | Capt. Zalmon Reed | Waterbury | |
| Amariah Plumb | | Hinman | Wounded and taken prisoner at St. Johns |
| Jedediah French | Capt. Read | Waterbury | |
| Joseph Thorp | Capt. Buell | Hinman | |
| Jehiel Comstock | Capt. Coit | Parsons | |

[*Comptroller's Office.*]

# CONTINENTAL REGIMENTS - 1776

## SEVENTEENTH REGIMENT — COL. HUNTINGTON

[*See Record of Connecticut Men in the Revolution, page 101.*]

### CAPT. BISSELL'S COMPANY.

An Ammunition Return of Cap$^t$ Ebenezer Fitch Bissells Company y$^e$ 17$^{th}$ Reg$^t$ New York May y$^e$ 15$^{th}$ 1776

Mens names that have Got Guns and other Ammunition

Serj$^t$ Cornelius Russell
Serj$^t$ John Roundey
Serj$^t$ Eleazer House
Serj$^t$ Hezek$^h$ Haydon
Corp$^l$ Sam$^{ll}$ Bordman
Corp$^l$ Aaron Porter
Corp$^l$ Sam$^{ll}$ Hall
Corp$^l$ Elijah Bordman
John Atwood
Will$^m$ Andruss
Ozias Atwell
Will$^m$ Arvin
Ephriem Alderman
Joshua Burgess
Shubell Cook
Will$^m$ Cradock
Elisha Case
Jedidiah Case
Ira Clark
John Chambers
Abner Fuller
Lemuel Fuller
Benjamin Fuller
Hezekiah Filley
Roger Filer
Reuben Flowers
Daniel Gilburt
Carmi Higley
Obed Higley
Erastus Humphrey
Joel Humphrey
John Humphrey
Jesse Halley
Jonath$^n$ Holaday
Jareth Ingraham
Henry Edwards
Phinihas Kellogg
Henery Kirkam
Samuel Kirkam
Nath$^{ll}$ Lamberton
Elijah Loomis
Sam$^{ll}$ Landers
George Lewardy
Elijah Lusk
James Lawrance
Isaac Merrell
Increas Mather
Alpheus Munsell
Daniel Moses
John Miller
Daniel Munsell
Frances Merrey
Isaac Mix
Elisha Messenger
Loammi Nearing
John Newbury
Daniel Olmsted
James Powers
Lewis Standley
John Smith
W$^m$ Shephard
Joseph Sedgwick
Alex$^r$ Thomson
Roswell Warner
Abner Warner
John Wilson
John White
John Whiting
Daniel Waller
Rhoderick Clark
Augustus Miller
John Flether

[*Connecticut Historical Society.*]

## NINETEENTH REGIMENT—COL. WEBB.

### CAPT. HALE'S COMPANY.

[See *Record of Connecticut Men in the Revolution, page 104.*]

A Pay Abstract of Capt. Hale's Company Colo. Webb's Regiment for yᵉ Month of April 1776. June 10ᵗʰ 1776

| Mens Names | Sum of Wages £ s d |
|---|---|
| Capt. Nathan Hale | 8 0 0 |
| Lieut. Alpheus Chapman | 5 8 0 |
| Lieut. John Elderkin | 5 8 0 |
| Ens. George Hurlbut | 4 0 0 |
| Sergᵗˢ Thomas Updike Fosdick | 2 8 0 |
| Stephen Hempsted | 2 8 0 |
| Francis Sage | 2 8 0 |
| Peter Robertson | 2 8 0 |
| Corpˡˢ Christopher Beebe | 2 4 0 |
| Asa Spink | 2 4 0 |
| Thomas Kingsbury | 2 4 0 |
| Christopher Woodbridge | 2 4 0 |
| Drumʳ Lemuel Maynard | 2 4 0 |
| Fifʳ William Willson | 2 4 0 |
| Privates Pigot Colin Adams | 2 0 0 |
| Ebenezer Allen | 2 0 0 |
| Alvin Ames | 2 0 0 |
| William Bacon | 2 0 0 |
| Guy Beckwith | 2 0 0 |
| Thaddeus Beebe | 2 0 0 |
| Gideon Beebe | 2 0 0 |
| Ephraim Beebe | 2 0 0 |
| Paul Beebe | 2 0 0 |
| Joseph Bolles | 2 0 0 |
| John Brown | 2 0 0 |
| Charles Brown | 2 0 0 |
| Eliphalet Button | 2 0 0 |
| Stephen Califf | 2 0 0 |
| David Canada | 2 0 0 |
| Silas Chapman | 2 0 0 |
| John Chappel | 2 0 0 |
| Alpheus Chappel | 2 0 0 |
| Joseph Church | 2 0 0 |
| William Clark | 2 0 0 |
| Thomas Cook | 2 0 0 |
| | £87 12 0 |
| Thomas Fargo | 2 0 0 |
| Timothy Fargo | 2 0 0 |
| Stephen Ginnings | 2 0 0 |
| Daniel Ginnings | 2 0 0 |
| Stephen Hall | 2 0 0 |

# CONTINENTAL REGIMENTS, 1776.

| Mens Names | Sum of Wages £ s d |
|---|---|
| Privates Enos Greenfield | 2 0 0 |
| Isaac Hammon | 2 0 0 |
| John Hand | 2 0 0 |
| Josiah Hand | 2 0 0 |
| Timothy Hedges | 2 0 0 |
| Henry Hopping | 2 0 0 |
| John Holmes | 2 0 0 |
| Lebbeus Houghton | 2 0 0 |
| Robert Johnson | 2 0 0 |
| Luther Martin | 2 0 0 |
| John Martin | 2 0 0 |
| Samuel Maynard | 2 0 0 |
| Jabez Maynard | 2 0 0 |
| Elkanah Meech | 2 0 0 |
| Matthew Melony | 2 0 0 |
| John Moltrop | 2 0 0 |
| Isaac Morgan | 2 0 0 |
| Josiah Osborn | 2 0 0 |
| William Parish | 2 0 0 |
| James Phillips | 2 0 0 |
| Daniel Plumbe | 2 0 0 |
| William Putnam | 2 0 0 |
| Arthur Robertson | 2 0 0 |
| Pharaoh Sharper* | 2 0 0 |
| Jeremiah Tallmadge | 2 0 0 |
| Nathaniel Tuttle | 2 0 0 |
| James Ward | 2 0 0 |
| Davidson Williams | 2 0 0 |
| Asher Wright | 2 0 0 |
| | £70 0 0 |

The Following Privates, being inlisted after the Month commenced, draw pay but for part of it.

| Names | When Inlisted | Days Serv⁼ | Sum |
|---|---|---|---|
| Samuel Ames | April 2d | 29 | 1 18 8 |
| Silas Holley | 23d | 8 | 0 10 8 |
| Ezra Smith | 20th | 11 | 0 14 8 |
| | | | 3 4 0 |
| | | | 87 12 0 |
| | | | 70 0 0 |
| | | Total | 160 16 0 |

A Return of Capt Hale's Company Col° Webb's Regiment giving the Stat[ ] of it morning and evening each Day. Beginning April 20th 1776.
[In addition to the names in the above pay abstract the following names appear.]

Diarea Elderkin
Henry Wardon
Thomas Merrit

---

* Evidently an error for Sharp, as the name is written Pharaoh Sharp in three other places in the same book.

An Account of the Arms, Amunition &c used by Capt Hale's Company [          ] Regiment in the Campain of 1776.

[In addition to the names in the above pay abstract and return the following names appear]

 Reynold Hooper
 Ezra Williams
 Simon Neil


An Account of Arms, Amunition and Accutrements Capt Hale's Company Col° Webb's Regiment

[In addition to the names in the above pay abstract the following names appear.]

 Isaac Brun June 29 1 Gun N226 bay$^t$ & Strap
 Eliphalet Robinson Mar. 4. 1 G. N. 45. 24r. 1 bay$^t$ & Car.b.
 Joseph Weeks Jun. 27 1 K. arms Compt:


Casualties in Capt. Hale's Company Col° Webb's Regiment.

1776
May 12 Ser$^t$ Thomas Updike Fosdick sent recruiting to the East end of Long Island & New London Instructions written not by Col° Webb but by his order.
   Jeremiah Tallmadge sent on command to the eastern part of Long Island after arms belonging to himself & some others of the Company Living near by him.
  28 Samuel Maynard Joined the Company
June 4 John Martin Joined the Company.
   8 Enos Greenfield returned from 12 Days command.
   Serg$^t$ Thomas Updike Fosdick returned from recruiting & joined the Company.
  29 Jeremiah Tallmadge returned having been detained at home by Sickness.

*[Connecticut Historical Society.]*

## SIZE ROLL OF CAPT. HALE'S COMPANY.

[The following roll being imperfect the headings given are assumed and may not be correct.]

| [ Names ] | [ Age Y | M | Height F | I ] | [ Place of Enlistment State | Town ] | [ Birthplace State | Town ] | [ Date of Enlistment ] |
|---|---|---|---|---|---|---|---|---|---|
| [ ] Robertson | | | | | Ibid | New London | Ibid | New London | |
| [ ] Sharp | 25 | 10 | 5 | 9¾ | New York | | | | March 1 |
| Jeremiah Tallmadge | 28 | 6 | 5 | 8¼ | New York | | | | March 1 |
| James Ward | 24 | 7 | 5 | 8½ | Connecticut | New London | Rhode Island | Newport | Nov. 15 |
| Davidson Williams | 21 | 2 | 5 | 6½ | Connecticut | New London | Connecticut | New London | March [ ] |
| Henry Worden | | | | | Ibid | Stonington | | | [ ] |
| Asher Wright | 22 | | 5 | 9½ | Ibid | Coventry | Connecticut | Coventry | Dec. 26 J [ ] |
| John Chappel | 55 | 7 | 5 | 7½ | Ibid | New London | | | March 27 Apr [ ] |
| Silas Chapman | 16 | 8 | 5 | 4 | Ibid | | | New London | March 28 |
| Joseph Church | 17 | 10 | 5 | 6½ | Ibid | | | | 30 |
| Samuel Ames Jun^r | 21 | 6 | 5 | 9½ | Ibid | | | | April 2 |
| Elkenah Meech | 16 | 6 | 5 | 9¾ | Ibid | Groton | | Groton | 1 |
| Thomas Merrit | | | | | | | | | March 9 |
| Nathaniel Tuttle | | | 5 | 7¾ | New York | | | | 1 |
| *Robert Johnson | | | 5 | 6 | Connecticut | New London | Connecticut | New London | Nov. 15 |
| Corp^l Christopher Woodbridge | 20 | 10 | 5 | 8 | Ibid | Stonington | | Stonington | 15 |
| Silas Halley | | | | | | | | | Apr. 28 |
| Ezra Smith | | | | | | | | | 20 |
| Simon Neil | | | | | | | | | |
| Ezra Williams | | | | | | | | | |
| Joseph Weeks | | | | | | | | | |

* This entry is crossed out in the original

[*Connecticut Historical Society.*]

## CAPT. PERRIT'S COMPANY.

[*See Record of Connecticut Men in the Revolution, page 104.*]

[Capt. Peter Perrit, Lieut. Joseph Hull, "and the Non Commissioned Officers and Matrosses of his Company Shewing to this Assembly that they were taken Prisoners of War the 16th of Novem' 1776 while in Continental Service" were granted certain allowances by special act of the General Assembly.]

Pay Table Office June 12th 1784
John Lawrence Esq. Treas'
    Sir

    Please to secure to the following Persons the Payment of the Sums annexed to their Names being for Service in the Army before January 1st 1780 agreably to a Special Act of Assembly in fav' of Cap' Peter Perritt passed in May 1784......

Eleazer Wales Com  

Cap' Peter Perrit
Lieu' Joseph Hull
Serj' Jam' Yatman
"   Jon' Stricland
"   Thomas Hinkley
Corp' Sam' Peck
"   Preserve Edgcomb
"   Landon Smith
"   Jn° Hambleton
Jonathan Beecher
Jer' Norton
Benjamin Doll
James Burn
Ephraim Jackson
Lewis Clark
Andrew Yeumons
William Jones
Jn° Davis
Charles Walles
Gideon White
William Lock
Joseph Harrope
Jn° Bartrum
Jeremiah Durkee
Benjamin Harris

Jn° Colter
Shubael Johnson
Nathan Andrus
Jn° Wood
Francies Danaty
Richard Read
Jn° Camron
Benj' Pease
Daniel Haridon
Thomas Lawson
Samuel Lowell
Nathan Horton
William Whipple
Jon' Barnett
Mahu Tupper
Charles Brown
Francies Garrow
Jabez Sperry
Asa Beach
William Sanders
Adam Voss
William Gorden
Isaac Waterhouse
Jn° Pease
Asa Johnson

[*State Library, Revolution 17.*]

## COL. BURRALL'S REGIMENT.

*[See Record of Connecticut Men in the Revolution, page 110.]*

### FIELD AND STAFF.

We the Subscribers being Col[ll] Lieu[t] Coll[ll] Major Chaplain Adjutant Quarter Master Surgeon and Surgeons Mate Acknowledge to have Rec[d] of Epap[s] Bull Duputy Pay Master of the Connecticut Battallion Rais'd by Virtue of the Governors Proclamation of the 27[th] of Jan[y] 1776 — the Sums Affixt to our Names being our first Months Pay for Entering into S[d] Service as Witness our hands. Feb[y] 24[th] 1776.

| | | |
|---|---:|---:|---:|
| Col[ll] Charles Burrall Fifty Dollars | £ 15. | 0. | 0 |
| L[t] Col[ll] Natha[l] Buell forty Dollars | 12. | 0. | 0 |
| Maj[r] John Sedgwick thirty three Dollars & one third of a Dollar | 10. | 0. | 0 |
| Ammi R. Robbins Chaplin Twenty six Dollars & ⅔ | 8. | 0. | 0 |
| Thos. Converse Auj[t] Eighteen Dollars & ⅓ | 5. | 10. | 0 |
| Zerah Beech Quarter Master Eighteen Dollars & ⅓ | 5. | 10. | 0 |
| Edward Sutton twenty five Dollars Surgeon | 7. | 10. | 0 |
| Isaac Swift thirteen dollars & ⅓ & 10/ for Blanket Surg[s] Mate | 4. | 10. | 0 |
| | 68. | 0. | 0 |

*[Connecticut Historical Society.]*

[The Regimental Commissary book adds the following names and information.]

Jn[o] Bigelow, captain of a company of Matrosses which formed a part of the regiment and went with the other companies at least as far as Albany.

Adonijah Strong, lieutenant in Bigelow's company and regimental commissary.

Reuben Murry, lieutenant in Swift's company.
Solomon Story, lieutenant in Throop's company.
Captain Swift's company contained at least 83 men.

*[Comptroller's Office.]*

## CAPT. DOWNS' COMPANY.

A Pay Role of Cap$^t$ David Downs's Comp$^y$ being the 1$^{st}$ Comp$^y$ in Colo$^{ll}$ Charles Burrell's Battallion. We the Subscribers whose Names are underwritten having Enter'd & Enlisted ourselves into the Connecticut Battallion Rais'd by virtue of y$^e$ Governors Proclamation dated the 27$^{th}$ of Jan$^y$ 1776, under the Command of Colo$^{ll}$ Charles Burrell, to Reinforce the Northern Army, Ack$^s$ to have Rec$^d$ of Epap$^s$ Bull duputy Paymaster to S$^d$ Battallion the Sums Affixt to our Names who have Sign'd hereuntoo for our first Months pay Bounty pay for Blankets & Napsacks as Carryed out in the Collum of Am$^t$  Witness our hands March 7$^{th}$ 1776.

| Names & Quality | Time Enlisted | | Names & Quality | Time Enlisted | |
|---|---|---|---|---|---|
| David Downs Cap$^t$ | Jan$^y$ | 19 | James Laughlane | | 26 |
| Adonijah Griswold | | 23 | Abner Goodrich | | 3 |
| David Doty Liu$^t$ | | 23 | Enos Pettit | | 27 |
| Samuel Johnson | | 23 | Isaac Chamberlin | | 3 |
| David Rusco Serg$^t$ | Feb$^y$ | 1 | Lawrance Knickerbacor | | 1 |
| David Strong " | | " | Reuben Willis | | 3 |
| Anthony Hoskins Serj | | " | John Reen | | 20 |
| Oliver Hatch " | | 14 | Jethro Delano | | 6 |
| David Goodrich Jun. Corpor | | 1 | Stephen Wilcox | | 12 |
| Obadiah Matthews " | | 3 | W$^m$ Hyde | | 4 |
| Oliver Crocker " | | 1 | Judah Bill | | 3 |
| Sam$^{ll}$ Southworth " | | 2 | Charles Gillet Sen$^r$ | | 1 |
| James Bruester | | 1 | David Manning Jun$^r$ | | " |
| Abner Buck drum$^r$ | | 6 | Cyrus Fillmore | | 12 |
| Nath$^{ll}$ Tyler Fifer | | 1 | Edward Bumpus | | 29 |
| Isaac Pardee | | 1 | Henry Ingram | | 6 |
| Benjamin Macintire | | " | W$^m$ Goodrich Weller | | 1 |
| David Randall | | 4 | Elijah Bennett | | 6 |
| Caleb Jewett Jun$^r$ | | 1 | Simeon Runo | | 10 |
| Jonas Knapp | | 3 | Edmon Hunt | | 4 |
| Elisha Ticknor | | " | John Churcher | | 8 |
| Nath$^l$ Calkins | | 1 | Eleazer Norton | | 6 |
| Simon Whitcomb | | 13 | Ephram Toby | | 3 |
| Sam$^l$ Wright | | 10 | Michael McKee | | 4 |
| James Hambleton | | 8 | Adonijah Pangbourn | | 5 |
| Daniel Parsons | | 1 | Ezra Chapman | | " |
| Isaac Persons | | " | Edward Richmernd | | 10 |
| Joshua Hambleton | | 10 | Amasa Warner | | " |
| Jacob Maxum | | 1 | Tho$^s$ Slitwill | | 1 |
| W$^m$ Williams | | 10 | Elijah Hurlburt | | 8 |
| Samuel Gray | | 6 | Jonas Adams | | " |
| Jesse Goodrich | | 20 | James Clary | Mar$^h$ | 1 |
| Asa Rice | | 3 | Rosel Roberts | Feb | 5 |
| Benjamin Youngs | | 8 | Peter Armstrong | | 8 |
| Jehiel Smith | | " | Isaac Lamb | | 10 |
| Joel Chafe | | " | John Fisk | | 1 |
| Elijah Jackson | | 6 | John Hall | | 4 |
| Joseph Doty | | 3 | Sam$^{ll}$ Brown | | 12 |
| John Jackson Jun$^r$ | | 6 | Dan Smith | | 8 |
| Josiah Stronge | | " | James Barker | | 29 |
| Joseph Calkin | | 3 | Jeduthan Gray | | 5 |
| Asa Hoskins | | 2 | Dan$^{ll}$ Stuard | | 4 |
| Charles Gillet | | 7 | Sam$^{ll}$ Goodrich | | 6 |

[*Connecticut Historical Society.*]

## CAPT. STEVENS' COMPANY.

A Pay Role of Cap¹ John Stevens's Company being the 2ⁿᵈ Company in Co¹¹ Charles Burrells Battallion. We the Subscribers whose Names are underwritten having Enter'd into & Enlisted ourselves into the Connecticut Battallion Rais'd by virtue of the Governors Proclamation dated the 27ᵗʰ of Janʸ 1776 under the Command of Co¹¹ Charles Burrell to Reinforce the Northern Army, Acknoᵍ to have Recᵈ of Epapˢ Bull duputy Paymaster to Sᵈ Battallion the Sums Affixt to our Names, who have Sign'd hereunto for our first Months pay Bounty & pay for Blankᵗˢ & Napsacks as Carryed out in the Colum of Amᵗ Witness our hands — March 1776 —

| Names & Quality | Time Enlisted | | Names & Quality | Time Enlisted | |
|---|---|---|---|---|---|
| Jnᵒ Stevens Capᵗ | Janʸ | 19 | John Hewit | | 27 |
| Jesse Kimball Liuᵗ | | 23 | Randol Hewit | | " |
| Matthew Patterson | | 23 | Willard Kingsbury | | 19 |
| Bayze Wells Esn | | 23 | Phinihas Heath | | 9 |
| David Fellows | | 24 | Sippo Negro | | 24 |
| Rufus Paine Serj. | Febʸ | 24 | Daniel Janeways [?] | Janʸ | 29 |
| Cornelus Flower Segᵗ | | 5 | Medad Newel | Febʸ | 9 |
| Jeddidiah Smith Cor¹¹ | | 19 | Jabez Lewes | Janʸ | 24 |
| Elisha Hosmer Corp | | 5 | Jonathan Davis | Febʸ | 9 |
| Samuel Green Drum | Janʸ | 24 | Samuel Steel | | 5 |
| Zachariah Porter Fifer | Febʸ | 19 | Eleazer Fisher | | 4 |
| Samuel Simmons | | " | Abraham Webster | | 5 |
| David Baldwen | | " | Isaiah Gridley | | 4 |
| Joseph Allen Tanner | | 6 | Eliphas Steel | | 5 |
| Daniel Everest | | 21 | Amos Shepard | | 4 |
| Elisha Bradford | | 6 | Titus Merrel | | 5 |
| Hezekiah Barce | | 15 | Ebnezear Sedgwick | | 5 |
| Ruben Dean | | " | Eldad Kellogg | | 5 |
| Ephram Simons | | 19 | John Ledgyrd | | 4 |
| John Cowle | | 6 | Simeon Dupe | | 4 |
| Thomas Fleming | | 15 | Julus Davis | | 4 |
| John Waterhouse | | " | Jack Negro | | 8 |
| James Claray | | 6 | Uriah Abᵐˢ Bailey | | 27 |
| John Spaulding | Janʸ | 24 | Jacob Wheeler | | " |
| Thoˢ Gilbert | | 22 | Josiah Eaglestone | | " |
| Stephen Fellows | | " | Wᵐ Wealer | | " |
| Olover Stevens | | " | Amaziah Palmeter | | " |
| Edward Bow | | 24 | Walter Whaling | | " |
| Obel Fellows | | 29 | Zadock Hawley | | " |
| Josiah Cleveland | | 24 | Joseph Foot | March | 5 |
| Ananias Pauridge | | " | Abner Spencer | Febʸ | 27 |
| Samuel Pierce | | " | Paulis Abune | | " |
| John Green | | 29 | Jonas Cleveland | Apˡ | 13 |
| William Chamber | | 24 | Phineas Stephens | Febʸ | 5 |
| Samuel Fitch | | 29 | Simeon Heath | | 15 |
| Zebulon Stevens | | 24 | Sam¹¹ Fellow | March | 2 |
| David Preston | Febʸ | 15 | Seth Raymond | | 8 |
| Benjᵃ Stevens | | 19 | John Evens | | 2 |
| Jehial Burr | | 15 | Enos Lyon | | 12 |
| Elias Lee | | 19 | John Harrington | | " |
| Aaron Lawrence | Janʸ | 24 | Joseph Henderson | | 19 |
| John Squier | | 29 | John McGoon | | 22 |
| Benjᵃ Hewit | Febʸ | 26 | Ebenʳ Evert Foot | | 5 |
| Epheram Hewit | | 27 | | | |

[*Connecticut Historical Society.*]

## CAPT. AUSTIN'S COMPANY.

A Pay Role of Cap! Aaron Austin's Comp^y being the 3^rd Comp^y in Colo^ll Charles Burrells Battalion. We the Subscribers whose Names are Underwritten having Enter'd & Enlisted ourselves into the Connecticut Battallion Rais'd by Virtue of the Governors Proclamation dated the 19^th of Jan^y 1776, under the Command of Colo^ll Charles Burrell to Reinforce the Northern Army Ack^s to have Rec^d of Epap^s Bull, duputy Paymaster to Said Battallion the Sums Affixt to our Names who have Sign'd hereunto for our first Months pay Bounty & pay for Blankets & Napsacks as Carryed out in the Collum of Am^t Witness our hands   March 1776.

| Names & Quality | Time Enlisted | | Names & Quality | Time Enlisted | |
|---|---|---|---|---|---|
| Cap^t Aaron Austin | Jan^y | 19 | Benajah Abro, Negro | | 10 |
| Moses Shepard Liu^t | | 23 | Benj^n Abro, Negro | | " |
| Asahel Hodge Lieu^t | | 23 | Benj^n Ball | | 1 |
| William Steel Ensign | | " | Thomas Gardiner | | 8 |
| James Benham Ser | Feb^y | 1 | James Pike | | 6 |
| James Austin Serg^t | | 1 | Dan^ll Fisher | | " |
| John Alford " | | 1 | Jesse Ives | | 6 |
| Seth Spencer " | | 6 | Usebius Austin | | 6 |
| Abraham Catting Cor^l | | " | Jn^o Sweet | | 6 |
| Zamri Skinner " | | " | James Spencer | | 6 |
| Leveret Kellogg " | | " | David Humphrey | | 20 |
| Normand Filer " | | " | George Frazier | | 12 |
| Elias Benham drumer | | " | Jn^o Marr | | 12 |
| Matthias Hurlburt fifer | | " | Josiah Russel | | 8 |
| Aaron Fay | | " | Abraham Coval | | 6 |
| Eli Andrus | | 6 | Abel Tyler | | 6 |
| Job Marsh | | 8 | Ezra Spencer | | 6 |
| Benj^n Frizby | | 9 | Joseph Kellogg | | 6 |
| Martin Wilcox | | 7 | Asa Griswold | | 10 |
| Benj^n Gaylord | | 1 | Hamlin Jonson | | 8 |
| Isaac Bradly | | 8 | Joshua Thomson | | 1 |
| Nehemiah Merrells | | 6 | Benj^n Barber | | 8 |
| Jn^o Hale | | 8 | White Griswold | | 10 |
| W^m Seymour | | 6 | Jn^o Matthews | | 8 |
| Reuben Warren | | 9 | Eliphelet Alford | | 8 |
| Dan^ll Kelcy | | 8 | Jabez Frisby | | 8 |
| W^m Taylor | | 10 | Elijah Scott | | 1 |
| Martin Kellogg | | 10 | Elijah Loomis | | 6 |
| Jn^o Steel | | 8 | Joseph Hally | | 9 |
| Roderick Hopkins | | 6 | Enos Scott | | 1 |
| George Hopkins | | " | Joel Castel | | 9 |
| Noah Kellogg | | 6 | Amasa Scott | | 6 |
| Benj^n Parsons | | 9 | Seth Meacham | | 9 |
| Hezekiah Olcott | | 6 | Moses Nash | Ma^ch | 25 |
| John Stanclift | | 6 | John Nearing | | 20 |
| Sam^ll Pike | | 6 | Phinehas Shepard | | 25 |
| Joseph Ives | | 6 | David Goff | | 24 |
| Elias Merrells | | 10 | Ezra Edgcomb | | 26 |
| Jonas Webb | | 1 | | | |

[*Connecticut Historical Society.*]

## CONTINENTAL REGIMENTS, 1776.

## CAPT. STODDARD'S COMPANY.

A Pay Role of Cap[t] Luther Stoddard's Company being the 6[th] Company in Colo[ll] Charles Burrells Battallion. We the Subscribers whose Names are underwritten having Enter'd into & Enlisted ourselves into the Connecticut Battallion Rais'd by virtue of the Governor's Proclamation dated the 27 day of Jan[y] 1776, under the Command of Colo[ll] Charles Burrell to Reinforce the Northern Army Acknowledge to have Rec[d] of Epap[s] Bull duputy Paymaster to Said Battallion the Sums affixt to our Names who have Sign'd hereunto for our first Months Pay Bounty & Pay for Blankets & Knapsacks as carryed out in the Collum of Am[t] Witness our hands. Feb[y] 1776 —

| Names & Quality | Time Enlisted | | Names & Quality | Time Enlisted | |
|---|---|---|---|---|---|
| Luther Stoddard Cap[t] | Jan[y] | 19 | Elezar Fuller | Jan[y] | 29 |
| Eleazer Claghorn 1 Liu[t] | | 23 | Joseph Culver | Feb | 11 |
| Tho[s] Converse Lieu[t] | | 23 | Benjamin Everest | | 6 |
| John Hollenbeak Ensign | | 23 | Timothy Holabird Ju[r] | | 7 |
| William Paterson Serg[t] | Feb[y] | 6 | Nethaniel Root | | 9 |
| Rufus Whitney Serg[t] | | 2 | Moses Bishop | | 8 |
| Sam[ll] Richmond | | " | Jasper Grinnel | | 9 |
| Asahel Kellogg Serg[t] | | 7 | Rial Bingham | | 7 |
| Oliver Church Corpo[l] | | 2 | Ebenezar Burch | | 2 |
| Michael Brooks | | " | Aaron Curtice | | 7 |
| Edmund Grandey Corp[l] | | 8 | Eleanah Cleavland | | 7 |
| John McClean Drum[r] | | 2 | Joseph Cowles | | 7 |
| Jacob McClean fifer | Jan[y] | 29 | Samuel Wilcox | | 7 |
| Charles Evarts Clerk | Feb[y] | 7 | William Robartson | | 16 |
| Samuel Kelsey | | 8 | Robert Whitcomb | | 2 |
| Ebur Evarts | | 7 | Elisha Mix | | 8 |
| Stephen Hawley | | " | John Musson | | 22 |
| Thomas Edwards | | 2 | Seth Hills | Jan[y] | 30 |
| John Rose | | 7 | Nathan Carter | Feb[y] | 12 |
| Isaac Bird | | 6 | John Thomson Ju[r] | Jan[y] | 29 |
| Sylvenus Tousley | | 6 | Ambrous Collins | | " |
| James Bradley | | 6 | Nathan Norton | Feb[y] | 2 |
| Timothy Capen | | 2 | Asher Smith | Jan[y] | 30 |
| Joshua Hide | | 10 | John Grigry | Feb[y] | 4 |
| Samuel Williams | | 6 | Lewis Hinman | | 2 |
| Curtis Chappel | | 2 | George Deer | | 8 |
| Billy Blinn | | 7 | James Rogers | | 21 |
| Samuel Waterhouse | | 8 | Dan[ll] Cady | | " |
| Fraderick Stevens | | 6 | Jonathan Sweet | | 18 |
| Isaac Hugg | | 8 | Tho[s] E. Munson | | 9 |
| Jesse Bishop | | " | Isaac Trowbridge | | 22 |
| Elenezar Birck | | 2 | Jonathan Richmond | | 12 |
| William Hinsdale | | 7 | Asaph Nichols | | 21 |
| Jesse Grandey | | 7 | Champion Ackly | | 11 |
| Joshua Jewell Ju[r] | | 2 | Isaac Smith | | 2 |
| Elisha Everest | | 6 | Benj[a] Vaughn | | 7 |
| Joseph Hawley | | 7 | Noah Nichols | | 8 |
| Russell Hunt y[e] 2[d] | | " | Jonathan Chipman | | 6 |
| Billy Munger Ju[r] | | 2 | Dan[ll] Wilcox | Jan[y] | 29 |
| Abraham Barthrong | | " | Jonathan Ensign | Feb[y] | 7 |
| William Blinn | | 7 | Robert Jones Ju[r] | | 18 |
| Elijah Marsh | | 17 | Jn[o] Prevett | March | 8 |
| Joel Tuttle | | 20 | Niel McNiel | Ap[l] | 15 |
| Timothy Woodford | | 7 | Francis Freeland | | " |
| Henry Hull | | 2 | Elijah Collins | Feb[y] | 28 |
| Daniel Fuller | | 6 | | | |

[*Connecticut Historical Society.*]

## CAPT. PARMELEE'S COMPANY.

A Pay Role of Cap$^t$ Oliver Parmelee's Comp$^y$ being the 7$^{th}$ Comp$^y$ in Colo$^{ll}$ Charles Burrell's Battallion — We the Subscribers whose Names are underwritten having Enter'd & Enlisted ourselves into the Connecticut Battallion Rais'd by Virtue of the Governors Proclamation dated the 27$^{th}$ of Jan$^y$ 1776, under the Command of Colo$^{ll}$ Charles Burrell, to Reinforce the Northern Army Ack$^g$ to have Rec$^d$ of Epap$^s$ Bull duputy Paymaster to 8$^d$ Battallion, the Sums Affixt to our Names who have Sign'd hereuntoo for our first Months Pay Bounty Pay for Blankets and Napsacks, as Carryed out in the Collum of Am$^t$ Witness our hands    March 1776 —

| Names & Quality | Time Enlisted | | Names & Quality | Time Enlisted | |
|---|---|---|---|---|---|
| Oliver Parmelee Cap$^t$ | Jan$^y$ | 19 | Jonah Goram | | 8 |
| Nathan Stoddard Lu$^t$ 1$^{st}$ | | 23 | Gideon Nichols | | " |
| Asahel Hurd Liut. | | 23 | Sam$^{ll}$ Galpen | | " |
| Reub$^n$ Calkin Ens | | 23 | Elijah Northrup | | 26 |
| Sam$^{ll}$ Peet  Serj$^t$ | Feb$^y$ | 8 | John Hally | | " |
| Stephen Spary | " | " | Dan$^{ll}$ Taylor | | 8 |
| James Smith | " | " | Caleb Whealer | | 26 |
| Michael Goodrich | | 4 | Amos Clark | | " |
| Dan$^{ll}$ Tucker Cor$^{ll}$ | | 8 | James Hannah | | 26 |
| Asahel Weller | " | " | David Runnell | | 29 |
| W$^m$ Torrence | " | " | Abraham Hill | | 10 |
| Charles Jennings | " | 4 | Philip Shattuck | | 4 |
| Eli Baldwin drum$^r$ | | 8 | Hezekiah Churchell | Ma$^h$ | 2 |
| Justus Gregroy fifer | Mar$^h$ | 1 | Noah Turrell | Feb$^y$ | 8 |
| William Beamont | Feb$^y$ | 16 | Ezckal Slate | | 6 |
| Benj$^a$ Peet | | 26 | Asahel Bissel | | 10 |
| Dan$^{ll}$ Tucker Ju$^r$ | | 8 | Elisha Goodrich | | 6 |
| Jeremiah Finch | | 26 | Matthew Parker | | 18 |
| Josiah Sweet | | 16 | Elijah Brace | | 4 |
| Stephen Smith | | 26 | Nath$^{ll}$ Richards | | 10 |
| Caleb Nichols | | 9 | Elisha Calkins | | 4 |
| Dan$^{ll}$ Dudly | | 26 | Dan$^{ll}$ Elmer Ju$^r$ | Ma$^h$ | 1 |
| John Root | | 8 | Elnathan Botsford | Feb$^y$ | 4 |
| Jn$^o$ Barns Ju$^r$ | | 26 | Amos Weller | | 10 |
| Reuben Smith | | 8 | W$^m$ Page | | " |
| Dan$^{ll}$ Warner | " | " | Thos Wainwright | | " |
| Robert Warner | " | " | Heman Gibbs | | 4 |
| Abijah Stoddard | " | " | John Doud | | 6 |
| Jn$^o$ Baldwin | " | " | John Sawyer | | 5 |
| Simeon Taylor | Feb$^y$ | 8 | Sam$^{ll}$ Hurlburt Ju$^r$ | | 10 |
| Dan$^{ll}$ Brown | | 26 | Dan$^{ll}$ Elmer Ju$^r$ | Ma$^h$ | 1 |
| Phinhas Hill | | 9 | Isaac Fisher | Feb$^y$ | 4 |
| Rich$^d$ Dale | March | 11 | Jn$^o$ Clark | Ma$^h$ | 1 |
| Cyrenus Stodard | Feb$^y$ | 9 | Sam$^{ll}$ Holms | | 1 |
| Josiah Churchell | Ma$^h$ | 2 | Joshua Culvar | Feb$^y$ | 4 |
| Thaddeus Stoddard | Feb$^y$ | 8 | Jonathan Norris | Ma$^h$ | 1 |
| Aner Adee | | 9 | Aaron Culver | Feb$^y$ | 4 |
| Dan$^{ll}$ Stilson | " | " | Preston Halbisk [?] | | 26 |
| Benj$^a$ Avery | " | " | W$^m$ Norton | | " |
| Michael Robbin | | 15 | Justice Hurd | | " |
| John Fitz Gerald | | 26 | John Hurd | | " |
| Tho$^s$ Munn | | 8 | Joshua Hurd | | " |
| Josiah Hooker | | 26 | Phinehas Clark | | " |
| W$^m$ Lamphear | | 10 | | | |

[*Connecticut Historical Society.*]

CONTINENTAL REGIMENTS, 1776.

## CAPT. WATSON'S COMPANY.

A Pay Role of Capᵗ Titus Watson's Compʸ being the 8ᵗʰ Compʸ in Colˡˡ Charles Burrell's Battallion — We the Subscribers whose Names are underwritten having Enter'd into & Enlisted ourselves into the Connecticut Battallion Rais'd by virtue of the Governor's Proclamation dated the 27ᵗʰ of Janʸ 1776 under the Command of Colˡˡ Charles Burrell to Reinforce the Northern Army, Ackˢ to have Recᵈ of Epapᵗ Bull deputy Paymaster to 8ᵈ Battallion the Sums Affixt to our Names, who have Sign'd hereunto for our first Months pay Bounty & pay for Blankets & Napsacks as Carryid out in the Collum of Amᵗ Witness our hands — March 1776 —

| Names & Quality | Time Enlisted | | Names & Quality | Time Enlisted | |
|---|---|---|---|---|---|
| Titus Watson Capᵗⁿ | Janʸ | 19 | Samuel Wolcott | Febʸ | 16 |
| Andrew Moor 1ˢᵗ Lᵗ | | 23 | Amos Phelps | Janʸ | 29 |
| John Rily 2ᵈ Lᵗ | | 23 | Asahel Case | Febʸ | 6 |
| Charles Wright Enⁿ | | 23 | Samˡˡ Mills Juʳ | | " |
| Elkanah Phelps Serjᵗ | Febʸ | 1 | Nathaniel Balcam | | " |
| Jarad Abernethy " | | " | Eli Filley | | " |
| Joseph Butler Serjᵗ | | " | Joseph Jones | | 1 |
| Josiah Whitney " | | " | Abram Knap | | 16 |
| Thos Curtis Corporal | | " | Caleb Aspenwall | Janʸ | 29 |
| Adam Mott " | | " | Levi Hotchkiss | Febʸ | 16 |
| Stephen North " | | 6 | Joel Grant | | 1 |
| David Wright " | | 1 | Amasa Parker | Janʸ | 29 |
| Silas Seward fifer | | " | Justus Squier | Febʸ | 1 |
| Isaac Williams | | 6 | Charles Walter | | " |
| Heman Watson | | 1 | Jonathan Wheaten | | 6 |
| Joseph Preston | | 3 | Seth Hill | | " |
| Benjamin Murooy | | 24 | Jonathan Deming | | " |
| Thomas Wiar | | 1 | Hose Willocks Juʳ | | 1 |
| Nathaniel Clark | Janʸ | 29 | Abel Butler | | 6 |
| Ambrose Beech | Febʸ | 6 | Seth North | | 6 |
| Jonathan Munger | | 1 | William Gillit | | 1 |
| Ichabod Tuttle | | " | Joel Hamblen | Janʸ | 29 |
| Samˡˡ Kellogg | | " | John Bristoll Jr | Febʸ | 1 |
| Nathaniel Field | | " | Samuel Barden | | 16 |
| Seth Hayden | | " | Robert Macksun | | 16 |
| Israel Beech | | " | Joseph Phelps | | 1 |
| Jacob Williams | | 6 | Joseph Knap | | " |
| Gibbens Wentworth | Janʸ | 29 | Asa Hewit | | " |
| Shuble Wentworth | Febʸ | 26 | John Walter | | " |
| Brotherton Seaward | Janʸ | 29 | Thomas Johnson | Janʸ | 29 |
| Wait Deming | Febʸ | 6 | Edward Fuller | | " |
| Stephen Goodwin Junʳ | | 1 | Roger Orvis | Febʸ | 6 |
| Rufus Thrall | | 15 | Simeon Mills | March | 5 |
| Bille Hatch | Janʸ | 29 | Abjah North | Febʸ | 6 |
| Samuel Gaylord | Febʸ | 6 | Chester Bingham | Janʸ | 29 |
| Isaac Butler | Janʸ | 29 | John Clark | | " |
| Elijah Pettibon | | " | John Curtis | | " |
| John Gillit | Febʸ | 26 | Reuben Wilkinson | Febʸ | 6 |
| Serajah Comstock | Janʸ | 29 | Seth Stanard | | " |
| Nicholas Holt | | " | Martin Allen | | " |
| Wᵐ Leech | | " | Darius Gibbs | | " |
| Alexander Leech | | " | Spencer Gibbs | | " |
| Moses Turner | Febʸ | 26 | Abel Norton | | " |
| Samˡˡ Bishop | | 1 | Joel Miller | | " |
| Nathan Tubbs | Janʸ | 29 | Geo. Hudson | | ' |

[*Connecticut Historical Society.*]

## CAPT. THROOPE'S COMPANY.

A Pay Roll of the Company Commanded by Cap'. Benj'. Throope in the Connecticut Battalion, Destined to Serve in the Province of Quebec

| Names | When entered the Service | Names | When entered the Service |
|---|---|---|---|
| Benj'. Throope Captain | | Sherman Gardner Corporal | Jan'y 20 |
| Solomon Story 1st Lieutenant | | Ebenezer Leonard | " |
| Thomas Bill 2nd " | | John Tiffany Jun' " | " |
| Jacob Fox Ensign | | Samuel Loomer Drummer | " |
| Jesse Brown Sergeant | Jan'y 20 | John Lydleman Jun' Fiffer | " |
| John Pember " | " | Ammon Fortune Private | " |
| Frances Fulton " | " | Samuel Davis | " |
| John Avery " | " | Elijah Palmer | " |
| Samuel Lothrop " | " | | |

[*State Library, Hebard Papers.*]

## COL. ELMORE'S REGIMENT.

### CAPT. WOODBRIDGE'S COMPANY.

*[See Record of Connecticut Men in the Revolution, page 113.]*

A Pay Roll of Cap$^t$ Theodore Woodbridge' Company in Col Elmores in the Service of the United States of America — From the 16$^{th}$ Day of April 1776 — to the 31$^{st}$ Day of July both Days included

| Officers Non Commission:d Officers & Privates Names | | Time of Inlisting or Reingageing | in what Company last Campaign | Number of Days in Service |
|---|---|---|---|---|
| Theodore Woodbridge Cap$^t$ | | april 16$^{th}$ 1776 | | 107 |
| Uriah Church First Lieut | | " | Cap$^t$ Woodbridge | 107 |
| Samuel Elmore 2$^d$ Lieut | | " | | 107 |
| Trial Tanner Ensign | | " | Cap$^t$ Woodbridge | 107 |
| James Doal Serj$^t$ | | " | " | 107 |
| William Hart " | | " | | 107 |
| Isaac Pardee " | | May 11$^{th}$ | Cap$^t$ Downs | 82 |
| Barnabas Payne " | | June 6$^{th}$ | | 56 |
| John Henderson Corp$^l$ | | Apr 16$^{th}$ | Cap$^t$ Woodbridge | 107 |
| Benjamin Gidding " | | June 6$^{th}$ | | 56 |
| Daniel Driggs " | | " | | 56 |
| Samuel Spencer " | | " | | 56 |
| Titus Allyn | Private | " | | 56 |
| Samuel Benjamin | " | " | | 56 |
| Azariah Bill | " | " | | 56 |
| Simeon Blyn | " | " | | 56 |
| Bartholomew Barret | " | " | | 56 |
| John Bell | " | " | | 56 |
| Thomas Brechin | " | " | | 56 |
| Noah Chappel | " | June 1$^{st}$ | | 61 |
| Silas Crippen | " | June 6$^{th}$ | | 56 |
| Jonathan Culver | " | " | | 56 |
| John Cain | " | " | Cap$^t$ Cooper | 56 |
| John Call | " | April 16$^{th}$ | Cap$^t$ Woodbridge | 107 |
| Joseph Chandler | " | " | " | 107 |
| William Chidester | " | June 6$^{th}$ | | 56 |
| Jonathan Chidester | " | " | | 56 |
| John Doal | " | June 7$^{th}$ | Cap$^t$ Woodbridge | 55 |
| Samuel Dickinson | " | June 6$^{th}$ | | 56 |
| Benjamin Darling | " | " | | 56 |
| Gershom Flagg | " | May 24$^{th}$ | Cap$^t$ Root | 69 |
| David Gold | " | June 6$^{th}$ | | 56 |
| John Goodrich | " | " | | 56 |
| Samuel Hall | " | April 16$^{th}$ | Cap$^t$ Woodbridge | 107 |
| Ebenezer Hastings | " | " | " | 107 |
| John Harrison | " | " | " | 107 |
| Erastus Hills | " | June 6$^{th}$ | | 56 |
| John Hubbart | " | " | | 56 |
| Seth Hamilton | " | " | | 56 |
| Phinehas Kingsbery | " | June 1$^{st}$ | | 61 |

| Officers Non Commission:d Officers & Privates Names | | Time of Inlisting or Reingageing | in what Company last Campaign | Number of Days in Service |
|---|---|---|---|---|
| Ebenezer Leech | Private | April 16th | Capt Woodbridge | 107 |
| John Moody | " | May 16th | Capt Parmalee | 77 |
| Abner Manley | " | June 6th | " | 56 |
| Sampson Marble | " | " | " | 56 |
| John Manley | " | " | " | 56 |
| David Rood | " | | | |
| William Ruston | " | " | | 56 |
| David Rice | " | " | | 56 |
| Thomas Watkins | " | April 16th | Capt Woodbridge | 107 |
| Levi Waller | " | June 6th | | 56 |
| Samuel Willcocks | " | " | | 56 |
| Samuel Wire | " | May 24th | Capt Woodbridge | 69 |
| Austen Wells | " | June 6th | | 56 |
| James Warren | " | " | | 56 |
| Thomas Tibbals Drumr | | April 16th | Capt Woodbridge | 107 |
| Joseph Gilbert Fifer | | June 6th | | 56 |

Capt Theodore Woodbridg — his Account Current with United States.
Augt 19th 1776 To Majr General Schuylers Warrant on the Pay Master general — £429 = 11 .. 6 .. ⅔
To Jonathan Trumble Jur Esqr P. M. genll in N. York Department

Sr:

Be Pleased to pay unto Capt Theodore Woodbridge the Sum of four hundred twenty-nine pounds eleven Shillings Six pence two thirds of one penny N. York Curency for which payment this with his Receipt thereon Endowed Will be to you Sufficient Voucher

Given under my hand at head Quarters
Albany Augt 19-1776

[*Connecticut Historical Society*.]

## CAPT. WOODBRIDGE'S COMPANY.

A Roll of Cap$^t$ Woodbridgs Company in Co$^{ll}$ Elmores Reg$^t$ for Overplus Bounty Inlisted upon Gen$^{ll}$ Worsters Order Given in Canada : Albany Aug$^t$ 24$^{th}$ 1776

| Mens Names | | Overplus Money for Bounty | Mens Names | | Overplus Money for Bounty |
|---|---|---|---|---|---|
| James Doal | Serj$^t$ | £0 16/ 0d. | Samuel Dickenson | Private | 16/ |
| William Hart | " | 16/ | Benjamin Darling | " | 16/ |
| Isaac Pardee | " | 16/ | Gershom Flagg | " | 16/ |
| Barnebas Payne | " | 16/ | David Gold | " | 16/ |
| John Henderson | Corp$^l$ | 16/ | John Goodrich | " | 16/ |
| Benjamin Giddings | " | 16/ | Sam$^{ll}$ Hall | " | 16/ |
| Sam$^{ll}$ Spencer | " | 16/ | Ebenezer Hastings | " | 16/ |
| Daniel Driggs | " | 16/ | John Harrison | " | 16/ |
| Thomas Tibbals | Drum$^r$ | 16/ | Erastus Hills | " | 16/ |
| Joseph Gilbert | Fifer | 16/ | John Hubbert | " | 16/ |
| Titus Allen | Private | 16/ | Seth Hambleton | " | 16/ |
| Sam$^{ll}$ Benjamin | " | 16/ | Phinehas Kingsbury | " | 16/ |
| Azariah Bill | " | 16/ | Ebenezer Leech | " | 16/ |
| Simeon Blyn | " | 16/ | John Moody | " | 16/ |
| Bartholomew Barret | " | 16/ | Abner Manley | " | 16/ |
| John Bell | " | 16/ | Sampson Marble | " | 16/ |
| Tho$^s$ Brechan | " | 16/ | John Manly | " | 16/ |
| Noah Chappel | " | 16/ | William Ruston | " | 16/ |
| Silas Crippan | " | 16/ | David Rice | " | 16/ |
| Jonathan Colver | " | 16/ | Thomas Watkins | " | 16/ |
| John Cain | " | 16/ | Levi Waller | " | 16/ |
| John Call | " | 16/ | Sammuel Wilcox | " | 16/ |
| Joseph Chandler | " | 16/ | Sam$^{ll}$ Wire | " | 16/ |
| William Chidester | " | 16/ | Austin Wells | " | 16/ |
| Jonathan Chidester | " | 16/ | James Warren | " | 16 |
| John Doal | " | 16/ | | | |

[*Connecticut Historical Society.*]

# CONNECTICUT LINE 1777-1781.

## OFFICERS.

[*See Record of Connecticut Men in the Revolution, pages 145-830.*]

The Arrangement of the Connecticut Line
Arrangement of the Connecticut Line rec<sup>d</sup>
P Brown 8<sup>d</sup> Oct<sup>r</sup> 79

### First Regiment

| Rank | | Names | | Date of Commissions |
|---|---|---|---|---|
| Colonel | | Josiah Starr | | 27<sup>th</sup> of May 1777 |
| L<sup>t</sup> Col<sup>o</sup> | | David F. Sill | | 5<sup>th</sup> of March 1777 |
| Major | | Chris<sup>r</sup> Darrow | | 15<sup>th</sup> April " |
| Captains | 1 | Eliphalet Holmes | | 1<sup>st</sup> January 1777 |
| | 2 | John Shumway | | " " |
| | 3 | Will<sup>m</sup> Richards | | " " |
| | 4 | Ithamar Harvey | | 1<sup>st</sup> of January 1778 |
| | 5 | Ebenezer Perkins | | " " |
| | 6 | Ezra Selden | | " " |
| Cap<sup>t</sup> Lieu<sup>t</sup> | | Enoch Reed | | 1<sup>th</sup> June 1778 |
| Lieut | 1 | Henry Hill | | 1<sup>st</sup> Janu<sup>y</sup> 1777 |
| | 2 | David Dorrance | | " 1778 |
| | 3 | Richard Douglass | | " " |
| | 4 | John Tiffany | | 6<sup>th</sup> Feb<sup>ry</sup> " |
| | 5 | Will<sup>m</sup> Colfax | | 18<sup>th</sup> March " |
| | 6 | James Lord | | 1<sup>st</sup> June " |
| | 7 | Simeon Avery | | " " |
| | 8 | Ezra Lee | | " " |
| Ensigns | 1 | Darius Peck | to rank as 2<sup>d</sup> Lieut 6<sup>th</sup> Feb<sup>ry</sup> " |
| | 2 | Ichabod Spencer | " | 29<sup>th</sup> May " |
| | 3 | Rufus B. Able | " | 1<sup>st</sup> June " |
| | 4 | Tho<sup>s</sup> Anderson | " | " " |
| Ensigns | 5 | Will<sup>m</sup> Tracy | | 30<sup>th</sup> July 1777 |
| | 6 | Robert Allen | | 1<sup>st</sup> November " |
| | 7 | Reuben Saunderson | | 29<sup>th</sup> Decemb<sup>r</sup> " |
| | 8 | Josiah Tiffany | | 1<sup>st</sup> Jan<sup>y</sup> 1778 |
| | 9 | Joseph Fellows | | 1<sup>st</sup> June " |
| Adjutant | | Simeon Avery | | |
| P. Master | | James Lord | | |
| Q. Master | | Ezra Lee | | |
| Surgeon | | Albigence Walds | | |
| Mate | | Sam<sup>l</sup> Brown | | |

## Second Regiment

| Rank | | Names | | Date of Commissions |
|---|---|---|---|---|
| Colonel | | Zebulon Butler | | 13th March 1778 |
| Lt Colonel | | Isaac Sherman | | 1st Jany 1777 |
| Major | | Ames Walbridge | | 27th May " |
| Captain | 1 | Ichabod Hinckley | | 1st Jany " |
| | 2 | David Parsons | | " " |
| | 3 | Stephen Betts | | " " |
| | 4 | Erastus Wolcott | | 27th May " |
| | 5 | James Beebe | | 25th Decr " |
| | 6 | Henry TenEyck | | 13th May 1778 |
| Capt Lieut. | | Roger Alden | | 1st June " |
| Lieutenants | 1 | Benoni Shipman | | 27th May 1777 |
| | 2 | Timothy Taylor | | 1st Septr " |
| | 3 | Moses Cleaveland | | 7th Decemr " |
| | 4 | Peter Robertson | | 25th Decemr " |
| | 5 | James Andrews | | 29th " " |
| | 6 | Solomon Fenton | | 1st May 1778 |
| | 7 | Joseph Austin | | 1st June " |
| | 8 | John Mix | | 16th " " |
| Ensigns | 1 | Isaac Keeler | to rank as 2d Lieut | 27th May 1777 |
| | 2 | Jabez Parsons | " | 1st Septr " |
| | 3 | Eli Barnum | " | 7th Decemr " |
| | 4 | Saml Hicock | | 1st Septr " |
| | 5 | Israel Strong | | 7th Decemr " |
| | 6 | Josiah Buell | | 25th " " |
| | 7 | Willm Linn | | 29th " " |
| P. Master | - | Ichabod Hinckley | | |
| Adjutant | | John Mix | | |
| Qt Master | | Jabez Parsons | | |
| Surgeon | | Noah Coleman | | |
| Mate | | Jonathan G. Graham | | |

## Third Regiment

| Rank | | Names | | Date of Commissions |
|---|---|---|---|---|
| Colonel | | Samll Wyllys | | 1st of Jany 1777 |
| Lt. Colonel | | Thos Grosvenor | | 13th March 1778 |
| Major | | Wills Clift | | 15th Octor " |
| Captains | 1 | Daniel Allen | | 1st Jany 1777 |
| | 2 | Henry Champion | | " " |
| | 3 | Robert Warner | | " " |
| | 4 | John Barnard | | " " |
| | 5 | Wm Judd | | " " |
| | 6 | Edward Eells | | " " |
| Capt Lieut | | Elias Stilwel | | 1st June 1778 |
| Lieutenants | 1 | Jonathan Hart | | 1st Jany 1777 |
| | 2 | Peleg Heath | | " " |
| | 3 | Saml Richards | | " " |
| | 4 | Obadiah Gore | | " " |
| | 5 | Sylvanus Perry | | " " |
| | 6 | Charles Miller | | 14th April 1778 |
| | 7 | Silas Godale | | 25th " " |
| | 8 | Ralph Pomeroy | | 1st June 1778 |
| Ensigns | 1 | Hezekiah Hubbard | to rank as 2 Lieut | 1st Jany 1777 |
| | 2 | Elijah Ransom | " | " " |
| | 3 | Saml Gibbs | " | " " |
| | 4 | Theophilus Woodbridge | " | " " |
| | 5 | Reuben Pride | " | 11th Novr " |
| | 6 | Hezekiah Bailey | " | 14th April 1778 |
| | 7 | Prentis Hosmer | " | 25th " " |

CONNECTICUT LINE, 1777-1781.

| Rank | | Names | Date of Commissions |
|---|---|---|---|
| Ensigns | 8 | Alex<sup>r</sup> M<sup>c</sup>Dowel | 1<sup>st</sup> Jan<sup>y</sup> 1777 |
| | 9 | Will<sup>m</sup> Higgins | 23<sup>d</sup> July " |
| Adjutant | | Jonathan Hart | |
| P. Master | | Sam<sup>l</sup> Richards | |
| Qt Master | | Will<sup>m</sup> Higgins | |
| Surgeon | | John R<sup>d</sup> Watrous | |
| Mate | | Hezekiah Clarke | |

### Fourth Regiment

| Rank | | Names | Date of Commissions |
|---|---|---|---|
| Colonel | | John Durkee | 1<sup>st</sup> Jan<sup>y</sup> 1777 |
| Lt Colonel | | John Sumner | 27<sup>th</sup> May " |
| Major | | Benjamin Throop | 25<sup>th</sup> " 1778 |
| Captains | 1 | John Harman | 1<sup>st</sup> Jan<sup>y</sup> 1777 |
| | 2 | John M<sup>c</sup>Greigur | " " |
| | 3 | Nath<sup>ll</sup> Webb | " " |
| | 4 | Andrew Fitch | " " |
| | 5 | Rob<sup>t</sup> Hallam | 31<sup>st</sup> July " |
| | 6 | Seth Phelps | 25<sup>th</sup> May 1778 |
| Capt Lieut | | Sam<sup>l</sup> Clift | 1<sup>st</sup> June " |
| Lieutenants | 1 | Daniel Wait | 1<sup>st</sup> Janu<sup>y</sup> 1777 |
| | 2 | John Buel | 24<sup>th</sup> July " |
| | 3 | John Durkee | 31<sup>st</sup> " " |
| | 4 | Joseph Chapman | |
| | 5 | Simeon Belding | 25<sup>th</sup> May 1778 |
| | 6 | Pownal Deming | 15<sup>th</sup> Nov<sup>r</sup> " |
| | 7 | Charles Fanning | " " |
| | 8 | Edward Slaxt<sup>r</sup> Coleman | |
| Ensigns | 1 | Will<sup>m</sup> Adams to rank as 2<sup>d</sup> Lieut | 24<sup>th</sup> July 1777 |
| | 2 | Ezra Smith " | 31<sup>st</sup> " " |
| | 3 | Ebenezer Wales " | " " |
| | 4 | Andrew Griswold " | 15<sup>th</sup> Nov<sup>r</sup> " |
| | 5 | Silas Holt " | 13<sup>th</sup> Jan<sup>y</sup> 1778 |
| | 6 | Lebbeus Loomis " | 1<sup>st</sup> March " |
| Ensigns | 7 | Diah Hartshorn | 31<sup>st</sup> July 1777 |
| | 8 | Elias Robinson | 27<sup>th</sup> Decem<sup>r</sup> " |
| | 9 | James Hyde | " " |
| Adjutant | | Lebbeus Loomis | |
| Pay Master | | Will<sup>m</sup> Adams | |
| Qt Master | | Joseph Chapman | |
| Surgeon | | David Adams | |
| Mate | | Jonathan Knight | |

### Fifth Regiment

| Rank | | Names | Date of Commissions |
|---|---|---|---|
| Colonel | | Philip Burr Bradly | 1<sup>st</sup> Jan<sup>y</sup> 1777 |
| Lt Col<sup>o</sup> | | Jonathan Johnson | 15<sup>th</sup> April 1778 |
| Major | | Albert Chapman | 5<sup>th</sup> March " |
| Captain | 1 | Abner Prior | 1<sup>st</sup> Jan<sup>y</sup> 1777 |
| | 2 | Joseph Allen Wright | " " |
| | 3 | Josiah Lacy | " " |
| | 4 | Sam<sup>l</sup> Hait | " " |
| | 5 | Will<sup>m</sup> Greene | 17<sup>th</sup> March 1778 |
| | 6 | John St John | 25<sup>th</sup> May " |
| Capt Lieut | | Thaddeus Weed | 1<sup>st</sup> June " |
| Lieutenant | 1 | Elizah Chapman | 1<sup>st</sup> Jan<sup>y</sup> 1777 |
| | 2 | James Morris | " " |
| | 3 | David Strong | " " |
| | 4 | Roger Wadsworth | " " |
| | 5 | Edward Palmer | " " |

| Rank | | Names | | Date of Commissions |
|---|---|---|---|---|
| | 6 | Hezekiah Rogers | | 12th July 1777 |
| | 7 | Cornelius Higgins | | 17th March 1778 |
| | 8 | Thaddeus Keeler | | 25th May " |
| Ensigns | 1 | Cornelius Russel | to rank as 2d Lt | 15th Decemr 1777 |
| | 2 | Nehemiah Gerham | " | " " |
| | 3 | Othniel Clark | " | 1st Jany 1778 |
| | 4 | Willm Henshaw | " | 4th " " |
| | 5 | Daniel Bradly | " | 13th " " |
| | 6 | Job Smith | " | 9th May " |
| | 7 | Jasper Mead | " | 1st June " |
| Ensigns | 8 | Saml Deforest | | 15th Decemr 1777 |
| | 9 | David Beach | | 4th Jany 1778 |
| Adjutant | | Hezekiah Rogers | | |
| P. Master | | Willm Henshaw | | |
| Qt Master | | Jasper Mead | | |
| Surgeon | | Sempson | | |

### Sixth Regiment

| Rank | | Names | | Date of Commissions |
|---|---|---|---|---|
| Colonel | | Return Jonan Meigs | | 12th May 1777 |
| Lt Colonel | | Ebenezer Gray | | 15th Octor 1778 |
| Major | | Eli Levenworth | | 18th Septr 1777 |
| Captains | 1 | Jonas Prentice | | 1st Jany " |
| | 2 | Joseph Mansfield | | " " |
| | 3 | Elijah Humphry | | " " |
| | 4 | David Humphry | | " " |
| | 5 | Elisha Ely | | " " |
| | 6 | Eleazer Claghorn | | 19th April 1779 |
| Capt Lieut | | Stephen Potter | | " " |
| Lieutenant | 1 | David Starr | | 1st Jany 1777 |
| | 2 | Saml Still   A Barker | | " " |
| | 3 | Asa Lay | | " " |
| | 4 | David Hull | | " " |
| | 5 | Willm Smith | | " " |
| | 6 | John Ball | | 15 Novr 1778 |
| | 7 | Joseph Shaler | | " " |
| | 8 | John Mansfield | | 19th April 1779 |
| Ensigns | 1 | Charles Burret | to rank as 2d Lt | 1st Jany 1777 |
| | 2 | Levi Munson | " | " " |
| | 3 | John Trowbridge | " | " " |
| | 4 | Gideon Bailey | " | " " |
| | 5 | John Sherman | " | 17th Octr 1777 |
| | 6 | Giles Curtiss | " | 15th Novr " |
| | 7 | Elias Mather | " | 15th Novr 1778 |
| | 8 | Thos Farmer | | 15th Febry 1777 |
| Adjutant | | Samuel S. A. Barker | | |
| P. Master | | John Sherman | | |
| Qt Master | | Elias Mather | | |
| Mate | | Theodore Wadsworth | | |

### Seventh Regiment

| Rank | | Names | Date of Commissions |
|---|---|---|---|
| Colonel | | Heman Swift | 1st Jany 1777 |
| Lt Colo | | Hezekiah Holdridge | 25th May 1778 |
| Major | | Theodore Woodbridge | 10th Febry 1778 |
| Captains | 1 | Titus Watson | 1st Jany 1777 |
| | 2 | Stephen Hall | " " |
| | 3 | Aaron Stephens | " " |
| | 4 | Ebenezer Hills | 1st Septr " |
| | 5 | Thos Converse | 3d Novr " |

## CONNECTICUT LINE, 1777–1781.

| Rank | | Names | | Date of Commissions |
|---|---|---|---|---|
| | 6 | Ephraim Chamberlain | | 15th Novr 1778 |
| Capt Lieut | | Caleb Baldwin | | 1st June " |
| Lieutenant | 1 | John Holomback | | 1st Jany 1777 |
| | 2 | Charles Miel | | " " |
| | 3 | Saml Barnum | | " " |
| | 4 | Tryal Tanner | | 1st Septr " |
| | 5 | James Chapman | | 25th Octor " |
| | 6 | Stephen Billings | | 3d Novr " |
| | 7 | Phineas Grover | | 2d Decemr " |
| | 8 | James Barnes | | 15th Novr 1778 |
| Ensigns | 1 | Augustine Taylor | to rank as 2d Lt | 1st Jany 1777 |
| | 2 | Joseph Wilcox | " | 1 Septr " |
| | 3 | Willm Starr | " | 3d Novr " |
| | 4 | Thos Starr | " | 2d Decemr " |
| | 5 | Philemon Hall | " | 10th March 1778 |
| | 6 | Henry Dagget | " | 24th April " |
| Ensigns | 7 | James Bennit | | 1st Septr 1777 |
| | 8 | Talmadge Hall | | 25th Octr " |
| Adjutant | | Trial Tanner | | |
| P. Master | | Augustine Taylor | | |
| Qt Master | | Henry Dagget | | |
| Surgeon | | Launcelot Jacques | | |
| Mate | | Timothy Mather | | |

### Eighth Regiment

| Rank | | Names | | Date of Commissions |
|---|---|---|---|---|
| Colonel | | Giles Russel | | 5th March 1778 |
| Lt Colo | | Joseph Hart | | 18th Septr 1777 |
| Major | | David Smith | | 13th March 1778 |
| Captains | 1 | Saml Mattocks | | 1st Jany 1777 |
| | 2 | Paul Brigham | | " " |
| | 3 | Saml Comstock | | " " |
| | 4 | Theos Manson | | " " |
| | 5 | Nehemiah Rice | | 15th Novr " |
| | 6 | Saml Sanford | | 15th Decr " |
| Capt Lieut | | Daniel Barns | | 1st June 1778 |
| Lieutenants | 1 | Asahel Hodges | | 1st Jany 1777 |
| | 2 | Selah Benton | | " " |
| | 3 | Richard Sill | | 15th Decemr " |
| | 4 | Ephraim Kimberly | | 14th Febry 1778 |
| | 5 | David Judson | | 10th March " |
| | 6 | Nathll Jackson | | 20th " " |
| | 7 | Aaron Benjamin | | 7th May " |
| | 8 | Salmon Hubbel | | 19th May 1779 |
| Ensigns | 1 | John Strong | to rank as 2d Lt | 10th March 1778 |
| | 2 | Levi Hotchkiss | " | 21st " " |
| | 3 | John Hubbard | " | " " |
| | 4 | Eli Curtiss | " | 21st April " |
| Ensigns | 5 | Willm Beaumont | | 15th Decemr 1777 |
| | 6 | James Olmsted | | 24th " " |
| | 7 | Joshua Whitney | | 31st " " |
| Surgeon | | David Holmes | | |
| Mates | | Jedediah Eansworth | | |
| Adjutant | | Asahel Hodges | | |
| P. Master | | Richard Sill | | |
| Qt Master | | Willm Beaumont | | |

Officers on the Supernumerary List — To be especially recommended.

### 1st Regiment
| | |
|---|---|
| 1st Lieut. | Avery |
| 2d Lieut. | Hale |
| 3d Lieut. | Fox |
| 4th Lieut. | Tracy |
| 5th Lieut. | Spencer |

### 2d Reg't
| | |
|---|---|
| 1. Capt. | Manning |
| 2. Ensign | Stewart |

### 3d Reg't
| | |
|---|---|
| 1. Capt. | Abbey |
| 2. Lieut. | Sprague |
| 3. Lieut. | Durkee |

### 4th Reg't
| | |
|---|---|
| 1. Capt. | Bacon |

| | |
|---|---|
| 2. Capt. | Bill |
| 3. Lieut. | Bishop |
| 4. Lieut. | Cleaveland |

### 5th Reg't
| | |
|---|---|
| 1. Capt. | Childs |

### 6th Reg't
| | |
|---|---|
| 1. Capt. | Barker |
| 2. Capt. | Kirtland |
| 3. Lieut. | Potter |
| 4. Lieut. | Robertson |

### 7th Regt
| | |
|---|---|
| 1. Capt. | Beardsly |

### 8th Reg't
| | |
|---|---|
| 1. Capt. | Brown |
| 2. Lieut. | Mack |

[*State Library, Hobard Papers.*]

## PROMOTIONS.

List of promotions in the Conn. Line 1780 1781

| | | |
|---|---|---|
| David Dorrance | Capt. | July 1, 1780 |
| Richard Douglass | Capt. | Aug. 21, 1780 |
| Selah Benton | Capt. | Aug. 21, 1780 |
| Joshua Whitney | Lieut. | Aug. 21, 1780 |
| Richard Sill | Capt. | Apr. 22, 1781 |
| Josiah Tiffany | Lieut. | Apr. 22, 1781 |
| William Fowler | Ens. | Feb. 27, 1781 |
| Aaron Keelor | Ens. | Apr. 22, 1781 |
| Elijah Chapman | Capt. | June 20, 1780 |
| James Morris | Capt. | Apr. 1, 1779 |
| Thadeus Weed | Capt. | Aug. 27, 1780 |
| David Strong | Capt. | May 2, 1781 |
| William Henshaw | Lieut. | June 20, 1780 |
| Samuel DeForest | Lieut. | Aug. 27, 1780 |
| Timothy Allyn | Capt. | Feb. 10, 1781 |
| Nathan H. Whiting | Lieut. | Feb. 10, 1781 |
| Benjamin Dimmick | Lieut. | May 4, 1781 |
| Asa Lay | Capt. | Aug. 28, 1780 |
| Thomas Farmer | Lieut. | Sep. 8, 1780 |
| Elias Robinson | Lieut. | Oct 26, 1780 |
| William Higgins | Lieut. | Oct. 28, 1781 |
| William Lord | Lieut. | Dec. 6, 1781 |

The Gentlemen above named were appointed to the respective Offices annexed to their several Names at the Time specified in the List, as appears from the Minutes & Journal of His Excellency the Governor & Council of Safety.

Test
Jedediah Strong Clerk

[*State Library, Revolution 25.*]

# FIRST REGIMENT—COL. HUNTINGTON.

[*See Connecticut Men in the Revolution, page 145.*]

## CAPT. REED'S COMPANY.

Pay Roll of Cap$^t$ Reeds Company 1$^{st}$ Connecticut Reg$^t$ of Foot Commanded By Col$^o$ Josiah Starr, for November 1779.

| Names | Rank | Remarks |
|---|---|---|
| Enoch Reed | Cap$^t$ | |
| Ichabod Spencer | L$^t$ | |
| John Davol | Srg$^t$ | |
| John West | | |
| Thomas Leeds | Corp$^l$ | |
| David Fellows | | |
| Henry Worden | | |
| Thomas Frink | Drum | |
| James Satterlee | Fife | |
| James Alexander | Privat | |
| George Buttolph | | |
| Abell Brown | | |
| Dan$^l$ Browning | | |
| Sam$^l$ Butler | | |
| Augustus Clark | | |
| Elihu Church | | |
| Simeon Cadwell | | |
| Nathan Cottrill | | |
| Benoney Congdon | | Sick Absent |
| Amos Dennison | | |
| Nath$^l$ Fellows | | |
| James Griffing | | |
| Simon Hubbart | | Sick Absent |
| Thomas Henry | | |
| Hezk$^h$ Ingraham | | |
| W$^m$ Little | | |
| Valentine Lewis | | |
| James Philips | | |
| Oliver Rouse | | |
| Sam$^l$ Shelley | | |
| Dan$^l$ Smith | | |
| Grant Wickwire | | |
| Jo$^s$ Westland | | |
| Wait Worden | | |
| Shubal Cook | | |
| Carpenter Elliss | | |
| Elisha Lord | | Omitted in October |
| Reuben Phelps | | " |
| George Foot | | " |

E. Reed Cap$^t$

[*Connecticut Historical Society.*]

## SHORT TERM LEVIES, 1779.

Return of the Eight Months Men In the 1st Connecticut Regt in the year 1779

| Names | Town | Commencement of Service | Expiration of Service |
|---|---|---|---|
| Eli Starr | N. Milford | Novr 1 | Jany 15 |
| Jno Pulman | Preston | Octr 1 | 15 |
| Asa Woodroof | Hartford | 1 | 15 |
| Monmoth Simons | Horse Neck | 1 | 15 |
| Joseph Hinman | Canaan | 20 | 15 |
| Nathl Morriss | Waterbury | 16 | 15 |
| Elisha Lord | Salisbury | 1 | 15 |
| Reuben Phelps | Simsbury | 1 | 15 |
| George Foot | New Town | 1 | 15 |
| Seth Frink | Sharon | 19 | 15 |
| Jeremiah Fisher | Washington | 19 | 15 |

[*State Library, Revolution 16.*]

## SECOND REGIMENT—COL. BUTLER.

[*See Record of Connecticut Men in the Revolution, page 157.*]

### RETURN, 1779.

Return of the Non Commissioned Officers and Soldiers engaged for the war Specifying the Towns they Belong to and by whom Hired, In the 2nd Connecticut Reg.t Commanded by Zebulon Butler Colonel

| | | | |
|---|---|---|---|
| Nathaniel Booth | Stratford | Robert Chandler | Woodstock |
| Nathan Brown | Norwalk | Silas Phelps | Lyme |
| Joshua Geecocks | Fairfield | | |

Those in Major Walbridges Company

| | | | |
|---|---|---|---|
| Daniel Sherwood | Stratford | William Quirk | Summers |
| Benj.n Cady | Woodstock | Peter Stephens | Killingsworth |
| Amos Fuller | Fradricksburgh | William Taylor | Simsbury |
| John Fuller | Fairfield | Joshua Wheeler | Stafford |
| Nath.l Johnson | Greenfield | | |

Those in Capt Betts Company

| | | | |
|---|---|---|---|
| Aaron St John | Norwalk | Justin St John | Norwalk |
| Isaiah Betts | " | Thomas Black | New heaven |
| Aaron Reymond | " | Joseph Hait | Stanford |
| David Webb | Stanford | Uzual Knap | " |
| John Dickeson | " | Sam.ll Bush | " |
| John Kelley | Litchfield | Hezekiah Bracket | New heaven |
| Assa Hase | Woodbury | Christopher Tully | " |
| Selah Scoffield | Stanford | Joseph Clinton | Norwalk |
| John McNally | " | Thadeous Scofield | " |
| Jacob Wardwell | " | John Downing | Fairfield |

Return of Lieu.t Colonel Haits Company in the 2nd Connecticut Regiment of Foot Commanded by Zebulon Butler Esq.r Col.o of the Non Commis.d Officers and Soldiers who are engaged for the war Dec.r 12th 79

| | | | |
|---|---|---|---|
| Enoch Meriman | Wallingford | Sam.ll Gookins | Suffield |
| Richard Lord | Lyme | Sam.ll Henman | Stratford |
| George Hubard | Tolland | Nero Hawley | " |
| James Downs | Northstatford | Shelden Pater | Woodbury |
| Richard Austin | Suffield | Comma Simons | " |
| John Demmon | Waterbury | John Widger | Sea Brook |
| Daniel Evitt | N Stratford | Benj.n Weed | Stanford |
| Ceasar Edwards | Stratford | Sam.ll Whitney | Stratford |
| James Fuller | Suffield | | |

Return of the Non Commision'd officers and Soldiers Inlisted for the war in Cap.t Parsons Company in the 2nd Connecticut Regiment of Foot Commanded by Zebulon Butler Esq.r Col.o Dec.r 12th 79

| | | | |
|---|---|---|---|
| William Basset | Woodbury | John Avery | Norwalk |
| Abiather Evens | Hartford | David Bullin | Enfield |
| Daniel Winchel | Farmington | John Baker | Fairfield |

| | | | |
|---|---|---|---|
| Moses Ellsworth | East Windsor | Stephen Meeker | Redding |
| Nathan Elwood | Fairfield | Jonath[n] Parsons | Enfield |
| John Jemson | Enfield | Abraham Reymond | Norwalk |
| Patrick Hines | New London | Aaron Tharp | Fairfield |

### Those of Cap[t] Aldens Company

| | | | |
|---|---|---|---|
| Jaquess Harmon | Suffield | Joel Masher | Stratford |
| Thomas Wood | Stanford | Abraham Murry | Woodbury |
| John Downs | Stratford | Sam[ll] Manning | Stratford |
| Abraham Hawley | " | Galloway Peter | Woodbury |
| Abijah Perrey | " | Simeon Rood | Woodbury |
| Nath[ll] Beach | Fairfield | David Rymond | Fairfield |
| Richard Denrary | Stratford | Elijah Spear | Suffield |
| Phineas Granger | Suffield | Elihue Spear | " |
| Nathan Harslen | Stratford | Charles Stwart | Salem |
| David Hurd | " | Benj[n] Waklee | Stratford |
| Brestor Jude | Waterbury | James Shop | Woodbury |
| Peter Lewis | Stratford | Jana Turney | Stratford |
| Benoni Moss | Wallingsford | | |

### Those in Cap[t] Hinckleys Company

| | | | |
|---|---|---|---|
| Jonathan Luce | Tolland | Thomas Wilson | Horse Neck |
| Amos Harris | " | Peter Johnson | New haven |

### Those belonging to Cap[t] Wolcotts Company

| | | | |
|---|---|---|---|
| Caleb Orcutt | Willington | John Churcher | Fairfield |
| John Mitchel | Fairfield | Stephen Ludlow | Sea Brook |
| Gideon Nobels | Willington | William Reymond | Fairfield |
| Moses Allen | Fairfield | Tiras Turkens | Canterbury |
| John Ammit | New haven | Prince Negro | Norwinch |

### Those in Cap[t] Ten Eycks Company

| | | | |
|---|---|---|---|
| Ruben Beach | Stratford | Lewis Hurd | Stratford |
| Nathan Bradley | Fairfield | Abraham Couch | Greenfield |
| Jonah Cushman | Stafford | Joseph Porter | Fairfield |
| William Daskomb | Stratford | Daniel Potter | " |
| Joseph Harrap | Fairfield | Elias Shaw | Woodstock |
| James Hide | " | Jesse S[t] John | Norwalk |

J Hait L[t] Col[o] Com[dt]

[*State Library, Hebard Papers.*]

CONNECTICUT LINE, 1777-1781. 55

## SHORT TERM LEVIES, 1779.

Return of the Eight Months men that belong'd to the 2d Connecticut Regiment Commanded by [          ] 1779
[The expiration of the service of each man is Jany 15]

| Names | Town | Commencement of Service |
|---|---|---|
| Thomas Kettle | Providence R. I. | July 14 |
| Daniel Hoskins | Norfolk | Aug. 20 |
| John Mills | Groton | " |
| Benajah Tracey | Preston | July 14 |
| Daniel Thomas | Lebanon | " |
| Stephen Post | Salisbury | |
| Asa Prissnear | Hartford | " |
| | | 18 |
| Increase Waymend | | 23 |
| Moses Walsore | Harwington | Aug. 23 |
| Solomon Chitingdon | Killingsworth | July 28 |
| Gideon Roberts | Waterbury | Aug. 18 |
| Allen Lain | Middletown | 1 |
| Moses Bradley | N Haven | July 29 |
| Lenard Bishop | Guilford | 27 |
| Benj$^n$ Waters | Symsbury | Aug. 20 |
| Nathan Wordwell | Somers | 4 |
| Jonathan Amedown | Willington | July 5 |
| John Poole | Ashford | 29 |
| David Allen | | Aug. 8 |
| Joshua Hartshorn | Cornwall | July 20 |
| Sam$^l$ Davis | Litchfield | 7 |
| Sam$^l$ Lambart | Harwington | 15 |
| Oliver Gibbs | Cornwall | 15 |
| Benajah Smith | Norwich | Aug. 1 |
| Elnathan Beach | Cornwall | July 26 |
| Elijah Buck | Somers | Aug. 2 |
| Allen Clinton | Norwalk | 18 |
| Daniel Chapin | Somers | 25 |
| John Douning | Fairfield | 18 |
| Alpheus Pease | Somers | July 26 |
| Ruben Stephens | Stamford | Aug. 18 |
| Elijah Sexton | Somers | 24 |
| Joseph Scofield | Cornwall | July 26 |
| Joshua Wedge | Norwich | Aug. 1 |
| Moses Bradley | N Haven | July 27 |
| Caleb Atwater | " | 25 |
| Edward Griswold | Killingsworth | 28 |
| Solomon Evit | Guilford | 27 |
| Nath$^l$ Root | Canaan | Aug. 14 |
| Jeremiah Page | N. London | 8 |
| John Beckwith | " | 8 |
| Thom$^s$ McKnight | E. Windsor | 8 |
| Charles Elsworth | " | July 18 |
| Nath$^l$ Tharp | Fairfield | Oct. 1 |
| Edward Thomson | Symsbury | Aug. 20 |
| Amas Reed | Mansfield | July 31 |
| [   ] Hill | Tolland | Aug. 9 |
| [   ] Atwater | | July 20 |
| [   ] Moory | Killingaley | Aug. 8 |
| [   ] | Woodbury | Oct. 1 |
| [   ] | Ashford | Aug. 8 |
| [   ] | Norwalk | 10 |

| Names | Towns | Commencement of Service |
|---|---|---|
| John Wheeler | Norwalk | 10 |
| Daniel Smith | " | Oct. 12 |
| James Sellick | " | Aug. 14 |
| John Curch | Symsbury | " 20 |
| Increase Brainard | Haddam | July 27 |
| Richard Goff | N. London | Aug. 1 |
| Sam[l] Parlms (?) | Lyme | 1 |
| Ashbel Waller | Cornwall | 1 |
| Hait Scofield | Stamford | 18 |
| Timothy Scofield | Cornwall | 18 |
| Evins Chancy | Killingsworth | 18 |
| W[m] McFall | N. London | 18 |
| Calvin Fuller | Somers | 8 |
| Pierce Boney | Cornwall | July 25 |
| James Thresher | Stafford | Aug. 3 |
| Richard Bogs | Hebron | 3 |
| Benajah Brown | | June 25 |
| John Ausborn | N. Fairfield | Aug. 11 |
| Moses Coay (?) | Tolland | 1 |
| Derias Carlton | " | 1 |
| Tho[s] Foster | Guilford | July 27 |
| Abra[m] Grimes | Cornwall | Aug. 1 |
| Sam[l] Hubbard | Louden Mass. | 25 |
| [ ] | Guilford | 9 |
| Elijah Johnson | Tolland | July 20 |
| John Lade | " | Aug. 1 |
| Jesse Tinker | Haddam | July 27 |
| Jared Tozen (?) | Symsbury | 20 |
| Eli White | Cornwall | 26 |
| Beriah Wright | Symsbury | Aug. 28 |
| Stephen Wedge | Norwich | July 26 |
| [ ] White | Tolland | Sep. 29 |
| [ ] Selleck | Danbury | 1 |
| ]th[l] Ames | Stonington | Aug. 1 |
| Ruben Harrington | Stafford | 14 |
| Jeduthan Dimack | Mansfield | 1 |
| Joseph Newcomb | Lebanon | 1 |
| John Taylor | | 1 |
| James Wood | Scituate R. I. | 1 |

[*State Library, Revolution 16.*]

## THIRD REGIMENT—COL. WYLLYS.

[*See Record of Connecticut Men in the Revolution, page 168.*]

[The Connecticut Historical Society contains a collection of some two hundred interesting documents relating to this regiment, which, however, do not come within the scope of this volume. They are chiefly returns of the men serving in various companies at certain periods, and lists of clothing furnished to individual soldiers. The men signed receipts for each article of clothing, so that the autograph of almost every man in the regiment appears.]

### CAPT. DANIEL ALLIN'S COMPANY.

| Names | Residence | Names | Residence |
|---|---|---|---|
| Serg. Isaac Barrows | Killingly | James Dodge | Colchester |
| " Amasa Brown | Colchester | Will<sup>m</sup> Baker | " |
| " Ezra Beckwith | Windsor | Nicholas Ackley | " |
| " David Gibbs | " | Ezekiel Daniels | " |
| Corp. Sam<sup>l</sup> Allen | Ashford | Champlin Haris | |
| " John Fox | Colchester | Lucius Hulbert | Suffield |
| " W<sup>m</sup> Osborn | Hartford | Mark Filley | E. Windsor |
| " Ebenez<sup>r</sup> Cheeney | Ashford | Thomas Parsons | Windsor |
| Abijah Smith | " | Benj<sup>a</sup> Bawdell | Simsbury |
| William Waters | " | Benj<sup>a</sup> Hayse | " |
| Joshua Isham | Colchester | Jacob Holiday | " |
| Titus Prescott | Ashford | John Lain | Ashford |
| Peletiah Pomroy | Suffield | Joshua Knolton | " |
| Sam<sup>l</sup> Chapman | E. Hadam | Chester Rogers | " |
| John Farrow | Simsbury | Lemuel Barrows | Killingly |
| Robert Hall | Ashford | David Coy | Volintown |
| Peter Smith | " | John Roberts | Colchester |
| John Smith | Mansfield | W<sup>m</sup> Burnham | " |
| John Finigan | Danbury | Nathan Roberts | " |
| Silas Pease | Suffield | Aaron Chamberlin | " |
| Israel Osborn | E. Windsor | Joshua Isham | " |
| John Warren | Bolton | W<sup>m</sup> Isham | " |
| Daniel Wheeler | Suffield | Nehemiah Daniels | " |
| Amos Couch | Farmington | Elezer Russell | Ashford |
| Obadiah Brown | Ashford | Perley Hering | Kilingsley |
| Henry Lyon | " | Elezer Smith | Ashford |
| Caleb Conant | Mansfield | John Wakins | " |
| Nathan Scovil | Colchester | Stephen Eaton | " |
| Hezekiah Marks | Hebron | Jedediah Smith | " |
| Lewis Ackley | Colchester | James Jones | Colchester |
| Ebenez<sup>r</sup> Isham | " | Jonathan Isham | " |
| Elihu Mather | Windsor | John Hambleton | N. Fairfield |

[*Connecticut Historical Society.*]

## CAPT. HENRY CHAMPION'S COMPANY.

| | | | |
|---|---|---|---|
| Henry Champion | Colchester | Henry Evans | E. Hartford |
| Charles Miller | Hartford | Josiah Evans | E. Hartf[d] |
| Theo[s] Woodbridge | Simsbury | Comfort Foster | Windham |
| Amasa Brown | Colchester | Abner French | " |
| Homer Phelps | Hebron | Richard Ferman | Infield |
| Abner Chapman | Colchester | Aaron Fargo | Windsor |
| Abner Mark | Hebron | James Gray | Hartford |
| Daniel Wheeler | Suffield | Sam[l] Glass | Canterbury |
| Henry Brown | New Haven | Asahel Goodrich | Weathersf[d] |
| Joseph Copp | N. London | Champlin Harrison | Colchester |
| Joseph Rouse | Preston | Tho[s] Hill | Pomfret |
| Ezra Ames | " | Jona[th] Hill | " |
| Stephen Brumon | Farmington | James Keeney | E. Hartf[d] |
| Francis Baxter | Windsor | Silas Pease | Suffield |
| Jona[th] Brister | Milford | Comfort Ranney | Middletown |
| Eben[r] Brown | Waterbury | John strong | Chatham |
| John Brown | Coventry | Joseph Starkweather | Killingly |
| Zeph[h] Bates | E. Windsor | Micah Towsley | Suffield |
| Benj[a] Bullen | Union | Alex[r] Tompson | E. Windsor |
| Edw[d] Coburn | Windham | Aaron Ward | Middlet[n] |
| W[m] Chafee | Infield | Elias Wares | Glastenbury |
| W[m] Cook | Middletown | John Wright | Union |
| Ez[l] Daniels | Colchester | James Walker | " |
| Neh[h] Daniels | " | John Warren | Bolton |

[*Connecticut Historical Society.*]

Return of Non Effectives in Cap[t] Henry Champion's Company.

| | | | |
|---|---|---|---|
| Alex[r] M[c]Dowell | Glastenbury | Job Bennet | |
| Eli Bigelow | Colchester | Eph[m] Seeley | |
| David Elgar | E. Hartford | George Delaby | Union |
| W[m] Earl | Pomphret | Levi Loveland | Glastenbury |
| Eliakim Johnson | Wallingford | Levi Otis | N. Haven |

[*Connecticut Historical Society.*]

## CAPT. CHAMPION'S COMPANY.

A Return of the Non Commission'd officers and Soldiers inlisted in Cap[t] Henry Champion's Company in the Regiment Commanded by Col[o] Samuel Wyllys, with the places of their abode, the town for which inlisted & the names of the persons who have hired any of them.

| Names | Term of Inlistment | Place of abode | Casualties |
|---|---|---|---|
| Alex[r] M[c]Dowell | Dur[g] war | Glastenbury | Promoted to an Ens[n] |
| John Parker | 8 Years | Stratford | Deserted |
| [ ][m] Tompson | Dur[g] war | Bolton | |
| Israel Johnson | " | Colchester | |
| Daniel Whiting | " | " | |
| Elisha Brown | 8 Years | " | Dead |
| Patrick Murfey | Dur[g] war | Mass. | Deserted |
| Samuel Coe | 8 Years | Farmington | |
| Levi Frisby | Dur[g] war | Sinsbury | Dead |
| Thomas Collat | " | Farmington | |
| Jared Teuky (?) | " | New Haven | |
| Levi Fox | " | East Haddam | |

## CONNECTICUT LINE, 1777-1781.

| Names | Term of Inlistment | Place of abode | Casualties |
|---|---|---|---|
| John Charley | 8 Years | Killinglee | Dead |
| Josiah Barrows | " | " | Dead |
| Henry Cone | " | East Haddam | |
| David Clark | " | Simsbury | Dead |
| Joseph Andras | " | Chatham | |
| Eliphalet Lord | " | Windsor | |
| Wm Matthews | " | N. Y. State | |
| Zebª Woodruff | " | Farmington | Captivated by the Enemy |
| Micah Towsley | Durg war | Suffield | |
| [ ]siah Lindsey | 8 Years | Farmington | Dead |
| [ ]hn Johnson | " | " | |
| Obadiah Andras | " | " | |
| Stephen Brunson | " | " | |
| Ladwick Hodgkiss | " | " | |
| John Conner | Durg war | | |
| Daniel Powel | " | Hartford | Inlisted in 4th Georgia Battª |
| James A. Johnson | " | " | Deserted |
| Nathll Merrills | " | " | |
| Wm Higgins | 8 Years | Lyme | Promoted to Q M |
| Ezra Ames | Durg war | Norwich | |
| Elijah Mann | " | Mass. | |
| Abijah Gardiner | " | Rhode Island | |
| [ ]ick Thomas | 8 Years | Hartford | |
| Aaron Ward | Durg war | Middletown | |
| Daniel Judd | 8 Years | Colchester | |
| Gardiner Gilbert | " | Hebron | Discharged |
| Abijah Pratt | " | Colchester | |
| John Higgins | Durg war | Chatham | Dead |
| Gideon Cole | 8 Years | Wethersfield | |
| Luke Wadsworth | Durg war | Farmington | |
| Thomas Dick | 8 Years | Norwich | Deserted |
| Ephraim Judd | " | Colchester | |
| Asher Carty | Durg war | " | |
| Abner Chapman | 8 Years | " | |
| Alexr Porter | " | Hebron | |
| James Couch | Durg war | Farmington | Dead |
| Jonathan Bill | 8 Years | Colchester | |
| Hosea Gridley | Durg war | Farmington | |
| Edward Eli | 8 Years | Weathersfield | |
| David Enos | " | Farmington | |
| Elisha Heart | " | " | |
| Tim° Heart | " | " | |
| Seth (?) Knowles | " | Chatham | |
| [ ] Davis | " | Simsbury | Deserted (?) |
| Elisha Harwington | " | " | |
| Zeckry Prince | Durg war | " | |
| Thos Phelps | 8 Years | " | Deserted |
| Saml Lomis | Durg war | Colchester | |
| Eli Bigelow | " | " | |
| Daniel Wright | 8 Years | Glastenbury | |
| Eben' Welch | " | New Hamp. | |
| Reuben Hart | " | Farmington | |
| Charles Wampey | " | " | Dead |

West Point Febr 17th 1778

Henry Champion Capt

[*State Library, Hobard papers.*]

## CAPT. CHAMPION'S COMPANY.

Cap[t] Champion's Return of Officers & men during the war, as P Division Orders of December 7[th] 1779

| Names | Towns | Names | Towns |
|---|---|---|---|
| Henry Champion C[t] | Colchester | Neh[h] Daniels | Colchester |
| Charles Miller L[t] | Hartford | Henry Evans | East Hartford |
| Theo[s] Woodbridge L[t] | Simsbury | Jonah Evans | " |
| Abner Mack Corp[l] | Hebron | Aaron Fargo | Windsor |
| Dan[l] Wheeler " | Suffield | James Gray | Hartford |
| Joseph Copp Drum[r] | New London | Silas Pease | Suffield |
| Joseph Rouse Fifer | Preston | John Strong | Chatham |
| Ezra Ames | " | Micah Towstey | Suffield |
| Jonathan Brester | Milford | Elias Wares | Glastenbury |
| Eben[r] Brown | Waterbury | Aaron Ward | Middletown |
| W[m] Cook | Middletown | John Warren | Glasenbury |
| Ez[l] Daniels | Colchester | Henry Brown Corp[l] | New Haven |

Second River 12[th] Dec[r] 1779

H. Champion Cap[t]

*[State Library, Hebard papers.]*

## CAPT. EELLS' COMPANY.

A Return of Non Commissioned Officers and Soldiers in Cap[t] Edward Eells C[o] in the Reg[t] Commanded By Col[o] Samuel Wyllys with the Place of their abode the term for which Inlisted & the Names of the Persons who have hired any of them

| Names | Term | Place of abode |
|---|---|---|
| Benj[a] Bowers | 8 Years | Chatham |
| Peter Graves | " | Colchester |
| W[m] Combs | D war | |
| David Canida | 8 Years | Glastenbury |
| Benjamin Bowers | " | Chatham |
| Eben[r] Billings | " | Stonington |
| Gideon Chapman | " | Colchester |
| Charles Brown | " | Stonington |
| W[m] Tryon | D war | Weathersfield |
| James Morgain | 8 Years | Colchester |
| Aaron Carter | D war | " |
| James Dewey | " | Middletown |
| Robart Douglass | 8 Years | Colchester |
| Nathan Dodge | " | " |
| Stephen Dart | D war | " |
| David Elger | " | Hartford |
| Joseph Egleston | " | Windsor |
| Jacob Freeman | 8 Years | Colchester |
| Abr[m] Freeman | " | " |
| Joseph McHood | D war | Lyme |
| Dick Loomis | " | Weathersfield |
| Nath[al] Miller | 8 Years | " |
| Dick Molatto | " | " |
| Asahel Newton | " | Colchester |
| Jack Bulkley | D war | " |
| Jn[o] Nickalds | 8 years | Middletown |

## CONNECTICUT LINE, 1777-1781.

| Names | Term | Place of abode | |
|---|---|---|---|
| Syfax Negro | D war | Glastenbury | |
| Newport Negro | " | " | |
| Thos Pilgrim | 8 Years | Colchester | |
| Jno Robison | D war | Middletown | |
| Stephen Ranney | 8 Years | " | |
| Comfort Ranney | " | " | |
| Ezry Tryon | D war | Glastenbury | |
| Thos Watrous | " | Hartford | |
| Elias Wires | " | Glastenbury | |
| Thos Durfey | " | L. I. Prisnor | Inlisted 4 years Regt |
| Dunkin Read | " | Deserter | " |
| Oliver Ocain | " | Weathersfield | Deserted |
| Darby Connel | " | L. I. Prisnor | " |
| Mical McNe[ ] | [ ] | " | " |

[*State Library, Hebard papers.*]

## CAPT. ROBERT WARNER'S COMPANY.

| | | | |
|---|---|---|---|
| Robert Warner | Middletown | John Harris | Middletown |
| Hezekiah Hubbard | " | Charles Loveland | " |
| Daniel Whitney | Colchester | Joseph Lung | " |
| Levi Goodrich | Chatham | Willm Mathews | Farmington |
| Abner Hubbard | Middletown | Daniel Morgan | Middletown |
| Lemuel Potter | Farmington | Charles O. Martin | Chatham |
| Daniel Parks | Chatham | John Oakley | |
| Bethuel Goodrich | " | John Parks | Chatham |
| Jacob Wood Junr | " | Jesper Pratt | Saybrook |
| Huet Alvord | " | Samuel Pierce | Union |
| Abel Abels | " | Thomas Rohds | New Haven |
| David Butler | Middletown | Elijah Royce | Wallingford |
| Thomas Brown | Chatham | Samuel Simmons | Middletown |
| Ephraim Bowers | " | John Stilwell | New Haven |
| Wolcott Burham | Farmington | Josiah Steal | Farmington |
| Samuel Comstock | " | Jonathan Stocking | Chatham |
| Lamberton Clark | Middletown | Solomon Townsand | New Haven |
| Cornelius Dunham | Farmington | Jered Trickey | " |
| John Foster | Middletown | Jonathan Verrey | Chatham |
| David Foster | " | Jacob Wood | " |
| Joseph Graham | Chatham | John Wright | " [N. Y. |
| John Graham | " | Frances Wright | West Chester |
| Jonathan Goff | Middletown | David West | Chatham |
| Samuel Goff | Chatham | William Wickham | " |
| David Hull | Middletown | Benja Welton | Farmington |

[*Connecticut Historical Society.*]

## CAPT. ROBERT WARNER'S COMPANY.

Return of Non effectives who have Serv⁴ in the 4 C⁰ third Connecticut Reg⁴ Since January 1ˢᵗ 1777

| | Rank | When Ingag⁴ in Service | Town from which Inlisted | Trm of Service | Unmarried | Casualties |
|---|---|---|---|---|---|---|
| Elihue Mott | Private | May 26ᵗʰ 77 | Chatham | 8 Years | 1 | Died July 26ᵗʰ 77 |
| Paul Topping | " | Apr¹ 30ᵗʰ 77 | Middletown | " | 1 | died June 26ᵗʰ 77 |
| John Barkley | " | June 6ᵗʰ 77 | Weathersfield | D. Warr | 1 | " Decemʳ 25 78 |
| John McMullin | " | Janʳ 1ˢᵗ 77 | Middletown | 8 Years | 1 | disarted Apr¹ 21ˢᵗ 79 |
| John Towers | " | Febʳ 22ᵈ 77 | Windsor | " | 1 | " Novmʳ 3ᵈ 78 |
| Richard Clark | " | Apr¹ 25ᵗʰ 77 | Middletown | D. War | 1 | " August 8 79 |
| John Grogan | " | June 3ᵈ 77 | Weathersfield | " | 1 | " Sepʳ 22ᵈ 77 |
| Nicholas Charles | " | Janʳ 1ˢᵗ 77 | Hebron | 8 Years | 1 | Died Febʳ 2ᵈ 77 |
| Charles Wallis | " | March 11ᵗʰ 77 | | D. War | 1 | Disarted Apr¹ 2ᵈ 77 |
| Charles Brune | " | " 11ᵗʰ 77 | | " | 1 | " August 12ᵗʰ 77 |
| John Dousal | " | June 3ᵈ 77 | Weathersfield | " | 1 | " 3ᵈ 77 |
| John Hughs | " | " 6ᵗʰ 77 | | " | 1 | " July 9ᵗʰ 77 |
| Livenus Holt | " | Febʳ 28ᵗʰ 77 | Harwinton | " | 1 | died Decemʳ 9ᵗʰ 78 [Married |
| Samuel Smith | " | May 28ᵗʰ 77 | Middletown | D. War. | | Inlisted in 4ᵗʰ George Bat Sepʳ 1ˢᵗ 1777 |

R. Warner Capᵗ

[*Connecticut Historical Society.*]

## FOURTH REGIMENT—COL. DURKEE.

[See Record of Connecticut Men in the Revolution, page 132.]

### SHORT TERM LEVIES, 1777.

A Return of the N° of Eight M° Men that were in Col° Durkees Reg[t] 1777

| Privates Names | | Names of Cap[rs] |
|---|---|---|
| Nath[n] Draper | | Cap[t] Bills |
| John Gary | | " |
| W[m] Burroughs | | " |
| Elijah Smith | | " |
| Tho[s] Cheney | | |
| Jon° Orms | Died 4[th] Dec[r] 1777 | |
| Nath[n] Stowell | Inlist[d] for 3 years 30 Aug[t] | |
| Gideon Waters | Dischg[d] 27 Aug[t] | Cap[t] Harmons |
| Ezekiel King | Died 19 Sep[t] | |
| Daniel Palley | Died 1 Jany 1778 | |
| Zenas Kent | | |
| David Ens | | |
| Caleb Austin | | |
| Medad Pomeroy | | |
| Jo[s] King | | |
| Gideon Waters | | |
| Sam[l] Weaver | | |
| Abram Skinner | | |
| Ovorus Yeomans | | |
| Jon[a] Russell | | |
| Eleaz[r] Skinner | | |
| Sam[l] Pratt | | |
| Joshua Sumner | | |
| Jon[a] Reed | | Cap[t] Webb |
| Benj[a] Fuller | | " |
| Eliph[t] Colburn | | " |
| Jon[a] Webb | | " |
| W[m] Oliv | | |
| Eph[m] Durphee | Died 27 Dec[r] 1777 | |
| George Michal | " 26 Oct. " | |
| Richard Harvey | Enlisted During War 15 May | Cap[t] Lee |
| Ithamer Smith | " " " " | " |
| John Hill | | Cap[t] Fitch |
| Martin Stiles | | " |
| Edward Burns | | " |
| Aaron Hulet | | McGreguiers |
| Jacob Wilson | | " |
| Lem[l] Parkhurst | | " |
| Duthan Parkhurst | | " |
| Ja[s] Hawkins | | " |
| John Almey | | " |
| W[m] C | | " |

| Privates Names | | | Names of Cap$^{ts}$ |
|---|---|---|---|
| Jacob Kinney | | | Bacons |
| Jacob Averil | | | " |
| Jesse Fosset | | | " |
| Stephen Baker | | | " |
| Nahum Cady | | | " |
| Sam$^l$ Wright | | | " |
| Jonathan Cady | | | " |
| Phin$^s$ Stephens | | | " |
| Benj$^a$ Fosset | | | " |
| Ebenez$^r$ Besster | | | " |
| John Ames | Enlist$^d$ | 29 Dec$^r$ | |
| Jo$^s$ Morey | Died 4 | Sep$^t$ | |
| Andr$^w$ Hibberd | Enlist$^d$ | 27 " | |
| Moses Tracy | Enlist$^d$ | 27 " | |
| Sam$^l$ Coburn | Enlist$^d$ | 27 " | |
| Hannibal Bassul | | | |
| Zach$^a$ Waldo | | | Cap$^t$ Hallam |
| Roger Carey | | | |
| Jarod Lilly | | | |
| David Harvey | | | |
| Jesse Kimbal | } these 10 paid 27 Oct 1778 | | |
| Elijah Lilley | | | |
| Eliphas Cleveland | | | |
| Levy Kyesby | | | |
| Elijah Manning | | | |
| Joel Manning | | | |

[*Copy in Comptroller's Office.*]

## SHORT TERM LEVIES, 1779.

Return of the Eight M$^s$ Men that belonged to the 4$^{th}$ Conn$^t$ Reg$^t$ comm$^d$ by John Durkee Col: 1779

| Names | | Commencement of Service | Expiration of Service |
|---|---|---|---|
| Oliver Ladd | Coventry | Sept 20 | Jany 15 |
| David Noiles | Lyme | " 13 | " 15 |
| Jesse Foster | | Aug$^t$ 13 | " 15 |
| Tim$^o$ Tucker | R Island | " 16 | " 15 |
| Jon$^a$ Putney | Killingly | " 16 | " 15 |
| Henry Brown | " | " 16 | " 15 |
| Isaac Sweet | Voluntown | July 27 | " 15 |
| Jesse Childs | Killingly | Aug$^t$ 16 | " 15 |
| Lem$^l$ Falkner | Milford | " 2 | " 15 |
| Obed Gridley | Farmington | July 29 | " 15 |
| Willard Evans | | Aug$^t$ 13 | " 15 |
| Asher Williams | Norwich | Oct 4 | " 15 |
| William Parker | Killingly | " 4 | " 15 |
| John Adams | Coventry | " 1 | " 15 |
| John Howard | Deserted | | |
| Abel Baker | R Island | Aug$^t$ 16 | " 15 |
| John Morris | | June 21 | |
| Dan$^l$ Palmer | Stonington | Aug$^t$ 16 | " 15 |
| Tho$^s$ Condin | Woodstock | " 16 | " 15 |
| Amos Mansfield | N. Haven | July 28 | " 15 |
| Sol$^o$ Wilton | Farmington | " 28 | " 15 |
| W$^m$ Cramer | Saybrook | Aug$^t$ 16 | " 15 |

## CONNECTICUT LINE, 1777-1781.

| Names | | Commencement of Service | Expiration of Service |
|---|---|---|---|
| Isaac Rood | Killingly | Sept 15 | Jany 15 |
| Steph{a} Emerson | | Augt 10 | " 15 |
| Nehem{h} Hulet | Killingly | Sept 21 | " 15 |
| Asa Alger | " | Augt 16 | " 15 |
| Danl Bixbey | " | " 16 | " 15 |
| Moses Bixby | " | " 16 | " 15 |
| John Banford | Farming{tn} | " 2 | " 15 |
| Saml Bishop | Bolton | " 21 | " 15 |
| Lem{l} Foster | R Island | " 16 | " 15 |
| Ambrose Cleavland | " | " 16 | " 15 |
| David Hosmer | Killingly | " 16 | " 15 |
| Basok Heath | " | " 16 | " 15 |
| Lewis Leach | R. Island | " 16 | " 15 |
| Eph{m} Page | Branford | July 20 | " 15 |
| Silas Taft | Killingly | Augt 16 | " 15 |
| Saml Price | Danbury | Oct 22 | " 15 |
| Danl Wright | Farmington | July 29 | " 15 |
| Geo: Harris | | Oct 1 | " 15 |
| Thos Fox | Simsbury | July 15 | " 15 |
| Moses Robinson | Killingly | " 15 | " 15 |
| Oliver Brown | Stonington | Augt 16 | " 15 |
| Alpheus Bowers | | " 16 | " 15 |
| Abial Chafe | Ashford | " 18 | " 15 |
| Saml Chafe | Killingly | " 16 | " 15 |
| James Chafe | Woodstock | " 16 | " 15 |
| Hiram Chappel | Lebanon | " 16 | " 15 |
| Steph{a} Downing | Canterbury | " 16 | " 15 |
| Henry Franklin | Woodstock | " 16 | " 15 |
| Thos Galford | Farmington | July 29 | " 15 |
| Wm Harrington | Mansfield | Augt 16 | " 15 |
| James Knapp | N. Fairfield | " 14 | " 15 |
| Aaron Rologg | | July 81 | " 15 |
| Nath{n} Martin | Mansfield | Augt 16 | " 15 |
| Steph{n} Martin | Hebron | " 16 | " 15 |
| Richd Robinson | Windham | " 16 | " 15 |
| Henry Smith | Hf{d} | July 29 | " 15 |
| Micha Taylor | Killingly | Augt 16 | " 15 |
| David Walding | Windham | " 16 | " 15 |

[*Copy in Comptroller's Office.*]

## SHORT TERM LEVIES.

Return of the Eight Months Men that belonged to the 4th Connecticut Regiment commanded by John Durkee Colo 1779.

| Names | | Commenc{t} of Service | Expiration of Service |
|---|---|---|---|
| Benjamin Lines | N. Haven | June 28 | Jany. 15 |
| Thomas Simons | Plainfield | Augt 16 | " 15 |
| Stephen Wilbur | " | " 16 | " 15 |
| William Fullour | Windham | " 16 | " 15 |
| John Adams | Colchester | " 16 | " 15 |
| John Casye | | " 16 | " 15 |
| Benjn Williams | Voluntown | " 16 | " 15 |
| Elijah Herrick | Coventry | " 16 | " 15 |

| Names | | Commenc⁴ of Service | Expiration of Service |
|---|---|---|---|
| Oliver Webster | New Haven | Aug⁴ 16 | Jany. 15 |
| Cyrus Powers | Killingly | " 16 | " 15 |
| Joseph Munn | Farmington | " 21 | [ " ] |
| Cotton Evens | Woodstock | " 28 | " 15 |
| Thomas Shephard | Middletown | " 24 | " 15 |
| Elijah Cady | Killingly | " 26 | " 15 |
| William Allen | Norwich | " 26 | " 15 |
| Benjamin Strong | Woodbury | Novʳ 26 | " 15 |
| Edward Washbon | " | " 26 | " 15 |
| Ahial Answorth | Woodstock | Aug⁴ 16 | " 15 |
| William Merritt | Hebron | " 16 | " 15 |
| Eli Perce | Ashford | " 16 | " 15 |
| Elias Tracy | Preston | " 16 | " 15 |
| Freeman Burnham | | " 16 | " 15 |
| Benjⁿ Perry | Preston | " 16 | " 15 |
| Thomas Eldridge | Rhod Island | " 16 | " 15 |
| Joshua R———l | Ashford | " 16 | " 15 |
| Uriah Carpenter | " | " 16 | " 15 |
| Robert Sumner | | Aug⁴ 16 | " 15 |
| Samuel Perry | | July 29 | " 15 |
| Eleazer Whipple | Farmington | " 28 | " 15 |
| Elijah Carpenter | Woodstock | Aug⁴ 18 | " 15 |
| Nathaniel Nash | Norwalk | July 20 | " 15 |
| David Growse | Killingly | Sep⁴ 14 | " 15 |
| Stephen Johnson | Haddam | Aug⁴ 1 | " 15 |
| Thomas Gardner | Milford | " 16 | " 15 |
| Henry Bennitt | Voluntown | Aug⁴ 18 | " 15 |
| Manassah Cady | Killingly | " 16 | " 15 |
| Jeremiah Durkee | Windham | " 16 | " 15 |
| Jed. Gilbert | Pomfret | " 16 | " 15 |
| Rufus Gossord | Simsbury | Sep⁴ 18 | " 15 |
| Levi Gossord | Simsbury | " 18 | " 15 |
| Israel Farnam | | Aug⁴ 16 | " 15 |
| John Joyce | Woodstock | " 16 | " 15 |
| Wᵐ Leatch | Winchester | " 1 | " 15 |
| Levi Meeks | Waterbury | " 3 | " 15 |
| Wᵐ Palmister | Coventry | " 16 | " 15 |
| Simeom Robertson | Windham | " 16 | " 15 |
| David Weltch | Plainfield | " 7 | " 15 |
| Nathˡ Beecher | Farmington | July 29 | " 15 |
| Charles Childs | Woodstock | " 16 | " 15 |
| Seth Gary | | " 16 | " 15 |
| Wᵐ Johnson | " | " 16 | " 15 |
| James Russell | " | " 16 | " 15 |
| Moses Robinson | " | " 16 | " 15 |
| Henry Morris | " | " 16 | " 15 |
| Jaˢ Leygoit | " | " 16 | " 15 |
| Edward Foster | Middletown | " 29 | " 15 |
| Moses Beegbe | Woodstock | Sep⁴ 14 | " 15 |

[*State Library, Revolution 16.*]

## FIFTH REGIMENT—COL. BRADLEY.

[*See Record of Connecticut Men in the Revolution, page 193.*]

### SHORT TERM LEVIES, 1779.

Return of the Eight Months Men In the 5[th] Connecticut Regiment Commanded by P. B. Bradley Col° In the Year 1779.
The expiration of the service of each was Jan. 15, [1780].

| Name | Town | Date |
|---|---|---|
| Ebenez' Huntington | Woodbury | Aug. 31 |
| Jn° Porter | " | 31 |
| Stephen Childs | Killington | 16 |
| Nath¹ Bacon | Litchfield | Sep. 24 |
| Phineas Holcomb | " | 24 |
| Elijah Hays | " | 24 |
| Zenas Hays | " | 24 |
| Zebina Smith | Sharon | July 26 |
| Will[m] Trowbridge | N. Milford | 26 |
| Bela Hill | Winchester | 26 |
| Ezra Pratt | Symsbury | 26 |
| Nath¹ Griffin | " | 20 |
| Absalom Griffin | " | Sep. 27 |
| Dan¹ Ensign | Hartland | July 20 |
| Amos Holcomb | Simsbury | Sep. 12 |
| Dosa Holcomb | " | 12 |
| Phin° Holcomb | " | 12 |
| Hamlin Johnson | Harrington | 12 |
| Joseph Bradley | " | 12 |
| Isaac Broker | Symsbury | 12 |
| Abijah Scofeld | " | Ju[ ] 20 |
| James Chappel | Tolland | 20 |
| Isaac Eno | Symsbury | Nov. 27 |
| Orange Barns or Burns | Litchfield | May 15 |
| Return Byer | " | Aug. 15 |
| Joab Gillet | Simsbury | Sep. 30 |
| Jn° Winchel | Torrington | 24 |
| Cyrenus Knapp | Simsbury | 30 |
| Abijah Clemmonds | Litchfield | Nov. 24 |
| John Garratt | Symsbury | July 27 |
| John McMann 1[st] | " | Aug. 8 |
| Jn° McMann 2[d] | " | 8 |
| Nathan Odle | Fairfield | 23 |
| Will[m] Phelps | Symsbury | 15 |
| Simeon Holladay | " | 15 |
| Ezekiel Hays | " | 15 |
| Lemuel Messenger | " | 15 |
| Jacob Finch | Danbury | 17 |
| Thaddeus Wheelock | Ridgfield | 13 |
| Grove Lommis | Windsor | 28 |
| Zacheus Holcomb | Simsbury | Sep. 24 |
| Bradford Kellogg | Goshen | July 26 |

[*State Library, Revolution 16; also Copy in Comptroller's Office.*]

## RETURN.

A Return of the Non Commissioned Officers & Privates in the 5th Connec$^t$ Reg$^t$ who are engaged during the War, The Town to which they belong & by whom hired.

### 1$^{st}$ Company

| Names | Towns | Names | Towns |
|---|---|---|---|
| Martin Denslow Serg$^t$ Maj$^r$ | Windsor | Jason Crawford | Woodstock |
| Edward Fields Drum Maj | Fairfield | John Gould | Goshen |
|  |  | Gideon Hurlbut | Fairfield |
|  |  | Asbel Mason | Litchfield |
| Ambrose Filer Fife Maj |  | Joseph Norton | Goshen |
| Louden Bailey Serg$^t$ | Haddam | Giles Olcutt | Litchfield |
| Jaazmah Howe Corp$^l$ | Goshen | [         ] | " |
| Stephen Wheeler Serg$^t$ | New Milford | Osburn Parsons | Norwalk |
|  |  | John Rockwell |  |
| Calvin Jenkins Drum | Norwalk | Henry Smith | Litchfield |
| Putnam Catlin Fife | Litchfield | John Seely | " |
| Cash Africa | " | Josiah Whitney | Ridgefield |
| James Columbus | " | James Wright | Litchfield |
| Reuben Craw | " | Ephraim Wheeler |  |

### 2$^{nd}$ Company

Thomas Wilson    Hartford

### 3$^d$ Company

| | | | |
|---|---|---|---|
| Jonath$^n$ Ambler |  | Enos Pettit |  |
| Elias Balcom | New Hartford | Azor Patchen |  |
| Jacob Bateman | Horseneck | Jon$^a$ Russ | Sharon |
| Ben Boston | Meriden | Edward Runnels |  |
| John Burgoyn |  | Jon$^a$ Tobias | Sharon |
| Benj$^a$ Bennet |  | John Taylor | Horseneck |
| Daniel Davison | Stonington | John Taylor | New Hartford |
| Daniel Fenn |  | George Tankerd |  |
| Henry Keeler | Norwalk | Samuel Witherill | Stamford |
| Edw$^d$ McClanning |  | Coker Wiggins | " |
| Abijah Olmsted | Norwalk |  |  |

### 4$^{th}$ Company

| | | | |
|---|---|---|---|
| Amos Lawrence Serg$^t$ | Windsor | Joseph Whippell Corp$^l$ | Hartford |
| Dan$^l$ Bissell Serg$^t$ | " | George Anger | Middletown |
| Will$^m$ Anderson Corp$^l$ | Hartford | John Brangin | " |

### 4$^{th}$ Company

| | | | |
|---|---|---|---|
| Amos Lawrence Serg$^t$ | Windsor | Zebulon Hoskins | Windsor |
| Dan$^l$ Bissell Serg$^t$ | " | Obed$^h$ Lamberton | " |
| Will$^m$ Anderson Corp$^l$ | Hartford | Ephraim Loatwell | " |
| Joseph Whippell | " | Phillip Negro | Simsbury |
| George Anger | Middletown | Plymouth Negro | Windsor |
| John Brangin | " | Alvan Owen | " |
| Jeremiah Barrit [?] | Hartford | Daniel Porter | " |
| John Beecher [?] | Windsor | Jacob Pason | " |
| Cornelius Cahale | " | Grove Rockwell | Middletown |
| Ozias Cone | Middletown | Sherman Rawland | Windsor |
| David Daniels | Windsor | Eben$^r$ Woolworth | " |
| William Graves | Middletown | Christopher Welch | Middletown |
| Jesse Gilbert | " | Robert Weston | Windsor |

CONNECTICUT LINE, 1777-1781.

### 5th Company

| Names | Towns | Names | Towns |
|---|---|---|---|
| Jared Knap Serg[t] | Litchfield | Simon Crosby | Litchfield |
| Mark Mildren " | Farmington | John Farnum | " |
| Enos Barns " | Litchfield | W[m] Jackson | Norwalk |
| Rich[d] Cornell Drum | Middletown | John Mason | Litchfield |
| Eber Stocking Corp[l] | Chatham | Denis Parkiton | Stamford |
| Paul Price " | Litchfield | Sam[l] Stannard | Litchfield |
| Jude C. Brown | Windsor | Moses Scott | Norwalk |
| Ezra Bates | Stamford | Jon[a] Dykeman | Danbury |
| Ambrose Barns | Litchfield | Joseph Thompson | Malbury |

### 6th Company

| Names | Towns | Names | Towns |
|---|---|---|---|
| Isaac Odell Serg[t] | Fairfield | Isaiah Jones | Stamford |
| Stephen Hall " | Stratford | Isban Jennings | Fairfield |
| Elijah Patchen Corp[l] | Fairfield | Josiah French | Stratford |
| Will[m] Cummins " | " | John Ludeman | Danbury |
| Wakeman Hull " | " | David Morehouse | Fairfield |
| Hez[h] Meaker Drum | " | Eben[r] Meaker | " |
| Charles Burrit | Stratford | Joseph Moger | " |
| Dan[ll] Burr | Fairfield | Woolcot Patchen | " |
| Pink Clark | Stratford | John Parker | Stratford |
| John Chaps | " | Neh[h] Sherwood | Redding |
| Ephraim Chorse | " | Baruck Taylor | Fairfield |
| David Cogins | Fairfield | Aron Wailey | " |
| Peter Fegro | | Joseph Wallace | " |
| William Gould | Fairfield | | |

### 7th Company

| Names | Towns | Names | Towns |
|---|---|---|---|
| Samuel Mead Fife | Norwalk | Thomas Keeler | Ridgefield |
| John Ashley | Haddam | Baruck Nickerson | " |
| Eliph[t] Allen | Fairfield | Wiram Pond | Colchester |
| Joseph Boynton | Cape Ann | Enoch Sperry | Litchfield |
| Enos Barns | Litchfield | Sylvanus Scofield | Stamford |
| Timothy Gibbs | " | Benj[n] Tarbox | Lyme |
| [ ] | [ ] | Micajah Weeks | Redding |
| Jerem[h] Keeler | Ridgefield | Jabez Williams | " |

### 8th Company

| Names | Towns | Names | Towns |
|---|---|---|---|
| Henry Bacon Serg[t] | Pomfret | William Jones | Colchester |
| Elias Bigsby " | Reading | Elijah Phelps | Middletown |
| Nathan Coley Corp[l] | " | Clark Roberts | Windsor |
| Samuel Woodcock " | Litchfield | James Stanton | Ridgefield |
| Edmund Fowler Drum | Fairffeld | Enoch Sperry | New Haven |
| Truman French Fifer | North Stratford | Gregory Thomas | Norwalk |
| John Cordrick | [ ] | Thadeus Waugh | Litchfield |
| David Clark | Windsor | Nathan Winton | Fairfield |
| Abel Culver | Litchfield | Nathan White | [ ] |
| Isaac Grant | " | | |

### 9th Company

| Names | Towns | Names | Towns |
|---|---|---|---|
| John Ryon Serg[t] | | Jacob Lewis | |
| Samuel Waugh " | Litchfield | Gamaliel Parker | |
| James Knapp Corp[l] | Sharon | Thomas Reed | |
| Nath[ll] Tylar Drum | " | Nath[ll] Richards | |
| [ ] Davis Fife | Middletown | William Stuart | Sharon |
| [ ] | [ ] | William Smith | |
| | | [ ] | [ " ] |
| Daniel Elmore | Somers | Daniel Tobias | |
| Eleazar Gilson | " | Dennis Torrey | |
| William Jackways | | Ezekiel Whitney | Sharon |
| John Jackson | | Isaac Welden | |
| Noah Kelsy | Sharon | Zelophehad Williamson | |

J. Wright Cap[t] Comd.

[*State Library, Hebard Papers.*]

## SIXTH REGIMENT—COL. DOUGLAS.

[*See Record of Connecticut Men in the Revolution, page 205.*]

### CAPT. STEPHEN POTTER'S COMPANY.

Return of the Non Commisiond officers and Privates Ingaged for the war in Cap$^t$ S. Potters Company In the 6$^{th}$ Conn$^t$ Reg$^t$ Commanded by R J Meigs Col$^o$

| Mens Names | Rank | towns they Belong to |
|---|---|---|
| Sam$^l$ Brown | Serj$^t$ | Branford |
| James Gold Smith | " | Milford |
| Phinehas Squires | " | Durham |
| Sam$^l$ Hadley | Corp$^l$ | Branford |
| John Eberhard | " | " |
| Joel Potter | Drum | |
| George Cook | Fife | N haven |
| Chandler Benton | Privat | Guilford |
| Ezekiel Butler | " | Branford |
| David Roggers | " | " |
| Sam$^l$ Chapman | " | Fairfield |
| Elihu Cook | " | Wallingford |
| Benjamin Foord | " | " |
| Jonathan Foord | " | " |
| Pratt Jones | " | " |
| Charles London | " | " |
| Zenos Mix | " | " |
| John Parker | " | " |
| Amasa Tharp | " | " |
| Amos Tharp | " | " |
| Skylor Goddard | " | Durham |
| David Hull | " | Darbey |
| Joel M. Daniel | " | " |
| John Hancock | " | N haven |
| Anthony M. Daniel | " | " |
| Bennajor Woolcut | " | " |
| Amos Warnor | " | " |
| John Lerrow | " | Licthfield |
| Charles Purkines | " | Stanford |
| Isaac Robberts | " | Middletown |
| David Hungerford | " | " |
| Joseph Hawkings | " | Branford |
| Roswell Whedon | " | " |
| David Hodge | " | Milford |

Camp December 10$^{th}$ /80

[ *Connecticut Historical Society.* ]

CONNECTICUT LINE, 1777–1781.   71

## MAJ. LEAVENWORTH'S COMPANY.

Muster Roll of Major Eli Leavenworth Comp⁷ 6ᵗʰ Conn' Reg' in the Service of the United States of America Commanded by Col° Retwin J. Meigs for Oct' 1779

Commissioned { Major Eli Leavenworth Sep' 18/77
{ Lieu' Asa Lay Jan⁷ 1ˢᵗ/77 Prisoner of War
{ Lieu' Giles Curtiss Nov' 15/77

| Appoint⁴ | | Time | Remarks |
|---|---|---|---|
| | **Sergeants** | | |
| Feb⁷ 6/77 | Eliakim Strong | 3 y˟ | |
| " 17 | And" Andrews | 3 y˟ | |
| | Jair˟ Harrison | | On Com⁴ Middletown |
| | **Corporals** | | |
| Jan 31/77 | Hugh˟ Hinman | 3 y˟ | On Duty |
| | Luther Page | | |
| Ap⁷ 10/77 | Benj" Crampton | 3 y˟ | " |
| | **Drum** | | |
| Ja" 31/77 | Reuben Brown | 3 y˟ | |
| | **Fife** | | |
| Mar˟ 4 | Sam' Brown | 3 y˟ | |
| Inlisted | **Privates** | | |
| | Cesar Bagdon | | On Duty |
| | Sam' Barker | | |
| Feb⁷ 17 | Joel Bishop | 3 y˟ | " |
| | Paul Beebe | | |
| | Ja˟ Cooper | | On Com⁴ N River |
| | Tho˟ Cook | | sick in Camp |
| | W" Carr | | sick Fishkill July 16 |
| | Sharper Camp | | On Duty |
| " 6ᵗʰ | Amos Davis | 3 y˟ | " |
| | Ja˟ Dinah | | " |
| | Reuben Frisbic | | |
| May 20 | Jn° Francis | 3 y˟ | On Com⁴ Robinsons farm |
| | Jn° Garrett | | On Duty |
| | Dav⁴ Hitchcock | | " |
| Dec' 8/76 | Jn° Hatchet | 3 y˟ | |
| | And" Jack | | |
| | W" Johnson | | " |
| May 13/77 | Jn° Johnson | 3 y˟ | sick Wallingford May 11/78 |
| Mar˟ 3 | Nath" Kelsey | 3 y˟ | |
| | Jack Little | | |
| Feb⁷ 3⁴ | Phin˟ Meigs | 3 y˟ | On Duty |
| | Jn° Meeker | | sick in Camp |
| | Warren Murray | | |
| | Meade Merrils | | On Duty |
| | Phillip Niger | | sick at Branford Apr 11/79 |
| | Abr" Norton | | |
| | Nathan Palmer | | on Com⁴ w'ʰ Gen' Parsons |
| Feb⁷ 17/77 | W" Parker | 3 y˟ | |
| | Benj" Potter | | |
| | Jn° Peck | | |
| Ap' 18 | M˟ Robinson | 3 y˟ | sick at Fishkill Oct' 12 |
| Feb⁷ 6 | Sam' Seward | 3 y˟ | Brigade Waggoner |
| " 17 | Seth Strong | 3 y˟ | |
| | Jord" Smith | | On Com⁴ N° River |

## REVOLUTION ROLLS AND LISTS.

| Inlisted | Privates | Time | Remarks |
|---|---|---|---|
| May 7 | Selah Stedman | 3 y$^s$ | |
| | Abia' Squire | | On Duty |
| | London Sawyer | | On Duty |
| | Tho$^s$ Sanford | | " |
| | Tory Scranton | | |
| | Enos Tuttle | | " |
| | Jacob Towner | | " |
| May 14 | Sam$^l$ Teale | 3 y$^s$ | |
| | Jn$^o$ Voigson | | |
| | Rufus Wheedon | | |
| | Step$^n$ Wade | | |
| Dec$^r$ 10/76 | Sam$^l$ Wood | 3 y$^s$ | On Duty |
| | Tho$^s$ Wheeler | | |
| May 27/77 | Limbo Stannard | 3 y$^s$ | Dischargd Oct$^r$ 11 [    ] |

Nov$^r$ 3 1779 Musterd then Major Leavenworth's Comp$^y$ as specified in the above Roll

Jacob Jn$^o$ Lansing [?]

[*Connecticut Historical Society.*]

Return of the Eight Months Men In the 6 Connecticut Reg$^t$ In the Year 1779

| Name | Town | Commencement of Service | Expiration of Service |
|---|---|---|---|
| Jn$^o$ Linsley | Branford | July 20 | Jan$^y$ 15 |

[*State Library, Revolution 16.*]

## SEVENTH REGIMENT—COL. SWIFT.

[*See Record of Connecticut Men in the Revolution, page 217.*]

### CAPT. HILLS' COMPANY.

The following is the balance due to the State of Connecticut from Each Man as anexed to their Respective Names for States Cloathing Received of Cap$^t$ W$^m$ Redfield States Cloather by Cap$^t$ Eben$^r$ Hills and delivered to them by Sd Hills at diferant times before Nov$^r$ 1778 taken from accounts Receipts &c. with Remarks

| | | | | |
|---|---|---|---|---|
| John Cole | 2 | 2 | 0 | dead June 10 1778 |
| Grig Trumbul | 2 | 8 | 0 | discharged |
| Christopher Coffin | 0 | 14 | 6 | disarted Feby 17 1778 |
| Edward Booth | 0 | 12 | 0 | " December 1779 |
| David Wells | 2 | 0 | 0 | Exchanged for John Cobb |
| James Taylor | 1 | 16 | 0 | deserted June 27 1778 |
| Thomas Brooks | 1 | 9 | 0 | |
| Elijah Parker | 0 | 8 | 6 | deserted |
| John Colson | 0 | 14 | 6 | deserted May 2 1778 |
| Chiliab Palmer | 0 | 7 | 0 | |
| James Lanford | 0 | 8 | 6 | |
| Mingo Treet | 0 | 5 | 6 | discharged |
| Joel Botchford | 0 | 19 | 0 | |
| Prince Simbo | 0 | 6 | 0 | |
| Ichabod Wilkinson | 0 | 19 | 0 | discharged |
| David Dean | 0 | 11 | 6 | " |
| Elijah Parker | 0 | 8 | 6 | deserted Jan$^y$ 8 1779 |
| William Barnit | 1 | 9 | 1 | " August 2 1778 |
| Edward Goodyear | 0 | 7 | 0 | |
| Robart Nicols | 0 | 7 | 0 | |
| Daniel Averil | 0 | 8 | 6 | discharged |
| Jacob Galusha | 1 | 16 | 6 | " |
| Gad Taylor | 0 | 18 | 0 | |
| Thomas Brooks | 0 | 9 | 6 | |
| Ebenezer Keelor | 0 | 7 | 0 | |
| total | 22 | 12 | 1 | |

The above named Soldiers ware Serving in the 8$^{th}$ Comp$^y$ 7$^{th}$ Connec$^t$ Reg$^t$ at the time of Receiveing the above sd Cloathing

Eben$^r$ Hills Cap$^t$ In s$^d$ Reg$^t$

Kent Ap$^l$ 2$^d$ 1782

[*Connecticut Historical Society.*]

## RECRUITS.

Return of Men recruited for the United States of America

[The list here given appears to be of recruits for the seventh regiment of Connecticut Line, formation of 1777—1781, Heman Swift, Colonel, where the names are found in the printed *Record of Connecticut Men in the Revolution.* The names are here reprinted because of the added information of "where inlisted"; the dates of inlistment and term agree with the printed *Record* and are here omitted.]

| Mens Names | Where inlisted | Mens Names | Where inlisted |
|---|---|---|---|
| John Bingham | Windham | Andrew McClarry | Preston |
| Nathan Morgan | Stonington | Joseph Mezen | Windham |
| Jabez Rouse | Windham | Jonah Palmer | " |
| Asa Hebard | " | Jabez Pottage | " |
| James Kingsley | Norwich | Eleazer Robertson | " |
| Nathan Morgan | Windham | Joseph Reed | Windham |
| Andrew Warner | " | Jabez Rockwell | Stonington |
| Aaron Bailey | Norwich | Joseph Robbins | Windham |
| Elijah Backus | Windham | Adariah Simons | " |
| Walter Chace | " | John Spears | Preston |
| Mason Abbee | " | Elisha Stoddard | Groton |
| Zebulon Ames | Preston | Theodore Taylor | Glastenbury |
| Elias Kingham | Windham | John Taylor | " |
| Levi Bingham | " | Benone De Wolf | " |
| Elisha Baldwin | Preston | Ephraim Jerry | Windham |
| John Bill | Coventry | Amos Woodward | " |
| Samuel Burdain | " | David Young | " |
| Gershom Dunham | Windham | Charles Ripley | " |
| Ezekiel Dunham | " | Gideon Seartes | Glastenbury |
| Stephen Dunwell | Preston | David Yerrington | Preston |
| Robert Davison | " | William Placey | Windham |
| Ezekiel Daniels | Glastonbury | Charles Riley | Glastenbury |
| John Dugard | Preston | Gershom Treat | " |
| Caleb Fitch | Windham | Moses Scott | " |
| Uriah Heberd | " | Seth Eddy | Chatham |
| Timothy Hebard | " | Joseph Gladding | Seabrook |
| Eben' Heberd | " | Selah Griswould | " |
| Jed" Hebard | " | Reuben Taylor | Glastenbury |
| Samuel Hallows | " | Azariah Taylor | " |
| Richard Howard | " | Aaron De Wolf | " |
| Lemuel Herrick | Preston | Jacob Meach | Groton |
| Lebeus Herrick | Stonington | Ezekiah Rood | " |
| Joseph Jinnings | Windham | Salmon Treat | Preston |
| Cyrus Killam | Groton | Luther Jones | " |
| Elijah Linkon | Windham | Samuel Stubbs | Windham |
| Nathan Loveland | Glastonbury | John Jonson | Preston |
| Amos Loveland | " | Eleazer Westcoat | Cituate |
| Benj" Lamb | Windham | Jabez Shoals | Groton |
| Seth Larrabee | " | Edw" John Witt | Plainfield |
| John Leathercoat | " | | |

[*State Library.*]

Return of the Eight Months Men in the 7 Connecticut Reg' in 1779

| Name | Town | Commencement of Service | Expiration of Service |
|---|---|---|---|
| Joseph Lindsley | Cornwall | July 26 | Jan' 15 |

[*State Library, Revolution 16.*]

# EIGHTH REGIMENT—COL. SHERMAN.

[*See Record of Connecticut Men in the Revolution, page 229.*]

## RETURN, 1779.

Return of the Commission'd & Staff Officers Non Commission'd officers and Privates in the Eighth Connecticut Regiment Inlisted for during the war

| Names | Rank | Town they belong too |
|---|---|---|
| **1st Capt Compy** | | |
| Paul Brigham | Capt | Coventry |
| Richard Sill | Lieut & P.M. | Lyme |
| Nathll Thompson | Serjt | Coventry |
| Jonah Mallery | Corpl | Waterbury |
| Saml Granger | Private | Suffield |
| Benja Frizbee | " | Torringsford |
| Eliphilet Philips | " | New britton |
| Amos Temple | " | Stratford |
| Japhura Primas | " | " |
| Cash Palingtine | " | Lebanon |
| **6th Capt Compy** | | |
| Asahel Hodge | Capt | Harrington |
| Egbon Hubbell | Serjt | Fairfield |
| Burr Gilbert | Corpl | " |
| John Gilbert | Privates | Stratford |
| David Pendleton | " | " |
| Seth Buckley | " | Fairfield |
| Jno McKinsey | " | " |
| Simeon Persons | " | Farmington |
| Levi Persons | " | " |
| James Fostor | " | |
| Joseph Frudom | " | Waterbury |
| Patrick Linch | " | |
| Jno Frame | " | Windom |
| Wm Woodruff | " | Farmington |
| Eli Denslow | " | Milford |
| **4th Capt Compy** | | |
| Samuel Sanford | Capt | Milford |
| John Strong | Lieut | Woodbury |
| William Beamont | Ens & Qr Master | Lebanon or Woodbury |
| Heber Smith | Serjt | Stratford |
| Abiel Linley | " | Woodbury |
| Anthony Stoddard | Corporal | " |
| Julan Easton | Fifer | " |
| Amor Eadee | Private | " |
| Peter Bristoll | " | Milford |
| Jehial Bradley | " | Woodbury |
| Titus Minor | " | " |
| Jethro Toney | " | " |

| Names | Rank | Town they belong too |
|---|---|---|
| Daniel Tucker | Private | Woodbury |
| Abiel Wakeley | " | " |
| Nathan Walker | " | " |
| James Cebree J{r} | " | Milford |
| Abner Lee | " | Woodbury |
| Robert Freeman | " | Stratford |
| John Fontine | " | Waterbury |
| Pomp London | " | Woodbury |
| Elisha Walker | " | " |
| Simeon Taylor | " | " |
| James Hooker | " | " |
| Isaac Pollard | " | " |

### Lt Colo Comd{t} Company

| Names | Rank | Town they belong too |
|---|---|---|
| Selah Benton | Lieut | Stratford |
| John Hobart | " | Branford |
| Daniel Provost | Private | Stanford |
| Abraham Holley | " | " |
| David Bates | " | " |
| Jeremiah Blackman | " | Stratford |
| Elisha Pulford | " | " |
| Eli Stodard | " | Woodbury |
| Benjn Wheeler | " | " |
| London Goodluck | " | Stratford |

### 4th Capt Comp{y}

| Names | Rank | Town they belong too |
|---|---|---|
| Nehemiah Rice | Capt | Waterbury |
| Joshua Whitney | Ensign | Canaan |
| Ozias Elwell | Private | Waterbury |
| Abel Lewes | " | Wallingford |
| Ethiel Scott | " | Harwinton |
| Levi Hitchcock | " | Wallinford |
| Prince Hotchkiss | " | " |

### Majors Comp{y}

| Names | Rank | Town they belong too |
|---|---|---|
| David Smith | Major | Waterbury |
| David Judson | Lieut & B. Q{r} M. | Woodbury |
| John Gillet | Serj{t} | Milford |
| Elihu Sanford | | New Haven |
| Jonathan Davis | Corporal | Waterbury |
| Joseph Cutler | " | " |
| William Russel | Drumer | Stratford |
| Elijah Picksley | | Waterbury |
| Ozem Cook | Private | " |
| Reuben Culver | " | " |
| Samuel Eells | " | Milford |
| Joseph Martin | " | " |
| Jonathan Preston | " | Waterbury |
| Strong Sanford | " | New Haven |
| Silas Glasgow | " | Stratford |
| John Jones Wakeley | " | " |

### 5th Capt Comp{y}

| Names | Rank | Town they belong too |
|---|---|---|
| Daniel Barns | Capt | Farmington |
| James Olmsted | Ensign | Hartford |
| Abraham Clark | Serj{t} | " |
| David Dixon | | Woodbury |
| Thomas Wells | Corporal | Hartford |
| Thomas Spencer | " | " |
| Amos Clark | " | Woodbury |
| John Ducitt | Fifer | Windsor |

## CONNECTICUT LINE, 1777–1781.

| Names | Rank | Town they belong too |
|---|---|---|
| Rich<sup>d</sup> Case | Private | Hartford |
| Asa Seymour | " | " |
| Daniel Stevens | " | Woodbury |
| Amos Sanders | " | Stratford |
| David Reynolds | " | Woodbury |
| Stephen Ranney | " | " |
| Philamon Stedman | " | Hartford |
| Grove Kellogg | " | " |
| Hezekiah Goodwin | " | " |
| James Libberty | " | Woodbury |
| Abram Yellis | " | Waterbury |
| Job Uffott | " | Woodbury |
| Charles Hollister | " | Hartford |
| Aaron Olds | " | Woodbury |
| Reuben Hadlock | " | Hartford |
| Asher Hecock | " | Farmington |
| Samuel Lee | " | Woodbury |
| Enoch Thomas | " | " |
| Jared Dixon | " | " |
| Hezekiah Keeler | " | |
| Timothy Andruss | " | Hartford |
| Aquilla Sturgis | " | Woodbury |

### 2<sup>d</sup> Cap<sup>t</sup> Comp<sup>y</sup>

| Names | Rank | Town they belong too |
|---|---|---|
| Sam<sup>ll</sup> Comstock | Cap<sup>t</sup> | Norwalk |
| Ephraim Kimberly | Lieu<sup>t</sup> | Newton |
| Salmon Hubbel | " | Norwalk |
| Elijah Taylor | Serj<sup>t</sup> | " |
| Abel Baldwin | " | Newtown |
| Aaron Keeler | " | Norwalk |
| Matthew Marwin | Corporal | " |
| Moses Gilbert | " | " |
| William Brown | " | Stanford |
| Uriah Mead | Fifer | Norwalk |
| Stephen Hait | Drum<sup>r</sup> | " |
| John Bouton | Private | " |
| Isaac Baldwin | " | Newtown |
| David Bouton | " | Norwalk |
| Jack Botsford | " | Newtown |
| Alben Cole | " | Norwalk |
| Sam<sup>l</sup> Fairweather | " | Newtown |
| Peter Fairchild | " | " |
| Elijah Foot | " | " |
| Robert Freman | " | Waterbury |
| Sam<sup>l</sup> Green | " | Norwalk |
| Nathan Hubbel | " | Newtown |
| Timothy Hanford | " | Norwalk |
| Samuel Nichols | " | " |
| Abijah Prindle | " | Newtown |
| Zalmon Prindle | " | " |
| William Spurr | " | Boston |
| Isaac Smith | " | Norwalk |
| Josiah Taylor | " | " |
| Enoch Kellogg | " | " |
| Azur Patchen | " | " |
| Seth Hubbell | " | " |
| John Williams | " | " |
| Theophilus Mead | " | " |
| Josiah Green | " | " |

**Staff**

| Names | Rank | Town they belong too |
|---|---|---|
| Thomas Skinner | Surgeon | Colchester |
| Jedediah Eansworth | Mate | Canterbury |
| Samuel Hait | Q'r Master Serj't | Stanford |

N: B: The Light Infantry are not Included in this Return

Isaac Sherman Lieu't Col Com't

[*State Library, Hebard Papers.*]

## CAPT. MONSON'S COMPANY.

Return of Cap't Monsons Comp'y L't Inf'y Who are during the War 8th Reg't.

Cap't T. Monsons Return of Officers & Men during the War as pr Division Orders of Decemb'r 7th 79.

| Names | Town | Names | Town |
|---|---|---|---|
| Theop's Monson Cap't | New Haven | Isiah Moss | Wallingford |
| Aaron Benjamin L't | Stratford | Linus Moss | Waterbury |
| Salmon Hubbel " | Wilton | Alex'r Mills | Woodbury |
| Ebenez'r Shelly Serj't | Stratford | Jesse Mathews | Waterbury |
| John Fulford " | Waterbury | John McRowe | Stratford |
| John Fletcher Corp'l | Danbury | Nath'l Pardee | Norwalk |
| Moses Churchel Drum'r | Woodbury | David Parsons | Wilton |
| Alex'r Fairchild Fifer | Stratford | Justice Reynalds | Woodbury |
| Will'm Burnes Priv't | Coventry | Stephen Thompson | Waterbury |
| Will'm Bundy | Woodbury | Henman Wooster | Woodbury |
| George Fields | " | Asa Thaires | Waterbury |
| Sam'l Jackson | " | Daniel M'Rowe | Stratford |
| Uriah Keeler | Wilton | Peter Fairchild | New Town |
| Eli King | Suffield | Sam'll Fairwether | " |
| Thomas Lewis | Stanford | | |

2d River Decemb'r 12th 1779
T. Monson Cap't

[*State Library, Hebard Papers.*]

## SHORT TERM LEVIES, 1779.

Return of the Eight M's Men in the 8th Conn't Reg't Comn'd by Isaac Sherman Co'l for the year 1779

| Names | | Commencem't of Service | Expiration of Service |
|---|---|---|---|
| Edw'd Ensworth | Groton | Aug't 11 | Jany 15 |
| Tim'o Anderson | Windham | " 24 | " " |
| Johnson Cleveland | | " 16 | " " |
| Jo's Gray | Lebanon | " 16 | " " |
| Rufus Gibbs | Windham | " 24 | " " |
| Jesse Long | Coventry | " 16 | " " |
| Jon'th Stawson | | " 11 | " " |
| Augustus Stawston | E Windsor | " 24 | " " |
| Elisha Tucker | Coventry | " 16 | " " |
| Jesse Whitman | Killingly | " 16 | " " |
| Chas Warner | | " 16 | " " |
| Nath'n Blackman | Winchester | Sept 24 | " " |
| Christ'r Swan | Colchester | " 10 | " " |
| Adonij'h Crane | Windsor | Nov 1 | " " |
| Hez'h Lewis | Killingly | Aug't 16 | " " |
| Sam'l Norton | Farmington | July 29 | " " |

CONNECTICUT LINE, 1777-1781.

| Names | | Commencem{t} of Service | | Expiration of Service | |
|---|---|---|---|---|---|
| Jn° Paine | Windham | Augt | 16 | died Oct° | |
| Isaih Plank | Killingly | " | 16 | Jany | 15 |
| Jo{s} Woodford | Kensington | July | 29 | " | " |
| Asa Torrey | Lebanon | Augt | 16 | " | " |
| Jn° Sweet | Millington | " | 16 | " | " |
| Uriah Finney | Lebanon | " | 16 | " | " |
| Ja{s} Ball | Coventry | " | 16 | " | " |
| Geo. Bissell | " | " | 16 | " | " |
| Ja{s} Field | Saybrook | " | 12 | " | " |
| Ebenr Merritt | Fairfield | Oct | 1 | " | " |
| Lem{l} White | Coventry | " | 1 | " | " |
| Israel Wood | Stamford | Sept | 19 | Oct | 14 |
| Erie M{c}Pharson | " | " | 19 | Jany | 15 |
| Jn° Larkin | " | " | 19 | " | " |
| Jo{s} Boyd | Killingly | Augt | 16 | " | " |
| Selah Cook | Waterbury | " | 22 | " | " |
| Asa Davidson | Ashford | " | 16 | " | " |
| Amos Green | Killingly | " | 16 | " | " |
| Henry Green | " | Sept | 5 | " | " |
| Jn° Lovejoy | Plainfield | " | 5 | " | " |
| Saml Mobbs | " | Augt | 21 | " | " |
| Benja Sweet | Killingly | " | 16 | " | " |
| Saml Wait | Plainfield | " | " | " | " |
| Hez{h} Bonnet | Farmington | Nov | 1 | " | " |
| Thos Love | Killingly | Augt | 16 | " | " |
| Jn° Crammer | Woodbury | Sept | 1 | " | " |
| Lyman Mott | " | Augt | 16 | " | " |
| David Walker | " | Sept | 1 | " | " |
| Gulielmas Hodg | " | " | 1 | " | " |
| Deliverance Eastman | " | Nov | 1 | " | " |
| Chauncy Adkins | Farmington | Augt | 16 | " | " |
| Jn° Barns | " | " | 4 | " | " |
| Saml Ingraham | Farmington | July | 27 | " | " |
| Joel Lane | Voluntown | Augt | 7 | " | " |
| Saml Manson | " | July | 27 | " | " |
| Rayner Page | " | Augt | 2 | " | " |
| Amaziah Raymond | Pomphet | Augt | 16 | " | " |
| Elias Harp or Tharp | Farmington | " | 16 | " | " |
| Reuben Hill | Woodbury | Oct | 10 | " | " |
| Ira Mandwill | " | Sept | 22 | " | " |
| Benj Porter | " | " | 22 | " | " |
| Roswill Burnham | Windham | Augt | 16 | " | " |
| Saml Barns | Farmington | " | 17 | " | " |
| Ezekiel Curtis | " | " | 17 | " | " |
| Selah Deming | " | " | 17 | " | " |
| Israel Fitts | Windham | Augt | 15 | " | " |
| Beriah Foote | Harrington | July | 2 | " | " |
| Robt Huntington | Ashf{d} | Augt | 16 | " | " |
| Ja{s} Harden | " | " | 16 | " | " |
| Ebenr Littlefield | Windham | " | 16 | " | " |
| Elijah Lilley | " | " | 16 | " | " |
| Jerem{h} Neal | Farmington | July | 17 | " | " |
| Moses Parsons | " | Augt | 18 | " | " |
| Ja{s} Powers | " | July | 30 | " | " |
| Jn° Tossell | Woodbury | Sept | 10 | " | " |
| Ichabod Talmage | Farmg{n} | July | 17 | " | " |

[*Copy in Comptroller's Office.*]

## NINTH REGIMENT—COL. WEBB.

### SHORT TERM LEVIES, 1779.

[*See Record of Connecticut Men in the Revolution, page 245.*]

Abstract of Pay for the Six Months Recruits in the 9th Connect Regt from the Commencement to the Expiration of their Service. [With rolls for 1779.]

| Names | Towns | Commencement of Service | Expiration of Service |
|---|---|---|---|
| **Colonels Compy** | | | |
| Joseph Atwood | Wethersfield | 18 July | 4 Dec |
| Joseph Andrus | " | 7 Aug | " |
| James Antony | " | 18 July | " |
| Levy Bulkley | " | " | " |
| John Deming | " | " | 14 |
| David Deming | " | " | 4 |
| Abel Edgerton | Norwich | 23 | 14 |
| Hezekiah Hartshorn | " | " | " |
| Nehemiah H [ | | ] Aug | " |
| Robert Francis | Wethersfield | 18 " | 9 |
| Abraham Guthrie | Fairfield | 26 | 4 |
| Samuel Kent | Suffield | 28 July | " |
| Asa Lewis | Woodbury | 23 | 16 |
| Ezekiel Main | Reading | 26 Aug | " |
| Huit Olvord | Hebron | 23 July | 4 |
| Joseph Root | Woodbury | " | " |
| Francis Weaver | Middletown | 7 | 14 |
| **3d Company** | | | |
| Elisha Allyn | Windsor | 20 Sep | 4 Dec. |
| Bartholemew Arthur | Groton | 24 Aug | " |
| Stephen Burnham | Hartford | 13 | 17 |
| Charles Clark | Wethersfield | 18 | 4 |
| Samuel Castle | Chatham | 28 July | " |
| Rufus Gillet | Suffield | " | 13 |
| William Grey | Chatham | 1 Oct. | 14 |
| Nathaniel Hale | Wethersfield | 18 Aug | " |
| Isaac Johnston | Chatham | 23 July | " |
| Daniel Lee | " | " | 1 Oct. |
| Daniel Lyman | Labanon | " | 12 Dec. |
| Giddeon Phillips | Litchfield | 24 Aug | 9 |
| Samuel Robbins | Wethersfield | 18 | 20 Sep. |
| Tom Tommas. | Lebanon | 23 July | 12 Dec. |
| Nathaniel Tibbles | Washington | 24 Aug. | 4 |
| Josiah Tryon | Wethersfield | 18 | " |
| Jedediah Woodworth | Lebanon | 23 July | 2 |
| John Porter | " | " | 14 |
| Richard Robbins | Wethersfield | " | 12 |
| Jonah Stricklin | Middletown | 16 Aug. | 9 |
| Daniel Taylor | Hartford | 23 July | 16 |
| David Stillman | Wethersfield | 1 Oct. | 9 |
| Bigelow Waters | Hebron | 23 July | 14 |
| David Ward | Durham | 16 Aug | 9 |

## CONNECTICUT LINE, 1777-1781.

| Names | Towns | Commencement of Service | Expiration of Service |
|---|---|---|---|
| **Majors Comp<sup>y</sup>** | | | |
| Elijah Bemus | Hebron | 23 July | 18 Dec. |
| John Carrier | " | " | 14 |
| Benjamin Denilo | Suffield | " | 4 |
| Nathan Eluzzad [?] | Durham [?] | [ | ] |
| John Hurlburt | Wethersfield | 17 July | 4 |
| Eliphelot Hill | " | 16 Aug. | 14 |
| Russell Hill | Glastenbury | " | " |
| Daniel Holmes | Wethersfield | 23 July | 9 |
| George King | New Haven | 18 Aug. | 14 |
| Hazia Landon | Litchfield | 26 | 16 |
| Henry Moriner | Middletown | 18 July | 14 |
| James Shaw | Saybrook | 18 Aug | 9 |
| Dudley Tracey | Norwich | 25 July | 14 |
| James Tiley | Say Brook | 18 Aug. | " |
| [ | | | ] |
| David Wetherty | Wethersfield | 18 July | 4 |
| John Welch | Chatham | 28 | 14 |
| **4<sup>th</sup> Company** | | | |
| James Brown | Coventry | 23 July | 16 Dec. |
| Nathaniel Baldwin | Wethersfield | " | 14 |
| John Bailey | Haddam | 28 | 12 |
| Joseph Briggs | Suffield | " | 4 |
| Joseph Brooks | Danbury | 18 Aug. | 14 |
| Silas Crane | Durham | 16 | 16 |
| Joseph Flower | Wethersfield | 18 | 9 |
| Simeon Goodrich | " | " | " |
| Theodore Harrison | | 15 July | " |
| Barnabus Hall | Wallingford | 16 Aug. | 16 |
| Adney Gillet | Hartford | " | 4 |
| Jacob Miller | Durham | " | 9 |
| Josiah Prior | Middletown | 17 July | " |
| **L<sup>t</sup> Infantry Comp<sup>y</sup>** | | | |
| David Baxter | Glastenbury | 23 July | 14 Dec. |
| John Bliss | Lebanon | " | 4 |
| Asa Blush | Colchester | " | 17 |
| Elisha Card | Vollentown | " | 14 |
| Stephen Commens | Coventry | 25 | 9 |
| James Downer | Lebanon | 23 | 4 |
| John Follen | Glastenbury | " | " |
| Philer Goodrich | Wethersfield | " | 14 |
| Daniel Lane | Moodus | 17 | " |
| Justin Lumbard | Suffield | 28 | 14 |
| James Pratt | Wethersfield | 9 Aug. | 4 |
| John Smith | Suffield | 8 July | 14 |
| Elisha Smith | Middletown | 18 | 4 |
| **1<sup>st</sup> Company** | | | |
| Abel Baldwin | Waterbury | 16 Aug. | 14 Dec. |
| Amos Cook | Chatham | 17 July | 4 |
| Joseph Churchill | " | 18 Aug. | 16 |
| Uriah Finney | Lebanon | 23 July | 9 |
| Edward Fenn | Wallingford | 16 Aug. | 16 |
| Elnathan Gary | Lebanon | 28 July | 9 |
| Asahel Hall | Wallingford | 16 Aug. | 4 |
| Jesse Lyman | Lebanon | 23 July | 9 |
| John Gipson | Wethersfield | 18 Aug. | 14 |
| Aron Overton | Norwich | 23 July | 20 |
| Zenus Pieno | Lebanon | " | 4 |

| Names | Towns | Commencement of Service | Expiration of Service |
|---|---|---|---|
| Nathaniel Robarts | Chatham | 17 | 14 |
| John Rice | Wallingford | 18 Aug. | " |
| Amasa Stocking | Chatham | 17 July | 4 |
| Abel Spicer | Lebanon | 23 | 14 |
| Ephraim Spalding | Ashford | 16 Aug. | 9 |
| Silas Tracey | Washington | 23 | 4 |
| James Wilson | Middletown | 17 July | " |
| Aaron West | Chatham | " | " |
| Samuel Woolcut | Wallingford | 16 Aug. | 16 |
| David Welch | Plainfield | " | 17 |
| Jonathan Whipple | " | 23 Aug. | 14 |
| **L$^t$ Colonels Comp$^y$** | | | |
| Samuel Ames | Waterbury | 23 July | 14 Dec. |
| Daniel Avery | Cornwall | " | " |
| Joseph Austin | Middletown | 17 | 9 |
| John Codner | " | " | 4 |
| John Downes | Groton | 30 Aug. | 14 |
| Jonath$^n$ Hutchinson | Coventry | 23 July | 9 |
| Samuel Jones | Hebron | " | 4 |
| John Kirtland | Suffield | 28 | 14 |
| Allen Lane | Middletown | 17 | " |
| Joseph Lewis | Stratford | 28 | " |
| Jesse Morgan | Chatham | 1 Sep | " |
| Isaac Owen | Hebron | 23 July | 4 |
| **5$^{th}$ Company** | | | |
| Sylvanus Avery | Lime | 26 Aug. | 14 Dec. |
| William Almy | Volentown | 23 July | 14 |
| Ebenezar Clark | Labanon | " | 9 |
| Phinehas Dean | Chatham | 26 Aug. | 4 |
| Jacob Fenton | Lebanon | 17 July | 9 |
| Squire Goff | Colchester | 23 | 14 |
| Japhet Hanmon | " | 28 | 20 Nov |
| Sam$^l$ Kingsbury | Plainfield | 16 Aug. | 16 Dec. |
| Isaac Lacey | Fairfield | 17 July | 9 |
| George Little | Killingley | 16 Aug. | 14 |
| Thomas Marvell | Coventry | 23 July | " |
| Amos Ranney | Chatham | 17 | 4 |
| Jonah Thomas | Lebanon | 23 Aug. | " |
| Daniel Stoddard | Litchfield | 26 | 14 |
| Isaac Utter | New Milford | 18 | 4 |
| Stephen Williams | Fairfield | " | " |
| Ambrous Woodward | Lebanon | 17 July | 14 |
| Fredrick Woodward | " | 9 | " |
| **2$^{nd}$ Comp$^y$** | | | |
| Jonathan Francis | Wallingford | 15 Aug. | 14 Dec. |
| Fredrick Fuller | Wethersfield | 18 | 4 |
| Jason Gay | Fairfield | " | 14 |
| Clark Hide | Stratford | 15 | 19 |
| Charles Johnson | Wallingford | 18 | 20 Nov. |
| Benjamin Porter | Hartford | 20 | 4 Dec. |
| Elias Purple | E Haddam | 4 Oct | " |
| Elisha Perkins | Cheshire | 18 July | 9 |
| Paul Griffis | Killingsley | 15 Aug. | 14 |
| Peregrine Garner | Norwich | 31 | 4 |
| Jonathan West | Lebanon | 23 July | 4 Oct |

I do hereby certify that the above Pay abstract is just & true according to the best of my Knowledge.    Jn$^o$ P. Wyllys

Maj$^r$ Comd$^t$ 9$^{th}$ Connec$^t$ Reg$^t$

[*State Library, Revolution 16.*]

## COL. HAZEN'S REGIMENT.

### DESERTERS, 1779.

[*See Record of Connecticut Men in the Revolution, page 260.*]

A Return of sundry Deserters from Col. Moses Hazen's Regiment inlisted in the State of Connecticut, and returned to the Board of War, as a Part of that State's Quota, and not included in the Return delivered by Capt. Munson to the Assembly of that State.

| Names &c | | Town | Names &c | | Town |
|---|---|---|---|---|---|
| John Cornelius | Priv. | New Haven | Aaron Tuttle | Priv. | Ridgfield |
| Edward Gilbertson | " | " | Michael Welch | " | New Milford |
| Christopher Gale | " | Canaan | William Baker | " | Salisbury |
| Benjamin Hindman | " | Woodbury | James Daurough | | Stamford |
| John M\`Coy | " | New Haven | | | |

Moses Hazen Col.

[*State Library, Revolution 16.*]

# THREE MONTHS' REGIMENT—COL. WYLLYS.

## OFFICERS.

[On June 30, 1780, the Council of Safety in consequence of Gen. Washington's representations voted to raise 1000 men to serve for three months in the "Connecticut Line."]

The United States D$^r$ To the State of Connecticut, for Disbursements for the Pay &c of three Regiments under the Command of Col. Hezekiah Wyllys, for three Months, raised in consequence of a requisition from General Washington in June 1780.

| Companies | Regiments | Companies | Regiments |
|---|---|---|---|
| Field & Staff | Hez$^h$ Wyllys's | Cap$^t$ D. Godfrey | Sam$^l$ Canfield's |
| Cap$^t$ Smith | " | Cap$^t$ J. Carter | " |
| Cap$^t$ D. Stewart | " | Cap$^t$ E. Couch | " |
| Cap$^t$ B. Norris | " | Cap$^t$ A. Sloper | " |
| Cap$^t$ J. Green | " | Cap$^t$ A. Mills | " |
| Maj$^r$ J. Clark | " | Col. B. Richards | " |
| L$^t$ S. Smith | " | Maj$^r$ D. Cone | " |
| Cap$^t$ D. Johnson | " | Cap$^t$ E. Palmer | " |
| Cap$^t$ Mathew Grant | " | Cap$^t$ A. Hotchkiss | " |
| Field & Staff | Sam$^l$ Canfields | Cap$^t$ D. Collins | " |
| Cap$^t$ J. Pennoyer | " | Cap$^t$ S. Ely | " |
| Cap$^t$ Joseph Smith | " | Col. B. Richards | " |
| Cap$^t$ H. Hait | " | Cap$^t$ J. Brian | " |

[*Comptroller's Office, Haskell's Receipts.*]

## BOUNTY ROLLS.

Account of Bounties paid to recruits raised for 3 mo. to join the Continental Army in the year 1780 by Col. Jonathan Dimon Viz$^t$

Siras Hawley
Bille Lacey
T. Porter
S. Gregory
J. Meeker
D. Brown
D. Raymond
A. Wheeler
S. Ranny
D. Jennings 3d
T. Rynes
Samuel French
S. Scovil
Silas Dayton
G. Welles
N. Morehouse
John Lockwood 3d

J. Adams
Elias Sturges
J. Squire
C. Godfrey
S. Daten
Peter Winton
J. E. Olcott
A. Pillias
E. Sherwood
Elijah Raymond
Joseph Platt
J. Crowfeet
Jonas Platt
E. French
A. Cable
Waker Bates
D. Drew

[*State Library, Revolution 17.*]

CONNECTICUT LINE, 1777–1781.    85

Bounty Roll of the 3 mo. Men who joined the Continental Army from the 9th Reg. of Militia in the year 1780

Isaac Smith
Reuben Mead
John Morrel
Jonathan Read
Levi Sherwood
John Reymond
Jacob Richards
Samuel Waring Jr
Samuel Penoyer
Benjamin Reymond
Samuel Reynolds
Joseph Patchen
Isaac Hubbell
Gol[    ]kwood
[        ]eed
John Butler
Abraham Raymond
Isaac Reymond

Abraham Seymour
Stephen Reed
Daniel Mills
Eliakim Smith Jr
William Raymond
Ira Scott
Moses Gates
Samuel Hait
Gideon Weed
Gold Ferris
William Patchen
Joseph Gregory
Dodatey Hendrick
Matthew Betts
Jesse Taylor
Reuben Mead Jr
Jedediah Nash
Jonathan Platt

[*State Library, Revolution 17.*]

Account of Bounties paid to recruits raised for 3 mo. to join the Continental Army in the year 1780 by Colo Increase Mosely

Elijah Hinman
Andrew Graham
John Thomas &c
Justus Hinman &c
Benja Hitchcock Jr &c
John Graham
Wait Hinman
Dan Chatfield
Danl Squier
David Rumsey

Thomas Knapen
Gershom Holmes
Joseph Hamlin
Agur Beach
Reuben Miner
Noah Bunnell
Thaddeus Lacey
John Skeel
S. Ingraham

[*State Library, Revolution 17.*]

State of Connecticut To Nehemiah Beardsley Paymaster to the Men raised in the 16th Regiment for three months in the year 1780 Bounties to the Men & for Guns Blankets &c Dr July 1780

Matthew Olmstead
Thaddeus Whitlock
Ebenezer Moody
Daniel Rockwell
Eanos Rockwell
Uriah Raymond
Amos Griffin
Robert Wilson
Jeremiah Andrews
Thomas Neal
Elijah Hait
Sedeman Harrard
Dan Towner
Nathaniel Fuller
John Potter
David Hall
Job Jones
Jonathan Griffin
Elnathan Beers

Joseph Boughton
Eliphalet Peck
Amos Hoyt
James Platt
John Benedict
Samuel Hoit
John Barnum
Samuel Brown
Ezra Barnum
Oliver Clark
Joseph Thomas
Hezekiah Wetherbee
Asa Powers
Benjamin Rockwell
Peleg Finch
Oliver Burton
James Lincoln
Simeon Baldwin
Joseph Rockwell

Abner Judd
Jehiel Smith
John Fairchild
Abiel Prindle
Bennet Perry
Joseph Barnum
Enoch Fairchild
Jacob Keeler
Thomas Hodges

Moses Gray
Jabez Wakeman
Samuel Crane
Elizer Taylor
Silas Dunning
David Beers
Jonathan Benedict
Thomas Kellogg

[*State Library, Revolution* 17.]

## COL. FLOWER'S ARTIFICERS.

[*See Record of Connecticut Men in the Revolution, page 295.*]

A Return of the Names of the Officers & men in the Military Department at Springfield under the Direction of Col. Ezekiel Cheevers D Commissary General Military Stores and who are Lawfull Inhabitants of the State of Connecticut together with the time of their Engagements in the Department also the towns and Counties to which they Severally Belong.

| Names | Time of Engagement | Towns |
|---|---|---|
| John Collins D Commissary Military Stores | Jan. 1, 1777 | Wethersfield |
| Amasa Loomis Clerk Military Stores | Feb. 28, 1777 | Bolton |
| William Barton Caplain of Armory | Aug. 20, 1777 | Farmington |
| John Conant Asst Harness Maker | Apr. 20, 1779 | Mansfield |
| Jacob Sergants Armorer | May 13, 1779 | " |
| Rufus Payne " | Mar. 28, " | East Windsor |
| William Barton " | Apr. 1, " | Farmington |
| Ashbel Fox " | May 6, " | East Hartford |
| Michael Jenson " | " " | Colchester |
| Samuel Weaver " | Aug. 15, " | " |
| Hiram Roberts " | Oct. 6, " | Farmington |
| Joseph Barton " | Jan. 1, 1779 | " |
| Amasa Polley " | Sep. 1, " | Suffield |
| Henery Pooley " | Dec. 16, " | Farmington |
| Joseph Daley " | Dec. 1, 1778 | " |
| Ephraim Luce Harness Maker | Apr. 13, " | Sumers |
| David Davis " | May 5, 1779 | Mansfield |
| Ephraim Richardson " | June 8, 1779 | Coventry |
| Lemuel Southworth " | " 16, " | Mansfield |
| Abijah North Blacksmith | Oct. 20, " | Farmington |

These may Certifie that the officers & men contained on this Roll is Engaged in the Service of the United States of America for three years or During the War, & that they have not been absent from their Respective Duties unless by proper authority

Attest Ezek<sup>l</sup> Cheever D C G M S

[*State Library, Revolution 15.*]

## SOLDIERS DISCHARGED AND DESERTED.

The United States D$^r$ to the State of Connecticut for supplies to the families of Officers & Soldiers of the Connecticut Line who were discharged from or deserted the service before the first day of January 1780 & were not included in the settlement for depreciation on their pay: Viz$^t$

| Names of the Persons supplied | By what Town supplied | Names of the Persons supplied | By what Town supplied |
|---|---|---|---|
| Daniel Allen Cap$^t$ | Ashford | Phinehas Beardsley Cap$^t$ | New Fairfield |
| Jonathan Allen | New Haven | David Bewel | New Milford |
| John Adams | Farmington | Josiah Burrows | Stratford |
| William Andruss Artif. | East Windsor | Benj$^a$ Burnap | Windham |
| Thomas Abbe Cap$^t$ | Enfield | Abisha Bingham | " |
| Thomas Avery L$^t$ | Groton | Dan$^l$ Culver | New London |
| John Anthony | Wallingford | Timothy Cleaveland L$^t$ | Canterbury |
| Sam$^l$ Barker Cap$^t$ | Brandford | | |
| Abner Bacon " | Canterbury | Darius Cady | Stonington |
| William Bacon Artil$^y$ | Middletown | Reuben Carter | Canterbury |
| Eli Biggelow | Colchester | James Carter | Lebanon |
| Beriah Bill Cap$^t$ | Norwich | Marcus Cole Lieu$^t$ | Chatham |
| Robin Blanchard | Colchester | John Cole | Farmington |
| Nath$^l$ Bishop Lieut. | Norwich | Nathan Clapp | Coventry |
| Silas Baldwin | Derby | John Chapman | Say Brook |
| Caleb Baldwin L$^t$ | Killingsworth | David Clark serj$^t$ | New Haven |
| Henry Baldwin | Say Brook | Asahel Clark Ens$^n$ | Woodstock |
| Jon$^a$ Brown Cap$^t$ | Farmington | Elijah Churchill | East Windsor |
| Charles Brown | Stonington | Ames Curtiss | Farmington |
| Oliver Brown | " | Phinehas Camp | Woodbury |
| James Barns L$^t$ | New Fairfield | John Conlee | Glastenbury |
| David Barns | Wallingford | Walter Chase | Haddam |
| Increase Brainard | Haddam | Ebenezer Church | Woodbury |
| Stephen Buckland Cap$^t$ | Hartford | Joseph Cone | Middletown |
| | | Noah Coleman Doct. | Lebanon |
| Asa Burnham | Litchfield | Josh$^a$ Chappel | New London |
| Joseph Burnham I. C. | Lyme | Comfort Chappel | " |
| | | Curtiss Chappel | Salisbury |
| Asa Burnham | Preston | Jon$^a$ Corwin | Norwich |
| Humphrey Ball | Lebanon | Selah Corwin | " |
| Jon$^a$ Blackman | " | John Comstock | Say Brook |
| Elijah Blackman Cap$^t$ | Middletown | W$^m$ Lock Collins | Stratford |
| | | Robert Davison | Greenwich |
| Ebenezer Blake | " | Stephen Downing | Canterbury |
| Edward Benton Serj$^t$ | Guilford | Christopher Downing | |
| Gideon Bailey L$^t$ | Haddam | | Norwich |
| Robert Bailey | " | Thomas Duffe | Fairfield |
| Jon$^a$ Beeman | East Windsor | Josh$^a$ Disborough | " |
| Friend Beeman | Washington | Titus Dutton | Waterbury |
| Boanerges Beebe | New London | Sam$^l$ Dealing | Glastenbury |
| Edward Brind | Haddam | Stephen Davis | Waterbury |
| John Burk | Milford | Israel Dayton Artif$^r$ | New Haven |

## CONNECTICUT LINE, 1777-1781.

| Names of the Persons supplied | By what Town supplied | Names of the Persons supplied | By what Towns supplied |
|---|---|---|---|
| Moses Dowd | Guilford | Joseph C. Hawley | New Milford |
| David Deming Lieut | Hartford | Rufus Hyde | Lyme |
| Daniel Die | Kent | John Hudson | Stonington |
| Daniel Dodge | Lyme | James Hull | Waterbury |
| Nathan Dodge | Colchester | Stephen Hull | Woodbury |
| James Dewy | Middletown | Champlin Harris, alias Harrison | Colchester |
| Joseph Dickerman | New Haven | | |
| William Drinkwater | New Milford | Frederick Harden Artif[r] | New Haven |
| Benj[n] Durkee Lieut | Windham | | |
| Jeremiah Durkee | " | Rich[d] Hunt | " |
| Zebulon Dudley | Say Brook | Tho[s] Hiscox | Stonington |
| Miles Dunbar | Waterbury | Hawk's Son | " |
| Solomon Douglas | New London | W[m] Heacock | Waterbury |
| Everet Eams | Danbury | David Heacock | Woodbury |
| Sam[l] Evans Jun[r] | Hartford | John Hastings | Wallingford |
| Isaac Evans | Preston | James Stoughton | Union |
| Ezra Edgcomb | New Hartford | Daniel Hendry | New London |
| Vine Elderkin Cap[tn] | Windham | Lemuel Hitchcock L[t] | Willinton |
| Jack Freeman | Colchester | W[m] Hambden | Woodstock |
| Samson Freeman | Glastenbury | Joseph Jones | Brandford |
| Providence Freeman | New London | Thomas Jones | Wallingford |
| John Fox | Colchester | Henry Jones | New London |
| Jacob Fox Lieu[t] | Norwich | Elnathan Jennings | Chatham |
| Nehemiah Fowler | Fairfield | Robert Johnston | Sharon |
| Caleb Fowler Corp[l] | Guilford | Dan[l] Judd Serj[t] | Colchester |
| Sam[l] French | Fairfield | Nathan P. Jackson L[t] | Fairfield |
| John Fenton | Willington | John Jordan | Washington |
| Reuben Farnum | Windham | M. Jacobs | Norwich |
| Francis Fillets | Woodbury | Usell Knapp | Stanford |
| John Garret | New Hartford | Thomas Kinning | New Fairfield |
| Elihu Geer | Chatham | Tho[s] Kirtland Cap[t] | Say Brook |
| Richard Giddens | " | John Kirrit | Symsbury |
| D. Tubbs Gardner | Norwich | W[m] Lane | New London |
| W[m] Green Cap[t] | Hartford | Levi Lee | " |
| Robert Green | Voluntown | Elisha Lee Cap[t] | Lyme |
| Nath[l] Gates Lieu[t] | Canterbury | Moses Loomis | East Windsor |
| Joseph Graham | Chatham | Sam[l] Lockwood Cap[t] | Greenwich |
| Ephraim Goodrich | Wethersfield | Levi Loveland | Glastenbury |
| Simeon Graves | Waterbury | Samuel Lucas | Hartford |
| Azariah Grant | East Windsor | Allen Leet | Killingsworth |
| Sam[l] Gross | Lebanon | John Lines | New Haven |
| Phinehas Granger | Suffield | Ebenezer Lewis | Wallingford |
| Sam[l] Gorham | Stratford | Sam[l] Lewis serj[t] | Waterbury |
| W[m] Hall | Ashford | Willet Larrabee | Salisbury |
| Sam[l] Hall Corp[l] | Killingsworth | Sylvester Minor | New London |
| Nath[l] Hall | Waterbury | James Minor | " |
| W[m] Hall Artif[r] | New London | Andrew Minor | Tolland |
| Elihu Hubbard | Chatham | W[m] Mackhall | New London |
| W[m] Harrison | Lyme | Cyprian Merrills | Farmington |
| Aaron Hale Lieut | Chatham | Thomas Mercy | Ashford |
| Cornelius Higgins | " Haddam | Enoch Miller | Chatham |
| Levi Hotchkiss | " Derby | W[m] M[c]Corne | " |
| Ithamar Harvey Cap[t] | East Haddam | George Mitchel | Norwich |
| Simeon Hagar serj[t] | Enfield | Stephen Meeker | Redding |
| Titus Hayes | Hartford | Noah Murray serj[t] | Kent |
| Joseph Hannabal | Groton | M[c]Dowal Ens. | Glastenbury |
| Joseph Hannabal | Stonington | John M[c]Donald | Groton |

| Names of the Persons supplied | By what Town supplied | Names of the Persons supplied | By what Town supplied |
|---|---|---|---|
| Sam¹ Mattocks Cap¹ | Hartford | David Rice | Willington |
| Orlando Mack Lieut | Hebron | Peter Stevens jr | Canterbury |
| James McKensey | Stonington | Roswel Stevens | Farmington |
| Jedediah Mackinborough | Hebron | Elias Seymour | New Hartford |
| | | John Shipman | Say Brook |
| John Main jun' | Kent | Sam¹ Shipman Serj¹ | " |
| Dan¹ Munger | Litchfield | Jaspar Stannard | " |
| Alexander McCoy | Lyme | Geo. Smith Ens. | Hartford |
| Comfort Marks | Middletown | Job Smith Ens. | Ridgefield |
| Wm Munson Capᵗⁿ | New Haven | Sam¹ Smith Artif. | Waterbury |
| Joseph Moulthrop | " | James Smith | Windham |
| Lewis Martin | " | Wm Shaw | Canterbury |
| John Moss | " | Benjᵃ Shaw | " |
| Wm Manning Captⁿ | Woodstock | Timothy Stark | Colchester |
| Urane Nickerson | Greenwich | Stephen Stark | " |
| Briston Negro | Say Brook | Stephen Stark | Hebron |
| Cuff Negro | Colchester | James Simmons | Stonington |
| Colonel Oswald | Farmington | Robert Swift | Groton |
| Timothy Oharra | New London | Benajah Strong | Lebanon |
| Wm Ollin | Norwich | Daniel Seward | Milford |
| Israel Patten Lieut | New Haven | Wm Seward | " |
| David Pelton | Groton | Sam¹ S. Squier | Farmington |
| Levi Price | Cornwall | David Spencer Lᵗ | East Haddam |
| Rufus Price Lᵗ | Tolland | Obadiah Spencer | Hartford |
| Thomas Picket | Danbury | James Sally | East Haddam |
| Dan¹ Perkins jun' | Enfield | Wm Smithers | Glastenbury |
| Peter Peas Serj¹ | Glastenbury | Aaron Suntsimons | Groton |
| Jacob Pomp | Groton | John Spears | " |
| Zebulon Peck | Goshen | States Spears | " |
| Silas Peck jun' | Lyme | Josep Sharp | Milford |
| Darius Peck | Norwich | Wm Shortman | Groton |
| Benjᵃ Pomeroy Doct | Hebron | John Shelley | Litchfield |
| Lazarus Puffer | " | Josiah Stone | " |
| Sylvanus Perry | Killingley | David Stone | Wallingford |
| Eben' Perry Serj¹ | Windham | Jonah Sizer | Middletown |
| Jonas Prentice Captⁿ | New Haven | Ezekiel Sandford | Waterbury |
| Jeremiah Parmelee Captⁿ | New Haven | Wm Sherman | New Haven |
| | | Chauncey Sperry | " |
| Eliab Parker | Waterbury | Nath¹ Sturdevant | Norfolk |
| Alpheus Polley | Lebanon | John Sydleman | Norwich |
| Andrew Patterson | Tolland | Sam¹ Spicer | " |
| Jonᵃ Pardee | Waterbury | Asa Starkweather | " |
| Dan¹ Pendleton Artifʳ | " | Elisha Stowel | Pomfret |
| John Robinson | Middletown | Obadiah Sears | Preston |
| Jared Robinson Lieut | New Haven | Constant Searl | Stonington |
| Sam¹ Robinson Q M | " | Nath¹ Suncheman | " |
| Simeon Robinson jun' | Windham | Prince Summit | Voluntown |
| | | James Sprague | Union |
| Abial Roberts | Waterbury | Stephen Scovill | Waterbury |
| Jeremiah Roswell | Danbury | Absalom Thomas | New London |
| Laban Riggs | Derby | James Thomas | New Haven |
| Sam¹ Raymond | Redding | John Taylor | New Hartford |
| Amos Rowe | Farmington | David Tomlinson Ens. | |
| Simeon Rouse | Preston | | Derby |
| Reuben Reed | Norwich | John Treat | Glastenbury |
| John Roach | Lyme | Ezekiel Tuttle | Waterbury |
| Nathan Root Lᵗ | Willington | Timothy Tuttle | " |

| Names of the Persons supplied | By what Town supplied | Names of the Persons supplied | By what Town supplied |
|---|---|---|---|
| Hezekiah Tuttle | Waterbury | Thomas Wiard | Goshen |
| Hezekiah Tracy Lieut | Norwich | Hammon Way | Hartford |
| | | W<sup>m</sup> Walter Art: | New Haven |
| Isaiah Wright | Hebron | W<sup>m</sup> Ward | Lebanon |
| Ezekiel Wright | Norwich | Martin Wade | Lyme |
| Joseph Weeks | New London | W<sup>m</sup> Whitely | New Milford |
| Henry Whiting P M<sup>r</sup> | Derby | Josh<sup>a</sup> Wedge | Norwich |
| Uriah Wise | Cornwall | Walter Warden | Stonington |
| Thomas Wooster Cap<sup>t</sup> | New Haven | Oliver Woodward | Windsor |
| | | Joseph West | Windham |
| Richard Watrous | Derby | Benj<sup>a</sup> Western Ens. | Weathersfield |
| Jon<sup>a</sup> Webb | Norwich | Albigence Waldo | Windham |
| Stephen Welton jun<sup>r</sup> | Waterbury | Michael Welch | Washington |
| Joshua Webster | Glastenbury | Gael Landor | New Haven |

[*Comptroller's Office, Haskell's Receipts.*]

# CONNECTICUT LINE, 1781-1783.

## FIRST REGIMENT—COL. DURKEE.

[*See Record of Connecticut Men in the Revolution, page 315.*]

### SHORT LEVIES, 1781.

The United States D' To the State of Connecticut, For the Pay of sundry Persons who joined the 1st Regiment, as short Levies in the Year 1781. Viz'

| Names | when entered the Service 1781 | when Discharged |
|---|---|---|
| Seth Garnsey | July 28 | Dec. 14 |
| Daniel Pierce | Aug. 30 | " 30 |
| Amos Westland | July 10 | " 19 |
| Benjamin Cushman | Aug. 31 | " 26 |
| Zebulon Hawkins | June 27 | " 31 |
| Benjamin Wood | " 27 | " 25 |
| Caleb Edson | Aug. 8 | " 15 |
| James Morgan | June 1 | " 29 |
| Josiah Terry | July 2 | " 29 |
| Seth Geary | Sept. 3 | " 28 |
| Nathan Fairchild | " 10 | " 25 |
| John B. Emmes | " 14 | " 25 |
| Araunah Kilborne | " 1 | " 25 |
| Elijah Griswold | Aug. 24 | " 31 |
| John Wilcoxon | July 1 | " 19 |
| Jabez Bottom | " 30 | " 14 |
| Thomas Peck | Aug. 27 | " 25 |
| Nath¹ Sabins | " 18 | " 25 |
| Derby Donavin | July 10 | " 31 |
| John Green | " 7 | " 25 |
| Cudgoe Shepard | " 1 | " 25 |
| Joseph Pratt | Aug. 10 | " 13 |
| William Fuller | " 27 | " 25 |
| Josiah Rogers Dodge | " 27 | " 14 |
| Daniel Perkins | " 18 | " 25 |

| Names | when entered the Service 1781 | when Discharged |
|---|---|---|
| Ichabod Blackman | July 13 | Dec. 25 |
| John Spencer | Sept. 14 | " 31 |
| Ephraim Babcock | July 1 | " 28 |
| Philip Perkins | Aug. 18 | " 19 |
| Solomon Brooks | " 21 | " 30 |
| Stephen Simmons | July 3 | " 12 |
| William Austin | " 1 | " 31 |
| Bernard Bagley | " 12 | " 25 |
| Thomas Evans | Sept. 11 | " 29 |
| Robert Hammond | " 5 | " 25 |
| Aaron Baxter | " 1 | Nov. 28 |
| Stephen Commins | July 10 | Dec. 25 |
| Timothy Green | Aug. 18 | " 25 |
| Thomas Marble | " 22 | " 30 |
| Roswell Beach | July 1 | " 25 |
| Nehemiah Blackman | Sept. 7 | " 28 |
| Jack Gregory | Aug. 23 | " 31 |
| Samuel Brewster | " 15 | " 27 |
| John Cumbo | July 19 | " 30 |
| Aaron Kellogg | Aug. 14 | " 31 |

[*Comptroller's Office, Haskell's Receipts.*]

## SHORT LEVIES, 1782.

Pay Roll of the eight Months Men who served in the 1st Connecticut Regiment in the Year 1782

| Names | Time of Inlistment | Time of Discharge |
|---|---|---|
| John Ayer | Apr. 8 | Dec. 25 |
| Isaac Snow | 22 | 9 |
| John Whitcomb | 28 | 29 |
| Samuel Cole | 28 | 9 |
| Mark Hamblin | May 1 | 9 |
| Henry Waldo | Apr. 22 | 28 |
| Willm Knapp | 23 | Feb. 1783 |
| David Hull 2d | May 3 | " |
| James Heart | Nov. 1 | Dec. 17 |
| Chas Rice | " | 5 |
| Fred Smith | " | 20 |
| Ebenr Doolittle | " | 31 |
| Elijah Northrop | " | 9 |
| Joseph West | " | 13 |
| Zaccha Doud | " | 5 |
| Bemmir(?) Morgan | Apr. 15 | Jan. 1 |
| David alias Daniel Pease | " | " |
| Amos Holden | 7 | |
| Jonn Fosket | May 1 | Jan. 1 |
| Jack Gregory | Apr. 24 | " |
| Emanus Lilley | May 4 | Nov. 15 |
| John Green | June 10 | Jan. 1 |
| Jonah Webb | Nov. 1 | " |
| Caleb Barrows | " | " |
| Willm Coltrain | " | " |

## CONNECTICUT LINE, 1781–1783.

| Names | Time of Inlistment | Time of Discharge |
|---|---|---|
| Eben<sup>r</sup> Cobuck | Nov. 1 | Jan. 1 |
| Rob<sup>t</sup> Follett | " | " |
| Elip<sup>t</sup> Burnham | " | " |
| Jacob Norton | " | Nov. 22 |
| Wolcott Burnham | May 14 | Dec. 9 |
| Ira Cannon | 8 | Nov. 16 |
| Ezra Tupper | June 7 | Sept. 23 |
| James Hopkins | 12 | Dec. 8 |
| Levi Parker | 22 | " |
| David Carpenter | 1 | Nov. 5 |
| Daniel Bird | Nov. 1 | Dec. 16 |
| Step<sup>n</sup> Moucher | " | 6 |
| Will<sup>m</sup> Davis | " | " |
| Asael Hull | " | Nov. 5 |
| Amasa Ingham | " | Dec. 31 |
| Asa Burr | " | 6 |
| Daniel Pick | " | Nov. 5 |
| John Butler | May 4 | 17 |
| Shubal Snow | 30 | Jan. 1 |
| Hezekiah Davison | " | " |
| John Blocker | " | Aug. 19 |
| Jesse Peck | 13 | Jan. 1 |
| Tho<sup>s</sup> Fox | 6 | Dec. 9 |
| James Kennedy | Nov. 1 | Jan. 1 |
| Moses Allyn | " | Dec. 5 |
| Elisha Marshall | " | 6 |
| Will<sup>m</sup> Reed | " | " |
| Jed<sup>h</sup> Cox or Coc | " | 29 |
| Isaac Boxford | " | " |
| Sam<sup>l</sup> Andrews | " | 28 |
| Jon<sup>a</sup> Egglestone | " | Nov. 29 |
| Arnold Worden | Apr. 15 | Jan. 1 |
| Elias Tracey | 22 | " |
| Phin<sup>s</sup> Hulett | 1 | " |
| Joseph Morgan | 26 | Nov. 17 |
| Bethuel Norton | 1 | 16 |
| Ezra Bates | 26 | Jan. 1 |
| Joshua Martin | July 16 | |
| Sam<sup>l</sup> Martin | " | |
| Tho<sup>s</sup> Rindge | | |
| Lemuel Barber | Nov. 1 | Dec. 5 |
| Sam<sup>l</sup> Cook | " | " |
| Abel Barnes | " | " |
| Jachish Holcomb | " | " |
| Fred. Avery | Apr. 14 | Jan. 1 |
| Benj<sup>n</sup> Ward | May 18 | " |
| Solom<sup>n</sup> Howard | 1 | " |
| John Conolly | June 21 | " |
| Noah Spencer | Nov. 1 | " |
| John Robinson | " | " |
| Will<sup>m</sup> White | " | " |
| Israel Frisby | " | " |
| Abrah<sup>m</sup> Tomkins | " | " |
| Sam<sup>l</sup> Collins | " | " |
| Edmund Griswold | " | " |
| Thomas Watson | " | " |
| Elijah Howard | May 1 | Dec. 5 |

| Names | Time of Inlistment | Time of Discharge |
|---|---|---|
| James Morse | Apr. 8 | Dec. 3 |
| John Martin | May 16 | 6 |
| David Pratt | June 10 | 9 |
| Gad Page | May 6 | 29 |
| Sylvanus Pease | May 19 | 9 |
| John Ford | Apr. 1 | " |
| Edw<sup>d</sup> Holmes | Nov. 1 | 7 |
| Josiah Rockwood | " | 16 |
| Amos Rich | " | 28 |
| Solomon Cone | " | 18 |
| Prince Crosby | " | 31 |
| Peter Maranday | " | 9 |
| Elisha Carrell | " | 5 |
| Shipman Clark | " | " |
| Joseph Cromb | Apr. 1 | Nov. 24 |
| Joseph Howe | 16 | Dec. 20 |
| Gilbert Hatch | 26 | Jan. 1 |
| Amos Starkweather | " | Dec. 9 |
| Elisha Dyer | May 1 | Jan. 1 |
| Joel Mack | 27 | " |

[*State Library, Revolution 25.*]

CONNECTICUT LINE, 1781-1783.

## SECOND REGIMENT—COL. SWIFT.

[*See Record of Connecticut Men in the Revolution, page 322.*]

### CAPT. CALEB BALDWIN'S COMPANY.

Return of Capt Baldwins Compy Specifying the time they have to serve.

| Names | Term y | m | Names | Term y | m |
|---|---|---|---|---|---|
| Serj Hall | War | | Eleazer Baldwin | 1 | 6 |
| Serj Meigs | War | | Eli Hull | 1 | 6 |
| Serj Turner | 1 | 7 | John Warrin | War | |
| Corpl Call | War | | Cornelius Chittenden | 1 | 7 |
| Corpl Mix | War | | Joel Gaylord | War | |
| Corpl Sillick | War | | Nathan Teall | 1 | 8 |
| J. Airey Dr | 1 | 1 | Amasa Warner | War | |
| J. Coon Fifer | War | | Robart Watkins | 1 | 6 |
| Benjamin Knapp | 1 | 5 | Call Fruman | War | |
| Hilderick Barritt | War | | John Wright | 1 | 9 |
| Samuel Lynds | 1 | 7 | Cuff Smith | 1 | 7 |
| David Cole | War | | Joel Willcon | 1 | 8 |
| Jonah Carter | 1 | 6 | Whala Springger | 1 | 7 |
| Reuben Stevens | War | | Samuel Rucket (?) | 1 | 6 |
| John Griswold | 1 | 8 | Ezeriah Canfield | War | |
| Joel Spencer | 1 | 6 | Solomon Chittenden | 1 | 7 |
| Robart Hull | 1 | 5 | | | |

[The remainder of the roll is missing.]

[*Connecticut Historical Society.*]

## SHORT LEVIES, 1781.

The United States Dr To the State of Connecticut for the Pay of sundry Persons who joined the second Regiment as short Levies in the Year 1781.

| Names | when entered the Service | when Discharged |
|---|---|---|
| Reuben Morey | July 31 | Dec. 12 |
| Samuel Stanliff | " 31 | " 81 |
| Ashbel Olmstead | Aug. 21 | " 24 |
| Samuel Nye | " 7 | " 13 |
| Samuel Dimmock | " 7 | " 20 |
| John Dimmock | " 7 | " 30 |
| Lothrop Burgiss | " 16 | " 7 |
| Joshua Simmons | " 7 | " 13 |
| Taman Kimball | " 16 | " 20 |

# REVOLUTION ROLLS AND LISTS.

| Names | when entered the Service | when Discharged |
|---|---|---|
| Samuel Tibbals | July 11 | Dec. 31 |
| Richard Skinner | " 12 | " 24 |
| Increase Brainard | " 12 | " 12 |
| George Healy | Aug. 27 | " 12 |
| Abel DeForrest | " 27 | " 12 |
| Thomas Newcomb | " 5 | " 30 |
| William Harris Fox | " 6 | " 30 |
| Timothy Linsey | July 31 | " 12 |
| Ephraim Hull | Aug. 21 | " 12 |
| Anthony Sizer | " 21 | Nov. 21 |
| Uriah Finney | " 16 | Dec. 12 |
| Nathan Gregory | " 29 | " 31 |
| Timothy Rundalls | July 27 | " 24 |
| Joseph Mead | " 27 | " 24 |
| Josiah Apley | " 31 | " 31 |
| Samuel Church | " 9 | " 13 |
| Nathan Hinman | Aug. 27 | " 12 |
| John McClentock | " 7 | " 31 |
| Jonathan Talbott | July 9 | " 13 |
| Silas Leonard | Aug. 3 | Jan. 4 |
| Noah Munroe | " 21 | Dec. 31 |
| James Lincoln | " 21 | " 31 |
| John Benidict | " 27 | " 12 |
| Matthew Barnum | " 27 | " 30 |
| Elihu Judd | " 29 | " 12 |
| Phineas Taylor | " 29 | " 12 |
| Benjamin Peck | " 27 | " 31 |
| William Coltrain | " 16 | " 14 |
| Jannah Sutliff | July 11 | " 12 |
| Elias Johnson | Aug. 24 | " 27 |
| Grove Loomiss | " 21 | " 24 |
| Isaac Mead | July 27 | " 13 |
| Timothy Herrington | Aug. 16 | " 13 |
| Abner Moses | July 13 | Nov. 18 |
| Idem | April 25 | June 11 |
| William Tisdale | July 12 | Dec. 30 |
| Phineas Gorham | Aug. 2 | " 24 |
| Caleb Bailey | July 11 | " 21 |
| Andrew Chidester | Aug. 27 | " 12 |
| Dan¹ (for Matthew) Hubbard | July 11 | " 31 |
| James Fuller | Aug. 16 | " 20 |
| Jeremiah Tharp | " 29 | " 31 |
| Phineas Smith | " 27 | " 31 |

[*Comptroller's Office, Haskell's Receipts.*]

## CONNECTICUT LINE, 1781–1783.

## DESERTIONS, 1781, 1782.

List of deserters from the 2d Connecticut Regt Commanded by Colonel Swift from the 1st of Jany 1781 to the 31st July 1782

| Names | Time Deserted 1781 | Names | Time Deserted 1781 |
|---|---|---|---|
| Ephraim Cohorse | Jan. 28 | Ebenezr Drinkwater | July 19 |
| Benja Tarbox (late Q Mr Serj) | Feb. 1 | Moses Dutton | " |
| | | David Andrus | Aug 9 |
| Jonah Jones | Mar. 16 | Jesse Smith | " |
| John Smith | Feb. 22 | Hiram Wm Howard | Sep. 4 |
| Abraham Gillet | Apr. 10 | Stephen Jones | Oct. 31 |
| Cocher Wiggins | Apr. 1 | Christopher Blake | Oct. 11 |
| John Taylor (of N. Hartford) | Jan. 1 | Samuel Lummis | Nov. 18 |
| | | | 1782 |
| John Condrick | Apr. 8 | Peter Surdan | Feb. 11 |
| Charles Goodwin | May 2 | Aaron Culver | Mar. 5 |
| Abraham Quakenbush | May 4 | William Jackson | Apr. 10 |
| Thomas Reed | Jan. 1 | Isaac Squires | " |
| Isaac Fisher | May 20 | Daniel Davidson | " |
| Noah Fulford | May 30 | Samuel Sturdivant | June 3 |
| John Springer | June 26 | Joseph Ross | June 21 |
| Samuel Whitney | July 1 | Thomas Allen | " |
| Henry Stevens | " | Jeremiah Wheaton | July 17 |
| Prince Cato | June 20 | Elipht Allen | July 21 |
| Elipht Nickerson | Aug. 1 | James Tobias | " |
| Elisha Bradford (late Corporal) | July 14 | George States | July 22 |
| | | John Ashley | " |
| John Dennison | Aug. 5 | | |

H. Swift Col.

[*State Library, Revolution 25.*]

## THIRD REGIMENT—COL. WEBB.

[*See Record of Connecticut Men in the Revolution, page 331.*]

### FIRST COMPANY—CAPT. BULKLEY.

Roll and Muster of the First Company in the 3rd Conn. Regiment Commanded by Colonel Samuel B. Webb.

| Ranks | Names | Term of Inlistment | Casualties | Alterations since last Muster |
|---|---|---|---|---|
| Captain | Edward Bulkley | 1st Jan 1777 | | |
| Lieut | Daniel Bradley | 20 July 1780 | In Connecticut | On Recruiting Service |
| Serg$^t$ Major | Jonathan White | D. W. | | Transfered to the Roll of Field & Staff 25$^{th}$ Ap$^l$ 82 |
| Q. M. Serg$^t$ | Simon Griffin | D. W. | | |
| Serg$^t$ | Elijah Bordman | D. W. | | |
| " | Darius Orcutt | 1 Year & 6 | 21$^{st}$ Feb. 1782 at Nyack D. Ferry | |
| " | Moses Griswold | D. W. | | |
| " | Daniel Sizer | D. W. | | |
| Corporal | Hezekiah Nott | D. W. | | |
| " | Thomas Stanley | D. W. | | |
| " | Gideon Goff | D. W. | | |
| Drum Major | David Pratt | D. W. | | " " " |
| Fife Major | John Kirkum | D. W. | | " " " |
| Drummer | Moses Hatch | D. W. | | " " " |
| " | David Lindsey | D. W. | | " " " |
| Fifer | Asa Squire | D. W. | | |
| " | William Armstrong | D. W. | | |
| | Daniel Bushnell | D. W. | | |
| | Abraham Belding | D. W. | | |
| | Jonathan Bullock | 1 Year & 8 Months | | |
| | Simeon Barnes | | | Discharged 13 Ap$^l$ 82 |
| | Jeremiah Bennet | 1 Year & 8 Months | 12$^{th}$ Ap$^l$ 82 on the lines | |
| | John Ballard | 1 & 11 | | |
| | Ward Colton | 1 & 8 | 22 Feb. 82 on the lines | |
| | Moses Coy | 1 & 9 | | |
| | Robert Chandler | 1 & 8 | | |
| | Daniel Dunham | 1 & 10 | | |
| | Joseph Douglass | 1 & 9 | 12$^{th}$ Ap$^l$ 82 on the lines | |

CONNECTICUT LINE, 1781-1783.

| Ranks | Names | Term of Inlistment | Casualties | Alterations since last Muster |
|---|---|---|---|---|
| | Alphred Dresser | 1 & 8 | 7th Feb '82 Pomphret in Conn. by Col. Grosvenor's order | |
| | Jack Freeman | | | |
| | Brince Freeman | | | |
| | Cato Freeman | | | |
| | Stephen Fox | | | |
| | Samuel Herrington | | | |
| | Arunah Hackley | | | |
| | Samuel Lyon | | | |
| | Daniel Mosley | | | |
| | David Peck | | | |
| | Nathaniel Price | | | |
| | Joseph Preston | | | |
| | Joseph Pease | | | |
| | Samuel Roberts | | | |
| | Reuben Roberson | | | |
| | Abel Stowel | | | |
| | Samuel Stowel | | | |
| | Nathaniel Stowel | | | |
| | John Smith | | | |
| | Joseph Treat | | | |
| | Hezekiah Wheeler | | | |
| | Peter Whitney | | | |
| | Joseph Willson | | | |

I certify the above Roll to be the true State of said Company the 25th Day of April 1782

Edward Bulkley Cap't.

[*Edward Bulkley, New Haven.*]

# EIGHTH COMPANY—CAPT. ROGERS.

[*See Record of Connecticut Men in the Revolution, page 336.*]

Size Roll of Captain Rogers's Company 8$^d$ Connecticut Regiment

| Mens Names | Age | Size Feet | Inches | Born | Residence | Complection | Eyes | Hair | When | Inlistments Term | What Town |
|---|---|---|---|---|---|---|---|---|---|---|---|
| Serj$^t$ Richard Lord | 31 | 5 | 7 | Lyme | Lyme | Dark | Dark | Brown | March 77 | D War | Willington |
| William Basset | 39 | 5 | 10½ | N. Haven | Water Town | Light | Light | D Brown | Feb. 1777 | D War | Watertown |
| Ablather Evans[1] | 40 | 5 | 9 | Hartford | Hartford | Dark | Dark | Dark | Feb. 1777 | " | Hartford |
| Peter Stalker[2] | 27 | 5 | 11 | Fairfield | Fairfield | Dark | Dark | Dark | Aug. 1777 | " | Fairfield |
| Reuben Beach | 24 | 5 | 11 | " | Stratford | Light | Light | Brown | Mar. 1, 1777 | " | Stratford |
| Henry Hull | | | | | | | | | | | |
| Thomas Wells | 28 | 5 | 7¾ | Hartford | Hartford | Fair | Grey | Light | Apr. 15, 1777 | D War | Hartford |
| Corp Jesse St John | 22 | 5 | 9½ | Norwalk | Norwalk | Dark | Dark | Black | Mar. 15, '78 | D War | Norwalk |
| James Crane | 22 | 5 | 9 | Saybrook | Goshen | Light | Light | Dark | Dec. 26, 1780 | 3 years | Goshen |
| Amasy Grenold[3] | 27 | 5 | 5 | Saybrook | Salsbury | Light | Grey | Brown | Apr. 1777 | D War | Salsbury |
| Nicholas Howell[4] | 46 | 5 | 4½ | Sandy Cruse | N. Haven | Dark | Black | Black | Jan. 1777 | D War | N. Haven |
| Reuben Carter | 31 | 5 | 11½ | Canterbury | Canterbury | Dark | Black | Black | Mar. 11, '77 | D War | Canterbury |
| Drummer John Avery | 17 | 5 | 5 | Norwalk | Norwalk | Light | Light | Dark | Mar. 1779 | D War | Norwalk |
| William Kane[5] | 16 | 5 | 2 | Fraderickburg, N. Y. | N. Milford | Light | Grey | Brown | Feb. 1, 1781 | 8 years | N. Milford |
| Fif Frederick Whipple[6] | 17 | 5 | 4½ | Norwich | Norwich | Dark | Dark | Black | Feb. 1781 | D War | Norwich |
| Isaac Higgans[7] | 17 | 5 | 7 | Stratford | Stratford | Light | Light | Brown | July 5, 1781 | 8 years | Fairfield |
| Private Anor Adee | 22 | 5 | 11 | Woodbury | Woodbury | Dark | Grey | D Brown | May 12, 1777 | D War | Woodbury |
| Reuben Adams | 16 | 5 | 5 | Voluntown | Voluntown | Light | Light | Brown | Dec. 20, 1780 | 8 years | Voluntown |

CONNECTICUT LINE, 1781-1783.

| Name | Age | Height | Birthplace | Complexion | Eyes | Hair | Enlistment | Term | Residence |
|---|---|---|---|---|---|---|---|---|---|
| Ephraim Bates[3] | 30 | 5 | Colchester | Light | Light | Light | May 1, 1781 | 8 years | Litchfield |
| Ephraim Burgess | 41 | 5 | Harwich, Mass. | Light | Light | Light | Feb. 1, 1781 | 8 years | Enfield |
| William Burrus | 21 | 5 | Killingly | Light | Light | Dark | Jan. 1, 1781 | 8 years | Killingly |
| Odas Butts | 17 | 6 | Canterbury | Light | Light | L B | Mar. 15, '82 | 1 year | Canterbury |
| Comfort Chapman[3] | 21 | 5 | Norwich | Light | Light | Dark | Feb. 1, '81 | 8 years | Norwich |
| Eliphalet Carpenter | 17 | 8 | Woodstock | Light | Light | L Brown | Jan. 9, 1781 | 8 years | Woodstock |
| David Clark | 24 | 5½ | Wethington Mass. | Light | Dark | Dark | Feb. 1777 | D War | |
| Ephraim Coy | 21 | 5 | Union | Light | Light | Light | April 1777 | 8 years | N. Haven |
| John Dingly | 21 | 10 | Preston | Light | Light | Brown | Nov. 1781 | D War | Windham |
| James Duggan | 36 | 5 | Windham | Dark | Dark | Dark | Jan. 1, 1781 | 8 years | Canterbury |
| Moses Elsworth | 34 | 8½ | Ireland | Dark | Light | L Brown | April 1777 | D War | E. Windsor |
| Jonathan Edwards[10] | 23 | 7¾ | E. Windsor | Light | Dark | L Brown | Jan. 1777 | D War | Milford |
| Samuel Eells[11] | 25 | 9½ | Rochester, Mass. | Light | Light | L Brown | April 1777 | D War | |
| Aron Eaton | 19 | 10 | Milford | Light | Light | L Brown | Apr. 8, 1782 | 1 year | Danbury |
| Thomas Frink | | 7 | No. 1, N. H. Conn. | | | | | | |
| Amos Holden | 30 | | Glastenbury | Dark | Grey | Light | June 15, 1782 | 8 years | Bolton |
| Samuel Hull | 16 | 5 | Milford | Dark | | Black | Feb. 1, 1781 | 8 years | N. Milford |
| Philip Hill[13] | 39 | 5 | Lebanon | Light | Light | D Brown | Jan. 1, '81 | 8 years | Lebanon |
| David Hammond | 17 | 4¼ | Woodstock | Light | Light | L Brown | Mar. 15, 81 | 8 years | Woodstock |
| Jacob Haladay | 24 | 4½ | Simsbury | Light | Dark | L Brown | Dec. 18, '80 | 8 years | Simsbury |
| David Hodge[15] | 27 | 7½ | Milford | Dark | Dark | D Brown | Apr. 1, 77 | D War | Milford |
| Joel Hait | 25 | 4½ | Stamford | Light | Light | L Brown | Feb. 77 | D War | Stanford |
| Samuel Jenkins | 17 | 8 | Norwalk | Dark | Dark | D Brown | June 1780 | D War | Norwalk |
| Justin St John | 34 | 8 | N. Haven | Light | Light | Black | Mar. 1777 | D War | Norwalk |
| Chandler Judd | | 5 | | | | | | | |
| Jedediah Kimball[14] | 33 | 5 | Norwich | Dark | Dark | Dark | Mar. 15, '81 | 8 years | Norwich |
| Uriah Keeler | 28 | 10 | Norwalk | Light | Grey | Light | Apr. 19, '77 | D War | Norwalk |
| Abner Lord | 20 | 8 | Lime | Light | Light | L Brown | | D War | |
| James Liberty | 31 | 5 | N. Y. City | Black | Black | Black | April '77 | D War | Woodbury |
| Weight Lewis[15] | 21 | 6 | N. Town | Dark | Dark | Dark | May 1, '79 | D War | N. Town |
| Joel Mosher | 21 | 6 | Stratford | Light | Light | L Brown | April '77 | D War | Stratford |
| David Matteson[16] | 23 | 6 | N. London | Light | Light | D Brown | Feb. 1, '81 | 8 years | Norwich |
| Abraham Murrey | 44 | 10 | Providence, R. I. | Dark | Dark | Dark | April '77 | D War | Stratford |

Occupation.— [1]C & Joiner [2]Taylor [4]Hatter [6]Joiner [9]Carpenter [10]Cocker (?) [11]Cooper
[3]Cooper [13]Shoe Mak[r] [16]C Winder
[7]Weaver [12]Weaver [8]Weaver [14]C Warner

## REVOLUTION ROLLS AND LISTS.

| Mens Names | Age | Size Feet | Inches | Born | Residence | Complection | Eyes | Hair | When | Inlistments Term | What Town |
|---|---|---|---|---|---|---|---|---|---|---|---|
| Private Stephen Meigs | 18 | 5 | 8 | Guilford | Guilford | Light | Light | Brown | May 1780 | D War | Guilford |
| Peter Mix | 25 | 5 | 7 | Ginea | Durham | Black | Black | Black | May 5, '77 | D War | Branford |
| Cato Negro | 18 | 5 | 9 | E. Windsor | E. Windsor | Black | Black | Black | July 5, '81 | 3 years | E Windsor |
| Aron Parks | 16 | 5 | 8½ | Preston | Ashford | Light | Light | L B | Nov. 26, '80 | D War | Ashford |
| Joseph Phinney[1] | 30 | 5 | 9 | Lebanon | Lebanon | Light | Light | Dark | Jan. 1 '81 | 3 years | Lebanon |
| Thomas Palmer | 22 | 5 | 10 | Hartford | Rockehill | Dark | Dark | Dark | Apr. 10, '83 | 3 years | N. Milford |
| Ebenezer Platt | 18 | 5 | 5 | Danbury | Danbury | Light | Light | Red | Apr. 10, '83 | 1 year | Danbury |
| James Raymond | 17 | 5 | 10½ | Canterbury | Canterbury | Dark | Dark | Dark | Mar. 15, '83 | 1 year | Canterbury |
| Ethiel Scott | 22 | 5 | 5 | Waterbury | Harwinton | Light | Grey | Light | Apr. 19, '79 | D War | |
| William Short | 20 | 5 | 6½ | Killingly | Killingly | Light | Light | L B | Mar. 6 '81 | 3 years | Killingly |
| Sariel Squires | 19 | 5 | 7½ | Ashford | E. Windsor | Dark | Dark | D B | Apr. 20, '82 | Dec. 81, '82 | E. Windsor |
| Darius Trusdell | 30 | 5 | 11 | Pomfret | Woodstock | Dark | Dark | Dark | Jan. 11, '81 | 3 years | Woodstock |
| Enos Tuttle[2] | 24 | 5 | 7 | Norwalk | Norwalk | Dark | Black | Black | Aug. 15 '78 | D War | Norwalk |
| Stephen Thompson | 23 | 5 | 8 | N. Haven | Waterbury | Dark | Black | Black | Mar. 1777 | D War | Waterbury |
| Amos Temple | 21 | 5 | 6 | Stratford | Stratford | Copper | Black | Black | June 1777 | D War | Stratford |
| Eli Tuller | 42 | 5 | 4½ | Simsbury | Simsbury | Dark | Dark | Dark | Jan. 21, '81 | 3 years | Simsbury |
| Johnson Tiff | 17 | 5 | 11½ | Simsbury | Simsbury | Dark | Dark | L B | Jan. 11, '81 | 3 years | Simsbury |
| John F. Tone | 24 | 5 | 4½ | Germany | Volunton | Light | Light | L B | Jan. 5, '81 | 3 years | Voluntown |
| Jethro Toney | 28 | 5 | 7 | Woodbury | Woodbury | Copper | Dark | Black | April '77 | D W | Woodbury |
| William Waterbury[3] | 25 | 5 | 7½ | Stamford | Stamford | Red | Grey | Brown | Apr. 11 '77 | D War | Stanford |
| Nathan Walker | 16 | 5 | 8 | Woodbury | Woodbury | Light | Blue | L Brown | Sep. 1777 | D War | Woodbury |
| Cato Wilborn | 21 | 5 | 2½ | Ginea | Durham | Black | Black | Black | May 1777 | D War | Durham |

Occupation.—[1] Weaver  [2] Shoe Maker  [3] Weaver

Size Roll of the 8th Company 3d Connecticut Regiment for the year 1782

Other monthly muster rolls in the same volume show that the regiment was commanded by Col. Samuel B. Webb; that the Captain was Hezekiah Rogers; and that the following persons were at sundry times Lieutenants: John Hobart, William Lynn, John Mix, Nathan H. Whiting, Benjamin Dimmick.

[*State Library, Hebard Papers.*]

## SHORT LEVIES, 1781.

The United States Dr To the State of Connecticut, for the Pay of sundry Persons who joined the third Regiment as short Levies, in the year 1781 — Viz —

| Names | when entered the Service | when Discharged |
|---|---|---|
| Noah U. Norton | July 5 | Oct. 16 |
| John Dailey | " 23 | Dec. 14 |
| Lemuel Gillet | " 20 | " 13 |
| Abiel Hinsdale | " 20 | " 24 |
| Timothy Catlin | " 15 | Sept. 9 |
| Josiah Gaylord | " 16 | Dec. 13 |
| Jesse Seymour | " 11 | Oct. 3 |
| Joseph Rogers | " 15 | Nov. 29 |
| Jonathan Wright | " 30 | Dec. 31 |
| Eleazer Payne | " 28 | " 13 |
| Elias Bascomb | " 28 | " 31 |
| Joseph Allen Junr | Sept. 7 | " 23 |
| Isaac Snow | " 7 | " 24 |
| Russell Pratt | " 7 | " 16 |
| Robert Follet | Aug. 29 | " 16 |
| Moses Wright | July 29 | Jan. 1 |
| Nathan Hovey | Aug. 23 | Dec. 1 |
| Jonathan Babcock | July 27 | " 25 |
| Jonathan Pasco | " 30 | " 8 |
| William Leach | Aug. 1 | " 13 |
| Christopher Willoughbey | Sept. 8 | Nov. 12 |
| Ebenezer Rockwell | Aug. 5 | " 12 |
| Simeon (for Elijah) Hunt | July 27 | Dec. 8 |
| Bliss Willoughbey | " 26 | " 13 |
| Joseph Bacon | " 27 | " 24 |
| John Ives | Sept. 8 | " 12 |
| George Burrows | " 8 | Oct. 3 |
| Noah Barber Junr | July 29 | Dec. 2 |
| Hervy Whiting | " 15 | " 24 |
| William Mattison | Aug. 26 | " 30 |
| Jonathan Bemont | " 8 | " 25 |
| Charles Warner | July 27 | " 18 |
| Benjamin Loomiss | Aug. 11 | Nov. 25 |
| Daniel Eaton | " 8 | Dec. 24 |
| John Marsh | " 27 | " 24 |
| Michael Freeman | " 26 | " 24 |
| Caleb Burrows | " 20 | " 26 |
| Joseph Allen | " 7 | " 31 |
| Samuel Kimball | July 15 | " 16 |
| William Porter | " 27 | " 24 |
| Ephraim Kingsbury | " 27 | Nov. 28 |
| James Carpenter | " 27 | Dec. 21 |
| Josiah Fassett | Sept. 5 | " 24 |
| Reuben Grant | July 24 | " 26 |
| Helmont Kellogg | " 15 | " 24 |
| Tracey Cleveland | Sept. 5 | " 13 |
| Stephen Long | July 27 | " 30 |
| Abner Richmond | " 27 | " 13 |
| Archelaus Deane | Oct. 10 | " 13 |
| Samuel Strong | July 24 | " 30 |
| Hezekiah Grant | " 24 | " 24 |
| Ashley Rathburn | Aug. 26 | " 14 |
| Harba Childs | July 27 | " 29 |

[Comptroller's Office, Haskell's Receipts.]

## SHORT LEVIES, 1782.

Return of Levies who served in the 3ᵈ Connecᵗ Regmᵗ part of the Year 1782

| Names | Commencᵗ of Pay | Expiration |
|---|---|---|
| Jacob Haskell | May 1 | Dec. 29 |
| Samuel Bliss | 6 | " |
| Samuel Parks | Apr. 20 | " |
| John Bliss | May 1 | " |
| Moses Barnard | Apr. 17 | " |
| Bereiah Bliss | 27 | " |
| Daniel Lyman | " | " |
| John Haskell | June 5 | " |
| Andrew Hazen | May 16 | " |
| Joshua Olmsted | June 17 | 9 |
| Noah Norton | July 1 | " |
| David Hubble | " | " |
| George Foott | Apr. 27 | 20 |
| Nehemiah Seeley | 30 | 9 |
| Amos Gustin | June 10 | 10 |
| Daniel Knight | May 1 | 26 |
| Benoni Robbins | " | 22 |
| Janna Willcox | " | 28 |
| Elisha Catlin | 23 | 28 |
| Ebenez Durffee | Apr. 29 | 5 |
| Elijah Durffee | May 13 | 9 |
| Noah Kesley | Apr. 19 | 24 |
| Jacob Fenton | 29 | 9 |
| James Bliss | May 15 | 5 |
| Hezʰ Terrell | Apr. 24 | 31 |
| Nehemiah Barnes | June 29 | 31 |
| Edward Duncan | May 11 | " |
| Charles Lewis | " | " |
| Aaron Wayley | June 3 | " |
| Zacheus Gillett | May 9 | 10 |
| Benoni Gillett | " | " |
| Nathan Fenton | June 6 | 9 |
| Sorel Squire | " | 31 |
| Nathaniel Conant | 20 | 6 |
| Levi Hall | May 4 | 31 |
| Simeon Stimpson | Feb. 3 | Nov. 8 |
| Daniel Jackson | May 15 | Dec. 9 |
| Miles Bennett | " | " |
| Jonathan Beamont | July 17 | 6 |
| Nathan Potter | Apr. 29 | Oct. 7 |
| Royal Manton | July 1 | Nov. 7 |
| Adonijah Chapman | Apr. 15 | Oct. 2 |
| Wᵐ Cooke | June 1 | " |
| Jonathan Curtiss | Apr. 9 | June 12 |
| Reubin Clark | 1 | Aug. 11 |
| Ebenʳ Chapman | May 24 | Oct. 2 |
| David Gardner | Apr. 13 | " |
| David Hawley | May 11 | Dec. 15 |

[*State Library, Revolution 25*]

# FOURTH REGIMENT—COL. BUTLER.

[*See Record of Connecticut Men in the Revolution, page 337.*]

## RETURN, 1781.

Return of the Non Commiss⁴ Officers & Men in the 4ᵗʰ Conn¹ Reg¹

| Names | Rank | Date of Inlistments | Term they Engag'd for | Town for which they Serve |
|---|---|---|---|---|
| Edw. Miller | Serg Mr | Apl 19 '77 | War | Middletown |
| Oliver Munn | Fife | Marh 7 '79 | " | " |
| Geo. Doolittle | Sergt | May 1 '78 | " | " |
| Jabez Atkins | Private | | " | " |
| Willm Bacon | " | | " | " |
| Saml Frothingham | " | | " | " |
| Jona Tayler | " | Jany 1 '77 | " | " |
| Joseph Willis | " | | " | " |
| Aaron Rawles | " | | " | " |
| John Codner | " | July 2d '81 | 6 Months | " |
| Leml Wilcox | " | | War | " |
| Michl Maloney | " | July 14 '81 | 6 Months | " |
| Jona Hubbard | " | Apl 1st '77 | War | " |
| Natl W Benton | " | June 1 '80 | " | " |
| Jacob Gilson | " | Jany 17 '77 | " | " |
| Isaac Roberts | " | Marh 16 '80 | " | [        ] |
| Peter Freeman | " | | " | |
| Cuff Liberty | " | Marh 1 '78 | [        ] | " |
| Phila Freeman | " | | | " |
| Cuff Freeman | " | | | " |
| Zacha Stow | " | Marh 12 '78 | | " |
| Saml Lucas | Sergt | Jany 31 '77 | | Durham |
| Gida Chittendon | " | Octr 9 '77 | | " |
| Phina Squires | " | May 5 '77 | " | " |
| Natl Brown | F Majr | Decr 13 '77 | " | " |
| [ ]ry[ ]ssetter* | Sergt | Jany 1 '77 | [    ] | " |
| John [ ]shop † | Corpl | Decr 25 '77 | " | " |
| Miles Cook | Drum | Apl 1 '80 | | " |
| Silas Stanbrough | fife | Jany 31 '81 | 3 Years | " |
| Leml Stanbrough | Drum | Feby 2d '81 | 3 Years | " |
| Schuyler Goddard | Prive | Feby 1 '78 | War | " |
| John Meeker | " | Feby 27 '77 | " | " |
| Willm Johnson | " | May 24 '77 | " | " |
| Asher Squire | " | May 5 '77 | " | " |
| Dudley Squire | " | June 15 '81 | 1 Year | " |
| Willm Carr | " | Apl 1 '77 | War | " |
| Warren Murray | Corp. | Feby 10 '77 | " | " |
| Robt Carr | Prive | Jany 31 '81 | 3 Years | " |
| Natl Clark | " | Feby 9 '81 | 3 Ys | " |
| Jona Loveland | " | Marh 15 '81 | 3 Ys | " |

* Bryant Rossetter      † John Bishop

| Names | Rank | Date of Inlistments | Term they Engag'd for | Town for which they Serve |
|---|---|---|---|---|
| Eben' Carr | Priv⁰ | Jan⁷ 31 '81 | 3 Years | Durham |
| Clement Carr | " | " | " | " |
| Sharp Camp | " | Dec' 1 '77 | War | " |
| Cato Wilbrow | " | Mar² '77 | " | " |
| Ahim² Punderson | Serg¹ | Dec' 13 '76 | " | N. Haven |
| David Alcock | " | Jan⁷ 1 '77 | " | " |
| Edw⁴ Baker | " | Nov' 24 '76 | " | " |
| Geo. Cook | fife | Feb⁷ 1 '77 | " | " |
| [          ]ld* | fife | Dec' 13 '76 | " | " |
| [       ]d | Corp¹ | Mar² 1 '77 | " | " |
| [    ] Howell † | " | Dec' '76 | " | " |
| [           ] | Private | Ap¹ '77 | " | " |
| [           ] | " | Nov' '76 | " | " |
| [    ]ael Dodge | " | Ap¹ '77 | " | " |
| Amos Frost | [    ] | [    ]'77 | " | " |
| John O Briant | | '77 | " | " |
| Abel Stockwell | | '78 | " | " |
| Asahel Salmon | [    ] | [    ]'77 | " | " |
| Moses Potter | " | '77 | " | " |
| Ambrose Smith | " | | " | " |
| Amos Tinker | " | | " | " |
| Jared Blakslee | " | | " | " |
| Martin Clark | " | Fe[ | " | " |
| Ja⁸ Sales | " | Jan⁷ 27 '77 | " | " |
| Benajah Bracket | " | Aug[ ] '79 | " | " |
| Medad Potter | " | | " | " |
| Abr^m Cooper | " | | " | " |
| Hez^h Bracket | " | | " | " |
| Steph² Shattuck | Serg¹ | | " | " |
| Amos Mallery | " | | " | " |
| Rob¹ Marsh | Private | | " | " |
| Ward Peck | " | | " | " |
| Elijah Wolcut | " | | " | " |
| Tim⁷ Mansfield | " | Jan⁷ 10 '77 | " | " |
| Dav⁴ Bradley | " | | " | " |
| Will^m Cook | " | | " | " |
| Rob¹ Climet | " | | " | " |
| Abr^m Sugden | " | Feb⁷ 8 '77 | " | " |
| Eph^m Thomas | " | | " | " |
| Jesse Smith | Serg¹ | Jan⁷ 4 '77 | " | " |
| Daniel Moss | Private | Jan⁷ 1 '77 | " | " |
| Sam¹ Thomas | " | Dec' 14 '76 | " | " |
| Augus^ts Peck | " | Dec' 14 '77 | " | " |
| Thomas Sanford | " | May 20 '77 | " | " |
| Anthony M Daniel | " | July 6 '78 | " | " |
| Benajah Wolcut | " | Jan⁷ 20 '78 | " | " |
| Amos Warner | " | July 6 '80 | " | " |
| Caleb Blakslee | Drum' | Aug¹ 10 '79 | " | " |
| Simeon Bishop | Private | | " | " |
| Elnathan Tolles | " | | " | " |
| Dav⁴ Eagleston | " | | " | " |
| Jn⁰ Nales | " | May 2 '78 | " | " |
| Bristol Baker | " | May '77 | " | " |
| And^w Tack | " | May '77 | " | " |
| Jack Little | " | | " | " |
| Lewis Martin | " | | " | " |

\* Charles Mansfield  † Nicholas Howell

CONNECTICUT LINE, 1781–1783.

| Names | Rank | Date of Inlistments | Term they Engag'd for | Town for which they Serve |
|---|---|---|---|---|
| Sharp Rogers | Private | Feb⁷ '77 | War | N. Haven |
| Jess⁰ (?) Sill * | " | | " | " |
| Ezekiel Toppand | " | Dec⁷ 13 '76 | " | " |
| Hector Williams | " | | " | " |
| Jabez Lord | " | May 1 '78 | " | " |
| Abrᵐ Johnson | " | Decʳ 14 '76 | " | " |
| John Wilson | " | Febʳ 1 '77 | " | " |
| Rᵈ L[ ]nsberry † | " | | " | " |
| Jer. Wooding | " | May 10 '77 | " | " |
| Jaˢ Goldsmith | Sergᵗ | Febʳ 10 '77 | " | Milford |
| Willᵐ Ovitt | " | | " | " |
| John Belding | Private | | " | " |
| Elijah Bryan | " | | " | " |
| Timʸ Johnson | " | | " | " |
| Phinehas Johnson | " | | " | " |
| John Peck | " | | " | " |
| Davᵈ Hodge | " | Apˡ 12 '77 | " | " |
| Ichabod Walden | " | Janʸ 27 '81 | " | " |
| Benjⁿ Pritchard | " | Apˡ 1 '77 | " | " |
| John Stewart | " | Janʸ 1 '77 | " | " |
| Jared Hitchcock | Corpˡ | Apˡ 25 '77 | " | " |
| Abel Hitchcock | " | May '77 | " | " |
| Isaac Northrup | " | Apˡ 25 '77 | " | " |
| Joseph Goldsmith | Private | | " | " |
| Titus Hine | " | | " | " |
| Benjⁿ Burns | " | | " | " |
| Willᵐ Goldsmith | " | Apˡ 15 '77 | " | " |
| Job Cesar | " | Marʰ '77 | " | " |
| [ ]be | " | | " | " |
| [ ]rus | " | Novʳ '76 | " | " |
| [ ]hapman | " | May '77 | " | " |
| [ ] Gibbs ‡ | " | May '77 | " | " |
| ]lˡᵐ Soʃ ]ₛ § | " | Marʰ '77 | " | " |
| ]ongo Z[ | " | Maʰ '77 | " | " |
| Juba Freeman | " | May '77 | " | " |
| Jasper Jones | " | Novʳ 24 '76 | " | Stratford |
| Gershom Bardsly | " | [ ] 30 '77 | " | " |
| David Hawley | " | [ ] '81 | 6 Months | " |
| Benjⁿ Treadwell | " | [ ] '81 | 3 Years | " |
| Isaac Hawley | " | [ ] '81 | 6 Months | " |
| Joseph Wakely | " | | War | " |
| Sam Gregory | " | July [ ] '81 | 6 Months | " |
| Natˡ Clark | " | July 5, '81 | 6 Months | " |
| Henʸ Baley | " | | War | " |
| Hezʰ Mitchel | " | July 28 '81 | 6 Months | " |
| Samˡ Chapman | " | Marʰ. 19 '79 | War | Fairfield |
| Asa Sherwood | fife | | " | " |
| Joseph Elwood | Privᵉ | Janʸ 1 '81 | 3 Years | " |
| Isaac Higgins | " | July 5 '81 | 3 Yˢ | " |
| David Jones | " | | War | " |
| Ned Freedom | " | May '78 | " | " |
| Stepⁿ Hall | Sergᵗ | Janʸ 10 '81 | 3 Years | " |
| Enos Tuttle | Privᵉ | | War | Norwalk |
| John Parrot | " | July 21 '78 | " | " |
| John Rogers | " | Apˡ '78 | " | " |
| Solᵒ Soutice | " | | " | " |

* Jeffʸ (?) Sill   † Richard Lounsberry   ‡ Peter Gebbs   § Willᵐ Sowers

REVOLUTION ROLLS AND LISTS.

| Names | Rank | Date of Inlistments | Term they Engag'd for | Town for which they Serve |
|---|---|---|---|---|
| Jonⁿ Newman | Priv⁰ | Jan⁷ 1 '81 | 3 Y⁸ | Ridgefield |
| Harry Williams | " | Feb⁷ '81 | War | " |
| Benjⁿ Bennit | Serg¹ | Nov⁷ 25 '76 | " | " |
| Jacob Patchen | Private | Mar⁵ 1 '81 | 3 Y⁸ | Reading |
| Josiah Hendrick | " | Jan⁷ 1 '81 | 3 Y⁸ | " |
| Dan¹ Couch | " | Jan⁷ 1 '81 | 3 Y⁸ | " |
| Jaˢ Dixon | " | | War | " |
| Wᵐ Dewen | " | Aug¹ 24 '81 | 6 Months | " |
| Ezra Ketcham | " | | War | Danbury |
| Jeremiah Rosel | " | May 1 '78 | " | " |
| Edwᵈ Goddard | Corp¹ | May 5 '79 | " | " |
| Brigs Ingersol | Private | June 25 '81 | 6 Months | New Milford |
| Nat¹ Porter | " | | War | " |
| Thadˢ Jacklin | " | July '81 | 6 Months | " |
| Willᵐ Cain | Fife | Feb⁷ 1 '81 | 3 Y⁸ | " |
| Jnᵒ Davenport | Corp¹ | | War | " |
| Jnᵒ Murray | Private | July 13 '81 | 6 Months | " |
| Salmon Bostick | " | | War | " |
| Damon R Converse | " | July 13 '81 | 6 Months | " |
| Hanford Newell | " | July 5 '81 | 6 Months | " |
| Benjⁿ Ruggles | " | July 5 '81 | 6 Months | " |
| Jared Hotchkiss | " | July 3 '81 | 6 Months | " |
| Sam¹ Nichols | " | July 2 '81 | 6 Months | " |
| Solᵒ Warner | " | July 3 '81 | 6 Months | " |
| Joseph Tomlinson | " | March 20 '77 | War | Derby |
| John Hatchet | " | Jan⁷ 20 '77 | " | " |
| Eli Hull | " | Mar⁵ 10 '80 | " | " |
| Willᵐ Smith | " | | " | " |
| Prince Freeman | " | Feb⁷ 1 '81 | War | " |
| Edwᵈ Warren | " | | 6 Months | " |
| Jaˢ Canada | " | | " | " |
| Joseph White | " | | " | " |
| Dan¹ Brown | Serg¹ | Nov⁷ 25 '76 | " | " |
| Ebenʳ Durand | Private | Jan⁷ 1 '78 | " | " |
| Ebenʳ Botchford | " | July 7 '81 | 6 Months | " |
| Reubⁿ Chapman | " | Feb⁷ 19 '81 | 3 Y⁸ | " |
| Reubⁿ Blake | " | Feb⁷ 20 '78 | War | " |
| Thoˢ Phillips | " | Dec⁷ 27 '76 | " | " |
| Shub¹ Johnson | " | Feb⁷ '77 | " | " |
| Ezra Foot | " | | " | " |
| David Hull | " | Mar⁵ 20 '78 | " | " |
| Jonⁿ Brown | " | Nov⁷ 24 '76 | " | " |
| Richᵈ Pitts | " | Dec⁷ 27 '80 | 3 Y⁸ | " |
| Sam¹ Bristol | " | July 17 '81 | 6 Months | Woodbury |
| John Herrick | Corp¹ | Nov⁷ 24 '76 | War | " |
| Zachⁿ How | Private | July '81 | 6 Months | " |
| Joseph Brooks | " | Aug¹ 18 '81 | 6 Months | " |
| Amos Davis | " | Jan⁷ 1 '81 | 3 Years | " |
| Justus Taylor | " | June 20 '81 | 3 Y⁸ | Washington |
| Wᵐ Lament | " | June 15 '81 | 3 Y⁸ | " |
| Eleazer Curtiss | " | June 11 '81 | 6 Months | " |
| John Davidson | " | May 1 '78 | War | " |
| Ezekiel Newton | " | June 22 '81 | 6 Months | " |
| John Jordan | " | Aug¹ 17 '81 | 6 Months | " |
| Isaac Davidson | Serg¹ | | War | " |
| John McLean | " | May 19 '77 | " | Salisbury |
| Jacob McLean | " | Feb⁷ 15 '78 | " | " |

## CONNECTICUT LINE, 1781–1783.

| Names | Rank | Date of Inlistments | Term they Engag'd for | Town for which they Serve |
|---|---|---|---|---|
| [Will]iam¹ Tarry | Serg¹ | May 21 '77 | War | Salisbury |
| [ ]ᵃ Bradley * | " | May '77 | " | " |
| [ ] Hull † | " | March 1 '78 | " | " |
| [ ]enton | Private | | " | " |
| [ ] Cool ‡ | " | | " | " |
| [ ] Griswold | " | | " | " |
| [ ] Griswold | " | | " | " |
| [ ] Whitney | " | | " | " |
| [A]sa Owen § | " | May 8 '78 | " | " |
| Champⁿ Ackley | Corp¹ | | " | " |
| Wᵐ Tupper | Q M [ ] | May 28 '77 | " | " |
| Daniel Hull | Corp | | " | " |
| Martin Tubbs | " | Febʸ 15 '77 | " | " |
| Phinehas Strong | " | May 14 '77 | " | " |
| Jonᵃ Hull | " | Feb [ ] '78 | " | " |
| Simeon Meigs | Privᵉ | May 5 '77 | " | " |
| Wᵐ Yates | " | May 7 '77 | " | " |
| Amasa Grinnol | Corp¹ | May '77 | " | " |
| Artemas Blodget | Privᵉ | May '77 | " | " |
| Curtiss Chappel | " | | " | " |
| Himan Cool | " | Febʸ '77 | " | " |
| Natˡ Emorson | " | May '77 | " | " |
| Wᵐ Eldredge | " | June '78 | " | " |
| Hʸ Fitzgerald | " | May '77 | " | " |
| Benjⁿ Graves | " | May '77 | " | " |
| Willᵐ White | " | May 10 '77 | " | " |
| Bille Munger | " | Apˡ '78 | " | " |
| John Lerow | " | Marʰ 16 '77 | " | Litchfield |
| Isaac Cluff | " | Decʳ 5 '76 | " | " |
| Samˡ Rossetter | " | | " | " |
| John Bricks | " | May '78 | " | " |
| Joseph Colyer | " | | " | " |
| Phinehas Parker | " | July 1 '78 | 6 Months | Watertown |
| Alexʳ Judd | " | | War | " |
| Medad Merrills | " | June 5 '78 | " | Waterbury |
| Elkanah Smith | " | July 10 '81 | 6 Months | " |
| Barnˢ Clark | " | | War | " |
| Jonah Webb | " | July 4 '81 | 6 Months | Cheshire |
| David Barns | " | Janʸ 1 '77 | War | " |
| Joel Barns | " | Febʸ 27 '81 | 3 Years | " |
| Samˡ Stone | " | Febʸ 1 '81 | War | " |
| Reuben Moss | Corp¹ | Apˡ 3 '77 | War | " |
| Benjⁿ Bristol | " | Febʸ 20 '77 | War | " |
| Amos Mix | Privᵉ | | War | " |
| Edmond Fields | Serg¹ | Marʰ 1 '78 | War | Wallingford |
| Joseph Clark | " | Febʸ 1 '77 | " | " |
| Danˡ Bradley | " | | " | " |
| Isaac Parker | " | Apˡ '77 | " | " |
| Samˡ Collins | " | May 5 '77 | " | " |
| Abrᵐ Parker | Corp¹ | | " | " |
| Edmᵈ Merriam | " | May 20 '77 | " | " |
| Ephᵐ Merriam | fife | May 5 '77 | " | " |
| Jotham Rice | Privᵉ | Febʸ 9 '77 | " | " |
| Timᵒ Parker | " | Apˡ 14 '77 | " | " |
| Willᵐ Prout | " | Marʰ 2 '78 | " | " |
| John Parker | " | Febʸ 9 '77 | " | " |

\* Zenas Bradley    † Henry Hull    ‡ Isaac Cool    § Asa Owen

REVOLUTION ROLLS AND LISTS.

| Names | Rank | Date of Inlistments | Term they Engag'd for | Town for which they Serve |
|---|---|---|---|---|
| Joel Cook | Corp¹ | May 10 '77 | War | Wallingford |
| Johnson Cook | Priv° | Jan⁷ 20 '77 | " | " |
| Warren Cook | " | | " | " |
| Jotham Hall | " | | " | " |
| Thad° Todd | " | Ap¹ '77 | " | " |
| Moses Hale | " | Mar^h 2 '78 | " | " |
| Orange Munson | Drum | Feb⁷ 10 '78 | " | " |
| Cha° Merriman | D Maj^r | Jan⁷ 23 '77 | " | " |
| Nash Yale | Priv° | Ap¹ 1 '77 | " | " |
| Lemuel Cook | " | June 30 '81 | 6 Months | " |
| Pratt Jones | " | Feb⁷ 10 '78 | War | " |
| Cha° London | " | Feb⁷ 15 '78 | " | " |
| Elihu Cook | " | Mar^h 7 '77 | " | " |
| Amasa Thorp | " | June 21 '77 | " | " |
| Amos Thorp | " | June 21 '77 | " | " |
| Zenas Mix | " | June 1 '77 | " | " |
| Benj^a Ford | " | Jan⁷ 5 '78 | " | " |
| Jon^a Ford | " | Jan⁷ 12 '78 | " | " |
| David Atkins | " | | " | " |
| Jn° Verguson | " | Ap¹ 25 '77 | " | " |
| Elisha Bishop | " | | " | " |
| Ja° Coban | " | Ap¹ 3 '77 | " | " |
| Isaac Hawley | " | Aug⁴ 6 '81 | 6 Months | " |
| Levi Robinson | " | | War | " |
| Jesse Vose | Corp¹ | Mar^h 1 '78 | " | " |
| Lent Munson | Drum | Mar^h '78 | " | " |
| Dick Freedom | Private | Mar^h '78 | " | " |
| Sam¹ Brown | Serg⁴ | Feb⁷ 2 '77 | " | Branford |
| Luther Page | " | Ap¹ 21 '77 | " | " |
| Jairus Harrison | " | Ap¹ 21 '77 | " | " |
| Rufus Whedon | " | May 9 '77 | " | " |
| Sam¹ Wardell | fife | Jan⁷ 16 '78 | " | " |
| [J]l Potter * | Drum | Ap¹ 1 '77 | " | " |
| [Je]iel Smith † | Private | | " | " |
| [ ] Potter | " | | " | " |
| [ ] Butler | " | May '77 | " | " |
| [ ] Palmer | " | May '77 | " | " |
| [J]on^a Finch ‡ | " | Ap¹ 1 '77 | " | " |
| Ezekiel Butler | " | Feb⁷ 10 '78 | " | " |
| Jordan Smith | " | Ap¹ 26 '77 | " | " |
| David Rogers | " | Feb⁷ 10 '78 | " | " |
| Joseph Hawkins | " | June 7 '78 | " | " |
| Roswell Whedon | " | Dec⁷ 14 '76 | " | " |
| Hermon Rose | Corp¹ | Feb⁷ 12 '77 | " | " |
| Hen⁷ Johnson | Private | Ap¹ '77 | " | " |
| Sam¹ Barker | Serg⁴ | Jan⁷ 1 '81 | 3 Years | " |
| John Eberhard | " | Jan⁷ 7 '77 | War | " |
| Sam¹ Hoadley | Corp¹ | Feb⁷ 2 '77 | " | " |
| Ja° Cooper | Priv° | Ap¹ 3 '77 | " | " |
| John Garrett | " | Mar^h 8 '77 | " | " |
| Reuben Frisbie | " | Feb⁷ 18 '77 | " | " |
| Will^m Cooper | fife | Dec⁷ 1 '77 | " | " |
| Ziba Robinson | Private | | 6 Months | " |
| Cesar Bagdon | " | Ap¹ '77 | War | " |
| James Dinah | " | May '77 | " | " |
| Prince George | " | Feb⁷ '77 | " | " |

\* Joel Potter   † Jehiel Smith   ‡ Jonathan Finch

## CONNECTICUT LINE, 1781-1783.

| Names | Rank | Date of Inlistments | Term they Engag'd for | Town for which they Serve |
|---|---|---|---|---|
| Peter Lion | Private | June '77 | War | Branford |
| Pomp Liberty | " | Mar^h '77 | " | " |
| Peter Mix | " | Mar^h '77 | " | " |
| Joseph Otis | " | Mar^h '77 | " | " |
| Dick Violet | " | Mar^h '77 | " | " |
| Heman Rogers | Corp^l | Ap^l 25 '77 | " | " |
| David Dowd | Private | Feb^y 1 '78 | " | Guilford |
| Tim^y Scranton | " | Ap^l 12 '77 | " | " |
| Tim^y Stevens | " | | " | " |
| Benj^n Watrous | " | | " | " |
| Joel Johnson | " | Feb^y 18 '81 | 3 Years | " |
| Tim^y Shelley | " | July 5 '81 | 6 Months | " |
| Ab^r Norton | " | Ap^l 6 '77 | War | " |
| Tho^s Wheeler | Corp^l | Ap^l 10 '77 | " | " |
| John Lewis | Private | July '81 | 6 Months | " |
| Jehiel Munger | " | July 5 '81 | 6 Months | " |
| Presto Kelsey | " | July 5 '81 | 6 Months | " |
| Chand^r Benton | " | Mar^h 7 '77 | War | " |
| Isaiah Atkins | Corp^l | | " | " |
| H^y M^cLean | Private | | " | " |
| Benj^n Welton | " | May '77 | " | " |
| Eber Hall | " | Ap^l 2 '81 | 6 Months | " |
| Jehiel Dowd | " | Feb^y 1 '80 | War | " |
| Steph^n Meigs | " | May 1 '80 | " | " |
| Bart^l Rawlinson | " | Mar^h 9 '81 | 3 Years | " |
| Reub^n Rawlinson | " | Mar^h 5 '81 | 3 Y^s | " |
| Ira Atkins | " | Ap^l 3 '81 | 3 Y^s | " |
| Reuben Everts | " | Feb^y 1 '81 | 3 Y^s | " |
| Gilbert Graves | " | Feb^y 1 '81 | 3 Y^s | " |
| Jehiel Wilcox | " | Feb^y 1 '81 | 3 Y^s | " |
| Dan^l Newton | " | July '81 | 6 Months | " |
| Zach^s Dowd | " | July 5 '81 | 6 Months | " |
| Dav^d Thompson | Serg^t | Jan^y 25 '77 | War | " |
| Torry Scranton | " | May '77 | " | " |
| Tho^s Cook | Private | | " | Killingsworth |
| Will^m Wellman | " | | " | " |
| Jesse Graham | Drum | | " | Say Brook |
| Joseph Whittlesey | Priv^e | Dec^r 18 '80 | 3 Years | " |
| Giles Clark | " | July 2 '81 | 6 Months | " |
| Ja^s Grant | " | Feb^y 1 '81 | 3 Years | " |
| Gid^n Buckingham | " | Feb^y 1 '81 | 3 Y^s | " |
| Sam^l Comstock | " | Mar^h 1 '81 | 3 Y^s | " |
| Rob^t Newell | " | Jan^y 1 '81 | 3 Y^s | " |
| Oliver White | " | Apr. 21 '77 | War | " |
| Cyrus Graham | " | Feb^y 1 '77 | " | " |
| Simon Hough | " | July 1 '81 | 1 Year | " |
| Rich^d Stokes | " | July 6 '81 | 6 Months | " |
| Tho^s Freeman | " | | War | " |
| Cons^t Chapman | Serg^t | Jan^y 1 '81 | 3 Years | " |
| John Lay | Private | Jan^y 15 '81 | 3 Y^s | Lyme |
| Rufus Holdridge | Drum | Mar^h 1 '81 | 3 Years | Groton |
| Cato Robinson | Private | Ap^l '77 | War | " |
| John Nugen | " | Jan^y 10 '77 | " | Stonington |
| Sam^l Hill | " | Jan^y 29 '81 | 6 Months | Lebanon |
| Benj^n Bissel | " | June 29 '81 | 6 Months | " |
| Nathan Law | " | Jan^y 1 '81 | 1 Year | " |
| Benj^n Bissel | " | July 4 '81 | 6 Months | " |

| Names | Rank | Date of Inlistments | Term they Engag'd for | Town for which they Serve |
|---|---|---|---|---|
| [ ]erry Reed | Private | Jan⁷ 16 '81 | 3 Years | Lebanon |
| [ ]nj ͣ Bennit | " | June 4 '81 | 6 Months | " |
| [ ] Wadsworth | " | June 29 '81 | 6 Months | " |
| [ ] Moulton | " | June 12 '81 | 1 Year | " |
| [ ] Hill | " | Feb⁷ 8 '81 | 3 Years | " |
| [ ]d Davidson | " | Feb⁷ 8 '81 | 3 Years | " |
| [ ]ep ͣ Buckingham | " | July 25 '81 | 6 Months | " |
| Ezekiel Lyman | " | July 26 '81 | 6 Months | " |
| Dan¹ Puffer | " | July 26 '81 | 6 Months | " |
| Prince Williams | " | June 26 '81 | 6 Months | " |
| Ja ͣ Sharp | " | June 30 '81 | 6 Months | " |
| Joseph Abby | " | Jan⁷ 4 '81 | 3 Years | Windham |
| Daniel Neff | " | July 3 '81 | 6 Months | " |
| Abner Lilley | " | Dec⁷ 15 '80 | 3 Years | " |
| Asa Cleaveland | " | June 25 '81 | 6 Months | " |
| Dan¹ Woodward | " | Nov⁷ 24 '80 | 3 Years | " |
| Phillip H Stish | " | June 1 '78 | War | " |
| Juba Dyer | " | Feb⁷ '81 | 3 Years | " |
| Prince Johnson | " | Dec⁷ 1 '80 | 3 Years | " |
| John Dingley | " | | War | " |
| Elisha Back | " | Mar ͪ 3 '81 | 3 Years | " |
| Salathiel Neff | " | June 3 '81 | 6 Months | " |
| James Dean | " | Mar ͪ 20 '81 | 2 Years | " |
| Jesse Gilbert | " | | War | " |
| Chester Lilley | " | July 1 '81 | 6 Months | " |
| Elias Upton | " | July 1 '81 | 6 Months | " |
| Lothrop Frink | " | Nov⁷ 24 '80 | 3 Years | " |
| Enos Robins | " | June 26 '81 | 1 Year | " |
| Nat¹ Abby | " | Jan⁷ 15 '81 | 3 Years | " |
| Cha ͣ Ripley | " | Dec⁷ 25 '80 | 3 Y ͣ | " |
| Eleaz⁷ Robinson | " | Nov⁷ 25 '80 | 3 Y ͣ | " |
| Jedediah Hibbard | " | Dec⁷ 4 '80 | 3 Y ͣ | " |
| Oliver Parish | " | July 1 '81 | 6 Months | " |
| Zacheus Hovey | " | July 3 '81 | 6 Months | " |
| James L Flint | Serg ͭ | May 1 '78 | War | " |
| Sol⁰ Bixbee | Private | May 1 '81 | 3 Years | Stafford |
| Elijah Norton | " | July 1 '81 | 6 Months | Hebron |
| Henry Booth | Serg ͭ | Mar ͪ 1 '81 | 3 Y ͣ | Coventry |
| And ʷ Peters | Priv ͤ | Feb⁷ 8 '81 | 3 Y ͣ | " |
| Jon ͣ Ball | " | Feb⁷ 7 '81 | 3 Y ͣ | " |
| Jesse Peck | " | July 10 '81 | 6 months | Canterbury |
| Sol⁰ Goff | " | Feb⁷ 20 '81 | 3 Y ͣ | E ͭ Haddam |
| Ansel Patterson | " | Jan⁷ 2 '81 | 3 Y ͣ | " |
| John Lee | " | Ap¹ 6 '81 | 3 Y ͣ | Ashford |
| Allen Prior | Serg ͭ | Jan⁷ 1 '81 | War | Windsor |
| Tim⁰ Hoskins | Private | Dec⁷ 21 '81 | 3 Y ͣ | " |
| Calvin Wilson | " | Feb⁷ 20 '81 | 3 Y ͣ | " |
| Elihu Mather | Serg ͭ | Jan⁷ 1 '81 | War | " |
| Jn⁰ Rowley | Private | Jan⁷ 1 '81 | 3 Y ͣ | " |
| Sampson Cuff | " | Jan⁷ 1 '81 | 3 Y ͣ | " |
| John Hosmer | " | Jan⁷ 1 '77 | War | Hartford |
| Uri Hungerford | fife | Mar ͪ '81 | War | Farmington |
| Roswell Cook | Drum | Jan⁷ 22 '81 | " | " |
| Ichabod Bailey | Priv ͤ | Nov⁷ 10 '76 | " | " |
| Josiah Cole | " | Dec⁷ 7 '76 | " | " |
| Jn⁰ Horlehoy | " | | " | Simsbury |
| Ja ͣ Eldridge | " | Jan⁷ 2 '81 | 3 Y ͣ | " |

## CONNECTICUT LINE, 1781-1783.

| Names | Rank | Date of Inlistments | Term they Engag'd for | Town for which they Serve |
|---|---|---|---|---|
| Dan¹ White | Priv² | July 1 '81 | 6 Months | Southington |
| Jam⁸ Powers | " | July 6 '81 | 6 Months | " |
| Nathan Beacher | " | Feb⁷ 1 '81 | 6 Months | " |
| Dav. Andrews | Fife | Jan⁷ 1 '81 | War | " |
| Ja⁸ Powers | Private | | " | " |
| Zeb¹ Dudley | " | Dec' 20 '80 | 3 Years | " |
| Elijah Bailey | " | July 1 '81 | 6 Months | " |
| Joseph Beacher | " | July 7 '81 | 6 Months | " |
| John Wellman | " | June 30 '81 | 6 Months | " |
| Isaac Hill | " | July 6 '81 | 6 Months | Ripton |
| Will¹ Bailey | " | | War | Haddam |
| Jacob Rowell | " | July 1 '81 | 6 Months | Springfield |
| Jack Arrabas | " | Nov' '77 | War | Fishkill |
| W¹ Smith | " | | " | Wyoming |
| Leonard Cole | " | | " | " |
| Matt⁷ Grace | " | | " | Fredericksburgh |

| S. Major | Q. M. Serg¹ | D. Major | Fife Maj' | Sergeants | Music | R. & file | Total |
|---|---|---|---|---|---|---|---|
| 1 | 1 | 1 | 1 | 40 | 20 | 389 | 453 |

Eben' Gray L' [   ]
& Com 4ᵗʰ C[   ]

[*Connecticut Historical Society.*]

## SHORT TERM LEVIES, 1781.

Return of Men Engaged for 6 Months 4 Conn¹ Reg¹ Commanded by Col⁰ Zebulon Butler for 1781.

All ranking as privates

| Names | Commen¹ of Service | Time of Discharge | |
|---|---|---|---|
| Benj⁴ Bissell | June 29 | Jan. 1 '82 | |
| Eleazer Curtiss | July 11 | Dec. 8 '81 | |
| Jared Hotchkiss | July 3 | " 12 | |
| Samuel Hills | June 29 | " 26 | |
| Zacheus Hovey | July 3 | Jan. 1 '82 | |
| Sam¹ Nichols | July 2 | | Sick Virginia |
| Elijah Norton | July 1 | Nov. 1 '81 | |
| Oliver Parrish | July 1 | Dec. 24 | |
| Sol⁰ Warner | July 3 | " 26 | |
| Daniel Newton | July 2 | " 13 | |
| Thad⁴ Jacklin | July 12 | " 13 | |
| Salathiel Neff | July 3 | " 20 | |
| Michael Maloney | July 14 | " 26 | |
| John Codnor | July 2 | " 31 | |
| Nathan Beacher | July 1 | " 30 | |
| Preston Kelsey | July 5 | " 2 | |
| Jehiel Munger | July 5 | " 24 | |
| Jonah Webb | July 4 | " 22 | |
| Benj⁴ Bennet | July 4 | " 30 | |
| Heman Woodworth | June 29 | Nov. 26 | |
| Benj⁴ Bissell | July 4 | Dec. 18 | |
| Sam¹ Bristol | July 17 | Dec. 12 | |
| Wolcut Blakley | July 17 | Jan. 1 '82 | |
| Giles Clark | July 2 | Dec. 24 '81 | |
| James Powers Jr. | July 16 | Dec. 11 | |
| Joseph Beecher | July 7 | Dec. 31 | |
| Jesse Peck | July 10 | Dec. 8 | |
| Asa Cleaveland | June 30 | Dec. 16 | |
| Brigs Ingorson | June 25 | " 14 | |
| Ezekiel Lyman Jr. | June 26 | " 23 | |
| Daniel Puffer | June 26 | " 27 | |
| Prince Williams | June 26 | Jan. 1 '82 | |
| Benj⁴ Ruggles | July 5 | Dec. 23, '81 | |
| Hanford Nichols | July 5 | Dec. 31 | |
| Tim⁰ Shelly | July 5 | Dec. 12 | |
| John Maney or Murray | July 13 | Dec. 25 | |
| Damon R Converse | July 13 | | |
| Daniel Neff | July 2 | Dec. 25 | |
| Phinehas Parker | July 1 | " 12 | |
| Daniel Wright | July 1 | " 12 | |
| John Wellman | June 30 | " 12 | |
| Elijah Bailey | July 1 | " 24 | |
| John Lewis | June 30 | " 24 | |
| Zach⁴ Dowd | July 3 | Jan. 1 '82 | |
| Chester Lilly | July 3 | Dec. 24 '81 | |
| Elias Upton | July 1 | " 24 | |
| Eben' Botchford | July 7 | Nov. 27 | |
| Lemuel Cook | June 30 | Jan. 1 '82 | |
| Sam¹ Gregory | July 10 | " | |
| Ezekiel Newton | June 22 | " | |
| Zachariah How | June 22 | Nov. 16 '81 | |

## CONNECTICUT LINE, 1781–1783.

| Names | Commen<sup>t</sup> of Service | Time of Discharge |
|---|---|---|
| Joseph Brooks | Aug. 18 | Jan. 1 '82 |
| Isaac Hill | July 6 | " |
| David Hawley | July 8 | Nov. 24 '81 |
| Isaac Hawley | July 5 | Nov. 10 |
| John Jordan | Aug. 17 | Jan. 1 '82 |
| W<sup>m</sup> Dervan | Aug. 24 | " |
| Zechariah Mitchel | July 28 | " |
| Step<sup>n</sup> Buckingham | July 25 | Dec. 31 '81 |
| Jacob Rowel | July 1 | Dec. 1 |
| James Thorp | June 30 | Dec. 29 |
| Richard Stokes | July 5 | "  12 |
| Nehemiah Clark | July 5 | "  22 |
| Elkanah Smith | July 10 | Jan. 1 '82 |
| Ziba Robinson | July 10 | " |
| Isaac Hawley | Aug. 16 | " |

Jn<sup>o</sup> Sherman P M 4<sup>th</sup> Conn<sup>t</sup> Reg<sup>t</sup>

[*State Library, Revolution 25; Comptroller's Office, Haskell's Receipts.*]

## SHORT TERM LEVIES, 1782.

Short Levies 4 Conn<sup>t</sup> Reg<sup>t</sup> (filed " 1782 ")

Samuel Androus
Moses Allyn
Daniel Burr
Abel Barns
Lemuel Barber
Caleb Burrows
Jeddiah Coe
Elisha Cone
Solomon Cone
James Cook
Solomon Cole
Job Cole
William Coltrain
Job Cole
Robert Follet
Israel Frisby
William Davis
Ebenezer Doolittle
Zephaniah Dowd
Edmund Griswold
Joel Gurnsey
James Hart

Increase Holcomb
Abner Hall
Asahel Hall
Chandler Judd
Elisha Marshall
Peter Morando
Stephen Moshier
Jacob Norton
Elijah Northrup
Daniel Peet
Charles Rice
Isaac Rexford
John Robinson
William Reed
Joseph Rockwell
Amos Rich
Jared Smith
Noah Spencer
Jonah Webb
Thomas Watson
William White
Joseph Wert

[*State Library, Revolution 25.*]

REVOLUTION ROLLS AND LISTS.

## DESERTERS, 1781, 1782.

A Return of the Deserters from the 3d & 4th Connecticut Regim's since the Return for Settlm't of their Pay for the Service of 1780

| Names | Regt | Time when | Towns they belong to |
|---|---|---|---|
| Samuel B Hotchkiss | 3d | 1 Feb. '81 | Wallingford |
| Stephen Herrington | " | 2 Mar. 81 | Norwich |
| Daniel Pelton | " | 16 Apr. 82 | Chatham |
| Nehemiah Daniels | " | 4 May 81 | Colchester |
| Robert Freeman | " | 20 June 81 | Hartford |
| Elias Crow | " | 5 July 81 | " |
| Benjamin Kenny | " | 19 July 81 | " |
| Samuel Goff | " | 1 Jan. 82 | Chatham |
| Hezekiah Phelps | " | 30 Mar. 82 | Symsbury |
| Jehiel Gibbs | " | 30 Mar. 82 | Somers |
| William Flowers | " | 10 Apr. 82 | Hartford |
| Henry Watton | " | 11 Apr. 82 | Danbury |
| Gilbert Whitney | " | 11 Apr. 82 | Symsbury |
| Josiah Evans | " | 11 Apr. 82 | Hartford |
| John Hamilton | " | 20 Apr. 82 | New Fairfield |
| Jacob Hurd | 4th | 1 Jan. 81 | Plainfield |
| John Grant | " | 14 Feb. 81 | Europe |
| Lot Chace | " | 14 Feb. 81 | Plainfield |
| Recompense Woodworth | " | 1 Jan. 81 | Lebanon |
| Serg. Elijah Spafford | " | 15 July 81 | Windham |
| Lemuel Chester | " | 19 July 81 | Norwich |
| Roswell Crocker | " | 20 July 81 | " |
| John Barker | " | 1 Sep. 81 | Pomfret |
| Isaac Bassett | " | 26 Nov. 81 | Canterbury |
| John Winship | " | 1 Dec. 81 | Norwich |
| Philimon Tiffany | " | 1 Feb. 81 | Lyme |
| Samuel Thompson | " | 21 Feb. 82 | Canterbury |
| John Casey Dr | " | 30 Mar. 82 | Providence |
| William Racke | " | 2 Apr. 82 | Bolton |
| Andrew Gay | " | 11 Apr. 82 | Stonington |
| Enos Mix | " | 21 June 82 | Wallingford |
| Austin Brown | " | 25 July 82 | Hebron |

The above is a true Extract from the Regimental Book
         Thos Grosvenor Lieut Col Com.
Camp Aug. 15, 1782

[*State Library, Revolution 25.*]

## FIFTH REGIMENT—LT.-COL. SHERMAN

[*See Record of Connecticut Men in the Revolution, page 343.*]

### SHORT TERM LEVIES, 1781.

Pay roll of the Short levies that serv'd in the 5th Connecticut Regiment (commanded by Lt Colo Comdt Isaac Sherman) in the year 1781.

| Names | Commencement of pay | Time in Service Mo | Days |
|---|---|---|---|
| Bishop Crammer | June 7 | 5 | 24 |
| William Johns or Jones | 20 | 6 | 5 |
| Elisha Frost | July 16 | 5 | |
| Thomas Turner | 5 | 5 | 15 |
| Simeon C. Stoddard | Aug. 3 | 4 | 8 |
| Benjamin Chapman | 16 | 3 | 15 |
| William Gregory | 24 | 3 | 6 |
| Thomas Wakely | 1 | 3 | 18 |
| Alexr Baxter | July 14 | 5 | 11 |
| John Fenton | 1 | 5 | 12 |
| Daniel Root | 14 | 5 | 18 |
| Stephen Simons | 14 | 5 | 5 |
| Adino Chapman | 18 | 5 | 16 |
| Amasa Hutchinson | 14 | 5 | |
| Jonah Cook | 5 | 2 | 1 |
| Jared Cone Jr. | 12 | 4 | 26 |
| Peletiah Alford | 22 | 4 | 21 |
| Levi Scovill | 5 | 5 | 7 |
| Ashbel Upson | 5 | 5 | 24 |
| Benjamin Hall | 5 | 5 | 19 |
| Gideon Barnes | Oct. 26 | 1 | 29 |
| Samuel Dart | July 7 | 5 | 5 |
| Daniel Williams | 5 | 5 | 19 |
| Elijah Porter | 15 | 4 | 29 |
| Benjamin Gaylord | 3 | 5 | 10 |
| Asahel Hodge | 10 | 5 | 6 |
| Ephraim Smith | 5 | 5 | 13 |
| Benjamin Loomis | 1 | 5 | 24 |
| John Tucker | 1 | 5 | 29 |
| David Hummiston | 1 | 5 | 29 |
| Enoch Sherman | Aug. 5 | 4 | 13 |
| Ephm Moorhouse | 28 | 3 | 21 |
| Caleb Terrill | Sep. 8 | 3 | 4 |
| Appleton Hollister | June 1 | 6 | 14 |
| Consider Hanks | 28 | 6 | 2 |
| Benja Stacy Evans | July 3 | 5 | 27 |
| Simeon Booth | 1 | 5 | 6 |
| Benoni Stiles | 1 | 5 | 16 |
| Joseph Emerson | 10 | 5 | 15 |
| Thaddeus Osburn | 1 | 5 | 29 |
| Allen Carpenter | 22 | 4 | 28 |

REVOLUTION ROLLS AND LISTS.

| Names | Commencement of pay | Time in Service Mo | Days |
|---|---|---|---|
| James Dunham | July 2 | 5 | 26 |
| Phillip Kibbee | 1 | 5 | 25 |
| Philip Manning | 1 | 5 | 25 |
| Caleb Thomas | 22 | 5 | 9 |
| Ebenezer Avery | 1 | 5 | 12 |
| Daniel Fowler | 1 | 8 | 14 |
| John Skinner | 1 | 6 | |
| Abiel Grant | 1 | 5 | 24 |
| Alpheus Russel | 14 | 3 | 9 |
| Frederick Kibbee | 14 | 5 | 8 |
| Daniel Edwards | 26 | 4 | 22 |
| Henry Waldo or Waldon | 1 | 5 | 28 |
| Nathan Hovey | 4 | 4 | 26 |
| Daniel Woodward | June 28 | 5 | 11 |
| Elijah Fantom | July 1 | 6 | |
| Jonathan Hill | 12 | 5 | 20 |
| James Johnston | 7 | 5 | 14 |
| Pliny Green | 6 | 5 | 26 |
| John Clark | 5 | 4 | 19 |
| Elijah Hurd | Aug. 16 | 2 | 17 |
| Caleb Rowell | 16 | 4 | 17 |
| David Hubbell | 22 | 3 | 8 |

Manoah Crowell entered service Aug. 26, discharged Dec. 18
John White      "      July 2,    "      "   31
Samuel Calkins  "      Aug. 7     "      Oct. 19
John Miller     "       "   7     "      Nov. 30
Asahel Osborn   "      July 30    "      Dec. 30

N. B. Jared Cone & James Johnston Rec[d] 2 months pay hard money in Virginia

Benj[a] Throop Maj[r] Comd[t] of y[e] 5[th] Conn[t] Reg[t]

[*State Library, Revolution 25; Comptroller's Office, Haskell's Receipts.*]

CONNECTICUT LINE, 1781–1783. 121

## LIGHT INFANTRY, 1781

[*See Record of Connecticut men in the Revolution, page 351.*]

Pay abstract of the Infantry who Marched to the Southard under the Command of the Marq$^s$ De la Fayette and were Omitted in the Abstract for February 1781.

| Names | Rank | Fro | To | |
|---|---|---|---|---|
| John P. Wyllys | Major | Feb. 1 | Mar. 1 | |
| **Infantry C°** | | | | |
| Roger Welles | Capt. | Feb. 1 | Mar. 1 | |
| William Lynn | Lieut. | " | " | |
| Jacob Kingsbury | Ens. | " | " | |
| Lewis Hurd | Serj. | " | " | |
| Silas Phelps | " | " | " | |
| Reubin Beach | " | " | " | |
| James Wasson | " | " | " | |
| Stephen Meeker | " | " | " | |
| John Downs | Priv. | " | " | |
| David Lounsbury | Corp | " | " | |
| Stephen Butler | " | " | " | |
| David Bullen | " | " | " | |
| Benjamin Dix | " | " | " | |
| Joseph Clinton | " | " | " | |
| Daniel Winchell | Fifer | " | " | |
| John Dixon | Drum. | " | " | |
| John Allyn | Priv. | " | " | |
| Noah Barnum | " | " | " | |
| Ichabod Goodrich | " | " | " | |
| Benjamin Kirkum | " | " | " | |
| Jonathan Miller | " | " | " | |
| Bryon Montigou | " | " | " | |
| Nathaniel Beach | " | " | " | |
| Vaniah Fox | " | " | " | |
| Samuel Gookins | " | " | " | |
| Seth Gregory | " | " | " | |
| James Hide | " | " | " | |
| Jedediah Kimball | " | Jan. 15 | Apr. 1 | |
| Sheldon Potter | " | Feb. 1 | Mar. 1 | |
| Samuel Whitney | " | " | " | |
| Jeremiah Cunnell | " | Jan. 1 | Apr. 1 | |
| Jacob Achor | " | Feb. 1 | Mar. 1 | |
| Hondrick Baile | " | Jan. 1 | Apr. 1 | |
| John Barnum | " | Feb. 1 | Mar. 1 | |
| Edward Burghes | " | " | " | |
| Reubin Cadwell | " | " | " | |
| William Chadwick | " | " | " | |
| Jeremiah Chamberlain | " | " | " | Deserted |
| Allyn Corning | " | " | " | |

| Names | Rank | From | To | |
|---|---|---|---|---|
| Allyn Evens | Priv. | Feb. 1 | Mar. 1 | |
| Remb. Filley | " | " | " | |
| David Hurd | " | Jan. 1 | Apr. 1 | |
| Joseph Johnson | " | Feb. 1 | Mar. 1 | |
| David Robbarts | " | " | " | |
| Isaiah Smith | " | " | " | |
| Justin S$^t$ John | " | " | " | |
| Ezra Tryon | " | " | " | |
| Samuel Vallet | " | " | " | |
| Benjamin Wakeley | " | " | " | |
| Joshua Wheeler | " | " | " | |
| Joseph Hand | " | " | " | Deserted |
| Seth Stannard | " | " | " | |
| Samuel Manning | " | " | " | |
| Samuel Pulford | " | " | " | |
| David Williams | " | " | " | |
| Joel Mashier | " | " | " | |
| Samuel Hinman | " | " | " | |
| Eben$^r$ Huntington | L$^t$ C$^o$ | | | |
| Stephen Betts | Cap. | | | |
| Nathan H. Whiting | Lieut. | | | |

. . . . .

Hopkins C$^o$ continued

| | | | | |
|---|---|---|---|---|
| Stephen Gavett | Priv. | Jan. 16 | Mar. 1 | |
| Ephraim Harrey | " | Jan. 1 | Apr. 1 | |
| John Pearle | " | Feb. 15 | " | |
| James Anderson | " | Mar. 1 | " | |
| Thomas Brewer | " | Feb. 27 | " | |
| Garner Cleveland | " | Jan. 1 | " | |
| Ichabod Downing | " | Mar. 1 | " | |
| Daniel Davis | " | " | " | Deserted |
| David Spencer | " | Jan. 1 | " | |
| Jacob Strong | " | Feb. 1 | " | |
| Edmund Shelly | " | Feb. 18 | " | |
| Joseph Smith | " | Jan. 1 | " | |

Capt. Walkers C$^o$

| | | | | |
|---|---|---|---|---|
| Samuel Barden | Priv. | Jan. 1 | Apr. 1 | |
| John Clarke | " | " | " | |
| Benjamin Durfee | " | " | " | |
| John Fagin | " | " 22 | " | |
| Mason Green | " | Feb. 14 | " | Deserted |
| Joel Hamlin | " | Jan. 1 | " | Deserted |
| Jabez Morten | " | " 11 | " | |
| Lemuel Stanclift | " | Feb. 26 | " | |
| Jonathan Simons | " | Mch. 1 | " | |
| William Scheeswick | " | Feb. 4 | " | |
| Seth Dodge | " | Jan. 1 | " | |
| Reubin Dodge | " | " | " | |
| Joshua Fuller | " | Feb. 1 | " | |
| Heman Hatch | " | Jan. 1 | " | |
| Henry Ponds | " | Feb. 7 | " | |
| Chester Upham | " | Jan. 1 | " | |
| Jacob Weight 1st | " | " | " | |
| Jacob Weight 2d | " | " | " | |
| Hubbard Burrous | " | Mar. 25 | " | |

CONNECTICUT LINE, 1781-1783.

Allyn's Cº

| Names | Rank | From | To | |
|---|---|---|---|---|
| [ ] | Priv. | Jan. 4 | Apr. 1 | |
| [ ] | " | Feb. 1 | " | |
| [ ] Beebee | " | Jan. 29 | " | |
| [ ] Chaffee | " | Feb. 6 | " | |
| [ ] Eggleston | " | Jan. 29 | Mar. 6 | |
| Benedict Eggleston | " | Jan. 1 | Apr. 1 | |
| Simeon Fox | " | Jan. 3 | Mar. 25 | |
| Bassett Fox | " | Jan. 15 | " | |
| Jabez Edgcomb | " | Mar. 1 | Apr. 1 | |
| David Gardner | " | " | " | |
| Jacob Gillet | " | Jan. 17 | " | |
| Cudjo Holmes | " | Jan. 1 | " | |
| John G. Holcomb | " | Jan. 1 | Mar. 6 | |
| [ ] Horton | " | Jan. 29 | Apr. 1 | |
| [ ] Kingsley | " | Jan. 16 | Mar. 25 | |
| Eliel London | " | Jan. 17 | Apr. 1 | |
| Elias Meason | " | Jan. 1 | Mar. 25 | |
| Nathan Mallery | " | Jan. 19 | Apr. 1 | |
| John Mills | " | Mar. 1 | " | |
| James Neason | " | Jan. 1 | Mar. 25 | |
| Robin Neason | " | Jan. 8 | Apr. 1 | |
| Isaac Nellson | " | Jan. 1 | Mar. 25 | |
| Daniel Perkins | " | " | Mar. 6 | |
| Isaiah Pratt | " | Mar. 5 | Apr. 1 | |
| Adonijah Rose | " | Jan. 1 | Mar. 25 | |
| John Robertson | " | Mar. 1 | Apr. 1 | |
| [ ] Sharp | " | " | " | |
| Ebenezer Shaw | " | Jan. 1 | " | |
| David Taylor | " | " | Mar. 6 | |

Cap Betts Cº

| Names | Rank | From | To | |
|---|---|---|---|---|
| Anthony DeFlorus | Dm | Jan. 12 | Apr. 1 | |
| Jonathan Brown | Priv. | Jan. 1 | " | |
| Parley Cay | " | Jan. 19 | " | |
| Joseph Davis | " | Jan. 1 | Mar. 28 | |
| David Dix | " | " | " 26 | |
| Edward Freeman | " | Mar. 17 | Apr. 1 | |
| Benjamin Greenslit | " | Feb. 3 | Mar. 28 | |
| John Gates | " | Jan. 1 | Mar. 28 | |
| Abel Gutherie | " | " | Apr. 1 | |
| Jason Gay | " | Feb. 1 | " | |
| Robert Holdridge | " | Jan. 1 | Mar. 28 | |
| David Jackson | " | Feb. 28 | Mar. 26 | |
| Theophilus Luther | " | Jan. 1 | Apr. 1 | Deserted |
| Joseph Lawson | " | Jan. 19 | " | |
| William Moore | " | Jan. 1 | " | |
| Jesse Olmsted | " | Jan. 8 | " | |
| Jacob Pettingall | " | Feb. 6 | Mar. 6 | |
| Asaph Pettengall | " | Feb. 6 | Mar. 28 | |
| Samuel Peters | " | Jan. 1 | Apr. 1 | |
| Abel Stimson | " | Jan. 29 | " | |
| Daniel S'John | " | Jan. 1 | " | |
| David Thompson | " | Jan. 19 | " | |
| James Thompson | " | " | " | |
| Chester Waterman | " | Jan. 1 | Mar. 28 | |
| Thomas Warden | " | Jan. 15 | Apr. 1 | |
| Phinehas Granger | " | Jan. 1 | " | |

### Cap Rileys Comp.

| Names | Rank | From | To | |
|---|---|---|---|---|
| Richard Dammorg | Priv. | Jan. 1 | Mar. 24 | Prisoner |
| Jonathan Luce | " | " | Apr. 1 | |
| Ozias Barker | " | Feb. 6 | Mar. 24 | |
| Benj* Cady | " | Jan. 1 | Apr. 1 | |
| John Kimball | " | Feb. 1 | " | |
| Marshall Keyes | " | Jan. 1 | " | |
| Jared Kimball | " | Feb. 1 | " | |
| Jabez Kirtland | " | Jan. 27 | " | |
| Phinehas Knight | " | Feb. 3 | " | |
| Joshua Reynolds | " | " | Mar. 24 | |
| James Miner | " | Feb. 23 | " | |
| John Munsill | " | Feb. 1 | " | |
| Levi Munsill | " | Feb. 6 | " | |
| Joel Hide | " | Feb. 5 | " | |
| Ichabod Wording | " | Jan. 1 | Apr. 1 | |
| Joseph Cockeel(?) | " | " | Mar. 26 | |
| [           ] | " | " | [       ] | |
| [       ] Latham | " | Jan. 17 | Apr. 1 | |
| George Seeley | " | Feb. 3 | " | |
| David Chester | " | Jan. 8 | " | |
| Abijah Downing | " | Mar. 1 | " | |
| Eliezer Hatch | " | Feb. 1 | " | |
| Sylvenus Gage | " | " | " | |
| Ichabod West | " | " | " | |
| Jacob Robbins | " | " | " | Deserted |
| Noah Merrills | " | Jan. 15 | " | |
| Nathan Tubbs | " | Jan. 1 | " | |
| John Wheeler | " | Mar. 1 | " | |
| Joseph Cheney | " | | | |

### Cap. Williams Cº

| Names | Rank | From | To |
|---|---|---|---|
| Joel Clarke | Fifer | Jan. 1 | Apr. 1 |
| Jedediah Adams | Priv. | " | " |
| Christopher Avery | " | Feb. 2 | " |
| Hezekiah Catlen | " | Jan. 29 | " |
| Nathaniel Gates | " | Jan. 1 | " |
| Silas Glass | " | " | " |
| Pileman Kirkum | " | " | " |
| Eliakim Seward | " | " | " |
| Charles Walters | " | " | " |
| Joseph Burrous | " | Feb. 3 | " |
| Samuel Fargo | " | Jan. 1 | " |
| Jim Holt | " | Mar. 2 | " |
| Elijah Fayer | " | Mar. 1 | " |
| Selah Hart | " | Mar. 5 | " |
| Peter Holt | " | Jan. 1 | Mar. 1 |
| Abijah Smith | " | " | Apr. 1 |

### Cap Parson's Cº

| Names | Rank | From | To |
|---|---|---|---|
| James Crane | Priv. | Jan. 1 | Apr. 1 |
| Frederick Whipple | " | Feb. 1 | Mar. 2 |
| Reubin Addams | " | Jan. 1 | Apr. 1 |
| Eph^m Burghes | " | Feb. 1 | Mar. 6 |
| William Burrous | " | Jan. 1 | Apr. 1 |
| Elias Carpenter | " | Jan. 9 | Mar. 26 |
| Eliphalet Carpenter | " | Jan. 1 | " |

## CONNECTICUT LINE, 1781-1783.

| Names | Rank | From | To | |
|---|---|---|---|---|
| Comfort Chapman | Priv. | Feb. 1 | Mar. 3 | Deserted |
| Joseph Phinney | " | " | Mar. 29 | |
| Jacob Halladay | " | Jan. 1 | Mar. 6 | |
| Phillip Hills | " | Feb. 1 | Mar. 29 | |
| Andrew Hausey | " | Mar. 1 | Mar. 30 | |
| David Matterson | " | Feb. 1 | Mar. 3 | |
| Aaron Parks | " | Jan. 1 | Apr. 1 | |
| William Short | " | Mar. 6 | " | |
| Reubin Smith | " | Feb. 1 | " | |
| Johnson Tiff | " | Jan. 11 | " | |
| David Hammond | " | Mar. 13 | " | |
| Darius Trusdale | " | Jan. 11 | Mar. 26 | |
| Eli Tullar | " | Jan. 15 | Apr. 1 | |
| John F. Jone | " | Mar. 1 | Mar. 30 | |
| Thomas Poghcegh | " | Feb. 4 | Mar 22 | Deserted |
| Arcules Ames | " | Mar. 1 | Apr. 1 | |

[*State Library, Revolution 25.*]

## VARIOUS REGIMENTS.

### LEVIES, 1782.

Return of Certificates Rec<sup>d</sup> from Sundry Pay Masters for payment of Levies in 1782.

A List of Certificates lodged in this Office by L<sup>t</sup> John Sherman Agent for the 2 Connecticut Regiment which Cert<sup>s</sup> are signd by Jn<sup>o</sup> Peirce Esq drawn in favour of the following persons who were short Levies in s<sup>d</sup> Reg<sup>t</sup> in 1782

Jonah Steckland
Abijah Batterson
Gilbert McGeer
David Brooks
Roswell Clark
Edward Gibbs
Nathaniel Parker
Jeremiah Rumsey
John Booth
Simeon Saxon
Oziel Richmond
William Norton
Asahel Sawyer
Richard Bishop
Charles Squires
Isaac Olcutt

Daniel Cowen
John Cowen
Samuel Patchers
Samuel Shipman
Niles Gideon
Abijah Elswood
Elijah Rood
Abraham Couch
Otis Ensign
John Ives
Solomon Johnson
Chipman Clark
Abisha Bard
Abisha Forbes
Daniel Bliss

A List of Certificates lodged in this Office by Lieu<sup>t</sup> Nathan Beers Agent for the 8<sup>d</sup> Connecticut Reg<sup>t</sup> which Cert<sup>s</sup> are Signd by John Pierce Esq<sup>r</sup> drawn in favour of the following Persons who were Short Levies in said Reg<sup>t</sup> in 1782

Jacob Haskell
Samuel Bliss
Samuel Parks
John Bliss
Moses Barnard
Beriah Bliss
Daniel Lyman
John Haskell
Adrew Hazen
Joshua Olmsted
Noah Norton
David Hubble
George Foot
Nehemiah Seeley
Amos Gustin
Daniel Knight
Benoni Robbins

Janna Wilcox
Elisha Catlin
Ebenezer Dufee
Elijah Duffee
Noah Kesley
Jacob Fenton
James Bliss
Hezekiah Torrell
Nehemiah Barnes
Edward Duncan
Charles Lewis
Aaron Wayley
Zacheus Gillett
Benoni Gillett
Nathan Fenton
Sarel Squires
Nathaniel Conant

CONNECTICUT LINE, 1781-1783.

Levi Hall
Simeon Stimson
Daniel Jackson
Jonathan Beamont
Miles Bennet
William Mitchel
Charles Minor
Amos Clark
David Hubbard
Solomon Ranny
Benjamin Webster
Neal McNeal

Gideon Russell
Jesse Thomas
Elijah Andrus
Elijah Kilby
James Packerr (?)
George Michel
Daniel Root
Samuel Peck
Jesse Terry
Thomas Marble
Stacy Evens
John Vaughn

A list of Certificates lodged in this Office by L$^t$ John Sherman Agent for the 4 Conn$^t$ Regiment which Certificates are signd by John Pierce Esq drawn in favour of the following persons who were short Levies in 4$^{th}$ Reg$^t$ in 1782

Moses Allen
Jedediah Coe
Elisha Marshall
Elisha Cone
William Reed
Peter Meranda
William Davis
Isaac Rexford
Daniel Peck
Stephen Mosher
Israel Frisby
Jacob Norton
John Robinson
Jonah Webb
Robert Follet
William Coltrain
Caleb Barrows
Solomon Cone
James Hart
Edmond Griswold
Daniel Bird
Amos Rich
Abner Hall
Asahel Hall or Hull
Charles Rice
Jared Smith
James Cook
Solomon Cole
Samuel Andrus
Abel Barnes
Noah Spencer
Lemuel Barber
Thomas Watson
Joseph Rockwell

Job Cole
Ebenezer Doolittle
Joseph West
Elijah Northrop
Zephaniah Dowd
Joel Gurnsey
Chandler Judd
William White
Increase Holcomb
Job Cole
James Burrill
Joseph Buratt
Abijah Beach
Eliphas Burnham
Elijah Beard
Ebenezer Chubbuck
Gideon Dunham
Samuel Elwell
Jonathan Eagliston
Ebenezer Elwell
Abisha Forbes
Philo Gibb
Elisha Hickum
Abraham Tomkins
William Turner
Jonathan Sheperd
Pely Simons
Samuel Nichols
Gurdon Molton
John McCarty
Stephen Luddenton
Abner Lilley
Nathan Law
Amaziah Ingraham

John Perries Certificates lodged in Pay Table Office by Jn° Sherman Agent for payment of Levies in 5th Conn. Regiment.

John Dawning
William Mitchell
Charles Miner
Amos Clark
David Hubbard
Solomon Ranney
Benjamin Webster
Neal McNeal
Gideon Russell
Jesse Thomas
Elijah Andrus
Elijah Kibbee

James Patchin
George Mitchel
Daniel Root
Samuel Peck
Jesse Toney
Thomas Marble
Stacey Evens
John Vaughn
Amos Westland
Roswell Lamphere
Ashbel Webster
John Clark

[*Comptroller's Office.*]

# CONNECTICUT LINE, 1783.

## THIRD REGIMENT—COL. WEBB.

[See *Record of Connecticut Men in the Revolution, page 267.*]

## EIGHTH COMPANY—CAPT. ROGERS.

[In the volume of *Hebard Papers* the monthly returns of this company for a year previous to February 1783 can be seen.] Roll and Muster of the 8th Company 3d Connecticut Regiment Commanded by Col° [8] B Webb for the Month of February 1783

| Ranks | Names | Term of Inlistment | Time since last Muster, or Inlistment | Casualties |
|---|---|---|---|---|
| Captain | Hezekiah Rogers | | December 5 1783 | |
| Lieut[1] | John Hobart | | January 1 1783 | [ ? ] |
| " | William Lynn | | | |
| Ens" | Aron Keeler | | January 26 1783 | Furlough'd Febry 26 83 |
| Sergeant | Richard Lord | D W | December 5 1783 | " by his Excellency Jany 8 83 |
| " | William Bassett | " | January 26 1783 | Sick Hartford Feby 1 83 |
| " | Abiather Evens | " | December 5 1783 | |
| " | Peter Stalker | " | January " " | |
| " | Reuben Beach | " | | Furlough'd March 7 83 |
| " | Henery Hull | " | April 3 1783 | Sick Connet April 2 83 |
| " | Thomas Wells | " | January 26 1783 | |

9

# REVOLUTION ROLLS AND LISTS.

| Ranks | Names | Term of Inlistment | Time since last Muster, or Inlistment | Casualties |
|---|---|---|---|---|
| Corporal | Jesse St John | D W | January 26 1783 | |
| " | James Crane | 9 M 12 D | October 18 1783 | |
| " | Amasa Grenold | D W | January 26 1783 | |
| " | Nicholas Howell | " | " | |
| " | Reubin Carter | " | " | |
| Drummer | John Avery | " | " | |
| " | William Kane | 11 M 6 D | December 5 1782 | Furlough'd by his Excellency Jan 8 83 |
| Fifer | Frederick Whipple | D W | January 26 1783 | |
| " | Isaac Higgins | 16 M 6 D | " | |
| Privats | Aner Adee | D W | " | |
| " | Frank Buck | " | " | |
| " | John Dingly | " | December 5 1782 | Sick N Winsor June 30 82 |
| " | Moses Elsworth | " | August 10 1783 | |
| " | Samuel Ells | " | January 26 1783 | |
| " | Thomas Frink | " | " | |
| " | Jonathan Edwards | " | " | |
| " | Joel Hait | " | December 5 1782 | |
| " | David Hodge | " | January 26 1783 | |
| " | Samuel Jinkens | " | " | |
| " | Uriah Keeler | " | " | |
| " | Abner Lord | " | " | |
| " | James Liberty | " | September 11 1783 | |
| " | Wait Lewis | " | January 26 1783 | |
| " | Stephen Meigs | " | " | |
| " | Joel Mosher | " | " | |
| " | Peter Mix | " | December 5 1783 | Connet with Capt Walker Jany 83 |
| " | Abraham Murry | " | June 14 1783 | Sick Ashford Febry 24 83 |
| " | Aaron Parks | " | January 26 1783 | |
| " | Justin St John | " | " | |
| " | Ethiel Scott | " | December 5 1783 | Furlough'd March 8 83 |
| " | Enos Tuttle | " | January 26 1783 | Furlough'd March 8 83 |
| " | Amos Temple | " | " | |
| " | Stephen Thomson | " | " | |

## CONNECTICUT LINE, 1783.

| | | | | | |
|---|---|---|---|---|---|
| Private | Jethro Toney | | D W | January 26 1783 | |
| " | Nathan Walker | | " | " | |
| " | William Waterbury | | " | " | |
| " | Cato Wilborow | | | " | |
| " | Reubin Adams | 9 M 11 D | | | |
| " | Esaias Butts | 10 M 7 D | | | |
| " | Ephraim Bates | 10 M 28 D | | June 14 1783 | |
| " | William Burrus | 9 M 28 D | | January 26 1783 | Sick Connet Oct' 2 83 |
| " | Ephraim Burgess | 10 M 28 D | | " | |
| " | Eliphelet Carpenter | 9 M 26 D | | " | |
| " | John F. Tone | 10 M 8 D | | " | |
| " | Amos Holden | 27 M | | " | |
| " | Philip Hill | 11 M 28 D | | | |
| " | David Hammond | 12 M 6 D | | December 5 1783 | |
| " | Samuel Hull | 10 M 28 D | | January 26 1783 | |
| " | Jacob Haladay | 9 M 9 D | | | |
| " | Chandler Judd | 1 M | | January 26 1783 | Burring Line |
| " | Jedediah Kimball | 12 M 9 D | | " | |
| " | David Matterson | 10 M 28 D | | " | |
| " | Cato Negro | 15 M 28 D | | " | |
| " | Thomas Palmer | 25 M 28 D | | " | |
| " | Joseph Pheney | 10 M 28 D | | " | |
| " | Ebenezer Platt | 1 M 18 D | | " | |
| " | James Raymond | 1 M 7 D | | " | |
| " | Aron Eaton | 1 M 11 D | | | |
| " | William Short | 12 M 6 D | | | |
| " | Johnson Tiff | 10 M 4 D | | December 5 1783 | Sick Connet Decem' 8 83 |
| " | Darius Trueadll | 10 M 4 D | | " | Furlough'd by his Excellency Jany 3 88 |
| " | Eli Tuller | 10 M 4 D | | | |
| " | James Duggan | 9 M 28 | | January 26 1783 | |
| " | Brestor Negro | | | " | |

I certify the above Roll to be the true State of said Company this 13th Day of March 1783
John Hobart Lieu'

[State Library, Hobard papers.]

# STATE TROOPS, 1775.

[*See Record of Connecticut Men in the Revolution, page 330.*]

### LIEUT. LAY'S COMPANY.

[This company was ordered raised by the Council of Safety, Sept. 14, 1775.]

Lieut Lee Lays Pay Roll for Soldiers at Lyme Jan$^y$ 1776.
Soldiers at Lyme 1775, settled 1776
Entered into Service 20$^{th}$ Oct$^r$

|  | Days |
|---|---|
| Lieut. Lee Lay | 65 |
| Sergt Benj$^a$ Higgins | 65 |
| Fifer Sam$^l$ Fosdick | 41 |
| Lem$^l$ Rogers | 65 |
| Paul Cooley | 65 |
| Phineas Huntley | 65 |
| Abner Smith | 64 |
| Martin Lee | 65 |
| Elisha Way | 65 |
| Silvanus Clark | 57 |
| Elisha Merrow | 57 |
| W$^m$ Mather | 41 |
| Ezra Lee | 41 |
| Elias Mather | 41 |
| Alex$^r$ Hyde | 41 |
| Geo. R. Lewis | 41 |

[*State Library, Revolution 6.*]

# STATE TROOPS, 1776.

[*See Record of Connecticut Men in the Revolution,* pages 381–386.]

## SICK BILLS.

[Names of soldiers extracted from a volume of "Sick Bills," 1776, being itemized accounts of the expenses of individual soldiers during sickness.]
Levies in Jan'y 1776 for 2 Months

| Name | Company | Regiment | Remarks |
|---|---|---|---|
| Abiel Crandle | Capt. Solomon Willes | Douglas | |
| Lieut. Lazarus Ives | Capt. Richards | Wadsworth | |
| Jonathan Tuttle Jr. | Capt. Peas | Douglas | |
| Isaac Newell Jr. | Capt. Noadiah Hooker | Wadsworth | Of Farmington |
| Zoeth Eldridge | Capt. Peas | Douglas | Of Willington |
| Jedediah Olcott | Capt. Prior | Wolcott | |
| Roswell Goodrich | Capt. Jonathan Hale | " | |
| Zechariah Kelsey | Capt. Prior | " | |
| Lieut. Samuel Pierce | " | " | |
| Jabez Chapman Jr. | Capt. John Willey | Wadsworth | |
| Elijah Whiton | Capt. Solomon Willes | Douglas | |
| Richard Spelman | Capt. Couch | Wadsworth | Of Durham |
| Samuel Lucas | | | Not ill |
| David Smith | Capt. Shepard | Wadsworth | |
| Giles Curtiss | Capt. Isaac Cook | Ward | |
| Chauncey Rowlee | Capt. Benjamin Richards | Wadsworth | |
| David Bunce | Capt. Prior | Wolcott | |
| James Whiton | Capt. Benjamin Clark | Douglas | |
| George Kimberly | Capt. Noah Fowler | Ward | |
| Dr. Robert Usher | | Wadsworth | Not ill |
| Ens. Michael Brunson | | " | |
| Corp¹ Ebenezer Kilby | Capt. Hezekiah Welles | Wolcott | |
| John Thomas | Capt. Willey | Wadsworth | |
| Elijah Porter | Capt. Jonathan Welles | " | |
| Richard Risley | " | " | |
| Theodore Keeney | " | " | |
| Corpl. Joseph Porter | " | " | Died |
| Aaron Clark | " | " | Died |

[*Comptroller's Office.*]

# FIRST REGIMENT—COL. WADSWORTH.

[*See Record of Connecticut Men in the Revolution, page 386.*]

## OFFICERS.

Coll James Wadsworth First Reg at Cambridge Winter of 1776— Roll of Capt Joseph Blagues Company & the Commis Officers of the Reg$^t$.

The officers of the first Reg$^t$ of Militia under the Command of Coll James Wadsworth Jan 1776

1
Capt John Willey
Lt John Skinner
Lt Ithamar Harvey
Ens Roger Phelps
   2$^{nd}$ Comp
Capt John Couch
Lt Simeon Parsons
Lt Joseph Newton
Ens Samuel Camp
3
Capt Eliph$^t$ Bulkley
Lt Solomon Tarbox
Lt John Treadway
Ens Eliph$^t$ Chamberlain
4
Capt Joseph Blague
Lt Joseph Churchill
Lt Jacob Wetmore
Ens Timothy Clark

5
Capt Jeremiah Mason
Lt Andrew Waterman
Lt Joel Chamberlain
Ens Elias Bliss
6
Capt Jared Shepard
Lt Edw$^d$ Ells
Lt David Smith 2$^d$
Ens Jabez Brooks
7
Capt Jesse Morse
Lt Tho$^s$ Shepard
Lt Asa Beebe
Ens Miles Hull
8
Capt Benj Richards
Lt Lazarus Ives
Lt Moses Foot
Ens Michael Brunson

[*Copy in Comptroller's Office, location of original unknown.*]

## CAPT. BLAGUE'S COMPANY.

Roll of Capt Joseph Blagues Company, at Cambridge in Winter & Spring of 1776
  The Commissiond officers are given in No 4
  Time of Enlisting Jan$^y$ 25 '76
  Time of Marching Feb. 8
  Discharged April 6
  Days in Service from 73 down to 69

Serj$^t$ Samuel Tuels (?)
  Nicholas Ames
  John Johnson
  Benj Cornell
Corp$^l$ Gershom Hinkley
  Jos Pelton
  Amos Clark
  Andrew Norton

Drummer Daniel Hamlin
Fifer Daniel Starr
Privates Atkins, Joel
  Atkins, Isaac
  Burton, Samuel
  Brown, Thomas
  Boardman, Timothy
  Bunn, Paul

## STATE TROOPS, 1776.

Privates Boardman, Nathan
Clark, Daniel
Cook, Gideon
Cook, Joshua
Clark, Stephen
Cone, Joseph
Cone, Hubb Daniel
Crittendon, Gideon
Cande, Theophilus
Cotton, Elisha
Doolittle, Thomas
Dana, Charles
Duncan, James
Davis, John
Doud, Richard
Gray, William
Goodwin, John
Griffith, Joseph
Gilbert, Allen
Gilbert, Williams
Hubbert, Gideon
Hurd, Thomas
Hale, Benjamin
Hall, Timothy
Harris, Joseph
Hulett, Joseph
Johnson, Isaac

Privates Lane, John
Miller, Giles
Pelton, Jonathan
Parks, Daniel
Penfield, Jesse
Penfield, Simeon
Prior, Jesse
Plumb, Jesse
Rogers, Timothy
Reed, Jonathan
Redfield, Samuel
Robbins, John
Stocking, Eber
Strickland, Stephen
  Jan 26 Discharged April 6
Stocking, Marshall
Stiles, Beriah
Story, John
Shepard, John
Sage, Michael
Stone, Joseph
Ufford, Eliakim
Wilcox, Comfort
White, William
Wetmore, Josiah
Willcox, John
Wood, Joel

[*Copy in Comptroller's Office, location of original unknown.*]


## COL. SWIFT'S BATTALION.

[*See Record of Connecticut Men in the Revolution, page 391.*]

---

### STRATFORD SOLDIERS.

[Arms delivered to Stratford soldiers under the command of Capt. Elijah Beach, in Col. Swifts regiment bound for the Northern Department, July 1776.]

to What Soldier delivered
James Downs
Samuel Edwards
Will<sup>m</sup> Winwright
Pheleg Sunderlin
John Crawford

to What Soldier delivered
Joseph Burton Jr
William Burton
Thomas Weathers
Nathanel Booth
Gideon Peet

[*State Library, Revolution 6.*]

## CAPT. LACEY'S COMPANY.

A List of the Minute Men Return'd to Col. Hinman by Cap$^t$ David Leavenworth Feb$^y$ 5$^{th}$ 1776.

James Reynolds
James B. Reynolds
Samuel Hurd
Daniel Hurd
Ebenezer Lacey
Ebenezer Thomas Jr
George Newton Jr
Adam Hurd
Thaddeus Lacey
Abraham Post
Simeon Hurd
John Mallery Jr
Timothy Castle
Isaac Thomas
Asahel Booth
James Morehouse
Azariah Eastman
Samuel Blakeley
Aaron Olds
Benjamin Eastman
William Torrance
John Thomas
Samuel Torrence Jr
Jedidiah Elderkin
Noah Woodward Jr

Edward Collens
Thomas Torrence
Joseph Torrence
Eldad Baker
Lovewel Hurd
Hezekiah Reynolds
Ezra Lacey
Simeon Hurd Jr
Steph Hurd
Henry Wakeley
Curtis Hurd
Thomas Canfield
John Austin Norton
David Rumsey
Seth Mitchel
Noah Frisbie Jr
Phinehas Baker
William Castle
Isaac Blakeley
Eliphaz Worner
Noah Frisbie
Israel Miner
Asahel Frisbie
Abner Hurd
William Norton

Thadeus Lacey Cap$^t$ of 8$^d$ Company

[Indorsed] List of Roxbury Minute Company

[*State Library, Revolution 6.*]

## FIRST BATTALION—COL. SILLIMAN.

[*See Record of Connecticut Men in the Revolution, page 393.*]

### STRATFORD SOLDIERS.

[Arms delivered to Stratford soldiers under the command of Capt. George Benjamin, in Col. Gold Sellick Silliman Regiment bound for New York, July 1776.]

To what Soldier delivered
Curtis Judson
Barnibas Cuningham
John Megraugh
John Downing
Elihu Mawwee

To what Soldier delivered
William Grant
Abner Elger
David Barlow Jr
Pink Clarke

[*State Library, Revolution 6.*]

## SECOND BATTALION—COL. GAY.

[*See Record of Connecticut Men in the Revolution, page 395.*]

### SEVENTH COMPANY—CAPT. WELLES.

Apprisement of the Soldiers guns under Com$^d$ of Cap$^t$ Sam$^l$ Welles

| Soldiers Names | Soldiers Names |
|---|---|
| Cap$^t$ Sam$^l$ Welles | Joseph Bidwell |
| Abraham Tallcott | Jon$^{th}$ Gains |
| George Tallcott | Leu$^t$ Tho$^s$ Hollister |
| Rich$^d$ Smith | Serj$^t$ Aaron Hubbard |
| Jesse Churchel | Elijah Hubbard |
| Josiah Lumis | Josiah Brooks |
| Josiah Stevens | Sam$^l$ Daniels |
| Serj$^t$ Benj$^a$ Stevens | Joseph Churchel |
| Benj$^a$ Howard | Eliz$^r$ Hubbard |
| Frances Nichalson | Ebez$^r$ Benton |
| Barnabas Fuller | Sam$^l$ Hills Jun$^r$ |
| Thomas Brooks | W$^m$ Densmore |
| Ashbil Webster | Timothy Stevens |
| Steven Couch | Aaron Hollister |
| Peter Stevens | Josiah Hollister |
| David Hubbard | Timothy Wood |
| John Morley | John How |
| Jon$^{th}$ Loveland | Elemuel Tubbs |
| David Nigh fifer | Hez$^h$ Wickham |
| Edward Potter | Nathan Nichalson |
| Elijah Covel | Tho$^s$ Morley |
| Jon$^{th}$ Covel | Elez$^r$ Goodale |

Glastenbury 18$^{th}$ 1776
Samuel Welles Cap

[*State Library, Revolution 6.*]

### SEVENTH COMPANY—CAPT. WELLES.

An account of 12 Blankets hired or impress$^d$ by the Select Men of Glastenbury & delivered to Soldiers of Cap$^t$ Sam$^l$ Wells's Comp$^y$ Col$^o$ Gay's Reg$^t$ 1776.

| to whom delivered | their Casulties |
|---|---|
| Benj$^a$ Howard | Lost with him when he died supposed buried in it |
| Rich$^d$ Smith | Lost in Retreat from Turtle Bay Sep. 15, 1776 |
| Joseph Brooks | " " " |
| Benj$^a$ Hale | Buried with him |
| Stephen Couch | Lost in Retreat above mentioned |
| Jesse Churchill | No account of & to be paid for |
| Elihu Smith | Lost in sd Retreat |
| Josiah Hollister | " " |
| Jon$^{th}$ Gains | " " |
| Josiah Loomis | Shot to pieces |
| Lem$^l$ Tubbs | No account of & to be paid for |
| Tho$^s$ Morley | Lost in sd Retreat |

[*State Library, Revolution 6.*]

## LOST GUNS.

An account of the Guns that were Lost in the Reg[t] late Col Gays while in the Continental Service under the Comand of Gen[l] Washington A D 1776

### Capt Stanlys Comp[y]

| Mens Names & what Companies they belonged to | What Place Guns lost at |
|---|---|
| Ambrus Sloper | on Long Island |
| Dan[l] Darens | " |
| Eli Pardy | " |
| John Park | " |
| Tho[s] Powers | " |
| John Thorp | on York Island in Retreat |
| John Andrus | "  " |
| John Doty | "  " |
| Amos Hawley | "  " |
| Sam[l] Lee | "  " |
| Asahel Newel | "  " |
| Josiah Smith | "  " |
| Lemuel Wyard | "  " |
| Ira Judson | "  " |
| Samuel Hitchcock | in North River crossing River |
| Josiah Mix | in Baggage Waggon |
| Nath[l] Shepherd | " |
| Gideon Porter | in A'munition Cart |
| Mark Newel | in Baggage Waggon |

### Capt Jellits Comp[y]

| | |
|---|---|
| David Phelps | in Baggage Waggon |
| Jonathan Eccleston | " |
| Oliver Case | " |
| Zenas Hayse | " |
| Simeon Holliday | " |
| Ehud Fuller | " |
| Obed Lamberton | in Trenches |

### Capt Rogers Comp[y]

| | |
|---|---|
| Simeon Barns | in B Waggon |
| Dan[l] Harris | " |
| James Willson | in Y. Island |
| John White | B Waggon |
| Benj[a] Carrier | " |
| William Fellows | on L. Island |
| Nehemiah Smith | B. Wagon |
| George White | " |
| John Whitnay | L Island |
| Sam[l] Franklin | " |
| Simeon Rude | B. Waggon |
| David Douglas | N. York in Retreat |
| Daniel Coo[ ] | Y. Island   " |
| Tho[s] Hamlin | "    " |
| Peter Pratt | "    " |
| Sluman Ables | B. Waggon |
| David Simons | " |
| Daniel Potter | " |
| William Jaquies | " |
| Asa Smith | " |
| David Franklin | " |

## STATE TROOPS, 1776.

### Capt Goodwins Company

| Mens Names & what Companies they belonged to | What Place Guns lost at |
|---|---|
| Lieut. Scovil | Y. Island in Retreat |
| Searg<sup>t</sup> Lockwood | B. Waggon |
| Joseph Gaylord | " |
| Joseph Gillet | " |
| Solomon Morse | Staten when on Guard |
| Levi Norton | B. Wagon |
| Bradford Kellogg | In Retreat York Island |
| Ebenez<sup>r</sup> Scovil | " " |
| Joel Gaylord | B. Wagon |
| Ananias Porrage | " |

### Capt Bradleys Company

| | |
|---|---|
| James Peat | Died on Long Island |
| Lieut. Blakesley | at White Plains when sick |
| Eli Easmon | Stolen on N. York |
| Sam<sup>l</sup> Stannard | in Retreat N. York |
| Josiah Hatch | Stolen at Hackensack |
| James Corby | B. Waggon |
| [     ] Norton | |
| David Rumsy | Armourers Shop L. Island |
| Isaac Blakesly | B. Waggon |
| John Preston | Y. Island |

### Capt Woolcotts Company

| | |
|---|---|
| Ebenz<sup>r</sup> Foot | Crossing N. River |
| Gideon Drake | " |
| William Jones | B. Waggon |
| Alexander Korton | " |
| Roz<sup>ll</sup> Pryor | " |
| John Stely | " |
| Abner Slade | " |
| John Thompson | " |

### Cap<sup>t</sup> Wells's Company

| | |
|---|---|
| Ens. Reuben Phelps | B. Wagon |
| Thomas Brook | " |
| Josiah Brook | " |
| Jonathan Covel | " |
| Elias Chapin | " |
| Sam<sup>l</sup> Danolds | " |
| John Hungerford | " |
| Sam<sup>l</sup> Kibby | " |
| Jonathan Loveland | " |
| Josiah Loomis | " |
| Fransis Nickinson | " |
| John Phelps | " |
| Lemuel Tubbs | " |

### Cap<sup>t</sup> Wilsons Company

| | |
|---|---|
| Aron Bristol | York Island Retreat |
| Abel Bristol | " " |
| Benajah Heydon | B Wagon |
| Sam<sup>l</sup> Hinsdale | " |
| Rufus Johnson | " |

[*State Library, Revolution 6.*]

# COAST GUARD.

## CAPT. SALTONSTALL'S COMPANY.

A Return of Those Intitl[d] to a Bounty in the Company of Matross[s] Commanded by Nath[l] Saltonstall

| Names | Time of Inlistment | | Whose Company Came out of |
|---|---|---|---|
| Nath[l] Saltonstall Cap | July | 1776 | |
| Nath[l] Coit Jr Capt Lieut. | July | 11 | |
| Daniel Starr 1 Lieut | | 11 | |
| Daniel Dee 2 Lieut | | 23 | Capt. Kirtland's |
| Tho[s] Jones 1 Serj. | | 12 | |
| Moses Fergo 2 Serj. | | 14 | |
| John Chapman 3 Serj. | | 14 | |
| Nath[l] Hempsted Jr 1 Corp. | | 12 | |
| John Woodward 2 Corp. | | 14 | |
| Jon[a] Miner 3 Corp. | | 26 | Capt Kirtland's |
| Manuel Boix 1 Gunner | | 14 | |
| George Rogers Drummer | | 12 | |
| Gurdon F. Saltonstall Fifer | | 10 | |
| John Howard Gunner | | 12 | |
| Jeremiah Culver " | | 12 | |
| Joseph Sharp " | | 12 | |
| Thomas Mossett " | | 12 | |
| John Buell " | | 26 | Capt. Kirtland's |
| John Walker " | | 27 | |
| Jonathan Miner " | | 12 | |
| Abner Beebe Matross | | 12 | |
| Samuel Mason " | | 12 | |
| Nath[l] Tharp | | 12 | |
| Ebenezer Colfax | | 12 | |
| James Holt | | 13 | |
| Nathan Spicer | | 14 | |
| Jonathan Comstock | | 14 | |
| Thomas Hopkins | | 14 | |
| Ethiel Plant | | 23 | Capt. Kirtland's |
| Robert Latimer | | 23 | |
| Gideon Chapman | | 23 | |
| Isaac Oliver | | 23 | |
| John Bolles 4[th] | | 23 | |
| John Clerk | | 26 | Capt. Shapley's |
| Peter Stannard | | 26 | Capt. Kirtland's |
| Titus Teal | | 26 | " |
| William Stevens | | 26 | " |
| William Bartholemew | | 26 | " |
| Asa Baker Jr | | 27 | |
| Palsey Baker | | 27 | Capt. Shapley's |
| John Baker | | 27 | " |
| Jeremy Bayley | | 26 | Capt. Kirtland's |
| Thomas Quinley | | 27 | Capt. Shapley's |

STATE TROOPS, 1776. 141

| Names | Time of Inlistment | Whose Company Came out of |
|---|---|---|
| Benj<sup>a</sup> Jones | 26 | Capt Kirtland's |
| Asa Denison | 26 | " |
| John Tredaway | 27 | Capt. Mather's |
| Joshua Griffing | 27 | " |
| Jeremiah Blake | 27 | " |
| Josiah Church | 27 | " |
| Augustus Lewis | 26 | Capt. Kirtland |
| Nath<sup>l</sup> Emerson | 26 | " [for Duty |
| John Hues | 14 | Discharged 29 being unfit |
| Aaron Jones | Aug. 10 | Capt. Kirtland |

[Indorsed] Cap<sup>t</sup> Nath<sup>l</sup> Saltonstals Pay Roll of Matross Company at New London.

[*State Library, Revolution 6.*]

## ENS. UFFOOT'S COMPANY.

A Pay Roll for the First Months pay of Ensign Samuel Uffoots Guard in Stratford

Ensign  
Serj<sup>nt</sup>  
Nathan M<sup>c</sup>Cune  
Josiah Hawley  
John Uffoot  
Benjamin Uffoot  
Joseph Beers  
John M<sup>c</sup>Cune  

William Osborn  
Joseph Prunwugh  
Stephen Frost  
Andrew Paylon  
Ephraim M<sup>c</sup>Cune  
Joseph Burritt  
Charles Burrough  
Samuel Patterson  

[*State Library, Revolution 6.*]

## THIRD BATTALION—COL. ENOS.

[*See Record of Connecticut Men in the Revolution, page 484.*]

## CAPT. BLACKMAN'S COMPANY.

An acc<sup>t</sup> of Prest Guns &c in Cap<sup>t</sup> Elijah Blackmans C<sup>o</sup> with the names of possesors &c Jany 23 1777

Possesors of Guns &c  
W<sup>m</sup> Colton  
Benah Cone  
Tho<sup>s</sup> Norton  
Allin Lane  
Chris<sup>r</sup> Whitehead  
Josh<sup>a</sup> Monroe  
Sim<sup>o</sup> Ranny  
David Clark  
Comfort Ranny  
Nath<sup>l</sup> Ranny J<sup>r</sup>  
Dan<sup>l</sup> Robberds  
Ja<sup>s</sup> Johnson  
Sam<sup>l</sup> Griffin  

Possesors of Guns &c  
Benj<sup>a</sup> Babbit  
Bennit Eglestone  
Jo<sup>s</sup> Bacon J<sup>r</sup>  
W<sup>m</sup> Stow  
John Gill  
Allin Ward  
Lamberton Clark J<sup>r</sup>  
Comfort Marks  
Ebenez<sup>r</sup> Robberds Fifer  
Ebenez<sup>r</sup> Bacon  
Steph<sup>n</sup> Robberds  
Ashbel Cornwell  

[*Copy in Comptroller's Office.*]

## COLS. ELY'S AND ENOS' REGIMENTS.

[*See Record of Connecticut Men in the Revolution, page 614.*]

### BOUNTIES.

The United States D[r] To the State of Connecticut, for Bounty paid to the Subalterns in Col. Ely & Enos's Regiments in 1777, for extra Services. Viz.

| Officers Names | Reg[ts] | Officers Names | Reg[ts] |
|---|---|---|---|
| L[t] John Chick | Col. Enos | L[t] A. Baldwin | Enos's |
| L[t] W[m] Morris | Ely's | L[t] Dan[l] Leffingwell | " |
| L[t] Asa Bacon | " | Ens[n] Joshua Gates | " |
| L[t] E. Taylor | " | L[t] Charles Goodwin | Enos's |
| L[t] Joseph Hale | " | Ens[n] John Francis | " |
| Ens[n] Dav[d] Scranton | " | L[t] Josiah Cleaveland | Ely's |
| L[t] Ezra Benedict | Enos's | L[t] Nath[l] Bingham | " |
| L[t] Noah Judson | " | Ens[n] John Wiley | " |
| L[t] Stephen Dodge | " | Ens[n] L. Gaylord | Enos's |
| Ens[n] W[m] Torrance | " | Ens[n] Job Smith | " |
| L[t] Ich[a] Bozworth | Ely's | L[t] Jn[o] Prudden | " |
| L[t] John Shipman | " | L[t] N. West | Ely's |
| Ens[n] Jn[o] Shipman 2[d] | " | L[t] B. Trowbridge | Enos's |
| L[t] Sam[l] Hozard | " | L[t] R. Chapman | Ely's |
| L[t] L. Grosvenor | " | | |

[*Comptroller's Office, Haskell's Receipts.*]

### CAPT. PETTIBONE'S COMPANY.

An Account of the Arms Accoutrements &c that are going in Servis in Cap[t] Abel Pettibones Comp[a] with the prises thereto July 18[th] 1777.

Capt. Abel Pettibone
Ens. John Chick
Sr. Jededi[a] Olcott
  Asahel Andrus Jr
  Obed Higley
  Elihu Case 2[d]
  Joseph Presson
  Eber Higley
  Asa Hays
  George Northway
  Roswel Case
  Jacob Davis 3[d]
  William Andrews Jr
  Noah Humphry
  Israel Tullar
  Richard Lilley Jr
  Eli Alderman

Daniel Olmsted Jr
Joel Barber Jr
Jonathan Alderman Jr
Judah Case
Amos Slarter
Jeremiah Willcox
Carmi Holcomb
Matthew Grifen Jr
Salmon Burr
Seth Grifen
Phineas Comstock
Eber Moor
Joseph Holcomb Jr
Serg[t] Nath[ll] Holcomb
James Slarter
Jonathan Andrus
Daniel Roe

[*State Library, Revolution 11.*]

## CAPT. ROBINSON'S COMPANY.

A Role of a Company in the State of Rhode Island in October A. D. 1777 Commanded by Abner Robinson Capt.

Capt Abner Robinson
Lieut Samuel Campbell
Lieut Joseph Coye
Ensign Abijah Fuller
Serj$^t$ James Robinson
Serj$^t$ Nathan Robinson
Serj$^t$ Daniel Fobes
Serg$^t$ Joseph Burnam
Serg$^t$ Josiah Collins
Corpl Samuel Cook
Corpl Asa Royce
Corpl Elijah Simons
Corpl Daniel Denison
Fifer Uriah Kingsley
    Jared Allen
    Jonathan Avery
    Isaac Abbe
    Joseph Ashley
    Samuel Ashley
    Benjamin Burnit
    Ethan Barrows
    Daniel Badcock
    Jonathan Burnit
    Elias Blanchard
    John Beamis
    Thomas Crosby
    Joseph Cary
    Oliver Cary
    Abner Church
    Edmon Conent
    William Cummins
    James Clark
    Thomas Coye

William Clark
William Durkee
Solomon Durkee
William D. Foster
James Fletcher
Moses Fith
John Flint
Amaziah Fisk
Ambros Grow
Abiel Holt
Jonathan Hovey
Richard Ingorsoll
William Loomis
Jonathan Loomis
Eleazer M$^c$Call
Benjamin Molton
Elijah Miller
Stephen Ormsby
John Ormsby
Vaniah Palmer
Jacob Preston
Eber Robinson
Reuben Robinson
Uriah Roundy
William Rindge
Solomon Robins
Amaziah Storrs
Abner Webb
Frederick J. Whiting
Joseph Waldo
Samuel Whiting
William Young

[*State Library, Hebard Papers.*]

# STATE TROOPS, 1777.

## COL. McCLELLAN'S REGIMENT.

### SIMSBURY SOLDIERS

[This regiment was raised for one month's service by a resolve of the General Assembly passed in August, and by further vote of the Council of Safety, September 23.]

Simsbury Sept$^r$; 8$^{th}$ 1777

We the Subscribers Soldiers belonging to a Reg$^t$; to be Commanded by Sam$^{ll}$ M$^c$Clellan Co$^l$; have Each of us Rec$^d$ of Cap$^t$ Jon$^a$ Humphry one Fire lock with Bayonet which Each of us am Accountable for witness Our hands —

| | |
|---|---|
| Salem Burr | Chattwil Parsons |
| Nathaniel Butler | Jonathan Bidwell Junr |
| Stephen Rowely | Pelatiah Cadwell |
| Stephen Goodrich | Timothy Case |
| Eli Hoskins | Charles Humphry |
| John Latimer | Solomon Humphy |
| Daniel Rowel | Abel Case |
| Timothy Woodbridg | Kaswell Halel (?) |
| Francsis Salter | Jedidiah Holcomb |
| James Larrenc | Thomas Colton |
| Israel Case | Martin Humphy |
| Theodore Hilleyer | James McNall |
| Elihu Case | Daniel Graham J |
| Thomas wildor | William Willcocks |
| David Phelps Ju$^r$ | Francis Garrett Jr |
| Joel Slater | Hosea Case Jr |
| Aaron Webster | George Hills |
| Ashbel Webster | Dan Case |
| Theodore Cadwell | Asher Humphry |
| Asa Gillet | John Nearing |
| Aaron Brown | David Thomas |
| Asa Hubbard | Charles Willcocks |
| Samuel Holton | David Messenger |

Elijah Holcomb
Charls Dewolf
Elisha Pering
Dan Dibol
Peter Holcomb
Thomas Whiton

George Cornish
Benoni Humphry
Levi Godard
Ebenezer Holcomb
Thomas Allyn

arms red. of Capt woodbridge receipted by Capt. Humphry to him for Lieut. Johnson men viz

Salah Jackson
Samuel Wood
Joseph Johnson

David Sears
Isaac Johnson
Abraham Griffeth

Simeon Hollady not receipted } have got receipts for the
Seth Holcomb        "       }        same Return⁴.

[*Connecticut Historical Society.*]

Simsbury 8ᵗʰ Octʳ 1777.

We the Subscribers soldiers in a Regᵗ; to be Commanded by Samuel MᶜClellan Esq Colʲ have recᵈ; of Capᵗ Jonᵃ Humphry the Several Sums Annexed to Our Respective Names, as part of our Pay or Bounty Recᵈ pʳ us.

Israel Case
Joel Slater
James McNall
Daniel Rowel
John Latimer
Eli Hoskins
Elisha Pering
William Roberts
Asher Humphry
Daniel Graham
Jehiel Wells (?)
Simeon Halladay
David Messenger
William Roberts
Elisha Pering
Simeon Holaday
George Hills
Timothy Woobrig
James McNall
Thomas Whiton
Charles Dᵉ Wolf
Isreail Case
Joel Slater
Israel Case
Timothy Woodbridge
Eli Hoskins
Daniel Rowel
John Latimer
Danel Grahom Jr
James Mc Nall
Seba Moses
John Nearing

Giles Humphry
Ithamer Colton
Francis Garritt Jr
Willam Roberts
Jehiel Wild (?)
Jedidiah Holcom
Timothy Woodbridge
Joel Slater
Phineas Holcomb
Daniel Dibble
Thomas Wilder
David Thomas
Israel Case
James Larrenc
Roswell Noble
Timothy Woodbridge
Timothy Woodbridge
Jehel Willcocks
Ithamer Colton
Jedidiah Holcomb
Daniel Rowel
John Latimer
George Cornish
Francis Garrit
Giles Humphry
Asher Humphry
Seth Holcomb
Micah Case
Charls Dolph
Simeon Halladay
Dan Dibbel
George Hills

## STATE TROOPS, 1777.

Dan Case
George Cornish
Benoni Humphry
Timothy Case
Daniel Grimes
Phinehas Holcomb
Michiel Case
Charls Dewolf
Abraham Griffen
John Latimer
Daniel Rowel
Isaac Johnson
Ithamar Colton
Jehiall Willcoks
James Lawrence
George Cornish
Joseph Johnson
Samuel Wood
Benoni Humphry
L$^t$. John Johnson
Elisha Pering
Benoni Humphry
Eli Hoskins
Israel Case
Thomas Whiton
Theodore Hillyer
Jedediah Holcomb
John Nearing
Samul Colton
Asher Humphry
Jed Holcomb
John Latimer
Daniel Rowel
David Sears
Thomas Allyn
Salem Burr
Chattwil Parsons
Theodore Cadwell
Pelatiah Cadwell

Francis Garrit
Elihu Case
Salah Jackson
Isaac Johnson
David Sears
David Thomas
Eli Hoskins
Stephen Rowely
Daniel Rowel
Timothy Case
Hosea Case
Abel Case
Timothy Woodbridge
Charles Willcocks
James M$^c$Naal
Dan$^{ll}$: Graham
John Lattimore
David Messenger
Phineas Holcomb
Joel Slater
Charles Humphry
James Larrance
Thomas Wilder
Israel Case
Samuel Colton
Aaron Webster
Aaron Brown
Seba Moses
Dan Case
George Hills
William Roberts
Joel Cornish for
   George Cornish
William Roberts
Benj$^a$ Holcomb
Benj$^a$ Holcomb
   for money r$^d$. by En$^s$ Hum
Martin Humphy

                              Simsbury Oct$^r$: 8$^{th}$ 1777

    Rec$^d$ of Cap$^t$ Jon$^a$ Humphy Eighteen pounds Eight Shillings L mony as a Bounty or advance pay to Raise a Company of men in a Reg$^t$ to be Commanded by Sam$^{ll}$ M$^c$Clellan Esq$^r$ Col which I am to acc$^t$ for £18 8 0
                                            p$^r$ me Benj$^a$ Holcomb Leut

                              Simsbury Oct$^r$ 8$^{th}$ 1777

    Rec$^d$ of Cap$^t$ Jon$^a$ Humphy Thirty pounds L money as a Bounty or advance pay for the Raising of a Company of men in a Reg$^t$ to be Commanded by Sam$^{ll}$ M$^c$Clellan Esq$^r$ Co$^l$ which I am to Acc$^t$ for £30
                                       p$^r$ me Martin Humphy Ensn
                                         [*Connecticut Historical Society.*]

    We the subscribers have Rec$^d$ of Cap$^t$ Jon$^a$ Humphry the full of Our Wages that was Due to us from the Town of Simsbury for service in an Expedition to providance in October Last in a Reg$^t$ Rais$^d$ by the state of

Connec[t] Commanded by Sam[ll] M[c]Clellen Esq[r] Co[l] & in S[d] Humphrys Company rec[d] p[r] us Simsbury March 24[th] 1778.

Timothy Case
Peter Holcomb Jr
Levi Gosard
Dan Case
Benoni Humphry
Joel Slater
Asher Humphry
James Hills for George
Francis Garrit for Son
Hosea Case Jur
Charles Willcocks
Thomas Wilder
Abel Case
Aaron Willcoks
David Thomas
Giles Humphry
Timothy Woodbridge
William Willcocks
James McNall
David Phelps
Seba Moses
Ebenezer Holcomb
George Cornish
Elijah Holcomb
John Nearing
Israel Case
Roswell Noble
Charles Humphry
James Larrance
Daniel Graham
Elihu Case
David Adams Jr
   for William Roberts
Samuel Miller for
   Jehial Willcocks
      two pound aight

[*Connecticut Historical Society.*]

# MILITIA REGIMENTS, 1776.

## FIRST REGIMENT (?) — COL. WOLCOTT.

[*See Record of Connecticut Men in the Revolution, page 449.*]

### CAPT. HYDE'S COMPANY.

[This company was inlisted as an independent company. See records of the Council of Safety August 16, 1776.]

A Travel Role of Cap$^t$ Walter Hydes Company in Col$^o$ Erastus Woolcot's Reg$^{mt}$ of Militia from Lebanon To New York

| Mens Names | Distance Traveled | Mens Names | Distance Traveled |
|---|---|---|---|
| Cap$^t$ Walter Hyde | miles 150 | Stephen Payne | 150 |
| Lieu$^t$ Samuel Fuller | 150 | Silas Nye | 150 |
| Lieu$^t$ John Vaughn | 150 | Dan Terrey | 150 |
| Doct$^r$ Andrew Metcalf | 150 | Whighting Backus | 150 |
| Sarj$^t$ Thomas Bingham | 150 | Samuel Woodard | 150 |
| Sarj$^t$ Joseph Abel | 150 | Jeriah Wright | 150 |
| Sarj$^t$ Robert Cambell | 150 | Solomon Wright | 150 |
| Serj$^t$ Eliphalet Barker | 150 | Joseph Bissel | 150 |
| Serj$^t$ Joseph Leech | 150 | Elijah Phelps | 150 |
| Corp$^{rl}$ Joseph Throop | 150 | Joseph Phelps | 150 |
| Corp$^l$ Elisha Doubleday | 150 | Daniel Smalley | 150 |
| Corp$^l$ Jabez Foster | 150 | Abraham Merifield | 150 |
| Corp$^l$ Benj$^a$ Throop | 150 | Daniel Rockwell | 150 |
| Drum$^r$ Daniel Hyde | 150 | Moses Hyde | 150 |
| Fif$^r$ Jacob Clark | 150 | Thomas Slooman | 150 |
| Samuel Hyde | 150 | Nehemiah Payne | 150 |
| Ezekiel Fitch | 150 | John Mackswell | 150 |
| Elisha Seabury | 150 | Dan Metcalf | 150 |
| James Baley | 150 | Ebeneazer Metcalf | 150 |
| Samuel Baley | 150 | Thomas Gross | 150 |
| Cumfort Bruster | 150 | Elijah Palmer | 150 |
| Bezelial Badger | 150 | | |
| Dan Clark | 150 | | Miles 6750 |
| Jonathan Blackman | 150 | | |

Camp Near Kings Bridge Sep$^{tr}$ 21$^{st}$, 1776
Joseph Leech Clark
John Vaughan Lieut

[*Connecticut Historical Society.*]

## THIRD REGIMENT—COL. JOHN ELY.

[*See Record of Connecticut Men in the Revolution, page 450.*]

### CAPT. HOLMS' COMPANY.

Capt Thomas Holms Roll to North Castle New York 1776 under Colo Ely

| | £ | s | d | | | £ | s | d | |
|---|---|---|---|---|---|---|---|---|---|
| Capt Holms | 5 | 1 | 4 | | Jeremiah Wheler | 1 | 5 | 4 | |
| Lt Billings | 3 | 8 | 5 | | John Wheler Geer | 1 | 5 | 4 | |
| Doct Babcock | 3 | 8 | 5 | | Amos Morgan | 1 | 5 | 4 | |
| Serg Coats | 1 | 10 | 5 | | John Utley | 1 | 5 | 4 | |
| Corp Miner | 1 | 7 | 10 | 2 | Jedediah Randall | 0 | 13 | 4 | |
| Corp Wheler | 1 | 7 | 10 | 2 | Joseph Wheler | 1 | 5 | 4 | |
| Joshua Wilcox | 1 | 5 | 4 | | Joshua Grant | 1 | 5 | 4 | |
| Amos Miner | 1 | 5 | 4 | | Stephen Main | 1 | 5 | 4 | |
| David Miner | 1 | 5 | 4 | | Amos Wheler | 1 | 5 | 4 | |
| Isaac Williams | 1 | 5 | 4 | | John Ayers | 1 | 5 | 4 | |
| Isaac Williams 2nd | 1 | 5 | 4 | | Amos Solomon | 1 | 5 | 4 | |
| Nat Williams | 1 | 5 | 4 | | Benedick Arons | 1 | 5 | 4 | |
| Jonathan Morgan | 0 | 13 | 4 | | | | | | |
| | | | | | | 39 | 1 | 8 | |
| | | | | | Sauce money | 1 | 9 | 3 | |
| | | | | | | 40 | 10 | 11 | |
| | | | | | Benedicks | 1 | 6 | 5 | |
| | | | | | | 39 | 4 | 6 | |

whole Sause money while under Coll Ely is /15ᵈ per mon Except 2 men /3ᵈ

December the 14th A D 1776

    Recd of Sanford Billing Four pounds Nine Shilling & Four pence L Money Being part of Capt Thomas Holms Decasd wages Due while under Collonel Ely at North Castle

                                        Sam. Holms administoratr

[A receipt for wages and sauce money signed by the men of the company is with this roll.]

[*Connecticut Historical Society.*]

# FOURTH REGIMENT—COL. WHITING.

[*See Record of Connecticut Men in the Revolution, page 449.*]

## CAPT. WHEELER'S COMPANY.

Cap$^t$ Nath$^l$ Wheelers Pay Roll for the C$^o$ under his command Belonging to the 4$^{th}$ Reg$^t$ of Militia of the State of Conn$^t$ under command of Col$^o$ Ichb$^d$ Lewis in a Campaign at New York

| Mens Names | Entered into Service 1776 | Discharg$^d$ and left the Service allowing 4 Days to get Home. | | Mo. | Dys. |
|---|---|---|---|---|---|
| Cap$^t$ Nath$^l$ Wheeler | Aug$^t$ 10 | Sep$^t$ | 23 | 1 | 13 |
| Jo$^s$ Curtis  Serg$^t$ | " 10 | " | 15 | 1 | 5 |
| Stiles Judson  " | " 10 | " | 20 | 1 | 10 |
| David Thompson " | " 10 | " | 10 | 1 | — |
| John Whiting  " | " 10 | " | 12 | 1 | 2 |
| Josiah Peek Corp$^l$ | " 10 | " | 10 | 1 | — |
| W$^m$ Brooks | " 10 | " | 15 | 1 | 5 |
| Curtis Beardsley | " 10 | Aug$^t$ | 28 | 0 | 18 |
| Joel Judson | " 24 | Sep$^t$ | 18 | 0 | 24 |
| Silas Judson Drum$^r$ | " 10 | " | 10 | 1 | — |
| Andrew Curtis | " 10 | " | 13 | 1 | 3 |
| Nath$^n$ Birdsey | " 10 | " | 10 | 1 | — |
| Elnath$^n$ Wilcockson | " 10 | " | 5 | 0 | 25 |
| Judson Peek | " 10 | " | 0 | 1 | — |
| Lewis Curtis | " 10 | " | 10 | 1 | — |
| Abel Booth | " 10 | " | 20 | 1 | 10 |
| Ja$^s$ Kirtland | " 10 | " | 23 | 1 | 13 |
| Abr$^m$ Curtis | " 10 | " | 9 | 1 | — |
| Steph$^n$ Lewis | " 10 | " | 9 | 1 | — |
| Ja$^s$ Shearman | " 10 | " | 18 | 1 | 18 |
| Thad$^s$ Curtis | " 10 | " | 8 | 0 | 28 |
| Jo$^s$ Frost | " 10 | " | 15 | 1 | 5 |
| Abel Judson | " 10 | " | 17 | 1 | 7 |
| Abel Walker | " 10 | " | 12 | 1 | 2 |
| Sam$^l$ Wheeler | " 10 | " | 10 | 1 | — |
| Job Peek | " 10 | " | 10 | 1 | — |
| Agur Curtis | " 10 | " | 15 | 1 | 5 |
| Isaac Curtis | " 10 | " | 8 | 0 | 28 |
| Nehem$^h$ Thompson | " 10 | " | 29 | 1 | 19 |
| Abel Fairchild | " 10 | " | 17 | 1 | 7 |
| Ebenez$^r$ Birdsey | " 10 | " | 29 | 1 | 19 |
| Ebenez$^r$ Curtis | " 10 | " | 8 | 0 | 28 |
| John Bardslee | " 10 | " | 19 | 1 | 9 |
| Ja$^s$ Peck | " 10 | " | 20 | 1 | 10 |
| Ja$^s$ Judson | " 10 | " | 20 | 1 | 10 |
| Steph$^n$ Curtis | " 10 | " | 20 | 1 | 10 |
| Elias Wells | " 10 | " | 10 | 1 | 6 |
| Ja$^s$ Wells | " 10 | " | 19 | 1 | 9 |
| Johon Beers | " 10 | " | 20 | 1 | 10 |

| Mens Names | Entered into Service 1776 | Discharg{d} and left the Service allowing 4 Days to get Home. Mo. Dys. |
|---|---|---|
| Robt Curtis | Augt 10 | Sept 15  1   5 |
| Phine{s} Beers | " 10 | "  29  1  19 |
| Saml Curtis | " 10 | "  20  1  10 |
| Silas Curtis | " 10 | "  12  1   2 |
| Abel Booth J{r} | " 10 | "  20  1  10 |

[*Copy in Comptroller's Office.*]

## FOURTEENTH COMPANY — CAPT. GODFREY.

A Ration Abstract for Capt Danl Godfrey{s} C{o} in Col. Saml Whiting{s} Reg{t} of Militia which enter{d} upon Guard in Greens Farms. By order pursuant to Genl Stillmans Order in Decr 1776 —

| Names | Time of Marching | Time of Discharge |
|---|---|---|
| Danl Godfrey Capt | Decr 5 | Decr 17 |
| Jo{s} Bennett Ens{n} | " 5 | " |
| Jonah Squire Serg{t} | " 5 | " |
| David Morehouse | " 5 | " |
| Joel Gilbert Corp{l} | " 5 | " |
| Joshua Disbrow " | " 5 | " |
| Bradley Dean Fifer | " 5 | " |
| Jesse Morehouse | " 5 | " |
| John Andrews J{r} | " 5 | " |
| Isaac Disbrow | " 5 | " |
| Gideon Couch | " 5 | " |
| Thos Nash Couch | " 5 | " |
| Danl Bradley Junr | " 5 | " |
| Thos Burnett J{r} | " 5 | " |
| John Disbrow | " 5 | " |
| Benjn Allen | " 5 | " |
| Amos Gray | " 5 | " |
| David Raymond | " 5 | " |
| Isaac Elwood | " 5 | " |
| John Crasman | " 5 | " |
| Esra Thorp | " 5 | " |
| Jared Duncan | " 5 | " |
| Henry Winkley | " 5 | " |
| Steph{n} Dickman | " 5 | " |
| Christ{r} Godfrey | " 5 | " |
| Jon{a} Beers | " 5 | " |
| Nath{n} Ogden | " 5 | " |
| Wm Batterson | " 5 | " |
| Ichab{d} Canfield | " 5 | " |
| Elias Bennett | " 5 | " |
| Sturges Burr | " 5 | " |
| Benjn Sol{o} Couch | " 5 | " |
| Wm Bennett | " 5 | " |
| Justus Disbrow | " 5 | " |
| Riab Beers | " 5 | " |
| Straton Briant | " 5 | " |
| Justus Smith | " 5 | " |

[*Copy in Comptroller's Office.*]

## SIXTH REGIMENT—COL. CHESTER.

[*See Record of Connecticut Men in the Revolution, page 449.*]

### CAPT. WELLS' COMPANY.

An abstract of Cap$^t$ Chester Wells Company in Col Chesters Reg$^t$ from the time of Enlistment untill march$^d$ July 1776

| Names | When Inlisted | When marched |
|---|---|---|
| Capt. Chester Wells | June 20 | July 10 |
| Lt. Edw$^d$ Bulkley | 20 | 10 |
| Lt. Eben$^r$ Wright | 20 | 18 |
| Ens. Jon$^a$ Stoddard | 20 | 10 |
| Serj. John Fraims | 20 | 10 |
| " Cha$^s$ Curtiss | 20 | 10 |
| " Oliver Treat | 20 | 10 |
| " Jos. Andrews | 20 | 10 |
| Fife Jo. May | 20 | 10 |
| Drum Sim Dickinson | 20 | 10 |
| Corp. Fred. Robbins | 20 | 10 |
| " Lem$^l$ Woodhoop | 20 | 10 |
| " Rob$^t$ Warner | 20 | 10 |
| " Elijah Bordman | 20 | 10 |
| Priv. Eli Tryon | 20 | 10 |
| Ashbil Riley | 20 | 10 |
| Jos. Adams | 24 | 10 |
| Sam$^l$ Andrews | 24 | 10 |
| Eben Bigelow | 24 | 10 |
| Henry Brown | 24 | 10 |
| Abr$^a$ Blin | 26 | 10 |
| Tho$^s$ Blackwell | 24 | 10 |
| Moses Belden | 21 | 10 |
| Fra$^s$ Bulkley | 24 | 10 |
| Jon$^a$ Brooks | Aug. 5 | Aug. 17 |
| Leo$^d$ Bordman | June 24 | July 10 |
| O Burnham | 24 | 10 |
| Jared Brace | 24 | 10 |
| Tho$^s$ Clark | Aug. 5 | Aug. 17 |
| Joseph Crain | June 24 | July 10 |
| James Curtiss | 24 | 10 |
| Joshua Cone | 24 | 10 |
| Jos. Combs | 24 | 10 |
| Jos. Curtiss | 24 | 10 |
| William Curtiss | 24 | 10 |
| Roger Clapp | 24 | 10 |
| Cha$^s$ Churchill | July 8 | Aug. 7 |
| Joel Caatch | Aug. 5 | 17 |
| Rich$^d$ Demming | June 24 | July 10 |
| Eph$^m$ Demming | 24 | 10 |
| Simeon Demming | 24 | 10 |
| Sam$^l$ Dix | 24 | 10 |
| Benj$^a$ Dix | 24 | 10 |

| Names | When Inlisted | When marched |
|---|---|---|
| Jesse Dix | Aug. 5 | Aug. 17 |
| Edmond Dorr | 28 | 10 |
| Waitstill Dickinson | 25 | 10 |
| Josiah Dickinson | 5 | 17 |
| Ozias Dickinson | 5 | 17 |
| William Dilling | 5 | 17 |
| Abel Fullar | June 28 | July 10 |
| John Fraines | 24 | 10 |
| John Furbs | 24 | 10 |
| Isaac Goodrich | 24 | 10 |
| Jeh[a] Goodrich | 22 | 10 |
| John Goodrich | 24 | 10 |
| Hosea Goodrich | Aug. 5 | Aug. 17 |
| Simon Griffin | July 1 | July 9 |
| Moses Griswold | June 24 | 10 |
| Silas Hurlburt | 24 | 10 |
| James Hatch | 24 | 10 |
| Eben[r] Kilbey | July 1 | 9 |
| David King | June 26 | 10 |
| Stephen Kellogg | 24 | 10 |
| Mitchell Kingman | Aug. 5 | Aug. 17 |
| Levi Loveland | July 1 | July 9 |
| Luman Lary | 4 | 24 |
| Sam[l] Lawson | Aug. 5 | Aug. 17 |
| Sol[o] Lattimer | 5 | 17 |
| Hosea Millar | June 24 | July 10 |
| James Murpy | 24 | 10 |
| John Minor | July 1 | 15 |
| Rich[d] Montague | June 24 | 10 |
| Zeb[n] Myggott | July 4 | 12 |
| Hez[a] Nott | June 21 | 10 |
| W[m] Rood | Aug. 5 | Aug. 17 |
| Jos. Rood | June 24 | July 10 |
| John Russell | 26 | 10 |
| Sam[l] Rockwell | 24 | 10 |
| Oswell Rockwell | 24 | 10 |
| Enoch Stoddard | 24 | 10 |
| Sam[l] Stoddard | Aug. 5 | Aug. 17 |
| John Stoddard | 5 | 17 |
| Zach[a] Seymour | 5 | 17 |
| Zach[a] Seymour Jr | July 12 | July 20 |
| James Smith | June 24 | 10 |
| Cha[s] Treat | 24 | 10 |
| John Woodhouse | 24 | 10 |
| Elisha Wolcott | 24 | 10 |
| William Wolcott | 24 | 10 |
| Elizur Wolcott | 24 | 10 |
| Eben[r] Wells | 24 | 10 |
| Elisha Wells | 24 | 10 |
| Sion Wentworth | 24 | 10 |
| Elisha Webster | Aug. 5 | Aug. 17 |
| Dan[l] Warner | June 24 | July 10 |
| Jos. Wheeler | 24 | 10 |
| Joshua Wells | Aug. 5 | Aug. 17 |
| Joseph Wright | June 24 | July 10 |
| Sam[l] Woodhouse | 24 | 10 |

[*State Library, Revolution 32.*]

## MILITIA REGIMENTS, 1776.

A Pay Roll of Cap$^t$ Chester Wells C$^o$ in Col$^o$ Chesters Reg$^t$ from their arrival in New York to the 1$^{st}$ Day of Oct$^{br}$ Including 6 day$^s$ to Travel 120 M$^l$

| Names & Rank | Time when arri$^d$ in N York 1776 | Time when Dead, Desert$^d$ or Discharged | M$^s$ & Days in Service M$^s$ Dy$^s$ |
|---|---|---|---|
| Cap$^t$ Chester Wells | July 10 | | 2 27 |
| Edw$^d$ Bulkley Lieut | " 10 | | 2 27 |
| Ebenez$^r$ Wright " | " 18 | | 2 19 |
| Jon$^a$ Stoddard Ensign | " 10 | Sep$^t$ 3 | 2 22 |
| John Francis Serg$^t$ | " 10 | " " | 2 27 |
| Cha$^s$ Curtis " | " 10 | Aug$^t$ 3 | 1 20 |
| Ja$^s$ Andrus " | " 10 | | 2 27 |
| Oliv$^r$ Treat " | " 10 | Aug$^t$ 19 | 1 16 |
| Lem$^l$ Woodhouse Corp$^l$ promot$^d$ Aug$^t$ 24 | " 10 | | 2 27 |
| Fred$^k$ Robbins promot$^d$ Aug 20 | " 10 | | 2 27 |
| Rob$^t$ Warner Corp$^l$ | " 10 | | 2 27 |
| Elijah Boardman " | " 10 | | 2 27 |
| Joseph May Fifer | " 10 | | 2 27 |
| Simeon Dickison Drum$^r$ | " 10 | Sep$^t$ 3$^d$ | 2 27 |
| Joseph Adams Private | " 10 | | 2 27 |
| Sam$^l$ Andrus | " 10 | | 2 27 |
| Alvin Bigelow | " 10 | | 2 27 |
| Henry Brown | " 10 | | 2 27 |
| Abr$^m$ Blin | " 10 | | 2 27 |
| Tho$^s$ Wilson Buknel | " 10 | | 2 27 |
| Moses Belding | " 10 | | 2 27 |
| Francis Bulkley | " 10 | | 2 27 |
| Jon$^a$ Brooks | Aug$^t$ 15 | | 1 22 |
| Lincord Boardman | July 10 | | 2 27 |
| Orrin Burnham | " 10 | | 2 27 |
| Jered Bunce | " 10 | | 2 27 |
| Tho$^s$ Clark | Aug$^t$ 15 | | 1 22 |
| Jo$^s$ Crane | July 10 | | 2 27 |
| James Curtis | " 10 | | 2 27 |
| Joshua Cone | " 10 | | 2 27 |
| Ja$^s$ Combs | " 10 | | 2 27 |
| Jo$^s$ Curtis | " 10 | | 2 27 |
| W$^m$ Curtis | " 10 | | 2 27 |
| Cha$^s$ Churchel | " 20 | | 2 17 |
| Roger Clap | " 10 | | 2 27 |
| Joel Conch | Aug$^t$ 15 | | 1 22 |
| Rich$^d$ Deming | July 10 | | 2 27 |
| Eph$^m$ Deming | " 10 | | 2 27 |
| Simeon Deming | " 10 | | 2 27 |
| Samuel Dix | " 10 | | 2 27 |
| Benj$^a$ Dix | " 10 | | 2 27 |
| Jesse Dix | Aug$^t$ 15 | | 1 22 |
| Edmond Dorr | July 10 | | 2 27 |
| Waitstill Dickerson | " 10 | | 2 27 |
| Osias Dickerson | Aug 15 | | 1 22 |
| Josiah Dickerson | " 15 | | 1 22 |
| W$^m$ Dilkins | " 15 | | 1 22 |
| Jo$^s$ Whealor | July 10 | | 2 27 |
| Joshua Wells | Aug 15 | | 1 22 |
| Abel Fuller | July 10 | | 2 27 |
| John Francis | " 10 | | 2 27 |
| John Farles | " 10 | | 2 27 |

| Names & Rank | Time when arri[d] in N York | Time when Dead, Desert[d] or Discharged | M[o] & Days in Service M[o] Dy[s] |
|---|---|---|---|
| | 1776 | | |
| Isaac Goodrich | July 10 | | 2 27 |
| John Goodrich | " 10 | | 2 27 |
| Hozea Goodrich | Aug[t] 15 | | 1 22 |
| Simeon Griffin | July 10 | | 2 27 |
| Moses Griswold | " 10 | | 2 27 |
| Silas Hurlburt | " 10 | | 2 27 |
| Ja[s] Hatch | " 10 | | 2 27 |
| Ebenez[r] Kilby | " 10 | | 2 27 |
| David King | " 10 | | 2 27 |
| Steph[n] Kellogg | " 10 | | 2 27 |
| Mitchell Kingman | Aug[t] 15 | | 1 22 |
| Levi Loveland | July 10 | | 2 27 |
| Lumon Long | " 20 | | 2 17 |
| Sam[l] Lawson | Aug[t] 15 | | 1 22 |
| Sol[o] Lattimer | " 15 | | 1 22 |
| Hosea Miller | July 10 | | 2 27 |
| Ja[s] Murfy | " 10 | | 2 27 |
| John Miner | " 10 | | 2 27 |
| Rich[d] Montigue | " 10 | | 2 27 |
| Zebelon Maggott | " 10 | | 2 27 |
| Heze[h] Nott | " 10 | | 2 27 |
| W[m] Roads | Aug[t] 15 | | 1 22 |
| Jo[s] Roads | July 10 | | 2 27 |
| John Russell | " 10 | | 2 27 |
| Sam[l] Rockwell | " 10 | | 2 27 |
| Oswell Rockwell | " 10 | | 2 27 |
| Enoch Stoddard | " 10 | | 2 27 |
| Sam[l] Stoddard | Aug[t] 15 | | 1 22 |
| John Stoddard | " 15 | | 1 22 |
| Zacheriah Seymour | " 15 | | 1 22 |
| Zachr[h] Seymour J[r] | July 20 | | 2 17 |
| Ja[s] Smith | " 10 | | 2 27 |
| Eli Tryon Corp[l] 20[th] Sep[t] | " 10 | | 2 27 |
| Cha[s] Treat | " 10 | | 2 27 |
| John Woodhouse | " 10 | | 2 27 |
| Sam[l] Woodhouse | " 10 | | 2 27 |
| Elisha Woolcott | " 10 | | 2 27 |
| W[m] Woolcott | " 10 | | 2 27 |
| Elizur Woolcott | " 10 | | 2 27 |
| Ebenez[r] Wells | " 10 | | 2 27 |
| Zion Wintworth | " 10 | | 2 27 |
| Elisha Wells | " 10 | | 2 27 |
| Elisha Webster | Aug[t] 15 | | 1 22 |
| Dan[l] Warner | July 10 | | 2 27 |
| Jo[s] Wright | " 10 | | 2 27 |
| Ashbell Riley promot[d] to Drum[r] Sep[t] 4 | " 10 | | 2 27 |

[*Copy in Comptroller's Office.*]

MILITIA REGIMENTS, 1776. 157

## SIXTH COMPANY—LIEUT. ANDRUSS.

A Pay Roll of the Sixth Company in the Sixth Regiment of Militia Commanded by Lieu' Stephen Andruss, for service Done in New York in August & September Last with wages and Milage and sauce money when Entered & when Discharged.

| Mens Name and Quality. | When Entered at York | When Discharged. | Wages L. s. d. f. | Travil Money s. d. | Sauce Money. d. | Total of each man's money. L. s. d. |
|---|---|---|---|---|---|---|
| | August | September | | | | |
| Lieu' Stephen Andruss | 20th | 11th | 8 18 1 | 19 8 | 1/10 | 6 9 7 |
| Sarj' Melitiah Nye | " | 24th | 3 8 10 1 | 19 8 | 2/11 | 4 11 5 |
| " Jared Hollister | " | 24th | 3 8 10 1 | 18 8 | 2/11 | 4 11 5 |
| " Joseph Churchel | " | 11th | 2 8 1 2 | 19 8 | 1/10 | 3 9 7 |
| " Isaac Tallcot | " | 6th | 1 18 4 | 19 8 | 1/5 | 2 19 5 |
| Corp' John Wire | " | 24th | 3 8 2 | 19 8 | 2/11 | 4 5 9 |
| " Nehimiah Hollister | " | 11th | 2 2 10 3 | 19 8 | 1/10 | 3 4 4¾ |
| " Ruben Risley | " | 11th | 2 2 10 3 | 19 8 | 1/10 | 3 4 4¾ |
| " Henry Huxford | " | 11th | 2 2 10 3 | 19 8 | 1/10 | 3 4 4¾ |
| Drum' David Fox | " | 11th | 2 2 10 3 | 19 8 | 1/10 | 3 4 4¾ |
| Fifer David Hollister | " | 11th | 2 2 10 3 | 19 8 | 2/11 | 3 4 4¾ |
| Charles Andruss | " | 24th | 2 17 4 | 19 8 | 1/10 | 3 13 11 |
| John Andruss | " | 11th | 2 0 0 | 19 8 | 2/11 | 3 1 6 |
| David Andruss | " | 24th | 2 17 4 | 19 8 | 2/11 | 3 19 11 |
| Benjiman Andruss | " | 24th | 2 17 4 | 19 8 | 2/11 | 3 19 11 |
| Levi Brooks | " | 24th | 2 17 4 | 19 8 | 2/11 | 3 19 11 |
| Samuel Covill | " | 24th | 2 17 4 | 19 8 | 2/11 | 3 19 11 |
| Philip Covill | " | 24th | 2 17 4 | 19 8 | 1/10 | 3 19 11 |
| Elisha Couch | " | 11th | 2 0 0 | 19 8 | 2/11 | 3 1 6 |
| Ebenezer Fox | " | 24th | 2 17 4 | 19 8 | 1/10 | 3 19 11 |
| Israel Fox | " | 11th | 2 0 0 | 19 8 | 1/10 | 3 1 6 |
| Isaac Fox | " | 11th | 2 0 0 | 19 8 | 2/11 | 3 1 6 |
| Stephen Fox | " | 24th | 2 17 4 | 19 8 | 2/11 | 3 19 11 |
| Joseph Goodale | " | 24th | 2 17 4 | 19 8 | 2/11 | 3 19 11 |
| Timothy Goslee | " | 24th | 2 17 4 | 19 8 | 2/3 | 3 19 11 |
| Aron Gosse | " | 16th | 2 6 8 | 19 8 | 2/3 | 3 8 7 |
| David Hubburd | " | 16th | 2 6 8 | 19 8 | 2/3 | 3 8 7 |
| Joseph Hubburd | " | 11th | 2 0 0 | 19 8 | 1/10 | 3 1 6 |
| Israel House | " | 24th | 2 17 6 | 19 8 | 2/11 | 3 19 11 |
| Elisha How | " | 11th | 2 0 9 | 19 8 | 1/10 | 3 11 0 |
| William Holdrath | " | 16th | 2 6 8 | 19 8 | 2/3 | 3 8 7 |
| William House | " | 11th | 2 0 0 | 19 8 | 1/10 | 3 1 6 |
| Lazarus House | " | 24th | 2 17 4 | 19 8 | 2/11 | 3 19 11 |
| Appleton Holmes | " | 24th | 2 17 4 | 19 8 | 2/11 | 3 19 11 |
| Elisha Hills | " | 24th | 2 17 4 | 19 8 | 2/11 | 3 19 11 |
| Ichabod Hollister | " | 24th | 2 17 4 | 19 8 | 2/11 | 3 19 11 |
| George Hollister | " | 24th | 2 17 4 | 19 8 | 2/11 | 3 19 11 |
| Israel Hills | " | 6th | 1 18 4 | 19 8 | 1/5 | 2 14 5 |
| Frary Hale | " | 24th | 2 17 4 | 19 8 | 2/11 | 3 19 11 |
| Isaac Hale | " | 24th | 2 17 4 | 19 8 | 2/11 | 3 19 11 |
| Daniel House | " | 11th | 2 0 0 | 19 8 | 1/10 | 3 1 6 |
| Joseph Hills | " | 24th | 2 17 4 | 19 8 | 2/11 | 3 19 11 |
| Abner House | " | 24th | 2 17 4 | 19 8 | 2/11 | 3 19 11 |
| Isaac Keeney | " | 24th | 2 17 4 | 19 8 | 2/11 | 3 19 5 |
| Elizur Lovland | " | 6th | 2 17 4 | 19 8 | 1/5 | 2 14 5 |
| Pelitiah Lovland | " | 24th | 1 18 4 | 19 8 | 2/11 | 3 19 11 |
| Levi Loveland | " | 24th | 2 17 4 | 19 8 | 2/11 | 3 19 11 |
| Samuel Risley | " | 24th | 2 17 4 | 19 8 | 2/11 | 3 19 11 |
| Ruben Sparks | " | 11th | 2 0 0 | 19 8 | 1/10 | 3 1 6 |

# REVOLUTION ROLLS AND LISTS.

| Mens Names and Quality. | When Entered at York | When Discharged. | Wages L. s. d. f. | Travil Money s. d. | Sauce Money. d. | Total of Each man's money. L. s. d. |
|---|---|---|---|---|---|---|
| | August | September | | | | |
| Samuel Smith | 20th | 16th | 2 6 8 | 19 8 | 2/3 | 3 8 7 |
| Ezekiel Skinner | " | 24th | 2 0 0 | 19 8 | 2/11 | 3 19 11 |
| Lemuel Stratton | " | 11th | 2 17 4 | 19 8 | 2/11 | 3 1 6 |
| Jonathan Treet | " | 11th | 2 0 0 | 19 8 | 1/10 | 3 1 6 |
| Isaac Tubbs | " | 24th | 2 17 4 | 19 8 | 2/11 | 3 19 11 |
| John Welles | " | 11th | 2 0 0 | 19 8 | 1/1 | 3 1 6 |
| Peleg Welden | " | 24th | 2 17 4 | 19 8 | 2/10 | 3 19 11 |
| Nehimiah Wire | " | 16th | 2 6 8 | 19 8 | 2/6 | 3 8 7 |
| Joseph Wares | " | 24th | 2 17 4 | 19 8 | 2/11 | 3 19 11 |
| John Wickham | " | 11th | 2 0 0 | 19 8 | 1/10 | 3 1 6 |

Lieut Stephen Andruss Roll to pay of his Men With. 1777. Feb. 25th

[*Dwight A. Andrews, Hartford.*]

## TWELFTH REGIMENT—COL. HOSFORD.

[*See Record of Connecticut Men in the Revolution, page 450.*]

### OFFICERS.

A Return of the Officers & Men that Serv$^d$ Under Col$^o$ Obadiah Hosford at West Chester Sept$^r$ 1776 Viz

| | | No. of Men | | | No. of Men |
|---|---|---|---|---|---|
| Cap$^t$. David Tarbox | per Roll | 28 | Cap$^t$. Ephraim Carpenter | Roll | 85 |
| Cap$^t$. David Miller | " | 85 | Cap$^t$. James Pineo | " | 35 |
| Cap$^t$. Andrew Waterman | " | [80] | Cap$^t$. John Wells | " | 86 |
| Cap$^t$. Eb$^r$. Hutchinson | " | 41 | | | |
| Cap$^t$. Dan$^l$ Dewey | " | 33 | | | 304 |
| Cap$^t$. Joshua Phelps | " | 30 | | | |

[*State Library, Revolution 6.*]

### CAPT. TARBOX'S COMPANY.

A List of Cap$^t$ David Tarbox C$^o$ in Reg$^t$ who march$^d$ by order to East Chester Sept last (filed Hosfords Reg$^t$)

| | | |
|---|---|---|
| David Tarbox | Cap$^t$ | Diah Stark |
| Sol$^o$ Tarbox | Lieu$^t$. | Dan$^l$ Waters |
| Elisha Beach | Ens$^n$ | Hez$^h$ Cutting |
| Caleb Root | Serg$^t$ | Jon$^a$ Dunham |
| Christ$^r$ Crouch | " | John Birg |
| Jo$^a$ Waters | " | John Taylor |
| Jo$^s$ Pepoon | " | Joshua Bigelow |
| Benj$^n$ Pepoon | Corp$^l$ | Lawrence Powers |
| Jared Allen | " | W$^m$ Darby |
| Levy Washborn | " | Zenas Tarbox |
| John Kellogg | " Desert$^d$ Oct 18 | Hazel Crandel |
| Joel Jones | Drum$^r$ | Alex$^r$ Phelps |
| Sam$^l$ Jones | Fifer | Nath$^l$ Pease |
| David Skinner | | Zebedee Cutting |

Jere$^h$ Mason Maj$^r$

[*Copy in Comptroller's Office.*]

## CAPT. MILLER'S COMPANY.

A List of Cap$^t$ David Millers C$^o$ L$^t$ Col. Obediah Hosfords Reg$^t$ that march$^d$ in Sept$^r$ 1776 to East Chester to join Gen$^l$ Washington's Army.

| Names | | Names |
|---|---|---|
| David Miller | Cap$^t$ | John Huxford |
| Sol$^a$ Phelps | Lieut | Epafrus Loveland |
| W$^m$ Burt | Ens$^n$ | Elisha Watrous |
| Jonah Root | Serg$^t$ | Benj$^n$ Chamberlain |
| Eleaz$^r$ Carter | " | Asa Loomis |
| Sam$^l$ Finley | " | Ja$^s$ Mackarel |
| David Blush | " | Abr$^m$ Skinner 3$^d$ |
| Israel Foot J$^r$ | " | David Strong |
| Tho$^s$ Carrier J$^r$ | Corp$^l$ | Jon$^a$ Willis |
| Ebenez$^r$ Coleman | " | Tho$^s$ Hills |
| Benj$^n$ Darbee | Fifer | David Kellogg |
| Libbius Hills | Drum$^r$ | Reuben Curtis |
| Adonij$^h$ Strong | | Benajah Jones |
| Cha$^s$ Edy | | Dan$^l$ Loveland |
| Jeded$^h$ Edgerton | | Jacob Ingraham |
| Silvenus Norket | | Asa Fuller |
| John Dewey | | Hezekiah Kneland |

Jerem$^h$ Mason Maj$^r$
Gideon Waters Desert$^d$. Oct 24

[*Copy in Comptroller's Office.*]


## CAPT. WATERMAN'S COMPANY.

A List of Capt Andrew Waterman Company in Lef$^t$ Colo Obediah Hosford Regm$^t$

| | | | |
|---|---|---|---|
| Andrew Waterman | Capt | Bela Devenport | |
| Elihu Thomas | Left | Mark Fowler | |
| Jacob Mackaul | Ensn | Amos Fowler | |
| Joseph Lomis | Sargt | Daniel Ingraham | |
| Simon Abel | Sargt | Benjamin Kinne | |
| Dijah Fowler | Sargt | James Lothrop | |
| Isaiah Loomis | Sargt | Dan Lee | |
| Aaron Thorp | Corp | Thomas L Hyde | |
| Otis Bigelow | Corp | Simeon Puffer | |
| Jesse Brown | Corp | Sam$^{ll}$ Robbinson | |
| William Hyde | Drum$^r$ | John Whitman | |
| Olliver Strong | fifer | Sam$^{ll}$ Wattles Jr | |
| John Bartlet | | Vetch Williams Jr | |
| William Bentley | | Joseph W Bissel | |
| Caleb Chappel | | Joseph Bartlet Jr | |
| Benjamin Dike | | | |

Jeremiah Mason Maj$^r$

[*State Library, Revolution 6.*]

## CAPT. HUTCHINSON'S COMPANY.

Cap¹ Eleaz' Hutchinsons C° Militia under Comman⁴ Col. Hosford⁸ Reg¹ State Conn¹

| Names | | |
|---|---|---|
| Eleaz' Hutchinson | . | Cap¹ |
| Paul Brigham | . | Lieut |
| Tho⁸ Terril | . | Ensign |
| John Henry | . | Serg¹ |
| Dan¹ White | . | Serg¹ |
| Aaron Swetland | . | " |
| Eliph¹ Hendy | . | " |
| Adonij^h White | . | Corp¹ |
| Jabez Loomis | . | " |
| Jo⁸ Kingsbury | . | " |
| Eph Beemas | . | " |
| Eleaz' Hutchinson | . | Drum' |
| Sam¹ Jones | . | Fifer |
| W^m Blackman | | |
| Jon^a Badcock | | |
| W^m Bowles | | Desert⁴ Sep¹ 28 return⁴ Nov' 8 |
| Adam Bingham | | |
| Reuben Bill | | |
| Levi Buell | | |
| Dan¹ Badcock | | " " " " |
| Josiah Burnap | | " " " " |
| David Brown | | |
| Asariah Bell | | " " " " |
| Tim° Cowles | | " " " " |
| Alex' House | | |
| Ja⁸ House | | |
| Ja⁸ Hawkins | | |
| Isahel Jones | | |
| Benj^a Jones | | |
| Abiath' Lyman | | " " " " |
| Eleaz' Lomiss | | |
| Sam¹ Perkins | | |
| Jacob Fox | | |
| Benj^a Sprague | | |
| Ebenez' Sweetland | | " " " " |
| Elisha Sprague | | " " " " |
| Jo⁸ Savary | | |
| Jon^a Savary | | |
| David Townsen | | " " " " |
| Jon^a Townsen | | |
| Tho⁸ Tomson | | " " " " |

*[Copy in Comptroller's Office.]*

## CAPT. DEWEY'S COMPANY.

A List of Cap¹ Dan¹ Deweys C° in L¹ Col° O. Hosfords Reg¹ that marched to East Chester Sep¹ 1776 to join Gen¹ Washington's Army

| | | | |
|---|---|---|---|
| Dan¹ Dewey | Cap¹ | Elisha Hutchinson | Serg¹ |
| And^w Huntington | L¹ | Annis Fitch | " |
| W^m Mordock | Ens^a | Eleaz' Manning | " |
| Cha⁸ Swift | Serg¹ | Tim° Allen | " |

Jo⁸ Robinson Corp¹
Tho⁸ Laws "
Ezek¹ Loomis "
Gersh^m Clark Drum^r
Andr^w Hide Fifer
Nath^n Lee
Peletiah Holbrook
David Potter
Ja⁸ Tickour
Rodolph⁸ Wacker
John Arnold
Sam¹ Beemon
Rich^d Lyman

Beriah Sprague
Jon⁸ Bliss
Jon⁸ Edgerton
Gurdian geer
David Metcalf
Isaih Loomis
Asa Tiffeny
Adonijah Crocker
Benj^a Tilden
Gideon Clark
Isaih Tiffeny
Asell Clark

Jer^h Mason Maj^r
[*Copy in Comptroller's Office.*]

## CAPT. PHELPS' COMPANY.

A List of Cap¹ Joshua Phelps C° in Lieut Col° Obadiah Hosfords Reg¹ that March^d by order to Eastchester in Sep¹ 1776 to join Gen¹ Washington's Army

Joshua Phelps Cap¹
Sam¹ Tyler Lieut
Roger Phelps Ens^n
Asa White Serg¹
John Gilbert "
Steph^a Barber "
Aaron Phelps "
David Strong Corp¹
Roswell Phelps "
David Carver "
Abel Bissel "
David Barber Drum^r
Beniah Phelps Fifer
Asa Boles
Amos Phelps J^r

Andrew Man
Eph^m Phelps
Sam¹ Phelps
Inereas Porter
Joshua Phelps J^r
Joel Porter
Ja⁸ Pratt
Jon⁸ Tarbox
Obed^h White
Phinehas Strong
Silvester Garner
Tim° Phelps J^r
John Gillet
Dan¹ Phelps
Obediah Phelps

Jere^h Mason Maj^r
[*Copy in Comptroller's Office.*]

## CAPT. CARPENTER'S COMPANY.

A List of Cap¹ Eph^m Carpenters C° in Col° Hosfords Reg¹ who march^d by order to East Chester Sep¹ 1776

Eph^m Carpenter Cap¹
Dan¹ Clark Lieut
Israel Williams Ens^n
Oliv^r Bill Serg¹
Malicha Thomas "
Joshua Carpenter "
Johiel Williams "
Cha⁸ Williams "
Amos Porter Corp¹
Jacob Clark "
Tabin Bosworth "
John Williams "

Roswell Clark Drum^r
Edw^d Luther
Israel Bliss
Ja⁸ Gay
Dan¹ Wilcox
Eliph¹ Abel
Jon⁸ T Bissell
Abiel Bajcom
Hosea Birge
Amos Clark
Jon⁸ Cole
Joel Chamberlin

MILITIA REGIMENTS, 1776.     163

Rufus Lamb
Roswell Richardson
Noah Roberds
John Torry
Tim⁰ Waters
Jaˢ Webster

Wᵐ Webster
Ephᵐ Wilcox
Jared Clark
Eleazer Bill
Andrew Clark

[*Copy in Comptroller's Office.*]

## CAPT. PINEO'S COMPANY.

A List of Capt James Pineo Company in Left Colo Hosford Regiment that Marched by order To East chester To Join General Washintons Army

James Pineo Capt
Elias Bliss Left
Daniel Dunham Ensn
James Woodworth Sargᵗ
Samuel West Sargᵗ
Henry Bliss Sergᵗ
Joseph Hatch Corpl
Eldad Hunt Corpl
Benoni Loomis Cor
Rufus Collins Drummer
Jabez Persons fifer
Eliot Porter
Joseph Solland
Josiah Thomas
Samˡˡ Allen
John Joy
Jesse Wright
David Boles

Ephrm Hills
Edward Hawkins
John Holbrook
Elisha Warner
William White
Eleazer Collins
Zelotis Collins
Joshua Woodworth
Elijah Chappel
Samˡˡ Boston
Bethewell Newcomb
Jonathⁿ Bissell
Fadrick White
Josiah Dewey
David Treadway
Joseph Demon
Samuel Guile

Jeremiah Mason Majʳ

[*State Library, Revolution 6.*]

## CAPT. WELLS' COMPANY.

A List of the 8ᵗʰ Company in the 12ᵗʰ Regiment of Melisha in the State of Conecticut that Marchᵈ to West Chester in Sepʳ in 1776

Capt John H Wells
Lieutenant William Tallcott
Ensign Simeon Dunham
Daniel Bushnell
David Post
Sargᵗ Alexsander White
Gad Tallcott
Daniel Chapman          Deserted
Corpˡ Eliphalet Youngs
Jehial Wilcox
Elihu Wells
Druʳ Samuel Peters
Fifer Ashel Gilbert     Deserted
Jonothan Hutchinson
Daniel Root
Joseph Hutchinson
Jeremiah Brown
Zachariah Perren

Isireal Hutchinson
Joshua Root
David Norton
Eli Phelps
Ezekiel Write
Joseph Peters           Deserted
Ellis Luther
Isarel Skiner
Abel Write              Deserted
Joseph Martin
Samuel Ingham
Zadock Man              Deserted
Josiah Mack
John Post
Adenijah Skiner
Elisha Phelps
John Perren
Ezekiel Root

Test John H Wells Capᵗ
Jeremiah Mason Majʳ

[*State Library, Revolution 6.*]

## SEVENTEENTH REGIMENT—COL. SHELDON.

[*See Record of Connecticut Men in the Revolution, page 449.*]

### DESERTERS.

List of Deserters from 17 Milit[a] Reg[t] on Service at N. York Aug[t] 1776 each of whom had 20/ advanc[d] before their March for which they are now Debtors to the State

| | |
|---|---|
| Moses Bartholomew | of Cap[t] Barns C[o] |
| Jn[o] Malsby | " " |
| Abner Hancock | " " |
| Bela Graves | " " |
| Sam[l] Renner | " " |
| Jn[o] Griswold | " " |
| Isaac Bartholomew | " " |
| Benj[a] Doolittle | of Cap[t] Osborns C[o] |
| Steph[n] Plant | " " |
| Benj[a] Bissel | " " |
| Josiah Stone | " " |
| Jonas Leach | of Cap[t] Loomiss C[o] |
| Noah Beach | " " |
| Rich[d] Leech | " " |

[*Copy in Comptroller's Office.*]

## EIGHTEENTH REGIMENT—COL. PETTIBONE.

### SIMSBURY MINUTE MEN.

[Simsbury men belonging to the 1st Company in the 18th Regiment of Militia, Abel Pettibone Captain, Jonathan Pettibone Colonel, who "inlisted to serve as Minute-Men for the Defence of this and the adjoining Colonies" June 11, 1776.]

Ehud Tuller
Ahijah Pettibone
Noah Humphry Jr
Isaac Alderman
Joel Tuller
Ozios Phelps
Joel Case
Isaac Willcocks
Richard Humphry

John Alderman
James Cornish Jun[r]
Aaron Willcocks
Sarrid Thomas
Elisha Willcok
Eli Alderman
Isak Allen
Elijah Tuller

[The following names found upon the back of the same paper appear to be a further record of inlistments.]

David Phelps
Sedose Willcoks
Jo[s] Foot
Jo[s] Goodwine
Dudly Pettibone

Caleb Case
Sam[ll] Goodwine
Peres Maskel
Moses Case
Jon[a] Case

[*L. W. Bigelow, Simsbury.*]

MILITIA REGIMENTS, 1776. 165

## NINETEENTH REGIMENT—LIEUT.-COL. PITKIN.

[*See Record of Connecticut Men in the Revolution, page 450.*]

### CAPT. FITCH'S COMPANY.

A Pay Roll of Cap.<sup>t</sup> James Fitch's Company Commanded by Maj.<sup>r</sup> Nath.<sup>ll</sup> Terry to 1.<sup>st</sup> of Octb.<sup>r</sup> Inclusive.

| Names | Arrival in New York Aug. 1776 | Days added on 144 Miles from N. Y. | Discharged | Days Service |
|---|---|---|---|---|
| Capt. James Fitch | 24 | 7 | | 46 |
| Lieut Elisha Kibbe | 24 | 7 | Sep.<sup>r</sup> 6.<sup>th</sup> | 27 |
| Ensign Daniel Elsworth | 24 | 7 | | 46 |
| Serj.<sup>t</sup> Ichabod Wadsworth | 24 | 7 | | 46 |
| Serj.<sup>t</sup> Daniel Warner | 24 | 7 | 6.<sup>th</sup> | 27 |
| Serj.<sup>t</sup> Gurdon Elsworth | 24 | 7 | | 46 |
| Serj.<sup>t</sup> Daniel Day | 24 | 7 | | 46 |
| Clerk Daniel Porter | 24 | 7 | 20.<sup>th</sup> | 41 |
| Corp.<sup>l</sup> John Craw Jr. | 24 | 7 | | 46 |
| Corp.<sup>l</sup> Silas Reed | 24 | 7 | 20.<sup>th</sup> | 41 |
| Corp.<sup>l</sup> Rufus Cleaveland | 24 | 7 | | 46 |
| Corp.<sup>l</sup> Edward Paine | 24 | 7 | | 46 |
| Drum.<sup>r</sup> Sam.<sup>ll</sup> Pierson Jr. | 24 | 7 | | 46 |
| Fifer Eb.<sup>r</sup> Pinney | 24 | 7 | | 46 |
| Eliphas Bartlet | 24 | 7 | | 46 |
| Edmund Bragg | 24 | 7 | | 46 |
| Sam.<sup>l</sup> Bartlet | 24 | 7 | | 46 |
| Simeon Belknap Jr. | 24 | 7 | | 46 |
| Joseph Campbell | 24 | 7 | | 46 |
| Adonijah Day | 24 | 7 | 3.<sup>rd</sup> | 24 |
| Jonathan Damon | 24 | 7 | 3.<sup>rd</sup> | 24 |
| Jedediah Durphy or Durfy | 24 | 7 | | 46 |
| John Damon | 24 | 7 | | 46 |
| Nathan Hall | 24 | 7 | | 46 |
| Elijah Farnam or Farmon | 24 | 7 | | 46 |
| Thomas Kennedy | 24 | 7 | 6.<sup>th</sup> | 27 |
| Elijah Kingsbury | 24 | 7 | | 46 |
| David McCray | 24 | 7 | 8 | 24 |
| Benja Lewis | 24 | 7 | | 46 |
| John Lovett | | | Deserted | |
| James Lovett | | | Deserted | |
| William Kinney | 24 | 7 | | 46 |
| James Kinney | | | Deserted | |
| William McCray | 24 | 7 | | 46 |
| Nathan McQuavy or MCurthy | 24 | 7 | | 46 |
| Tho.<sup>s</sup> McKnight | 24 | 7 | | 46 |
| Isaac Newton | 24 | 7 | | 46 |
| John Newhall | 24 | 7 | | 46 |
| Andrew Pimber | 24 | 7 | 3.<sup>rd</sup> | 24 |
| John Parker | 24 | 7 | 6.<sup>th</sup> | 27 |

| Names | Arrival in New York Augt. 1776 | Days added on 144 Miles from N. Y. | Discharged | Days Service |
|---|---|---|---|---|
| Jonathan Porter | 24 | 7 | | 46 |
| Daniel Person | 24 | 7 | | 46 |
| Ephraim Pierson | 24 | 7 | | 46 |
| Lemuel Pinney | | Deserted | | |
| Hezekiah Russell | 24 | 7 | 6th | 27 |
| Lothrop Shirtleff | 24 | 7 | | 46 |
| Wiliam Spear Jr. | 24 | 7 | | 46 |
| John Wallace | 24 | 7 | 6th | 27 |
| James Wallace | 24 | 7 | 3rd | 24 |
| William Wallace | 24 | 7 | 6th | 27 |
| Lemuel West | 24 | 7 | | 46 |

[*Connecticut Historical Society.*]

## TWENTY-FIRST REGIMENT—COL. DOUGLASS.

[*See Record of Connecticut Men in the Revolution, page 450.*]

### CAPT. SMITH'S COMPANY.

Pay Role of Cap$^t$ W$^m$ Smiths Company in Co$^{ll}$ J. Douglas Reg$^t$ who joind the American army in the State of New York Sep$^t$. 1776

| Mens Names | Miles to & from Camp | | Entred Service | Dischargd | |
|---|---|---|---|---|---|
| Cap$^t$ W$^m$ Smith | | | 7$^{th}$ Sept$^r$ | Nov$^r$ | 20 |
| Ensi Peter Davison | | | " | Nov | 9 |
| Sarj Na$^t$ Cogwell | 272 | | " | Nov | 20 |
| Sarj John Stevens | 272 | | " | Nov | 10 |
| Sarj W$^m$ Cushman | 160 | | | | |
| Cor. Deleno Peirce | 272 | | " | Nov | 20 |
| Cor. Nathan Deans | 272 | | " | Nov | 20 |
| Col. Walter Boman | 272 | | " | Nov | 10 |
| Cor. John Baker | 272 | | " | Nov | 20 |
| David Thayer | 272 | | " | Nov | 6 |
| Jonathan Pike | 272 | | " | Nov | 8 |
| Ward Woodard | 272 | | " | Nov | 9 |
| John Ashcraft | 272 | | " | Nov | 20 |
| W$^m$ Foster | 112 | | " | Dead Nov | 4 |
| W$^m$ Ashcraft | 272 | Absent Carting 1 month | " | Nov$^r$ | 20 |
| Caleb Adams | 272 | | " | Oct | 10 |
| Jonathan Copland | 272 | | " | Oc$^t$ | 12 |
| Eleazer Litchfield | 272 | | " | Nov | 20 |
| Silas Adams | 272 | | " | Sep$^t$ | 30 |
| Increse Huit | 272 | | " | Oc$^t$ | 10 |
| Jonas Baker | 272 | | " | Nov | 20 |
| Stephen Huit | 272 | | " | Nov | 20 |
| Elisha Fitch | 112 | | " Enlisted Sep$^t$ | | 21 |
| James Cleavland Ju | 112 | | " " " | | 24 |
| Uriah Holt | 112 | | " " " | | 21 |

[*Connecticut Historical Society.*]

### CAPT. CADY'S COMPANY.

A Pay Roll of Cap$^t$ David Cady$^s$ Company in Co$^{ll}$ Douglass$^s$ Rig$^t$ Who Join'd The American Army In the State of Newyork Sep$^t$ 1776.

| Mens Names | Engag$^d$ in Service | Miles to and From Camp | Deserted | Discharg$^d$ | Time in Service m d |
|---|---|---|---|---|---|
| Cap$^t$ D : Cady | Sep$^t$ 7$^{th}$ 1776 | | | Nvo$^r$ 20 | 2 21 |
| Liu$^t$ Co$^l$ Day | | | | " | 2 21 |
| Ens$^n$ Na$^t$ Spaulding | | | | " | 2 21 |
| Serg$^t$ Jo$^n$ Roberts | | 288 | | " | 2 21 |
| " Will$^m$ Graves | | | Sep$^t$ 26$^{th}$ | " | |
| " Jed$^h$ Bennet | | | " | | |
| " Jon$^m$ Day | | | " | | |
| Clark Sil$^s$ Huchans | | | " | | |

168   REVOLUTION ROLLS AND LISTS.

|  | Engag'd in Service | Miles to and From Camp | Deserted | Discharg'd | Time in Service m d |
|---|---|---|---|---|---|
| Corp'l Step'n Rude |  |  | Sep't 26th |  |  |
| " Abner Day |  |  |  | Sep't 28 | 0 29 |
| " Corn'ss Whitney |  |  | " |  |  |
| Fif'r Ros'l Fairman |  | 288 |  | Nov. 20 | 2 21 |
| Will'm Spaulding |  | 288 |  | Nov. 20 | 2 21 |
| Uriah Kee |  | 288 |  | Nov. 9 | 2 10 |
| Henry Sparks |  | 288 |  | Nov. 20 | 2 21 |
| John Sparks |  | 288 |  | Nov. 20 | 2 21 |
| Jam's Dixson |  | 288 |  | Nov. 7 | 2 8 |
| Step'n Grover |  | 288 |  | Sept. 27 | 0 28 |
| John Bush |  | 288 |  | Sep 30 | 1 1 |
| Icah'd Sparks |  | 288 |  | Nov. 20 | 2 21 |
| John Moffitt |  | 288 |  | Nov. 20 | 2 21 |
| And'w Moffitt |  | 288 |  | Oc't 6th | 1 7 |
| Jo'n Stedman |  | 288 |  | Nov 20 | 2 21 |
| Seth Short |  | 288 |  | Nov. 5 | 2 6 |
| Elim Hulet |  | 288 |  | Nov. 9 | 2 10 |
| Ezek'l Walan |  |  | " |  |  |
| Joseph Whitney |  |  | " |  |  |
| Ezra Huchans |  |  | " |  |  |
| Shub'l Huchans |  |  |  |  |  |
| Mathi's Whitney |  |  | " |  |  |
| Thos Bordon |  |  | " |  |  |
| Joshua Eaton |  |  | " |  |  |

N. B. The Above Company Found Themselves 19 Guns 19 Blankets and 19 Knapsacks &c         Test

David Cady Cap't

[*Connecticut Historical Society*.]


## CAPT. ANDREW BACKUS' COMPANY.

Travil Pay Role of Cap't Andrew Backus Company in Co'll John Douglas Rig't Who Joind the Amarican army in the State of New York Sep't 1776.

|  | When Engaged | Miles travil to & from Camp |
|---|---|---|
| Cap't Andrew Backus |  |  |
| Liu't Joshua Dunlap |  |  |
| Sarj't Nathan Dean | Sep't 7. 1776 | 280 |
| Sarj't Joseph Spaulding |  | " |
| Sarj't John Cleavland |  | " |
| Sarj't Silas Spalding |  | " |
| Q'rm Sarj't John Peirce |  | " |
| Cor Robert Car |  | " |
| Cor Ezra Spalding |  | " |
| Fifer Stephen Backus |  | " |
| Squier How |  | " |
| David Atterton |  | " |
| Thomas Antrum |  | " |
| Joseph Robinson |  | " |

## MILITIA REGIMENTS, 1776. 169

| | When Engaged | Miles travil to & from Camp |
|---|---|---|
| Abijah Dean | . | 280 |
| James Hawkins | . | " |
| Timothy Babcock | . | " |
| Ezra Warren | . | " |
| Nathaniel Barnet | . | " |
| Nathaniel Marsh | . | " |
| Daniel Spalding | . | " |
| David Carter | . | " |
| Andrew Herick | . | " |
| Moses Barnet | . | " |
| Henry Head | . | " |
| Lemuel Warren | . | " |
| Daniel Moredock | . | " |
| Joshua Hall | . | " |
| James How | . | " |
| William Thompson | . | " |
| James Stromthorn [?] | . | 180 |
| | | 8020 |

Premium for 83 men including Aaron Wheetor & Na<sup>hl</sup> Hewlet who marched with the Rig<sup>t</sup> & taken Sick & was not Returnd with the Rest of y<sup>e</sup> Rig<sup>t</sup>

Test Andrew Backus Captain

*[Connecticut Historical Society.]*


## CAPT. TIMOTHY BACKUS' COMPANY.

Mileage Roll of Cap<sup>t</sup> Tim<sup>o</sup> Backus Company of Volunteers In Co<sup>ll</sup> Jn<sup>o</sup> Douglass's Reg<sup>t</sup> of Melitia From the State of Connecticutt

| Mens Names | Miles to & from Camp | Mens Names | Miles to & from Camp |
|---|---|---|---|
| Cap<sup>t</sup> T. Backus | | Jona<sup>h</sup> Downing | 295 |
| L<sup>t</sup> Jo<sup>s</sup> Raynsford | | Tho<sup>s</sup> Dimmick | " |
| En<sup>s</sup> Jo<sup>s</sup> Leach | | William Dyar | " |
| Serg<sup>t</sup> Sam<sup>ll</sup> Felch | 295 | James Durfee | " |
| " Josiah Dewey | " | Nathan Fish | " |
| " Caleb Faulkner | " | John Hough | " |
| Corp<sup>l</sup> Jn<sup>o</sup> Curtiss | " | Asa Leffingwell | " |
| Corp<sup>l</sup> Levi Adams | " | Abel Lyon | " |
| Drum<sup>r</sup> Jon<sup>a</sup> Davis | " | Josiah Munrow | " |
| Elihu Adams | " | Simeon Parke | " |
| Nehemiah Adams | " | John Simms | " |
| John Adams | " | Jo<sup>s</sup> Safford | " |
| Silas Allen | " | Zacheriah Waldo | " |
| Jo<sup>s</sup> Buth | " | | |
| Nath<sup>l</sup> Clark | " | Total | 7875 |

*[Connecticut Historical Society.]*

## CAPT. BACON'S COMPANY.

A Travil Abstract of Cap.t Benj.a Bacon's Company in Col. Jn. Douglass Regiment North Castle Nov.r 1776.

| Mans Names | Miles Travil to & from Camp | Mans Names | Miles Travil to & from Camp |
|---|---|---|---|
| Cap.t B. Bacon |  | Phinehas Lester | 295 |
| L.t J. Adams |  | Oliver Tyler | " |
| Sarg. D. Foster | 295 | Ebenezer Ransome | " |
| " J. Park | " | Thadeus Palmer | " |
| " B. Moore | " | Nathaniel Luce (?) | " |
| " S. Bacon | " | Ebenezer Smith | " |
| Corp. J. Bacon | " | John Brown | " |
| " J. Bradford | " | Ezekiel Park | " |
| " J. Clark | " | Roswell Parish | " |
| F. L. Bingham | " | Robert Stephens | 135 |
| F. W. Brown | " | Lemuel Stephens | " |
| George Austin | " | Joseph Rainsford | " |
| James Adams | " | Josiah Bradford | " |

Premiums to L.t & Cap.t and 24 men £26.

[*Copy in Connecticut Historical Society.*]

## LIEUT. PARKE'S COMPANY.

Pay Roll of L.t Robart Parke Company in Col Douglas Reg.t who Joind the American army in the Stat of Newyork Sep.t

| Mens Names | Entered Service | Miles to and From Camp | Deserted | Discharged | Time in Service m d | |
|---|---|---|---|---|---|---|
| L.t Robart Parke | Sep 7. 1776 |  |  | Nov. 7 | 2 | 8 |
| Sarg.t David Eames |  | 288 |  | Nov. 9 | 2 | 10 |
| Sarg.t Thomas Dixson |  | 288 |  | Nov. 20 | 2 | 21 |
| Sarg.t John Eames |  | 288 |  | " | 2 | 21 |
| Corp John Gaston |  | 288 |  | Nov. 10 | 2 | 11 |
| Corp Peleg Mateson |  | 288 |  | Nov. 9 | 2 | 10 |
| Job Green |  | 288 |  | Nov. 10 | 2 | 11 |
| Joshua Thrall |  | 288 |  | Nov. 20 | 2 | 21 |
| Job Talbat |  | 288 |  | " | 2 | 21 |
| Moses Barret |  | 120 |  | Died Oct. 10 | 1 | 8 |
| Reuban Marshal |  | 288 |  | " 10 | 2 | 11 |
| David Hatch |  |  | Sep.t 26 |  |  |  |
| William Vaughn |  | 288 |  | Oct. 10 | 1 | 11 |
| Isaac French |  | 288 |  | Nov. 9 | 2 | 10 |
| Jonathan Chilson |  |  | Sep.t 26 |  |  |  |
| Amaziah Parke |  | 288 |  | Nov. 20 | 2 | 21 |
| William Williams |  | 288 |  | Nov. 8 | 2 | 9 |
| Archabel Dorranc |  | 288 |  | Nov. 20 | 2 | 21 |
| Comfort Slack |  | 288 |  | Nov. 7 | 2 | 8 |

Payed the Above Deserters £1. 0. 0 Each

N. B: The Above Company Found themselves 17 Guns 17 Blankets 17 Knapseks        Tho.s Dixson Serg.t

Elisha Hall and Gideon Tower Rec.d 20.s each & were left sick on the Road & Returnd home & nothing Drawn for them

Jan.y 31. 1777        Test Robert Parke Lieut

[*Connecticut Historical Society.*]

MILITIA REGIMENTS, 1776. 171

## CAPT. PALMER'S COMPANY.

A Roal of Capt Palmer Company that march to Westchester September y⁰ 7ᵗʰ those names as followeth that is intitled to a Premium

Capt Joseph Palmer
Sargt Pelik Randall
Sargt William Gallup
Sargt John Wylie
Sargt John Huston
Sargt Daniel Hopkins
Cor Nehemiah Parks
Cor Nicolas Randal
Cor Cyrus Keney
  Joseph Egliston
  Robart Wylie

William Stuard
Brintnell Robins
Daniel Fish
Henry Nuton
Jonathan Palmer
Stevene Ray
Seth Morgin
Ruben Babcock
Peter Morgin
Benjamin Rods
Christopher Randal

test by Joseph Palmer Capt
January yᵉ 16 AD 1777

[Another copy adds the following to the names on the above roll:]
New Haven Sept 12ᵗʰ 1776

Phineas Edwards
Benjamin Palmer

Samuel Kinne Corporal
Jarius Palmer

These marched from Voluntown 9ᵗʰ Sept to New Haven and arrived on the 12 & to Strafford 14ᵗʰ Sepᵗ & to fairfield 15ᵗʰ Sept with our Packs I. E. we carried all our packs

[A receipt for wages adds the following names:]
Joseph Randall
Moses Fish

Matthew Newton
Thomas Stewart

[*Connecticut Historical Society.*]

## CAPT. HEBBARD'S COMPANY.

A Ration Role of Capᵗ Wm Hebbard Company in Col John Douglass Regment in the State of Connecticut Who marched to New London Sepᵗ the 2 day A D 1776

| Mens Names | Number of days in Carvis | Mens Names | Number of days in Carvis |
|---|---|---|---|
| Capt. Wᵐ Hebbard | 5 | Jams Butt | 5 |
| Leut. Joseph Burgus | 5 | Isaac Backes | 4 |
| Ens. Stephen Dowing | 5 | Paul Harris | 4 |
| Sar. Wᵐ Foster | 5 | Samuel Harris | 4 |
| Sar. Ebenezer Deains | 4 | Joshua Ramond | 4 |
| Sar. Aleck Gorden | 5 | Lee Wodard | 5 |
| Corp. Joseph Dimack | 5 | Eliphet Farnam | 5 |
| Corp. Samuel Hovey | 5 | Joseph Dewey | 5 |
| Drumer John Brown | 4 | Joseph Botton | 4 |
| John Hebbard Jr. | 5 | Silus Glass | 5 |
| Wm Hebbard Jr. | 4 | John Hebbard | 4 |
| Ebenezer Butt | 5 | Samuel Parish | 4 |
| John Butt | 5 | Isaac Fuller | 4 |
| Cyrus Manard | 5 | | |

[*State Library, Revolution 6.*]

## CAPT. HEBBARD'S COMPANY.

A Travel Abstract of Cap¹ Wᵐ Hebbards Company In Co¹¹ John Douglass Regt North Castle November 1 1776

Test    Joseph Burgs Leuᵗ.

| | Miles to & From Camp | | Miles to & From Camp |
|---|---|---|---|
| Capᵗ Wilᵐ Hebbard | | Ebenʳ Butt | 295 |
| Lᵗ J. Burges | | Stephᵃ Farnam | " |
| Enˢ S. Downing | | Eliphᵗ Farnam | " |
| Segᵗ M. Goodell | 295 | Sils Glass | " |
| Sergᵗ J. Dimock | " | Danⁱˡ Herington | " |
| Coʳ S. Hovey | " | Sirˢ Manord | " |
| " J. Hebbard | " | Jason Rood | " |
| Fʳ Wilᵐ D. Foster | " | Lee Woodard | " |
| Jnᵒ Butt | " | Jo Dewa | " |
| Jams Butt | " | | |

[*Connecticut Historical Society.*]

## CAPT. BUTT'S COMPANY.

A Return of a Company of Minute men Raisᵈ in May 1776 in the 21ˢᵗ Regᵗ in the State of Connecticut and Commanded by Sherebiah Butt Capᵗ of the 2ᵈ Militia Company in 8ᵈ Regᵗ

| Mens Names | Days spent in Service | Mens Names | Days spent in Service |
|---|---|---|---|
| Capt Shebᵇ Butt | 9 | Warren Williams | 2 |
| Lt John Adms | 4 | Joshua Bradfoad | 2 |
| Lt Jos Burges | 4 | Jacob Staples | 2 |
| Ens Pᵗ Davidson | 5 | John Cleaveland | 2 |
| S James Delop | 2 | Thoˢ Herris | 2 |
| S Benj Morse | 2 | Rufus Downing | 2 |
| S Levi Downing | 2 | Ebʳ Butt | 7 |
| S Jonᵃˢ Day | 1 | Solomon Adams Jr | 2 |
| S John Stevens | 2 | Rufus Hebbard | 2 |
| C Jos Adams | 2 | John Butt | 2 |
| C Corlˢ Adams | 2 | Phineas Downing Jr | 2 |
| C Samˡˡ Hovey | 2 | John Lilley | 1 |
| C Delino Pierce | 2 | Lee Woodward | 1 |
| F James Leach | 2 | John Stedman | 1 |
| Danˡˡ Herrick | 2 | Amasa Hutchins | 1 |
| Elijah Parke | 2 | George Little | 1 |
| John Butt Jr | 2 | Ezra Hutchins | 1 |
| Gideon Butt | 2 | Stephen Hewit | 2 |
| Jesse Adams | 2 | Joshua Miles | 2 |
| Ebʳ Berstow | 2 | Jesse Miles | 2 |
| Joˢ Adams 3ᵈ | 1 | Ebʳ Simons | 2 |
| Oliver Tiler | 2 | Joˢ Gorum | 1 |
| John Bradford | 2 | Nathan Dean | 1 |
| Simˡ Benjamins | 2 | Joˢ Baker | 1 |

[*State Library, Revolution 11.*]

## MAJOR SHELDON'S REGIMENT.

[*See Record of Connecticut Men in the Revolution, page 480.*]

### CAPT. BULL'S COMPANY.

Pay Rool for Cap! Tho! Bulls Company of Light Horse When Ordered to New York in July 1776

| Mens Names & Rank | Time when marched | When Discharged or Returned home |
|---|---|---|
| Thoˢ Bull Capᵗ | July 4 | July 20 |
| James Judson Leuᵗ | " | " |
| Agur Curtis Cornet | " | " |
| Gideon Martin Qurʳ | " | " |
| Isaiah Gilbert Copˡ | " | " |
| John Edwards Copˡ | " | " |
| Solomon Hurd Copˡ | " | " |
| Thoˢ Parmile Copˡ | " | " |
| James Karsen Clerk | " | " |
| Robert Clark Trumpᵗ | " | " |
| Elezur Dudley Trumpᵗ | " | " |
| Silas Hicok | " | " |
| Solomon Conisey | " | " |
| Solomon Robinson | " | " |
| Daniel Judd | " | " |
| Ichabod Stoddard | " | " |
| Matthew Loggan | " | " |
| Jeremiah Burton | " | " |
| Wait Curtis | " | " |
| Joseph Clark | " | " |
| David Leavit | " | " |
| Moses Hawley | " | " |
| John Clark | " | " |
| Nathan Dudley | " | " |
| Benjⁿ Durkee | " | " |
| Simeon Cole | " | " |
| Timᵗʰ Goodrich | " | " |
| Thoˢ Thompson | " | " |
| Caleb Austin | 6 | " |
| David Judson | 6 | " |
| Walker Mallery | 4 | " |
| Danˡˡ Sherman | " | " |
| Elnathan Gilbert | " | " |
| Peter Walker | " | " |
| John Abernathey | " | " |
| Asa Curtis | " | " |
| Wᵐ Robinson | " | " |
| Simeon Mitchel | 6 | " |
| Chapman Judson | " | " |
| Samˡˡ Woodman | " | " |
| Truman Hurlbut | " | " |
| Ezekiel Lewis | 6 | " |

[*State Library, Revolution 27.*]

## GROTON HILL FORT GUARD.

[See *Record of Connecticut Men in the Revolution*, page 617.]

### CAPT. MOTT'S COMPANY.

A Pay Role of Cap¹ Edward Mott's Company Stationed at Groton 1776

| Mens Names | Time of Inlistment | Time when Discharged or turned over |
|---|---|---|
| Edward Mott Capt | Feb. 16 | July 4 |
| Oliver Coit 1 Lt | " | " |
| Wᵐ Latham 2 Lt | " | " |
| Wᵐ Whitney Ens. | " | " |
| Serj. John James | 28 | " |
| Serj. Lemuel Wethey | " | " |
| Serj. Elisha Perkins | Mar. 1 | " |
| Serj. Benjⁿ Hilliard | Feb. 27 | " |
| Clark Jedʰ Whitney | 26 | " |
| Corp. Levi Tracy | 27 | " |
| Corp. Peris Tracy | 28 | " |
| Corp. Joseph Bentley | Mar. 1 | " |
| Corp. Ephraim Herrick | Feb. 27 | " |
| Drum. Thoˢ Leach | Mar. 1 | " |
| Fifer Jnᵃ Averil | 5 | " |
| Fifer Robert Latimer | 4 | " |
| John Austin | 1 | " |
| Nathan Avery | 4 | " |
| Zebulon Button | Feb. 27 | " |
| Danˡ Benit | 28 | " |
| Abiel Benjamin Jr. | Mar. 4 | " |
| Silas Brewster | Feb. 26 | " |
| Thoˢ Brooks | Mar. 10 | " |
| John Baley Jr | 4 | " |
| Paul Burrows | " | " |
| Elisha Burrows | May 13 | " |
| Hugh Brown | Mar. 4 | " |
| Richard Burnet | " | " |
| Joshua Baker | " | " |
| Isaac Coit | Feb. 29 | " |
| Farwell Coit | 28 | " |
| Benjⁿ Clark | Mar. 1 | May 18 |
| James Comstock | 4 | July 4 |
| Fairbanks Church | " | " |
| James Culver | " | " |
| Charles Chester | " | " |
| Eldridge Chester | " | " |
| Joseph Davis | Feb. 28 | " |
| David Edgcomb | Apr. 11 | " |
| James Fish | Mar. 4 | " |
| John Gates | 1 | " |
| Thoˢ Giles | June 8 | " |
| Lemuel Geer | Feb. 28 | " |
| Oliver Gates | " | " |

## MILITIA REGIMENTS, 1776.

| Mens Names | Time of Inlistment | Time when Discharged or turned over |
|---|---|---|
| Zephaniah Hartshorn | Mar. 4 | July 4 |
| Jonathan Hartshorn | " | " |
| Beriah Hartshorn | June 24 | " |
| Thoˢ Harris | Mar. 1 | " |
| Danˡ Harris | " | " |
| Josiah Harris | Feb. 28 | " |
| Asaph Jones | 26 | " |
| Luther Jones | " | " |
| George Jeffords | Mar. 4 | " |
| Rober Langworthy | 1 | " |
| Joseph Latham 2ⁿᵈ | " | " |
| Daniel Latham | " | " |
| Joseph Latham 4ᵗʰ | 4 | Apr. 18 |
| Cary Latham | Apr. 18 | July 4 |
| Jasper Latham | Mar. 4 | " |
| Joseph Latham 5ᵗʰ | 1 | " |
| Amos Latham | Apr. 28 | " |
| David Lamb | Mar. 4 | " |
| Ephraim Morgan | 2 | " |
| Joshua Meech | Feb. 26 | " |
| Jacob Meech | 27 | " |
| Pero Moody | Mar. 4 | " |
| Moses Park | Feb. 26 | " |
| Rufus Park | " | " |
| Levi Park | 27 | " |
| John Ray Jr. | Mar. 4 | " |
| Richard Otis | Feb. 28 | " |
| Ezekiel Rude | 26 | " |
| Benjᵃ Richards | 27 | " |
| Rufus Rix | Mar. 9 | " |
| Nathan Rix | " | " |
| Lemuel Smith | 1 | June 24 |
| Ephraim Starkweather | 2 | July 4 |
| David Stanton | " | " |
| Asa Stanton | " | " |
| Samˡ Sabin | 1 | " |
| Richmond Tracy | 7 | " |
| Cyrus Tracy | 1 | " |
| Bela Tracy | " | " |
| Absalom Thompson | " | " |
| Ephraim Wethey | 7 | " |
| Henry Walton | 1 | " |
| Adin Wilbur | 4 | " |
| Henry Wethey | 1 | " |
| Elijah Wethey | Feb. 28 | " |
| Peter Williams | Mar. 4 | " |
| Simeon William | 8 | " |
| John Wood Jr | " | " |
| Thoˢ Wells | " | " |
| Wate Wells | " | " |
| John Whitney | " | " |
| Ezekiel Yarrington | Feb. 27 | " |
| Elisha York | 26 | " |
| William Manning | Mar. 11 | Apr. 28 |
| Seth Frink | 2 | 11 |

[*State Library, Revolution 6.*]

# MILITIA REGIMENTS, 1777.

## DANBURY RAID.

[*See Record of Connecticut Men in the Revolution, page 492.*]

### OFFICERS.

The United States D$^r$ To the State of Connecticut, for Services &c of Militia in the Danbury Alarm in April 1777. Viz.—

| Bills & Accounts | Remarks |
|---|---|
| Cap$^t$ D. Judson | 13$^{th}$ Reg$^t$ |
| L$^t$ D. Phelps | Col. J. Humphries |
| Cap$^t$ N. Gilbert | |
| Col. J. P. Cook | his Reg$^t$ |
| Cap$^t$ C. Raymond | |
| Col. J. Thomson | his Reg$^t$ |
| Cap$^t$ S. Morehouse | Col. J. Meads |
| Cap$^t$ Tho$^s$ Fenn | 10$^{th}$ Reg$^t$ |
| Cap$^t$ N. Seeley | Col S Whitings |
| Cap$^t$ Elijah Case | |
| Col. Sam$^l$ Whiting | his Regt |
| En$^s$ Jona. Filley | 1st Reg$^t$ |
| Cap$^t$ A. Brimsmade | 4$^{th}$ " |
| Cap$^t$ E. Russell | Col Thomsons |
| Cap$^t$ N. Wheeler | Col. S. Whitings |
| Cap$^t$ E. Hinman | Col. J. Moseleys |
| Daniel Lyman | |
| John Crane | Col. T. Cooks |
| Col. E. Abel | |

[*Comptroller's Office, Haskell's Receipts.*]

## CAPT. PLATT'S COMPANY.

A pay Roll of Capt. Dan Plattses Company of the 7th Regiment in the State of Conetecut Commanded by W<sup>m</sup> Worthington Esq Leut. Cornel who march<sup>t</sup> in the Larram as far as New haven on April 27<sup>th</sup> A D 1777
Entered Sarvis Apriel 27 — Sarvis 5 Days

Capt. Dan Platts
Leut. Elijah Scovel
Ens. Sam<sup>l</sup> Doty
Sar. Israel Done
Sar. Asa Pratt
Sar. Ruben Pratt
Sar. Jesse Pratt
Cor. James Comstock
Cor. Daniel Pratt
Cor. Sam<sup>l</sup> Bushnel
Cor. Sam<sup>l</sup> Parker
  Benjamin Williams Jr.
  Frances Bushnel
  Jesse Pratt 2<sup>d</sup>
  Ashbel Clark
  Zephemiah Pratt
  Phinis Pratt
  Abraham Pratt Jr.
  Stephen Starkey
  Joseph Glading

Ebenezar Williams
Noah Scovel Jr.
Jered Buckingham
Taber Pratt
Jorge Shaw
Bemond Clark
James Utter
William Buckley
Nathan Southard
David Beebe Pratt
James Hamblen
Marten Dibble
Josiah Post
Isaac Webb
William Southard
Gideon Pratt
John Williams 2d
James Shaw
Ezra Pratt
Abraham Buckley

[*State Library, Revolution 6.*]

## CAPT. STARKEY'S COMPANY.

A Pay Roll of Cap<sup>t</sup> Timothy Starkeys Company the 7<sup>th</sup> Company of the alarm List of the 7<sup>th</sup> Regiment of the State of Connecticut Commanded by Lieu<sup>t</sup> Con<sup>l</sup> William Worthington Esq<sup>r</sup>.
Marcht in the alarm to New haven april y<sup>e</sup> 27<sup>th</sup> A D 1777
Time of Service 5 Days

Capt. Timothy Starkey
Lieut. Noah Platts
Ins. John Bull
Sert. Simon Hough
Sert. Phinehas Bushnel
Sert. John Pratt
Sert. Edw<sup>d</sup> Bull
Clark Edmon Pratt
Cor. Jonth<sup>n</sup> Pratt
Cor. John Platts
Cor. Daniel Bushnell
Cor. David Williams
  Sam<sup>l</sup> Pratt

Jacob Haydon
Daniel Chalker
Jn<sup>o</sup> Handley Bushnell
Jeremiah Kelcy
Benj<sup>n</sup> Handy
Edmond Snow
Jn<sup>o</sup> Williams
Abr<sup>m</sup> Pratt
Et[    ] Pratt
Selden Chalker
Lem<sup>l</sup> Bushnell
Job Buckley
Sam<sup>l</sup> Steavens

[*State Library, Revolution 6.*]

## SECOND REGIMENT—COL. THOMPSON.

### ALARM LISTS.

A List of the Names of the Subaltins in the Alarm Lists in the 2d Reg't

| | | | |
|---|---|---|---|
| Jonah Bradley Lieut<br>John Austin Ens | 1st | John Dibble Lieut<br>Enoch Newton Ens | 10th |
| Benj Freen Lieut<br>John Fowler Junr Ens | 2d | Ebenezer Trusedel Lieut<br>Asel Harrison Ens | 11th |
| Sam'l Hoadley Lieut<br>Ferrington Harrison Ens | 3d | Dan'l Chatfield Lieut<br>David Woodrose Ens | 13th |
| Joseph Loveland Lieut<br>Abraham Smith Ens | 4th | Isaac Sherman Kimberly Lt<br>Timothy Hoadly Ens | 14th |
| Henry Daggett Lieut<br>John Pierpoint Ens | 5th | Joel Bradly Lieut<br>Alling Ives Ens | 15th |
| John Smith Lieut<br>John Powel Ens | 6th | Jesse Beecher Lieut<br>Jacob Hotchkiss Ens | 16th |
| Jared Robertson Lieut<br>Dan'l Smith Ens | 7th | Elisha Booth Lieut<br>Caleb Alling Ens | 17th |
| Sam'l Smith Lieut<br>Lemuel Humphrevile Ens | 8th | Jabez Prechard Lieut<br>Levi Tomlinson Ens | 18th |
| Jonathan Dayton Lieut<br>Thomas Humiston Ens | 9th | | |

New Haven ye 24 of May 1777

[*State Library, Hebard Papers.*]

## FOURTH REGIMENT—COL. WHITING.

[*See Record of Connecticut Men in the Revolution, page 514.*]

### OFFICERS.

A Ration Bill of the Officers in Col. Sam[l] Whitings Regiment of Guards being the 4[th] Regiment of Militia in the State of Connecticut and Raised for the defense of Said State in March 1777 And Stationed at Fairfield & Stratford &c By Order of Brigadier Gen[l] Silliman

| Names | Time of Entering into the Service | | Time when Discharged | |
|---|---|---|---|---|
| S. Whiting Esq Col. | Apr. | 3 | Aug. | 2 |
| Ab[m] Gould Lt. Col. | Mar. | 6 | Apr. | 7 |
| Jonathan Dimon Major | | 7 | | 22 |
| P. Hendrick & Lewis Adjutant | | 7 | Aug. | 2 |
| T. Smedley & Benedict Q[r] master | | 7 | | 2 |
| Elijah Abel Capt. | | 6 | Apr. | 22 |
| Sam[l] Seelye Lieut. | | 7 | Mar. | 22 |
| Nathan Seelye Lieut. | | 22 | Apr. | 22 |
| Daniel Dimon Ens. | | 6 | Mar. | 22 |
| Nathan Bennitt Ens. | | 22 | Apr. | 22 |
| Zache[h] Coe Capt. | | 7 | | 9 |
| William Thomson Lieut. | | 7 | | 21 |
| Solomon Booth Ens. | | 7 | | 22 |
| Eph[m] Curtis Lieut. | | 23 | | 22 |
| Beach Tomlinson Capt. | | 6 | Mar. | 22 |
| Eph[m] Lyon Lieut. | | 6 | | 22 |
| Enoch Lewis Ens. | | 7 | | 22 |
| Eben[r] Hill Capt. | | 7 | Apr. | 22 |
| Lewis Goodsell Lieut. | | 7 | | 22 |
| D. Dimon Ens. | | 23 | | 22 |
| Jabez Wheeler Capt. | Apr. | 7 | | 22 |
| Daniel Bennitt Lieut. | | 8 | | 22 |
| Seth Seelye Ens. | | 8 | | 22 |
| James Booth Capt & Company as per abstract | | 956 Days | | |
| Joseph Birdsey Capt. | | 5 | | 11 |
| Jedd[n] Mills Ens. | | 5 | | 11 |
| Thom[s] Nash Capt. | | 5 | | 23 |
| Eben Jesup Ens. | | 5 | | 23 |
| Jonath[n] Squire Ens. | | 5 | | 23 |
| George Burr Capt. | | 4 | | 22 |
| David Williams Lieut. | | 4 | | 22 |
| Albert Sherwood Ens. | | 4 | | 22 |
| Steph[n] Thorp Capt. | | 8 | | 22 |
| Job Bartram Lieut. | | 8 | | 22 |
| David Wheeler Ens. | | 8 | | 22 |
| Zalmon Reed Capt. | Mar. | 7 | Mar. | 22 |
| Daniel Duncan Lieut. | | 7 | | 22 |
| Dan[l] Sanford Ens. | | 7 | | 22 |
| William Hawley Lieut. | Apr. | 8 | Apr. | 22 |
| Phin[s] Sherman Lieut. | | 7 | | 13 |
| Steph Thorp Capt. | | 23 | | |

## MILITIA REGIMENTS, 1777.

| Names | Time of Entering into the Service | Time When Discharged |
|---|---|---|
| Lewis Goodsell Lieut. | Apr. 23 | July 22 |
| Nathan Seelye Lieut. | 23 | 22 |
| Eliph' Thorp Capt. | Mar. 23 | 22 |
| Stephen Wakeman Lieut. | 23 | 22 |
| John Olmsted Ens. | 23 | Apr. 22 |
| Daniel Dimon Ens. | Apr. 23 | July 22 |
| Edmond Leavenworth Capt | May 15 | 22 |
| Sam¹ Patterson Lieut. | 16 | 22 |
| Solomon Booth Lieut. | 22 | June 17 |
| Judson Burton Ens. | 16 | July 22 |
| Abrah<sup>m</sup> Brinsmade Capt. | Apr. 7 | Apr. 22 |
| Steph<sup>n</sup> Bourroughs Capt | 8 | 13 |
| Woolcutt Hawley Serjt. | May 15 | July 22 |
| Capt. Dan¹ Godfrey as per abstract 1776 | Dec. 5 76 | Dec 17 '76 |

[*State Library, Revolution 6.*]

## CAPT. BOOTH'S COMPANY.

A Ration Role of Cap' James Booths Company of Guards Which were Detach<sup>d</sup> from the 4<sup>th</sup> Regiment of Melitia for that Purpose, Pursuant to Order From G. Sillick Silliman Brigadier General &c.

| Mens Names | Number of Days in service | Mens Names | Number of Days in service |
|---|---|---|---|
| Capt. James Booth | 15 | John Sherman | 18 |
| Lieut. Samuel Patterson | 18 | Lewis Curtiss | 15 |
| Ens. Judson Burton | 15 | Nathan Osborn | 18 |
| Serg. David Thompson | 15 | James Coe | 18 |
| Serg. Elihew Curtiss | 15 | Abner Beers | 15 |
| Serg. Stephan Beers | 15 | Benjamin Wells | 15 |
| Serg. John Peck | 18 | Isaac Curtiss | 18 |
| Corpl. Abijah Booth | 18 | James Sherman | 15 |
| Corpl. Josiah Peck | 15 | Judson Peck | 15 |
| Corpl. David Curtiss | 15 | Ebenezer Curtiss | 18 |
| Corpl. Aaron Judson | 18 | Joseph Deforest | 15 |
| Fifer William Tomlinson | 8 | John Beardslee | 15 |
| Joel Judson | 15 | James Judson | 18 |
| Ephraim Willcockson | 15 | William Hilliard | 15 |
| Thomas Stratton | 18 | George Lewis | 15 |
| William Southworth | 18 | Benjamin Gorham | 15 |
| Edmund Curtiss | 10 | John Wells | 18 |
| Samuel Burritt | 18 | Abner Elgur | 15 |
| Robert Curtiss | 15 | Jeremiah Curtiss | 18 |
| John Booth | 15 | Samuel Ward | 18 |
| Elihew Judson | 15 | Ebenezer Hubbil | 18 |
| Abner Curtiss | 15 | Josiah Walker | 15 |
| Elnathan Wheeler | 15 | David Barlow | 18 |
| John McGraw | 18 | Ephraim Burton | 15 |
| Nathan Beardslee | 18 | Josiah Beers | 10 |
| Samuel Osborn | 18 | John E. Olcott | 10 |
| Andrew Curtiss | 15 | John Wayland | 10 |
| Daniel Curtiss | 18 | Henry Beardslee | 10 |
| William Judson | 18 | Henry Curtiss | 10 |
| Jonathan Tongue | 15 | John Whiting | 18 |
| Jabes Curtiss | 18 | Joseph Frost | 15 |

[Indorsed] Capt. James Booth's Ration Roll Company of Guards from the 11 Regiment Militia April 1777.

[*State Library, Revolution 6.*]

## TWELFTH REGIMENT—COL. MASON.

### GUARD.

A Pay Abstract for a gard kept in Lebanon By order of Colonel Jeremiah Masen Col° of the 12th Rigment in the State of Conecticut Gard Began Augt 19, 1777

| Mens Names | Number of Nights | Mens Names | Number of Nights |
|---|---|---|---|
| Jam⁸ Bayley | 11 | Jams Diskill | 11 |
| Thos Groos | 11 | Nehimʰ Payn | 11 |
| Isaac Gillit | 11 | Josh Hutchenson | 10 |
| Samˡ Gay | 11 | John Vaughan | 10 |

[These men were guarding a building containing Continental stores.]

[*State Library, Revolution 11.*]


## MAJ. WOODRUFF'S VOLUNTEERS.

[*See Record of Connecticut Men in the Revolution, page 514.*]

### OFFICERS.

Retaind Rations Due to Major Woodruff Regᵗ of Volunteers from Conecticut from October 13ᵗʰ to October 22ᵗʰ 1777

| | Rations | | Rations |
|---|---|---|---|
| Major Judah Woodruff | 30 | Ensⁿ Nathaniel Lewis | 3 |
| Adjᵗ Simean Newel | 20 | Capᵗ John Porter | 20 |
| Q Master Elijah Lewis | 10 | Leuᵗ Elisha Scott | 10 |
| Capᵗ Amos Barns | 20 | Ensⁿ Joseph Woodford | 10 |
| Leuᵗ Samuel Adams | 10 | Capᵗ Ambris Sloper | 20 |
| Capᵗ Matthew Cowles | 20 | Leuᵗ Joel Potter | 10 |
| Leuᵗ Samuel Wiliams | 10 | Leuᵗ Simean Fullor | 5 |
| Capᵗ Hezekiah Gridley | 20 | Ens John Clark | 10 |
| Leuᵗ Thomas Hungerford | 10 | Capᵗ Abraham Pettibonc | 6 |
| Capᵗ Samuel Upson | 6 | Ensⁿ Samuel Hotchkiss | 10 |
| Leuᵗ Isaac Cleavland | 10 | | |

[*Connecticut Historical Society.*]

# MILITIA REGIMENTS, 1778.

## COL. McCLELLAN'S REGIMENT.

[*See Record of Connecticut Men in the Revolution, page 543.*]

### PETITION.

ʃ To the Honorable General Assembly of the State of Connecticut now sitting at Hartford Octo<sup>r</sup> Sessions 1778. The Petition of the Commission Officers, Non Commission Officers and Soldiers in the Battalion under the Command of Col° Samuel M°Clellan being one of the Battallions Included in the Two Brigades Raised by Order of the Gen<sup>l</sup> Assembly at their Adjourned Sessions in Feb<sup>ry</sup> 1778. Sheweth.

That Wee Were Raised while an Act of this State was Existing Regulating the Prices of Labour Produce &c and upon the Faith and Footing of said Act and had such Wages and Allowances as while s<sup>d</sup> Act Continued were Just and Reasonable. But that since s<sup>d</sup> Act has been Repeal'd the Prices of the Various Necessaries of Life are so Enhanced as that Our Wages and Allowances are by no means an Adequate Reward for Our services.

We Therefore Pray your Honors to take Our Case into your Wise Consideration and Grant such an Addition to Our Wages and Allowances as shall be adequate to the Reward we Expected when we Entered said service. Justice is all Wee Ask. Wee doubt not your Honors will Grant Our Reasonable Request, and wee as in Duty Bound Shall Ever Pray. Dated at New London Octo<sup>r</sup>. 1778.

| | | | |
|---|---|---|---|
| Elisha Chapman<br>Daniel Tilden<br>Lee Lay<br>Abner Robinson<br>Squier Hills<br>William Whitney | } Capt<sup>s</sup> | Daniel Larned Lt<br>Sam<sup>l</sup> Capron Lt<br>Ambros Bawldwin Lt<br>Asahel Harrison Ens<br>Joshua Gates Ens<br>George Gallup Ens<br>Obad<sup>h</sup> Child Ens<br>Zechariah Parker Ens | |
| Aron Hale<br>Gam<sup>ll</sup> Ripley<br>Phinehas Peck<br>Nehemiah Smith<br>Lem<sup>ll</sup> Grosvenor<br>Will<sup>m</sup> Morriss<br>Aaron Cleaveland<br>John Frink<br>Ezra Root | } Lieut<sup>s</sup> | Benj<sup>a</sup> Billins Serg<sup>t</sup> Ma'j<sup>r</sup><br>Justis Johnson<br>John Arnold<br>Eliakim Stannard<br>Joseph Baldwin<br>Moses Hyde<br>Aseph Goodale | } Serjeants |

Noah Day ⎫
Jabez Foster
Dan Lee
Silas Ackla ⎬ Serjeants
William Sheldon
John Colt ⎭
Jonathan Downning ⎫
James Clark
Jeremiah Durkee
Vaniah Palmer
Moses Amadown
Eben' Kindal
Benj[a] Carpenter ⎬ Serjeants
John Gilbart
Nehemiah Gallup
Rufus Brown
Pain Kinman
John Fox
Elisha Converce ⎭
Francis Clark D Major
Sam[ll] Wise ⎫
Darias Learned ⎬ Drummers
Darias Fuller ⎭
Rementon Sears ⎫
Rufus Parks
Jabez Brainard
Darias Leskomb ⎬ Fifers
Jacob Holt
John Green
Rufus Felton ⎭
Joseph Colbet ⎫
Amos Brainard
John Welch
Radireck Platts
Sam[ll] Beamont
Elisha Sabin
Issachar Graves
Thomas Peake
Elijah Bennet
Joseph Turner
Lemuel Clark ⎬ Corpo-
Amos Randol      rals
Gamalel Huntington
Elisha Boman
Samuel Linchon
Amos Smith
Soloman Robins
Jabez Cheesebrook
James Fletcher
Woodbury Starkweather
Elias Babcock
Elkanah Huet
Jacob Meach ⎭
   Privates
Samuel Arnold
Felix Augru (?)
Jonathan Baldwin
David Bishop
Heman Balwin

Jonathan Bushnull
Zachariah Branaird
Ruben Bushnull
Richard Bialey
Ephiream Bushnull
John Benjamin
Senas Balwin
Robert Clark
Dimetrus Cook
Caleb Chapman
John Carter
Sam[ll] Church
Joseph Clark
Olive Clark
John Field
John Tuller
Elisha Goff
Ithial Harrison
Nathan Harrison
Eben' Hamistond
Jacob Hurd
Phileman Harrison
Rufus Harrison
Joel Houd
Asahel Hull
Dan[ll] Ingham
Stephen Johnston
Ruben Keley
Joel Keley
Christ[o] Masunall
Ithael Munson
James Nichols
Eben' Waid
James Utter
James Spencer
Daniel Ray
David Sears
Micahel Smith
Joathan Smith
Mat[w] Scofel
Jacob Savage
Jehial Tod
Nathan Wilcocks
William White

William Alton
Nath[ll] Allen
Joseph Boid
Samuel Burnall
Epheriam Barrit
Lyman Childs
Cyrus Chafee
Jonathan Converse
Elias Carpenter
Seth Cutler
Noah Davenport
David Hosmer
John Moffat
Joseph Russell

## MILITIA REGIMENTS, 1778.

Moses Wylder
Ambermarle Stone

John Adams
Roswell Bennet
Abial Bill
John Burt
James Burnham
Joseph Carey
Phineas Downing
Solomon Durkee
Oliver Flint
Elijah Pharnum
George Goram
Robert Gager
Roswell Green
Elijah Huntington
Gershom Haill
Dan[ll] Herrick
Asahel Herrick
Paul Harriss
Eben[r] Kingsley
Eben[r] Luce
Elijah Lilley
Roswell Manning
Asher Morgan
Benj[a] Manning
Eliphalet Ormsby
William Parish
Oliver Parish
Roswell Parish
Chester Pool
Jon[a] Robinson
Ebor Robinson
Richard Robinson
Eben[r] Robins
Dan[ll] Ringe
Lem[ll] Stephens
Oliver Smith
James Smith
David Smith
Abnor Webb
William Wailes
Amos Woodward
Timothy Winter

Philarman Androus
Peter Ayres
Cherub Abel
Richard Bogue
Nhth[ll] Baker
Cromell Bennet
Will[m] Butler
Abel Bennet
Cyrus Cone
Abel Edgerton
Dan[ll] Ellis
Alpheus Foster
Amos Fox

W[m] Foresider
Dan Gillit
Richard Greenfield
Asahel Harvey
Moses Huntly
Zadock Huntly
Amos Ingraham
Stephen Lee
John Manwaring
John Mitchel
Naman Mosher
Benj[a] Peck
John Perigo
Joseph Ransom
Stephen Richenson
Richard Rogers
Gideon Rogers
Theo. Rathbone
David Shattock
Clemment Stebbens
Elijah Spencer
Ebenezer Staples
Emmon Spencer
Francis Smith
Joseph Steward
John Starling
Nath[ll] Starr
Zebadiah Scott
Eleazer Tubbs
Asa Watson
Timo. Wright
Daniel Wright

Ezekiel Waterman
Abraham Warner
Ruel Woodworth
Thomas Anderson
Will[m] Anderson
Thomas Brag
Peter Button
James Brown
Sam[ll] Brown
Robert Baker
Eli Brown
Rufus Barnard
Nath[ll] Babcock
Elijah Carpenter
David Carpenter
Nath[ll] Conant
Jeremiah Cunnil
Parly Dean
Humphrey Davenport
Asahel Eastman
Ebenezer Eaton
Ebenezer Eastman
Marvirick Eaton
Jedediah Fay
Elijah Fenton
Edward Holmes

Eliphlet Huntington
Bazalileen Hopkins
Christopher Huntington
Elijah Hunt
Ezeriah Hall
Ezekil Kellogg
Amisa Ladd
Dan[ll] Olds
Ebeneze Oen
Shubal Presson
Thomas Russell
William Rice
Jon[a] Rice
Abijah Smith
Phillip Squire
Elijah Squire
Levi Snow
Silas Snow
Rufus Tyler
Ebenezer Whiton
George Austin
Barthilmus Arthur
Jesse Brown
Walter Branch
John Billings
Asa Bawdish
David Bellus
Robart Crary
Joseph Crary
Peter Culver

Robort Dixon
Asahel Fish
David Fish
William Fagens
Robart Geer
Jacob Gallup
Levi Gallup
W[m] Hethe
Crandal Holley
Henrey Hewit
Azariah Hillard
Simeon Jones
Stephen Kimey
David Lewis
Tubal Moody
Elijah Meech
Hubbard Mason
Henrey Main
Jerimiah Main
Samuel Newton
Joseph Price
Daniel Ruff
Gilbart Tracy
Salmon Treat
John Tift
Ebenezer Witter
Ichabud Worden
Benjamin Williams
Icabud Palmer
Aden Swan

[*State Library, Revolution 13.*]

# GUARDS.

## HARTFORD GUARD.

A Pay Roll of the Guard in the Town of Hartford to Guard Sundry Offices in S<sup>d</sup> Town as p<sup>r</sup> Act of the General Assembly of the State of Connecticut in the Month of Fabruary Anno Dom 1778

| | Time when Inlisted | Time in Service Months | Days |
|---|---|---|---|
| Lieut Tho<sup>s</sup> Sloan | March 12 | 2 | 24 |
| Sarj W<sup>m</sup> Collyer | 12 | 2 | 24 |
| Sarj. Nath<sup>n</sup> Goodwine | 12 | 2 | 24 |
| Serj. Nathen Wadworth | 16 | 2 | 20 |
| Drummer Theoder Goodwine | 19 | 2 | 17 |
| Phifer James Cook | 22 | 2 | 10 |
| W<sup>m</sup> Pratt | 12 | 2 | 24 |
| George Pratt | 14 | 2 | 22 |
| George Wadsworth | 14 | 2 | 22 |
| Robert Waterman | 14 | 2 | 22 |
| Caleb Church | 16 | 2 | 20 |
| Joal Boyington | 16 | 2 | 20 |
| Frederick Lorde | 16 | 2 | 20 |
| Samuel Hall | 16 | 2 | 20 |
| W<sup>m</sup> Lord | 16 | 2 | 20 |
| Oliver Clapp | 19 | 2 | 17 |
| Mosses Dickinson | 19 | 2 | 17 |
| W<sup>m</sup> Watson | 19 | 2 | 17 |
| Jo<sup>n</sup> Pantrey Goodwine | 19 | 2 | 17 |
| David Peirce | 19 | 2 | 17 |
| Ashbel Dodd | 20 | 2 | 16 |
| Whiting Seymor | 20 | 2 | 16 |
| Neamiah Cadwall | 20 | 2 | 16 |
| Calvin Wooding | 20 | 2 | 16 |
| Dorus Warron | 20 | 2 | 16 |
| Timothy Church | 20 | 2 | 16 |
| Jason Howell | 20 | 2 | 16 |
| Levi Curtiss | 22 | 2 | 14 |
| Tho<sup>s</sup> Bunce | 22 | 2 | 14 |
| Jona<sup>th</sup> Olcott | 22 | 2 | 14 |
| Frederick Standly | 22 | 2 | 14 |
| Isrel Wadsworth | 22 | 2 | 14 |
| James Butler | 22 | 2 | 14 |
| Haz. Seymor | 22 | 2 | 14 |
| Daniel Sheldon | 24 | 2 | 12 |
| Sam<sup>l</sup> Church | 24 | 2 | 12 |

[*State Library, Revolution 11.*]

## OFFICE GUARD.

A pay Roll of the Garde for Garding the Treasurrs and Loan Offices Office of the Secretary and Pay Tabel Office Apointed by General Assembly of the Governer and Company of the State of Connecticut Holden at Hartford May 1778 — from June 1st to Novr 5 Inclusive

Leut. Thos Sloan
Sert Joseph Pratt
Ser Levi Curtis
Ser Fradrick Standley
Drummer Thoa Bunce
Phifr Freeman Seymour
David Parce
Wm Watteson
Ashbell Dodd
Timothy Church
Mosses Dickinson
Neamiah Cadwall
Normand Bunce
Isaac Oakes
Uriah Shippard
Normand Clapp
Richard Hood
John Bardwall
Saml Hall

Samul Chipman
Danniel Shaldon
Doris Warron
Fradrick Lord
James Mookler
Ebezr Moor
Saml Church
Rodrick Larkim
David Goodwine
John Tiel
John Panr Goodwine
Robert Watterman
Neamiah Cadwall
Benjaman Townshand
Robert Nivens
Jonathan Olcott
Haz Seymor
Joseph Barnerd

[*State Library, Revolution 11.*]

## CONVENTION TROOPS GUARD.

The United States Dr To the State of Connecticut for services &c. of Militia guarding the Convention Troops through said State in 1778, when they marched from Massachusetts to Virginia — viz —

| Bills & Accounts | Remarks |
|---|---|
| Capt Moses Forbs | Guarding Convention Troops |
| Capt E. F. Bissell | " |
| Capt Lemuel Roberts | " |
| Capt Chester Wells | " |
| Capt W. Gibbs | " |
| Capt Isaac Pomeroy | " |
| Capt Wm Burrell | " |
| Capt Adonh Griswold | " |
| Ensa John Reynolds | " |
| Capt Hezh Parsons | " |
| Col. Noah Phelps | " |
| Capt Ozias Pettibone | " |
| Lt Seth Smith | " |
| Capt N. Kellogg | " |
| Capt Jona. Wells | " |

[*Comptroller's Office, Haskell's Receipts.*]

# MILITIA REGIMENTS, 1779.

## TRYON'S INVASION.

[*See Record of Connecticut Men in the Revolution, page 549.*]

### CAPT. HOLBROOK'S COMPANY.

A Return of the Horses Employed for the Use of Cap$^t$ Daniel Holbrook Jun$^r$ Company of Melitia in Col$^o$ Edward Russels Reg$^t$ On A Larm from Derby to New Haven & from Derby to Fairfield in the Month of July A D 1779 Under Command of Maj$^r$ Nathan Smith

| Mens Names | No Miles | Mens Names | No Miles |
|---|---|---|---|
| Daniel Holbrook J$^r$ Capt | 76 | Jonathan Hitchcock | 28 |
| Joseph Riggs Ju$^r$ Lieut | 88 | Roberd Pope | 28 |
| Thadeus Baldwin Ens | 48 | Abel Peirson | 28 |
| Hezekiah Johnson Serj$^t$ | 28 | Enoch French | 10 |
| Dorman Coe Clark | 28 | Joseph Johnson Jun$^r$ | 28 |
| Joseph Parson Corp$^l$ | 28 | Enos Bradley Jun$^r$ | 10 |
| Moses Hotchkiss Corp$^l$ | 28 | Shelden Curtis | 10 |
| Abraham Peirson Corp$^l$ | 10 | Truman Loveland | 10 |
| Zepheniah Tucker Drm | 28 | Richard Mansfield | 28 |
| Ashel Johnson | 10 | Ethel Keeney | 28 |
| Nathanel Johnson J$^r$ | 28 | Leveret Hotchkis | 28 |
| Thadeus Kene | 10 | Ashbel Loveland | 18 |
| Gideon Johnson J$^r$ | 28 | Abraham Downs J$^r$ | 28 |
| Israel French J$^r$ | 28 | Abenezer Dagget | 18 |
| Moses Wheler | 28 | Ebenezer Chatfield | 18 |
| Samuel Allen | 28 | Micael Clark | 18 |
| Amos Johnson | 28 | Edmon Clark | 28 |
| Medad Keeney | 10 | Joseph Picket | 18 |
| John Wheler | 10 | Nathan Wheler | 28 |
| Amos Parson | 28 | Abel Wheler | 10 |
| Samuel Johnson | 28 | Charles French | 18 |
| Frances French | 10 | James Beard | 10 |

[*State Library, Revolution 16.*]

## CAPT. BIRDSEY'S COMPANY.

A pay Role of Cap$^t$ Joseph Birdsey Company In Co$^l$ Whiting Regiment in a tower; at the Alarm at New Haven and from Their to Fairfield which was five Days in Scarvice   July 9$^{th}$ 1779 Entred Service

Capt. Jo. Birdsey
Leut. Luke Sumner
Ens. Blackman
Clark Wooster
Ser. Ep$^h$ Wooster
Ser. Lins (?) Thompson
Ser. Sam. Beard
Ser. M. Wheeler
Cor. N. Deforest
Cor Step$^n$ Beardslee
Cor. Ebe$^r$ Beardslee
Cor. Wi$^{ll}$ Curtiss
Jo. Munson Drm
Lins (?) Beardslee
Ben Beardslee
Curtiss Fairchild

John Gilbart
Cal. Levans (?)
Sam. Hide
Eph. Mitchel
Edm. Thulford
David Wilson Jor
Abr$^h$ Thompson
Tho. Gilbart
Abijah Wells
Jo. Larkings
Joso. (?) Clark
Hez Curtiss
Nathan Blackman
Gideon Levensworth
Gideon Beard

[*State Library, Revolution 16.*]

## CAPT. BENJAMIN'S COMPANY.

A Pay Abstract for horse hire of Capt$^n$ John Benjamin's Company of the 4 Regiment of Alarm List of Militia, in the New Haven & Fairfield Alarms, also Pay & Subsistance for three Men Omitted in the Pay Abstract now on File in Pay Table Office, Hartford.   Stratford December 8$^{th}$ 1779

| Mens Names | Time entered service | Days in service | Number of miles out |
|---|---|---|---|
| Capt John Benjamin | July 5 | 4 | 26 |
| Lieut Samuel Patterson | 5 | 4 | 26 |
| Serg$^t$ Ezra Elgar | 5 | 4 | 10 |
| Serg$^t$ Hezekiah Burritt | 5 | 4 | 26 |
| Corpl Samuel Ward | 5 | 4 | 26 |
| John Brooks Esq | 5 | 4 | 26 |
| Sam$^l$ Burton | 5 | 4 | 26 |
| Nathan$^l$ Lamson Jun$^r$ | 5 | 4 | 26 |
| Samuel Wells | 7 | 2 | 10 |
| Isaac Gorham | 5 | 4 | 10 |
| Samuel Curtiss | 5 | 2 | 14 |
| Josiah Curtiss | 5 | 4 | 26 |
| Abijah M$^c$Cune | 5 | 4 | 26 |
| Darius Folsom | 7 | 2 | 10 |
| John Hubbil Jun$^r$ | 7 | 2 | 10 |
| Stephen Porter | 5 | 2 | 14 |
| Samuel Burritt | 6 | 3 | 26 |
| Benjamin Brooks | 7 | 2 | 10 |
| John Hubbil | 7 | 2 | 10 |
| Nathaniel Lamson | 7 | 2 | 10 |
| Abijah Brooks | 7 | 2 | 10 |
| Joseph Prince | 7 | 2 | 10 |
| Isaac Brooks | 5 | 4 | 10 |
| Omitted before, | | | |
| Solomon Plant | 5 | 2 | 14 |
| Stephen Cunningham | 7 | 2 | 14 |
| Nathan Dagget | 7 | 2 | 10 |

[*State Library, Revolution 16.*]

## LIEUT. PORTER'S COMPANY.

A Horse Mileage Roll of Lieut Aaron Porter's Compy in ye Sixth Regt Ordered to N. Haven July 5th 1779.

| Mens Names | No Miles | Mens Names | No Miles |
|---|---|---|---|
| Lieut Aaron Porter | 30 | Fifer Abijah Porter | 30 |
| Ens Solo. Dunham | " | William Kelsey | " |
| Corpl John Kelsey | " | Solo. Dunham Jr. | " |
| Corpl Saml North | " | | |

[*State Library, Revolution 16.*]

## CAPT. LANDON'S COMPANY.

Guilford     State of Connecticut     Dr
For horse hire for the 2d Compy Alarm list in the 7 Regt to New Haven on an Expedition July 5th 1779 Commd by Col Wm Worthington

| | | | | | |
|---|---|---|---|---|---|
| David Landon | | 15 Miles | David Hull | | 15 Miles |
| Daniel Norton | | " | Asher Seward | | " |
| Nathaniel Ruggles | | " | Edward Benton | | " |
| Pitman Collins | | " | John Scovill | | " |
| Wilmot Goldsmith | | " | Jared Grifting | | " |
| Elishua Reves | | " | Daniel Tuthill | | " |
| John Ingraham | | " | Nathaniel Ingraham | | " |
| Demetius Cook | | " | | | |

David Landon Capt.

[*State Library, Revolution 16.*]

## CAPT. ROBINSON'S COMPANY.

A pay Roll for Horse Travel of Capt James Robinsons Company in Colle Cooks Regt of Militia when call'd for the Relief of New-Haven July 5th A D 1779 and also for the Releif of Fairfield July 8th 1779

| Mens Names | No Miles | Mens Names | No Miles |
|---|---|---|---|
| Lt. Simeon Parsons | 40 | Benjamin Ames | 20 |
| Ens. John Johnsons | 20 | Elnathan Stevens | 20 |
| Serjt. Jeremiah Butler | 20 | Rejoice Camp | 20 |
| Serjt. Joseph Parsons | 40 | John Curtiss | 20 |
| Serjt Jacob Clark | 20 | Richard Spelman | 40 |
| Corl. Asher Canfield | 40 | Ozias Picket | 20 |
| Corl. Joseph Tibbals | 20 | William Chauncy | 40 |
| Daniel Coe | 40 | Titus Canfield | 40 |
| Timothy Coe | 40 | Ebenezer Tibbals | 20 |
| Asher Coe | 20 | James Robinson | 40 |
| David Parsons | 40 | James Curtiss | 20 |
| Abial Baldwin | 20 | | |

[*State Library, Revolution 16.*]

## CAPT. CAMP'S COMPANY.

A pay Roll for Horses Travel of Capt Sam¹ Camps Company Col Cooks Regt of Militia when Calld for the Relief of New Haven July 5th 1779 and also for the Relief of Fairfield July 8th 1779

| Mens Names | N° Miles | Mens Names | N° Miles |
|---|---|---|---|
| Capt Sam¹ Camp | 40 | Elihu Goodrich | 40 |
| Lt Sam¹ Hart | 40 | Seth Graves | 40 |
| Ser Joseph Wright | 40 | David Graves | 20 |
| Ser Eli Crane | 20 | John Nois Wadsworth | 20 |
| Ser Abraʰᵐ Scranton | 40 | Wilᵐ Wadsworth | 20 |
| Cor Gordon Hull | 20 | Enoch Henman | 20 |
| Cor James Hickcox | 20 | John Hull | 20 |
| Cor Charles Parmele | 40 | Charles Hull | 20 |
| Dr Nathaniel Hickcox | 20 | Gad Hall | 20 |
| Abram Bartlit | 20 | John Norton | 20 |
| Zebulon Bishop | 20 | Joel Parmele | 20 |
| Jabez Chalker | 20 | Selah Strong | 20 |
| Elihu Crane | 20 | Thomas Strong | 40 |
| Ozias Camp | 20 | Ichabod Scrantom | 20 |
| Sam¹ Camp | 20 | Steven Spencer | 20 |
| Jonathan Wells | 20 | Asher Wright | 20 |
| Gilbert Catlin | 20 | Reubin Bishop | 20 |

[*State Library, Revolution 16.*]

## CAPT. COLLINS' COMPANY.

A Milage Roll for The Horses in the New haven & Fairfield Alarms July 5th & 7th last For the 5th Company of the Alarm list in the 10th Regᵗ.

| Mens Names | N° Miles | Mens Names | N° Miles |
|---|---|---|---|
| Dan Collins Capt | 38 | Wᵐ Merriam | 19 |
| James Haugh Lt | 38 | Joseph Merriam | 38 |
| Brinton Hall Ens | 19 | Yale Bishop | 38 |
| Sam¹ Hall Serj | 38 | John Barns | 38 |
| Benjamin Merriam | 38 | John Ives | 38 |
| Amos Ives Serjt | 19 | Abel Curtiss | 19 |
| John Merriam Serjt | 38 | Timothy Ives | 38 |
| Daniel Janes Corpl | 19 | Timothy Foster | 19 |
| Ezra Rice Corpl | 38 | John Miles | 19 |
| Sanburn Ford fifer | 38 | Caleb Merriman | 19 |
| John Couch | 38 | Moses Hall | 19 |
| Bezaleel Ives | 38 | Elisha Scovil | 38 |
| Jesse Merriam | 19 | Jared Benham | 38 |
| Stephen Perkins | 19 | Moses Hall Juʳ | 19 |
| James Cabon | 38 | Insign Haugh | 19 |
| Benjᵃ Hart | 38 | Daniel Hall | 19 |
| Sam¹ Johnson | 38 | Isaac Hall | 19 |
| Titus Merriam | 38 | | |

[*State Library, Revolution 16.*]

## MILITIA REGIMENTS, 1779.

### CAPT. NORTON'S COMPANY.

A Pay Roll for Horse Travel of Capt Charles Nortons Company Col Thaddeus Cooks Reg^mt being the 10th Regiment of Melitia in the State of Connecticut when Call'd for the Relief of Newhaven July 5th 1779, and also for the Relief of Fairfield July 8th A D 1779

| Mens Names | No Miles | Mens Names | No Miles |
|---|---|---|---|
| Capt. Charles Norton | 20 | Joseph Chidsey | 20 |
| Ens. Joseph Smith | 40 | Timothy Hall | 20 |
| Serjt. John Jones | 40 | Heth Camp | 20 |
| Serjt. Phinehas Parmele | 20 | Israel Burritt | 20 |
| Serjt. Jonathan Cruttenden | 20 | Sylvanus Hull | 20 |
| Corpl. Stephen Norton | 40 | William Lucas | 20 |
| John Canfield | 40 | Thomas Lyman | 20 |
| John Curtiss | 20 | Daniel Meeker | 20 |
| Noadiah Grave | 40 | Noah Norton | 20 |
| Elnathan Norton | 20 | John Norton | 20 |
| John Newton | 20 | Burwell Newton | 40 |
| Joseph Southworth | 20 | Benjamin Pickett | 20 |
| Thomas Strong | 20 | Samuel Squire | 20 |
| James Arnold | 40 | Abel Tibbals | 20 |
| Samuel Bartlet | 20 | David Ward | 20 |
| Elnathan Camp | 40 | Job Camp | 20 |
| Jesse Crane | 20 | Reuben Bishop | 20 |

[*State Library, Revolution 16.*]

### CAPT. HOUGH'S COMPANY.

A Milage Abstract for Horse Travil in the Alarms at New Haven & Fairfield July 5th and 7th 1779 for the 6th Militia Company in the 10th Regiment.

John Hough Capt.
Nathaniel Merriam Lt.
Thos. Foster Ens.
Serj. Joseph Edwards
" Timothy Hall
" Jonth^s Yale
" Comfort Butler
" Giles Griswould
Marshal Merriam
Elisha Merriman
Phinehas Hall
Phinhas Lyman
Edward Collins
Enos Hall
Daniel Mekye
Jn° Morgan
Caleb Merriman
Thos. Spencer
Amasa Merriam
Giles Foster
Ozius Foster

Jeremiah Ferrington
Simeon Perkins
Ameton Yale
Elijah Scovil
Elijah Yeomans
Elisha Curtis
Wyllys Mekye
John Yale
Moses Way
Jesse Merriman
Abner Way
Israel Hall
Wyllys Bishop
Daniel Yale
Nathaniel Yale
Asa Brown
David Scovil
Samuel Merriam
John Robinson
Samuel Rice

[*State Library, Revolution 16.*]

## CAPT. STANLEY'S COMPANY.

A Pay Abstract of Cap$^t$ Abraham Stanley's Company in Col Thaddeus's Reg$^t$ for Horses Travel in two Alarms as far as New Haven Viz. One to New Haven on the fifth of July 1779, and the other for Fairfield on the Eighth of July 1779

Cap. Abraham Stanley
Lieu. Solomon Doolittle
Ens. Benjamin Preston
Serg. Charles Hull
Serg. Elihu Yale
Serg. John Davidson
Serg. Daniel Parker
Serg. Abner Rice
Corp. Jotham Gaylord
Corp. David Johnson
Corp. Joel Rice
Corp. Isaac Doolittle
Drum. Ebenezer Moss
  Samuel Ives
  Joseph Doolittle Jr.
  John Doolittle
  Jedediah Button
  Charles Parker
  Joel Hough

Joshua Parker
Oliver Doolittle
Lent Hough
John Lewis
Caleb Merriman
Ebenezer Hull
Eliakim Parker
Stephen Beach
William Atwater Jr
Nicholas Jones
Jonathan Johnson
Daniel Hitchcock
Abel Ward Atwater
Jehiel Rice Jr
Abijah Ives
James Prout
Levi Parker
Francis Wilcox

        Abraham Stanley Ju$^r$ Cap$^t$
        Wallingford August 13, 1779

[*State Library, Revolution 16.*]


## CAPT. CLARK'S COMPANY.

Pay Role for Horse travel Capt James Clarks Company 16$^{th}$ Reg$^t$ Commanded by Nehemiah Beardsley Esq$^r$ Col$^o$ on an Expedition to Fairfield Norwalk Danbury &c 16$^{th}$ July 1779

**Names of Persons who Rode Horses**
James Clark Capt
Elijah Wood Lieut
Thad$^{us}$ Barnum Ens.
Aaron Stone Serg.
Nathan Starr Serg
Seth Crofoot Serg.
Daniel Hoyt Serg.
Benj$^a$ Wood Corp.
Elnathan Gregory Drum
Joshua Benedict
James Crary
Stephen Curtis
Joseph Crofoot

**Names of Persons who Rode Horses**
Amos Hoyt
Agur Hoyt
Stephen Peck
Stephen Scovil
Eli Sanford
Daniel Stone
William Stone
Joel Stone
Jonathan Taylor
Abraham Waring
Benj$^a$ S. Rockwell
Joseph Wood
James Lincoln

[*State Library, Revolution 16.*]

## CAPT. OLMSTED'S COMPANY.

Pay Roll for Horse travle of Cap$^t$ David Olmsted's Company in Col$^a$ Nehemiah Bardsleys Reg$^t$ Whilest on Alarm at Fairfield

David Olmsted Capt
Job Smith Leut
Jered Olmsted Ens
Abijah Benedict Serj
James Scott Serj
Jacob Nash Serj
Ebenezer Hauley Cl
Corp John Benedict
Corp Trowbridge Bennett
Corp Nathan Hoyt
  Ezra Nash
  Benjimin Keeler
  John Gilbert
  Jonathan Hoyt
  Alexander Resseguie

Nathan Smith
Ezra Mead
Mathew Olmsted
Robert Wilson
Jesse Benedict
Hial Morris
Nathan Kellogg
Josiah Osbourn
Gamaliel Benedict
Mathew Keeler
Jonathan Nash
Jeremiah Dauchy
Josiah Northrop
Abijah Seymour
James Follet

[*State Library, Revolution 16.*]

## CAPT. ABEL BOTSFORD'S COMPANY.

Pay Role for Hors travel Capt Abel Botsford Company Commanded by Abel Baldwin Let. in the 16$^{th}$ Rigment Commanded by Nehemiah Bardsle Esq. Colo on an Expedition to Fairfield Norrowolk and Canon Newtown July 8$^{th}$ 1779

Let. Abel Baldwin
Serj. Nirum Botsford
Serj. Ezckel Beers
Serj. Edward Blackman

Cor. Ely Whelor
Cor. Elijah Baldwin
Daniel Turrel
Zalmon Burret

[*State Library, Revolution 16.*]

## CAPT. RICHARD SMITH'S COMPANY.

A Rool for Hors Travel, Capt Richard Smith's Company 16$^{th}$ Regt Commanded by Nehemiah Bardsley Esq Col$^o$ on an Expedition to Fairfield & Norwalk    Newbury August y$^e$ 9$^{th}$ 1779

Lieut Dibbl
Ens Marwin
Segt Starr
Sergt Nearin
Sergt Bostwick
Corp Keeler
Corp David Keeler
  Joshua Northrup
  Benjamin A. Ruggles
  Comfor Ruggles
  Isaac Lockwood
  Liverus Dunning
  Joseph Nearin

Eli Smith
Bostwick Ruggles
Samuel Dunning
John Bostwick
George Clark
Ruben Taylor
Amiel Camp
Shermon Smith
John Peck
Jonathan Beacher
Peter Hubbell
Samuel Cobet

[*State Library, Revolution 16.*]

## CAPT. JOSEPH SMITH'S COMPANY.

Pay Role for Horse travel of Capt Joseph Smith of y[e] 16[th] Reg[t] Comanded by Nehemiah Beardley Col on an Expedition to Norwalk &c July 1779

Capt. Joseph Smith
Liut. Timothy Buggles
Ens. Marles Warner
Seg. Isaas Gray
Seg. Eli Trowbridg
  Jeial Smith
  Wll[m] Nicols
  Samuel Ruggles
  Ashbel Ruggles
  John Kimberley
  Garshum Jackson
  Nathan Camp
  Ezra Duning
  Jeremiah Lockwood

Job Bunnell
Joseph Thomblenson
Ruben Talor
Andrew Northrup
Joshua Northrup
Joel Judson
David Smith
Jered Baldwin
Thad Baldwin
Ager Stevens
Levi Murrwin (?)
Ebenezer Barnum
Caleb Stevens

[*State Library, Revolution 16.*]

## CAPT. PENFIELD'S COMPANY.

A Pay Role for Horse Travel Cap[t] Peter Penfield Company 16[th] Regiment Commanded by Nehemiah Beardsley Esq[r] Col. on an Expedition to Fairfield & Norwalk &c New fairfield July 17[th] 1779

Peter Penfield Capt
Sarj. Eliphalet Brush
  " Joseph Bearse
  " Janas Brush
Abel Trowbridge
Zadock Barnum Corp
Abel Corier
Abel Hodges Jr
Asa Disbrow
Elijah Bearse

Newcomb Bearse
Sam[ll] Crane
Lem[ll] Pardee
Oliver Trobridge
Gideon Beardsley Jr.
Gideon Hubbell
Asel Hambleton
Tho[s] Brush
Wail Bull

[*State Library, Revolution 16.*]

## CAPT. ELIJAH BOTSFORD'S COMPANY.

A Pay Roll for Horse Travel Capt Elijah Botsford Company 16[th] Regiment Commanded by Col Nehem[h] Beardsley in an Expedition in the State of New York July 1779

Capt Elijah Botsford
Lieut Matth[w] Curtis
  Nathan Plats

Ezra Sherman
Moses Bardsley

A Pay Roll of a Corps Belonging to 8[d] Company in an Expedition to Fairfield Norwalk &c

        Capt Elijah Botsf[d]
        Lieut Math[w] Curtis

[*State Library, Revolution 16.*]

MILITIA REGIMENTS, 1779.   197

## CAPT. JABEZ BOTSFORD'S COMPANY.

Pay Role for Horse Travil Cap$^t$ Jabez Botsfords Company 16 Redg$^t$ Commanded by Nehemiah Bardsley Colonel on an Expedition to Fairfield and from there to Norwalk and Stamford

Jabez Botsford Capt
Henry Fairman Lt
Joshua Hatch Ens
Amos Barrett Serg
Asa Cogswell Serg

Abraham Bennett Cor
Enoch Hubble Cor
Silas Huble
Fitch Kimberly

[*State Library, Revolution 16.*]


## CAPT. PARDEE'S COMPANY.

A Pay Role for Horse travel Belonging to the 6$^{th}$ Alarm List Company in New fairfield in the 16$^{th}$ Redgment of Connecticut Militia Commanded by Nehemiah Bardsley Col. at a Late Expedition to Fairfield Norwalk for the defence of this and the Rest of the United States of America July 7$^{th}$ 1779

Stephen Pardee Capt
Daniel Smith Lieut
Sarg. Seth Trobridg
Corp. Squier (?) Wakeman
Corp. Moses Gray
P$^r$ Moses Knap
  Abel Hodges
  John Smith

Luis Hall
Thomas Brush
John Gorham
Elisha Hobbard
Eli Stevens
Benjamin Stevens
Josiah Bardsley

[*State Library, Revolution 16.*]


## CAPT. GIDDINGS' COMPANY.

Pay Role for Horse travel Capt W$^m$ Giddings Comp$^y$ in 16$^{th}$ Regt Militia Commanded by Nehemiah Beardsley Esq$^r$ Col$^o$ to Fairfield Norwalk Stamford New Fairfield July 8$^{th}$ 1779

Zephan$^h$ Briggs Liut
Benj$^a$ Picket Ens
Joseph Phelps
Amos Hubbell
Tho$^s$ Dunk
John Gorham
Hezekiah Bosworth
Joseph Eastman

Shadrack Hubbell
Aaron Smith
Josiah Hungerford
Noble Bennet
Nehemiah Seelye
Alexand$^r$ Stewart
John Page
Isaiah Babcock

[*State Library, Revolution 16.*]

## LIEUT. SEELEY'S COMPANY.

Pay Role for Horse Travil Liu$^t$ James Seelyes Company 16$^{th}$ Rig$^t$ Commanded by Nehemiah Bardsley Esq Colo on an Expedition to Fairfield Danbury Norwalk &c July 16$^{th}$ 1779

James Seelye Liut.
John Andrews Ens.
Nathaniel Hoyt Serj.
Oliver Benedict Serj.
Matthew Barnum Corp.
Nathaniel Barnum

Luke Roberds
Eliakim Starr
Silas Taylor
David Barnum
Benjami Martin
Joshua Starr

[State Library, Revolution 16.]

## CAPT. WILDMAN'S COMPANY.

Pay Roll for horse Travel Cap Daniel Wildman's Company of Alarm List 16$^{th}$ Reg$^t$ commanded by Co$^l$ Neh$^h$ Beardsly on an Expedition to Fairfield Norwalk &c July 1779

Dan$^l$ Wildman Cap
Theop$^s$ Bened$^t$ Ens
Caleb Baldwin
Tim$^o$ Ketcham
Major Taylor
Benj$^n$ Crosby
Eleazer Bened$^t$
Comfort Wildman
Sela Gregory
Jonas Benedict
Jon$^h$ Starr

Jacob Finch
Levi Stalker
Philip Corbin
Alex$^r$ Stuart
Lem$^l$ Wood Ju$^r$
Obed Wildman
Sam$^l$ Baldwin
Abijah Starr
Comfort Hoyt
Eleazer Taylor
Daniel Wood

[State Library, Revolution 16.]

## CAPT. SHUTE'S COMPANY.

A Pay Abstract for Capt Richard Shutes Company in Col. Bardsley Reg$^t$ of Militia of the State of Connecticut for hors travel in an Expedition to fairfield Norwalk &c A D 1779

Richard Shute Capt
Benj$^a$ Boughton Lieut
Jared Patchin Ens
David Peirce Sarj
Ely Boughton Sarj
Paul Hamelton Sarj
Samuel Stevens Corp
Eleazor Benedict Corp
John Barnum Drum
Ebenezer Nichols fifer
John Barnum Jr.
Judah Barnum Jr.
Asel Benedict
Nathan Barhan (?)
Abraham Benedict Jr.
William Comes

Samuel Cook
Nathan Gregory Jr
Enos Hoyt
Ezra Hobbol
Tho$^s$ Judd Jr.
Abner Judd
Jacob Judd
Silas Peirce
Peter Starr
Eleazer Starr
Forod Stevens
Eleazer Weed
Samuel Wildman Jr
David Wildman Jr
Daniel Boughton

[State Library, Revolution 16.]

MILITIA REGIMENTS, 1779. 199

## CAPT. HUBBELL'S COMPANY.

Pay Role For Horse travil Capt<sup>n</sup> W<sup>m</sup> G. Hubbell's Comp in 16<sup>th</sup> Reg<sup>t</sup> Militia Commanded by Nehemiah Beardsley Esq<sup>r</sup> Col<sup>o</sup> in an Expedition to Fairfield Norwalk & Stamford New Fairfield July 8<sup>th</sup> 1779

W<sup>m</sup> G. Hubbell Capt
W<sup>m</sup> Phelps Ens
John Penfield  Serj
Eben<sup>r</sup> Buck     "
Berzilla Brown  "
Sam<sup>l</sup> Stewart Corp
Benj<sup>a</sup> Bennet
David Gorham
Jeremiah Mead
Bennet Sill
Abel Page
James Gorham
Isaiah Hungerford
Ezra Hungerford
Joseph Eastman

Aaron Perry
Isaac Tripp
Stephen Stewart
Abel Lamphear
Sam<sup>l</sup> Richardson
George Higgins
John Sturdavant
Nath<sup>ll</sup> Squire
Obadiah Tibits
Silvenus Palmetur
Stephen Sherwood
Joseph Giddings
John Gould
Eph<sup>m</sup> Conger

[*State Library, Revolution 16.*]


## CAPT. HICKOK'S COMPANY.

Pay Roll for Horse travil Capt Daniel Hickoks Company 16<sup>th</sup> Regiment Commanded by Nehemiah Beardsly Esq<sup>r</sup> Col on An Expedition to Fairfield Danbury 9<sup>th</sup> July A D 1779

Daniel Hickok Capt
Joseph Elmor Lieut
Mathew Starr Ens.
Benajah Benedict Serg
Eliphalet Ferry Serg
Moses Vail Serg
Daniel Platt Corp
Benjamin Peeck Fif
William Benedict
Moses Benedict
Seth Benedict
Daniel Crowfut
Samuel Hoyt
James Hoyt
Lazerus Barnum
Daniel Barnum

Eden Andrus
Eliphalet Peck
James Platt
Samuel Benedict
Ebenezer Judd
John Holcomb
Benajah Hoyt
Eliud Taylor
Samuel Taylor
John Taylor
Elihu Judd
Stephen Trowbridge
Amos Starr
Samuel Starr
Nathan Wallor

[*State Library, Revolution 16.*]

## CAPT. BARNUM'S COMPANY.

A Pay Abstract for Horse travel Belonging to the 4 Alarm List Company in Danbury in the 16 Redgment of Militia in the State of Connecticut Commanded By Nehemiah Bardsley Col. In a Late Expidition to Farfield Norwalk &c for the Defence of this State and the Rest of the United States of Amaricah, July the 7 1779

Officers and Soldiers names That Rode on Horse Back

Richard Barnum Cap.
Nathaniel Barnum Lieut.
Serg. Thaddeus Mourhouse
Serg. Miles Boughton
Serj. Matthew Wilkee (?)
Clerk John Lindsley
Corp. Justus Hoyt
Corp. Lemuel Lindsley
Drum. Amos Knap
Priv. David Boughton
Matthew Boughton
Noble Benedict
Calub Church
Benjamin Curtis
Daniel Grigory

Nathan Grigory
Hezekiah Gray
John Hoyt
Noah Hoyt
Jonathan Hoyt
Jonathan Hays
Elnathan Knap
Matthew Lindsley
James Lindsley
David Picket
Noah Starr
John Starr
Ezra Stevens
Samuel Weed
Isaac Wildman

[*State Library, Revolution 16.*]

## CAPT. HINE'S COMPANY.

A Pay Abstract of Capt. Isaac Hines Company in Col⁰ Nehemiah Bardsley Regt: Militia in yᵉ State of Connecticut for Horse Travil in Alarm to Fairfield Bedford & Norwalk

Dated Ridgefield July 1779.

| Mens Names | Miles Travil | Mens Names | Miles Travil |
|---|---|---|---|
| Capt Isaac Hine | 20 | Ebenezer Price | 20 |
| Lieut David Scott | 20 | John Benedict | 20 |
| Ensn John Keeler | 20 | Samuel Fairbanks | 20 |
| Clerk James Rockwell | 20 | David Olmsted 2ᵈ | |
| Serjᵗ Hugh Cane | 20 | Stephen Hard | 10 |
| Sergᵗ Samuel Olmsted | 20 | Aaron Northrup | 10 |
| Serjᵗ Abram Nash | 20 | Timothy Kecler | 10 |
| Serjᵗ James Resseguie | 20 | Ezekiel Wilson | 10 |
| Corpl Daniel Smith | 20 | Seth Lee | |
| Corpl Samuel Smith | 20 | Aaron Hull | 20 |
| Corpl Gabriel Bennet | 10 | Thadeus Sturgis | 20 |
| David Hoyt | 20 | James Lusey | |
| John Morris | 20 | Ebenezer Jones | |
| Jacob Smith 2ᵈ | 20 | Elijah Kellogg | 20 |
| Thomas Hauley | | Silas Hall | 10 |
| Daniel Olmsted | 20 | Benjamin Smith | 10 |
| Jehial Bouton | 20 | Timothy Keeler 2ᵈ | 20 |
| David Stjohn | 20 | Gideon Scott | 20 |
| Daniel Kellogg | | John Baldwin | 10 |
| Amos Baker | 20 | Daniel Dean | 20 |
| Theodore Rockwill | 20 | Elijah Weedg | 10 |
| Benjamin Sherwood | 20 | Joseph Stebbins | 10 |
| Robert Edmond | 20 | | |

[*State Library, Revolution 16.*]

MILITIA REGIMENTS, 1779.     201

## CAPT. WAUGH'S COMPANY.

A Pay Abstract for the Horse Travel of Capt Alex^d Waughs Company in the 17th Reg^t of Militia of the State of Connecticut who March'd on a sudden emergency to oppose the Enemy; who were burning Fairfield & Norwalk on July 10th A D 1779

| Mens Names | N° Miles | Mens Names | N° Miles |
|---|---|---|---|
| Alex^d Waugh Capt | 50 | Andrew Woodruff | 50 |
| David Stoddard Lt | 50 | Sol. Woodruff | 20 |
| Abner Cone Ens | 50 | Sam^ll Woodruff | 50 |
| Sergt. Benj. Webster | 50 | John Woodruff | 50 |
| Serj. Clark Royce |  | Reuben Webster | 50 |
| Serj. Solomon Linly | 50 | Elijah Webster | 50 |
| Serj. Friend Dickinson | 50 | John Waterbury | 50 |
| Corpl. Aaron Gibbs | 50 | Ezekiel Graves | 50 |
| Corpl. John Osborn | 50 | Seba Canfield | 50 |
| Corpl. Jeremiah Riggs | 50 | Joshua Hide | 50 |
| Corpl. James Griffis | 50 | Asa Page | 50 |
| Abner Baldwin | 50 | Jo. Barber | 50 |
| Samuel Bernard |  | Zadok Seelye | 50 |
| Stephen Brown | 50 | Abel Page | 50 |
| Benj. Baker | 50 | Moses Munson | 50 |
| Benj. Birge | 50 | Alex^d M^cNeil | 50 |
| Truman Beamon | 50 | Eliada Orton | 50 |
| Nathaniel Benton | 50 | Oliver Dickinson | 50 |
| Jesse Bartholomew | 50 | John Bissell | 50 |
| Reuben Page | 50 | Sam^ll Catlin | 50 |
| Stephen Baldwin | 50 | Moses Barns | 50 |
| Daniel Clark | 50 | Abel Barns | 20 |
| Isaac Catlin | 50 | Serj. Nath^a Munson | 20 |
| Levi Coe | 50 | William Lewis | 20 |
| Charles Collens | 50 | Benj. Throop | 20 |
| John Carter | 50 | Zach^y Johnson | 20 |
| Oliver Churchill | 50 | Ezekiel Borden | 20 |
| Bradley Catlin | 50 | Hezekiah Agard | 20 |
| Simeon Gibbs | 50 | Ahijah Warren | 20 |
| Uri Goodwin | 50 | Reuben Landon | 20 |
| Jacob Green | 50 | Jeremiah Osborn | 20 |
| Oliver Gibbs | 50 | Jesse Stoddard | 20 |
| Solomon Harrison | 50 | Jarey Kilborn | 20 |
| John How | 50 | Benjamin Barns | 20 |
| Harris Jones | 50 | John Metcalf | 20 |
| Samuel Jones | 50 | Asa Morey | 20 |
| Helmont Kellogg | 50 | Aahel Dickinson | 20 |
| Griffin Kinnion | 50 | Stephen Judson | 20 |
| William Little | 50 | Zophar Beach | 50 |
| Samuel Little | 50 | John Russell | 50 |
| Timothy Linly | 50 | Isaac Thomson | 50 |
| James Landon | 50 | Isaac Horsford | 50 |
| Samuel Orton | 50 | Reuben Barns | 50 |
| Darius Orton | 50 | Seely Way | 20 |
| Isaac Osborn | 50 | Daniel Page | 20 |
| Amos Parmeley | 50 | David Wetmore | 20 |
| Moses Peck | 50 | Bela Graves | 20 |
| Joseph Sanford | 50 | Stephen Plant | 20 |
| Abel Saunders | 50 | Luther Mason | 50 |
| Ezekiel Trumbul | 50 | George Bull | 50 |
| Asher Thorp | 50 |  |  |

Stephen Plant 2 Days in Service     John Bissell 4 Days in Service
[This company was in service at Horse Neck in July and August, 1779, under Andrew Adams, Lieut.-Colonel Commander.]

[*State Library, Revolution 16.*]

## CAPT. PHELPS' COMPANY.

A Pay Abstract for the Horses that went in Service in Cap¹ Josiah Phelps' Comp^y in Col. Phelps' Reg¹ of Militia Ordered by Co¹ Epaphras Sheldon in a Tour to Norwalk July 9th 1779

Horses Sent Back at Wilton Being 60 Miles Travel

**Mens Names**
Capt Josiah Phelps
Lieut Eph^m Bancroft
Ens Jona^th Kettell
Serjt Jacob Tyler
" Seth Lockwood
" Amos Webster
" Timothy Hale
Corp Thomas Skiner
" Solomon Moss
" Seth Meacham
" Amos Bush or Beech
Elijah Andrus
Levi Benedick
Jacob Benton
Francis Beech
Oliver Bissel
Elijah Bill
Hezekiah Bissel
Ichabod Brown
Russel Burr
William Brown
Asahel Barbur
Brewin Beech
Ambrose Blakesly
Eben' Johnson
Thom Cook
Ichabod Chapins
Will^m Cook
Elisha Catlin
Gad Ely
John Frisbie
Silas Gridley
George Griswold
Andw Gleason
Asa Griswold
Simeon Humphry

**Mens Names**
Gideon Hurlbard
Noah Humphry
John Hurlbard
Benoni Johnson
Nathan Keley
Abraham Loomis
Epaphras Loomis
Eph^m Loomis
Joseph Loomis
Grove Loomis
Brigadore Loomis
Joseph Wooden
Elisha Gaylord
Ens. Bissel
Isaiah Loomis
Oliver Loomis
Jonas Leech
Roswel Marshel
Israel Merriman
Benjamin Mills
Jesse Murrain
Remembrance North
Eber Norton
Elisha Norton
Gideon Peck
Noah Preston
Tim^th Kay
Robert Rood
Ebenezer Smith
David Smith
Jesse Smith
Medad Taylor
Moses Wilcox
John Winchel
John Wilcox
Hervy Whiting

Horses Sent Back at New Milford Being 30 Miles

Mihael Bull
David Mansfield
Abner Perkins
Benj^a Butler
Eliphalet Bristol

Moses Wilcox 2^d
Elijah Catlin
Andw Austin
John Strong
Lieut Eli Wilson

[*State Library, Revolution 16.*]

## FIFTEENTH REGIMENT—LIEUT.-COL. STANLEY.

### CAPT. HALL'S COMPANY.

A Pay Abstract for Capt Asaph Halls Company in Col. Gad Stanlys Regt for Hors Travel Who Was ordered to Ride to Horse Neck by Col Epaphras Sheldon in August 1779 for the Defense of the State of Connecticut.

Capt Asaph Hall
Lt Nath$^{ll}$ Bull
Ensn David Goff
Sergt Chancy Beech
Corpl Jonathan Miller
  Alen Kellogg
  Ira Phelps
  Joseph Baley
  Israel Smith
  Oliver Wilcox

Ruben Barber
Sam$^{ll}$ Tyler
Jonathan Cook
Sam$^{ll}$ Phelps
Noah Gleason
Stephen Thomson
Sam$^{ll}$ Weston
John Weston
Nathan Davis

[*State Library, Revolution 16.*]

## EIGHTEENTH REGIMENT—COL. PHELPS.

### CAPT. BATES' COMPANY.

September y$^e$ 7$^{th}$ A D 1779 to Joel Moor Clark of y$^e$ Second Company of Alaram List in Simsburey in the State of Connecticut Greting

Persuant to orders you are heareby Commanded to Deracte Richard Gay    Ephram Adams    Nath Winchil    Ezekiel Phelps Juny    Barnabus Meacham    Jams Luis    David Clark    Obediah Moore    Joseph Griswold    Isaac Broker    John Horskins    Isaac Moor    Rane Cossit    John Check    Wm Shepard    Adonijah Holcomb    Silas Holcomb    Mathew Griffin Juny    Ephraim Holcomb    Hezakiah Holcomb    Joshua Holcomb    Thomas Spring    Josiah Toping    Asa Hilyer    Benjah Dibol    David Holcomb    John Vallants    Elnathan Lamson    Juda Hays    Rebert Fields,    Aron Duey    Abijah Phelps    Elijah Phelps    Seth Viets    Noah Phelps    Silvanus Bartlet    John Miller to Aquipt them Selves with arms and aconterments and hold them Selves in Readeynes to march at y$^e$ Shortest Notis for y$^e$ Defence of this this State

                                      Lemuel Bates Capt

[*Charles W. Bates, East Granby.*]

## DETACHED SERVICE.

### LIEUT. HEPBURNE'S COMPANY.

This may certify that Peter Hepburne Command [     ]

Jos Davidson
Daniel Burn
James Goldsmith
Sam B Smith
John W<sup>m</sup> Gillit
Benajah Smith
David Miles
Jene Stow

Theoph<sup>s</sup> Smith
Garrit DeWitt
Henry Lenimey (?)
Tiret Bull
Eben<sup>r</sup> Oviat
Henry Bull
Jos. Whiting

Each of them served as Matrosses in the Fort at Milford A. D. 1779 and therefore have their Hea[ ] abated from their Lists Viz<sup>t</sup> Eighteen pounds from each of them James Goldsmith only excepted his Son being under 21 years of age

Milford 28<sup>th</sup> April 178[ ]

[*State Library, Revolution 16.*]

### MIDDLETOWN GUARD.

A Pay Rolle for Guarding Six Brass Field Pieces in Middletown from the 3<sup>d</sup> of August 1779 to the 15<sup>th</sup> of September.

| | | |
|---|---|---|
| Elihu Cotton | . . | 20 Nights |
| Timothy Cornwell | . | 14 " |
| Noah Higbe | . . | 8 " |
| Andrew Bacon | . . | 15 " |
| George Adkins | . . | 15 " |

| | | |
|---|---|---|
| John Hollit | . . | 15 Nights |
| Abel Sizer | . . | 15 " |
| Prince Winban | . . | 15 " |
| Aaron Robards | . . | 15 " |

[*State Library, Revolution 16.*]

# FIRST LIGHT HORSE REGIMENT—MAJ. HART.

[*See Record of Connecticut Men in the Revolution, page 443.*]

## SECOND TROOP—CAPT. WOODRUFF.

A Pay Abstract of Capt Enoch Woodruff Troop of Horse while in State Service at Greenwich for Extra Expense A D 1779

    Enoch Woodruff Capt
    Andrew Clark, Express to Fairfield
    Michael Taintor
    Wilford Johnson
    Isaac Lane, Express to Hartford
    Timothy Gilbard
    Eber Ward, Express to Stanford
    Jonas Larence, Express to Fairfield
    Solomon Stanton, Express to Fairfield
    Lemuell Martin
    John Ables
    Lent Kough
    Abner Tharp
    Jacob Morgan
    Jesse Cook
    Daniell Willard
    Nathan Basset, Express to Norwalk
    Abram Buckley
    Benj[a] Weeb, Express to Wilton Canon &c
    Ozias Phelps
    Sam[ll] Hays
    Gabrel Flowers
    Pineas Coe
    David Giddins, Express to Fairfield

                                              [*State Library, Revolution 16.*]

## VARIOUS COMPANIES.

### SERVICE WITH CONTINENTAL ARMY.

The United States D$^r$ To the State of Connecticut, for the Service &c of Militia, ordered to joyn the Continental Army in 1779, Viz : —

| Bills & Acct$^s$ | Remarks |
|---|---|
| Cap$^t$ Uriel Holmes . | Col. B. Hutchins Reg$^t$ |
| Cap$^t$ Peter Curtis . | 15$^{th}$ Reg$^t$ |
| Cap$^t$ Aaron Kelcy . | Maj$^r$ N. Smiths |
| Cap$^t$ J. Forward . | Col. B. Hutchins |
| Cap$^t$ Noble Hine . | Col. S. Canfields |
| Cap$^t$ Divan Berrys . | Maj$^r$ N. Smiths |
| Cap$^t$ I. Lewis . | " |
| Col. B. Hutchins | |
| Cap$^t$ Joseph Dart . | Col. A. Tylers Reg$^t$ |
| Cap$^t$ D. Olmstead . | Col. S. Canfields |
| Cap$^t$ E. Hinman . | " |
| Gen$^l$ A. Ward | |
| Cap$^t$ J. Wright . | Col. Gallops |
| Cap$^t$ J. Johnson . | " |
| Cap$^t$ J. Wyllys . | " |
| Cap$^t$ Amos Woodward . | Col. Gordons |
| Cap$^t$ Caleb Handee . | " |
| Cap$^t$ John Swan . | Col. Gallups |
| Cap$^t$ O. Spicer . | " |
| Col. N. Gallup | |
| Cap$^t$ A. Waterman . | Col. O. Johnsons |
| Cap$^t$ W$^m$ Frissel . | Col. J. Gordons |
| Cap$^t$ A. Loomis . | Col. H. Wyllys |
| Col. H. Wyllys | |
| Cap$^t$ E. Botsford . | Col. S. Canfield |
| Cap$^t$ R. Abbe . | Col. H. Wyllys |
| Cap$^t$ J. Converse . | Col S. Chapmans. |
| Cap$^t$ Charles Smith . | Maj$^r$ J. Davenports |

[*Comptroller's Office, Haskell's Receipts.*]

### SERVICE WITH COUNT D'ESTAING.

The United States D$^r$ To the State of Connecticut, for the service &c of Militia orderd to Co-operate with Count De Estang in 1779 — Viz.—

| Bills & Accounts | Remarks |
|---|---|
| Col. James Gordon | |
| Cap$^t$ J. Gray . | Col. S. Canfields |
| Col. S Canfield | |
| Cap$^t$ J. Burton | " |
| Cap$^t$ J. Gillet . | Col. R. Newbury |
| Cap$^t$ E. Moseley | Col. J. Gordons |

MILITIA REGIMENTS, 1779.   207

Bills & Accounts
Cap<sup>t</sup> D. Hitchcock .
Cap<sup>t</sup> Moses Gilbert .
Cap<sup>t</sup> N. Waterman .
Cap<sup>t</sup> B. Buell . .
Cap<sup>t</sup> J. Green
Cap<sup>t</sup> B. Buell .
Cap<sup>t</sup> C. Wells .

Remarks
Col. Tylers
                "
Col. Gallup
Col. J. Mason

            "
    .   .   .   Col. H. Wyllys
[*Comptroller's Office, Haskell's Receipts.*]

## MILITIA SERVICE.

The United States D<sup>r</sup> To the State of Connecticut for the service of State Troops & Militia [between the 1<sup>st</sup> April & 1 Nov<sup>r</sup>] raised for the defence of the State & allowed by Act of Congress December 28<sup>th</sup> 1779 computed according to the Continental establishment of Pay [and rations as per resolution of Congress of 2 & 6 June 1778].

(The statements in brackets were added in pencil in a different hand. It is not stated for how long any of these companies served. A few of them also served before or after the period April 1,—Nov<sup>r</sup> 1, 1779.)

Officers Pay Rolls
Cap<sup>t</sup> Lee Lay . . . .   [Guard Lyme]
Cap<sup>t</sup> John Williams . . .   "    Fort Griswold]
Cap<sup>t</sup> William Howard . .   [coast guard Newbury Regt 1777]
Cap<sup>t</sup> Isaac Howe . . .   [Meads Reg<sup>t</sup>]
Cap<sup>t</sup> Odle Close . . .   [Guard Horseneck May 1779]
Cap<sup>t</sup> Charles Smith . . .   [Comp<sup>y</sup> Horseneck]
Cap<sup>t</sup> Reuben Bostwick . .   [Horseneck Alarm]
L<sup>t</sup> Col<sup>o</sup> Samuel Canfield . .              "
Cap<sup>t</sup> D. Leavenworth . .   [Coast guard]
Col<sup>o</sup> Roger Newberry . .   [field & staff N. London]
Cap<sup>t</sup> George Terrill . .   [Coast guard Horseneck]
Cap<sup>t</sup> Edward Payne . . .   [Company at New London]
Cap<sup>t</sup> John Porter . . .   [Coast guard Horseneck]
Cap<sup>t</sup> Samuel Bronson . .          "          "
Col<sup>o</sup> Noadiah Hooker . .          "          "   field & staff]
Cap<sup>t</sup> Divan Berry . . .          "          "
Cap<sup>t</sup> Judah Woodruff . .          "          "
Cap<sup>t</sup> Lemuel Bates . . .          "          "
Cap<sup>t</sup> Giles Miller . . .          "          "
Cap<sup>t</sup> N. Chapman . . .   [Company Horseneck ——]
Cap<sup>t</sup> Charles Norton . .   [Company N. Haven alarm]
      "           "           .          "   Fairfield alarm]
Cap<sup>t</sup> J. Robinson . . .          "   N. Haven   "
      "           "           .          "   Fairfield   "
Cap<sup>t</sup> Samuel Camp . . .          "   New Haven  "
      "           "           .          "   Fairfield   "
Ensign Joseph Smith , . .   [Coast guards]
Col<sup>o</sup> Hezekiah Wyllys . .   [Coast guards]
Cap<sup>t</sup> Josiah Phelps         Cap<sup>t</sup> Roger Riley
Cap<sup>t</sup> Amos Barnes          Cap<sup>t</sup> John Hugh
Cap<sup>t</sup> Timothy Clark        Cap<sup>t</sup> Dan Collins
Cap<sup>t</sup> Solomon Sage         Col<sup>o</sup> Andrew Adams
Cap<sup>t</sup> Nathan Gilbert       Serj<sup>t</sup> James Payson
Cap<sup>t</sup> Jared Shepperd       Cap<sup>t</sup> James Stoddard
Cap<sup>t</sup> Samuel Hart          Cap<sup>t</sup> David Phelps

### Officers Pay Rolls

Cap⁺ Elizur Hale
Cap⁺ Elizur Hubbard
Cap⁺ David Hitchcock
Cap⁺ Nath¹ Bunnell
Cap⁺ Miles Hull
Cap⁺ Robert Martin
Cap⁺ David Hitchcock
Cap⁺ Ephraim Cook
L⁺ Nathan Hurd
Cap⁺ Nathan Hine
Cap⁺ Amos Wetmore
Cap⁺ John Wetmore
Cap⁺ Joseph Kellogg
Cap⁺ Joseph Blague
Cap⁺ Jacob Witmore
Cap⁺ George Hubbard
Cap⁺ Jabez Brooks
Cap⁺ Othniel Williams
Cap⁺ George Phillips
Cap⁺ Daniel Stewart
Cap⁺ Daniel Clark
Cap⁺ Othniel Williams
Cap⁺ Thomas Giddings
Cap⁺ Elizur Hubbard
Cap⁺ Augustus Collins
Cap⁺ Oliver Stanley
Cap⁺ Caleb Hall
Cap⁺ Abraham Stanley
Cap⁺ Miles Johnson
Cap⁺ Thomas Shepard
L⁺ Daniel Holt
Cap⁺ Abraham Stanley
Cap⁺ Joseph Carew
Col° Samuel Abbot
Majʳ Asa Bray
Cap⁺ Simeon Sheldon
Cap⁺ Hezekiah Gridley
Cap⁺ Job Case
L⁺ Thomas Phelps
Col° Comfort Sage
Cap⁺ Enos Hawley
Col° Comfort Sage
Cap⁺ Samuel Osborn
L⁺ Stephen Goodrich
Col° Howel Woodbridge
Cap⁺ Neheṁ Laurence
Cap⁺ James Burton
Col° N. Beardsley
Cap⁺ Richard Smith
Cap⁺ Elijah Botsford
Cap⁺ A. Botsford
Cap⁺ Jabez Botsford
Cap⁺ James Clark
Cap⁺ Isaac Hine
Cap⁺ Richard Barnum
Cap⁺ William Giddings
Cap⁺ Daniel Wildman
Cap⁺ Richard Shute

### Officers Pay Rolls

Cap⁺ William G. Hubbell
Cap⁺ Stephen Pardee
Cap⁺ Knowles Sears
Cap⁺ Peter Penfield
Cap⁺ Daniel Hickock
Cap⁺ Joseph Smith
L⁺ James Seeley
Cap⁺ David Olmsted
Cap⁺ Timothy Judson
Cap⁺ Jonah Foster
Cap⁺ William Willson
Cap⁺ Ephraim Barnum
Cap⁺ Joseph Bottom
Cap⁺ Abel Burritt
Cap⁺ Elijah Hazen
L⁺ Abner Mosley
Cap⁺ Jesse Curtiss
L⁺ Abner Moseley
Ensign Enoch Scribner
Cap⁺ Nath¹ Gilbert
Cap⁺ Jonathan Farrand
Cap⁺ Jesse Curtiss
Ensⁿ Sol° Martin
Cap⁺ Stephen Seymour
Cap⁺ Elijah Backus
Cap⁺ Nehemiah Tinker
Cap⁺ David Hinman
Cap⁺ Thomas Giddings
Cap⁺ Uriel Holmes
Cap⁺ John Williams
Cap⁺ Elijah Avery
Cap⁺ John Williams
Cap⁺ John Dixon
Cap⁺ Daniel Brainard
Cap⁺ Joseph Dart
Col° John Penfield
Cap⁺ Jonathan Case
Cap⁺ Elias Bliss
Cap⁺ N. Bunnell
Cap⁺ Amos Wetmore
Cap⁺ Lemuel Roberts
Cap⁺ Elisha Chapman
Cap⁺ Eliphalet Curtiss
Cap⁺ Reuben Sikes
Cap⁺ Samuel Felt
Cap⁺ Israel Converse
Majʳ Abiel Pease
Cap⁺ Stephen Roberts
Cap⁺ Jedediah Amedown
Cap⁺ Ezra Kinney
Cap⁺ James Morgan
Cap⁺ Joseph Bordman
Cap⁺ Jonathan Bush
Cap⁺ Gilbert Dudley
Cap⁺ William Giddings
Cap⁺ Abraham Fuller
Cap⁺ Abner Mallery
Cap⁺ James Averill

MILITIA REGIMENTS, 1779.

Officers Pay Rolls
Cap¹ N. Barber
Cap¹ Lazarus Ruggles
Cap¹ Benjamin Stone
Cap¹ Abel Botsford
Cap¹ Jotham Curtiss
Cap¹ Nath¹ Barnes
Cap¹ William Cogswell
Cap¹ Ebenezer Couch
Cap¹ Jotham Curtiss
L¹ Barth¹ Pond
Cap¹ Noble Hine
Cap¹ Joseph Isham
Cap¹ Reuben Bostwick
Col⁰ Samuel Canfield
Cap¹ Adam Hurlbut
Serj¹ Ebenezer Thomas
L¹ Reuben Blakesley
Ensⁿ James Porter
Cap¹ Alexʳ Waugh
Cap¹ Jared Dudley
Cap¹ Nath¹ Hall
Cap¹ Benjᵃ Richards
Cap¹ John Woodruff
Cap¹ Phineas Castle
L¹ Thomas Dutton
Cap¹ Thomas Fenn
Cap¹ Joseph Garnsey
Col⁰ Noah Phelps
Cap¹ Arch. McNeal
Cap¹ Elisha Edgerton
Cap¹ Isaac Johnson
Cap¹ Josiah King
Cap¹ Aaron Horsford
Cap¹ Reuben Stone
Cap¹ Miles Beach
Cap¹ Samuel Rockwell
Cap¹ Reuben Rose
Cap¹ David Barber
Cap¹ Amasa Mills
Col⁰ Jonathan Dimon
Lieu¹ Aaron Porter
Cap¹ L. Hotchkiss
Cap¹ Asa Yale
Cap¹ Joseph Bacon
Cap¹ Josiah Terrill
Cap¹ Charles Wright
Cap¹ Abijah Hall
Cap¹ Jonathan Kilborne
Cap¹ Elias Graves
Cap¹ John Lewis
Cap¹ Kezin Gridley
Cap¹ Elisha Scott
Cap¹ Peter Curtiss
Cap¹ Abel Brace
Majʳ Elihu Kent
L¹ Nathan Noble
Cap¹ Nehemiah Brainard
Cap¹ Samuel Hubbard

Officers Pay Rolls
Cap¹ Samuel Brooks
Cap¹ John Smith
Cap¹ James Lusk
Cap¹ Hezekiah Wells
Cap¹ Chester Wells
L¹ James Arnold
Col⁰ William Worthington
Cap¹ Amos Barnes
Cap¹ B. Stoddard
Cap¹ Asaph Hall
Cap¹ Zeb Taylor
Cap¹ M. Smith
Cap¹ A. Burr
Ensign Wright
Cap¹ Jabez Wright
Cap¹ Matthew Cole
Cap¹ Zeb Taylor
Cap¹ Seth Peirce
Cap¹ Asaph Hall
Cap¹ Benjamin Mills
Cap¹ Ebenezer Fletcher
Cap¹ Adonijah Burr
Cap¹ Ambrose Sloper
Cap¹ Roger Moore
Cap¹ Jonathan Cady
Cap¹ Nehemiah Waterman
Cap¹ J. Raynsford
Cap¹ Samuel Wheat
Cap¹ Jonathan Cady
Cap¹ Benjᵃ Mills
Cap¹ N. Waterman
Cap¹ Samuel Upson
Cap¹ Daniel Cone
Cap¹ Z. Hungerford
Cap¹ N. Jewit
Cap¹ Israel Spencer
Cap¹ William Cone
Cap¹       Phelps
Cap¹ Jacob Hinsdale
Cap¹ David Wood
Cap¹ Odle Close
L¹ James Austin
L¹ Nathaniel Mead
Cap¹ Odle Close
Cap¹ Caleb Mead
Cap¹ John Allyn
Cap¹ John Deshon
Gen¹ Selah Heart
L¹ Thomas Powers
Serj¹ John Colt
Cap¹ Amos Barnes
Cap¹ Amos Beecher
L¹ Ezra Dibble
Cap¹ Josiah Fowler
L¹ John Thrall
Cap¹ Benoni Smith
Cap¹ Samuel Wells
Cap¹ Samuel Peck

14

### Officers Pay Rolls

Cap<sup>t</sup> Timothy Clark
Cap<sup>t</sup> Matthew Cole
Cap<sup>t</sup> Ambrose Sloper
Cap<sup>t</sup> John Langton
Cap<sup>t</sup> Joseph Forward
Cap<sup>t</sup> Thomas Bidwell
Cap<sup>t</sup> Samuel Williams
Cap<sup>t</sup> Elijah Hinman
Cap<sup>t</sup> Ziba Hunt
Cap<sup>t</sup> Asa Bray
Cap<sup>t</sup> John Perkins
Cap<sup>t</sup> Abraham Stanley
Cap<sup>t</sup> Caleb Hall
Cap<sup>t</sup> Oliver Stanley
Cap<sup>t</sup> Dan Collins
Cap<sup>t</sup> Samuel Hays
Cap<sup>t</sup> Daniel Lyon
Cap<sup>t</sup> Matthew Smith
Cap<sup>t</sup> Peter Mills
Cap<sup>t</sup> Lewis Mills
Cap<sup>t</sup> Lewis Mallett
L<sup>t</sup> Noah Porter
L<sup>t</sup> Asa Cooley
Cap<sup>t</sup> Jesse Curtiss
Col<sup>o</sup> Oliver Smith
Ens<sup>n</sup> Joseph Babcock
L<sup>t</sup> John Williams
Cap<sup>t</sup> Daniel Lankton
Cap<sup>t</sup> Josiah Baldwin
Cap<sup>t</sup> William Stanton
Cap<sup>t</sup> John Breed
Cap<sup>t</sup> Josiah Baldwin
Cap<sup>t</sup> Job Wright
Cap<sup>t</sup> Isaac Bronson
Col<sup>o</sup> Hezekiah Sabin
Cap<sup>t</sup> J. Bronson
Col<sup>o</sup> Seth Smith
Cap<sup>t</sup> Jed Chapman
Cap<sup>t</sup> Simeon Lay
Cap<sup>t</sup> Isaac Bronson
Cap<sup>t</sup> Benjamin Richards
Cap<sup>t</sup> Aaron Kelcey
Cap<sup>t</sup> Bez<sup>a</sup> Bristol
Maj. Gen<sup>l</sup> O. Wolcott
Cap<sup>t</sup> John Pennoyer
Cap<sup>t</sup> John Willey
Col<sup>o</sup> Gad Stanley
Col<sup>o</sup> E. Storrs
Cap<sup>t</sup> Dan Bouton
Cap<sup>t</sup> C. Raymond
Cap<sup>t</sup> N. Gilbert
Cap<sup>t</sup> Reuben Scofield
L<sup>t</sup> Eliphalet Seeley
L<sup>t</sup> Joel Hays
Col<sup>o</sup> Gad Stanley
Cap<sup>t</sup> Allen Cooper
Cap<sup>t</sup> Caleb Mix
Cap<sup>t</sup> Timothy Starkey

### Officers Pay Rolls

Cap<sup>t</sup> Thomas Shepard
Cap<sup>t</sup> Timothy Munger
Cap<sup>t</sup> Stephen Palmer
Cap<sup>t</sup> Jesse Goodyear
Cap<sup>t</sup> Benjamin Baldwin
Cap<sup>t</sup> Bryan Stoddard
Cap<sup>t</sup> Jesse Billings
Cap<sup>t</sup> Nathaniel Harriss
Col<sup>o</sup> E. Worthington
Cap<sup>t</sup> Jabez Perkins
Cap<sup>t</sup> N. Hall
Cap<sup>t</sup> John Breed
Cap<sup>t</sup> Benjamin Clark
L<sup>t</sup> Ichabod Palmer
Cap<sup>t</sup> Christopher Leffingwell
Cap<sup>t</sup> David Hough
Cap<sup>t</sup> Chrs. Leffingwell
Cap<sup>t</sup> David Landon
Cap<sup>t</sup> Benajah Leffingwell
Cap<sup>t</sup> Ichabod Miller
Maj<sup>r</sup> N. Brown
Cap<sup>t</sup> Shubael Griswold
Col<sup>o</sup> Epa<sup>s</sup> Sheldon
Cap<sup>t</sup> Epa<sup>s</sup> Loomis
Lieut Miller
B. General And<sup>w</sup> Ward
Cap<sup>t</sup> Amos Smith
Maj<sup>r</sup> John Belding
L<sup>t</sup> Timothy Lockwood
L<sup>t</sup> Nathan Sloson
Cap<sup>t</sup> Jesse Bell
Cap<sup>t</sup> Ebenezer Ferris
Cap<sup>t</sup> Richard Deshon
Cap<sup>t</sup> Jeremiah Halsey
Cap<sup>t</sup> Ebenezèr Witters
Cap<sup>t</sup> Jonathan Warring
L<sup>t</sup> Justus Buck
Ensign Allen Smith
Cap<sup>t</sup> James Barker
Cap<sup>t</sup> James Lindsley
Cap<sup>t</sup> Edward Shipman
L<sup>t</sup> Hoadley
Cap<sup>t</sup> Isaac Howe
Col<sup>o</sup> William Worthington
Cap<sup>t</sup> John Hills
Cap<sup>t</sup> Joseph Loveland
Cap<sup>t</sup> Thomas Horsey
Cap<sup>t</sup> Seth Pierce
Cap<sup>t</sup> Jabez Wright
Cap<sup>t</sup> Abraham Foot
Cap<sup>t</sup> Daniel Holbrook
Cap<sup>t</sup> Amos Barnes
Cap<sup>t</sup> Samuel Peck
Cap<sup>t</sup> Charles Smith
Col<sup>o</sup> John Mead
L<sup>t</sup> Elijah Bruster
Cap<sup>t</sup> Joshua Dunlap
Cap<sup>t</sup> Stephen Lyon

## MILITIA REGIMENTS, 1779.

Officers Pay Rolls

Col° Dyer Throop
Cap¹ Simeon Edgerton
Cap¹ Joseph Whitmore
Cap¹ Amaziah Rust
Col° Marshfield Parsons
Cap¹ C. Allen
Cap¹ Samuel Osborne
Cap¹ Noah Kellogg
Cap¹ Jesse Ford
Cap¹ M. Gilbert
Col° William Worthington
Cap¹ John Isham
Cap¹ Bethuel Treat
Cap¹ Ruluff Dutcher
Cap¹ Jared Cone
Cap¹ William Howard
Cap¹ Joseph Sanford
Cap¹ Ebenezer Smith
Cap¹ Augur Curtiss
Col° Jonathan Wells
Maj¹ Thomas Bull
Cap¹ Silas Dunham
Cap¹ Daniel Platt
Cap¹ Silas Dunham
Cap¹ John Wood
Cap¹ Israel Seymour
Cap¹ Joseph Woodford
Cap¹ Thomas Giddings
Col° Samuel Mott
Cap¹ Samuel Leffingwell
Cap¹ Ebenezer Barnard
Cap¹ Eliphalet Bulkley
Cap¹ Samuel Brooks
Cap¹ Samuel Gates
Cap¹ Thomas Bidwell
Cap¹ Ladwick Hotchkiss
Cap¹ Elisha Toby
Cap¹ Shubael Griswold
Cap¹ Isaac Hall
Cap¹ John Riggs
Cap¹ Bradford Steel
Cap¹ Daniel Chatfield
Cap¹ David Phelps
Cap¹ David Beecher
Cap¹ Peter Perkins
Cap¹ Amos Hallam
Cap¹ Amos Main
Col° Nathan Gallup
Cap¹ Benjamin Summer
Col° Joseph Abbott
Lieu¹       Hughes
Cap¹ Stephen Smith
L¹ William Lay
Cap¹ Issachar Bates
Cap¹ Jeremiah Bradley
Serj¹ Giddeon Brockway
Col° Edward Russell
Cap¹ Benoni Smith

Officers Pay Rolls

L¹ Lawrence Clinton
Cap¹ Noah Ives
Cap¹ Elijah Hazen
Cap¹ Samuel Jones
Cap¹ Othniel Williams
Cap¹ Elnathan Nichols
Cap¹ Enoch Woodruff
Corp¹ Elisha Edgerton
Cap¹ Jonathan Dayton
Col° Jonathan Dimon
Cap¹ James Borton
Cap¹ Robert Wells
Maj¹ Ichabod Norton
Cap¹ Warham Gibbs
Cap¹ Samuel Wells
Cap¹ Phineas Sherman
Ensign Eben° Morehouse
Cap¹ Stiles Judson
Cap¹ Samuel Uffott
Cap¹ Charles Churchill
Cap¹ Richard Shute
Cap¹ Nathaniel Copley
Cap¹ Abel Burritt
Cap¹ Dan Collins
Gen¹ Erastus Wolcott
Corp¹ Nathan Goodspeed
Corp¹ Silvanus Cone
Cap¹ Richard Wait
Lebbeus Beckwith
L¹ Silvanus Smith
Cap¹ Odel Close
Cap¹ Samuel Wells
Maj¹ John Davenport
Cap¹ Benj⁴ Peck
Cap¹ Noah Fowler
Cap¹ Thomas Wheeler
L¹ Ichabod Brown
Cap¹ William Whitney
Cap¹ A. M°Neal
Cap¹ Peter Johnson
Cap¹ John Mix
Serj¹ John Percival
Lieu¹ John Crane
Cap¹ Josiah Fowler
Cap¹ Nathaniel Bunnell
Cap¹ Miles Hull
Cap¹ Lewis Mallett
Cap¹ Jehial Bryan
Cap¹ Benajah Holcomb
Cap¹ N. Hutchins
Serj¹ James Davidson
Cap¹ Aaron Hosford
Cap¹ Hubbard Burrus
Corp¹ S Hartshorne
Samuel Wright
Cap¹ Oliver Spicer
Cap¹ John Waterhouse
     John Munroe

### Officers Pay Rolls

Peter Grant
Ephraim Kelley
Cap' Elisha Graham
Cap' Benjamin Clark
Cap' Eliphalet Lockwood
Cap' Jabez Gregory
L' Isaac Foot
L' Arnold Hazelton
Cap' Jesse Starkweather
Cap' Jesse Bell
L' John Bean
L' Justus Buck
L' Col° Jonathⁿ Baldwin
Cap' J. Bronson
Col° I. Baldwin
Cap' Moses Seymour
Cap' John Shipman
Cap' Lemuel Lamb
Cap' Amos Jones
Cap' Daniel Bouton
Serj' Henry Wood
L' Jacob Bunnell
L' Joseph Bennett
Serj' William Hall
Cap' C. S' John
Cap' David Hitchcock
Allen Lane
Ebenezer Coe
Cap' Ezra Kinnee
Col° Increase Moseley
L' Peter Hepburne
Col° Thomas Belden
Cap' John Green
Serj' Wolcott Hawley
Cap' Oliver Stanley
Cap' Nehemiah Tinker
Serj' Solomon Stoddard
Cap' Benjamin Stone
Cap' Eli Butler
Cap' Daniel Godfrey
Cap' Benjamin Dean
Cap' David Phelps
Cap' Elijah Seymour
Cap'ˢ Smith & Kimberley
Cap' Seth Demming
Cap' Daniel Tyler
Cap' Phineas Bradley
E. Ledyard
Cap' Jesse Raymond
L' Gamaliel Taylor
Cap' O. Marvin
Cap' Eliakim Smith
Cap' Absalom Williams
Daniel Abbott
Isaac Tucker
Cap' Benjamin Green
Cap' Eben. Lathrop

### Officers Pay Rolls

Cap' Moses Stevens
Cap' S. Marshall
L' Isaac Abell
Cap' Jared Cone
Cap' E. Thorp
Cap' R. Richards
L' A. Porter
Cap' Solomon Morehouse
Cap' Knowles Sears
Cap' E. Lathrop
Cap' George Peck
Cap' William Giddings
Cap' Elijah Palmer
Ensign Simeon Hiscox
Col° Samuel Whiting
Cap' Reuben Scofield
Cap' Uriah Raymond
Col° Levi Wells
Cap' I. Stanton
Cap' James Smith
Cap' Peter Perit
Cap' Benjᵃ Summers
Cap' John Allen
Cap' John Pettibone
Cap' S. Keelor
Cap' John Yeates
Col° Matthew Mead
Lemuel Nichols
Corp' Charles Buckley
Cap' Enos Hawley
Cap' Adam Shapley
Cap' William Latham
Cap' Daniel Tilden
Cap' Briant Stoddard
Cap' Everts
Cap' Enos Hawley
Majʳ William Ledyard
Cap' Andrew Hyllyer
Cap' Josiah Bradley
Col° Phineas Porter
Cap' Nathan Hine
Noah Wells
L' Achors Sheffields
Cap' Absalom Williams
Billious Kirtland
Cap' Benjamin Richards
L' Eben. Whitney
Cap' Benjᵃ Hickock
Majʳ Ezra Starr
Anthony Annable
Cap' Jabez Beebe
Cap' John Hempstead
Cap' Abell Hall
Cap' Caleb S' John
Cap' Daniel Allen
Lieu' John Curtis

[*Comptroller's Office, Haskell's Receipts.*]

# MILITIA REGIMENTS, 1780.

## SIX MONTHS REGIMENT.

[Although noted as recruits for the Continental Army the men named in this and the two following lists appear to have been raised to serve as Militia rather than in the "Line" or State regiments. See the doings of the Council of Safety May 30, 1780.]

Account of Bounties paid to recruits raised for 6 mo. to join the Continental Army in the year 1780, by Col° Increase Moseley. Viz$^t$

Elisha Noble
Daniel Ouer
Asahel Ives
Amos Booth
Hezekiah Whitney
Luman Brownson
Johnson Wheeler
Joseph Ferry
Amos Davis
Benj$^a$ Buckingham
Nathaniel Beecher
Nathaniel Geer

Noah Smith Jr.
Agur Hinman
S. Tracy
G. Phillips
Reuben Hill
Elizur Wheeler
Enos Hinman
John Royce
Matthew Reynolds
Caleb Scott
Ezekiel Beeman
Joel Hinman

[*State Library, Revolution* 17.]

Account of Bounties paid to recruits raised for 6 mo. to join the Continental Army in the year 1780 by Colonel Jonathan Dimon. Viz$^t$

Lemuel Chatfield
Roman Negro
W. Hurd
Samuel French
Joseph Mitchel
Peter Roes
J. Colver
Jack Gregory
Josiah Burroughs
James Hurlburt
Alen (?) Smith
W$^m$ (?) Ward
Joseph Lewis

William Sissen
J. Wheeler
Richard Bangs
N. Hinman
J. Dimon Jr
E. Sherwood
E. Seyley
Aby Batter
S. Downs
Benj. Bennet
Justus Whitlock
Joseph Battson

[*State Library, Revolution* 17.]

A Bounty Roll of the 6 mo. men who joined the Continental Army from Col° John Meads Reg' of Mil* in the Year 1780
Justus Hait
John Mead Col° and Muster Master of the Recruits & 3 months men from the 9th Reg'

[*State Library, Revolution* 17.]

## MILITIA AT WEST POINT.

The United States D' To the State of Connecticut for sundry Expenditures &c. of Militia, who served at West Point, in the Year 1780

| Bills & Accounts | Remarks |
|---|---|
| Cap' N. Smith | Col. E. Russell's Reg' |
| Cap' J. Lusk | Col. Hutchins |
| Cap' C. Norton | J. Richards |
| Cap' M. Mills | Hutchins |
| Cap' D. Brainerd | |
| Maj' J. Cooks | |
| Cap' D. Clark | Sages |
| Col. B. Hutchins | |
| Cap' N. Hayden | Wells |
| Col. J. Wells | |
| Cap' A. Loomis | Wells |
| Cap' R. Abbee | " |
| Cap' J. Cooke | " |
| Cap' Abel Brace | Hutchins |
| Cap' C. Churchill | Wells |
| Cap' Gansey | B. Richards |
| Col. B. Richards | |
| Cap' A. Pettibone | Hutchins |
| Ens" H. Hines | B. Richards |
| Cap' W. Coggswell | Moseleys |
| Cap' A. Griswold | |
| Cap' J. Brian | Russells |

[*Comptroller's Office, Haskell's Receipts.*]

# MILITIA REGIMENTS, 1781.

## FOURTH REGIMENT—LIEUT.-COL. COMD. DIMON.

### ADJ. JUDSON'S COMPANY.

A Pay Abstract for a Guard Ordered from the 4 Reg$^t$ in Connecticut for the purpose of Colecting all the Delinctuants within 8$^d$ Reg$^t$ and ware Commanded By Nathaniel Judson Adgt of 8$^d$ Reg$^t$ who was apointed August the 24$^{th}$ 1781 to take Command of 8$^d$ guard which Service continued By turns until Nov. 28$^{th}$ 1781

| Mens Names | Number of Days in Service | Mens Names | Number of Days in Service |
|---|---|---|---|
| Nath$^{ll}$ Judson Adj | 34 | Philow Hird | 3 |
| Edmund Pulford Srgt | 19 | Othenial French | 9 |
| Edmund Curtiss Srgt | 14 | Beach Lewis Junr | 12 |
| Isaac Beach | 17 | James Duning | 14 |
| Selah Burrouss | 16 | Joel Gilbert | 3 |
| James Bardslay | 9 | Lemuel Judson | 11 |
| Eph$^m$ B. Hubbert | 9 | Nathan Thompson | 4 |
| Nath$^{ll}$ Sherman | 8 | Sam$^l$ F Mills | 3 |
| Sirus Hawley | 9 | | |

[*State Library, Revolution 25.*]

# EIGHTH REGIMENT — COL. SMITH.

[*See Record of Connecticut Men in the Revolution, page 577.*]

## CAPT. MORGAN'S COMPANY.

A Pay abstract of Cap$^t$ John Morgan's Company in Col. Oliver Smith's Reg$^t$ who Marched upon Alarm on the 6$^{th}$ Day of Sep. 1781. [Invasion of New London.]

| Mens Names | Days in service | Mens Names | Days in service |
|---|---|---|---|
| John Morgan Capt. | 8 | Ralph Williams | 2 |
| W$^m$ Williams Lt. | 8 | Nathan Avery | 3 |
| Chris$^r$ Morgan Ens. | 8 | Stephen Morgan | 3 |
| Benadam Gallup Sarj. | 8 | David Annew | 8 |
| Tho$^s$ Morgan Sarj. | 8 | Amos Brown | 3 |
| Amos Allyn Sarj. | 8 | Jabez Perkins | 3 |
| Phineus Fanning Sarj. | 8 | Simeon Barnes | 3 |
| Jesse Gallup Clerk | 8 | Seth Williams | 3 |
| Ephraim Allyn Corp. | 8 | Simeon Brown | 3 |
| W$^m$ Brown Corp. | 8 | Joseph Thomson | 3 |
| Isaac Morgan Corp | 8 | Elisha Brown | 3 |
| Daniel Nickerson | 3 | Silas Lamb Jr. | 3 |
| W$^m$ Heath | 8 | Jacob Perkins | 3 |
| Abel Newton | 8 | Joshua Elderkin | 3 |
| Isaac Williams | 8 | Benj$^n$ Gray | 8 |
| Jedediah Morgan | 8 | Rufus Williams | 3 |
| Sam$^l$ Williams 4 | 8 | Benj$^n$ Stedman | 2 |
| Nathan$^l$ Brown Jr. | 8 | John Dixson Jr | 2 |
| Stephen Park | 8 | Nehemiah Barnes | 1 |
| Joseph Williams | 8 | Ezekiel Brown | 2 |
| W$^m$ Morgan | 8 | Robert Dixson | 2 |
| David Allyn | 8 | Elkanah Hewit | 2 |
| Henry Gallup Jr. | 8 | | |

[*State Library, Revolution 25.*]

# MILITIA REGIMENTS, 1782.

## CAPT. MARVIN'S COMPANY.

A Pay abstract of Cap' Ozias Marvins Company of Coast guard Ordered To Be Raised by the town of Norwalk for the Defence of S^d Town in Feb^r 18^th 1782

| Mens Names | | Time when Entered service | Time when discharged |
|---|---|---|---|
| Ozias Marvin Cap. | | Feb. 18 | Aug. 1 |
| John Byxbe Ens. | | " | " |
| Thomas Hyatt Sarj. | | 19 | " |
| Sam^l Hyatt " | | " | " |
| Nathan Fillow " | | 20 | " |
| Daniel Eversley " | | Mar. 3 | " |
| Elijah Fitch | Corp. | 1 | " |
| Nathaniel Benedict " | | Apr. 1 | " |
| Jacob Jinnings " | | Mar. 8 | June 20 |
| Sam^l Seymour " | | 1 | Aug. 1 |
| Will^m Bouton Private | | 9 | " |
| Daniel Seymour | | 19 | " |
| Joseph Waring | | Feb. 20 | " |
| James Waring | | " | " |
| Ozias Marvin Jr | | 19 | " |
| Stephen Hyatt | | 20 | " |
| Stephen Marvin | | " | June 20 |
| Mathew Hanford | | " | " |
| Thomas Penneoyr | | " | " |
| Azor Fillow | | " | |
| Peter Tuttle | | " | Apr 21 |
| John Rull | | May 5 | Aug. 1 |
| James Jelloff | | Feb. 20 | May 15 |
| Jesse Taylor | | " | Apr. 25 |
| Stephen Fillow | | May 12 | June 20 |
| Will^m Fitch | | Feb. 21 | " |
| Levi Taylor | | " | Aug. 1 |
| Noah Nash | | " | " |
| Edmond Tuttle | | " | June 20 |
| Josiah Gregory | | Apr. 3 | " |
| Isaac Fillow | | Mar. 4 | Aug. 1 |
| Huttun Smith | | " | " |
| Will^m Mott | | " | " |
| David Comstock | | " | " |
| Isaac Hyatt | | " | " |

REVOLUTION ROLLS AND LISTS.

| Mens Names | Time when Entered service | Time when discharged |
|---|---|---|
| Enoch Benedict | Mar. 4 | Aug. 1 |
| James Fitch | " | " |
| Will<sup>m</sup> Smith | " | " |
| John Eversley | " | June 20 |
| James Hoyt | " 12 | " |
| John Betts Jr. | " | " |
| Levi Sherwood | " 18 | " |
| Jesse Bennidict | " | " |
| Hopkins Byxbee | Feb. 20 | Aug. 1 |
| Elijah Jones | " | " |
| Sam<sup>l</sup> Bowton | " | " |
| Enoch Wareing | " | " |
| John Byxbee | " | June 20 |
| Daniel Hoyt | " | " |
| Sam<sup>l</sup> Brown | " | " |
| Stephen Bowton | " | " |
| Jesse Waring | " | " |
| John Kellogg | Mar. 1 | Aug. 1 |
| Wolcut Downs | " | " |
| Isaac Raymond | " | " |
| Will<sup>m</sup> Salmas | 5 | " |
| Job Hoyt | 1 | " |
| John Raymond | " | " |
| Ira Bowton | 6 | " |
| Walter Hoyt | 5 | " |
| Peter Quinturd Jr | 22 | " |
| Jonathan Hoyt | 21 | " |
| Nath<sup>l</sup> Raymond Jr | 9 | June 20 |
| Stephen Wood | " | " |
| Eleazor Bedient | 1 | " |
| Stephen Picket | 10 | " |
| Ezra Picket | " | " |
| David Seymour | 1 | Aug. 1 |
| Calub Curtis | " | " |
| Ruben Olmsted | " | " |
| Mordica Bedient | 3 | " |
| David Bennet | 1 | June 20 |
| Jiles Fitch | " | " |
| Sam<sup>l</sup> Gregory | 3 | " |
| Jeremiah Will<sup>ms</sup> | 5 | " |
| Abraham Hurlbat | " | " |
| John Seymour | Apr. 1 | " |
| Uriah Raymond | " | " |
| Nathaniel Raymond | " | " |
| Nathan Benedict | " | Aug. 1 |
| John Seymour Jr | " | " |
| James Seymour | " | " |
| Hezekiah Raymond | " | " |
| Hezekiha Sillik | Apr. 3 | June 20 |
| Charles Sillick | " | " |
| Evert Quintard | " | " |
| Mathew Betts | 6 | " |
| Lemuel Brooks | 1 | Aug. 1 |

[*State Library, Revolution 32.*]

# MILITIA REGIMENTS.

## FOURTH REGIMENT.

### CAPT. BOOTH'S COMPANY.

A Ration Roll of Cap¹ Ja⁸ Booths C⁰ of guards which were detached from the 4ᵗʰ Reg¹ of Militia for that purpose pursuant to order from G. S. Silliman Brig' Gen¹.

| Names | N° of Days in Service | Names | N° of Days in Service |
|---|---|---|---|
| Ja⁸ Booth Cap¹ | 15 | John Sherman | 18 |
| Sam¹ Patterson Lieut | 18 | Lewis Curtiss | 15 |
| Judson Burton Ensⁿ | 15 | Nathⁿ Osborn | 18 |
| David Thompson Serg¹ | 15 | Ja⁸ Coe | 18 |
| Elihew Curtiss " | 15 | Abner Beers | 15 |
| Stephen Beers " | 15 | Benjᵃ Wells | 15 |
| John Peck " | 18 | Isaac Curtiss | 18 |
| Abijah Booth Corp¹ | 18 | Ja⁸ Sherman | 15 |
| Josiah Peck " | 15 | Judson Peck | 15 |
| David Curtiss " | 15 | Ebenez' Curtis | 18 |
| Aaron Judson | 18 | Ja⁸ Deforest | 15 |
| Wᵐ Tomlinson Fifer | 8 | John Beardslee | 15 |
| Joel Judson | 15 | Ja⁸ Judson | 18 |
| Ephᵐ Wilcockson | 15 | Wᵐ Hilliard | 15 |
| Thoˢ Stratton | 18 | George Lewis | 15 |
| Wᵐ Southworth | 18 | Benjⁿ Gorham | 15 |
| Edmund Curtiss | 10 | John Wells | 18 |
| Sam¹ Burnet | 18 | Abner Elgur | 15 |
| Rob¹ Curtiss | 15 | Jeremʰ Curtiss | 18 |
| John Booth | 15 | Sam¹ Ward | 18 |
| Elihew Judson | 15 | Ebenez' Hubbil | 18 |
| Abner Curtiss | 15 | Josiah Walker | 15 |
| Elnathⁿ Wheeler | 15 | David Barlow | 18 |
| John McGraw | 18 | Ephᵐ Burton | 15 |
| Nathⁿ Beardslee | 18 | Josiah Beers | 10 |
| Sam¹ Osborn | 18 | John E. Olcott | 10 |
| Andrew Curtiss | 15 | John Wayland | 10 |
| Dan¹ Curtiss | 18 | Henry Beardslee | 10 |
| Wᵐ Judson | 18 | Henry Curtis | 10 |
| Jonᵉ Tongue | 15 | John Whiting | 18 |
| Jabez Curtiss | 18 | Joˢ Frost | 15 |

[*Copy in Comptroller's Office.*]

## VARIOUS REGIMENTS.

[The dates in the following lists are the dates when the bills were rendered, and do not necessarily show the time of service.]

### HARTFORD GAOL GUARD.

The United States D$^r$ To the State of Connecticut, for services &c of Militia, guarding Prisoners in Hartford Goal &c & Continental Stores in sundry Places &c. Viz:—

| Date | | Bills & Accounts | Remarks |
|---|---|---|---|
| 1778 | Aug$^t$ 14 | Ens$^n$ B. Hudson | Guard$^s$ Hartford Goal |
| | Dec 5 | " | " |
| 1779 | Feb$^ry$ 12 | " | " |
| | Aug$^t$ 11 | " | " |
| | " | Ens$^n$ W$^m$ Barnard | " |
| | Dec$^r$ 14 | " | " |
| 1780 | April 3 | " | " |
| | June 12 | Ens$^n$ W$^m$ Barnard | " |
| | Aug$^t$ 30 | " | " |
| 1781 | Feb$^ry$ 5 | " | " |
| | Nov$^r$ 17 | Ens$^n$ W$^m$ Barnard | " |
| 1782 | May 3 | " | " |
| 1784 | July 26 | " | " |
| 1779 | July 9 | Serg$^t$ E. Denslow | Guard$^s$ Hospital Stores |
| | Aug$^t$ 16 | Ens$^n$ Dan$^l$ Haydon | " |
| | Sep$^t$ 24 | Cap$^t$ John Lewis | Guard$^s$ Stores in Waterbury |
| 1780 | April 5 | Serg$^t$ E. Stoughton | Guard$^s$ Hospital Stores |
| | Sep$^t$ 15 | William Emmons | Guard$^s$ Military Stores |
| 1781 | Jan$^ry$ 1 | Serg$^t$ Levi Clark | |
| | 31 | L$^t$ H. Dwight | Guard$^s$ Prisoners |
| | March 10 | Ens$^n$ Sam$^l$ Hugins | " |
| | April 17 | Serg$^t$ E. Stoughton | Guard$^s$ Hospital Stores |
| | May 19 | Serg$^t$ Josiah Smith | Guard$^s$ Prisoners |
| 1782 | March 14 | L$^t$ Sam$^l$ Lattimer | " |
| 1781 | Nov$^r$ 16 | Moses Willson | Guard$^s$ Hospital Stores |
| | Dec$^r$ 1 | John Johnson | Guard$^s$ Prisoners |
| | 29 | Serg$^t$ Job Cooke | " Powder |
| 1783 | Feb$^ry$ 11 | Moses Willson | " Hospital Stores |
| | May 19 | Cap$^t$ Hamlin Dwight | " Prisoners |
| | 30 | Simeon Huntington | " Naval Prisoners |

[*Comptroller's Office, Haskell's Receipts.*]

### SERVICE AT THE NORTHWARD.

The United States D$^r$ To the State of Connecticut for sundry Expenditures for Bounties, extra Allowances, Wages &c of Troops from said State who served at the Northward. Viz:—

| Date | | Bills & Acc$^ts$ | Remarks |
|---|---|---|---|
| 1777 | Dec$^r$ 24 | Cap$^t$ Jona. Calkins | Col. J Lattimers Reg$^t$ |
| | " | Cap$^t$ Amos Jones &c | " |

## MILITIA REGIMENTS. 221

| Date | | | Bills & Acct[s] | Remarks |
|---|---|---|---|---|
| 1778 | Jan[ry] | 24 | Cap[t] Tarbal Whitney | Col. T Cooks |
| | | 30 | Cap[t] Elip[t] Curtis | Bennington Alarm |
| | Feb[ry] | 5 | Cap[t] Ichab[d] Norton | Gen[l] Wolcotts Brigade |
| | | 17 | Cap[t] John Allen | Col. N. Hookers |
| | | " | Cap[t] James Stoddard | " |
| | | 18 | Col. Seth Smith | |
| | | 27 | Cap[t] Edw[d] Shipman | Col. T. Cooks Reg[t] |
| | | 28 | " | " |
| | March | 5 | Samuel Hays | Bennington Alarm |
| | | 12 | Joel Hays | " |
| | | 19 | Cap[t] Benj. Hutchins | " |
| | | 23 | Col. N. Hooker | " |
| | April | 7 | Cap[t] Asahel Holcomb | " |
| | | 11 | Cap[t] Giddings | " |
| | | 16 | Cap[t] Adon[b] Burr | " |
| | | 28 | Cap[t] Asa Bray | " |
| | | 30 | L[t] Elijah Case | " |
| | | " | Ens[n] Sam[l] Benning | " |
| | May | 16 | Col. Epa[s] Sheldon | Under Gen[l] Gates |
| | | 29 | Cap[t] Joseph Forward | Bennington Alarm |
| | | 30 | Cap[t] Tho[s] Bidwell | " |
| | June | 9 | Cap[t] Moses Seymour | Gen[l] Wolcotts Brigade |
| | | 25 | Cap[t] Ich[d] Norton | " |
| | July | 9 | Maj[r] Thomas Bull | Sundry Acct[s] |
| | Aug[t] | 12 | Cap[t] Nathan Smith | Col. T. Cooks Reg[t] |
| | Sep[t] | 7 | Charles Kellogg P. M. | Col. J. Lattimers |
| | Oct[r] | 15 | L[t] Samuel Hart | Col. T. Cooks |
| 1779 | Jan[ry] | 12 | Jonah Scofield | Col. J. Lattimers |
| | | 22 | Stephen Scott | Woosters '75 |
| | | 29 | Col. Joshua Porter | Gen[l] Wolcotts Brigade |
| | May | 20 | Derias Spalding | Col. J. Lattimers '77 |
| 1778 | Mar. | 23 | Cap[t] Asa Bray | Gen[l] O. Wolcotts Brigade |
| 1781 | June | 20 | Col[o] Samuel Mott | " |
| 1783 | Mar | 25 | David Trumbull | " |
| 1785 | Dec | 17 | Noah Phelps | |
| 1787 | Nov. | 5 | Lieut. Stephen Goodrich | Col[o] T Cooks Reg[t] |
| " | Sep[t] | 24 | Edward Mott | |

[*Comptroller's Office, Haskell's Receipts.*]

## SERVICE IN RHODE ISLAND.

The United States D[r] to the State of Connecticut for sundry Expenditures for Bounties, Extra Allowances, Wages &c of Militia from said State, who served in the State of Rhode Island. Viz:—

| Date | | | Bills & Acct[s] | Remarks |
|---|---|---|---|---|
| 1789 | Jan[y] | 21 | Col. Sam[l] M[c]Clellan | his Reg[t] in 1777 |
| | Feb[y] | 25 | Col John Ely | " |
| | Ap[l] | 6 | L[t] Daniel Dee | |
| | Dec[r] | 17 | Cap[t] Moses Stevens | Col. Oliver Smiths Reg[t] |
| | | " | Cap[t] Timo[y] Percival | " |
| | | " | Cap[t] Richard Pitkin | " |
| | | 31 | Cap[t] David Miller | " |
| 1779 | Jan[y] | 7 | Cap[t] Joseph Cutler | " |
| | | " | Cap[t] John Arnold | " |
| | | 26 | Col. W[m] Worthington | his Reg[t] |
| | April | 9 | Col. Oba[h] Johnson | " |

| Date | | | Bills & Accts | Remarks |
|---|---|---|---|---|
| 1779 | June | 5 | Cap$^t$ J. Chamberlain | his C$^o$ Drogoons |
| | Aug$^t$ | 24 | Cap$^t$ J. Churchill | Worthingtons Reg$^t$ |
| | Sept$^r$ | 29 | Col. Sam$^l$ Chapman | his Reg$^t$ |
| 1780 | Jan$^ry$ | 25 | Cap$^t$ Elias Graves | Col. Tylers |
| 1781 | Jan$^y$ | 4 | Cap$^t$ Dan$^l$ Tyler | Matross C$^o$ |
| | March | 16 | Cap$^t$ W$^m$ Whitney | Col. Smiths Reg$^t$ |
| | May | 22 | | " |
| | | 31 | Cap$^t$ Caleb Hendee | Col. E. Storrs |
| | June | 26 | Col. James Gordon | |
| | | 27 | L$^t$ Elias Palmer | Col. O. Smith |
| | | 4 | Cap$^t$ Sam$^l$ Thomson | Col. E. Storrs |
| | Aug$^t$ | 29 | Cap$^t$ Peter Keith | Col. J. Gordons |
| | Sept$^r$ | 20 | Cap$^t$ Timo$^y$ Backus | Volunteers |
| | | 24 | Cap$^t$ Amos Woodward | Col. J. Gordons |
| | Oct$^r$ | 14 | Cap$^t$ Abner Adams | Col. S. M$^c$Clellans |
| | Nov$^r$ | 8 | Cap$^t$ Titus Bailey | Col J. Gordons |

[*Comptroller's Office, Haskell's Receipts.*]

## SERVICE AT PEEKSKILL.

The United States D$^r$ To the State of Connecticut for sundry Expenditures for Bounties, extra Allowances, Wages &c of Militia from said State who served with the Main Army at and near Peekskill in the State of New York — Viz :

| Dates | | | Bills & Accounts | Remarks |
|---|---|---|---|---|
| 1777 | Sep$^t$ | 10 | John Robbins | |
| | | 17 | David Little | |
| | | 29 | Cap$^t$ Miles Johnson | Col. Noadiah Hookers Reg$^t$ |
| | Oct | 24 | Cap$^t$ Amasa Loomis | Col. Nath$^l$ Terrys Regt |
| | Nov$^r$ | 1 | Col. John Chester | |
| | | 5 | Wethersfield S. Men | |
| | | " | Cap$^t$ Oliver Stanley | |
| | | 12 | S$^t$ John Cook | |
| | | 18 | Glassenbury S. Men | |
| | | 25 | Maj$^r$ Gad Stanly | { Field & Staff, Cap$^t$ Nortons & Slopers C$^o$ |
| | | 26 | Cap$^t$ Peter Vial | |
| | Dec$^r$ | 3 | Cap$^t$ John Allen | |
| | | " | James Stoddard | |
| | | 5 | Cap$^t$ Josiah Converse | Col. Hez$^h$ Wyllys Reg$^t$ |
| | | 8 | John Hurlbutt Q. M. | " |
| | | 9 | Col. Hez$^h$ Wyllys | " |
| | | 10 | Cap$^t$ Benj. Allyn | |
| 1778 | Jan$^ry$ | 8 | Hanley Bushnel | |
| | | 9 | Cap$^t$ Giles Pettibone | |
| | | 20 | Cap$^t$ Eliz. Hubbard | Col. Thomas Beldings Reg$^t$ |
| | | 22 | Col. Joseph Thomson | 2$^d$ Regiment |
| | | 29 | Cap$^t$ Oliver Stanley | Sundry Acc$^t$ |
| | | 30 | Cap$^t$ Ab$^m$ Fuller | Col. Increase Moselys Reg$^t$ |
| | | " | Col. Samuel Whiting | |
| | | " | Cap$^t$ Elisha Hall | |
| | Feb$^ry$ | 3$^d$ | Col. Hez$^h$ Wyllys | 1$^{st}$ Reg$^t$ |
| | | 4 | Col. Tho$^s$ Belding | |
| | | 26 | Cap$^t$ Dan Collins | |
| | | " | L$^t$ Jabez Hamlin | Col. Increase Moselys Reg$^t$ |
| | | 27 | Col. Hez$^h$ Wyllys | 1$^{st}$ Reg$^t$ |

## MILITIA REGIMENTS.

| Dates | | Bills & Accounts | Remarks |
|---|---|---|---|
| 1778 Feb'y | 28 | Col. Noadiah Hooker | |
| March | 4 | Cap' Noah Webster | Col. Nath' Terrys Reg' |
|  |  | L' John Hough | Col. Jona. Baldwins |
|  | 5 | Col. Baz<sup>a</sup> Ives | " |
|  | 6 | Col. Nath' Terry | |
|  | 19 | Cap' Judah Woodruff | 15<sup>th</sup> Reg' |
| April | 3 | Maj<sup>r</sup> Ab<sup>m</sup> Tyler | |
|  | 6 | Col. W<sup>m</sup> Worthington | 7<sup>th</sup> Reg' |
|  | 9 | Cap' Thom<sup>s</sup> Fenn | 16<sup>th</sup> " |
|  |  | L' Thomas Dutton | " |
|  | 10 | Cap' Jonathan Bull | Governors guard |
|  | 17 | Cap' Timo<sup>y</sup> Gaylor | |
|  | 24 | Ens<sup>n</sup> Lucius Tuttle | Col. Jona. Baldwins Reg' |
|  | " | Cap' Nath' Bunnel | " |
|  | " | Cap' Eph<sup>m</sup> Cook | " |
|  | " | Cap' Jesse Moss | " |
|  | " | Cap' Ambrose Hine | " |
|  | " | Maj<sup>r</sup> W<sup>m</sup> Hart | His L' Dragoons |
|  | 28 | Col. Sylvanus Graves | |
| May | 19 | Cap' Jared Shepard | Col. Beldens Reg' |
|  | 21 | L' James Arnold | 7<sup>th</sup> Reg' |
|  | 22 | Col. J. P. Cook | his Reg' Oct. 1777 |
|  | " | " | " Aug<sup>t</sup> |
|  | " | " | " " |
|  | 27 | Col. Charles Burrell | " |
|  | 29 | L' Thomas Dutton | Col. J. Baldwins Reg' |
| June | 1 | L' Hanford | Col. J. Meads |
|  | 2 | Col. Increase Moseley | his Reg' Oct. 1777 |
|  | " | " | " Danbury Al<sup>m</sup> '77 |
|  | 5 | Maj<sup>r</sup> Judah Woodruff | his Reg' |
|  | " | Ens<sup>n</sup> Lem' Hotchkiss | " |
|  | " | Cap' Nath' Wales | Wards |
|  | 10 | Cap' Paul Yates | Col. Increase Moseleys Reg' |
|  | 20 | L' Woodruff & Cornet Griswold | } Maj<sup>r</sup> Harts Reg' L' Dragoons |
| July | 6 | Charles Kellogg P. M. | 10<sup>th</sup> Reg' |
|  | 22 | Cap' Sam' Camp | " |
| Aug' | 10 | Col. Roger Newberry | his Reg' |
|  | 26 | Cap' Charles Norton | Col. Jona. Baldwins |
|  | " | Cap' James Robinson | " |
|  | 27 | Charles Kellogg P. M. | 18<sup>th</sup> Reg' |
|  | 28 | " | Col. J. Cooks Reg' |
| Sept<sup>r</sup> | 3 | Maj<sup>r</sup> Tho<sup>s</sup> Bull | his Reg' L' Dragoons |
|  | " | " | " |
|  | 5 | Charles Kellogg P. M. | Col. Comfort Sages Reg' |
|  | 7 | " | Col. Roger Newburys |
|  | 9 | " | Cap' Strongs C<sup>o</sup> |
|  | " | " | Col. John Humphrys Reg' |
|  | " | " | Maj<sup>r</sup> Jabez Hills |
|  | 11 | Serj' Joseph Brace | |
|  | 17 | Cap' Josiah King | Col. Roger Newburys Reg' |
|  | 19 | Cap' Nathan Chapman | Col. Increase Moseleys Reg' |
|  | 28 | Cap' Dav<sup>d</sup> Leavensworth | |
| Nov<sup>r</sup> | 4 | Gen' James Wadsworth | Sundry Bills |
|  | " | Cap' Phin<sup>s</sup> Castle | |
|  | 5 | L' Elijah Cook | Col. Roger Newburys Reg' |
|  | 6 | Nathan Sloson | |
|  | 12 | Cap' Adon<sup>h</sup> Burr | Col. Increase Moseleys Reg' |

| Dates | | Bills & Accounts | Remarks |
|---|---|---|---|
| 1778 Nov<sup>r</sup> | 24 | Col. Comfort Sage | his Reg<sup>t</sup> Supernum<sup>y</sup> |
| " | " | " | " |
| Dec<sup>r</sup> | 22 | Cap<sup>t</sup> Jesse Curtis | Col. Jona. Baldwins Reg<sup>t</sup> |
| | " | " | |
| | | Cap<sup>t</sup> Jotham Curtis | " |
| | | Cap<sup>t</sup> Stephen Seymour | " |
| 1779 Jan<sup>ry</sup> | 9 | Charles Kellogg P. M. | |
| | | " | Col. Increase Moseleys |
| | 21 | Cap<sup>t</sup> Zach. Case | Col. Tho<sup>s</sup> Beldens Reg<sup>t</sup> |
| | | Col. Comfort Sage | his Reg<sup>t</sup> |
| | | Cap<sup>t</sup> Josiah Converse | Col. N. Terrys |
| | 22 | Amos Ives | Col. Baldwins |
| | 29 | Col. Increase Moseley | 13<sup>th</sup> Reg<sup>t</sup> |
| | | " | " |
| Feb<sup>ry</sup> | 2 | Samuel Bishop | |
| | | Cap<sup>t</sup> Aaron Foot | Col. N. Hookers Reg<sup>t</sup> |
| | 4 | Cap<sup>t</sup> Miles Johnson | Col. J. Baldwins |
| | 23 | Cap<sup>t</sup> Oliver Stanley | |
| | 26 | L<sup>t</sup> Eaton Jones | 17<sup>th</sup> Reg<sup>t</sup> |
| March | 10 | Cap<sup>t</sup> Elijah Hinman | 13<sup>th</sup> Reg<sup>t</sup> |
| | | Cap<sup>t</sup> Eben<sup>r</sup> Smith | " |
| | | L<sup>t</sup> Asa Hinman | " |
| | | Cap<sup>t</sup> David Hinman | " |
| | | Ens<sup>n</sup> Joseph Sanford | " |
| | | Cap<sup>t</sup> Caleb Mix | " |
| April | 3 | Cap<sup>t</sup> Asa Bray | Col. Hookers Reg<sup>t</sup> |
| | | Cap<sup>t</sup> J. Norton | |
| | 13 | Cap<sup>t</sup> Joseph Viall | 17<sup>th</sup> Reg<sup>t</sup> |
| | | Cap<sup>t</sup> John Osborn | " |
| | | Cap<sup>t</sup> Amos Barns | " |
| | 14 | Cap<sup>t</sup> James Stoddard | Col. Increase Moseleys |
| May | 18 | Cap<sup>t</sup> W<sup>m</sup> Cogswell | " |
| | | Col. Comfort Sage | his Reg<sup>t</sup> |
| | 21 | Cap<sup>t</sup> Eben<sup>r</sup> Couch | Col. Increase Moseleys |
| | 22 | Cap<sup>t</sup> W<sup>m</sup> G. Hubbel | 16<sup>th</sup> Reg<sup>t</sup> |
| June | 3 | Cap<sup>t</sup> Job Case | Guarding Cannon |
| April | 9 | " | " |
| June | 3 | " | " |
| | 4 | Cap<sup>t</sup> Isaac Bronson | Col. J. Baldwins Reg<sup>t</sup> |
| | 10 | Cap<sup>t</sup> Judah Woodruff | 15<sup>th</sup> Reg<sup>t</sup> |
| | 30<sup>th</sup> | Cap<sup>t</sup> Nathan Hine | 18<sup>th</sup> " |
| | | Cap<sup>t</sup> D. Leavensworth | Col. S. Whitings |
| | | Cap<sup>t</sup> Nathan Hine | 13<sup>th</sup> Reg<sup>t</sup> |
| July | 31 | Cap<sup>t</sup> John Strong | 17<sup>th</sup> " |
| Aug<sup>t</sup> | 11 | Cap<sup>t</sup> Nathan Chapman | 18<sup>th</sup> " |
| | 24 | Cap<sup>t</sup> Nathan Hine | Col. S. Whitings Reg<sup>t</sup> |
| | | Cap<sup>t</sup> Abner Mallery | 13<sup>th</sup> |
| | 27 | Cap<sup>t</sup> Enos Hawley | " |
| | | | " |
| | | Col. Comfort Sage | his Reg<sup>t</sup> |
| | 31 | Cap<sup>t</sup> Peter Penfield | Col. J. F. Cooks Reg |
| | " | " | 16<sup>th</sup> |
| | " | Cap<sup>t</sup> David Olmstead | " |
| | " | Cap<sup>t</sup> James Clark | " |
| | " | Cap<sup>t</sup> Dan<sup>l</sup> Hickocks | " |
| | " | Cap<sup>t</sup> Rich<sup>d</sup> Shutes | " |
| | " | Cap<sup>t</sup> Rich<sup>d</sup> Smith | " |
| | " | Cap<sup>t</sup> Elijah Botsford | " |
| | " | Cap<sup>t</sup> A. Botsford | " |

## MILITIA REGIMENTS.

| Dates | | Bills & Accounts | Remarks |
|---|---|---|---|
| 1779 Aug‡ | 31 | Cap‡ W⁽ᵐ⁾ G. Hubbel | 16ᵗʰ |
| " | " | Ens⁽ⁿ⁾ Henry Whitney | " |
| " | " | Col. N. Beardsley | " |
| " | " | | " |
| Sept‡ | 1 | Cap‡ Jona. Farrand | 18ᵗʰ |
| " | " | Cap‡ Elijah Hazen | " |
| " | 10 | Cap‡ Benj. Stones | " |
| " | " | Cap‡ Joseph Carter | " |
| " | " | Cap‡ Eben‡ Couch | " |
| " | " | Cap‡ Noble Hine | " |
| " | " | L‡ Morgan Noble | " |
| " | " | Cap‡ Ab⁽ᵐ⁾ Fuller | " |
| " | 17 | Cap‡ Miles Beach | 17ᵗʰ |
| " | " | Cap‡ Reuben Stone | " |
| " | " | Cap‡ Jabez Wright | " |
| " | " | Col. Medad Hills | " |
| " | 21 | Col. Jona. Dimon | 4ᵗʰ |
| " | 22 | Cap‡ David Hinman | 18ᵗʰ |
| " | 23 | Maj‡ Elijah Abel | 4ᵗʰ |
| " | 24 | Cap‡ Abel Brace | 18ᵗʰ |
| Oct‡ | 1 | Cap‡ Jacob Hinsdale | 17ᵗʰ |
| " | 14 | Cap‡ Elijah Hinman | 18ᵗʰ |
| " | 15 | Cap‡ Timothy Stanley | Col. Hills Reg‡ |
| " | 16 | Cap‡ Adam Hurlbut | Col. Increase Moseleys Reg‡ |
| " | 20 | Ens‡ Sam‡ Carter | " |
| " | " | Cap‡ Peter Mills | " |
| " | 22 | Gen‡ O. Wolcott | |
| " | " | Col. Benj Richards | |
| " | 27 | Cap‡ John Strong | 17ᵗʰ Reg‡ |
| " | " | Corp‡ John Whiting | Guards Military Stores |
| " | 29 | Cap‡ Abel Botsford | Col. P. Beardsleys Reg‡ |
| " | " | Gen‡ James Wadsworth | |
| Nov‡ | 5 | Cap‡ Bethuel Treat | Col. Sam‡ Whiting |
| " | 9 | Cap‡ Eben‡ Smith | Col. Increase Moseleys Reg‡ |
| " | " | Cap‡ Jos. Sanford | " |
| " | 10 | Maj‡ Tho⁽ˢ⁾ Bull | |
| " | " | Cap‡ Augur Curtis | Maj‡ T. Bulls Reg‡ |
| Dec‡ | 7 | Col. Jona. Dimon | |
| " | 20 | Cap‡ Benj. Nichols | Co Jona. Dimon's Reg‡ |
| 1780 Jan‡⁽ʸ⁾ | 14 | Cap‡ Isaac Howe | Col. John Mead |
| Feb‡⁽ʸ⁾ | 8 | Col. Increase Moseley | his Reg‡ |
| March | 1 | Cap‡ Dan‡ Holbrook | Col. Tylers Reg‡ |
| " | 16 | Cap‡ Dan‡ Godfrey | Col. Sam‡ Whitings Reg‡ |
| " | 30 | Col. Thad‡ Cooke | his Reg‡ |
| May | 25 | Col. Sam‡ Whiting | |
| June | 6 | Cap‡ Noble Hine | Col. J. Moseleys Reg‡ |
| 1779 Jan‡⁽ʸ⁾ | 28 | Cap‡ John Tomlinson | 2ᵈ Reg‡ |
| " | " | Jona. Bartholemew | |
| 1781 March | 7 | Cap‡ Benj. Hutchins | 18ᵗʰ |
| May | 9 | Cap‡ Abner Malley | Col. J. Moseleys |
| June | 4 | Cap‡ Paul Yates | " |
| 1783 Aug‡ | 12 | L‡ Benj. Seeley | |
| Oct | 16 | Col. Benj. Richards | |
| 1784 May | 7 | Clark Roys | |
| 1785 Jan‡⁽ʸ⁾ | 11 | Cap‡ A. Barns | |
| 1782 June | 15 | Cap‡ E. Sumner | |
| 1787 June | 29 | Cap‡ J. Stoddard | Col. N. Hookers '77 |
| Aug‡ | 28 | Suntry Acct⁽ˢ⁾ | " '77 |

[*Comptroller's Office, Haskell's Receipts.*]

## SERVICE IN WEST CHESTER.

The United States D$^r$ To the State of Connecticut, for sundry Expenditures for Bounties, extra Allowances, Wages &c of Troops from said State who served with the Army in West Chester County in the State of New York. Viz:

| Dates | | | Bills & Acc$^t$ | Remarks |
|---|---|---|---|---|
| 1778 | May | 21 | Ens$^n$ Nath$^l$ Weed | Col. Roots Reg$^t$ |
| | | 29 | Cap$^t$ U. Raymond | Col. John Meads |
| | July | 1 | Cap$^t$ Silv. Knapp | " |
| | Nov$^r$ | 4 | Cap$^t$ Mills Hull | Col. S Graves |
| 1779 | Jan$^y$ | 16 | Cap$^t$ C. Churchill | 2$^d$ Reg$^t$ |
| | | 19 | Cap$^t$ Isaac Howe | Col. John Meads Reg$^t$ |
| | | 26 | Bouton J. Scofield | Maj$^r$ John Davenport |
| | | 28 | Cap$^t$ Uriah Raymond | Col. John Meads |
| | | " | Col. Stephen S$^t$ John | |
| | Feb$^y$ | 18 | Cap$^t$ John Smith | Col. Increase Moseleys |
| | March | 10 | Cap$^t$ Robert Martin | " |
| | April | 2 | Cap$^t$ Adam Hurlbut | Col. John Meads Reg$^t$ |
| | | 8 | Cap$^t$ Asa Bray | Col. Roger Enos's |
| | | 8 | Cap$^t$ Joseph Smith | Col John Meads |
| | | 14 | Cap$^t$ Ozias Marvin | " |
| | May | 22 | Cap$^t$ Adonijah Burr | Col. Increase Moseleys |
| | | 26 | Cap$^t$ Silvanus Knapp | Col. John Meads |
| | | 27 | Cap$^t$ John Ensign | Col. J. Moseleys |
| | | 28 | Cap$^t$ Caleb S$^t$ John | Maj$^r$ J. Hills Dragoons |
| | June | 3 | Cap$^t$ Nathan Gilbert | Col. John Meads |
| | | 7 | Cap$^t$ Knowles Sears | " |
| | Sep$^t$ | 1 | Cap$^t$ Clap Raymond | " |
| | | " | Cap$^t$ Ozias Marvin | " |
| | | 21 | Cap$^t$ John Gray | Col. Samuel Whitings |
| | | " | Cap$^t$ David Olmstead | Col. Jona. Dimon |
| | | " | Cap$^t$ Joseph Birdsey | " |
| | | " | Cap$^t$ David Wood | " |
| | | " | Cap$^t$ Comfort Hoyt | " |
| | Oct | 1 | L$^t$ N. Mead | Col. John Meads |
| | | 20 | Cap$^t$ Peter Mills | " |
| | Nov$^r$ | 3 | Cap$^t$ Silv$^s$ Marshall | Rangers |
| | | 13 | Cap$^t$ El$^m$ Smith | Col. John Meads |
| | | 16 | Cap$^t$ David Hitchcock | 10$^{th}$ Reg$^t$ |
| 1780 | May | 8 | Cap$^t$ Stiles Judson | Col John Meads |
| | | 22 | Cap$^t$ George Peck | " |
| 1778 | Jan$^y$ | 28 | Silvanus Mead | Rangers |
| 1779 | Ap$^l$ | 13 | Cap$^t$ Jona. Waring | Maj$^r$ J. Davenports |
| 1787 | Sep$^t$ | 13 | Cap$^t$ John Skinner | his Command |

[ *Comptroller's Office, Haskell's Receipts.* ]

## SERVICE IN NEW YORK.

The United States D$^r$ to the State of Connecticut for sundry expenditures for Bounties, extra Allowances, Wages &c of Troops from said State who served with the Main Army in New York and places Adjacent: Viz:

| Dates | | | Bills & Acct$^s$ | Remarks |
|---|---|---|---|---|
| 1777 | Sep$^t$ | 26 | Col. Jona. Fitch | his Reg$^t$ |
| | Oct | 24 | Cap$^t$ Isaac Hall | |

## MILITIA REGIMENTS.

| Dates | | Bills & Accts | Remarks |
|---|---|---|---|
| 1778 | Janry 10 | Col. Neheh Beardsley | |
| | Mar. 19 | Col. Roger Newbury | his Regt |
| | April 28 | Capt Saml Thomson | Col. E. Storrs |
| | May 22 | John Kellogg | Capt Tarboxs Co |
| | 25 | Lt Jona. Whiting | |
| | 29 | Lt Saml Abbott | |
| | June 4 | Capt Jona. Calkins | 3d Regt |
| | " | Capt John Morse | 10th |
| | 5 | Col. Jona. Pettibone | his Regt |
| | 6 | Col. Hoel Woodbridge | Lexington Alarm |
| | 24 | Col. Saml Whiting | Militia to Maroneck |
| | " | " | Enos Battalion |
| | " | Col. Increase Moseley | Bradleys & Webbs Pattalions 1776 |
| | Augt 22 | Col. Matthew Talcot | 28d |
| | 27 | Majr Simeon Strong | 15th |
| | Oct 23 | Eleazer Scripture | 22d |
| | Novr 6 | Col. Ebenr Gay | his Regt |
| 1779 | Apl 8 | Capt Asa Bray | Col. Thadds Cooks Regt |
| | 12 | Capt Seth Seymour | Col. John Meads |
| | 13 | Genl John Douglass | |
| 1777 | Novr 17 | Capt John Watson | Col. Thadds Cooks Regt |
| 1779 | May 4 | Capt Amah Wright | Col. Enos's |
| 1783 | Feby 7 | Capt J. Chamberlain | Volunteers |
| | 8 | Genl John Mead | his Regt |
| | 13 | Col. Saml Chapman | " |
| | May 20 | Col. Ebenr Williams | " |
| | 30 | Baza Beebe | |
| | " | Nehe. Lewis | |
| 1784 | June 2 | Lt Col. Dyer Throop | his Regt |
| | " | Col. O. Hosford | |
| | " | Majr John Ely | 3d Regt |
| 1785 | Janry 19 | Elijah Hide | his Dragoons |
| | Febry 25 | Jesse Root Esqr | Volunteers |
| | Decr 29 | Col. Benj. Hinman | his Regt |
| 1786 | Jany 24 | Col. Elizur Talcott | his Regt |
| 1787 | July 16 | Col. George Pitkin | " |
| | 30 | Capt James Robinson | Baldwins |
| | " | Capt J. Hickoxs | " |
| | Augt 24 | Col. Saml Coit | his Regt |
| | Sept 13 | Capt M. Kirtland | |

[*Comptroller's Office, Haskell's Receipts.*]

## SERVICE AT WESTMORELAND.

The United States, To the State of Connecticut Dr for sundry Expenditures for extra Allowances, Wages &c. of Militia who served at Westmoreland. Viz.—

| Date | | Bills & Accounts | Remarks |
|---|---|---|---|
| 1778 | Octr 21 | Capt Daniel Gore | Mila Westmoreland |
| | 31 | Col. Nathan Dennison | " |
| 1779 | May 22 | Capt Wm H. Smith | " |
| | " | Lt Daniel Gore | " |

[*Comptroller's Office, Haskell's Receipts.*]

## SUNDRY SOLDIERS.

Names of Sundry Soldiers whose Rect⁸ are on File 1778

| | |
|---|---|
| Josiah Brinsmade | date unknown |
| L' Phineas Grover | 1778 |
| Luther Jones | 1778 |
| Co¹ Roger Enos at Horseneck in | 1778 |
| Ezekiel Rood | 1778 |
| Jacob Meach | 1778 |
| Salmon Treat | 1778 |
| Jo⁸ Gladding | 1778 |
| Selah Griswold | 1778 |
| A Taylor | 1778 |
| Aaron D Wolf | 1778 |
| Seth Eddy | 1778 |
| Reuben Taylor | 1778 |
| Gershom Treat | 1778 |
| George Trumbull | 1778 |

[*Copy in Comptroller's Office.*]

# NAVAL RECORD.

[*See Record of Connecticut Men in the Revolution, page 605.*]

## BRIG "MINERVA"

### CAPT. HALL'S MEN.

1775 A Muster Roll and Pay Roll for the Brigantine Minerva Fitted out on the Acc$^t$ of the Colony of Connecticut By Order of his Hon$^r$ the Gov$^r$ and Com$^{tee}$ of Safety for the Defence of said Colony Viz$^t$

| Names of Officers and Men | Quality | When Inlisted | When Discharged or Deserted |
|---|---|---|---|
| Giles Hall | Captain | Aug. 2 | 1776 Jan. 26 |
| James Hopkins | 1$^{st}$ Lt. | Aug. 14 | Dec. 19 |
| Thompson Phillips | 2$^d$ Lt. | Sep. 14 | Dec. 19 |
| William Pluymert | Master | Aug. 22 | Dec. 17 |
| William Warner | 1$^{st}$ Mate | Aug. 24 | Dec. 26 |
| John Cotton | 2$^d$ Mate | Aug. 12 | Dec. 26 |
| Tho$^s$ Lamb | Clark | Sep. 4 | 1776 Jan. 26 |
| Andrew Johonnot | Stewart | Sep. 11 | 1776 Jan. 20 |
| Gregory Powers | Boaswain | Aug. 14 | Dec. 26 |
| Benj$^n$ Cranston | Gunner | Aug. 31 | Dec. 19 |
| William Miles | Gunners Mate | Aug. 15 | Dec. 19 |
| George Lewis | Carpenter | Sep. 10 | Nov. 5 |
| Richard Dickerson | Pilote | Sep. 16 | Dec. 25 |
| John Harris | Carpenters Mate | Aug. 15 | Dec. 26 |
| Jacob Gibson | Mariner | Aug. 14 | Nov. 25 |
| Will$^m$ Thomas | Marine | Aug. 15 | Nov. 9 |
| Tho$^s$ Dande | Mariner | Aug. 15 | Nov. 20 |
| William Warner | Cook | Aug. 16 | Dec. 16 |
| Jesse Higgins | Mariner | Aug. 17 | Oct. 17 |
| Jonathan Tinker | " | Aug. 17 | Nov. 10 |
| Jeremiah Branard | " | Aug. 22 | Dec. 25 |
| Giles Cone | " | Aug. 22 | Dec. 16 |
| John Russell | " | Aug. 24 | Dec. 16 |
| John Chipman | " | Aug. 22 | Dec. 23 |
| Aaron White | " | Aug. 27 | Dec. 19 |
| Jerediah Norton | " | Aug. 28 | Dec. 25 |

| Names of Officers and Men | Quality | When Inlisted | When Discharged or Deserted |
|---|---|---|---|
| George Pelton | Mariner | Sep. 4 | Oct. 24 |
| Joseph Burn | " | Sep. 12 | Dec. 19 |
| George Lucas | " | Sep. 15 | Dec. 19 |
| Sam¹ Johnson | " | Sep. 21 | Dec. 18 |
| Stephen Lee | " | Sep. 21 | Dec. 23 |
| James Griffin | " | Sep. 22 | Nov. 17 |
| Edward Tryon | " | Oct. 3 | Dec. 19 |
| Peter Granger | " | Oct. 3 | Dec. 19 |
| Dave Whittlecey | " | Oct. 7 | Dec. 19 |
| Giles Gill | " | Oct. 9 | Dec. 26 |
| Walter Spooner | " | Oct. 12 | Dec. 19 |
| Derny Butler | " | Aug. 26 | Sep. 26 |
| Zebediah Mix | Marine | Aug. 22 | Dec. 25 |
| Elisha Ward | " | Aug. 24 | Dec. 19 |
| Peter a Negro Man | " | Aug. 25 | Dec. 23 |
| Gift a Negro Man | " | Aug. 25 | Dec. 19 |
| John Theaf | " | Aug. 25 | Oct. 17 |
| William Casheen | " | Aug. 25 | Nov. 18 |
| Richard Hunt | " | Aug. 25 | Nov. 10 |
| Phillip Mahan | " | Aug. 26 | Oct. 15 |
| Ebenz' Savage | " | Aug. 27 | Dec. 19 |
| Philip Aspell | " | Aug. 27 | Dec. 16 |
| James McDavid | " | Aug. 30 | Dec. 18 |
| Edward Griswold | " | Aug. 31 | Nov. 19 |
| James Johnson | " | Aug. 31 | Oct. 25 |
| George Stow | " | Sep. 5 | Dec. 19 |
| Stephen Jordan | " | Sep. 5 | Dec. 23 |
| Joseph Graum | " | Sep. 5 | Dec. 23 |
| Sam¹ Torry | " | Sep. 6 | Dec. 19 |
| John Wright | " | Sep. 11 | Nov. 18 |
| John Coult | " | Sep. 18 | Dec. 23 |
| Jacob Hail | " | Sep. 12 | Nov. 5 |
| John Elderkin | " | Oct. 3 | Dec. 19 |
| John Allen | " | Oct. 3 | Dec. 19 |
| James Fisher | " | Oct. 11 | Nov. 11 |
| John Lucas | Boaswains Mate | Aug. 24 | Suspended Nov. 8 |
| David Hall | Mariner | Sep. 12 | Suspended Nov. 8 |
| James Johnson | " | Aug. 21 | Ran away Oct. 14 |
| Rouben Bailey | " | Aug. 26 | Ran away Dec. 5 |
| Timothy Bailey | " | Aug. 26 | Ran away Dec. 5 |
| Peter Gantly | Marine | Aug. 26 | Ran away Sep. 10 |
| George Spencer | " | Aug. 29 | Ran away Dec. 5 |
| Nath¹ Witmore | " | Aug. 30 | Ran away Oct. 15 |
| Philemon Roberts | " | Aug. 30 | Ran away Oct. 15 |
| John Nickolas | " | Sep. 5 | Ran away Dec. 6 |
| Moses Pelton | " | Sep. 12 | Ran away Dec. 6 |

Capt Gills Halls Pay Roll of the Brig Minerva January 25th 1776.

[*State Library, Revolution 9.*]

## BRIG "DEFENCE".

[See *Record of Connecticut Men in the Revolution*, page 593.]

### CAPT. HARDING'S MEN.

A Pay List of Cap Harding' men belonging to the Brigg Defence Colony Service

| Time of Entry | Mens Names | Rank | Time of payment |
|---|---|---|---|
| 1776 | | | |
| May 24 | Nathan Tupper | Marene | July 24 |
| June 15 | James Young | Seam | Nov. 15 |
| Mar. 13 | Benj<sup>a</sup> Gold | Boy | " |
| " | W<sup>m</sup> Burnett | " | " |
| " | Eleazer Buckly | " | " |
| " | Francis Swords | " | " |
| " | Seth Bur | " | " |
| July 1 | Anthony Manuel | Seam | " |
| May 29 | W<sup>m</sup> Hooks | " | " |
| " | Jn<sup>o</sup> Mitts | " | " |
| " | Jon<sup>a</sup> Alden | Sailm | " |
| " | Vallintine Skiff | Seam | " |
| Aug. 9 | Tho<sup>s</sup> Menter | " | " |
| 18 | W<sup>m</sup> Murry | " | " |
| Nov. 8 | Josiah Willey | " | " |
| " | Jn<sup>o</sup> Holms | " | " |
| 10 | James Alden | " | " |
| Aug. 20 | Prosper Brown | Q<sup>r</sup> mas<sup>tr</sup> | " |
| " | Sam<sup>n</sup> Balden | Seam | " |
| " | Robert Fowler | " | " |
| " | Christopher Lewis | " | " |
| " | Jn<sup>o</sup> Davis | " | " |
| " | W<sup>m</sup> Shelden | " | " |
| " | Abbe Spicer | " | " |
| 28 | Pelatiah Peas | " | " |
| " | Stephen Peas | " | " |
| July 1 | Tho<sup>s</sup> Morris | " | " |
| Aug. 20 | John Bond | " | " |
| " | Lebbeus Quy | " | " |
| May 29 | Moses Cam | " | " |
| Aug. 20 | James Davis | " | " |
| " | Turner Harding | | " |
| 28 | West Daggett | Boy | " |
| 20 | Jn<sup>o</sup> Kazer | Seam | " |
| " | Benj<sup>a</sup> Rockwell | " | " |
| May 18 | Tho<sup>s</sup> Crandal | " | Aug. 15 |

[State Library, Revolution 9.]

A Pay List of Capt Harding's Men Belonging to the Brig Defence Colony Service

| When Entered into the Service | Mens Names | Rank | Time of Payment | Time of Discharge |
|---|---|---|---|---|
| 1776 | | | | |
| Mar. 6 | Joseph Whitemore | Seaman | Nov. 15 | |
| " | Jn° May | " | " | |
| " | Guillam Veale | Cockswain | " | |
| " | Thomas Graystock | Seaman | " | |
| 21 | Martin Patchin | " | " | |
| 17 | Edward Brown | " | " | |
| May 7 | George Moyer | " | " | |
| Apr. 10 | George Negro | " | " | |
| Mar. 12 | Gabril Allin | " | " | |
| " | Russil Disbrow | " | " | |
| May 1 | Jonª Poor | " | " | |
| 21 | Jonª Colkins | " | " | |
| " | Jonª Jervis | Qtʳ Gunʳ | " | |
| " | Nathaniel Jervis | Seaman | " | |
| June 25 | Wᵐ Bolton | " | " | |
| Mar. 6 | Joseph Bartran | " | " | |
| June 7 | David Norton | " | | Nov. 8 |
| Mar. 25 | Henery Disbrow | Mareen | | Oct. 18 |
| " | James Judson | " | | Aug. 29 |
| 6 | Oliver Midelbrooks | Seaman | | Nov. 8 |
| 21 | Ezekiel Canfield | " | | " |
| April 10 | James Barton | " | | July 22 |
| May 26 | Jn° Connor | " | | " |
| 21 | Ebinezar May | Qtʳ Gunʳ | | Oct. 2 |
| 18 | Zephaniah Hatch | Seaman | | July 23 |
| Mar. 21 | Morris Griffin | " | | June 22 |
| " | Thomas Reed | " | | 27 |
| Apr. 10 | Richard Hunt | Mareen | | July 29 |
| Mar. 18 | Josiah Walker | " | | Oct. 15 |
| May 24 | Abraham Sturgis | Boy | | Nov. 9 |
| " | Abraham Cable | Mareen | | 8 |
| 29 | Robert Crage | Gunʳ Mᵗ | | Aug. 23 |
| " | Isaac Cottle | Seaman | | Nov. 8 |
| Mar. 10 | Israel Clefford | Mareen | | Oct. 12 |
| Aug. 21 | James Greer | Seaman | | Nov. 10 |
| Mar. 10 | Gideon Wells | Surgeon | | Aug. 20 |
| 13 | Richardson Minor | Armʳ | | July 28 |

[*State Library, Revolution 9.*]


A Pay List of Capᵗ Hardings Men Belongˢ to the Brig Defence Colony Service

| Time of Entry in the Service | Mens Names | Rank | Time of Payment |
|---|---|---|---|
| 1776 | | | |
| Mar. 6 | Joseph Squire | Lieut Marmes | Nov. 15 |
| 10 | Thomas Elwood | 1ˢᵗ Serjᵗ | " |
| " | Nehemiah Whiting | 2ᵈ " | " |
| " | Joseph Minor | 3ᵈ " | " |
| " | James Jennings | 4ᵗʰ " | " |
| " | Charles Mans | 5ᵗʰ " | " |

NAVAL RECORD. 233

| Time of Entry in the Service | Mens Names | Rank | Time of Payment |
|---|---|---|---|
| 1776 | | | |
| Mar. 15 | David Parret | Mareen | Nov. 15 |
| 21 | Isaac Elwood | " | " |
| " | John Still | " | " |
| April 11 | Francoes Woodburn | " | " |
| Mar. 16 | Benjamin Darrow | Boy | " |
| " | George Battison | Mareen | " |
| " | Abraham Buckley | Seaman | " |
| 18 | Gideon Allin | Mareen | " |
| 6 | Nathan Squire | " | " |
| 24 | Samuel Taylor | " | " |
| " | Samuel Raymong | " | " |
| " | Stephen Hays | " | " |
| " | David Meaker | " | " |
| " | Giulbard Dudley | " | " |
| " | David Patchin | " | " |
| 10 | Joseph Battison | " | " |
| Nov. 8 | Francoes Butler | Seaman | " |
| 9 | Joseph L. Rowley | " | " |
| " | Peter Curtis | " | " |
| " | Wm Williams | " | " |
| June 7 | Silas Dagget | " | Discharged July 24 |
| " | Jno Hazelton | Qr Gunr | " " |
| " | Cornelius Dunham | Seaman | " |
| " | Barzilla Luce | " | " |
| " | Samuel Norris | " | " |
| June 15 | Simeon Spencer | Armr Mt | " |
| 5 | Calob Dyar | Qtr Gunr | " |

[*State Library, Revolution 9.*]

A Pay List of Capta Hardings Officers & men belongs to the Brigg Defence Collony Service

| 1776 | Mens Names | Rank | Time of Payment | |
|---|---|---|---|---|
| Feb. 24 | Seth Harding | Capt | Nov 15 | |
| Mar 3 | Eebnr Bartram | 1st Lieut | " | |
| 10 | Samll Smedly | 2d Lieut | " | |
| Apr. 1 | Josiah Burnham | Master | " | |
| Aug. 20 | Henry Billings | 3d Lieut | " | |
| Mar. 4 | Edward Bebe | 1st Mate | " | |
| Apr. 12 | Jesse Geacoks | 2d Mate | " | |
| Mar. 13 | David Lewis | Boatsn | " | |
| May 18 | Thos Hutchenson | Gunr | " | |
| Mar. 13 | Justis Plum | Mate | | Discharged Oct 15 |
| " | Jona Darrow | Carpentr | " | |
| 6 | Curtis Reed | Steward | " | |
| Aug. 20 | Simon Calkins | Copper | " | |
| May 29 | James Moor | Cook | " | |
| Mar. 13 | John Warsan | Carptm | " | |
| " | Isaac Squires | Yeoman | " | |
| May 28 | Laurance Martin | " Bs | " | |
| 8 | Sam Asband | Gr " | " | |
| Mar. 10 | John Chatfield | Pilote | " | |
| June 7 | Nathan Daggett | " | " | |

REVOLUTION ROLLS AND LISTS.

| 1776 | | Mens Names | Rank | Time of Payment |
|---|---|---|---|---|
| June | 25 | Eben' Nicholson | Capt Clark | Nov. 15 |
| Mar. | 18 | Shearman Lewis | 1st Qr Mt | " |
| " | | Jonª Silsby | 2d Qr M | " |
| " | | Andrew Thorp | 3d " | " |
| " | | David Jinings | 4th " | " |
| June | 8 | George Newcomb | 5th " | " |
| July | 1 | John Lewis | 6th " | " |
| Mar. | 10 | Ezra Bushnal | Surgn Mate | " |
| | 25 | Henry Taylor | B Mate | " |
| | 6 | Wm Higgins | 1st Mate | " |
| Apr. | 15 | Asail Smith | 1st p. Mast. | " |
| Mar. | 10 | Rial M House | Phifer | " |
| | 12 | Simon Desbrow | Sea m | " |

[*State Library, Revolution 9.*]

1776 A List of the Dead & Desertd from Capt Harding in brigg Defence Collony Service

| Time of Entry | | Mens Names | R or Desertd | | In Service Months | Days |
|---|---|---|---|---|---|---|
| March | 6 | James Young Copper | July | 22 | 4 | 16 |
| | | George Gee | Aug | 5 | 4 | 29 |
| | 17 | John Steward | | 23 | 5 | 6 |
| April | 11 | Richard Fry | July | 14 | 3 | 3 |
| May | 8 | Jared Ervin | Aug. | 23 | 3 | 15 |
| | 24 | Peter Thorp | " | | 2 | 29 |
| | 30 | Edward Ingraham | " | | 2 | 23 |
| | 1 | John Brown | " | | 3 | 22 |
| | | Solomon Brown | " | | 3 | 22 |
| | 12 | Joseph Thomas | June | 21 | 1 | 9 |
| July | 1 | John Basson | Aug | 1 | 1 | 0 |
| | | James Maden | | | 1 | 0 |
| March | 6 | Wm Harrison | Died | | 3 | 17 |

[*State Library, Revolution 9.*]

# NORTHERN DEPARTMENT.

## CAPT. CHAPEL'S COMPANY.

Pay Roll of Captain Fredrick Chapels Company of Seamen, raised in the State of Connecticut, for the Naval Service on the Lakes in the Northern Department commencing on the day of their Inlistment & ending the 25 Day of Sept' [1776] Inclusive agreeable to encouragement of first M° advance wages, Including also Billeting Money, traveling Expenses, Premiums for entering the Service, Blankets, Guns, Cartouch Boxes, Knapsacks and Belts.

| Names | When entered the service | Names | When entered the service |
|---|---|---|---|
| Fredrick Chapel Capt | Aug. 9 | Ephraim Hotchkiss | Aug. 26 |
| Ephraim Goldsmith Lt | 18 | Robert Hotchkiss | " |
| Stephen G. Thatcher Lt | " | Joseph Cooper | " |
| Samuel Little Seaman | " | Nathaniel Stacey | " |
| John Miller | " | Samuel Tharp | " |
| James Benham | " | Clement Tuttle | " |
| John Martin | " | Eliada Parker | " |
| Joseph Hosmer | 25 | Eliakim Parker | " |
| Stephen Willson | " | Joshua Parker | " |
| John Wilson | " | Levi Parker | " |
| Reuben Hadlock | " | Ebenezer Merry | " |
| Fredrick Standley | " | Reuben Judd | " |
| Benjamin Almstead | " | Samuel Holmes | " |
| Benjamin Kenney | " | Abraham Hays | " |
| John Wilcott | " | Nehemiah Knap | " |
| Joseph Wise | " | Samuel Morwin | 23 |
| Benjamin Osborn | " | John Gardner | 26 |
| Thomas Mix | " | James Taylor | " |
| Amos Potter | " | Edward Neile | " |
| William Ives | " | John Kelly | " |
| Benjamin Cook | " | William Briggs | " |
| Abraham Sugdon | " | John Knap | " |
| Elenozer Alling | | | |

[*State Library, Revolution 32.*]

## CAPT. HAWLEY'S COMPANY.

Pay Roll of Captain David Hawley's Company of Seamen raised in the State of Connecticut for the Naval Service of the American States in the Northern Department, commencing on the Day of their inlistment & ending the 25 Septem 1776 agreeable to encouragement of first M° advance

REVOLUTION ROLLS AND LISTS.

wages, Including also Billeting money, Traveling Expences, Premiums for entering the Service, Blankets, Guns, Cartouch Boxes, Knapsacks & Belts.

| Names | When entered the Service | Names | When entered the Service |
|---|---|---|---|
| David Hawley Capt | Aug 9 | John Hayes | Aug 24 |
| John Fairweather Lieut | 19 | William Duncomb | " |
| Ephraim Hawley " | " | Abner Hendricks | " |
| Michael Jennings Sea | " | John Lyon | " |
| Samuel Hawley " | " | Samuel Daniels | 25 |
| Andrew Patterson | 24 | Samuel French | " |
| Jesse Burr | " | Peter Butler | " |
| Joseph Mather | " | Levy Goodrick | " |
| William Brothwell | " | Sam¹ Freedswell | " |
| Mel Wahlee | " | Edmund Pulford | " |
| Samuel Hendricks | " | George Leemon | " |
| Enoch Lacey | " | Darius Fisher | " |
| Daniel Winifred | " | Squire Breadsley | " |

[*State Library, Revolution 32.*]

## GALLEY "TRUMBULL".

[*See Record of Connecticut Men in the Revolution, page 594.*]

### CAPT. WARNER'S COMPANY.

A Pay Roll of Captain Seth Warners Company of Seamen raised in the State of Connecticut for the naval Service on the lake in the Northern department, commencing on the day of their enlistments and ending when they were discharged being Nov: 25, 1776 including Billiting money traveling expence premium for ent[s] the Service Blanket Money, Gun, Cartouch box Knapsack &c &c agreable to encouragement.

| Names | | When entered the Service | When left the Service and for what reason |
|---|---|---|---|
| Seth Warner | Cap. | Aug. 12 | Nov 17 Dischd. |
| Josiah Canfield | Seaman | 13 | Prom[d] Sep. 9 |
| " | 2 Lt | Sep. 9 | Disch[d] wounded in Hospitl Nov. 25 |
| Job Wheeler | Seaman | Aug. 15 | Prom[d] Sep. 9 |
| " | Mate | Sep. 9 | Disch[d] Nov. 25 |
| Giles Cone | Seaman | Aug. 25 | Prom[d] Sep. 9 |
| " | Boatswain | Sep. 9 | Disch[d] Nov. 25 |
| Simon Hough | Seaman | Aug. 15 | Prom[d] Sep. 9 |
| " | Capt. clerk | Sep. 9 | Disch[d] Nov. 25 |
| Samuel Ames | Seaman | Aug. 15 | Prom[d] Sep. 9 |
| " | Carpenter | Sep. 9 | Disch[d] Nov. 25 |
| Amos Bates | Seaman | Aug. 15 | Prom[d] Sep. 9 |
| " | Carp[ts] Mate | Sep. 9 | Disch[d] Nov. 25 |
| Thomas Fitch | Seaman | Aug. 18 | Prom[d] Sep. 9 |
| " | Steward | Sep. 9 | Disch[d] Nov. 25 |
| Ebenezer Squires | Seaman | Aug. 15 | " |
| David Warner | " | 18 | " |
| Joseph Barbee | " | 15 | " |
| Pascal Deangalis | " | 18 | " |
| Peter Negro | " | 29 | " |
| George Puffer | " | Sep. 1 | " |

[*State Library, Revolution 6.*]

## SCHOONER "SPY".

[*See Record of Connecticut Men in the Revolution, page 593.*]

### CAPT. NILES' MEN.

Schooner Spy Acc$^t$ Wages Oct$^r$ 8$^{th}$ 1776
Schooner Spy to Robert Niles for sund$^y$ Persons wages by him paid Viz

|  |  | | |
|---|---|---|---|
| Rob$^t$ Niles | Capt | from Jan. 8 | Oct. 8 |
| Timothy Parker | Lieut | " | " |
| Zebadiah Smith | | " | " |
| Benj$^a$ Mortimore | Boatsw$^n$ | " | " |
| Ret$^n$ Moore | Clerk | " | " |
| John Lessieur | Cook | " | " |
| Eber Blakesley | Gun$^r$ | " | " |
| Ezekle Sayers | Seaman | " | " |
| John Hall | " | " | " |
| Archibald Nails | " | " | " |
| John Tucker | " | " | " |
| W$^m$ Rambow | Boats$^n$ Mate | " | " |
| James Devenport | Seaman | " | " |
| John Johnson | " | " | " |
| John Gaylord | Marine | " | " |
| W$^m$ Swan | " | " | " |
| W$^m$ Devall | Seaman | " | " |
| Stephen Squire | " | " | " |
| Josiah Carew | Carpenter | " | " |
| Zephaniah Tapping | Seaman | " | " |
| David Hand | Marine | " | " |
| David Bowers | Seaman | " | " |
| Luther Hildreth | " | " | " |
| W$^m$ Goldsmith | Off$^r$ Marines | " | " |
| Caleb Brown | Marine | " | " |
| Lewis Chatfield | Seaman | " | " |
| John Gan | " | " | " |
| Ezekiel Miller | Marine | " | " |
| W$^m$ Covel | Pilot | Aug. 13 | " |
| John Tisaker | Seaman | " | Sep. 9 |
| Joseph Hally | " | " | Oct. 8 |
| W$^m$ Sprigs | " | 22 | Sep. 14 |
| John Nails | " | " 13 | " 19 |
| Hen$^y$ Walker | " | " | " |
| Thom$^s$ Coffin | " | " | Oct. 8 |
| Manuel Swazey | " | " | Sep. 9 |
| W$^m$ Gardner | Marine | " | " 19 |
| Jaquin Ferdenands | | " 22 | Oct. 8 |
| Silas Clement | | " | " |
| Rich$^d$ Baxter | | " | Sep. 8 |
| James Gowdy | | " | Oct. 8 |
| Dan$^{ll}$ Toomy | | " 25 | Sep. 18 |
| Anthony Bonscourse | | " | " |
| Tho$^s$ Etherly | | " | " |

[*State Library, Revolution 9.*]

## NAVAL RECORD.

Schooner Spy to Robert Niles for Sundry Persons Wages by him paid Viz Janʸ 8 1777

| Name | Role | From | To | m | d |
|---|---|---|---|---|---|
| Robert Niles | Capt. | Oct. 8 | to Jan. 8, 1777 | 3 | |
| Timothy Parker | Lieut | " | " | 3 | |
| Zebadiah Smith | Master | " | " | 3 | |
| Benjⁿ Mortimore | Boatswain | " | Dec. 8 | 2 | |
| Eben Blakesley | Gunner | " | Jan 8 | 3 | |
| Retⁿ Moore | Clerk | " | " | 3 | |
| Josiah Cary | Carpenter | " | " | 3 | |
| John Lasseur | Cook | " | " | 3 | |
| Wᵐ Gold Smith | Serjant Marines | " | " | 3 | |
| Wᵐ Rumbow | Boatswains Mate | " | " | 3 | |
| John Johnson | Seaman | " | Nov. 29 | 1 | 21 |
| Ezekle Sayers | " | " | Nov. 18 | 1 | 9 |
| Archibald Nails | " | " | Jan. 8 | 3 | |
| John Hall | " | " | " | 3 | |
| James Davenport | " | " | " | 3 | |
| Wᵐ Swan | Boy | " | " | 3 | |
| John Gaylord | Marine | " | " | 3 | |
| Wᵐ Davall | Seaman | " | " | 3 | |
| David Hand | Marine | " | Dec 26 | 2 | 18 |
| Stephen Squire | Seaman | " | Jan. 8 | 3 | |
| Caleb Brown | Marine | " | " | 3 | |
| Zephaniah Tapping | Seaman | " | " | 3 | |
| David Bowen | " | " | " | 3 | |
| Luther Hildreth | " | " | " | 3 | |
| William Covel | Pilot | " | " | 3 | |
| Thomas Coffin | Seaman | " | " | 3 | |
| Joseph Holley | " | " | " | 3 | |
| John Tucker | " | " | " | 3 | |
| John Gan | " | " | " | 3 | |
| Ezekle Miller | Marine | " | " | 3 | |
| James Goudy | Seaman | " | " | 3 | |
| Lewis Chatfield | " | " | " | 3 | |

[*State Library, Revolution 9.*]

Schooner Spy to Robert Niles For Sundʸ persons wages by him paid Viz

|  |  |  |
|---|---|---|
| Robert Niles | Capᵗ | fᵐ Janʸ 8 to May 8 1777 |
| Nathˡˡ Barns | Mate | March 26 to " 14 |
| Thoˢ Rice | 2ᵈ Mate | " 12 to Apr 12 |
| Willᵐ Higgins | | Febʸ 28 to " 28 |
| Ezekiel Sayers | | March 5 to " 21 |
| Stephen Squire | | " 5 to " 18 |
| John Tucker | | Janʸ 8 to Febʸ 22 |
| John Tucker | | Febʸ 22 to May 14 |
| David Bowers | | March 5 to " 14 |
| John Anthony | | " 5 to " 14 |
| Richard Stewart | | " 12 to " 14 |
| William Swan | | Janʸ 8 to Febʸ 21 |
| William Swan | | Febʸ 21 to May 14 |
| James Ford | | " 1 to " 14 |
| Josiah Carey | | |
| Jaquin Fernandes | | Jan 8 to Febʸ 8 |
| Jaquin Fernandes | | Febʸ 8 to May 14 |
| William Skinner | | March 15 to April 20 |

[*State Library, Revolution 9.*]

Schooner Spy to Robert Niles For Sund⁷ Persons Wages by him paid Viz

| Name | Rank | From | To |
|---|---|---|---|
| Robert Niles | Capt. | from May 8 | to Sep 26 1777 |
| Zebadiah Smith | Lieut. | 28 | " |
| Willm Harris | Master | 28 | " |
| Michael Pepper | Mate | 27 | " |
| Richd Stewart | Gunner | 26 | " |
| David Lewis | B. Swain | 26 | " |
| Peter Jeffers | Carpenter | 28 | " |
| John Robertson | Clark | 29 | " 29 |
| Jonath. Rudd | Stuard | " | Deserted |
| Jacob Kingsbury | Serjt | 28 | " |
| Willm Swan | Cook | 29 | " |
| Joseph Francis | B. Mate | 26 | " |
| Kingsbury Edgerton | . | 28 | " |
| Thos Wood | Seaman | 24 | " |
| Harris Tinker | " | 30 | " |
| Charles Turner | " | 30 | " |
| David Rogers | " | 30 | " 24 |
| Thomas Dandee | " | June 4 | " |
| Anthony Wolf | " | June 6 | " |
| Thomas Reed | " | June 12 | July 22 |
| Jacob Cooper | " | July 11 | Aug. 12 |
| John Williams | " | July 20 | Sep. 26 |
| Johan Leseur | " | Aug. 16 | " |
| Jooseph Webb | Boy | May 29 | " |

[*State Library, Revolution 9.*]

## CAPT. SMITH'S MEN.

Dr Schooner Spy to Zebadiah Smith for Sund⁷ wages by him paid Viz March 24 1778

| Name | Rank | From | To |
|---|---|---|---|
| Zebadiah Smith | Capt. | Oct. 16 1777 | to March 24 1778 |
| Asahel Smith | Leut. | Nov. 3 | to Feb. 27 |
| Benja Mortimore | Master | Oct. 20 | to 20 |
| James Elderkin | Gunner | " | to " |
| Jonathan Sachel | Boatswain | " | to Nov. 20 |
| Heny Boardman | Boatswains mate | " | to Feb. 22 |
| John Johnson | Cook | 81 | to " |
| Thos Wood | Seaman | Nov. 8 | to " |
| Minor Elderkin | Seaman | " | to " |
| Roger Avery | " | 12 | to " |
| John Parsons | Boy | 21 | to 27 |
| Wm Swan | Seaman | 18 | to " |
| Nathl Swan | " | 24 | to 24 |
| Jno Williams | " | 12 | to 22 |
| John Masters | " | " | to 28 |
| Willm Allen | Marine | 30 | to 20 |
| Saml R Smith | Clerk | Dec. 20 | to 22 |

[*State Library, Revolution 12.*]

The United States D$^r$ To the State of Connecticut for the Wages &c of sundry on board the Schooner Spy while prisoners in the service of the United States.

| | |
|---|---|
| Michael Pepper | Service on board the Schooner Spy |
| Cap$^t$ Robert Niles | " |
| James Brown | " |
| Solomon Hatch | " |
| Zephaniah Hatch | " |
| Cyrus Fanning | " |

[*Comptroller's Office, Haskell's Receipts.*]


## SLOOP "DOLPHIN".

[*See Record of Connecticut Men in the Revolution, page 593.*]


### MASTER NILES' MEN.

Sloop Dolphin to Robert Niles D$^r$ for Sundry Persons Wages by him Paid Viz

| | |
|---|---|
| Robert Niles Master | from Sep. 27 to Mar. 6, 1778 |
| Frederick Calkins Mate | from Oct. 12 to Feb. 25 |
| Peter Jeffers Capt | from Nov. 14 to Mar. 2 |
| John Leseur | from Oct. 8 to " 5 |
| John Paterson | from Nov. 15 to Feb. 24 |
| Cornelius Savage | from Oct. 6 to Mar. 6 |
| Zefeniah Hatch | from Nov. 14 to " 2 |
| Abner Bebee | from " 18 to " 2 |
| Joseph Webb | from " 26 to " 2 |
| James Treet | from Dec. 26 to Feb. 24 |
| Lawdin Higgins | from " 29 to " 18 |

[*State Library, Revolution 12.*]

## SLOOP "GUILFORD".

### CAPT. NOTT'S MEN.

A Pay Abstract for Capt Notts men on board the Sloop Guilford.

| Mens Names | Time Rec from | Time Rec up to | |
|---|---|---|---|
| Capt Will<sup>m</sup> Nott | Feb. 25 | June 29 | |
| Lieut W<sup>m</sup> M<sup>c</sup>Queen | Apr. 15 | " | |
| Lieut Dan<sup>l</sup> Mallery | Mar. 21 | " | |
| Sailing M<sup>r</sup> Dan. Miles | " | " | |
| Doct W<sup>m</sup> Fitch | Apr. 25 | " | |
| Mate W<sup>m</sup> Coggeshall | Mar. 24 | " | |
| Clarke John Dewitt | 17 | " | |
| Gunner Timothy Andrews | Apr. 15 | " | Disartd |
| Pilot W<sup>m</sup> Stuart | May 10 | " | |
| P Master Simeon Linley | " | " | |
| Armo<sup>r</sup> Bela Stone | Mar. 20 | " | |
| Harry Taylor Boats<sup>n</sup> | May 26 | " | |
| David Raymond Cook | " | " | Disartd |
| David Morris | Mar. 26 | " | |
| David Baldwain | " | " | |
| Job Clarke | Apr. 4 | " | |
| Sam. Burrell | May 10 | " | |
| Peter Pond | 21 | " | |
| W<sup>m</sup> Wolcott | 15 | " | Disartd |
| John Hall | 17 | " | |
| Will<sup>m</sup> Hall | 15 | " | Disartd |
| Acher Molthrop | June 8 | " | Disartd |
| Jacob Molthrop | " | " | |
| Levy Mallery | May 10 | " | Disartd |
| John Barns | June 17 | " | |
| Joseph Wheaton | May 19 | " | Disartd |
| James Goodrige | " | | |
| Peter Gabriel | Mar. 5 | | |
| Thomas V<sup>n</sup> Dosen | " | | |
| Peter Sisco | | | |
| Peter Nostrand | | | |
| Stephen Row | | | |

[An entry on the back of this Pay Abstract shows that it is for the year 1779 and that the vessel was lost during that year.]

[*State Library, Revolution 31.*]

## CAPT. HAWLEY'S MEN.

A Pay Roll of Cap$^t$ David Hawleys Company of Seamen on board the Sloop Guilford belonging to the State of Connecticut, 1779.

| Officers and Mens Names | | When Entered | When Discharged |
|---|---|---|---|
| David Hawley | Cap$^t$ | June 18 | July 8 |
| and from the 16 Aug. to the 8 Sep. — Court Enquiry Ended | | | |
| Will$^m$ M$^c$Queen | 1 Lieut | June 29 | July 11 |
| Dan$^l$ Mallery | 2 Lieut | " | " |
| Nathan Jackson | Lieut marines | 21 | " |
| Dan$^l$ Miles | Sailing master | 29 | " |
| John Dewett | Clerk | " | " |
| Simeon Linsly | prise master | " | " |
| Will$^m$ Steward | " | " | " |
| W$^m$ Coggswell | Mate | " | " |
| Dan$^l$ Jackson | Pilot | 22 | 6 |
| John Hawley | Gunner | 25 | " |
| John Ritch | Carpenter | 22 | " |
| Henry Tayler | Boatswain | 29 | 11 |
| Seth Barker | Serj marines | 25 | 6 |
| Nath$^l$ Jennings | " | " | " |
| Reuben Bostwick | Steward | " | " |
| Jonathan Saymour | G mate | " | " |
| John Hall | Boatswains mate | 29 | " |
| Benj Morrill | Carpenters mate | 25 | " |
| Sam$^l$ Siseoll | Cook | " | " |
| Jeffry Bur | Seaman | " | " |
| Peter Finch | " | " | " |
| Bela Stone | Armourer | 29 | 11 |
| John Meakor | " | 25 | 6 |
| Zebulon Wiscutt | " | " | " |
| Thomas Darrow | " | " | " |
| Richard Provost | " | " | " |
| John R Lockwood | " | " | " |
| Alvin Huatt | " | " | " |
| W$^m$ Jarvis | " | " | " |
| John Duncomb | " | " | " |
| Wakemon Burrtt (?) | " | " | " |
| David Lacy | Seaman | " | " |
| Abijah Gilbert | " | " | " |
| Adner Henerdricks | " | " | " |
| Peter Pond | Marine | " | " |
| Billay Finch | " | " | " |
| W$^m$ Holburton | " | " | " |
| Peter Rose | " | " | " |
| John Bostwick | " | " | " |
| John Barns | " | 29 | 11 |

[*State Library, Revolution 31.*]

## SHIP "OLIVER CROMWELL".

[*See Record of Connecticut Men in the Revolution, page 596.*]

### CAPT. ROBARTS' MEN.

Account of men inlisted by Cap$^t$ Elip$^t$ Robarts [for the Ship Oliver Cromwell]

| Mens Names | Capacites | Time of inlisting |
|---|---|---|
| W$^m$ Roberts | Seaman | September 1, 1776 |
| W$^m$ Mosley | Clarke of marenes | 2 |
| Moses Butler | Gunners mate | 2 |
| Step$^n$ Ward | Marine | 25 |
| Gurdin Burnham | Drummer | 26 |
| John Spencer | Sergnt | October 2 |
| James Bidwell | Seaman | September 15 |
| John Watkins | Marine | October 4 |
| William Allyn | " | 7 |
| James Patterson | " | 7 |
| John Brownley | " | 7 |
| Richd Risley | " | 7 |
| Jon$^t$ Arnold | " | 7 |
| Levi Risley | " | 7 |
| [ ] Robarts Jun$^r$ | " | 2 |
| David Porter | " | 7 |
| Jacob Gibson | " | 14 |
| Aaron Robarts | " | 14 |
| David Mackintosh | Yoman | November 10 |
| Benjamin Burnit | Marine | 8 |
| John Wilson | " | 8 |
| John Hale | " | 12 |
| W$^m$ Johnson | " | 7 |
| [ ] Fulorton | " | October 8 |
| W$^m$ Powell | " | 7 |
| David Bagley | Seaman | December 23 |
| Isaac Rogers | Marine | |
| Moses Porter | " | January 28, 1777 |
| John Steuart | Seaman | February 8 |
| Abel Davise | Marine | January 16 |

To Cash to men inlisted by others

Sam$^l$ Stratton
John Williams
Solomon Lord
Sam$^l$ Stodard
Adrial Simans
John Hartshorne
Heze Abbe Jr

Arad Simans
Steph$^n$ Both
Isaiah Rogers
John Shoart
John Robinson
David Hawkins
Henery Arnold

[*State Library, Revolution 9.*]

## CAPT. COIT'S MEN.

Feb. 1777 A List of Seamen on bord the Ship Oliver Cromwell D<sup>d</sup> in P<sup>r</sup> Cap<sup>t</sup> W<sup>m</sup> Coit

A List of Officers Seamen & Mareens

| | |
|---|---|
| W<sup>m</sup> Coit Esq<sup>r</sup> | Capt P |
| Micael Mullally | 1 Lt P |
| John Chapman | 2 " P |
| John Smith | 3 " P |
| Elefelett Roberts | Capt Marines P |
| John Prentice | 1 Lt P |
| Bela Elderkin | 2 Lt P |
| Levi Young | Master P |
| Tho<sup>s</sup> Chatfield | 1 Mate |
| Nath<sup>l</sup> Wilson | 2 " P |
| Allegence Waldo | Surgeon P |
| Tho<sup>s</sup> Gray | Mate |
| Luther Elderkin | Midshipman P |
| Jn<sup>o</sup> A Christophers | " |
| John Bailey | " P |
| Giles Hollester | " P |
| Selvenus Pinkham | " P |
| Rob<sup>t</sup> Newson | Boatswain P |
| Rob<sup>t</sup> Graige | Gunner P |
| Tho<sup>s</sup> Williams | Carpenter P |
| Tho<sup>s</sup> Winston | Capt Clerk P |
| Christopher Prince | Stewart P |
| W<sup>m</sup> Howard | Cooper P |
| Hugh Mathews | Cook |
| Solomon Lord | Serg<sup>t</sup> P |
| Jn<sup>o</sup> Spencer | " P |
| W<sup>m</sup> Moseley | Clerk Marines D |
| Tho<sup>s</sup> Setchele | Boatswains Mate |
| Jn<sup>o</sup> Dennice | 2 " " |
| Jn<sup>o</sup> Burns | Carpenters Mate P |
| Moses Butlers | Gunners " |
| Gurdon Burnham | Drummer R |
| David M<sup>c</sup>Ingtosh | Gunners Yeoman P |
| Tho<sup>s</sup> Jones | Pilot P |

Seamen

| | |
|---|---|
| Sam<sup>l</sup> Bassett | Jon<sup>a</sup> Miner |
| Jn<sup>o</sup> Rogers | Jn<sup>o</sup> Woolf R |
| Ja<sup>s</sup> Mathews | George Lord D |
| Jn<sup>o</sup> Robins | Edward Culver P |
| Tho<sup>s</sup> Roberts | Ben Short P |
| Sam<sup>l</sup> Stratton | Stephen D Woolf P |
| Jn<sup>o</sup> Smith R | John Merrow D |
| Jn<sup>o</sup> Adams R | Henry Cannady P |
| Tho<sup>s</sup> Bowen R | Ichabob Shiffield R |
| Hezekiah Baker R | Will<sup>m</sup> Fagands |
| Oliver Blossom R | John Heath P |
| Joseph Fisher P | John Tease P |
| Jotham Gardner R | Rob<sup>t</sup> Alsop James R |
| Tho<sup>s</sup> Holladay G | Thomas Smith P |
| Elijah Loveland R | Tho<sup>s</sup> Blin Harris R |
| Jn<sup>o</sup> Morrison P | Tho<sup>s</sup> Hampton P |
| W<sup>m</sup> Palmer R | Paul Long |
| Nath<sup>a</sup> Chase D | James Hill |
| Stephen Ward R | Edward Crow P |

Seamen
Reuben Godfrey P
Shubele Crowele D
Tho⁸ Etterly R
Stephen Blossom R
Joseph Frederick
William Dansey G
Ruben Smith
John Woobury
Ben Hussey P
Stephen Brooks R
Joseph King R
Geo Worthylake P
Bazaliel Beby P
Nathan Burrus
Wᵐ Harris D
John Randolp
Eben' Backus
James Bedwell D
Wᵐ Roberts P
Wᵐ Garrick  Murdred
Cornelius McPerson P
Josiah Ware R
Silas Daggett
John Collings R
John Linstrum Run
Stephⁿ Booth
Daniel Waggs S
Ezekael Lyon P
Samˡ Fosdick R
Thoˢ Vⁿ Duson R
Joseph Bailey R
Silvenus Smith
Job Hanniball
John Williams
Nathaniel Cowett P
Solomon Capee S
Joseph Pornett
Thoˢ Winston Clerk
Jonas Hultman
David Trueman

Marenes
Isaiah Rogers
John Spencer
Samˡ Robinson
Silas Flint
Thoˢ Holbrook
Samˡ Stoddard
Abel Woodworth
Pheneus Carew
Jacob Sawer D
Jonⁿ Jennings D
Nathⁿ S Calkings
Ezekel Dunham
John Hartsorn
Henry Williams Drowned
David Folger D
Frederick Curtice
Samˡ Curtice

Seamen
John Williams
Peter Hanson P
Peter Harry P
Jonathan Whelding P
Judah P. Spooner P
Ceaser Niles D
Henry Burnsides P
Thoˢ Nuchcold R
John Robinson R
Jarrus Alden R
Vollantyne Bunker D
Joseph Ewett R
Thoˢ Sinemon
Samˡ Gyer R
John Short R
Samˡ Boston
Joseph Hannibale P
Joseph Thatcher P
George Potague P
Boston Boston P
James Lanphere D
Charles Clark G
Oliver Done P
Simeon Debago P
Solomon Perpener P
John Dunking R
Selvenus Simes P
Thoˢ Shiverick P
Edwᵈ Hatch P
Wᵐ Bishop G
Timothy Weeks
Robinson Jones
John Lathergo R
Freeborn Bowes P
Moses Talmon P
Jonas Horsewett P
Zacceus Chase P
Abele Soppoosor
Job Bunker R

Marenes
Nathˡ Backus D
Jonⁿ Hubbard
Hezekiah Abby
Solomon Tracey
Elijah Shaford
Arad Simonds
Eleazer Welch
Adrial Simonds
John Williams R
Abner Follett D
Dearky Elderkin
Abijah Hutchingson S
John Dingley D
Abele Minor S
Wᵐ Capp P
Stephen Ward
David Hawkins P

## Marenes

John Watkins D
W<sup>m</sup> Allen R
James Patteson P
Will<sup>m</sup> Powell P
John Brownley P
Rich<sup>d</sup> Risley P
Jon<sup>a</sup> Arnould P
Levi Risley P
Elifelet Roberts Jun<sup>r</sup> D
David Porter P
Jacob Gibson D

### Boys

Duglass Chapman P
Joseph Merrils R
Asael Flint
David Young
Aron Roberts P
Elijah Ormsby
Charles Brown P
Vollantyne Chase P
W<sup>m</sup> Peat P
Ben<sup>a</sup> Sinemon
Jn<sup>o</sup> Robins

### Seamen

Henry Hunt P
John Hill P
Daniel Card P
Frederick Murfey P

## Marenes

Natha'l Fullerson D
Henry Arnold D
John Wilson R
Ben Burnett
John Hay
Hammond Sup
Thomas Williams
W<sup>m</sup> Johnson R
W<sup>m</sup> Marsh P
Abele Davis
Ben<sup>a</sup> Fowler P

### Boys

Tho<sup>s</sup> Robins
Jn<sup>o</sup> Baccus D
Jon<sup>a</sup> Burnett
Jn<sup>o</sup> Deming R
Tho<sup>s</sup> Doertes R
Joseph Fisher P
Jn<sup>o</sup> Grant D
Phineus Manfeld P Seaman
Tho<sup>s</sup> Parseval
Corn<sup>l</sup> Baxter   Seaman
Davis P

### Seamen

David Bagley P
Jn<sup>o</sup> Steward
Stephen Fox P

| | |
|---|---|
| Present | 85 |
| On Furlow | 68 |
| In Gaol | 4 |
| Run away | 41 |
| Discharged | 20 |
| Murdred | 1 |
| Drown<sup>d</sup> | 1 |
| Sick | 4 |
| | 219 |
| Not known | 13 |
| | 232 |

[*State Library, Revolution 9.*]

---

List of Officers and Men formerly belonging to the Ship Oliver Cromwell, and still on board, viz

John Chapman    Lieut            Judah P. Spooner
John Smith      "                John Rees
David Mackintosh { Yeoman of     Benjamin Hussy
                 { Powder Room   Frederick Curtis
Jonathan Setchell Quarter Master  Samuel Curtis
Henry Kennedy   Coxwain          George Worthylake
Edward Culver                    Abel Woodworth
William Marsh                    Douglas Chapman
Barzaleel Beeby  Armourer's Mate

[Indorsed] List of Men on Bord O. Cromwell who were in Capt Colts cruise.

[*State Library, Revolution 9.*]

A list of the Marines that have and do Belong to the Ship Oliver Cromwell William Coit Esq Commander

|  |  |  |
|---|---|---|
| Elifelett Roberts | Captn | Furlow |
| John Prentice | 1st Lieut | Present |
| Bela Elderkin | 2 " | Furlow |
| Solomon Lord | Sergant | " |
| John Spencer | | Present |
| Wm Moseley | Clerk | Dischargd |
| Gurdon Burnham | Drummer | Runaway |
| Isaih Rogers | Private | Present |
| John Spencer | " | Furlow |
| Saml Robinson | " | " |
| Silas Flint | " | " |
| Thos Holbrook | " | Present |
| Saml Stoddart | " | Furlow |
| Abel Woodworth | " | Small Pox |
| Phereus Carew | " | Furlow |
| Jacob Sawyer | " | Discharged |
| Nathl Calkings | " | " |
| Zekel Dunham | " | Furlow |
| John Hartshorn | " | Present |
| Henry Williams | " | Downed |
| Frederick Curtice | " | Present |
| Saml Curtice | " | " |
| Nathl Backus | " | Dischargd |
| Jona Hebard | " | Furlow |
| Hezekiah Abby | " | " |
| Solomon Tracey | " | " |
| Elijah Sparford | " | " |
| Arad Simonds | " | Present |
| Eleazer Welch | " | Furlow |
| Adrial Simonds | " | " |
| John Williams | " | " |
| Abner Follet | " | Discharged |
| Diarky Elderkin | " | Present |
| Abijah Hutchinson | " | " |
| John Dingley | " | Discharged |
| Abel Minor | " | Furlow |
| Wm Copp | " | Present |
| Stephen Ward | " | " |
| David Hawkins | " | |
| John Watkins | " | Discharged |
| Wm Allen | " | Runaway |
| James Patterson | " | Present |
| Wm Powell | " | Runaway |
| John Brownley | " | |
| Richd Risley | " | Present |
| Jona Arnold | " | " |
| Levi Risley | " | " |
| Elifelett Roberts Junr | " | Discharged |
| David Porter | " | Present |
| Jacob Gibson | " | Drumd Out |
| Nathl Fullerton | " | Discharged |
| Henry Arnold | " | " |
| John Wilson | " | Runaway |
| Bena Burnett | " | Present |
| John Hale | " | Runaway |
| Ammon Seep | " | Present |
| Thos Persevall | " | |

NAVAL RECORD. 249

| | | |
|---|---|---|
| Wᵐ Johnson | Private | |
| Wᵐ Marsh | " | Present |
| Abel Davis | " | |
| Benⁿ Fowler | " | Present |
| John Robins | " | Furlow |
| John Baccus | " | Discharged |
| Jonⁿ Burnett | " | Furlow |
| Thoˢ Doherty | " | Runaway |
| John Grant | " | Furlow |
| Pheneus Munsell | " | Discharged |
| Cornelius Baxter | " | |
| Jonⁿ Jennings | Fifer | Discharged |
| Wᵐ Roberts | Private | " |

[*State Library*, "*Revolution 9*."]

A List of Officers & Seamen Belonging & have Belong'd to the Ship Oliver Cromwell.

| | | |
|---|---|---|
| Wᵐ Coit Esqʳ | Capt. & Commander | Present |
| Michail Millally | 1 Lieut | " |
| John Chapman | 2 " | " |
| John Smith | 3 " | " |
| Levi Young | Master | " |
| Thoˢ Chatfield | 1 Mate | " |
| Nathaniel Wilson | 2 " | " |
| Albegence Waldo | Surgeon | " |
| Thomas Gray | " Mate | " |
| Luther Elderkin | Midshipman | " |
| Allen Christophers | " | " |
| John Bailey | " | " |
| Giles Hollister | " | " |
| Selvenus Pinkham | " | " |
| Robᵗ Graige | Gunner | " |
| Robᵗ Newson | Boatswain | " |
| Thoˢ Williams | Carpenter | " |
| Christopher Prince | Steward | " |
| Wᵐ Howard | Cooper | " |
| George Lord | Clerk | Discharged |
| Hugh Mathews | Cook | |
| James Hill | Boatswains Mate | Present |
| Moses Butler | Gunners Mate | " |
| David Mackingtosh | Gʳˢ Yeoman | " |
| Thoˢ Jones | Pilot | " |
| John Dennis | Bᵗ 2ᵈ Mate | in Gaol for Murder |
| Jonⁿ Setchell | Qutʳ Master | Present |
| Job Bunker | " | Runaway |
| John Smith | " | " |
| John Burns | Carpenters Mate | Present |
| Cornˡ McPerson | 2 " | " |
| John Woolf | Boatᵐˢ Yeoman | Runaway |
| Stephen De Woolf | Carpenters " | Present |
| Henry Cannady | Coxswain | " |
| John Merrow | Armorour | Discharged |
| James Lanphere Junʳ | Steward | " |
| David Folger | Boatswain | " |
| Edward Culver | Seaman | Present |
| Benⁿ Short | " | " |

|  |  |  |
|---|---|---|
| Ickebert Shiffield | Seaman | Runaway |
| W<sup>m</sup> Fagons | " | Present |
| John Heath | " | " |
| John Pease | " | " |
| Rob<sup>t</sup> Alsop James | " | Runaway |
| Tho<sup>s</sup> Smith | " | Present |
| Tho<sup>s</sup> Blin Harris | " | Runaway |
| Tho<sup>s</sup> Hampton | " | Present |
| Paul Long | " | " |
| Edward Crow | " | " |
| Reuben Godfrey | " | " |
| Shubell Crowele | " | Discharged |
| Tho<sup>s</sup> Etherly | " | Runaway |
| Stephen Blosson | " | " |
| W<sup>m</sup> Dansey | " | Present |
| Reuben Smith | " | Discharged |
| John Woobury | " | " |
| Ben<sup>n</sup> Hussey | " | Present |
| Steph<sup>n</sup> Brooks | " | Runaway |
| Joseph King | " | " |
| Geo. Wetherlegs | " | Present |
| Baz<sup>l</sup> Beby | " | " |
| Nathan Burrows | " | Sick in Small Pox |
| W<sup>m</sup> Harris | " | Discharged |
| John Randol | " | Present |
| Eben<sup>r</sup> Baccus | " | Discharged |
| James Biddell | " | " |
| W<sup>m</sup> Garrick | " | Murdered |
| Josiah Ware | " | Runaway |
| Silas Daggett | " | |
| John Collings | " | Runaway |
| John Linston | " | " |
| Stephen Booth | " | |
| Dan<sup>l</sup> Waggs | " | Sick and not fit for Duty |
| Ezekiel Lyon | " | Present |
| Sam<sup>l</sup> Fosdick | " | Runaway |
| Tho<sup>s</sup> V<sup>n</sup> Duson | " | " |
| Jos. Baylye | " | |
| Selevenus Smith | " | Present |
| Job Hanniball | " | |
| John Williams | " | Runaway |
| Solomon Corvett | " | |
| Solomon Capee | " | Runaway |
| Nath<sup>l</sup> Cowett | " | Present |
| Jos<sup>h</sup> Porrutt | " | Runaway |
| Tho<sup>s</sup> Winston | " | Present |
| Jonas Horswett | " | " |
| David Freeman | " | Runaway |
| John Williams | " | " |
| Peter Hanson | " | Present |
| Peter Harry | " | " |
| Jon<sup>a</sup> Welding | " | " |
| Judah P. Spooner | " | Present |
| Ceasar Niles | " | Discharged |
| Henry Burnside | " | Present |
| Tho<sup>s</sup> Nicholds | " | Runaway |
| James Alden | " | Discharged |

|  |  |  |
|---|---|---|
| Vallantyne Bunker | Seaman | Discharged |
| Sam¹ Bunker | " | Runaway |
| Josʰ Hewett | " | " |
| Thoˢ Cinnamon | " | Present |
| Sam¹ Geer | " | Runaway |
| John Short | " | " |
| Sam¹ Poston | " | " |
| Joseph Hanniball | " | |
| Joseph Thatcher | " | Present |
| Geo. Patague | " | " |
| Boston Boston | " | " |
| Chaˢ Clerk | " | " |
| Oliver Done | " | " |
| Simon Debago | " | |
| Solomon Popenah | " | Present |
| Selvenus Simms | " | " |
| John Demking | " | " |
| Thoˢ Shiverick | " | " |
| Edwᵈ Hatch | " | " |
| Wᵐ Bishop | " | Discharged |
| Timothy Weeks | " | Present |
| Robinson Jones | " | " |
| John Lathergo | " | Runaway |
| Freeborn Bowes | " | Present |
| Moses Talman | " | |
| Zacceus Chace | " | " |
| Abel Sapposorn | " | |
| Samᵒ Bassett | " | |
| John Mathews | " | |
| John Rogers | " | |
| Sam¹ Stratton | " | Present |
| John Adams | " | Runaway |
| Thoˢ Bowen | " | |
| Hezekiah Baker | " | Runaway |
| Joseph Fisher | " | Present |
| Jothan Gardner | " | Runaway |
| Thoˢ Holladay | " | Present |
| Elijah Loveland | " | Runaway |
| John Morrison | " | Present |
| Wᵐ Palmer | " | Runaway |
| Nathan Chase | " | Discharged |
| Stephen Ward | " | Runaway |
| Jonⁿ Minor | " | " |
| Timothy Murphey | " | " |
| Henry Hunt | " | " |
| Dan¹ Carr | " | " |
| John Hill | " | " |
| John Bagley | " | Present |
| John Steward | " | |
| Thoˢ Jones | " | Present |
| Abner Ransom | " | " |
| Peter Swain | . . . | " |
| Maning Stubbs | . . | " |
| Nathaniel Rowley | . . | " |
| Rob' Hatch | . . | " |
| Seth Swift | . . | |
| Boys | | |
| John Deming | . . | Runaway |
| Joseph Merrills | . . | Runaway |

### Boys

| | | |
|---|---|---|
| Duglass Chapman | | Present |
| Assel Flint | | On Furlow |
| David Young | | " |
| Aron Roberts | | Present |
| Elijah Ormsby | | On Furlow |
| Chaˢ Brown | | Present |
| Vollantyne Chase | | " |
| Wᵐ Peet | | " |
| Benⁿ Cinemon | | " |
| Peter Darrow Junʳ | | " |

[*State Library, Revolution 9.*]

## COMMANDER PARKER'S MEN.

Pay Roll of Officers & Men belonging to the Ship Oliver Cromwell 1777.

| Names | Qualities | Time of Entry | Time of Discharge |
|---|---|---|---|
| Timothy Parker | Lieutenant | April 14 | Oct. 14 |
| John Chapman | " | " | " |
| John Smith | " | " | " |
| Caleb Frisbie | Master | April 24 | " |
| Thomas Rice | Mate | May 8 | " |
| Stephen Lee | " | May 31 | " |
| Thomas Whelden | " | June 1 | Sep. 22 |
| David Pool | Boatswain | May 8 | Oct. 14 |
| David Mackentosh | Gunner | April 14 | " |
| William Marbell | Carpenter | " | " |
| Jonathan Woodworth | Midshipman | " | " |
| Shirman Lewis | " | " | " |
| Curtis Reed | " | " | " |
| Ralph Hoadley | " | April 27 | " |
| Andrew Morris | " | May 28 | " |
| Robert Alsop James | " | June 9 | " |
| Judah P. Spooner | Clerk | April 14 | " |
| Benjamin Ellis | Surgeon | " | " |
| Timothy Rogers | Surgeon's Mate | April 28 | " |
| John Craige | Boatswains Mate | May 8 | " |
| William Higgins | " | May 8 | " |
| James Elderkin | Gunner's Mate | April 14 | " |
| Phinehas Chapman | Carpenter's " | May 17 | Oct. 8 |
| Jonathan Setchell | Quartermaster | April 14 | Oct. 14 |
| Prosper Brown | " | May 16 | Sep. 22 |
| Samuel Adams | " | May 26 | Oct. 14 |
| Benjamin Smith | " | " | Sep. 22 |
| John Boyle | " | May 27 | Oct. 14 |
| William Baldwin | " | " | " |
| Peleg Hillman | " | June 1 | " |
| David Norton | " | " | Sep. 22 |
| Henry Parry | Cooper | May 26 | Oct. 14 |
| Epaphras Smith | Steward | April 14 | Sep. 22 |
| Henry Taylor | Cook | May 10 | Oct. 14 |
| Henry Kennedy | Coxswain | April 14 | " |
| Frederick Curtis | Master at Arms | " | Sep. 22 |
| Barzaleel Beebe | Armourer | " | Oct. 14 |
| William Kimbalin | Sailmaker | June 1 | " |
| John Negus | Armʳˢ Mate | May 2 | Sep. 22 |

| Names | Qualities | Time of Entry | Time of Discharge |
|---|---|---|---|
| Ephraim Herrick | Steward's Mate | April 14 | Oct. 14 |
| Joab Alden | Gunner's Yeoman | April 24 | Sep. 22 |
| Henry Hunt | Yeoman | May 27 | Sep. 22 |
| Josiah Walker | " | April 18 | " |
| Nathan Daggett | Pilot | May 19 | Oct. 14 |
| John Chatfield | " | April 14 | Sep. 26 |
| George Hillman | " | June 1 | Sep. 22 |
| John Rees | Seaman | April 14 | Died Sep. 1 |
| Edward Culver | " | " | Oct. 14 |
| Benjamin Hussey | " | " | " |
| George Worthylake | " | " | " |
| James N. Griffin | " | " | " |
| Samuel Silliman | " | " | " |
| Abel Woodworth | " | " | " |
| Timothy Teal | " | " | Sep. 22 |
| Zephaniah Hatch | " | " | " |
| Abel Lewis | " | " | " |
| Samuel Curtis | " | " | " |
| Arnold Kinyon | " | " | " |
| Philip Driscoll | " | " | " |
| James Hilliard | " | " | " |
| William Holmes | " | April 20 | " |
| Archelaus Barker | " | April 28 | Oct. 14 |
| Stephen Smith | " | " | " |
| Isaac Sharpe | " | May 2 | " |
| Theophilus Whaley | " | May 3 | " |
| Azariah Hilliard | " | " | " |
| Isaac Frisbie | " | May 5 | Sep. 22 |
| Teleman Cuyler | " | May 7 | Oct. 14 |
| Turtle Hunter | " | May 8 | " |
| Justus Harrison | " | " | Sep 22 |
| Butler Harrison | " | " | " |
| John Jacobs | " | May 10 | Oct. 14 |
| Henry Bowman | " | May 18 | Sep 22 |
| James Brown | " | May 26 | Oct. 14 |
| John Manuel | " | " | " |
| Charles Kenney | " | " | " |
| Felix Quin | " | " | " |
| Peter Grant | " | " | " |
| James Everett | " | " | " |
| William Odell | " | " | " |
| William Ingraham | " | " | " |
| William Hall | " | " | Sep. 22 |
| James Morris | " | " | " |
| Timothy Murphy | " | " | " |
| Robert Gordon | " | " | " |
| James McVey | " | " | " |
| James Ford | " | " | " |
| James Anderson | " | " | " |
| James Wall | " | " | " |
| William Harris | " | " | " |
| Joab Scranton | " | " | " |
| John Willard | " | " | " |
| Thomas Groundwater | " | " | " |
| Benjamin Rockwell | " | " | .. |
| Rosamus Laurence, Extra | " | May 31 | Oct. 14 |
| Anthony Swasey | " | June 6 | Sep 22 |
| William Teleder | " | " | " |

| Names | Qualities | Time of Entry | Time of Discharge |
|---|---|---|---|
| Michael Moore | Seaman | June 6 | Sep 22 |
| Richard Lillie | " | " | Oct. 14 |
| Patrick Conner | " | June 10 | Sep. 22 |
| John Taylor | " | July 8 | Oct. 14 |
| Boston Swain | " | June 13 | " |
| William Ellis | " | June 6 | Oct. 14 |
| William Lamb | " | July 26 | " |
| James Wimberley | " | July 22 | " |
| David Rogerson | " | " | " |
| John Mortimer | " | " | " |
| Thomas Burke | " | " | " |
| Robert Marks | " | " | " |
| Nathaniel Swan | Boy | April 14 | Oct. 14 |
| John Parsons | " | " | " |
| Douglas Chapman | " | " | " |
| Theophilus Fitch | " | April 20 | " |
| John Setchell | " | April 14 | " |
| Darius Brewster | " | May 11 | Sep 22 |
| Philo Lewis | " | May 1 | Oct. 14 |
| George Edwards | " | May 27 | " |
| Ivory Snow | " | May 26 | Sep. 22 |
| Sylvanus Daggett | " | June 6 | " |
| West Daggett | " | " | " |
| Thomas Jones | " | July 22 | Oct. 14 |
| John Cleverly | " | " | " |
| Run | | | |
| Thomas Wilson | Seaman | April 14 | |
| Thomas Graystock | " | " | |
| James Murray | " | May 27 | |
| Peleg McGuire | " | May 26 | |
| Thomas Aaron | " | May 3 | |
| James Goging | " | May 27 | |
| Alpheus Johnson | " | April 27 | |
| Henry Pierce | " | May 30 | |
| Obadiah Sears | " | May 8 | |
| Thomas Keney | " | April 20 | |
| Ebenezer Smith | " | May 5 | |
| John Rosson | " | May 26 | |
| Samuel Webster | " | April 20 | |
| Francis Jackson | " | " | |
| Nicholas Taaffe | " | April 22 | |
| Thomas Knowlton | " | April 24 | Disc[d] June 7 |
| William Russell | " | May 3 | " |
| James Day | Lieut. Marines | April 14 | Oct. 14 |
| William Marsh | Serjeant | " | Sep. 27 |
| Samuel Holt | " | May 18 | Sep. 22 |
| Henry Walton | Drummer | April 14 | " |
| John Walton | Fifer | May 18 | " |
| Nathaniel Jennings | Marine | April 14 | Oct. 14 |
| Nathan Jennings | " | " | " |
| John Easton Olcott | " | April 26 | " |
| Josiah Beers | " | " | Sep. 22 |
| Richard Kimball | " | April 27 | " |
| Elijah Spencer | " | " | " |
| Hendrick Pickle | " | April 14 | Oct. 14 |
| James Beers | " | May 1 | " |
| George Stilken | " | May 18 | Sep. 22 |
| Elihu Cook | " | May 2 | " |

## NAVAL RECORD.

| Names | Qualities | Time of Entry | Time of Discharge |
|---|---|---|---|
| John Linslie | Marine | May 2 | Oct. 14 |
| Timothy Huffman | " | " | Sep. 22 |
| Oliver Gates | " | May 18 | " |
| Robert Geer | " | May 9 | " |
| Noah Stevens | " | May 2 | " |
| Heli Foot | " | May 6 | " |
| John Mouterdier | " | May 26 | " |
| Timothy Hebbard | " | April 27 | " |
| Josiah Wolcott | " | May 27 | " |
| John Pullman | " | May 8 | " |
| Elnathan Dexter | " | May 2 | " |
| Jepthah Curtis | " | May 17 | " |
| Charles Dana | " | June 2 | " |
| Edmund Morris | " | May 7 | " |
| Samuel Bartholomew | " | May 18 | " |
| Asaph Pease | Yeoman | June 1 | " |
| James Calkins | Marine | May 5 | " |
| Henry Hunt | Seaman | May 27 | " |
| Samuel Foy | " | Aug. 22 | " |
| Daniel Green | " | " | " |
| Alexander Wood | Marine | April 14 | Oct. 14 |
| Thomas Rogers | " | May 5 | Sep. 22 |
| Josiah Frisbie | " | " | " |
| Thomas Holbrook | Seaman | May 18 | " |
| Seth Harding | | | |

[*State Library, Revolution 9.*]

Pay List for Ship Oliver Cromwell Timothy Parker Esqr Commander from 10th December 1777 to Sepr 10th 1778

| Names | Capacities | Time of Entry | When Discharged |
|---|---|---|---|
| Timothy Parker Esqr | Commander | 6 Dec. 1777 | 22 Sep. 1778 |
| John Chapman | first Lieutenant | 6th Decr 1777 | 10 Sep. 1778 |
| Caleb Frisbie | 2d " | 10th Decr 1777 | 10th Sep. 1778 |
| John Tillinghast | 3d " | 2d Feby 1778 | 11 June 1778 |
| Benjn Jones | Master | 12th March | 11 June 1778 |
| Andrew Morris | 1st mate to 12th June & then master | 10 Dec. 1777 | 10th September |
| Joseph Hubbard | 2d mate | 12th June 1778 | 10th |
| Curtis Reed | 3d " to 12th June and then first | 6th Dec. 1777 | 11th June 1778 |
| Ralph Hoadly | Midshipman to 12th June & then 3d Mate | 10th Dec. 1777 | 10th Sept. |
| Samuel Stow | Midshipman to 12th June & then 3d mate | 5th Jany. 1778 | 12th June |
| William Higgins | midshipman | 12th June | 10th Sept. |
| Samuel Bidwell | " | 10th Dec. 1777 | 10th " |
| Isaiah Cahoon | " | 6th Dec. 1777 | 10th " |
| Samuel Buffam | " | 5th Feby. 1778 | 10th Sep. |
| John Crage | Boatswain | 10th Dec. 1777 | 10th " |
| Thomas Tillinghast | " mate | 14th Dec. 1777 | Run 25th June 1778 |
| Samuel Lollard | 2d " | 2nd Feby 1778 | 10th Sep. |
| Thomas Wait Foster | Gunner | 9th Jany. | 10th " |
| Peter John Forrsster (?) | " mate | 12 Feby | 10th " |
| Edward Brasier | Yeoman | 18th Feby. | Run 1st June |
| Jacob Chandlor | Carpenter | 6th decr 1777 | 10th Sept |
| Amos Ranny | " mate | 5th Jany. 1777 | 20th June Run. |
| Timothy Boardman | | 6th Dec. 1777 | 10th Sep. 1778 |
| James Day | Capt Marlens | 15th | died 18th Apl. |
| Azeriah Hillyard | Sergt Marlens | 20th | 10th Sepr 1778 |
| Abel Woodworth | | | 10th " |
| Jabez Perkins 3d | Captain's Clark | 19th | 22d Sepr |
| Turtle Hunter | Coxswain (Say Sailmaker) | 18th Feby. 1777 | 10th Sepr |
| Samuel Holman | Steward | 6th Decr 1777 | 10th " |
| Thomas Smith | Qr Master | 11th Feby. 1778 | 10th Sepr |
| John Essex | | 18th March. | 1st June Run |

## NAVAL RECORD. 257

| Name | Role | Date | Status |
|---|---|---|---|
| Douty Randol | " | | 10th Sepr |
| Thomas Waples | " | 16th | 1st June Run |
| Chace Rogers | Cooper | 10th | 10th Sepr |
| Gideon Chapman | Doctrs Mate | 1st Jany. | 10th Sepr |
| Edmond Morris | Seman | 8th | " |
| Richard Rose | Marlen | 12th Decr 1778 | " |
| Jurden Smith | | " | " |
| Caleb Smith | Cook | 22d " | " |
| Archelus Barker | Seman | 14th Jany | " |
| Samuel Andrus | marlen | 14th Dec. 1777 | " |
| Joseph Smith | Seman | 22d " | " |
| Hutchins Bowden | " | 16th Jany. 1778 | " |
| Charles Bordman | Marlen | 26th | " |
| Ebenezer Baldwin | " | 14th | deserted |
| Eliphalet Roberts Junr | (") Seman | 23d Decr 1777 | " |
| John Henry | Marlen | 29th | 10th September |
| Levy Darling | , | 29th | 10th Sepr |
| Cruttenden Ward | Marlen | 3d Jany | 10th Sepr |
| Jeremiah Ward | " | 3d | 10th Sepr |
| Daniel Sandeforth | " | 3d | 10th Sepr |
| John Rogers 6th | Drummer | 4th | 10th |
| Chapman Simmons | Marlen | 20th | 10th |
| Thomas Croman | " | 20th | 10th |
| Jeremiah Thorp | " | 20th | 10th |
| Jonathn Waterhouse | " to ye 12 June. & then Gunners yewman | 10th 20th | 12th June & then Enter'd as Yewman |
| Daniel Hillyard | Marlen | 20th | 10th Sepr |
| John Wittlesey | " | 10th | 10th |
| John Welman | " | 20th | 10th |
| Roswell Lamphear | " | 20th | 10th |
| Nathl Riley | " | 30th | Deserted |
| John Batt | " | 20th | 10th Sepr |
| Roger Dyer | Seman | 20th | 10th Sepr |
| Joseph Miller | " | 20th | 10th |
| Anthony Woolf | " | 20th | 10th |
| Samuel Mackentash | " | 17th | Deserted |

17

| Names | Capacities | Time of Entry | When Discharged |
|---|---|---|---|
| John Drisco | Seman | 17th | Deserted |
| John Slattury |  | 26th | " |
| Jonas Park | Marlen | 30th |  |
| Levy Park | " | 30th |  |
| Pirum Ripley | " | 3rd Feby. |  |
| Joseph Starkweather | " | 3d | deserted 24th June |
| Giles Tracy | " | 3d | 10th Sepr |
| James Starkweather | " | 31st Jany. | 10th Sepr |
| Amasa Waterman (negro) |  | 9th Feby. | deserted 24th June |
| Chancy Smith | Seman | 15th Dec. 1777 | 10th Sepr |
| Hezekiah Goff | Marlen | 6th Dec. | 9th Sepr |
| John Rogers Junr | " | 6th Dec. | 1 July died at Boston. |
| Stephen Ward Junr | Marlen | 6th | 7th June |
| Philemon Roberts | " | 6th | 10th Sepr |
| Charles Plum | " | 6th | 10th |
| Stephen Ward | Marlen | 6th | Run 9th June |
| Benjn Gardnor | Stewards Mate. | 9th Jany 1778 | 10th Sepr |
| Moses Butlor |  | 6th Decr 1777 | 9th Sep. |
| John Griffin | Marlen | 6th " | 10th Sepr |
| Tombo Dea | " | 6th | 10th |
| Daniel Lee | " | 6th | Deserted |
| Daniel Starr | " | 6th | Run 9th June. |
| John Lamb | Seman | 6th Decr 1777 | 10th Sepr |
| John Blasdell | Seman | 5th Jany 1778 | Run 1st June. |
| Thomas Ridgway | Master of Arms. | 3rd March | 10th Sepr |
| Benjn Woodruff | Marien | 6th Decr 1777 | 10th |
| Wilson Rowlandson |  | 25th Febr 1778 | 10th |
| Edmond Dorr | Seman | 25th | 10th |
| William Bunce | Marlen | 25th | 10th |
| Ebenezer Tolcut | Seman | 25th. | 10th |
| Michael Dwire |  | 9th March | Run 8rd June. |
| George Runey |  | 5th | 9th Sepr |
| Samuel Johnson | Marlen | 5th | 9th Sepr |
| John Baker |  | 6th | 15th April killed |
| Elkanah Elmes | Seman | 6th | 10th Sepr |
| | | | Deserted |

## NAVAL RECORD.           259

| Name | Rank | Date | |
|---|---|---|---|
| Peter Gilbert | " | 7th March 1778 | " |
| Benjm Shetten | Marien | 24th Feby. | Sepr 9th |
| Nathl Oliver | " | 5th March | 9th |
| John Hedge | Seaman | 26th Jany | 9th |
| Benjm Wyett | " | " | Run |
| Thomas Mathews | " | 1st Feby. | " |
| Jotham Gardinor | " | 2nd Feby | " |
| Joseph Hovey | Marien | 3rd | 9th Sepr |
| Samuel Chace | Seaman | 11th | 9th |
| Boston Swain | " | 9th | 9th |
| Samuel Coombs | " | 19th | Run |
| James Mathews | " | 7th | 9th Sepr |
| Thomas Brimblecom | " | 10th Jany | 9th |
| Enoch Crowell | " | 25 Decr 1777 | Run 3rd July |
| Samuel Addams | Qr Master | 31st " | Sepr 10th |
| Simeon Post | Marien | 10th Feby 1778 | Run 2d July |
| Abraham Low | Seaman | 10th | 10th Sepr |
| William Jones | Marien | 10th | 10th |
| Samuel Williams | " | 13th | 9th |
| Stephen Payn | " | 26th | 10th |
| William Waterman | Seaman | 26th | 10th |
| William Swan | " | 12th Decr 1777 | 10th |
| John Setchel | " | 28th " | Run |
| John Parsons | Seaman | 23rd " | " |
| Wm Henry Wattles | Marien | 10th Jany. 1778 | 10th Sepr |
| Thomas Goodman | " | 25th | Run |
| Thomas Revers | " | 27th | 10th Sepr |
| Chandlor Wattles | " | 10th | 10th |
| Jabez Palmer | " | 10th | 10th |
| Eliphalet House Junr | " | 17th | 10th |
| Asa Lyman | | | |
| Joseph Allen | | | |
| Jesse Loomis | | | |
| Derias Waterman | | | |
| Jerard Allen | " | 3rd Feby. | 10th |
| Timothy Goodwin | " | 4th | 10th |

| Names | Capacities | Time of Entry | | When Discharged | |
|---|---|---|---|---|---|
| Neal Lathrop (Negro) | Marien | 7th | | 10th | |
| Ezekiel Fitch Junr | " | 20th Decr | 1777 | 10th | |
| Abijah Hutchinson | " | 25th " | | 10th | |
| Walter Hunt | " | 1st Jany. | 1778 | 10th Sepr | |
| Gladden Waterman | " | 10th Jany. | | 10th | |
| John Bliss | " | 10th | | 10th | |
| Josiah Woodworth | " | 10th | | 10th | |
| John Costney | ( " Corporal) | 20th Feby. | | 10th | |
| Samuel Wattles | Marien | 10th Jany. | | 10th | |
| Daniel Rockwell | " | 15th " | | 10th | |
| John Brichel | " | 29th | | 10th | |
| Joshua Boyinton | " | 20th | | 10th | |
| Benona Dick | " | 17th Feby. | | 10th | |
| Richard Hendrick (Negro) | " | 18th | | 10th | |
| Peter Molbone | Marien | Deserted | | 9th | |
| Cato Tyng (Negro) | Seman | 17th March. | | Deserted | |
| Francis Jarvis | Marien | 11th Febr | 1778 | 10th Sepr | 1778 |
| Bosaleel Beebie | Seman | 22d Decr | 1777 | 11th June | |
| Benjn Jones Junr | Armorer | 12th March | | 10th Sepr | |
| Dominique Tawain | Surgen | 1st " | | 10th | |
| Wm Byrnes | Seman | 19th | | 9th | |
| Hugh McMannes | Landman | 19th | | Run 3d June | |
| Thomas Williams | Seman | 29d | | " " | |
| John Wood | " | " | | " " | |
| John Killey | " | " | | 8th June | |
| William Lamb | Volunteer | 14th Jany. | | 10th Sepr | |
| George Lamb | " | 17th July | | 10th | |
| Daniel Malcolm | " | 8th | | 10th | |
| Isaac Frisbie | Cockswain | | | 10th | |
| George Jacobson | doctrs Mate | | | 10th | |
| Amos Harding | Seman | | | | |
| Alexander McLain | Boatswain's Mate | | | | |
| John Costney Entered Charles-town | Seman | 10th | | 10th | |

NAVAL RECORD.   261

| Name | Rank | Date | Notes |
|---|---|---|---|
| Solomon Siles | " | | { Run & did not Repair on board 10th Sepr |
| Wm Petty | " | | { Deserted & did not Repair on board 10th Sepr |
| William Davis | " | | { Deserted & did not Repair on board 10th Sepr |
| William Reymond | Seman | 11th | 10th |
| Israel Smith | " | 18th | 10th |
| Peter Parker | 5th Midshipman | 15th | 10th |
| John Knowles | 4th | 10th June | 10th |
| John H. Green | " deserted | 15th July | { Deserted & did not Repair on board 10th Sepr |
| Charles Howard | Seman | 10th | 10th |
| Thomas Smith Shipt in Charlestown | { Marien | 14th | 10th |
| Seth Higgins | Seman | 10th | 10th |
| Richard Nowlan | " | 18th | { Deserted & did not Repair on board 10th |
| Joseph Tee | " | 11th | 9th |
| James Risley | " | 26th June | " |
| Isrel Dyer | " | 21st July | " |
| Timothy Woodbridge | Midshipman | 20th | 10th Sepr |
| Daniel Hillyard | Gunners Yewman from | 12th June to | Deserted Ship |
| James Hanscum | Seman | 14th July to | 28rd Inst. Discharg'd |
| Philemon Roberts | Landsman was in the Brig from | 10 Inst. | " |
| John Whittlesey | " | " | " |
| James Starkweather | " | " | " |
| Joseph Starkweather | " | " | " |
| Josiah Woodworth | " | " | " |
| Daniel Rockwell | " | " | " |

Hartford Sepr 25th 1778 Personally appeared Timothy Parker Esqr Commander of the Ship Oliver Cromwell, & made Oath that according to his best knowledge & Belief the Pay Abstract by him exhibited & Subscribed of the Officers & Men belonging to Ship is Justly and truly made Out Sworn before James Church one Comrs P. Table.

[State Library, Revolution 21.]

## REVOLUTION ROLLS AND LISTS.

Pay List for Ship Oliver Cromwell, Timothy Parker Esq[r] Commander from 22[d] Sep[r] 1778 to y[e] Aug[t] 1779.

| Names | Capacities | Time of Entry | Time of Discharge |
|---|---|---|---|
| Timothy Parker | Captain | Sep. 11[th] 1778 | 11[th] Sep. 1779 |
| John Chapman | First Lieut | " 11[th] | 23[rd] Aug. 1779 |
| Zebadiah Smith | 2[nd] " | Decemb[r] 1[st] | " |
| Andrew Morris | 3[d] " | Sep. 11[th] | " |
| Curtis Reed | Sailing Master | Sep[t] 11[th] | " |
| Jabez Perkins y[e] 3[rd] | Cap[t] Mariens | Sep[t] 11[th] | " |
| Peter Lingdyon | Gunnor | March 15[th] 79 | " |
| John Crage | Boatswain | " 15[th] 79 | " |
| John Smith | Carpentor | " 15[th] 79 | " |
| Dominique Tawzin | Surgeon | Sep. 11[th] 1778 | " |
| Samuel Stowe | First Mate | 11[th] Oct. | " |
| William Palmer | 2[d] " | 10[th] April 1779 | 10[th] July died |
| John Knowles | 3[d] " | 15[th] Feb[y] | 6[th] June Killed |
| W[m] Howard | Midshipman | 10[th] May | 23[d] Aug. |
| Nath[ll] Stanton | " | 10[th] Decemb[r] 1778 | " |
| John Smith | " | | " |
| Gideon Chapman | " | 11[th] Sep[t] | " |
| Joshua Palmer | " | 10[th] April 1779 | " |
| Joseph Champlin | " | 10[th] May | 1[st] June |
| Robert Niles Jun[r] | Captain's Clerk | 25[th] Dec. 1778 | 23[d] Aug. |
| Jeremiah Chapman | Steward | 14[th] Dec 1778 | " |
| John Hunt | Cooper | 13[th] March 1779 | " |
| Jonathan Setchel | Sail Maker | 21[st] | " |
| Joseph King | Boatswains Mate | May 1[st] 1779 | " |
| Nathan Burch | Gunnors Mate | 31[st] March | " |
| John Lesure | Cook | 1[st] Feb[y] | " |
| Jesse Lester | Cockswain | Nov[r] 25[th] 1778 | " |
| Able Woodworth | Serg[t] Mariens | May 1[st] 1779 | " |
| Norman Morrison | " | 10[th] April | " |
| Abraham Acker | Carpentors Mate | 27[th] | " |
| Jasper Smith | Armourer | May 1[st] 1779 | " |
| Timothy Lynch | Seaman | Jan[y] 10[th] 1779 | " |
| George George | " | 10[th] Feb[y] | " |
| Walter Bottom | Stewards Mate | 15[th] April | " |
| Charles Millenor | Landsman | March 29[th] 1779 | " |
| John Setchel | Seaman | 28[th] | " |
| William Waterman | Landsman | 1[st] | " |
| Paul Bunn | Seaman | April 3[d] | deserted |
| Henry Calleway | Seaman | 21[st] | " |
| Solomon Dunham | Landsman | 21[st] | deserted |
| Samuel Thrasher | " | 21[st] | " |
| Daniel Butler | " | 21[st] | " |
| Allen Bidwell | | 21[st] | " |
| Levy Mallery | Seman | 22[d] | " |
| Edmond Morriss | " | 19[th] | " |
| Valentine Rockester | " | 22[d] | deserted |
| Daniel Robbins | Landsman | Jan[y] 17[th] | " |
| Asa Bellows | " | 29[d] | " |
| Ebenezer Allen | Landsman | April 19[th] 1779 | " |
| Calvin Davison | Seaman | March 26[th] | " |
| James Ash | Landsman | 17[th] | " |
| Alexander Young | Q[r] Master | May 1[st] | deserted |
| John Webb | Seaman | March 1[st] | " |
| Eph[m] Pumham | Landsman | 27[th] | " |
| Robert Field | Seaman | Ap[l] 15[th] | " |

| Names | Capacities | Time of Entry | Time of Discharge |
|---|---|---|---|
| A Francies | Seaman | Ap¹ 19th | deserted |
| Cull Cobus | " | 1st | 38d Aug. |
| Joseph Cutler | Master at Arms | April 20th | deserted |
| Joseph Keenne | Corperal Mariens | 20th | " |
| Frederick Andrus | Seaman | 20th | " |
| William Tyack | " | 25th | " |
| Alexand' Lowry | " | 25th | deserted |
| Peleg Sanford | " | 25th | deserted |
| Thomas Scott | Quarter Master | 27th | " |
| Hezekiah Meach | Landman | 27th | " |
| Israel Durfey | " | 27th | " |
| Christopher Brown | " | 28th | " |
| Abijah Fisk | Seaman | 29th | " |
| Philip Covel | Landman | May 1st | " |
| Micael Knox (?) | Seaman | April 25th | deserted |
| Benjª Unchous | Seaman | 27th | " |
| Joseph Squib | Landman | 28th | " |
| Bimeleck Uncas | " | 30th | " |
| James Bottom 3d | " | 7 Dec. 1778 | |
| Joseph Walker | Seaman | 14 Janʸ 1779 | deserted |
| Martin Ford | Landman | 14 " | deserted |
| Jonathan French Jun' | " | 20th " | " |
| Eliphalet Coburn | " | 20th " | " |
| Jabez Kingsley | " | 30 " | deserted |
| John Cary | " | 1 March | " |
| Jonathan Hill | " | 1 " | " |
| Benjamin Shelden | " | 15 Febʸ | " |
| Benony Dick | Seaman | 15 " | " |
| Philip Chuish | Landsman | 3 May | " |
| Charles Freeman | " | 6 " | deserted |
| James French | Seaman | 15 Febʸ | " |
| Jeremiah Bailey | " | 7 May | " |
| John Baldwin | " | 7 " | " |
| Samuel Ovit | " | 7 " | " |
| Jonah Wells | " | 7 " | " |
| William Buggee | Landsman | 6 " | deserted |
| Jonah Malbone | " | 11 " | " |
| Richmond Crandel | " | 15 April | " |
| James Burnham | Seaman | 15 " | " |
| Jacob Fobs | " | 1 May | " |
| Charles White | Boatswains Mate | 9 " | " |
| Willet Carpender | Landsman | 9 " | " |

Carried to another sheet.
[The other sheet is missing.]

[*State Library, Revolution 31.*]

Pay List for Ship Oliver Cromwell Timº Parker Esq' Commander

| | | | |
|---|---|---|---|
| John Richards | Seaman | 9 May 1779 to | 26 July died |
| Zebulon Cooper | Landsman | 10 " to | 28 Aug |
| Cruttendon Ward | Seaman | 15 Febʸ to | " |
| Benjª Fuller | Landsman | 20 Janʸ to | " |
| William Satterlee | Seaman | 14 May to | " |
| Thomas Stanton | Quarter-master | 28 April to | 7 June killed |
| Daniel Stanton 2d | Landsman | 10 May to | 28 Aug. |
| Daniel Stanton 3d | " | 10 " to | " |

| Name | Rank | From | To |
|---|---|---|---|
| Charles Cheeseborough | Quarter-master | 12 May | to 20 July died |
| William Billings | Landsman | 12 " | to 28 Aug. |
| Daniel Curtis | Seaman | 10 " | to " |
| Isaac Frisbee | " | 1 Dec[r] | to " |
| John Wellman | Landsman | 15 Feby. | to " |
| Eben[r] Robinson | Surgeons-Mate | 5 May | to " |
| William Malone | Quarter-Master | 15 " | to " |
| Benj[a] Dickerson | Landsman | 15 " | to " |
| Abner Beebe | Seaman | 15 " | to " |
| Michael Ewen | Quarter-master | 16 " | to 6 June killed |
| Simon Pembleton | Landsman | 16 " | to 28 Aug |
| John Pembleton | " | 16 " | to " |
| Jedediah Morton | Seaman | 1 April | deserted |
| Edward Barrett | " | 26 May | to 28 Aug[t] |
| John Moan | " | 26 " | to " |
| Jabez Luce | Landsman | 28 " | to " |
| William Aborn | Quarter Gunner | 28 " | deserted |
| Frederick Niles | Seaman | 28 " | to 28 Aug. |
| Simeon Starkweather | Landsman | 28 " | to " |
| Rufus Gardener | " | 28 " | to " |
| Retrieve Moore | Seaman | 26 " | to " |
| Eliphalet Covel | " | 29 " | to " |
| Michael Holland | " | 29 " | to " |
| Joseph Curtis | Landsman | 25 " | to " |
| John Walton | Seaman | 29 " | to " |
| Thomas Larkam | " | 29 " | to " |
| Norman Bunce | " | 29 " | to " |
| Daniel Clark | " | 29 " | deserted |
| William Young | Landsman | 29 " | " |
| Conklin Shadin | " | 21 " | to 28 Aug[t] |
| William Otis | " | 31 " | to " |
| Pharoh Sharper | " | 31 " | to " |
| Thomas Sprigs | " | 31 " | deserted |
| Isaac Heard | " | 31 " | to 28 Aug[t] |
| Guardin Wyyaung | Seaman | 31 " | to " |
| Daniel Winfield | " | 31 " | deserted |
| Simon Ray Ward | Midshipman | 20 " | to 28 Aug[t] |
| Eben[r] Colfax | " | 1 June | to " |
| John Chatfield | Pilote | 30 May | to " |
| Thomas Hancock | Seaman | 1 June | to " |
| Guy Palms | " | 1 " | died 10 July |
| James Jeffery | Landsman | 1 " | to 28 Aug[t] |
| Thomas Bolles 3[d] | " | 1 " | to " |
| William Fuller | " | 20 Jany. | to " |
| Bristow Palmer | " | | deserted |
| Clement Miner | " | 15 May | to 28 Aug[t] |

[*State Library, Revolution 31.*]

The following persons signed receipts for wages for service on board the Ship of War Oliver Cromwell.

William Lamb
John Chatfield
Hutchins Boden
Daniel Hillard
John Whittelsey

Dominioque Tawzin was taken prisoner and put on board prison ship at New York.

[*Connecticut Historical Society.*]

# PENSIONERS.

## HALF PAY.

[This and the following list are condensed from several lists by omitting all but a single reference to each name.]

The United States Dr To the State of Connecticut for disbursements for half pay for Troops wounded in the service of the United States Agreeably to Act of Congress August 26th 1776.

| Bills & Accounts | Remarks |
|---|---|
| Serjt Thomas Farnham | Col. C. Webbs Regt |
| Serjt Nathan Smith | Col. S. Sheldons " Dragoons |
| John Rood | Col. G. S. Sillimans " |
| Joel Ives Jr. | Col. Andrew Wards " |
| Benja Denslow | Col. Thadª Cooks " |
| Stephen Fellows | Col. Burrells " |
| Simeon Mills | Col. Burrells " '76 |
| Lt Elnathan Nichols | Danbury Alarm |
| Joseph Matson or Mattison | Col. Thadª Cooks Regt |
| Salmon Buell | Danbury Alarm |
| Serjt Lothrop Davis | Col. Starrs Regt, 1st Conn. |
| Artemas Johnson | Col. Woosters " |
| Justus Johnson | Danbury Alarm |
| William Edmonds | " |
| Stephen Everts | Col. Warners Regt |
| John Hutchinson | 1st Conn " |
| Seth Boardman | Col. Thadª Cooks " |
| Lemuel Demming | Col. Huntingtons " |
| Moses Raymond | Col. Saml Whitings " |
| Lt Thomas Avery | Col. Huntingtons " |
| Elijah Lincoln | Col. Swifts " |
| John Chilson | Col. Charles Webbs " |
| William Lucas | Col. Meigs " |
| Lt David Williams | Danbury Alarm |
| Nathaniel Church | Col. G. S. Sillimans Regt |
| William Tarball | Col. Durkees " |
| Ransford A. Ferris | Danbury Alarm |
| James St John | Col. Bradleys Regt |
| William Burrus | Col. S. B. Webbs " |
| Stephen Fellows | Col. Burrells " '76 |

| Bills & Accounts | Remarks |
|---|---|
| William Edmonds | Danbury Alarm |
| Isaac Richards | Col. Stephen S[t] Johns Reg[t] |
| Ozias Goodwin | Express Danbury Al[m] |
| Lieu[t] Aaron Kelcey | Col. Thad[s] Cooks Reg[t] |
| Isaac Trowbridge | Danbury Alarm |
| John Crane | " |
| Ezra Willcox | Col. Thad[s] Cooks Reg[t] |
| Amos Gray | Danbury Alarm |
| Nathaniel Austin | Col. Thad[s] Cooks Reg[t] |
| Seth Johnson | " |
| Serj[t] Jeremiah Markham | " |
| Roswell Franciss | " |
| Jonathan Bowen | " |
| E. & J. Sheldon | " |
| Levy Peck | Danbury Al[m] Sheldons Reg[t] |
| Asa Tyler | Col. John Chesters " |
| Joseph Mix for his son | 5[th] Connec[t] " |
| Richard Watrous | 6[th] " " |

[Comptroller's Office.]

The United States D[r] To the State of Connecticut for disbursements for half pay for Troops Wounded in the service of the State of Connecticut agreeably to Act of Assembly passed May 1777

| Bills & Accounts | Reg[ts] to which they belonged |
|---|---|
| Josiah Smith | Col. N. Hookers Reg[t] |
| Thomas Bristol | Col. Thad[s] Cooks " |
| Lent Ives | Col. M. Meads " or Col. John Meads |
| Constant Webb | Col. M. Meads " |
| George Lord | Col. M. Meads " or Col. John Meads |
| Zacheus or Zachariah Fargo | Militia N. London; Col. J. Lattimer's Reg[t] |
| Lemuel King | Col. Wells's Reg[t] |
| Wait Hinkley | Cap[t] Miels C[o] |
| David Squier | Fairfield Battery |
| William Osborne | Cap[t] D. Leavensworths C[o] |
| Justin Jennings | Brig Defence |
| Ens[n] And[w] Mead | Cap[t] Fitchs C[o] |
| Benj[a] Close | Cap[t] Fitchs C[o] |
| William Hodge | Col. N. Hookers Reg[t] |
| Tim[y] Bassett | 2[d] Militia " |
| Amos Mix | Col John Meads " |

[Comptroller's Office.]

## CIVIL LIST.

Names &c. of Connecticut soldiers entitled by reason of wounds or disabilities recieved in service to be placed upon the pension list

[The names here given are those not found in the pension list printed in Record of Connecticut Men in Revolution.]

| Name | Town from | Served in |
|---|---|---|
| John Williams | | |
| Nathan Ellis | | 1st Conn. Reg. |
| Lewis Hurd | | 3d Conn. Reg. |
| Sherman Gardner | | Invalid Corps. |
| Benoni Conel | | " |
| Richard P. Hallow | | " |
| Aaron Wilder | | " |
| Albert Bowman | | 5th Conn. Reg. |
| Lemuel Rich | | Invalid Corps. |
| John Kelly | | " |
| Theophilus Mead | | 8th Conn. Reg. |
| Jirah Carter | | 2d Conn. Reg. |
| Edward Benton | | Invalid Corps. |
| Richard Finney | | 3d Conn. Reg. |
| Benjamin Denslow | Suffield | Militia under Col. Thaddeus Cook [lass |
| Roswell Parish | Canterbury | Militia under Col. John Doug- |
| Lent Ives | Bristol | Col. Matthew Mead's Reg. |
| Lemuel Deming Jr. | East Hartford | Col. Huntington's Reg. |
| Isaac Finch | Stratford | Col. Samuel B. Webb's Reg. |
| Wiat Hinckley | Stonington | Gen. Waterbury's Brigade. |
| Stephen Hemstead | New London | Col. Webbs Reg.; Militia, 1781. |
| Benjamin Close | Greenwich | Independent Co. |
| Stephen Everts | Salisbury | Col. Warner's Reg. |
| William Edmond | Woodbury | Col. Increase Moseley's Reg. |
| Elnathan Nichols | Stratford | Gen. Arnold's Horse |
| Selah Scofield | Stamford | Col. Charles Webb's Reg. |
| Thomas Avery | Groton | 1st Conn. Reg. |
| John Rood | New Milford | Col. Silliman's Reg. |
| Grant Johnson | Stratford | Col. Heman Swift's Reg. |
| John Herren or Herron | Lyme | 1st Conn. Reg. |
| Park Avery Jr. | Groton | Militia |
| Robert Gallup | Groton | Fort Griswold |
| John Starr | Groton | Militia |
| Solomon Stark | Groton | Col. Lattimers Militia |
| Jabez Pembleton | Groton | Militia [Reg. |
| Joseph Waterman | Norwich | Gen. Jedediah Huntington's |
| Elisha Burrows | Groton | Col. John Ely's Reg. |
| Samuel Mills Jr. | Norfolk | Col. Charles Burrall's Reg. |
| William Barrows | Killingley | Col. Samuel B. Webb's Reg. |
| Lemuel Deming | East Hartford | |
| Oliver Bennitt | | Invalid Corps |
| John Starr | | |

[*Comptroller's Office.*]

## SCHEDULE OF PENSIONERS.

[Copied from a "Letter from the Secretary of War, communicating a transcript of the pension list of the United States —— June 1, 1813 —— Washington. 1813."]

| No. on the Roll | Names | Rank or Quality | Annual Stipend |
|---|---|---|---|
| 1 | Thomas Avery | lieutenant | $200 |
| 2 | Park Avery, Junior | " | 60 |
| 3 | Ebenezer Avery | corporal | 30 |
| 4 | David Atkins | private | 60 |
| 5 | Gad Asher | " | 60 |
| 6 | Abner Andruss | " | 60 |
| 7 | Daniel Avery | " | 36 |
| 8 | Amos Avery 2d | " | 30 |
| 9 | Theodore Andruss | " | 60 |
| 10 | Samuel Andrus | corporal | 45 |
| 11 | Smith Ames | private | 60 |
| 12 | Nathaniel Austin | " | 45 |
| 13 | Daniel Bouton | captain | 180 |
| 14 | Oliver Bostwick | ensign | 120 |
| 15 | Daniel Bushnell | private | 60 |
| 16 | Simeon Bishop | " | 60 |
| 17 | Salmon Buell | " | (dead) |
| 18 | William Burrows | " | 60 |
| 19 | Daniel Bill | " | 60 |
| 20 | Isaiah Bunce | " | 45 |
| 21 | Stephen Barnum | " | 60 |
| 22 | Samuel Burdwin | " | 60 |
| 23 | Benjamin Bennett | " | 24 |
| 24 | John Beardsley, junior | " | 60 |
| 25 | Jedediah Brown | " | 20 |
| 26 | Elisha Burrows | " | 15 |
| 27 | Isaiah Beaumont | " | 15 |
| 28 | Walter Burdick | " | 30 |
| 29 | Edward Bassett | " | 30 |
| 30 | William Bailey | " | 30 |
| 31 | Robert Bailey | " | 15 |
| 32 | Enos Blakesley | " | (dead) |
| 33 | David Blackman | " | 40 |
| 34 | Jonathan Bowers | corporal | 60 |
| 35 | Aner Bradley | sergeant | 30 |
| 36 | Oliver Burnham | " | 15 |
| 37 | Isaiah Buell | private | 45 |
| 38 | Joseph Button | " | 60 |
| 39 | Seth Boardman | " | 40 |
| 40 | William C. Beebe | " | 60 |
| 41 | Ebenezer Coe | captain | 240 |
| 42 | Richard Chamberlain | private | 44 |
| 43 | John Clark | " | 60 |
| 44 | Matthew Cadwell | " | 60 |

## PENSIONERS.

| No. on the Roll | Names | Rank or Quality | Annual Stipend |
|---|---|---|---|
| 45 | Benoni Connell | private | $60 |
| 46 | Jirah Carter | " | 60 |
| 47 | Timothy Ceasar | " | 60 |
| 48 | Benjamin Close | " | 48 |
| 49 | Amariah Chappell | " | 24 |
| 50 | Elisha Clark | " | 30 |
| 51 | Jonah Cook | " | 60 |
| 52 | Henry Cone | " | 60 |
| 53 | Simon Crosby | " | 40 |
| 54 | Nathaniel Church | " | 30 |
| 55 | Ebenezer Duran | " | 60 |
| 56 | George Dixon | " | 60 |
| 57 | Lemuel Denning, junior | " | 20 |
| 58 | Lothrop Davis | sergeant | 60 |
| 59 | Israel Dibble | private | 30 |
| 60 | Gershom Dormon | " | 60 |
| 61 | Joseph Dunbar | corporal | 45 |
| 62 | John Daboll | private | 7.50 |
| 63 | Stephen Everts | " | 40 |
| 64 | William Edmonds | " | 40 |
| 65 | Eliphalet Easton | " | 60 |
| 66 | Gideon Edwards | " | 60 |
| 67 | Stephen Fellows | sergeant | 60 |
| 68 | Thomas Farnham | " | 36 |
| 69 | John Fountaine | private | 60 |
| 70 | Aaron Farmar | " | 60 |
| 71 | Isaac Frink | " | 60 |
| 72 | Ransford A. Ferris | " | 60 |
| 73 | Zaccheus Fargo | " | 30 |
| 74 | Henry Filmore | " | 30 |
| 75 | Samuel French | " | 60 |
| 76 | Andrew Griswold | lieutenant | 160 |
| 77 | Sherman Gardner | private | 60 |
| 78 | Henry Gilner | " | 60 |
| 79 | Andrew Gallup | " | 40 |
| 80 | Robert Gallup | " | 15 |
| 81 | Richard P. Hallow | " | 60 |
| 82 | Jazaniah How | " | 60 |
| 83 | Stephen Hull | corporal | 30 |
| 84 | Joseph Harrup | private | 60 |
| 85 | Stephen Hempstead | " | 45 |
| 86 | Nero Hawley | " | 40 |
| 87 | Isee Hayt | " | 30 |
| 88 | John Herron | " | 30 |
| 89 | Eleazer Hudson | " | 45 |
| 90 | Ashbel Hosmer | corporal | (dead) |
| 91 | Nathan Hawley | " | 48 |
| 92 | Daniel Hewitt | sergeant | 20 |
| 93 | Isaac Higgins | private | (dead) |
| 94 | Thurston Hilliard | " | 20 |
| 95 | John Horsford | " | (dead) |
| 96 | Benjamin Howd | " | 45 |
| 97 | Elijah Hoyt | " | 30 |
| 98 | David Hubbell | " | 60 |
| 99 | Nathaniel Hewitt | " | 45 |
| 100 | Joel Hinman | " | 60 |
| 101 | David Hurd | " | 60 |

| No. on the Roll | Names | Rank or Quality | Annual Stipend |
|---|---|---|---|
| 102 | Charles Jones | private | $60 |
| 103 | Justus Johnson | " | 40 |
| 104 | Johuel Judd | " | 48 |
| 105 | Lent Ives | " | 80 |
| 106 | Caleb Jewett | " | 20 |
| 107 | William Johnson | " | 80 |
| 108 | Jared Knapp | sergeant | 60 |
| 109 | Lemuel King | private | 60 |
| 110 | Elisha Lee | captain | 240 |
| 111 | Peter Lewis | private | 60 |
| 112 | Phinehas Lake | " | 60 |
| 113 | William Leach | " | 60 |
| 114 | Christopher Latham, junior | " | 45 |
| 115 | John Ledyard | " | 45 |
| 116 | Naboth Lewis | " | 40 |
| 117 | Nathaniel Lewis | " | 15 |
| 118 | Samuel Lewis | corporal | 45 |
| 119 | Lee Lay | captain | 80 |
| 120 | Elijah Lincoln | corporal | 60 |
| 121 | Timothy Mix | lieutenant | 60 |
| 122 | Andrew Mead | ensign | 80 |
| 123 | Dan Mansfield | private | (dead) |
| 124 | Samuel Mitchell | " | 60 |
| 125 | Samuel Mills, junior | " | 80 |
| 126 | John Morgan 3d | " | 40 |
| 127 | Jacob Meach | " | 20 |
| 128 | James Morgan, junior | " | 80 |
| 129 | Joseph Moxley | " | 80 |
| 130 | Jeremiah Markham | sergeant | 60 |
| 131 | Allyn Marsh | corporal | 80 |
| 132 | Stephen Miner | qr. gunner | 80 |
| 133 | Elnathan Norton | private | (dead) |
| 134 | Mark Noble | " | 60 |
| 135 | David Orcutt | " | 60 |
| 136 | Joseph Otis | " | 30 |
| 137 | Thomas Picket | " | 60 |
| 138 | Alexander Phelps | " | 60 |
| 139 | David Pool | " | 60 |
| 140 | Thomas Parmelie | sergeant | 7.50 |
| 141 | Chandler Pardie | private | 52.50 |
| 142 | Daniel Preston | " | 20 |
| 143 | Obadiah Perkins | lieutenant | 96 |
| 144 | Enos Petott | private | 24 |
| 145 | John Rood | " | 48 |
| 146 | Jeremiah Ryan | " | 60 |
| 147 | Lemuel Rich | " | (transfd) |
| 148 | Moses Raymond | " | 60 |
| 149 | Oliver Rogers | " | 24 |
| 150 | David Ranney | " | 60 |
| 151 | Solomon Reynolds | " | 60 |
| 152 | Samuel Rossetter | " | 60 |
| 153 | Elijah Royce | " | 45 |
| 154 | Josiah Smith | " | 60 |
| 155 | Edward Stanton | " | 60 |
| 156 | Josiah Strong | " | 40 |
| 157 | John Starr | " | 40 |
| 158 | Selah Scoffield | " | 80 |

## PENSIONERS.

| No. on the Roll | Names | Rank or Quality | Annual Stipend |
|---|---|---|---|
| 159 | William Seymour | private | $240 |
| 160 | Benjamin Seely | " | 15 |
| 161 | William Starr | qr. master | 45 |
| 162 | Elihu Sabin | private | 40 |
| 163 | Samuel Sawyer | " | 30 |
| 164 | Thomas Shepherd | " | 15 |
| 165 | Amos Skeel | " | 60 |
| 166 | Heber Smith | sergeant | 60 |
| 167 | Aaron Smith | private | 15 |
| 168 | Edmund Smith | " | 30 |
| 169 | Samuel Stillman | " | 30 |
| 170 | Aaron Stephens | captain | 120 |
| 171 | Peter Smith | private | 48 |
| 172 | Elijah Sheldon | " | (dead) |
| 173 | John Smith | " | 48 |
| 174 | Moses Tracy | sergeant | 60 |
| 175 | William Tarball | corporal | 36 |
| 176 | Solomon Townsend | private | 60 |
| 177 | Aaron Tuttle | " | 40 |
| 178 | Jabez Tomlinson | " | 15 |
| 179 | Enoch Turner, junior | " | 60 |
| 180 | Levi Tuttle | " | 15 |
| 181 | Samuel Woodcock | sergeant | 60 |
| 182 | Constant Webb. | " | 36 |
| 183 | William Wilson | private | 60 |
| 184 | John Waklee | " | 60 |
| 185 | Joseph Waterman | " | 40 |
| 186 | Benjamin Weed, junior | " | 60 |
| 187 | Joseph Woodmansee | " | 60 |
| 188 | Thomas Williams | " | 20 |
| 189 | Jacob Williams | " | 15 |
| 190 | Richard Watrous | " | 45 |
| 191 | Jonathan Whaley | " | 15 |
| 192 | Ezra Wilcox | " | 15 |
| 193 | Azel Woodworth | " | 60 |
| 194 | Seth Weed | lieutenant | 72 |
| 195 | James Wayland | private | 40 |
| 196 | William Woodruff | corporal | 60 |
| 197 | Hezekiah Bailey | ensign | 60 |
| 198 | Isaac Durand | private | 30 |
| 199 | Joel Fox | " | 30 |
| 200 | Luke Guyant | " | 60 |
| 201 | Aaron Peck | " | 40 |
| | Total of annual stipends | | 9778.50 |

# APPENDIX

[Here are included several rolls received too late for insertion in their proper place, one that was omitted in arranging the material at hand, and a few individual records and miscellaneous items.]

## THIRD BATTALION—COL. ENOS.

See Page 141.

[*See Record of Connecticut Men in the Revolution, page 424.*]

### CAPT. GRISWOLD'S COMPANY.

The Marching Roll of Capt. Griswold's Company, March 4, 1777.

From Torrington
John Burr
Seth Coe
Charles Roberts
Ambrose Fyler
Jonathan Miller
Asaph Atwater
John Birge
Isaac Filley
Timothy Loomis
Ebenezer Bissell
Return Bissell

From Litchfield
Stephen Smith
Gideon Philips
Abel Catlin
Simeon Ross
Timothy Gibbs
Benjamin Stone
Ashbel Catlin
Calvin Bissell
Benjamin Palmer
John Way
Abner Baldwin
Philemon Wilcox
Solomon Linsley

From Torrington
Daniel Winchell
Frederick Bigelow
Cotton Mather
Benjamin Frisbie
Thomas Skinner
Nathaniel Barber
Timothy Kelsey
Thomas Matthews
Stephen Rossiter
Elisha Kelsey

From Litchfield
John Woodruff
Enoch Sperry
Dyer Cleaveland
Enos Bains
Solomon Harrison
Harris Hopkins
Timothy Linsley
Joel Taylor
John Bissell
Solomon Woodruff
Philo Woodruff
Simeon Gibbs
Bela Benton

From Cornwall
John Mebbins
Samuel Burton
Josiah Hopkins
Asahel Leet
Solomon Johnson
Henry Philemor
Samuel Emmons
Israel Dibble

From Cornwall
Thomas White
Elisha Demmen
James Wadsworth
Joshua Hartshorn
Noah Harrison
Asa Emmons
Jonathan Bell
Simeon North

[*Dwight C. Kilbourne, Litchfield.*]

## FIRST REGIMENT—MAJ. NEWBERRY.
### See Page 149.

[*See Record of Connecticut Men in the Revolution, page 449.*]

### FOURTH COMPANY—LIEUT. SEYMOUR.

August 14 1776. Received of Maj' Newbury for advance money Towards wages £67 : 0 :
15 : Marcht with 58 men including officers towards New York
16 Set sail from New Haven upon our way to New York
16 Arived att Newyork late 7 o'clock.
Hartford August 15, 1776.

| | |
|---|---|
| Ebenezer Belding . . . £1.00 | Gideon Butler J<sup>un</sup> £1.00 |
| Will<sup>m</sup> Hopkins . . . 1.00 | Ruben Judd . 1.00 |
| Jon<sup>th</sup> Sidgwick . . . 1.00 | Sam<sup>ll</sup> Merrill . 1.00 |
| Elizer Merrill . . . 1.00 | Ashbel Hosmer . 1.00 |
| Peter King . . . 1.00 | Ashbel Wells . 1.00 |
| Rosseter Belding . . . 1.00 | Jon<sup>th</sup> B. Balch . 1.00 |
| Elisha Mix . . . 1.00 | Joseph Brown . 1.00 |
| Oliver Kellogg . . . 1.00 | Ashbel Shepard . 1.00 |
| Noah Butler J<sup>r</sup> . . . 1.00 | Asa Goodman . 1.00 |
| Jon<sup>th</sup> Gilbert . . . 1.00 | Gideon Merrill . 1.00 |
| Ebenezer Seymour . . . 1.00 | Nath<sup>ll</sup> Braman . 1.00 |
| Richard Chapley . . . 1.00 | James Wadsworth 1 00 |
| Francis Smith . . . 1.00 | Moses Brace . 1.00 |
| Ebenezer Merry . . . 1.00 | Ichabod Lyman . 1.00 |
| Will<sup>m</sup> Whiting . . . 1.00 | Sam<sup>ll</sup> Stanly . 1.00 |
| Joel Lord . . . 1.00 | John Nott . 1.00 |
| Richard Goodman . . . 1.00 | Elihu Olmsted . 1.00 |
| Ens<sup>n</sup> George Kellogg . . . 1.00 | Tho<sup>s</sup> Olmsted . 1.00 |
| Isaac Webster . . . 1.00 | Sam<sup>ll</sup> Holmes . 1.00 |
| Joseph Butler | Henry Brace . 1.00 |
| Aaron Seymour . . . 1.00 | John Nash . 1.00 |
| John Spencer . . . 1.00 | Isaac Flower . 1.00 |
| Aaron Cadwell J<sup>un</sup>. . . 1.00 | Eben<sup>r</sup> Faxon . 1.00 |
| George Bidwell . . . 1.00 | Eben<sup>r</sup> Crosby . 1.00 |
| Enos Kellogg . . . 1.00 | Zach Kelsey . 1.00 |
| Stephen Skiner . . . 1.00 | John Wells J<sup>un</sup> . 1.00 |
| Jeduthan Cadwell . . . 1.00 | Moses Gaylord . 1.00 |
| Joseph Cadwell . . . 1.00 | Tho<sup>s</sup> Faxon . 1.00 |
| Aaron Cadwell . . . 1.00 | Solomon Ensign . 1.00 |

[There is an attestation in the book, signed by Sally S. Mills, stating that the within Document was a Journal and Roll of 58 men who served under her deceased Father, Charles Seymour, who was a Lieutenant in the army of the Revolution, and was found by her among his papers — dated January 26, 1887.]

[*Mary K. Talcott, Hartford.*]

## TENTH REGIMENT—COL. COOK.

See Page 183.

### CAPT. NORTON'S COMPANY.

List of those going to R. I under Command of Capt Charles Norton Aug 23 1778

Nathan Chittenden Serg'
Joseph Hall
Peter Peck
Liut James Peck
Jonathan Bartholomew
Benj Chittenden
John Lewis
Ward Johnson

Josiah Tuttle
Oliver Doolittle
Saml Barns
Saml Mattoon
Asahel Hull
Joseph Curtes Jr
Giles Cook

[*George M. Curtis, Meriden.*]

## TENTH REGIMENT—COL. COOK.

See Page 203.

### LIST OF MEN DETACHED.

Appraizal of Guns &c belonging to Cap Oliver Stanley Comp. for those detached June 13 1779

Roswell Beach
Moses Bartholomew
Ens Saml Culver

Dowey Daily
    in the Room of Dan Peck

Of those belonging to Cap Miles Johnsons Company Same time

Isaac Kirtland
Leml Cook
Giles Churchill
Hiue (?) Munson

Jesse Rice
Saml Barns
    went in Rices Room

Appointment of Horses Arms & Acq. of a Number draughted from Cap Isaac Halls Compy of Troop   Hill Hall 2ᵈ Master
Lent Hough                                                                 David Morgan

Appraizal of Guns &c belonging Capt Abraham Stanleys Company for those detached to go to Greenwich 13ᵗʰ June 1779

Reuben Horsford                       Beri Tuttle
Ichabod Barns                         Charles Johnson
Joel Doolittle                        Enos Benham Jr
Chas Preston                          in room of Wᵐ Atwater

Of those belonging to Capt Thos Shephards Company Same time

Amos Johnson                          Jacob Curtis
Amos Merriman                         Thos Andrus
Edw. Fenn Jr

Of those belonging to Capt Caleb Hall Same time

Danl Merwin                           Enos (?) Benham
Stephen Johnson                       Saml Rice
David Barns                           in room of Josiah Mix

Recᵈ of the Selectmen out of the Town Stock each of us half a pound Powder & sixteen Balls being detached to go to Greenwich 16ᵗʰ June 1779
                                      P  us Simon Frances
                                      Buller Ives

Wallingford

Appraisment of Arms &c Carried by men detached Aug 20 1779 from Capt John Houghs  2 Months Men

Jonathan Blakesley                    Simeon Perkins
  hired by Abner Way                  Osias Foster in the
Ens Thoˢ Foster                         room of Tim Foster
Asahel Yale in the                    Enos Hall
  room of Noah Yale                   Isral Hall

                Capt Thos Shepards Company
Robert Grannis                        Jonᵗʰ Francis

                Capt Ephraim Cooks Company
Elisha Wilmot                         Josiah Talmadge Jr
Gideon Curtes                         Thoˢ Gaylord
Robert Hotchkiss

                Capt Abraham Stanleys Comp
Joel Hough                            Zebulon Dudley
                                        hired by Cabb Merriman

                Capt Divan Berrys Comp
                Daniel Baldwin

                                      [*George M. Curtis, Meriden.*]

APPENDIX. 277

## SEVENTH REGIMENT—COL. WORTHINGTON.
### See Page 215.

### SECOND COMPANY—LIEUT. LEE.

[Guilford men summoned to serve as Sea Coast Guard at Sachem's Head, Guilford.]

Guilford February the 19th 1781
According to the within Writ I Have Summonsed the Following men to Guard under Lieu<sup>t</sup> Sam<sup>l</sup> Lee Viz Thelus Ward Ju<sup>r</sup> Caleb Everts for Six Days Friend Collins W<sup>m</sup> Barker John Leet Nehemiah Bradley Levy Lee Jared Bishop Nathan Redfield Wilmot Goldsmith Sam<sup>l</sup> Everts Ju<sup>r</sup> Isaac Parmele Thomas Griswold Ju<sup>r</sup> John Wick Sineus Dibble Reuben Shelley James Davis Ju<sup>r</sup> Joel Collens For three Days Each
                            John Starr Constable of Guilford
In addition to the Above I have summons<sup>d</sup> the following Persons to guard Namely Asael Murry Timothy Lee Eber Hall James Davis Jun<sup>r</sup> Russel (?) Stone James Bradley Joel Johnson Benjamin Hall Ju<sup>r</sup> Joel Parmele Isaac Parmele Thomas Griswold Ju<sup>r</sup> Levy Lee Treat Demming Reuben Shelly Medad Shelly John Leet Samuel Cruttenden Reuben Fowler John Stone Samuel Roberson Ju<sup>r</sup> John Johnson Ju<sup>r</sup> James Bradley William Barker Caleb Evarts Each of these garded three Days A Peace & James Bradley Six Days

                                                          [*E. C. Starr, Cornwall.*]

### SHORT LEVIES, 1782.

The following names appear in account and receipt books among many names already in print :

| Names | Service | Regiment |
|---|---|---|
| Rufus Hide | July 1 to Nov. 8 | |
| Neal M<sup>c</sup>Clean | May 21 to Dec. 6 | |
| John Miller | June 8 to Dec. 3 | 3d |
| Phineas Perkins | Apr. 30 to Sep. 21 | |
| Mark Hamlin | | 1st Conn. |
| Thomas Binge | | " |
| Joel Buckley | | Baldwins Artificers |
| Phineas Platt | | " |

                                                          [*Comptroller's Office.*]

## MISCELLANEOUS.

Justice Warner, Josiah Warner, Mark Warner & Timothy Scouval, where all Disafected Persons in Confinment, and Inlisted into the Service During the War, and Remaining disafected twas thought most Proper, for the good of the Service, they should procure Good men in their Stead, and Accordingly they Procured, William Heacock, Samuel Pribble, Patrick Snow, and Tabor Smith, and where accordingly Discharged.

[*State Library, Hebard Papers.*]

Rec$^d$ March 15$^{th}$ 1779 of Silvanus Starling one of the Select men of Stratford Fifty seven Pounds 12/ Shillings Lawful money which is in full for my Services and the persons under my Command in keeping Guard at North Fairfield In april 1777 Rec$^d$
        P  Stephen Middlebrook

[*Louis F. Middlebrook, Hartford.*]

To whom concern$^d$ permit the bearer Thomas Sharp of Newtown to pass unmolested to Stamford or Hors Neck and there joyn the Company Detached from Colo$^l$ Bordleys Regt
        pr Jabez Botsford J of peace
Newtown January ye 9 1781

[*William C. Sharpe, Seymour.*]

# ADDITIONS FROM RECORD OF CONNECTICUT MEN IN THE REVOLUTION.

[The following is taken from the official copy in the Adjutant-General's office.]

Page 9 For Thomas Tuder, read Daniel Tudor.
" 45 Ambrose Church died in service Aug. 22.
" " Stephen \ckley died Oct. 1.
" " Bethuel Fuller died Sep. 23.
" " Timothy Fuller died Oct. 17.
" 46 For John Mash, read John Mack.
" " Giles Gilbert died Sep. 22.
" " Moses Olmsted died Sep. 26, of East Haddam.
" 48 For William Ston (?), read William Stowe.
" 85 Phineas Lyman Tracy died Aug. 22.
" 89 For Abraham Filer, read Abraham Tyler.
" 109 Robert Sumner of Ashford in Capt. Daniel Allen's Co., Col. Ward's Regt.
" 326 Capt. Billings' Company ; add, Caleb Bailey, Haddam, enlisted June 24, 1781, for 6 months.
" 345 For John Mash, read John Mack.

## APPENDIX. 279

Page 471  Eli Moore also served as a private and Adjutant in Col. Roger Enos' regiment. His name appears on an abstract of rations due for the period from Oct. 8 to Nov. 15, 1777 — served as Adjutant 1st Connecticut regiment, commanded by Col. Roger Enos, joined June 25, 1778, name borne on the roll dated at Fort Clinton, Sept. 5, 1778.
" 501  Capt. Camp's Company; for Time of Marching, April 29, read March 29.
" "  Capt. Stoddard's Company; for Time of Marching, May 30, read March 30. Also same correction on the following page.
" 553  Hezekiah Bassett and Medad Atwater were both members 17th New Haven Company State Militia, British Invasion of New Haven, 1779.
" 611  Capt. Amos Smith, Washington, Conn., Captain of Artillery Co., State Militia, carpenter and farmer.
" 636  Absolom Pride, private Capt. Ebenezer Brewtsers Co., Col. Parsons Regt., from Oct. 1775 to Dec. 1776, in battles of Long Island, New York Island and Harlem Heights.
" 663  For John Mash, read John Mack.
" 664  For David Shepard, read Daniel Shepard.

# ERRATA.

Page 12. Transpose lines 12 and 13, beginning with word Officers.

Page 66. For Simeom Robertson, read Simeon Robertson.

Page 87. Line 13, for May 13, 1779, read May 13, 1777; line 17, for Michael Jenson, read Michael Jerison; line 19, for Oct. 6, read Oct. 1.

Page 165. For William Kinney, read William Kinney.

# INDEX.

Aaron, Thomas, 254.
Abbe, Heze, Jr., 244.
Abbe, Isaac, 14, 143.
Abbe, Isack, 14.
Abbe, R., 206, 214.
Abbe, Thomas, 88.
Abbee, Mason, 74.
Abbey, 50.
Abbot, Phillip, 14.
Abbot, Samuel, 208.
Abbott, Daniel, 212.
Abbott, Joseph, 211.
Abbott, Samuel, 227.
Abby, Hezekiah, 246, 248.
Abby, Joseph, 114.
Abby, Nathaniel, 114.
Abel, Cherub, 185.
Abel, E., 177.
Abel, Elijah, 180, 225.
Abel, Eliphalet, 162.
Abel, Joseph, 5, 149.
Abel, Simon, 160.
Abell, Isaac, 212.
Abels, Abel, 61.
Aberhart, John, 9.
Abernathey, John, 173.
Abernethy, Jarad, 39.
Able, Rufus B., 45.
Ables, John, 205.
Ables, Sluman, 138.
Aborn, William, 264.
Abro, Benajah, 36.
Abro, Benjamin, 36.
Abune, Paulis, 35.
Achor, Jacob, 121.
Acker, Abraham, 262.
Ackla, Silas, 184.
Ackley, Champion, 111.
Ackley, Lewis, 57.
Ackley, Nicholas, 57.
Ackley, Stephen, 278.
Ackly, Champion, 37.
Adams, Abner, 222.

Adams, Andrew, 201, 207.
Adams, Caleb, 167.
Adams, Corls, 172.
Adams, David, 47.
Adams, David, Jr., 148.
Adams, Elihu, 169.
Adams, Ephram, 203.
Adams, J., 84, 170.
Adams, James, 170.
Adams, Jedediah, 124.
Adams, Jesse, 172.
Adams, John, 64, 65, 88, 169, 185, 245, 251.
Adams, Jonas, 34.
Adams, Joseph, 153, 155, 172.
Adams, Joseph, 3d, 172.
Adams, Levi, 169.
Adams, Nehemiah, 169.
Adams, Parmeno, 7.
Adams, Pigot C., 28.
Adams, Reuben, 102.
Adams, Reubin, 131.
Adams, Samuel, 182, 252.
Adams, Silas, 167.
Adams, Solomon, Jr., 172.
Adams, William, 47.
Addams, Reubin, 124.
Addams, Samuel, 259.
Adee, Aner, 38, 130.
Adee, Anor, 102.
Adkins, Chauncy, 79.
Adkins, George, 204.
Adms, John, 172.
Africa, Cash, 68.
Agard, Hezekiah, 201.
Airey, J., 97.
Albany, 33, 42, 43.
Alcock, David, 108.
Alden, James, 231, 250.
Alden, Jarrus, 246.
Alden, Joab, 253.
Alden, Jonathan, 231.
Alden, Roger, 46, 54.

Alderman, Eli, 142, 164.
Alderman, Ephriem. 27.
Alderman, Isaac, 164.
Alderman, John. 164.
Alderman, Jonathan, Jr., 142.
Aldich, John, Jr., 1.
Alexander, James, 51.
Alford, Eliphelet, 36.
Alford, John, 36.
Alford, Peletiah, 119.
Alger, Asa, 65.
Allen, Amasa, 25.
Allen, Benjamin, 152.
Allen, C., 211.
Allen, Daniel, 14, 46, 88, 212, 278.
Allen, Daniel, Jr., 14.
Allen, David, 14, 55.
Allen, Ebenezer, 28, 262.
Allen, Eliphalet, 69, 99.
Allen, Isak, 164.
Allen, Jared, 143, 159.
Allen, Jerard. 259.
Allen, John, 212, 221, 222, 230.
Allen, Jonathan, 88.
Allen, Joseph, 105, 259.
Allen, Joseph, Jr., 105.
Allen, Martin, 39.
Allen, Moses, 54, 127.
Allen, Nathaniel, 184.
Allen, Phineas, 19.
Allen, Robert, 45.
Allen, Samuel. 57, 163, 189.
Allen, Silas, 169.
Allen, Thomas, 99.
Allen, Timothy, 161.
Allen, Titus, 43.
Allen, William, 14, 66, 240, 247, 248.
Allien, Benjamin, 1.
Allien, Christopher, 1.
Allin, Daniel, 57.
Allin, Gabril, 232.
Allin, Gideon, 233.
Allin, William, 14.
Alling, Caleb, 179.
Alling. Elenzoer, 235.
Allyn, 123.
Allyn, Amos, 216.
Allyn, Benjamin. 222.
Allyn, Chester, 23.
Allyn, David, 216.
Allyn, Elisha, 80.
Allyn, Ephraim, 216.
Allyn, John, 121, 209.
Allyn, Moses, 95, 117.
Allyn, Thomas, 146, 147.
Allyn, Timothy, 50.
Allyn, Titus, 41.

Allyn, William, 244.
Almey, John, 63.
Almstead, Benjamin, 235.
Almy, William, 82.
Alton, William, 184.
Alvord, Huet, 61.
Amadown, Moses, 184.
Ambler, Jonathan, 68.
Amedown, Jedediah, 208.
Amedown, Jonathan, 55.
Ames, 56.
Ames, Alvin, 28.
Ames, Arcules, 125.
Ames, Benjamin, 191.
Ames, Ezra, 58, 59, 60.
Ames, John, 64.
Ames, Nicholas, 134.
Ames, Samuel, 29, 82, 237.
Ames, Samuel, Jr., 31.
Ames, Smith, 268.
Ames, Zebulon, 74.
Amidown, Jedidiah, 14.
Ammidown, Jedediah, 14.
Ammit, John, 54.
Anderson, George, 14.
Anderson, James, 122, 253.
Anderson, Stephen, 14.
Anderson, Steven, 14.
Anderson, Thomas, 14, 45, 185.
Anderson, Timothy, 78.
Anderson, William, 68, 185.
Andras, Joseph, 59.
Andras, Obadiah, 59.
Andress, Samuel, 1.
Andrews, Andrew, 71.
Andrews, David, 115.
Andrews, James, 46.
Andrews, Jeremiah, 85.
Andrews, John, 198.
Andrews, John, Jr., 152.
Andrews, Joseph, 153.
Andrews, Samuel, 95, 153.
Andrews, Timothy, 242.
Andrews, William, 7.
Andrews, William, Jr., 142.
Androus, Philarman, 185.
Androus, Samuel, 117.
Andrus, Asahel, Jr., 142.
Andrus, David, 99.
Andrus, Eden, 199.
Andrus, Eli, 36.
Andrus, Elijah, 127, 128, 202.
Andrus, Frederick, 263.
Andrus, James, 155.
Andrus, John, 138.
Andrus, Jonathan, 142.
Andrus, Joseph, 80.
Andrus, Nathan, 32.

## INDEX.

Andrus, Samuel, 127, 155, 257, 268.
Andrus, Thomas, 19, 276.
Andrus, Timothy, 9.
Andruss, Abner, 268.
Andruss, Asa, 20.
Andruss, Benjiman, 157.
Andruss, Charles, 157.
Andruss, David, 157.
Andruss, John, 157.
Andruss, Stephen, 157, 158.
Andruss, Theodore, 268.
Andruss, Timothy, 77.
Andruss, William, 27, 88.
Anger, George, 68.
Annable, Anthony, 212.
Annew, David, 216.
Annibal, David, 16.
Answorth, Ahial, 66.
Anthony, John, 88, 239.
Antony, James, 80.
Antrum, Thomas, 168.
Apley, Josiah, 98.
Armstrong, Peter, 34.
Armstrong, William, 100.
Arnold, 267.
Arnold, Benedict, 23.
Arnold, Henery, 244.
Arnold, Henry, 247, 248.
Arnold, James, 17, 18, 19, 20, 22, 193, 200, 223.
Arnold, John, 162, 183, 221.
Arnold, Jonathan, 244, 248.
Arnold, Josiah, 22.
Arnold, Samuel, 184.
Arnould, Jonathan, 247.
Arons, Benedick, 150.
Arrabas, Jack, 115.
Arthur, Barthilmus, 186.
Arthur, Bartholemew, 80.
Arvin, William, 27.
Asband, Sam, 233.
Ash, James, 262.
Ashcraft, John, 167.
Ashcraft, William, 167.
Asher, Gad, 268.
Ashford, 25, 55, 57, 65, 66, 79, 82, 88, 89, 104, 114, 130, 278.
Ashley, John, 60, 99.
Ashley, Joseph, 143.
Ashley, Samuel, 143.
Aspell, Philip, 230.
Aspenwall, Caleb, 39.
Atkins, David, 112, 268.
Atkins, Ira, 113.
Atkins, Isaac, 134.
Atkins, Isaiah, 113.
Atkins, Jabez, 107.

Atkins, Joel, 134.
Atterton, David, 168.
Atwater, 55.
Atwater, Abel W., 194.
Atwater, Asaph, 273.
Atwater, Caleb, 55.
Atwater, Medad, 279.
Atwater, William, 276.
Atwater, William, Jr., 194.
Atwell, Ozias, 27.
Atwood, John, 27.
Atwood, Joseph, 80.
Augru, Felix, 184.
Augur, Philemon, 9.
Ausborn, John, 56.
Austin, Aaron, 36.
Austin, Amos, 16, 17, 22.
Austin, Andrew, 202.
Austin, Benjamin, 20.
Austin, Caleb, 63, 173.
Austin, George, 170, 186.
Austin, James, 36, 209.
Austin, John, 174, 179.
Austin, Joseph, 46, 82.
Austin, Nathaniel, 266, 268.
Austin, Richard, 53.
Austin, Usebius, 36.
Austin, William, 94.
Averil, Daniel, 73.
Averil, Jacob, 64.
Averil, Jonathan, 174.
Averill, Jacob, 18.
Averill, James, 208.
Averill, Nathaniel, 18.
Averill, Thomas, 19, 23.
Avery, 50.
Avery, Amos, 2d, 268.
Avery, Benjamin, 38.
Avery, Christopher, 124.
Avery, Daniel, 82, 268.
Avery, Ebenezer, 120, 268.
Avery, Elijah, 208.
Avery, Frederick, 95.
Avery, Jabez, 17, 22.
Avery, John, 40, 53, 102, 130.
Avery, Jonathan, 14, 143.
Avery, Nathan, 174, 216.
Avery, Park, Jr., 267, 268.
Avery, Roger, 240.
Avery, Simeon, 45.
Avery, Sylvanus, 82.
Avery, Thomas, 88, 265, 267, 268.
Ayer, John, 94.
Ayers, John, 150.
Ayres, Peter, 185.

Babbit, Benjamin, 141.
Babcock, 150.

Babcock, Benjamin, 16.
Babcock, Elias, 184.
Babcock, Ephraim, 94.
Babcock, Isaiah, 197.
Babcock, John, 25.
Babcock, Jonathan, 105.
Babcock, Joseph, 210.
Babcock, Nathaniel, 185.
Babcock, Ruben, 171.
Babcock, Timothy, 169.
Baccus, Ebenezer, 250.
Baccus, John, 247, 249.
Back, Elisha, 114.
Backes, Isaac, 171.
Backus, Andrew, 168, 169.
Backus, Ebenezer, 246.
Backus, Elijah, 74, 208.
Backus, Nathaniel, 246, 248.
Backus, Stephen, 168.
Backus, Timothy, 169, 222.
Backus, Whighting, 149.
Bacon, 50, 64.
Bacon, Abner, 88.
Bacon, Andrew, 204.
Bacon, Asa, 142.
Bacon, Benjamin, 170.
Bacon, Ebenezer, 141.
Bacon, Henry, 69.
Bacon, J., 170.
Bacon, Joseph, 105, 209.
Bacon, Joseph, Jr., 141.
Bacon, Nathaniel, 67.
Bacon, S., 170.
Bacon, William, 28, 88, 107.
Badcock, 12.
Badcock, Beriah, 5.
Badcock, Daniel, 3, 4, 143, 161.
Badcock, Jonathan, 161.
Badger, Bezelial, 149.
Badger, Jonathan, 14.
Bagdon, Cesar, 71, 112.
Bagley, Bernard, 94.
Bagley, David, 244, 247.
Bagley, John, 251.
Baile, Hondrick, 121.
Bailey, Aaron, 74.
Bailey, Caleb, 98, 278.
Bailey, Ebenezer, 3, 4.
Bailey, Elijah, 115, 116.
Bailey, Gideon, 48, 88.
Bailey, Hezekiah, 46, 271.
Bailey, Ichabod, 114.
Bailey, Jeremiah, 263.
Bailey, John, 81, 245, 249.
Bailey, Joseph, 246.
Bailey, Louden, 68.
Bailey, Robert, 88, 268.
Bailey, Rouben, 230.
Bailey, Timothy, 230.
Bailey, Titus, 222.
Bailey, Uriah A., 35.
Bailey, William, 115, 268.
Bains, Enos, 273.
Bajcom, Abiel, 162.
Baker, Abel, 64.
Baker, Amos, 200.
Baker, Asa, Jr., 140.
Baker, Benjamin, 201.
Baker, Bristol, 108.
Baker, Edward, 108.
Baker, Eldad, 136.
Baker, Hezekiah, 245, 251.
Baker, John, 53, 140, 167, 258.
Baker, Jonas, 167.
Baker, Joseph, 172.
Baker, Joshua, 174.
Baker, Lemuel, 12.
Baker, Nathaniel, 185.
Baker, Palsey, 140.
Baker, Phinehas, 136.
Baker, Robert, 185.
Baker, Stephen, 64.
Baker, William, 57, 83.
Balcam, Nathaniel, 39.
Balch, Jonathan B., 274.
Balcom, Elias, 68.
Balden, Samuel, 231.
Baldwen, David, 35.
Baldwin, 224, 227, 277.
Baldwin, A., 142.
Baldwin, Aaron, 9.
Baldwin, Abel, 77, 81, 195.
Baldwin, Abial, 191.
Baldwin, Abner, 201, 273.
Baldwin, Benjamin, 210.
Baldwin, Caleb, 49, 88, 97, 108.
Baldwin, Daniel, 276.
Baldwin, David, 242.
Baldwin, Ebenezer, 257.
Baldwin, Eleazer, 97.
Baldwin, Eli, 38.
Baldwin, Elijah, 195.
Baldwin, Elisha, 74.
Baldwin, Henry, 88.
Baldwin, I., 212.
Baldwin, Isaac, 77.
Baldwin, J., 223, 224.
Baldwin, Jacob, 6.
Baldwin, Jered, 196.
Baldwin, John, 38, 200, 263.
Baldwin, Jonathan, 184, 212, 223, 224.
Baldwin, Joseph, 183.
Baldwin, Josiah, 210.
Baldwin, Levi, 9.
Baldwin, Nathaniel, 81.

INDEX. 285

Baldwin, Samuel, 25, 198.
Baldwin, Silas, 88.
Baldwin, Simeon, 85.
Baldwin, Stephen, 201.
Baldwin, Thad, 196.
Baldwin, Thadeus, 189.
Baldwin, William, 252.
Baley, Henry, 109.
Baley, James, 149.
Baley, John, Jr., 174.
Baley, Joseph, 203.
Baley, Samuel, 149.
Ball, Benjamin, 36.
Ball, Humphrey, 88.
Ball, James, 79.
Ball, John, 48.
Ball, Jonathan, 114.
Ballard, John, 100.
Balwin, Heman, 184.
Balwin, Senas, 184.
Bancroft, Ephraim, 202.
Banford, John, 65.
Bangs, Richard, 213.
Banks, Ebenezer, Jr., 24.
Barbee, Joseph, 237.
Barber, Amaziah, 20.
Barber, Benjamin, 20, 36.
Barber, Daniel, Jr., 7.
Barber, David, 5, 162, 209.
Barber, Joel, Jr., 142.
Barber, Joseph, 201.
Barber, Lemuel, 95, 117, 127.
Barber, N., 209.
Barber, Nathaniel, 273.
Barber, Noah, Jr., 105.
Barber, Ruben, 203.
Barber, Simeon, 20.
Barber, Stephen, 162.
Barbur, Asahel, 202.
Barce, Hezekiah, 35.
Bard, Abisha, 126.
Barden, Samuel, 39, 122.
Bardslay, James, 215.
Bardslee, John, 151.
Bardsley, Josiah, 197.
Bardsley, Moses, 196.
Bardsly, Gershom, 109.
Bardwall, John, 188.
Barhan, Nathan, 198.
Barker, 50.
Barker, A., 48.
Barker, Archelaus, 253.
Barker, Archelus, 257.
Barker, Augustus, 9.
Barker, Eliphalet, 149.
Barker, James, 34, 210.
Barker, John, 118.
Barker, Ozias, 124.
Barker, Samuel, 9, 71, 88, 112.
Barker, Samuel S. A., 48.
Barker, Seth, 243.
Barker, Timothy, 9.
Barker, William, 277.
Barkley, John, 62.
Barlow, David, 181, 219.
Barlow, David, Jr., 136.
Barlow, Samuel, 23, 24.
Barnaba, James, 3.
Barnabee, James, 4.
Barnard, Ebenezer, 211.
Barnard, John, 46.
Barnard, Moses, 106, 126.
Barnard, Rufus, 185.
Barnard, William, 220.
Barnerd, Edward, Jr., 24.
Barnerd, Joseph, 188.
Barnes, Abel, 95, 127.
Barnes, Amos, 207, 209, 210.
Barnes, Gideon, 119.
Barnes, James, 49.
Barnes, Nathaniel, 209.
Barnes, Nehemiah, 106, 126, 216.
Barnes, Simeon, 100, 216.
Barnet, Moses, 169.
Barnet, Nathaniel, 169.
Barnett, Jonathan, 32.
Barney, Joseph, Sr., 25.
Barney, Joseph, Jr., 14.
Barnit, William, 73.
Barns, 164.
Barns, A., 225.
Barns, Abel, 117, 201.
Barns, Ambrose, 69.
Barns, Amos, 182, 224.
Barns, Benjamin, 201.
Barns, Daniel, 12, 49, 76.
Barns, David, 88, 111, 276.
Barns, Eliphalet, 9.
Barns, Enos, 69.
Barns, Ichabod, 276.
Barns, Isaac, 9.
Barns, James, 88.
Barns, Joel, 111.
Barns, John, 79, 192, 242, 243.
Barns, John, Jr., 38.
Barns, Moses, 201.
Barns, Nathaniel, 239.
Barns, Orange, 67.
Barns, Reuben, 201.
Barns, Samuel, 79, 275.
Barns, Simeon, 138.
Barns, Solomon, 9.
Barnum, Daniel, 199.
Barnum, David, 198.
Barnum, Ebenezer, 196.
Barnum, Eli, 46.

Barnum, Ephraim, 208.
Barnum, Ezra, 85.
Barnum, John, 85, 121, 198.
Barnum, John, Jr., 198.
Barnum, Joseph, 86.
Barnum, Judah, Jr., 198.
Barnum, Lazerus, 199.
Barnum, Matthew, 98, 198.
Barnum, Nathaniel, 198, 200.
Barnum, Noah, 121.
Barnum, Richard, 200, 208.
Barnum, Samuel, 40.
Barnum, Stephen, 268.
Barnum, Thaddeus, 194.
Barnum, Zadock, 196.
Barret, Bartholomew, 41, 43.
Barret, Moses, 170.
Barrett, Amos, 197.
Barrett, Edward, 264.
Barrit, Epheriam, 184.
Barrit, Jeremiah, 68.
Barritt, Hilderick, 97.
Barrows, Caleb, 94, 127.
Barrows, Ethan, 143.
Barrows, Isaac, 57.
Barrows, Josiah, 59.
Barrows, Lemuel, 57.
Barrows, William, 267.
Barstow, Joseph, 6.
Barstow, Michael, 4.
Bartholemew, Jonathan, 225.
Bartholomew, Benjamin, 9.
Bartholomew, Gideon, 9.
Bartholomew, Isaac, 164.
Bartholomew, Jesse, 201.
Bartholomew, Jonathan, 275.
Bartholomew, Moses, 164, 275.
Bartholomew, Samuel, 255.
Bartholomew, William, 140.
Barthrong, Abraham, 37.
Bartlet, Edmond, Jr., 1.
Bartlet, Eliphas, 1, 165.
Bartlet, John, 160.
Bartlet, Joseph, Jr., 160.
Bartlet, Samuel, 1, 165, 193.
Bartlet, Silvanus, 203.
Bartlet, Stephen, 1.
Bartlit, Abram, 192.
Barton, James, 232.
Barton, Joseph, 87.
Barton, William, 87.
Bartram, Ebenezer, 233.
Bartram, Job, 180.
Bartram, Joseph, 232.
Bartrum, John, 32.
Bascomb, Elias, 105.
Basset, Nathan, 205.
Basset, William, 53, 102.

Bassett, Edward, 268.
Bassett, Hezekiah, 279.
Bassett, Isaac, 118.
Bassett, Samuel, 245.
Bassett, Samo, 251.
Bassett, Timothy, 266.
Bassett, William, 129.
Basson, John, 234.
Bassul, Hannibal, 64.
Bateman, Jacob, 68.
Bates, Amos, 237.
Bates, David, 76.
Bates, Ephraim, 103, 131.
Bates, Ezra, 69, 95.
Bates, Issachar, 211.
Bates, Lemuel, 203, 207.
Bates, Reuben, 22.
Bates, Waker, 84.
Bates, Zephaniah, 58.
Batt, John, 257.
Batter, Aby, 213.
Batterson, Abijah, 126.
Batterson, William, 152.
Battison, George, 233.
Battison, Joseph, 233.
Battson, Joseph, 213.
Bawdell, Benjamin, 57.
Bawdish, Asa, 186.
Bawldwin, Ambros, 183.
Baxter, Aaron, 94.
Baxter, Alexander, 119.
Baxter, Cornl, 247.
Baxter, Cornelius, 249.
Baxter, David, 81.
Baxter, Francis, 58.
Baxter, Richard, 238.
Bayley, James, 182.
Bayley, Jeremy, 140.
Baylye, Joseph, 250.
Beach, Abijah, 127.
Beach, Agur, 85.
Beach, Asa, 32.
Beach, Ashbel, 20.
Beach, David, 48.
Beach, Eber, 21.
Beach, Elijah, 135.
Beach, Elisha, 159.
Beach, Elnathan, 55.
Beach, Isaac, 215.
Beach, Miles, 209, 225.
Beach, Nathaniel, 54, 121.
Beach, Noah, 164.
Beach, Reuben, 102, 129.
Beach, Reubin, 121.
Beach, Roswell, 94, 275.
Beach, Ruben, 54.
Beach, Stephen, 194.
Beach, Zophar, 201.

## INDEX.

Beacher, Jonathan, 195.
Beacher, Joseph, 115.
Beacher, Nathan, 115, 116.
Beamis, John, 143.
Beamon, Truman, 201.
Beamont, Jonathan, 106, 127.
Beamont, Samuel, 3, 184.
Beamont, William, 38, 75.
Bean. John, 212.
Bearce, William, 23.
Beard, Elijah, 127.
Beard, Gideon, 190.
Beard, James, 189.
Beard, Samuel, 190.
Beardslee, Ben, 190.
Beardslee, Ebenezer, 190.
Beardslee, Henry, 181, 219.
Beardslee, John, 181, 219.
Beardslee, Lins, 190.
Beardslee, Nathan, 181, 219.
Beardslee, Stephen, 190.
Beardsley, Curtis, 151.
Beardsley, Gideon, Jr., 196.
Beardsley, John, Jr., 268.
Beardsley, N., 208, 225.
Beardsley, Nehemiah, 21, 23, 24, 25, 85, 104, 195, 196, 197, 198, 199, 200, 227.
Beardsley, P., 225.
Beardsley, Phinehas, 88.
Beardsly, 50.
Bearse, Elijah, 196.
Bearse, Joseph, 21, 196.
Bearse, Newcomb, 196.
Beaumont, Isaiah, 268.
Beaumont, William, 49.
Bebe, Edward, 233.
Bebee, Abner, 241.
Beby, Bazaliel, 246, 250.
Beckwith, Ezra, 57.
Beckwith, Guy, 28.
Beckwith, John, 55.
Beckwith, Lebbeus, 211.
Bedford, 200.
Bedient, Eleazor, 218.
Bedient, Mordica, 218.
Bedwell, James, 246.
Beebe, Abner, 140, 264.
Beebe, Asa, 134.
Beebe, Barzaleel, 252.
Beebe, Bazaliel, 227.
Beebe, Bonnerges, 88.
Beebe, Christopher, 28.
Beebe, Ephraim, 28.
Beebe, Gideon, 28.
Beebe, Jabez, 212.
Beebe, James, 46.
Beebe, Joseph, 17.
Beebe, Paul, 28, 71.
Beebe, Reuben, 17.
Beebe, Thaddeus, 28.
Beebe, William C., 268.
Beebee, 123.
Beebie, Bosaleel, 260.
Beeby, Barzaleel, 247.
Beech, Ambrose, 39.
Beech, Amos, 202.
Beech, Brewin, 202.
Beech, Chancy, 203.
Beech, Francis, 202.
Beech, Israel, 39.
Beech, William, 22.
Beech, Zerah, 33.
Beecher, Amos, 209.
Beecher, Ashbel, 19.
Beecher, David, 211.
Beecher, Jesse, 179.
Beecher, John, 68.
Beecher, Jonathan. 19, 32.
Beecher, Joseph, 116.
Beecher, Nathaniel, 66, 213.
Beegbe, Moses, 66.
Beeman, Ezekiel, 213.
Beeman, Friend, 88.
Beeman, Jonathan, 88.
Beemas, Eph, 101.
Beemon, Samuel, 162.
Beers, Abner, 181, 210.
Beers, David, 86.
Beers, Elnathan, 85.
Beers, Ezekel, 195.
Beers, James, 254.
Beers, Jonathan, 152.
Beers, Johon, 151.
Beers, Joseph, 141.
Beers, Josiah, 181, 210, 254.
Beers, Nathan, 126.
Beers, Phinens, 152.
Beers, Riab, 152.
Beers, Stephan, 181.
Beers, Stephen, 210.
Belden, 223.
Bellen, Moses, 153.
Belden, Thomas, 212, 224.
Belding, Abraham, 100.
Belding, Ebenezer, 274.
Belding, John, 109, 210.
Belding, Moses, 155.
Belding, Rosseter, 274.
Belding, Simeon, 47.
Belding, Thomas, 222.
Belknap, Francis, 1.
Belknap, Simeon. Jr., 165.
Bell, Asariah, 101.
Bell, Jesse, 210, 212.
Bell, John, 41, 43.

Bell, Jonathan, 274.
Bellows, Asa, 262.
Bellus, David, 186.
Bemiss, Ephram, 2.
Bemont, Jonathan, 105.
Bemont, Samuel, 3, 4.
Bemus, Elijah, 81.
Bemus, Ephram, 3.
Benedick, Levi, 202.
Benedict, 180.
Benedict, Abijah, 195.
Benedict, Abraham, Jr., 198.
Benedict, Asel, 198.
Benedict, Benajah, 199.
Benedict, Eleazer, 198.
Benedict, Eleazor, 198.
Benedict, Enoch, 218.
Benedict, Ezra, 142.
Benedict, Gamaliel, 195.
Benedict, Jesse, 195.
Benedict, John, 85, 195, 200.
Benedict, Jonas, 198.
Benedict, Jonathan, 86.
Benedict, Joshua, 194.
Benedict, Moses, 199.
Benedict, Nathan, 218.
Benedict, Nathaniel, 217.
Benedict, Noble, 25. 200.
Benedict, Oliver, 198.
Benedict, Samuel, 199.
Benedict, Seth, 199.
Benedict, Theophilus, 198.
Benedict, William, 199.
Benham, 18.
Benham, Elias, 36.
Benham, Enos, 276.
Benham, Enos, Jr., 276.
Benham, James, 21, 36, 235.
Benham, Jared. 17, 20, 192.
Benham, Samuel, 18.
Benidict, John, 98.
Benit, Daniel, 174.
Benjamin, Aaron, 49, 78.
Benjamin, Abiel, Jr., 174.
Benjamin, Daniel, 12.
Benjamin, George. 136.
Benjamin, John, 184, 190.
Benjamin, Samuel, 41, 43.
Benjamins, Siml, 172.
Bennet, Abel, 185.
Bennet, Andrew, 23.
Bennet, Benjamin, 22, 68, 116, 199, 213.
Bennet, Cromell. 185.
Bennet, David, 218.
Bennet, Elijah. 184.
Bennet, Gabriel. 200.
Bennet, Jedediah, 167.
Bennet, Jeremiah, 100.
Bennet, Job, 58.
Bennet, Miles, 127.
Bennet, Noble, 197.
Bennet, Roswell, 185.
Bennett, Abraham, 197.
Bennett, Benjamin, 268.
Bennett, Elias, 152.
Bennett, Elijah, 34.
Bennett, Joseph, 152, 212.
Bennett, Miles, 106.
Bennett, Trowbridge, 195.
Bennett, William, 152.
Bennidict, Jesse, 218.
Benning, Samuel, 221.
Bennington, 221.
Bennit, Benjamin, 110, 114.
Bennit, James, 49.
Bennitt, Daniel, 180.
Bennitt, Henry, 66.
Bennitt, Nathan, 180.
Bennitt, Oliver, 267.
Bentley, Joseph, 174.
Bentley, William, 160.
Benton, Bela, 273.
Benton, Chandler, 70, 113.
Benton, Ebenezer, 137.
Benton, Edward, 88, 191, 267.
Benton, Jacob, 202.
Benton, Nathaniel, 201.
Benton, Nathaniel W., 107.
Benton, Selah, 49, 50, 76.
Benton, Zebulon, 23.
Bernard, Samuel, 201.
Berney, Joseph, 14.
Berry, Divan, 207, 276.
Berrys, Divan, 206.
Berstow, Ebenezer, 172.
Besster, Ebenezer, 64.
Bestow, Michael, 3.
Betts, 123.
Betts, Isaiah, 53.
Betts, John, Jr., 218.
Betts, Mathew, 218.
Betts, Matthew, 85.
Betts, Stephen, 46, 53, 122.
Betts, Thaddeus, 17.
Bewel, David, 88.
Bialey, Richard, 184.
Biddell, James, 250.
Bidwell, Allen, 262.
Bidwell, George, 274.
Bidwell, James, 244.
Bidwell, Jonathan, Jr., 145.
Bidwell, Joseph, 137.
Bidwell, Samuel, 256.
Bidwell, Thomas, 210. 211, 221
Bigelow, Alvin, 155.

# INDEX.

Bigelow, Eben, 153.
Bigelow, Eli, 58, 59.
Bigelow, Frederick, 273.
Bigelow, John, 33.
Bigelow, Joshua, 159.
Bigelow, Otis, 160.
Biggelow, Eli, 88.
Bigsby, Elias, 69.
Bill, 50.
Bill, Abial, 185.
Bill, Azariah, 41, 43.
Bill, Beriah, 63, 88.
Bill, Daniel, 16, 268.
Bill, Eleazer, 163.
Bill, Elijah, 202.
Bill, Gideon, 16.
Bill, John, 74.
Bill, Jonathan, 59.
Bill, Judah, 34.
Bill, Jude, 16.
Bill, Oliver, 162.
Bill, Reuben, 161.
Bill, Thomas, 2, 3, 40.
Billing, Sanford, 150.
Billings, 150.
Billings, Ebenezer, 60.
Billings, Henry, 233.
Billings, Jesse, 210.
Billings, John, 186.
Billings, Roger, 17.
Billings, Stephen, 49, 278.
Billings, William, 264.
Billins, Benjamin, 183.
Binge, Thomas, 277.
Bingham, Abisha, 88.
Bingham, Adam, 161.
Bingham, Chester, 39.
Bingham, F. L., 170.
Bingham, John, 74.
Bingham, Levi, 74.
Bingham, Nathaniel, 142.
Bingham, Rial, 37.
Bingham, Thomas, 149.
Birck, Elenezar, 37.
Bird, Daniel, 95, 127.
Bird, Isaac, 37.
Birdsey, Ebenezer, 151.
Birdsey, Joseph, 180, 190, 226.
Birdsey, Nathan, 151.
Birg, John, 159.
Birge, Benjamin, 201.
Birge, Beriah, 23.
Birge, Hosea, 162.
Birge, John, 273.
Bishop, 50.
Bishop, David, 184.
Bishop, Elisha, 112.
Bishop, Jared, 277.

Bishop, Jesse, 37.
Bishop, Joel, 71.
Bishop, John, 107.
Bishop, Lenard, 55.
Bishop, Moses, 37.
Bishop, Nathaniel, 88.
Bishop, Reuben, 193.
Bishop, Reubin, 192.
Bishop, Richard, 126.
Bishop, Samuel, 39, 65, 224.
Bishop, Simeon, 108, 268.
Bishop, William, 246, 251.
Bishop, Wyllys, 193.
Bishop, Yale, 192.
Bishop, Zebulon, 192.
Bissel, Abel, 162.
Bissel, Asahel, 38.
Bissel, Benjamin, 113, 164.
Bissel, Ensign, 202.
Bissel, Hezekiah, 202.
Bissel, Joseph, 149.
Bissel, Joseph W., 160.
Bissel, Oliver, 202.
Bissell, Benjamin, 116.
Bissell, Calvin, 273.
Bissell, Daniel, 68.
Bissell, E. F., 188.
Bissell, Ebenezer, 273.
Bissell, Ebenezer F., 27.
Bissell, George, 79.
Bissell, John, 201, 273.
Bissell, John P., 6.
Bissell, Jonathan, 163.
Bissell, Jonathan T., 162.
Bissell, Return, 273.
Bixbee, Solomon, 114.
Bixbey, Daniel, 65.
Bixby, Moses, 65.
Black, Thomas, 53.
Blackman, 190.
Blackman, David, 268.
Blackman, Edward, 195.
Blackman, Elijah, 88, 141.
Blackman, Ichabod, 94.
Blackman, Jeremiah, 76.
Blackman, Jonathan, 5, 88, 149.
Blackman, Nathan, 78, 190.
Blackman, Nehemiah, 94.
Blackman, William, 161.
Blackwell, Thomas, 153.
Blague, Joseph, 134, 208.
Blake, Christopher, 99.
Blake, Ebenezer, 88.
Blake, Jeremiah, 141.
Blake, Reuben, 110.
Blakeley, Isaac, 136.
Blakeley, Samuel, 136.
Blakesley, Asa, 19.

Blakesley, Eben, 239.
Blakesley, Eber, 238.
Blakesley, Enos, 268.
Blakesley, Jonathan, 276.
Blakesley, Reuben, 209.
Blakesley, Tilley, 139.
Blakesly, Ambrose, 202.
Blakesly, Isaac, 139.
Blakley, Wolcut, 116.
Blakslee, Caleb, 108.
Blakslee, Jared, 108.
Blaksley, Zealous, 10.
Blanchard, Elias, 143.
Blanchard, Robin, 88.
Blasdell, John, 258.
Blin, Abraham, 153, 155.
Blinn, Billy, 37.
Blinn, William, 37.
Bliss, Abraham, 4.
Bliss, Bereiah, 106.
Bliss, Beriah, 126.
Bliss, Daniel, 126.
Bliss, Elias, 134, 163, 208.
Bliss, Henry, 4, 163.
Bliss, Israel, 162.
Bliss, James, 106, 126.
Bliss, John, 81, 106, 126, 260.
Bliss, Jonathan, 3, 4, 162.
Bliss, Samuel, 106, 126.
Blocker, John, 95.
Blodget, Artemas, 111.
Blossom, Oliver, 245.
Blossom, Stephen, 246.
Blosson, Stephen, 250.
Blotchet, Roswell, 23.
Blush, Asa, 81.
Blush, David, 160.
Blyn, Simeon, 41, 43.
Boardman, Elijah, 155.
Boardman, Henry, 240.
Boardman, Lincord, 155.
Boardman, Nathan, 135.
Boardman, Seth, 265, 268.
Boardman, Timothy, 134, 256.
Boden, Hutchins, 264.
Bodwell, Benjamin, 7.
Boen, John, 14.
Boen, Joseph, 14.
Bogs, Richard, 56.
Bogue, Richard, 185.
Boid, Joseph, 184.
Boing, Christopher, 14.
Boix, Manuel, 140.
Boles, Asa, 162.
Boles, David, 163.
Boles, Lemuel, 14.
Bolles, John, 4th, 140.
Bolles, Joseph, 28.

Bolles, Thomas, 3d, 264.
Bolton, William, 232.
Bolton, 57, 58, 65, 87, 103, 118.
Boman, Elisha, 184.
Boman, Walter, 167.
Bond, Aaron, 12.
Bond, John, 231.
Bone, Samuel, 22.
Boney, Pierce, 56.
Bonnet, Hezekiah, 79.
Bonny, Jairus, 12.
Bonscourse, Anthony, 238.
Booth, Abel, 151.
Booth, Abel, Jr., 152.
Booth, Abijah, 181, 219.
Booth, Amos, 213.
Booth, Asahel, 136.
Booth, Edward, 73.
Booth, Elisha, 179.
Booth, Henry, 114.
Booth, James, 180, 181, 219.
Booth, John, 126, 181, 219.
Booth, Nathaniel, 53, 135.
Booth, Simeon, 119.
Booth, Solomon, 180, 181.
Booth, Stephen, 246, 250.
Borden, Ezekiel, 201.
Borden, Samuel, 20.
Bordley, 278.
Bordman, Charles, 257.
Bordman, Elijah, 27, 100, 153.
Bordman, Joseph, 208.
Bordman, Leod, 153.
Bordman, Samuel, 27.
Bordon, Thomas, 168.
Borton, James, 211.
Bostick, Salmon, 110.
Boston, Ben, 68.
Boston, Boston, 246, 251.
Boston, Samuel, 163, 246.
Boston, 6, 77.
Bostwick, 195.
Bostwick, John, 195, 243.
Bostwick, Levi, 21.
Bostwick, Oliver, 24, 268.
Bostwick, Reuben, 207, 209, 243.
Bosworth, Hezekiah, 197.
Bosworth, Ichabod, 5.
Bosworth, Tabin, 162.
Botchford, Ebenezer, 110, 116.
Botchford, Joel, 73.
Both, Stephen, 244.
Botsford, A., 208, 224.
Botsford, Abel, 195, 209, 225.
Botsford, E., 206.
Botsford, Elijah, 196, 208, 224.
Botsford, Elnathan, 38.
Botsford, Jabez, 197, 208, 278.

INDEX.    291

Botsford, Jack, 77.
Botsford, Mirum, 195.
Bottom, Jabez, 93.
Bottom, Jacob, 1.
Bottom, James, 3d, 263.
Bottom, Joseph, 208.
Bottom, Walter, 262.
Botton, Joseph, 171.
Boughton, Benjamin, 198.
Boughton, Daniel, 198.
Boughton, David, 200.
Boughton, Ely, 198.
Boughton, Joseph, 85.
Boughton, Matthew, 200.
Boughton, Miles, 200.
Bourroughs, Stephen, 181.
Bouton, Dan, 210.
Bouton, Daniel, 212, 268.
Bouton, David, 77.
Bouton, Jehial, 200.
Bouton, John, 77.
Bouton, William, 217.
Bow, Edward, 35.
Bowden, Hutchins, 257.
Bowen, Christopher, 14.
Bowen, David, 239.
Bowen, Jonathan, 266.
Bowen, Thomas, 245, 251.
Bowers, Alpheus, 65.
Bowers, Benjamin, 60.
Bowers, David, 238, 239.
Bowers, Ephraim, 61.
Bowers, Jonathan, 268.
Bowes, Freeborn, 246, 251.
Bowing, John, 14.
Bowing, Joseph, 14.
Bowles, William, 161.
Bowman, Albert, 267.
Bowman, Henry, 253.
Bowton, Ira, 218.
Bowton, Samuel, 218.
Bowton, Stephen, 218.
Boxford, Isaac, 95.
Boyd, Joseph, 79.
Boyington, Joal, 187.
Boyington, Joshua, 260.
Boyle, John, 252.
Boynton, Joseph, 69.
Bozwarth, Daniel, 14.
Bozworth, Ichabod, 142.
Brace, Abel, 209, 214, 225.
Brace, Elijah, 38.
Brace, Henry, 274.
Brace, Jared, 153.
Brace, Joseph, 223.
Brace, Moses, 274.
Bracket, Benajah, 108.
Bracket, Hezekiah, 53, 106.

Bradfoad, Joshua, 172.
Bradford, Elisha, 35, 99.
Bradford, J., 170.
Bradford, John, 172.
Bradford, Josiah, 170.
Bradley, 227, 265.
Bradley, Abraham, 139.
Bradley, Aner, 268.
Bradley, Daniel, 100, 111.
Bradley, Daniel, Jr., 152.
Bradley, David, 108.
Bradley, Enos, Jr., 189.
Bradley, James, 37, 277.
Bradley, Jehial, 75.
Bradley, Joseph, 67.
Bradley, Jeremiah, 211.
Bradley, Jonah, 179.
Bradley, Josiah, 212.
Bradley, Josiah, Jr., 1.
Bradley, Moses, 55.
Bradley, Nathan, 54.
Bradley, Nehemiah, 277.
Bradley, Oliver, 20.
Bradley, Peter, 24.
Bradley, Philip B., 67.
Bradley, Phineas, 212.
Bradley, Reuben, 1.
Bradley, Stephen, 1.
Bradley, Zenas, 111.
Bradly, Abijah, 9.
Bradly, Daniel, 48.
Bradly, Isaac, 36.
Bradly, Joel, 179.
Bradly, Philip B., 47.
Bradly, Zebulon, 10.
Brag, Thomas, 185.
Bragg, Edmond, 1.
Bragg, Edmund, 165.
Bragg, Thomas, 14.
Brainard, Amos, 184.
Brainard, Daniel, 208.
Brainard, Increase, 56, 88, 98.
Brainard, Jabez, 184.
Brainard, Nehemiah, 209.
Brainerd, D., 214.
Braman, Nathaniel, 274.
Branaird, Zachariah, 184.
Branard, Jeremiah, 229.
Branch, Walter, 186.
Branford, 25, 65, 70, 71, 72, 76, 88, 89, 104, 112, 113.
Brangin, John, 68.
Brasier, Edward, 256.
Braughton, John, 14.
Bray, Asa, 208, 210, 221, 224, 226, 227.
Breadsley, Squire, 236.
Brechan, Thomas, 43.

Brechin, Thomas, 41.
Breed, John, 210.
Brester, Jonathan, 60.
Brewer, Thomas, 122.
Brewster, Darius, 254.
Brewster, Ebenezer, 279.
Brewster, Jonathan, 6.
Brewster, Samuel, 94.
Brewster, Silas, 18, 174.
Brian, J., 84, 214.
Briant, John O., 108.
Briant, Straton, 152.
Brichel, John, 260.
Bricks, John, 111.
Briggs, Joseph, 81.
Briggs, William, 235.
Briggs, Zephaniah, 197.
Brigham, Paul, 49, 75, 161.
Brimblecom, Thomas, 259.
Brind, Edward, 88.
Brinsmade, A., 177.
Brinsmade, Abraham, 181.
Brinsmade, Josiah, 228.
Brister, Jonathan, 58.
Bristol, 267.
Bristol, Abel, 139.
Bristol, Aron, 139.
Bristol, Benjamin, 111.
Bristol, Bezaleel, 210.
Bristol, Eliphalet, 202.
Bristol, Samuel, 110, 116.
Bristol, Thomas, 266.
Bristoll, John, Jr., 39.
Bristoll, Peter, 75.
Britain, Samuel, 10.
Brockett, Titus, 21.
Brockway, Giddeon, 211.
Broker, Isaac, 67, 203.
Bronson, Isaac, 210, 224.
Bronson, J., 210, 212.
Bronson, Samuel, 207.
Brook, Josiah, 139.
Brook, Thomas, 139.
Brookline, 19.
Brooks, Abijah, 190.
Brooks, Benjamin, 190.
Brooks, David, 126.
Brooks, Elizur, 19.
Brooks, Isaac, 190.
Brooks, Jabez, 134, 208.
Brooks, John, 190.
Brooks, Jonathan, 153, 155.
Brooks, Joseph, 22, 81, 110, 117, 137.
Brooks, Josiah, 137.
Brooks, Lemuel, 218.
Brooks, Levi, 157.
Brooks, Michael, 37.
Brooks, Samuel, 209, 211.
Brooks, Solomon, 94.
Brooks, Stephen, 20, 246, 250.
Brooks, Thomas, 3, 4, 18, 73, 137, 174.
Brooks, Thomas, Jr., 19.
Brooks, Wickham, 17.
Brooks, William, 151.
Brothwell, William, 236.
Brown, 50.
Brown, Aaron, 145, 147.
Brown, Abell, 51.
Brown, Amasa, 57, 58.
Brown, Amos, 216.
Brown, Asa, 193.
Brown, Austin, 118.
Brown, Azariah, 4.
Brown, Benajah, 56.
Brown, Berzilla, 199.
Brown, Caleb, 238, 239.
Brown, Charles, 28, 32, 60, 88, 247, 252.
Brown, Christopher, 263.
Brown, D., 84.
Brown, Daniel, 16, 20, 38, 110.
Brown, David, 161.
Brown, Ebenezer, 58, 60.
Brown, Edward, 232.
Brown, Eli, 185.
Brown, Elisha, 58, 216.
Brown, Ezekiel, 216.
Brown, F. W., 170.
Brown, Henry, 58, 60, 64, 153, 155.
Brown, Hugh, 174.
Brown, Ichabod, 202, 211.
Brown, Isaac, 23.
Brown, James, 81, 185, 241, 253.
Brown, Jedediah, 268.
Brown, Jeremiah, 163.
Brown, Jessa, 40.
Brown, Jesse, 160, 186.
Brown, John, 28, 58, 170, 171, 234.
Brown, Jonathan, 1, 88, 110, 123.
Brown, Joseph, 10, 274.
Brown, Jude C., 69.
Brown, N., 210.
Brown, Nathan, 53.
Brown, Nathaniel, 107.
Brown, Nathaniel, Jr., 216.
Brown, Obadiah, 57.
Brown, Oliver, 65, 88.
Brown, P., 45.
Brown, Prosper, 231, 252.
Brown, Reuben, 71.
Brown, Rufus, 184.
Brown, Samuel, 10, 12, 34, 45, 70, 71, 85, 112, 185, 218.

INDEX. 293

Brown, Simeon, 216.
Brown, Solomon, 234.
Brown, Stephen, 201.
Brown, Thaddeus, 14.
Brown, Thomas, 61, 134.
Brown, William, 77, 202, 216.
Browning, Daniel, 51.
Brownley, John, 244, 247, 248.
Brownson, Asa, 24.
Brownson, Luman, 213.
Bruester, James, 34.
Brumon, Stephen, 58.
Brun, Isaac, 30.
Brune, Charles, 62.
Brunson, Beriah, 18.
Brunson, Michael, 133, 134.
Brunson, Stephen, 59.
Brush, Eliphalet, 196.
Brush, Janas, 196.
Brush, Jonas, 21.
Brush, Thomas, 196, 197.
Bruster, Cumfort, 149.
Bruster, Elijah, 210.
Bryan, Elijah, 109.
Bryan, Jehial, 211.
Buck, Abner, 34.
Buck, Ebenezer, 199.
Buck, Elijah, 55.
Buck, Frank, 130.
Buck, Joel, 19, 24.
Buck, Justus, 210, 212.
Buckingham, 114.
Buckingham, Benjamin, 213.
Buckingham, Gideon, 113.
Buckingham, Jered, 178.
Buckingham, Stephen, 117.
Buckland, Alexander, 1.
Buckland, Stephen, 88.
Buckley, Abraham, 178, 233.
Buckley, Abram, 205.
Buckley, Charles, 212.
Buckley, Job, 178.
Buckley, Joel, 277.
Buckley, Seth, 75.
Buckley, William, 178.
Buckly, Eleazer, 231.
Buel, John, 47.
Buell, B., 207.
Buell, Isaiah, 268.
Buell, John, 140.
Buell, John H., 2, 3.
Buell, Josiah, 46.
Buell, Levi, 161.
Buell, Nathaniel, 19, 20, 21, 25, 33.
Buell, Salmon, 265, 268.
Buffam, Samuel, 256.
Bugbe, Abihel, 14.

Bugbe, Amos, 14.
Buggee, William, 263.
Buggles, Timothy, 196.
Bucknel, Thomas W., 155.
Bulkley, Edward, 100, 101, 153, 155.
Bulkley, Eliphalet, 134, 211.
Bulkley, Fras, 153.
Bulkley, Francis, 155.
Bulkley, Jack, 60.
Bulkley, Levy, 80.
Bull, Edward, 178.
Bull, Epaphras, 33, 34, 35, 36, 37, 38, 39.
Bull, George, 201.
Bull, Henry, 24, 204.
Bull, Jeremiah, 24.
Bull, John, 178.
Bull, Jonathan, 223.
Bull, Michael, 202.
Bull, Nathaniel, 19, 203.
Bull, T., 225.
Bull, Thomas, 173, 211, 221, 223, 225.
Bull, Tiret, 204.
Bull, Wail, 196.
Bullen, Benjamin, 58.
Bullen, David, 121.
Bullin, David, 53.
Bullock, Jonathan, 100.
Bumpus, Edward, 34.
Bunce, David, 133.
Bunce, Isaiah, 268.
Bunce, Jered, 155.
Bunce, Norman, 264.
Bunce, Normand, 188.
Bunce, Thomas, 187, 188.
Bunce, William, 258.
Bundy, William, 78.
Bunker, Job, 246, 249.
Bunker, Samuel, 251.
Bunker, Vallantyne, 251.
Bunker, Vollantyne, 246.
Bunker Hill, 17, 24.
Bunn, Paul, 134, 202.
Bunnel, Abraham, 10.
Bunnel, John, 9, 25.
Bunnel, Nathaniel, 223.
Bunnell, Abraham, 16.
Bunnell, Jacob, 212.
Bunnell, Job, 196.
Bunnell, N., 208.
Bunnell, Nathaniel, 208, 211.
Bunnell, Noah, 85.
Bur, Jeffry, 243.
Bur, Seth, 231.
Buratt, Joseph, 127.
Burch, Ebenezar, 37.

Burch, Nathan, 262.
Burdain, Samuel, 74.
Burdick, Walter, 268.
Burdwin, Samuel, 268.
Burges, J., 172.
Burges, Jos, 172.
Burgess, Ephraim, 103, 131.
Burgess, Joshua, 27.
Burghes, Edward, 121.
Burghes, Ephraim, 124.
Burgiss, Lothrop, 97.
Burgoyn, John, 68.
Burgs, Joseph, 172.
Burgus, Joseph, 171.
Burham, Wolcott, 61.
Burk, John, 88.
Burke, Thomas, 254.
Burley, Aseph, 14.
Burley, Jacob, 14.
Burn, Daniel, 204.
Burn, James, 32.
Burn, Joseph, 230.
Burnall, Samuel, 184.
Burnam, Joseph, 143.
Burnap, Benjamin, 88.
Burnap, Josiah, 161.
Burnes, William, 78.
Burnet, Richard, 174.
Burnet, Samuel, 219.
Burnett, Ben, 247.
Burnett, Benjamin, 248.
Burnett, Jonathan, 247, 249.
Burnett, Thomas, Jr., 152.
Burnett, William, 231.
Burnham, Asa, 88.
Burnham, Eliphalet, 95.
Burnham, Eliphas, 127.
Burnham, Freeman, 66.
Burnham, Gurdin, 244.
Burnham, Gurdon, 245, 248.
Burnham, James, 185, 263.
Burnham, Joseph, 88.
Burnham, Josiah, 233.
Burnham, O., 153.
Burnham, Oliver, 268.
Burnham, Orrin, 155.
Burnham, Roswell, 79.
Burnham, Stephen, 80.
Burnham, William, 57.
Burnham, Wolcott, 95.
Burnit, Benjamin, 143, 244.
Burnit, Jonathan, 143.
Burns, Benjamin, 109.
Burns, Edward, 63.
Burns, John, 245, 249.
Burns, Orange, 67.
Burnside, Henry, 250.
Burnsides, Henry, 246.

Burr, A., 209.
Burr, Adonijah, 209, 221, 223, 226.
Burr, Asa, 95.
Burr, Daniel, 69, 117.
Burr, George, 180.
Burr, Jehial, 35.
Burr, Jesse, 236.
Burr, John, 273.
Burr, Russel, 202.
Burr, Salem, 145, 147.
Burr, Salmon, 142.
Burr, Sturges, 152.
Burrall, Charles, 33, 267.
Burrell, 265.
Burrell, Charles, 34, 35, 36, 37, 38, 39, 223.
Burrell, Samuel, 242.
Burrell, William, 188.
Burret, Charles, 48.
Burret, Elihu, 19.
Burret, Elishia, 19.
Burret, Zalmon, 195.
Burrill, James, 127.
Burrit, Charles, 69.
Burritt, Abel, 208, 211.
Burritt, Hezekiah, 190.
Burritt, Israel, 193.
Burritt, Joseph, 141.
Burritt, Samuel, 181, 190.
Burrough, Charles, 141.
Burroughs, Abner, Jr., 1.
Burroughs, Josiah, 213.
Burroughs, Stephen, 1.
Burroughs, William, 63.
Burroughs, Zebulon, 1.
Burrous, Hubbard, 122.
Burrous, Joseph, 124.
Burrous, William, 124.
Burrouss, Selah, 215.
Burrows, Caleb, 105, 117.
Burrows, Elisha, 174, 267, 268.
Burrows, George, 105.
Burrows, Josiah, 88.
Burrows, Nathan, 250.
Burrows, Paul, 174.
Burrows, William, 268.
Burrtt, Wakemon, 243.
Burrus, Hubbard, 211.
Burrus, Nathan, 246.
Burrus, William, 103, 131, 265.
Burt, John, 185.
Burt, William, 160.
Burton, Daniel, 21.
Burton, Ephraim, 181, 219.
Burton, J., 206.
Burton, James, 208.
Burton, Jeremiah, 173.
Burton, Joseph, Jr., 135.

Burton, Judson, 181, 219.
Burton, Oliver, 85.
Burton, Samuel, 134, 190, 274.
Burton, William, 135.
Bush, Amos, 202.
Bush, John, 168.
Bush, Jonathan, 208.
Bush, Samuel, 53.
Bushnal, Ezra, 234.
Bushnel, Frances, 178.
Bushnel, Hanley, 222.
Bushnel, Phinehas, 178.
Bushnel, Samuel, 178.
Bushnell, Daniel, 100, 163, 178, 268.
Bushnell, John H., 178.
Bushnell, Lemuel, 178.
Bushnull, Ephiream, 184.
Bushnull, Jonathan, 184.
Bushnull, Ruben, 184.
Buth, Joseph, 169.
Butler, 112.
Butler, Abel, 39.
Butler, Abel, Jr., 22.
Butler, Benjamin, 202.
Butler, Comfort, 193.
Butler, Daniel, 262.
Butler, David, 61.
Butler, Derny, 230.
Butler, Eli, 212.
Butler, Ezekiel, 70, 112.
Butler, Francoes, 233.
Butler, Gideon, Jr., 274.
Butler, Isaac, 39.
Butler, James, 187.
Butler, Jeremiah, 191.
Butler, John, 85, 95.
Butler, Joseph, 39, 274.
Butler, Matthew, 10.
Butler, Moses, 244, 249.
Butler, Nathaniel, 145.
Butler, Noah, Jr., 274.
Butler, Peter, 236.
Butler, Samuel, 51.
Butler, Stephen, 121.
Butler, Titus, 10, 16.
Butler, Walter, 10.
Butler, William, 185.
Butler, Zebulon, 46, 53, 107, 116.
Butlers, Moses, 245.
Butlor, Moses, 258.
Butt, Ebenezer, 171, 172.
Butt, Gideon, 172.
Butt, Jams, 171, 172.
Butt, John, 171, 172.
Butt, John, Jr., 172.
Butt, Sherebiah, 172.
Butten, Zebulon, 17.

Buttolph, George, 51.
Button, Eliphalet, 28.
Button, Jedediah, 194.
Button, Joseph, 268.
Button, Peter, 185.
Button, Zebulon, 174.
Butts, Esaias, 131.
Butts, Osias, 103.
Byer, Return, 67.
Byintun, Ebenezer, 10.
Byrnes, William, 260.
Byxbe, John, 217.
Byxbee, Hopkins, 218.
Byxbee, John, 218.

C., William, 63.
Caatch, Joel, 153.
Cable, A., 84.
Cable, Abraham, 232.
Cabon, James, 192.
Cadwall, Neamiah, 187, 188.
Cadwell, Aaron, 18, 274.
Cadwell, Aaron, Jr., 274.
Cadwell, Jeduthan, 274.
Cadwell, Joseph, 274.
Cadwell, Matthew, 268.
Cadwell, Pelatiah, 145, 147.
Cadwell, Reubin, 121.
Cadwell, Simeon, 51.
Cadwell, Theodore, 145, 147.
Cady, Benjamin, 53, 124.
Cady, Daniel, 37.
Cady, Darius, 88.
Cady, David, 167, 168.
Cady, Elijah, 66.
Cady, Jonathan, 64, 209.
Cady, Manassah, 66.
Cady, Nahum, 64.
Cahale, Cornelius, 68.
Cahoon, Isaiah, 256.
Cain, John, 41, 43.
Cain, William, 110.
Califf, Stephen, 28.
Calkin, Joseph, 34.
Calkin, Reuben, 38.
Calkings, Nathan S., 246.
Calkings, Nathaniel, 248.
Calkins, Elisha, 38.
Calkins, Frederick, 241.
Calkins, James, 255.
Calkins, Jonathan, 220, 227.
Calkins, Nathaniel, 34.
Calkins, Samuel, 120.
Calkins, Simon, 233.
Call, 97.
Call, James, 12.
Call, James, Jr., 12.
Call, John, 12, 41, 43.

Calleway, Henry, 262.
Cam, Moses, 231.
Cambell, Robert, 149.
Cambridge, 4, 17, 134.
Camp, Aaron, 17.
Camp, Amiel, 195.
Camp, Elnathan, 193.
Camp, Heth, 193.
Camp, Isaac, 19, 24.
Camp, Job, 103.
Camp, John, 17.
Camp, Nathan, 196.
Camp, Ozias, 192.
Camp, Phinehas, 88.
Camp, Rejoice, 191.
Camp, Samuel, 134, 192, 207, 223, 278.
Camp, Sharp, 108.
Camp, Sharper, 71.
Campbell, Joseph, 165.
Campbell, Mathew, 1.
Campbell, Samuel, 143.
Camron, John, 32.
Canaan, 20, 21, 22, 23, 52, 55, 76, 83, 195, 205.
Canada, David, 28.
Canada, James, 110.
Canada, 12, 13, 23, 43.
Cande, Theophilus, 135.
Cane, Hugh, 200.
Canfield, Asher, 191.
Canfield, Ezekiel, 232.
Canfield, Ezeriah, 97.
Canfield, Ichabod, 23, 152.
Canfield, John, 193.
Canfield, Josiah, 237.
Canfield, S., 206.
Canfield, Samuel, 84, 207, 209.
Canfield, Seba, 201.
Canfield, Thomas, 136.
Canfield, Titus, 191.
Canida, David, 60.
Cannady, Henry, 245, 249.
Cannon, Ira, 95.
Canterbury, 54, 58, 65, 78, 88, 89, 90, 102, 103, 104, 114, 118, 267.
Cape Ann, 69.
Capee, Solomon, 246, 250.
Capen, Timothy, 37.
Capp, William, 246.
Capron, Samuel, 183.
Car, Robert, 168.
Card, Daniel, 247.
Card, Elisha, 81.
Carew, Joseph, 208.
Carew, Josiah, 238.
Carew, Phereus, 248.
Carew, Phineus, 246.

Carey, Joseph, 185.
Carey, Josiah, 239.
Carey, Roger, 64.
Carlton, Derias, 56.
Carpender, Willet, 263.
Carpenter, Allen, 119.
Carpenter, Benjamin, 184.
Carpenter, David, 95, 185.
Carpenter, Eli, 1.
Carpenter, Elias, 124, 184.
Carpenter, Elijah, 66, 185.
Carpenter, Eliphalet, 103, 124.
Carpenter, Eliphelet, 131.
Carpenter, Ephraim, 159, 162.
Carpenter, James, 105.
Carpenter, Joshua, 162.
Carpenter, Nathan, 18, 22.
Carpenter, Uriah, 66.
Carr, Clement, 108.
Carr, Daniel, 251.
Carr, Ebenezer, 108.
Carr, Robert, 107.
Carr, William, 71, 107.
Carrell, Elisha, 96.
Carrier, Benjamin, 138.
Carrier, John, 81.
Carrier, Thomas, Jr., 160.
Carter, Aaron, 60.
Carter, David, 169.
Carter, Eleazer, 160.
Carter, J., 84.
Carter, James, 88.
Carter, Jirah, 267, 269.
Carter, John, 184, 201.
Carter, Jonah, 97.
Carter, Joseph, 225.
Carter, Nathan, 37.
Carter, Reuben, 88, 102.
Carter, Reubin, 130.
Carter, Samuel, 225.
Cartwright, Jonathan, 17.
Carty, Asher, 59.
Carver, David, 162.
Cary, John, 263.
Cary, Joseph, 143.
Cary, Josiah, 239.
Cary, Oliver, 143.
Case, Abel, 145, 147, 148.
Case, Asahel, 39.
Case, Caleb, 164.
Case, Dan, 145, 147, 148.
Case, Elihu, 145, 147, 148.
Case, Elihu, 2d, 142.
Case, Elijah, 177, 221.
Case, Elisha, 27.
Case, Hosea, 147.
Case, Hosea, Jr., 145, 148.
Case, Israel, 145, 146, 147, 148.

INDEX.    297

Case, Isreail, 146.
Case, Jedidiah, 27.
Case, Job, 6, 7, 208, 224.
Case, Joel, 164.
Case, John, Jr., 7.
Case, Jonathan, 164, 208.
Case, Judah, 142.
Case, Martain, 7.
Case, Micah, 146.
Case, Michiel, 147.
Case, Moses, 164.
Case, Oliver, 138.
Case, Richard, 77.
Case, Roswel, 142.
Case, Solomon P., 4.
Case, Timothy, 145, 147, 148.
Case, Zach., 224.
Casey, John, 118.
Casheen, William, 230.
Castel, Joel, 36.
Castle, Phineas, 209, 223.
Castle, Samuel, 80.
Castle, Timothy, 136.
Castle, William, 136.
Casye, John, 65.
Catlen, Hezekiah, 124.
Catlin, Abel, 273.
Catlin, Abraham, 21.
Catlin, Ashbel, 273.
Catlin, Bradley, 201.
Catlin, Elijah, 202.
Catlin, Elisha, 106, 126, 202.
Catlin, Gilbert, 192.
Catlin, Isaac, 201.
Catlin, Nathaniel, 20.
Catlin, Putnam, 68.
Catlin, Samuel, 201.
Catlin, Thomas, 20.
Catlin, Timothy, 105.
Cato, Prince, 99.
Catting, Abraham, 36.
Cay, Parley, 123.
Ceasar, Timothy, 269.
Cebree, James, Jr., 76.
Cesar, Job, 109.
Chace, Lot, 118.
Chace, Samuel, 259.
Chace, Walter, 74.
Chace, Zacceus, 251.
Chadwick, William, 121.
Chafe, Abial, 65.
Chafe, James, 65.
Chafe, Joel, 34.
Chafe, Samuel, 65.
Chafee, Cyrus, 184.
Chafee, William, 58.
Chaffe, Jonathan, 14.
Chaffee, 123.

Chalker, Daniel, 178.
Chalker, Jabez, 192.
Chalker, Selden, 178.
Chamber, William, 35.
Chamberlain, Benjamin, 160.
Chamberlain, Eliphalet, 134.
Chamberlain, Ephraim, 19, 49.
Chamberlain, J., 222, 227.
Chamberlain, Jeremiah, 121.
Chamberlain, Joel, 134.
Chamberlain, Richard, 268.
Chamberlin, Aaron, 57.
Chamberlin, Isaac, 34.
Chamberlin, Joel, 5, 162.
Chambers, John, 27.
Champion, Henry, 46, 58, 59, 60.
Champlin, Joseph, 262.
Chancy, Evins, 56.
Chandler, Joseph, 12, 41, 43.
Chandler, Robert, 53, 100.
Chandlor, Jacob, 256.
Chapel, Fredrick, 235.
Chapin, Daniel, 55.
Chapin, Elias, 139.
Chapins, Ichabod, 202.
Chapley, Richard, 274.
Chapman, Abner, 58, 59.
Chapman, Adino, 119.
Chapman, Adonijah, 106.
Chapman, Albert, 47.
Chapman, Alpheus, 28.
Chapman, Andrew, 5.
Chapman, Benjamin, 119.
Chapman, Caleb, 184.
Chapman, Christopher, 14.
Chapman, Comfort, 103, 125.
Chapman, Constant, 113.
Chapman, Daniel, 163.
Chapman, Douglas, 254.
Chapman, Douglass, 247, 252.
Chapman, Ebenezer, 106.
Chapman, Elias, 17.
Chapman, Elijah, 50.
Chapman, Elisha, 183, 208.
Chapman, Elizah, 47.
Chapman, Ezra, 34.           [262.
Chapman, Gideon, 60, 140, 257,
Chapman, Hoseah, 1.
Chapman, Jabez, Jr., 133.
Chapman, James, 49.
Chapman, Jed, 210.
Chapman, Jeremiah, 262.
Chapman, John, 88, 140, 245, 247,
  249, 252, 256, 262.
Chapman, Joseph, 47.
Chapman, N., 207.
Chapman, Nathan, 223, 224.
Chapman, Oliver, 1.

Chapman, Phinehas, 252.
Chapman, R., 142.
Chapman, Reuben, 110.
Chapman, S., 206.
Chapman, Samuel, 57, 70, 109, 222, 227.
Chapman, Silas, 28, 31.
Chapman, Thomas, 14.
Chappel, Alpheus, 28.
Chappel, Caleb, 160.
Chappel, Comfort, 88.
Chappel, Curtis, 37.
Chappel, Curtiss, 88, 111.
Chappel, Elijah, 163.
Chappel, Hiram, 65.
Chappel, James, 67.
Chappel, John, 28, 31.
Chappel, Joshua, 88.
Chappel, Joshua, Jr., 5.
Chappel, Noah, 41, 43.
Chappell, Amariah, 269.
Chaps, John, 69.
Charley, John, 59.
Charles, Nicholas, 62.
Charlestown, 260, 261.
Charter, George, 1.
Charter, John, Jr., 1, 25.
Chase, Jeremiah, 23.
Chase, Jonathan, 14.
Chase, Nathan, 245, 251.
Chase, Vollantyne, 247, 252.
Chase, Walter, 88.
Chase, Zacceus, 246.
Chatfield, Caleb, 21.
Chatfield, Dan, 85.
Chatfield, Daniel, 179, 211.
Chatfield, Ebenezer, 189.
Chatfield, John, 233, 253, 264.
Chatfield, Lemuel, 213.
Chatfield, Lewis, 238, 239.
Chatfield, Thomas, 245, 249.
Chatham, 58, 59, 60, 61, 62, 69, 74, 80, 81, 82, 88, 89, 118.
Chauncy, William, 191.
Check, John, 203.
Cheeney, Ebenezer, 57.
Cheeseborough, Charles, 264.
Cheeseborough, Thomas, 22, 23.
Cheesebrook, Jabez, 184.
Cheever, Ezekiel, 87.
Cheevers, Ezekiel, 87.
Cheney, Joseph, 10, 124.
Cheney, Thomas, 63.
Cheney, William, 14.
Cheshire, 82, 111.
Chester, Charles, 174.
Chester, David, 124.
Chester, Eldridge, 174.

Chester, John, 18, 19, 23, 153, 155, 222, 266.
Chester, Lemuel, 118.
Chick, John, 142.
Chidester, Andrew, 98.
Chidester, Jonathan, 41, 43.
Chidester, William, 41, 43.
Chidsey, Ephraim, 10.
Chidsey, Joseph, 193.
Chidsey, Street, 10.
Child, Obadiah, 183.
Childs, 50.
Childs, Charles, 66.
Childs, Harba, 105.
Childs, Jesse, 64.
Childs, Lyman, 184.
Childs, Stephen, 67.
Chilson, John, 265.
Chilson, Jonathan, 170.
Chipman, John, 229.
Chipman, Jonathan, 37.
Chipman, Samuel, 188.
Chitingdon, Solomon, 55.
Chittenden, Benjamin, 275.
Chittenden, Cornelius, 97.
Chittenden, Nathan, 275.
Chittenden, Solomon, 97.
Chittendon, Gideon, 107.
Chittenton, Abraham, 19.
Chorse, Ephraim, 69.
Christophers, Allen, 249.
Christophers, John A., 245.
Chubbuck, Ebenezer, 127.
Chuish, Philip, 263.
Church, Abner, 143.
Church, Ambrose, 278.
Church, Caleb, 187.
Church, Calub, 200.
Church, Ebenezer, 88.
Church, Elihu, 51.
Church, Fairbanks, 174.
Church, James, 261.
Church, Joseph, 28, 31.
Church, Josiah, 141.
Church, Nathaniel, 265, 269.
Church, Oliver, 37.
Church, Samuel, 98, 184, 187, 188.
Church, Timothy, 187, 188.
Church, Uriah, 12, 41.
Churchel, Charles, 155.
Churchel, Jesse, 137.
Churchel, Joseph, 137, 157.
Churchel, Moses, 78.
Churchell, Hezekiah; 38.
Churchell, Joseph, 81.
Churchell, Josiah, 38.
Churcher, John, 34, 54.
Churchill, C., 214, 226.

INDEX. 299

Churchill, Charles, 153, 211.
Churchill, Daniel, 17.
Churchill, Elijah, 88.
Churchill, Giles, 275.
Churchill, J., 222.
Churchill, Jesse, 137.
Churchill, Joseph, 134.
Churchill, Oliver, 201.
Cinemon, Benjamin, 252.
Cinnamon, Thomas, 251.
Cinnel, Jerimiah, 14.
Cituate, 74.
Claghorn, Eleazer, 37, 48.
Clap, Roger, 155.
Clapp, Nathan, 88.
Clapp, Normand, 188.
Clapp, Oliver, 187.
Clapp, Roger, 153.
Claray, James, 35.
Clark, Aaron, 133.
Clark, Abraham, 76.
Clark, Amos, 38, 76, 127, 128, 134, 162.
Clark, Andrew, 6, 163, 205.
Clark, Asahel, 88.
Clark, Asell, 162.
Clark, Ashbel, 178.
Clark, Augustus, 51.
Clark, Barnabas, 111.
Clark, Bemond, 178.
Clark, Benjamin, 133, 174, 210, 212.
Clark, Charles, 80, 246.
Clark, Chipman, 126.
Clark, D., 214.
Clark, Dan, 149.
Clark, Daniel, 135, 162, 201, 208, 264.
Clark, David, 59, 69, 88, 103, 141, 203.
Clark, Ebenezer, 82.
Clark, Edmon, 189.
Clark, Elisha, 269.
Clark, Francis, 184.
Clark, George, 195.
Clark, Gershom, 162.
Clark, Gideon, 162.
Clark, Giles, 113, 116.
Clark, Hezekiah, 20.
Clark, Ira, 27.
Clark, J., 84, 170.
Clark, Jacob, 149, 162, 191.
Clark, James, 5, 6, 143, 184, 194, 208, 224.
Clark, Jared, 163.
Clark, Jerom, 3, 4, 6.
Clark, Joel, 17, 23.
Clark, Joel M., 203.

Clark, John, 38, 39, 120, 128, 173, 182, 268.
Clark, Joseph, 111, 173, 184.
Clark, Joso., 190.
Clark, Lamberton, 61.
Clark, Lamberton, Jr., 141.
Clark, Lemuel, 3, 4, 184.
Clark, Levi, 220.
Clark, Lewis, 32.
Clark, Martin, 108.
Clark, Micael, 189.
Clark, Nathaniel, 20, 39, 107, 109, 169.
Clark, Nehemiah, 117.
Clark, Olive, 184.
Clark, Oliver, 85.
Clark, Othniel, 48.
Clark, Phinehas, 38.
Clark, Pink, 69.
Clark, Reuben, 20.
Clark, Reubin, 106.
Clark, Rhoderick, 27.
Clark, Richard, 62.
Clark, Robert, 173, 184.
Clark, Roswell, 126, 162.
Clark, Shipman, 96.
Clark, Silvanus, 132.
Clark, Smith, 23.
Clark, Stephen, 135.
Clark, Thomas, 4, 153, 155.
Clark, Timothy, 134, 207, 210.
Clark, William, 28, 143.
Clarke, Edmund, 24.
Clarke, Hezekiah, 47.
Clarke, James, 20.
Clarke, Job, 242.
Clarke, Joel, 124.
Clarke, John, 122.
Clarke, Pink, 136.
Clary, James, 34.
Cleaveland, 50.
Cleaveland, Aaron, 183.
Cleaveland, Asa, 114, 116.
Cleaveland, Dyer, 273.
Cleaveland, John, 172.
Cleaveland, Josiah, 142.
Cleaveland, Moses, 46.
Cleaveland, Rufus, 165.
Cleaveland, Timothy, 88.
Cleavland, Ambrose, 65.
Cleavland, Eleanah, 37.
Cleavland, Isaac, 182.
Cleavland, James, Jr., 167.
Cleavland, John, 168.
Cleavland, Rufus, 1.
Cleavland, Zenus, 1.
Clefford, Israel, 232.
Clement, Silas, 238.

Clemmonds, Abijah, 67.
Clemons, John, 23.
Clerk, Charles, 251.
Clerk, John, 140.
Cleveland, Eliphas, 64.
Cleveland, Garner, 122.
Cleveland, Johnson, 78.
Cleveland, Jonas, 35.
Cleveland, Josiah, 35.
Cleveland, Tracey, 105.
Cleverly, John, 254.
Clift, Samuel, 47.
Clift, Wills, 46.
Climet, Robert, 108.
Clinton, Allen, 55.
Clinton, Joseph, 53, 121.
Clinton, Lawrence, 211.
Close, Benjamin, 266, 267, 269.
Close, Odel, 211.
Close, Odle, 207, 209.
Cluff, Isaac, 111.
Clumb, Amariah, 21.
Coatney, John, 260.
Coats, 150.
Cony, Moses, 56.
Coban, James, 112.
Cobb, John, 73.
Cobet, Samuel, 195.
Cobuck, Ebenezer, 95.
Coburn, Edward, 58.
Coburn, Eliphalet, 263.
Coburn, Samuel, 64.
Cobus, Cull, 263.
Coc, Jedediah, 95.
Cochecks, Peter, 18.
Cochram, 16.
Cockeel, Joseph, 124.
Codner, John, 82, 107.
Codnor, John, 116.
Coe, Asher, 191.
Coe, Daniel, 101.
Coe, Dorman, 189.
Coe, Ebenezer, 212, 268.
Coe, James, 181, 219.
Coe, Jeddiah, 117.
Coe, Jedediah, 127.
Coe, Levi, 201.
Coe, Pineas, 205.
Coe, Samuel, 21, 58.
Coe, Seth, 273.
Coe, Timothy, 191.
Coe, Zacheriah, 180.
Coffin, Christopher, 73.
Coffin, Thomas, 238, 239.
Coggeshall, William, 242.
Coggswell, W., 214.
Coggswell, William, 243.
Cogins, David, 69.

Cogswell, Asa, 197.
Cogswell, William, 209, 224.
Cogwell, Nat, 167.
Cohorse, Ephraim, 99.
Coit, Farwell, 174.
Coit, Isaac, 174.
Coit, Nathaniel, Jr., 140.
Coit, Oliver, 174.
Coit, Samuel, 227.
Coit, William, 25, 245, 247, 248, 249.
Colbet, Joseph, 184.
Colburn, Daniel, Jr., 18.
Colburn, Eliphalet, 63.
Colchester, 57, 58, 59, 60, 61, 65, 69, 78, 81, 82, 87, 88, 89, 90, 103, 118.
Cole, Abner, 20.
Cole, Alben, 77.
Cole, Asa, 16.
Cole, David, 97.
Cole, Gideon, 59.
Cole, Job, 117, 127.
Cole, John, 73, 88.
Cole, Jonathan, 162.
Cole, Josiah, 114.
Cole, Leonard, 115.
Cole, Marcus, 88.
Cole, Matthew, 209, 210.
Cole, Samuel, 94.
Cole, Simeon, 173.
Cole, Solomon, 117, 127.
Coleman, Ebenezer, 160.
Coleman, Edward S., 47.
Coleman, Noah, 46, 88.
Coley, Nathan, 69.
Colfax, Ebenezer, 140, 264.
Colfax, William, 45.
Colkins, Jonathan, 232.
Collat, Thomas, 58.
Collens, Charles, 201.
Collens, Edward, 136.
Collens, Joel, 277.
Collings, John, 246, 250.
Collins, Ambrous, 37.
Collins, Augustus, 208.
Collins, D., 84.
Collins, Dan, 192, 207, 210, 211, 222.
Collins, Edward, 193.
Collins, Eleazer, 163.
Collins, Elijah, 37.
Collins, Friend, 277.
Collins, John, 87.
Collins, Josiah, 143.
Collins, Pitman, 191.
Collins, Rufus, 163.
Collins, Samuel, 95, 111.

INDEX. 301

Collins, William L., 88.
Collins, Zelotis, 163.
Collyer, William, 187.
Colson, John, 73.
Colt, John, 184, 209.
Colter, John, 32.
Colton, Ithamar, 147.
Colton, Ithamer, 146.
Colton, Samuel, 147.
Colton, Thomas, 145.
Colton, Ward, 100.
Colton, William, 141.
Coltrain, William, 94, 98, 117, 127.
Columbus, James, 68.
Colver, J., 213.
Colver, Jonathan, 43.
Colyer, Joseph, 111.
Combs, James, 155.
Combs, Joseph, 153.
Combs, William, 60.
Comes, William, 198.
Commens, Stephen, 81.
Commins, Stephen, 94.
Comstock, David, 217.
Comstock, James, 174, 178.
Comstock, Jehiel, 25.
Comstock, John, 16, 88.
Comstock, Jonathan, 140.
Comstock, Phineas, 142.
Comstock, Samuel, 49, 61, 77, 113.
Comstock, Serajah, 39.
Conant, Caleb, 57.
Conant, John, 87.
Conant, Nathaniel, 106, 126, 185.
Conch, Joel, 155.
Concord, 3.
Condin, Thomas, 64.
Condrick, John, 99.
Cone, Abner, 201.
Cone, Benah, 141.
Cone, Cyrus, 185.
Cone, D., 84.
Cone, Daniel, 19, 209.
Cone, Elisha, 117, 127.
Cone, Giles, 229, 237.
Cone, Henry, 59, 269.
Cone, Hubb D., 135.
Cone, Jared, 120, 211, 212.
Cone, Jared, Jr., 119.
Cone, Joseph, 88, 135.
Cone, Joshua, 153, 155.
Cone, Ozias, 68.
Cone, Phineas, 19.
Cone, Silvanus, 211.
Cone, Solomon, 96, 117, 127.
Cone, William, 209.
Conel, Benoni, 267.

Conent, Edmon, 143.
Congdon, Benoney, 51.
Conger, Ephraim, 199.
Conisey, Solomon, 173.
Conlee, John, 88.
Connel, Darby, 61.
Connell, Benoni, 269.
Conner, John, 59.
Conner, Patrick, 254.
Connor, John, 232.
Conolly, John, 95.
Converce, Elisha, 184.
Converse, Damon R., 110, 116.
Converse, Israel, 208.
Converse, J., 206.
Converse, James, 18.
Converse, Jesse, 18.
Converse, Jonathan, 184.
Converse, Josiah, 222, 224.
Converse, Thomas, 33, 37, 48.
Coo[ ], Daniel, 138.
Cook, 22.
Cook, Abraham, 10.
Cook, Amos, 81.
Cook, Benjamin, 235.
Cook, Caleb, 10.
Cook, Daniel, 20.
Cook, Demetius, 191.
Cook, Dimetrus, 184.
Cook, Elihu, 70, 112, 254.
Cook, Elijah, 223.
Cook, Ephraim, 208, 223, 276.
Cook, Ezekiel, 12.
Cook, George, 70, 108.
Cook, Gideon, 135.
Cook, Giles, 275.
Cook, Isaac, 18, 19, 20, 21, 22, 133.
Cook, Isaac, Jr., 16, 17, 24.
Cook, J., 223.
Cook, J. F., 224.
Cook, J. P., 177, 223.
Cook, James, 117, 127, 187.
Cook, Jesse, 21, 205.
Cook, Joel, 112.
Cook, John, 222.
Cook, Johnson, 112.
Cook, Jonah, 119, 269.
Cook, Jonathan, 203.
Cook, Joshua, 135.
Cook, Lemuel, 112, 116, 275.
Cook, Miles, 107.
Cook, Ozem, 76.
Cook, Roswell, 114.
Cook, Samuel, 10, 12, 95, 143, 198.
Cook, Selah, 79.
Cook, Shubal, 51.
Cook, Shubell, 27.

Cook, T., 177, 221.
Cook, Thaddeus, 191, 192, 193, 194, 227, 265, 266, 267, 275.
Cook, Thomas, 1, 28, 71, 113, 202.
Cook, Timothy, 1.
Cook, Warren, 112.
Cook, William, 58, 60, 108, 202.
Cooke, J., 214.
Cooke, Job, 220.
Cooke, Thaddeus, 225.
Cooke, William, 106.
Cooks, J., 214.
Cool, Himan, 111.
Cool, Isaac, 111.
Cooley, Asa, 210.
Cooley, Paul, 132.
Coombs, Samuel, 259.
Coon, J., 97.
Cooper, 41.
Cooper, Abraham, 108.
Cooper, Allen, 210.
Cooper, Jacob, 240.
Cooper, James, 71, 112.
Cooper, Joseph, 235.
Cooper, William, 112.
Cooper, Zebulon, 263.
Copland, Jonathan, 167.
Copley, Nathaniel, 211.
Copp, Joseph, 58, 60.
Copp, William, 248.
Copper, James Y., 234.
Corbett, James, Jr., 19.
Corbin, Philip, 198.
Corby, James, 139.
Cordrick, John, 69.
Corier, Abel, 196.
Cornelius, John, 83.
Cornell, Benjamin, 134.
Cornell, Richard, 69.
Corning, Allyn, 121.
Cornish, George, 146, 147, 148.
Cornish, James, Jr., 164.
Cornish, Joel, 147.
Cornwall, 23, 55, 56, 74, 82, 90, 91, 274.
Cornwell, Ashbel, 141.
Cornwell, Timothy, 204.
Corvett, Solomon, 250.
Corwin, Jonathan, 88.
Corwin, Selah, 88.
Cossit, Rane, 203.
Cottle, Isaac, 232.
Cotton, Elihu, 204.
Cotton, Elisha, 135.
Cotton, John, 229.
Cottrill, Nathan, 51.
Couch, 133.
Couch, Abraham, 54, 126.

Couch, Amos, 57.
Couch, Benjamin S., 152.
Couch, Daniel, 110.
Couch, E., 84.
Couch, Ebenezer, 209, 224, 225.
Couch, Elisha, 157.
Couch, Gideon, 152.
Couch, James, 59.
Couch, John, 134, 192.
Couch, Stephen, 137.
Couch, Steven, 137.
Couch, Thomas N., 152.
Coult, John, 230.
Coval, Abraham, 36.
Covel, Elijah, 137.
Covel, Eliphalet, 264.
Covel, Jonathan, 137, 139.
Covel, Philip, 263.
Covel, William, 238, 239.
Coventry, 16, 31, 58, 64, 65, 66, 74, 75, 78, 79, 81, 82, 87, 88, 114.
Covill, Philip, 157.
Covill, Samuel, 157.
Cowen, Daniel, 126.
Cowen, John, 126.
Cowett, Nathaniel, 246, 250.
Cowle, John, 35.
Cowles, Joseph, 37.
Cowles, Matthew, 182.
Cowles, Timothy, 161.
Coy, David, 57.
Coy, Ephraim, 103.
Coy, Moses, 100.
Coye, Joseph, 143.
Coye, Thomas, 143.
Cox, Jedediah, 95.
Cradock, William, 27.
Crage, John, 256, 262.
Crage, Robert, 232.
Craige, John, 252.
Crain, Joseph, 153.
Cramer, William, 64.
Crammer, Bishop, 119.
Crammer, John, 79.
Crampton, Benjamin, 71.
Crandal, Thomas, 231.
Crandel, Hazel, 159.
Crandel, Richmond, 263.
Crandle, Abiel, 133.
Crane, Adonijah, 78.
Crane, Elihu, 102.
Crane, Elijah, 24.
Crane, James, 102, 124, 130.
Crane, Jesse, 103.
Crane, John, 177, 211, 266.
Crane, Jonathan, 14.
Crane, Joseph, 155.

Crane, Samuel, 86, 196.
Crane, Silas, 81.
Crane, William, 18.
Cranston, Benjamin, 229.
Crary, James, 194.
Crary, Joseph, 186.
Crary, Robart, 186.
Crasman, John, 152.
Craw, John, Jr., 1, 165.
Craw, Reuben, 68.
Crawford, Jason, 68.
Crawford, John, 135.
Crippan, Silas, 43.
Crippen, Silas, 41.
Crittenden, Gilbert, 22.
Crittendon, Gideon, 135.
Crocker, Adonijah, 3, 4, 162.
Crocker, Oliver, 34.
Crocker, Roswell, 118.
Crofoot, Joseph, 194.
Crofoot, Seth, 194.
Croman, Thomas, 257.
Cromb, Joseph, 96.
Crosbey, Obed, 21.
Crosby, Benjamin, 198.
Crosby, Ebenezer, 274.
Crosby, Prince, 96.
Crosby, Simon, 69, 269.
Crosby, Thomas, 143.
Cross, Stephen, 18.
Crouch, Christopher, 159.
Crow, Edward, 245, 250.
Crow, Elias, 118.
Crowele, Shubele, 246.
Crowele, Shubell, 250.
Crowell, Enoch, 259.
Crowell, Manoah, 120.
Crowfeet, J., 84.
Crowfut, Daniel, 199.
Cruttenden, Jonathan, 193.
Cruttenden, Samuel, 277.
Cuff, Sampson, 114.
Culvar, Joshua, 38.
Culver, Aaron, 38, 99.
Culver, Abel, 69.
Culver, Daniel, 88.
Culver, Edward, 245, 247, 249, 253.
Culver, Eliakim, 10.
Culver, James, 174.
Culver, Jeremiah, 140.
Culver, Jonathan, 41.
Culver, Joseph, 37.
Culver, Peter, 186.
Culver, Reuben, 70.
Culver, Samuel. 275.
Cumbo, John. 94.
Cummins, William, 69, 143.

Cuningham, Barnibas, 136.
Cunnell, Jeremiah, 121.
Cunnil, Jeremiah, 185.
Cunningham, Stephen, 190.
Curch, John, 56.
Curtes, Gideon, 276.
Curtes, Joseph, Jr., 275.
Curtice, Aaron, 37.
Curtice, Frederick, 246, 248.
Curtice, Samuel, 246, 248.
Curtis, Abraham, 151.
Curtis, Agur, 151, 173.
Curtis, Andrew, 151.
Curtis, Asa, 173.
Curtis, Augur, 225.
Curtis, Benjamin, 200.
Curtis, Calub, 218.
Curtis, Charles, 155.
Curtis, Daniel, 264.
Curtis, Ebenezer, 151, 219.
Curtis, Eliphalet, 221.
Curtis, Elisha, 193.
Curtis, Ephraim, 180.
Curtis, Ezekiel, 79.
Curtis, Frederick, 247, 252.
Curtis, Henry, 219.
Curtis, Isaac, 151.
Curtis, Jacob, 276.
Curtis, James, 155.
Curtis, Jepthah, 255.
Curtis, Jesse, 224.
Curtis, John, 39, 212.
Curtis, Joseph, 151, 155, 264.
Curtis, Jotham, 224.
Curtis, Levi, 188.
Curtis, Lewis, 151.
Curtis, Matthew, 196.
Curtis, Peter, 206, 233.
Curtis, Reuben, 160.
Curtis, Robert, 152.
Curtis, Samuel, 152, 247, 253.
Curtis, Shelden, 189.
Curtis, Silas, 152.
Curtis, Stephen, 151, 194.
Curtis, Thaddeus, 151.
Curtis, Thomas, 39.
Curtis, Wait, [4]173.
Curtis, William, 14, 155.
Curtiss, Abel, 192.
Curtiss, Abner, 181, 219.
Curtiss, Ames, 88.
Curtiss, Andrew, 181, 219.
Curtiss, Augur, 211.
Curtiss, Charles, 153.
Curtiss, Daniel, 181, 219.
Curtiss, David, 181, 219.
Curtiss, Ebenezer, 181.
Curtiss, Edmund, 181, 215, 219.

Curtiss, Eleazer, 110, 116.
Curtiss, Eleazer, Jr., 18, 23, 24.
Curtiss, Eli, 49.
Curtiss, Elihew, 181, 219.
Curtiss, Eliphalet, 208.
Curtiss, Giles, 48, 71, 133.
Curtiss, Henry, 181.
Curtiss, Hezekiah, 190.
Curtiss, Isaac, 181, 219.
Curtiss, Jabes, 181.
Curtiss, Jabez, 219.
Curtiss, James, 153, 191.
Curtiss, Jeremiah, 181, 219.
Curtiss, Jesse, 208, 210.
Curtiss, John, 23, 169, 191, 193.
Curtiss, Jonathan, 106.
Curtiss, Joseph, 153.
Curtiss, Josiah, 190.
Curtiss, Jotham, 209.
Curtiss, Levi, 187.
Curtiss, Lewis, 181, 219.
Curtiss, Peter, 209.
Curtiss, Robert, 181, 219.
Curtiss, Samuel, 190.
Curtiss, William, 153, 190.
Cushman, Benjamin, 93.
Cushman, Jonah, 54.
Cushman, William, 167.
Cutler, Joseph, 76, 221, 263.
Cutler, Seth, 184.
Cutting, Hezekiah, 159.
Cutting, Zebedee, 159.
Cuyler, Teleman, 253.

Daboll, John, 269.
Dagget, Abenezer, 189.
Dagget, Henry, 49.
Dagget, Nathan, 190.
Dagget, Silas, 233.
Daggett, Henry, 179.
Daggett, Nathan, 233, 253.
Daggett, Silas, 246, 250.
Daggett, Sylvanus, 254.
Daggett, West, 231, 254.
Dailey, John, 105.
Daily, Dowey, 275.
Dale, Richard, 38.
Daley, Joseph, 87.
Daman, Edmund, 3, 4.
Dammorg, Richard, 124.
Damon, Aaron, 1.
Damon, John, 165.
Damon, Jonathan, 165.
Damon, Jonathan, Jr., 1.
Dana, Charles, 135, 255.
Danaty; Francies, 32.
Danbury, 56, 57, 65, 67, 69, 78, 81, 89, 90, 103, 104, 110, 118, 177, 194, 198, 199, 200, 223, 265, 266.
Dande, Thomas, 229.
Dandee, Thomas, 240.
Daniel, Anthony M., 70, 108.
Daniel, Ezekiel, 57.
Daniel, Joel M., 70.
Daniels, David, 68.
Daniels, Ezekiel, 58, 60, 74.
Daniels, Nehemiah, 57, 58, 60, 118.
Daniels, Samuel, 137, 236.
Danolds, Samuel, 139.
Dansey, William, 246, 250.
Darbee, Benjamin, 160.
Darby, William, 159.
Darens, Daniel, 138.
Darga, Asa, 12.
Darling, Benjamin, 41, 43.
Darling, Levy, 257.
Darrow, Benjamin, 233.
Darrow, Christopher, 45.
Darrow, Jonathan, 233.
Darrow, Peter, Jr., 252.
Darrow, Thomas, 243.
Dart, Joseph, 206, 208.
Dart, Samuel, 119.
Dart, Stephen, 60.
Daskomb, William, 54.
Daten, S., 84.
Datton, John, 12.
Dauchy, Jeremiah, 195.
Daurough, James, 83.
Davall, William, 239.
Davenport, Humphrey, 185.
Davenport, J., 206.
Davenport, James, 239.
Davenport, John, 110, 211, 226.
Davenport, Noah, 184.
Davidson, 114.
Davidson, Asa, 79.
Davidson, Daniel, 99.
Davidson, Isaac, 110.
Davidson, John, 110.
Davidson, James, 211.
Davidson, John, 194.
Davidson, Joseph, 204.
Davidson, Pt. 172.
Davinson, Robert, 88.
Davis, 59, 69, 247.
Davis, Abel, 249.
Davis, Abele, 247.
Davis, Amos, 71, 110, 213.
Davis, Daniel, 122.
Davis, David, 1, 87.
Davis, Jacob, Jr., 7.
Davis, Jacob, 3d, 142.
Davis, James, 231.

INDEX. 305

Davis, James, Jr., 277.
Davis, John, 32, 135, 231.
Davis, Jonathan, 35, 76, 169.
Davis, Joseph, 123, 174.
Davis, Julus, 35.
Davis, Lothrop, 265, 269.
Davis, Nathan, 203.
Davis, Samuel, 3, 4, 40, 55.
Davis, Stephen, 88.
Davis, William, 95, 117, 127, 261.
Davise, Abel, 244.
Davison, Asa, 15.
Davison, Calvin, 262.
Davison, Daniel, 68.
Davison, Hezekiah, 95.
Davison, Peter, 167.
Davison, Robert, 74.
Davison, Thomas, 15.
Davol, John, 51.
Dawning, John, 128.
Day, 167.
Day, Abner, 168.
Day, Adonijah, 165.
Day, Adonijah, Jr., 1.
Day, Charles, 1.
Day, Daniel, 165.
Day, James, 254, 256.
Day, Jonathan, 167, 172.
Day, Noah, 184.
Dayton, Israel, 88.
Dayton, Jonathan, 179, 211.
Dayton, Silas, 84.
Dea, Tombo, 258.
Deains, Ebenezer, 171.
Dealing, Samuel, 18, 88.
Dean, Abijah, 169.
Dean, Benjamin, 212.
Dean, Bradley, 152.
Dean, Daniel, 200.
Dean, David, 73.
Dean, James, 114.
Dean, Nathan, 168, 172.
Dean, Parly, 185.
Dean, Phinehas, 82.
Dean, Ruben, 35.
Deane, Archelaus, 105.
Deangalis, Pascal, 237.
Deans, Levi, 22.
Deans, Nathan, 167.
Dear, George, Jr., 22.
Debago, Simeon, 246.
Debago, Simon, 251.
Dee, Daniel, 140, 221.
Deer, George, 37.
"Defence," 231, 232, 233, 234, 266.
De Florus, Anthony, 123.
Deforest, James, 219.

Deforest, Joseph, 181.
Deforest, N., 190.
Deforest, Samuel, 48.
De Forrest, Abel, 98.
Delaby, George, 58.
Delano, Jethro, 34.
Delop, James, 172.
Deming, David, 80, 89.
Deming, Ephraim, 155.
Deming, John, 80, 247, 251.
Deming, Jonathan, 39.
Deming, Lemuel, 267.
Deming, Lemuel, Jr., 267.
Deming, Pownal, 47.
Deming, Richard, 155.
Deming, Selah, 79.
Deming, Simeon, 155.
Deming, Wait, 39.
Demking, John, 251.
Demmen, Elisha, 274.
Demming, Ephraim, 153.
Demming, Lemuel, 265.
Demming, Richard, 153.
Demming, Seth, 212.
Demming, Simeon, 153.
Demming, Treat, 277.
Demmon, John, 53.
Demon, Joseph, 163.
Denilo, Benjamin, 81.
Denison, Asa, 141.
Denison, Daniel, 143.
Dennice, John, 245.
Denning, Lemuel, Jr., 269.
Dennis, John, 249.
Dennison, Amos, 51.
Dennison, John, 99.
Dennison, Nathan, 227.
Denrary, Richard, 54.
Denslow, Benjamin, 265, 267.
Denslow, E., 220.
Denslow, Eli, 75.
Denslow, Martin, 68.
Densmore, William, 137.
Derby, 70, 88, 89, 90, 91, 110, 189.
Dervan, William, 117.
Desbrow, Simon, 234.
Deshon, John, 209.
Deshon, Richard, 210.
D'Estaing, N., 206.
Devall, William, 238.
Devenport, Bela, 160.
Devenport, James, 238.
Dewa, Jo. 172.
Dewen, William, 110.
Dewett, John, 243.
Dewey, Andrew, 2, 3.
Dewey, Daniel, 4, 159, 161.

Dewey, James, 60.
Dewey, John, 160.
Dewey, Joseph, 171.
Dewey, Josiah, 163, 169.
De Witt, Garrit, 204.
Dewitt, John, 242.
De Wolf, Aaron, 74.
De Wolf, Benone, 74.
De Wolf, Charles, 146.
Dewolf, Charls, 147.
De Woolf, Stephen, 249.
Dewy, James, 89.
Dexter, Elnathan, 255.
Dibbel, Dan, 146.
Dibbl, 195.
Dibble, Daniel, 146.
Dibble, Ezra, 209.
Dibble, Israel, 269, 274.
Dibble, John, 179.
Dibble, Marten, 178.
Dibble, Sineus, 277.
Dibol, Benjah, 203.
Dibol, Dan, 146.
Dick, Benona, 260.
Dick, Benony, 263.
Dick, Richard, 24.
Dick, Thomas, 59.
Dickenson, Samuel, 43.
Dickerman, Joseph, 89.
Dickerson, Benjamin, 264.
Dickerson, Josiah, 155.
Dickerson, Osias, 155.
Dickerson, Richard, 229.
Dickerson, Waitstill, 155.
Dickeson, John, 53.
Dickinson, Aahel, 201.
Dickinson, Friend, 19, 201.
Dickinson, Josiah, 154.
Dickinson, Mosses, 187, 188.
Dickinson, Oliver, 201.
Dickinson, Ozias, 154.
Dickinson, Samuel, 41.
Dickinson, Sim, 153.
Dickinson, Waitstill, 154.
Dickison, Simeon, 155.
Dickman, Stephen, 152.
Dickson, David, 16.
Die, Daniel, 89.
Dike, Benjamin, 160.
Dilkins, Williams, 155.
Dilling, William, 154.
Dimack, Jeduthan, 56.
Dimack, Joseph, 171.
Dimmick, Benjamin, 14, 50, 104.
Dimmick, Isack, 15.
Dimmick, Thomas, 169.
Dimmick, Tymothy, 14.
Dimmock, John, 97.

Dimmock, Samuel, 97.
Dimmuck, Isaac, 15.
Dimock, Edward, 25.
Dimock, J., 172.
Dimon, D., 180.
Dimon, Daniel, 180, 181.
Dimon, David, 16, 19, 23, 24.
Dimon, J., Jr., 213.
Dimon, Jonathan, 84, 180, 209, 211, 213, 215, 225, 226.
Dinah, James, 71, 112.
Dingley, John, 114, 246, 248.
Dingly, John, 103, 130.
Disborough, Joshua, 88.
Disbrow, Asa, 196.
Disbrow, Henery, 232.
Disbrow, Isaac, 152.
Disbrow, John, 152.
Disbrow, Joshua, 152.
Disbrow, Justus, 152.
Disbrow, Russil, 232.
Diskill, Jams, 182.
Dix, Benjamin, 121, 153, 155.
Dix, David, 123.
Dix, Jesse, 154, 155.
Dix, Samuel, 153, 155.
Dixon, David, 76.
Dixon, George, 269.
Dixon, James, 110.
Dixon, Jared, 77.
Dixon, John, 121, 208.
Dixon, Robort, 186.
Dixson, James, 168.
Dixson, John, Jr., 216.
Dixson, Robert, 216.
Dixson, Thomas, 170.
Doal, James, 12, 41, 43.
Doal, John, 12, 41, 43.
Dobbs Ferry, 100.
Dodd, Ashbel, 187.
Dodd, Ashbell, 188.
Dodge, 108.
Dodge, Daniel, 89.
Dodge, James, 57.
Dodge, Josiah R., 93.
Dodge, Nathan, 60, 89.
Dodge, Reubin, 122.
Dodge, Seth, 122.
Dodge, Stephen, 142.
Doertes, Thomas, 247.
Doggett, John, 4.
Doherty, Thomas, 249.
Doll, Benjamin, 32.
Dolph, Charls, 146.
"Dolphin," 241.
Donaldson, Samuel, 16.
Donavin, Derby, 93.
Done, Israel, 178.

# INDEX. 307

Done, Oliver, 246, 251.
Doolittle, Benjamin, 164.
Doolittle, Ebenezer, 94, 117, 127.
Doolittle, George, 107.
Doolittle, Ichabod, 16, 18, 21, 23, 24.
Doolittle, Isaac, 194.
Doolittle, Joel, 276.
Doolittle, John, 194.
Doolittle, Joseph, Jr., 194.
Doolittle, Oliver, 194, 275.
Doolittle, Solomon, 194.
Doolittle, Thomas, 135.
Dormon, Gershom, 269.
Dorr, Edmond, 154, 155, 258.
Dorranc, Archabel, 170.
Dorrance, David, 45, 50.
Doty, David, 34.
Doty, John, 138.
Doty, Joseph, 34.
Doty, Samuel, 178.
Douaal, John, 62.
Doubleday, Abner, 3, 4, 5.
Doubleday, Elisha, 149.
Doubleday, Joseph, 4.
Doud, John, 38.
Doud, Richard, 135.
Doud, Zaccheus, 94.
Douglas, David, 138.
Douglas, John, 17, 19, 22, 23, 133, 167, 168.
Douglas, Solomon, 89.
Douglas, William, 9, 22, 23, 24. 25, 70.
Douglass, 167.
Douglass, John, 16, 169, 170, 171, 172, 227, 267.
Douglass, Joseph, 100.
Douglass, Nathaniel, 21.
Douglass, Richard, 45, 50.
Douglass, Robert, 60.
Douning, John, 55.
Douning, Jonathan, 169.
Douset, Amas, 15.
Dowd, David, 113.
Dowd, Jehiel, 113.
Dowd, Moses, 89.
Dowd, Zaccheus, 113, 116.
Dowd, Zephaniah, 117, 127.
Dowens, Chauncey, 16.
Dowing, Stephen, 171.
Downer, Caleb, 1.
Downer, James, 81.
Downes, John, 82.
Downing, Abijah, 124.
Downing, Christopher, 88.
Downing, Ichabod, 122.
Downing, John, 53, 136.

Downing, Levi, 172.
Downing, Phineas, 185.
Downing, Phineas, Jr., 172.
Downing, Rufus, 172.
Downing, S., 172.
Downing, Stephen, 65, 88.
Downning, Jonathan, 184.
Downs, 41.
Downs, Abraham, Jr., 189.
Downs, David, 34.
Downs, James, 53, 135.
Downs, John, 54, 121.
Downs, S., 213.
Downs, Wolcut, 218.
Dowset, Amos, 15.
Dowset, Jonathan, 15.
Drake, Gideon, 139.
Draper, Nathan, 63.
Dresser, Alphred, 101.
Drew, D., 84.
Driggs, Daniel, 41, 43.
Drinkwater, Ebenezer, 24, 99.
Drinkwater, William, 89.
Drisco, John, 258.
Driscoll, Philip, 253.
Ducitt, John, 76.
Dudley, Elezur, 173.
Dudley, Gilbert, 208.
Dudley, Guilbard, 233.
Dudley, Jared, 209.
Dudley, Nathan, 173.
Dudley, Zebulon, 89, 115, 276.
Dudly, Daniel, 38.
Duey, Aron, 203.
Dufee, Ebenezer, 126.
Duffe, Thomas, 88.
Duffee, Elijah, 126.
Dugard, John, 74.
Duggan, James, 103, 131.
Dunbar, Joseph, 269.
Dunbar, Miles, 89.
Duncan, Daniel, 180.
Duncan, Edward, 106, 126.
Duncan, James, 135.
Duncan, Jared, 152.
Duncomb, John, 243.
Duncomb, William, 236.
Dunham, Cornelius, 61, 233.
Dunham, Daniel, 4, 100, 163.
Dunham, Ezekel, 246.
Dunham, Ezekiel, 74.
Dunham, Gershom, 74.
Dunham, Gideon, 127.
Dunham, James, 120.
Dunham, Jonathan, 159.
Dunham, Silas, 211.
Dunham, Simeon, 163.
Dunham, Solomon, 191, 262.

Dunham, Solomon, Jr., 191.
Dunham, Zekel, 248.
Duning, Ezra, 196.
Duning, James, 215.
Dunk, Thomas, 197.
Dunking, John, 246.
Dunlap, Joshua, 168, 210.
Dunning, Gideon, 21.
Dunning, Liverus, 195.
Dunning, Samuel, 195.
Dunning, Silas, 86.
Dunwell, Stephen, 74.
Dupe, Simeon, 35.
Duran, Ebenezer, 269.
Durand, Ebenezer, 110.
Durand, Isaac, 271.
Durfee, Benjamin, 122.
Durfee, James, 169.
Durfey, Israel, 263.
Durfey, Thomas, 61.
Durffee, Ebenez, 106.
Durffee, Elijah, 106.
Durfy, Jedediah, 1, 165.
Durfy, Joseph, Jr., 1.
Durham, 22, 70, 80, 81. 104, 107, 108, 133.
Durkee, 50, 265.
Durkee, Benjamin, 89, 173.
Durkee, Jeremiah, 32, 60, 80, 184.
Durkee, John, 47, 63, 64, 65, 93.
Durkee, Solomon, 143, 185.
Durkee, William, 143.
Durphee, Ephraim, 63.
Durphy, Jedediah, 165.
Dutcher, Ruluff, 211.
Dutton, Amos, 24.
Dutton, Moses, 99.
Dutton, Thomas, 209, 223.
Dutton, Titus, 88.
Dwight, H., 220.
Dwight, Hamlin, 220.
Dwire, Michael, 258.
D Wolf, Aaron, 228.
D Woolf, Stephen, 245.
Dyar, Calob, 233.
Dyar, William, 169.
Dyer, Elisha, 96.
Dyer, Isrel, 261.
Dyer, Juba, 114.
Dyer, Roger, 257.
Dykeman, Jonathan, 69.

Eadee, Amor, 75.
Eagleston, David, 108.
Eaglestone, Josiah, 35.
Eagliston, Jonathan, 127.
Eames, David, 170.
Eames, John, 170.
Eams, Everet, 89.
Eansworth, Jedediah, 49, 78.
Earl, William, 58.
Easmon, Eli, 139.
East Chester, 159, 160, 161, 162, 163.
East Haddam, 23, 57, 58, 59, 82, 89, 90, 114, 278.
East Hartford, 58, 60, 87, 267.
East Haven, 25.
East Windsor, 1, 54, 55, 57, 58, 78, 87, 88, 89, 103, 104.
Eastman, Asahel, 185.
Eastman, Azariah, 136.
Eastman, Benjamin, 136.
Eastman, Deliverance, 79.
Eastman, Ebenezer, 185.
Eastman, Joseph, 197, 199.
Eastman, Timothy, 15.
Easton, Eliphalet, 269.
Easton, Julan, 75.
Eaton, Ebenezer, 185.
Eaton, Joshua, 168.
Eaton, Marvirick, 185.
Eaton, Aron, 103, 131.
Eaton, Daniel, 105.
Eaton, Josiah, 15.
Eaton, Stephen, 57.
Eberhard, John, 70, 112.
Eccleston, Jonathan, 138.
Eddy, Seth, 74, 228.
Edgcomb, David, 174.
Edgcomb, Ezra, 36, 89.
Edgcomb, Jabez, 123.
Edgcomb, Preserve, 32.
Edgerton, Abel, 80, 185.
Edgerton, Elisha, 209, 211.
Edgerton, Jedediah, 160.
Edgerton, Jonathan, 162.
Edgerton, Kingsbury, 240.
Edgerton, Simeon, 211.
Edmond, Robert, 200.
Edmond, William, 267.
Edmonds, William, 265, 266, 269.
Edson, Caleb, 93.
Edwards, Ceasar, 53.
Edwards, Daniel, 120.
Edwards, George, 254.
Edwards, Gideon, 269.
Edwards, Henry, 27.
Edwards, John, 173.
Edwards, Jonathan, 103, 130.
Edwards, Joseph, 193.
Edwards, Phineas, 171.
Edwards, Samuel, 135.
Edwards, Thomas, 37.
Edy, Charles, 160.
[ ]eed, 85.

INDEX. 309

Eells, Edward, 46, 60.
Eells, Samuel, 76, 60.
Egeton, Joshua, 7.
Eggleston, 123.
Eggleston, Benedict, 123.
Egglestone, Jonathan, 95.
Egleston, Joseph, 60.
Eglestone, Bennit, 141.
Egliston, Joseph, 171.
Elderkin, Bela, 245, 248.
Elderkin, Dearky, 246.
Elderkin, Diarea, 29.
Elderkin, Diarky, 248.
Elderkin, James, 240, 252.
Elderkin, Jedidiah, 136.
Elderkin, John, 28, 230.
Elderkin, Joshua, 216.
Elderkin, Luther, 245, 249.
Elderkin, Minor, 240.
Elderkin, Vine, 89.
Eldredge, Daniel, 25.
Eldredge, William, 111.
Eldridge, Daniel, 14.
Eldridge, James, 114.
Eldridge, Thomas, 66.
Eldridge, Zoeth, 133.
Elgar, David, 58.
Elgar, Ezra, 190.
Elger, Abner, 136.
Elger, David, 60.
Elgur, Abner, 181, 219.
Eli, Edward, 59.
Eli, King, 78.
Eli, Tuller, 131.
Eliot, Joseph, 17.
Ellis, Benjamin, 252.
Ellis, Daniel, 185.
Ellis, Nathan, 267.
Ellis, William, 254.
Elliss, Carpenter, 51.
Ells, Edward, 134.
Ells, Samuel, 130.
Ellsworth, Charles, 23.
Ellsworth, Moses, 54.
Elmer, Daniel, Jr., 38.
Elmes, Elkenah, 258.
Elmor, Joseph, 199.
Elmore, Daniel, 69.
Elmore, Samuel, 16, 17, 41, 43.
Elswood, Abijah, 126.
Elsworth, Charles, 55.
Elsworth, Daniel, 165.
Elsworth, Daniel, 3d, 1.
Elsworth, Gurdon, 165.
Elsworth, Hezekiah, 1.
Elsworth, Moses, 103, 130.
Eluzzad, Nathan, 81.
Elwell, Ebenezer, 127.

Elwell, Ozias, 76.
Elwell, Samuel, 127.
Elwood, Isaac, 152, 233.
Elwood, Joseph, 109.
Elwood, Nathan, 54.
Elwood, Thomas, 232.
Ely, Elisha, 48.
Ely, Gad, 202.
Ely, John, 142, 150, 221, 227, 267.
Ely, S., 84.
Emerson, Joseph, 119.
Emerson, Nathaniel, 141.
Emerson, Stephen, 65.
Emmes, John B., 91.
Emmons, Asa, 274.
Emmons, Noadiah, 20.
Emmons, Samuel, 274.
Emmons, William, 220.
Emorson, Nathaniel, 111.
Enfield, 53, 54, 58, 88, 89, 90, 103.
Eno, Isaac, 67.
Enos, 227.
Enos, David, 59.
Enos, Roger, 18, 24, 141, 142, 226, 228, 273, 278.
Ens, David, 63.
Ensign, Daniel, 67.
Ensign, John, 226.
Ensign, Jonathan, 37.
Ensign, Otis, 126.
Ensign, Solomon, 274.
Ensworth, Edward, 78.
Ervin, Jared, 234.
Essex, John, 256.
Etherly, Thomas, 238, 250.
Etterly, Thomas, 246.
Europe, 118.
Evans, Abiather, 102.
Evans, Benjamin S., 119.
Evans, Henry, 58, 60.
Evans, Isaac, 89.
Evans, Jonah, 60.
Evans, Josiah, 58, 118.
Evans, Samuel, Jr., 89.
Evans, Thomas, 94.
Evans, Willard, 64.
Evarts, Caleb, 277.
Evarts, Charles, 37.
Evarts, Ebur, 37.
Evens, Abiather, 53, 129.
Evens, Allyn, 122.
Evens, Cotton, 66.
Evens, John, 35.
Evens, Stacey, 128.
Evens, Stacy, 127.
Everest, Benjamin, 37.
Everest, Daniel, 35.
Everest, Elisha, 37.

Everett, James, 253.
Everit, Eliphalet, 12.
Eversley, Daniel, 217.
Eversley, John, 218.
Everts, 212.
Everts, Caleb, 277.
Everts, Eber, 21.
Everts, Reuben, 113.
Everts, Samuel, Jr., 277.
Everts, Stephen, 265, 267, 269.
Evertun, William, 10.
Evit, Solomon, 55.
Evitt, Daniel, 53.
Ewen, Michael, 264.
Ewett, Joseph, 246.

Fagands, William, 245.
Fagens, William, 186.
Fagin, John, 122.
Fagons, William, 250.
Fairbanks, Samuel, 200.
Fairchild, Abel, 151.
Fairchild, Alexander, 78.
Fairchild, Curtiss, 190.
Fairchild, Enoch, 86.
Fairchild, James, 21, 22.
Fairchild, Jesse, 22.
Fairchild, John, 22, 86.
Fairchild, Nathan, 93.
Fairchild, Peter, 77, 78.
Fairfield, 53, 54, 55, 67, 68, 69, 70, 75, 79, 80, 82, 88, 89, 102, 109, 171, 180, 189, 190, 191, 192, 193, 194, 195, 196, 197, 198, 199, 200, 201, 205, 207, 266.
Fairman, Henry, 197.
Fairman, Roswell, 168.
Fairweather, John, 236.
Fairweather, Samuel, 77.
Fairwether, Samuel, 78.
Falkner, Lemuel, 64.
Fanning, Charles, 47.
Fanning, Cyrus, 241.
Fanning, Phineus, 216.
Fantom, Elijah, 120.
Fargo, Aaron, 58, 60.
Fargo, Samuel, 124.
Fargo, Thomas, 28.
Fargo, Timothy, 28.
Fargo, Zaccheus, 269.
Fargo, Zachariah, 266.
Fargo, Zacheus, 266.
Farles, John, 155.
Farmar, Aaron, 269.
Farmer, Thomas, 48, 50.
Farmington, 18, 24, 53, 57, 58, 59, 61, 64, 65, 66, 69, 75, 76, 77, 78, 79, 87, 88, 89, 90, 114, 133.
Farmon, Elijah, 165.
Farnam, Elijah, 165.
Farnam, Eliphet, 171.
Farnam, Eliphalet, 172.
Farnam, Israel, 66.
Farnam, Stephen, 172.
Farnham, Thomas, 265, 269.
Farnum, John, 69.
Farnum, Reuben, 89.
Farrand, Jonathan, 208, 225.
Farrin, Zebulon, 10.
Farrow, John, 57.
Fassett, Josiah, 105.
Faulkner, Caleb, 109.
Faxon, Ebenezer, 274.
Faxon, Thomas, 274.
Fay, Aaron, 36.
Fay, Jedediah, 185.
Fayer, Elijah, 124.
Fegro, Peter, 69.
Felch, Samuel, 169.
Fellow, Samuel, 35.
Fellows, David, 35, 51.
Fellows, Joseph, 45.
Fellows, Nathaniel, 51.
Fellows, Obel, 35.
Fellows, Samuel, 20.
Fellows, Stephen, 35, 265, 269.
Fellows, William, 138.
Felt, Samuel, 208.
Felton, Rufus, 184.
Fenn, Daniel, 68.
Fenn, Edward, 81.
Fenn, Edward, Jr., 276.
Fenn, Thomas, 177, 209, 223.
Fenton, Eleazer, Jr., 24.
Fenton, Elijah, 185.
Fenton, Jacob, 82, 106, 126.
Fenton, John, 89, 119.
Fenton, Nathan, 106, 126.
Fenton, Solomon, 46.
Ferdenands, Jaquin, 238.
Fergo, Moses, 140.
Ferman, Richard, 58.
Fernandes, Jaquin, 239.
Ferrington, Jeremiah, 193.
Ferris, Ebenezer, 210.
Ferris, Gold, 85.
Ferris, Peter, 12.
Ferris, Ransford A., 265, 269.
Ferry, Eliphalet, 199.
Ferry, Joseph, 213.
Field, James, 79.
Field, John, 184.
Field, Nathaniel, 39.

# INDEX.

Field, Robert, 262.
Fields, Edmond, 111.
Fields, Edward, 68.
Fields, George, 78.
Fields, Rebert, 203.
Filer, Abraham, 278.
Filer, Ambrose, 68.
Filer, Normand, 36.
Filer, Roger, 27.
Fillets, Francis, 89.
Filley, Eli, 39.
Filley, Elnathan, 24.
Filley, Hezekiah, 27.
Filley, Isaac, 273.
Filley, Jonathan, 177.
Filley, Mark, 57.
Filley, Remb., 122.
Fillmore, Cyrus, 34.
Fillow, Azor, 217.
Fillow, Isaac, 217.
Fillow, Nathan, 217.
Fillow, Stephen, 217.
Filmore, Henry, 269.
Filow, 22.
Finch, Billay, 243.
Finch, Isaac, 267.
Finch, Jacob, 67, 198.
Finch, Jeremiah, 38.
Finch, Jonathan, 112.
Finch, Peleg, 85.
Finch, Peter, 243.
Finigan, John, 57.
Finley, Samuel, 160.
Finney, Richard, 267.
Finney, Uriah, 79, 81, 98.
Fish, Asahel, 186.
Fish, Daniel, 171.
Fish, David, 186.
Fish, James, 174.
Fish, Moses, 171.
Fish, Nathan, 169.
Fisher, Darriel, 36.
Fisher, Darius, 236.
Fisher, Eleazer, 35.
Fisher, Isaac, 38, 99.
Fisher, James, 230.
Fisher, Jeremiah, 52.
Fisher, Joseph, 245, 247, 251.
Fishkill, 71, 115.
Fisk, Abijah, 263.
Fisk, Amaziah, 143.
Fisk, John, 34.
Fitch, 266.
Fitch, Andrew, 5, 47, 63.
Fitch, Annis, 161.
Fitch, Caleb, 74.
Fitch, Elijah, 217.
Fitch, Elisha, 167.

Fitch, Ezekiel, 149.
Fitch, Ezekiel, Jr., 260.
Fitch, Ichabod, Jr., 5, 20.
Fitch, James, 165, 218.
Fitch, Jesse, 1.
Fitch, Jiles, 218.
Fitch, Jonathan, 226.
Fitch, Josiah, 4.
Fitch, Samuel, 35.
Fitch, Theophilus, 254.
Fitch, Thomas, 237.
Fitch, William, 217, 242.
Fith, Moses, 143.
Fitts, Daniel, 15.
Fitts, Israel, 79.
Fitzgerald, Henry, 111.
Fitz Gerald, James, 18.
Fitz Gerald, John, 38.
Flagg, Gershom, 41, 43.
Fleming, Thomas, 35.
Fletcher, Ebenezer, 209.
Fletcher, James, 143, 184.
Fletcher, John, 78.
Flether, John, 27.
Flint, Asael, 247, 252.
Flint, James L., 114.
Flint, John, 143.
Flint, Oliver, 185.
Flint, Silas, 246, 248.
Flower, Cornelius, 35.
Flower, Isaac, 274.
Flower, Joseph, 81.
Flowers, Benjamin, 87.
Flowers, Gabrel, 205.
Flowers, Reuben, 27.
Flowers, William, 118.
Fobes, Daniel, 143.
Fobs, Jacob, 263.
Foster, Timothy, 192.
Folger, David, 246, 249.
Follen, John, 81.
Follet, Abner, 248.
Follet, James, 195.
Follet, Robert, 105, 117, 127.
Follett, Abner, 246.
Follett, Robert, 95.
Folsom, Darius, 190.
Fontine, John, 76.
Foord, Benjamin, 70.
Foord, Jonathan, 70.
Foot, Aaron, 224.
Foot, Abraham, 210.
Foot, Ebenezer, 10, 139.
Foot, Ebenezer E., 35.
Foot, Elijah, 77.
Foot, Ezra, 110.
Foot, George, 51, 52, 126.
Foot, Heli, 10, 255.

Foot, Isaac, 212.
Foot, Israel, Jr., 160.
Foot, Joseph, 35, 164.
Foot, Moses, 134.
Foote, Beriah, 79.
Foott, George, 106.
Forbes, Abisha, 126, 127.
Forbs, Elias, 10.
Forbs, Moses, 188.
Ford, Benjamin, 112.
Ford, James, 239, 253.
Ford, Jesse, 211.
Ford, John, 96.
Ford, Jonathan, 112.
Ford, Martin, 263.
Ford, Sanburn, 192.
Foresider, William, 185.
Forest, Samuel D., 50.
Forraster, Peter J., 256.
Fort Clinton, 278.
Fort Edward, 20.
Fort George, 20.
Fort Griswold, 207, 267.
Fortune, Ammon, 40.
Forward, J., 206.
Forward, Joseph, 210, 221.
Fosdick, Samuel, 132, 246, 250.
Fosdick, Thomas U., 28, 30.
Fosket, Jonathan, 94.
Fosset, Benjamin, 64.
Fosset, Jesse, 64.
Foster, Alpheus, 185.
Foster, Chauncey, 1.
Foster, Comfort, 58.
Foster, D., 170.
Foster, David, 61.
Foster, Edward, 66.
Foster, Giles, 193.
Foster, Jabez, 3, 4, 149, 184.
Foster, Jesse, 19, 64.
Foster, John, 61.
Foster, Jonah, 208.
Foster, Lemuel, 65.
Foster, Osias, 276.
Foster, Ozius, 193.
Foster, Stephen, 15.
Foster, Steven, 15.
Foster, Thomas, 56, 192, 276.
Foster, Thomas W., 256.
Foster, Tim, 276.
Foster, Wareham, 1.
Foster, William, 167, 171.
Foster, William D., 143, 172.
Fostor, James, 75.
Fountaine, John, 269.
Fowler, 18.
Fowler, Amos, 160.
Fowler, Benjamin, 247, 249.

Fowler, Caleb, 89.
Fowler, Daniel, 120.
Fowler, Dijah, 160.
Fowler, Edmund, 69.
Fowler, John, 5.
Fowler, John, Jr., 179.
Fowler, Josiah, 22, 209, 211.
Fowler, Josiah, Jr., 9.
Fowler, Mark, 160.
Fowler, Nehemiah, 89.
Fowler, Noah, 133, 211.
Fowler, Reuben, 277.
Fowler, Robert, 231.
Fowler, William, 24, 50.
Fox, 50.
Fox, Amos, 185.
Fox, Ashbel, 87.
Fox, Bassett, 123.
Fox, David, 157.
Fox, Ebenezer, 157.
Fox, Edward, 12.
Fox, Isaac, 157.
Fox, Israel, 157.
Fox, Jacob, 40, 89, 161.
Fox, John, 57, 89, 184.
Fox, Joel, 271.
Fox, Levi, 58.
Fox, Obediah, 23.
Fox, Simeon, 123.
Fox, Stephen, 101, 157, 247.
Fox, Thomas, 65, 95.
Fox, Vaniah, 121.
Fox, William H., 98.
Foy, Samuel, 255.
Fraims, John, 153.
Fraines, John, 154.
Frame, John, 75.
Frances, Simon, 276.
Francies, A., 263.
Francis, John, 71, 142, 155.
Francis, Jonathan, 82, 276.
Francis, Joseph, 240.
Francis, Robert, 80.
Franciss, Roswell, 266.
Franklin, David, 138.
Franklin, Henry, 65.
Franklin, Samuel, 138.
Frazier, George, 36.
Frederick, Joseph, 246.
Fredericksburg, 53, 102, 115.
Freedom, Dick, 112.
Freedom, Ned, 109.
Freedswell, Samuel, 236.
Freeland, Francis, 37.
Freeman, Abraham, 60.
Freeman, Benjamin, 17.
Freeman, Brince, 101.
Freeman, Cato, 101.

## INDEX.

Freeman, Charles, 263.
Freeman, Cuff, 107.
Freeman, David, 250.
Freeman, Edward, 123.
Freeman, Jack, 89, 101.
Freeman, Jacob, 60.
Freeman, Juba, 109.
Freeman, Michael, 105.
Freeman, Peter, 107.
Freeman, Phila, 107.
Freeman, Prince, 110.
Freeman, Providence, 89.
Freeman, Robert, 76, 118.
Freeman, Samson, 89.
Freeman, Thomas, 113.
Freen, Benjamin, 179.
Freman, Robert, 77.
French, Abner, 58.
French, Charles, 189.
French, E., 84.
French, Enoch, 189.
French, Frances, 189.
French, Isaac, 170.
French, Israel, Jr., 189.
French, James, 263.
French, Jedediah, 25.
French, Jonathan, Jr., 263.
French, Josiah, 69.
French, Othenial, 215.
French, Samuel, 84, 89, 213, 236, 269.
French, Truman, 69.
Frink, Isaac, 269.
Frink, John, 183.
Frink, Lothrop, 114.
Frink, Seth, 52, 175.
Frink, Thomas, 51, 103, 130.
Frisbee, Isaac, 264.
Frisbee, Jabez, 20.
Frisbie, Asahel, 136.
Frisbie, Benjamin, 273.
Frisbie, Caleb, 10, 252, 256.
Frisbie, Isaac, 253, 260.
Frisbie, John, 202.
Frisbie, Josiah, 255.
Frisbie, Noah, 136.
Frisbie, Noah, Jr., 136.
Frisbie, Reuben, 71, 112.
Frisbie, Titus, 10.
Frisby, Israel, 95, 117, 127.
Frisby, Jabez, 36.
Frisby, Levi, 58.
Frissel, William, 206.
Frizbee, Benjamin, 75.
Frizby, Benjamin, 36.
Frost, Amos, 108.
Frost, Elisha, 119.
Frost, Ephrim, 1.

Frost, Joseph, 151, 181, 219.
Frost, Josiah, Jr., 1.
Frost, Noah, 1.
Frost, Stephen, 141.
Frothingham, Samuel, 107.
Frudom, Joseph, 75.
Fruman, Call, 97.
Fry, Richard, 234.
Fulford, John, 78.
Fulford, Noah, 99.
Fulford, Titus, 24.
Fullar, Abel, 154.
Fuller, Abel, 155.
Fuller, Abijah, 143.
Fuller, Abner, 27.
Fuller, Abraham, 208, 222, 225.
Fuller, Amos, 53.
Fuller, Asa, 160.
Fuller, Barnabas, 137.
Fuller, Benjamin, 27, 63, 263.
Fuller, Bethuel, 19, 278.
Fuller, Calvin, 56.
Fuller, Daniel, 37.
Fuller, Darius, 184.
Fuller, Edward, 39.
Fuller, Ehud, 138.
Fuller, Elezar, 37.
Fuller, Fredrick, 82.
Fuller, Isaac, 171.
Fuller, James, 53, 98.
Fuller, John, 53.
Fuller, Joshua, 122.
Fuller, Lemuel, 27.
Fuller, Nathaniel, 85.
Fuller, Samuel, 149.
Fuller, Timothy, 278.
Fuller, William, 93, 264.
Fullerson, Nathaniel, 247.
Fullerton, Nathaniel, 248.
Fullor, Simean, 182.
Fullour, Stephen, 65.
Fulorton, 244.
Fulton, Frances, 40.
Furbs, John, 154.
Fyler, Ambrose, 273.

Gabriel, Peter, 242.
Gage, Sylvenus, 124.
Gager, Robert, 185.
Gains, Jonathan, 137.
Galaspy, William, 12.
Gale, Christopher, 83.
Gale, Samuel, 22.
Galford, Thomas, 65.
Gallop, 206.
Gallup, 206, 207.
Gallup, Andrew, 269.
Gallup, Benadam, 216.

Gallup, George, 183.
Gallup, Henry, Jr., 216.
Gallup, Jacob, 186.
Gallup, Jesse, 216.
Gallup, Levi, 186.
Gallup, N., 206.
Gallup, Nathan, 211.
Gallup, Nehemiah, 184.
Gallup, Robert, 267, 269.
Gallup, William, 171.
Galpen, Samuel, 38.
Galusha, Jacob, 73.
Gan, John, 238, 239.
Gansey, 214.
Gautly, Peter, 230.
Gardener, Rufus, 264.
Gardiner, Abijah, 59.
Gardiner, Thomas, 36.
Gardner, D. Tubbs, 89.
Gardner, David, 106, 123.
Gardner, John, 235.
Gardner, Jotham, 245.
Gardner, Jothan, 251.
Gardner, Sherman, 40, 267, 269.
Gardner, Thomas, 66.
Gardner, William, 238.
Gardnor, Benjamin, 258.
Gardnor, Jotham, 259.
Garner, Peregrine, 82.
Garner, Silvester, 162.
Garnsey, Joseph, 209.
Garnsey, Seth, 93.
Garratt, John, 67.
Garret, John, 89.
Garrett, Francis, Jr., 145.
Garrett, John, 71, 112.
Garrick, William, 246, 250.
Garrit, Francis, 146, 147, 148.
Garritt, Francis, Jr., 146.
Garrow, Francies, 32.
Gary, Benjamin, 4.
Gary, Elnathan, 81.
Gary, John, 63.
Gary, Seth, 66.
Gaston, John, 170.
Gates, 221.
Gates, Daniel, 19, 21.
Gates, John, 123, 174.
Gates, Joshua, 142, 183.
Gates, Moses, 85.
Gates, Nathaniel, 89, 124.
Gates, Oliver, 174, 255.
Gates, Samuel, 211.
Gavett, Stephen, 122.
Gay, Andrew, 118.
Gay, Asael, 4.
Gay, Asel, 3.
Gay, Ebenezer, 227.
Gay, Fisher, 137, 138.
Gay, James, 162.
Gay, Jason, 82, 123.
Gay, Richard, 203.
Gay, Richard, Jr., 24.
Gay, Samuel, 182.
Gaylor, Timothy, 223.
Gaylord, Benjamin, 21, 36, 119.
Gaylord, Elisha, 202.
Gaylord, Giles, 13.
Gaylord, Joel, 97, 139.
Gaylord, John, 238, 239.
Gaylord, Joseph, 139.
Gaylord, Josiah, 105.
Gaylord, Jotham, 194.
Gaylord, L., 142.
Gaylord, Moses, 274.
Gaylord, Samuel, 39.
Gaylord, Silas, 18, 19.
Gaylord, Thomas, 276.
Geacoks, Jesse, 233.
Gears, Benajah, 24.
Geary, Seth, 93.
Gebbs, Peter, 109.
Gee, George, 234.
Geecocks, Joshua, 53.
Geer, Benajah, 16, 17.
Geer, Elihu, 89.
Geer, Gurdian, 162.
Geer, John W., 150.
Geer, Lemuel, 174.
Geer, Nathaniel, 213.
Geer, Robart, 186.
Geer, Robert, 255.
Geer, Samuel, 251.
George, George, 262.
George, Prince, 112.
Georgia, 59, 62.
Gerham, Nehemiah, 48.
German, Charles, 19.
German, Peter, 19.
Germany, 104.
Gibb, Philo, 127.
Gibbs, Aaron, 201.
Gibbs, Darius, 39.
Gibbs, David, 57.
Gibbs, Edward, 126.
Gibbs, Heman, 38.
Gibbs, Jehiel, 118.
Gibbs, Levy, 1.
Gibbs, Oliver, 1, 55, 201.
Gibbs, Peter, 109.
Gibbs, Rufus, 78.
Gibbs, Samuel, 46.
Gibbs, Seth, 1.
Gibbs, Simeon, 201, 273.
Gibbs, Spencer, 39.
Gibbs, Timothy, 69, 273.

# INDEX. 315

Gibbs, W., 188.
Gibbs, Warham, 211.
Gibson, Jacob, 229, 244, 247, 248.
Giddens, Richard, 89.
Gidding, Benjamin, 41.
Giddings, 221.
Giddings, Benjamin, 43.
Giddings, Joseph, 199.
Giddings, Thomas, 208, 211.
Giddings, William, 197, 208, 212.
Giddins, David, 205.
Gideon, Niles, 126.
Gift, 230.
Gilbard, Timothy, 205.
Gilbart, John, 184, 190.
Gilbart, Thomas, 190.
Gilbert, Abijah, 243.
Gilbert, Allen, 135.
Gilbert, Amos, 21.
Gilbert, Ashel, 163.
Gilbert, Burr, 75.
Gilbert, Elnathan, 173.
Gilbert, Gardiner, 59.
Gilbert, Giles, 278.
Gilbert, Isaiah, 173.
Gilbert, Jedediah, 66.
Gilbert, Jesse, 68, 114.
Gilbert, Joel, 152, 215.
Gilbert, John, 75, 162, 195.
Gilbert, Jonathan, 274.
Gilbert, Joseph, 42, 43.
Gilbert, M., 211.
Gilbert, Moses, 77, 207.
Gilbert, N., 177, 210.
Gilbert, Nathan, 207, 226.
Gilbert, Nathaniel, 208.
Gilbert, Peter, 259.
Gilbert, Samuel, 19.
Gilbert, Thomas, 35.
Gilbert, Williams, 135.
Gilbertson, Edward, 83.
Gilburt, Daniel, 27.
Giles, Thomas, 174.
Gill, Giles, 230.
Gill, John, 141.
Gillet, Abraham, 99.
Gillet, Adney, 81.
Gillet, Asa, 145.
Gillet, Charles, 34.
Gillet, Charles, Sr., 34.
Gillet, Ebenezer, Jr., 3.
Gillet, Garshom, 3.
Gillet, Gershom, 4.
Gillet, J., 206.
Gillet, Jacob, 3, 4, 123.
Gillet, Joab, 67.
Gillet, John, 76, 162.
Gillet, Jonah, Jr., 138.

Gillet, Joseph, 139.
Gillet, Lemuel, 21, 105.
Gillet, Othniel, Jr., 20.
Gillet, Rufus, 80.
Gillett, Benoni, 106, 126.
Gillett, Zacheus, 106, 126.
Gillit, Dan, 185.
Gillit, Ebenezer, Jr., 2.
Gillit, Isaac, 182.
Gillit, John, 39.
Gillit, John W., 204.
Gillit, William, 39.
Gilner, Henry, 10, 269.
Gilson, Eleazar, 69.
Gilson, Jacob, 107.
Ginnings, Daniel, 28.
Ginnings, Stephen, 28.
Gipson, John, 81.
Gladding, Joseph, 74, 228.
Glading, Joseph, 178.
Glasgow, Silas, 76.
Glass, Samuel, 58.
Glass, Silas, 124.
Glass, Sils, 172.
Glass, Silus, 171.
Glastenbury, 22, 58, 59, 60, 61, 74, 81, 88, 89, 90, 91, 103, 137, 222.
Gleason, Andrew, 202.
Gleason, Noah, 203.
Godale, Silas, 46.
Godard, Levi, 146.
Goddard, Edward, 110.
Goddard, Schuyler, 107.
Goddard, Skylor, 70.
Godfrey, C., 84.
Godfrey, Christopher, 152.
Godfrey, D., 84.
Godfrey, Daniel, 152, 181, 212, 225.
Godfrey, Reuben, 246, 250.
Goff, David, 36, 203.
Goff, Elisha, 184.
Goff, Gideon, 100.
Goff, Hezekiah, 258.
Goff, Jonathan, 61.
Goff, Richard, 56.
Goff, Samuel, 61, 118.
Goff, Solomon, 114.
Goff, Squire, 82.
Goging, James, 254.
Gold, Benjamin, 231.
Gold, David, 41, 43.
Goldsmith, Ephraim, 235.
Goldsmith, James, 109, 204.
Goldsmith, Joseph, 109.
Goldsmith, William, 109, 238.
Goldsmith, Wilmot, 191, 277.
Goodale, Aseph, 183.

Goodale, Elezr, 137.
Goodale, Joseph, 157.
Goodell, M., 172.
Goodluck, London, 76.
Goodman, Asa, 274.
Goodman, Richard, 274.
Goodman, Thomas, 259.
Goodrich, Abner, 34.
Goodrich, Asahel, 58.
Goodrich, Bethuel, 61.
Goodrich, David, Jr., 34.
Goodrich, Elihu, 192.
Goodrich, Elisha, 38.
Goodrich, Ephraim, 89.
Goodrich, Ichabod, 121.
Goodrich, Hosea, 154.
Goodrich, Hozea, 156.
Goodrich, Isaac, 154, 156.
Goodrich, Jeha, 154.
Goodrich, Jesse, 34.
Goodrich, John, 41, 43, 154, 156.
Goodrich, Levi, 61.
Goodrich, Michael, 38.
Goodrich, Philer, 81.
Goodrich, Roswell, 133.
Goodrich, Samuel, 34.
Goodrich, Simeon, 81.
Goodrich, Stephen, 145, 208, 221.
Goodrich, Timothy, 173.
Goodrick, Levy, 236.
Goodrige, James, 242.
Goodsell, Lewis, 180, 181.
Goodsell, Samuel, 10.
Goodspeed, Nathan, 211.
Goodwin, Charles, 99, 142.
Goodwin, Hezekiah, 77.
Goodwin, John, 135.
Goodwin, Ozias, 266.
Goodwin, Samuel, 5.
Goodwin, Solomon, 23.
Goodwin, Stephen, 139.
Goodwin, Stephen, Jr., 39.
Goodwin, Timothy, 259.
Goodwin, Uri, 201.
Goodwin, Zebedee, 4.
Goodwine, David, 188.
Goodwine, John P., 187, 188.
Goodwine, Joseph, 164.
Goodwine, Nathan, 187.
Goodwine, Samuel, 164.
Goodwine, Theoder, 187.
Goodwine, Zebedee, 3.
Goodyear, Edward, 73.
Goodyear, Jesse, 210.
Gookins, Samuel, 53, 121.
Goram, George, 185.
Goram, Jonah, 38.
Gorden, Aleck, 171.

Gorden, William, 32.
Gordon, 206.
Gordon, J., 206, 222.
Gordon, James, 206, 222.
Gordon, Robert, 253.
Gore, Daniel, 227.
Gore, Obadiah, 46.
Gorham, Benjamin, 181, 219.
Gorham, David, 199.
Gorham, Isaac, 190.
Gorham, James, 199.
Gorham, John, 197.
Gorham, Phineas, 98.
Gorham, Samuel, 89.
Gorum, Joseph, 172.
Gosard, Levi, 148.
Goshen, 22, 23, 67, 68, 90, 91, 102.
Goslee, Timothy, 157.
Gosse, Aron, 157.
Gossord, Levi, 66.
Gossord, Rufus, 66.
Goudy, James, 239.
Gould, Abraham, 180.
Gould, John, 68, 199.
Gould, William, 69.
Gowdy, James, 238.
Grace, Matthew, 115.
Graham, Andrew, 85.
Graham, Cyrus, 113.
Graham, Daniel, 146, 147, 148.
Graham, Daniel, Jr., 145.
Graham, Elisha, 212.
Graham, Jesse, 113.
Graham, John, 61, 85.
Graham, Jonathan G., 46.
Graham, Joseph, 61, 89.
Grahom, Danel, Jr., 146.
Graige, Robert, 245, 249.
Grandey, Edmund, 37.
Grandey, Jesse, 37.
Granger, Peter, 230.
Granger, Phineas, 54.
Granger, Phinehas, 89, 123.
Granger, Samuel, 75.
Grannis, Isaac, 10.
Grannis, Robert, 276.
Grant, 12.
Grant, Abiel, 120.
Grant, Azariah, 89.
Grant, Hamilton, 15.
Grant, Hezekiah, 105.
Grant, Isaac, 69.
Grant, James, 15, 113.
Grant, Joel, 39.
Grant, John, 118, 247, 249.
Grant, Joshua, 150.
Grant, Matthew, 84.

# INDEX. 317

Grant, Peter, 212, 253.
Grant, Rewben, 105.
Grant, William, 136.
Graum, Joseph, 230.
Grave, Noadiah, 193.
Graves, Bela, 164, 201.
Graves, Benjamin, 111.
Graves, David, 192.
Graves, Elias, 209, 222.
Graves, Ezekiel, 201.
Graves, Gilbert, 113.
Graves, Issachar, 184.
Graves, Peter, 60.
Graves, S., 226.
Graves, Seth, 192.
Graves, Simeon, 89.
Graves, Sylvanus, 223.
Graves, William, 68, 167.
Gray, Amos, 152, 266.
Gray, Benjamin, 216.
Gray, Ebenezer, 48, 115.
Gray, Hezekiah, 200.
Gray, Isaas, 196.
Gray, J., 206.
Gray, James, 58, 60.
Gray, Jeduthan, 34.
Gray, John, 226.
Gray, Joseph, 78.
Gray, Moses, 86, 197.
Gray, Samuel, 34.
Gray, Thomas, 245, 249.
Gray, William, 135.
Graystock, Thomas, 232, 254.
Green, Amos, 10, 79.
Green, Benjamin, 212.
Green, Daniel, 1, 255.
Green, Henry, 79.
Green, J., 84, 207.
Green, Jacob, 18, 201.
Green, Job, 170.
Green, John, 13, 35, 93, 94, 184, 212.
Green, John H., 261.
Green, Josiah, 77.
Green, Mason, 122.
Green, Pliny, 120.
Green, Robert, 89.
Green, Roswell, 185.
Green, Samuel, 35, 77.
Green, Timothy, 94.
Green, William, 89.
Greene, William, 47.
Greenfield, Enos, 29, 30.
Greenfield, Richard, 185.
Greenfield, 53, 54.
Greenslit, Benjamin, 123.
Greenwich, 88, 89, 90, 205, 267, 276.

Greer, James, 232.
Gregory, Elnathan, 194.
Gregory, Jabez, 212.
Gregory, Jack, 94, 213.
Gregory, Joseph, 85.
Gregory, Josiah, 217.
Gregory, Justus, 38.
Gregory, Nathan, 98.
Gregory, Nathan, Jr., 198.
Gregory, S., 84.
Gregory, Sam, 109.
Gregory, Samuel, 116, 218.
Gregory, Sela, 198.
Gregory, Seth, 121.
Gregory, William, 119.
Grenold, Amasa, 130.
Grenold, Amasy, 102.
Grey, William, 80.
Gridley, Hezekiah, 182, 208.
Gridley, Hosea, 59.
Gridley, Isaiah, 35.
Gridley, Kezin, 209.
Gridley, Obed, 64.
Gridley, Silas, 202.
Grifen, Matthew, Jr., 142.
Grifen, Seth, 142.
Griffen, Abraham, 147.
Griffeth, Abraham, 146.
Griffin, Absalom, 67.
Griffin, Amos, 85.
Griffin, James, 230.
Griffin, James N., 24, 253.
Griffin, John, 258.
Griffin, Jonathan, 85.
Griffin, Mathew, Jr., 203.
Griffin, Morris, 232.
Griffin, Nathaniel, 67.
Griffin, Samuel, 141.
Griffin, Simeon, 156.
Griffin, Simon, 100, 154.
Griffing, James, 51.
Griffing, Jared, 191.
Griffing, Joshua, 141.
Griffing, Kirtland, 21.
Griffis, James, 201.
Griffis, Paul, 82.
Griffith, Joseph, 135.
Grigory, Daniel, 200.
Grigory, Nathan, 200.
Grigry, John, 37.
Grimes, Abraham, 56.
Grimes, Daniel, 147.
Grimes, Joseph, Jr., 7.
Grinnel, Jasper, 37.
Grinnol, Amasa, 111.
Griswold, 111, 223.
Griswold, A., 214.
Griswold, Adonijah, 34, 188.

Griswold, Andrew, 47, 269.
Griswold, Asa, 36, 202.
Griswold, Edmond, 127.
Griswold, Edmund, 95, 117.
Griswold, Edward, 55, 230, 273.
Griswold, Elijah, 93.
Griswold, George, 202.
Griswold, John, 97, 164.
Griswold, Joseph, 203.
Griswold, Moses, 100, 154, 156.
Griswold, Selah, 228.
Griswold, Shubael, 18, 19, 20, 21, 24, 210, 211.
Griswold, Thomas, Jr., 277.
Griswold, White, 36.
Griswould, Giles, 193.
Griswould, Selah, 74.
Groas, Thomas, 149.
Grogan, John, 62.
Groos, Thos., 182.
Gross, Jonah, 3, 4.
Gross, Samuel, 89.
Grosvenor, L., 142.
Grosvenor, Lemuel, 183.
Grosvenor, Thomas, 46, 101, 118.
Groton, 31, 55, 74, 78, 80, 82, 88, 89, 90, 113, 174, 267.
Groundwater, Thomas, 253.
Grover, Phineas, 49, 228.
Grover, Stephen, 168.
Grow, Ambros, 143.
Growse, David, 66.
Gudeahn, Dick, 21.
Guile, Samuel, 163.
Guilford, 18, 23, 24, 25, 55, 56, 70, 88, 89, 104, 113, 191, 277.
"Guilford," 242, 243.
Guinea, 104.
Gurnsey, Joel, 117, 127.
Gustin, Amos, 106, 126.
Gutherie, Abel, 123.
Guthrie, Abraham, 80.
Guy, John, 10.
Guyant, Luke, 271.
Gyer, Samuel, 246.

H[ ], Nehemiah, 80.
Hackensack, 139.
Hackley, Arunah, 101.
Hackly, Abel, 5.
Haddam, 56, 66, 68, 69, 81, 88, 89, 115, 278.
Hadley, Samuel, 70.
Hadlock, Reuben, 77, 235.
Hadlock, Stephen, 12.
Hagar, Simeon, 89.
Hail, Jacob, 230.
Haill, Gershom, 185.

Hait, Elijah, 85.
Hait, H., 84.
Hait, Joel, 103, 130.
Hait, John, 23.
Hait, Joseph, 53, 54.
Hait, Justus, 214.
Hait, Samuel, 47, 78, 85.
Hait, Stephen, 77.
Haladay, Jacob, 103, 131.
Halbisk, Preston, 38.
Hale, 50.
Hale, Aaron, 89.
Hale, Aron, 183.
Hale, Benjamin, 135, 137.
Hale, Elizur, 208.
Hale, Frary, 157.
Hale, Isaac, 157.
Hale, John, 36, 244, 248.
Hale, Jonathan, 133.
Hale, Joseph, 142.
Hale, Moses, 112.
Hale, Nathan, 28, 29, 30, 31.
Hale, Nathaniel, 80.
Hale, Robert, 15.
Hale, Samuel, 15.
Hale, Timothy, 202.
Halel, Kaswell, 145.
Hall, 97.
Hall, Abell, 212.
Hall, Abijah, 209.
Hall, Abner, 117, 127.
Hall, Asahel, 81, 117, 127.
Hall, Asaph, 203, 209.
Hall, Barnabus, 81.
Hall, Benjamin, 119.
Hall, Benjamin, Jr., 277.
Hall, Brinton, 192.
Hall, Caleb, 208, 210, 276.
Hall, Charles, 18, 19.
Hall, Daniel, 192.
Hall, David, 85, 230.
Hall, Ebenezer, 16.
Hall, Eber, 23, 113, 277.
Hall, Elisha, 170, 222.
Hall, Enos, 193, 276.
Hall, Ezeriah, 186.
Hall, Gad, 192.
Hall, Gilbert, 13.
Hall, Giles, 229.
Hall, Gills, 230.
Hall, Hiland, 20.
Hall, Hill, 2d, 276.
Hall, Isaac, 192, 211, 226, 276.
Hall, Israel, 193.
Hall, Isral, 276.
Hall, John, 1, 34, 238, 239, 242, 243.
Hall, Jonah, 17, 19.

INDEX. 319

Hall, Joseph, 275.
Hall, Joshua, 169.
Hall, Jotham, 112.
Hall, Levi, 106, 127.
Hall, Luis, 197.
Hall, Moses, 18, 192.
Hall, Moses, Jr., 192.
Hall, N., 210.
Hall, Nathan, 1, 165.
Hall, Nathaniel, 89, 209.
Hall, Philemon, 49.
Hall, Phinehas, 193.
Hall, Robert, 57.
Hall, Samuel, 13, 24, 27, 41, 43, 89, 187, 188, 192.
Hall, Silas, 200.
Hall, Stephen, 28, 48, 69, 109.
Hall, Street, 17, 20, 23.
Hall, Talmadge, 49.
Hall, Talmage, 25.
Hall, Timothy, 135, 193.
Hall, William, 89, 212, 242, 253.
Halladay, Jacob, 125.
Halladay, Simeon, 146.
Hallam, 64.
Hallam, Amos, 211.
Hallam, Robert, 47.
Halley, Jesse, 27.
Halley, Silas, 31.
Hallow, Richard P., 267, 269.
Hallows, Samuel, 74.
Hally, John, 38.
Hally, Joseph, 36, 238.
Halsey, Jeremiah, 210.
Hambden, William, 89.
Hamblen, James, 178.
Hamblen, Joel, 39.
Hambleton, Asel, 196.
Hambleton, James, 34.
Hambleton, John, 32, 57.
Hambleton, Joshua, 34.
Hambleton, Seth, 43.
Hamblin, Mark, 94.
Hamblin, William, Jr., 23.
Hamelton, Paul, 198.
Hamilton, John, 118.
Hamilton, Seth, 41.
Hamistond, Ebenezer, 184.
Hamlin, Daniel, 134.
Hamlin, Jabez, 222.
Hamlin, Joel, 122.
Hamlin, Joseph, 85.
Hamlin, Mark, 277.
Hamlin, Thomas, 138.
Hamlin, William, 21, 22.
Hamlinton, Duke, 22.
Hammon, Isaac, 29.
Hammond, David, 103, 125, 131.

Hammond, Robert, 94.
Hampton, Thomas, 245, 250.
Hanchet, 12.
Hanchet, Oliver, 18, 19, 20, 21, 23.
Hanchin, 13.
Hancock, Abner, 164.
Hancock, John, 70.
Hancock, Thomas, 264.
Hand, David, 238, 239.
Hand, John, 29.
Hand, Joseph, 122.
Hand, Josiah, 29.
Hande, Caleb, 15.
Handee, Caleb, 206.
Handy, Benjamin, 178.
Hanfield, Benjamin, 15.
Hanford, 223.
Hanford, Mathew, 217.
Hanford, Timothy, 77.
Hanks, Consider, 119.
Hanmon, Japhet, 82.
Hannabal, Joseph, 89.
Hannah, James, 38.
Hannibale, Joseph, 246.
Hanniball, Job, 246, 250.
Hanniball, Joseph, 251.
Hanscum, James, 261.
Hanson, Peter, 246, 250.
Hard, Stephen, 200.
Harden, Frederick, 89.
Harden, James, 79.
Harding, Amos, 260.
Harding, Seth, 231, 232, 233, 234, 255.
Harding, Turner, 231.
Haridon, Daniel, 32.
Haris, Champlin, 57.
Harlem, 279.
Harman, John, 47.
Harmon, Jaquess, 54.
Harmon, John, 63.
Harp, Elias, 79.
Harrap, Joseph, 54.
Harrard, Sedeman, 85.
Harrey, Ephraim, 122.
Harrington, John, 35.
Harrington, Ruben, 56.
Harrington, William, 65.
Harris, Amos, 54.
Harris, Benjamin, 32.
Harris, Champlin, 89.
Harris, Daniel, 138, 175.
Harris, George, 65.
Harris, John, 61, 229.
Harris, Joseph, 135.
Harris, Josiah, 175.
Harris, Paul, 171.
Harris, Samuel, 171.

Harris, Thomas, 175.
Harris, Thomas B., 245, 250.
Harris, William, 240, 246, 250, 253.
Harrison, Asahel, 9, 183.
Harrison, Asel, 179.
Harrison, Butler, 253.
Harrison, Champlin, 58, 89.
Harrison, Ferrington, 179.
Harrison, Ithial, 184.
Harrison, Jairus, 71, 112.
Harrison, Jarius, 10, 16.
Harrison, John, 13, 41, 43.
Harrison, Justus, 253.
Harrison, Nathan, 184.
Harrison, Noah, 274.
Harrison, Phileman, 184.
Harrison, Rufus, 184.
Harrison, Solomon, 201, 273.
Harrison, Theodore, 81.
Harrison, William, 89, 234.
Harrison, Wooster, 10.
Harriss, Nathaniel, 210.
Harriss, Paul, 185.
Harrope, Joseph, 32.
Harrup, Joseph, 269.
Harry, Peter, 246, 250.
Harslen, Nathan, 54.
Hart, 223.
Hart, Benjamin, 192.
Hart, James, 117, 127.
Hart, Jonathan, 46, 47.
Hart, Joseph, 49.
Hart, Reuben, 59.
Hart, Samuel, 192, 207, 221.
Hart, Selah, 124.
Hart, William, 12, 41, 43, 205, 223.
Hartford, 16, 18, 19, 21, 23, 52, 53, 55, 57, 58, 59, 60, 61, 65, 68, 76, 77, 80, 81, 82, 88, 89, 90, 91, 102, 104, 114, 118, 129, 183, 187, 188, 190, 205, 220, 261, 274.
Hartland, 67.
Hartshorn, Beriah, 175.
Hartshorn, Diah, 47.
Hartshorn, Hezekiah, 80.
Hartshorn, John, 248.
Hartshorn, Jonathan, 175.
Hartshorn, Joshua, 55, 274.
Hartshorn, Zephaniah, 175.
Hartshorne, John, 244.
Hartshorne, S., 211.
Hartsorn, John, 246.
Harvey, Asahel, 185.
Harvey, David, 64.
Harvey, Ithamar, 45, 89, 134.
Harvey, Richard, 63.
Harvey, Robert, Jr., 23.
Harwich, Mass., 103.
Harwington, Elisha, 59.
Harwinton, 18, 20, 55, 62, 67, 75, 76, 79, 104.
Hase, Aasa, 53.
Haskell, Jacob, 106, 126.
Haskell, John, 106, 126.
Hastings, Ebenezer, 13, 41, 43.
Hastings, John, 89.
Hatch, Bille, 39.
Hatch, Billy, 17, 20.
Hatch, David, 170.
Hatch, Edward, 246, 251.
Hatch, Eliezer, 124.
Hatch, Gilbert, 96.
Hatch, Heman, 122.
Hatch, James, 154, 156.
Hatch, Joseph, 163.
Hatch, Joshua, 197.
Hatch, Josiah, 139.
Hatch, Moses, 100.
Hatch, Oliver, 34.
Hatch, Robert, 251.
Hatch, Solomon, 241.
Hatch, Zefeniah, 241.
Hatch, Zephaniah, 232, 241, 253.
Hatchet, John, 71, 110.
Hatchway, John, 18.
Haugh, Insign, 192.
Haugh, James, 192.
Hauley, Ebenezer, 195.
Hauley, Thomas, 200.
Hausey, Andrew, 125.
Hawk, 89.
Hawkings, Joseph, 70.
Hawkins, David, 244, 246, 248.
Hawkins, Edward, 163.
Hawkins, James, 63, 161, 169.
Hawkins, Joseph, 112.
Hawkins, Zebulon, 93.
Hawley, Abraham, 54.
Hawley, Amos, 138.
Hawley, David, 106, 109, 117, 235, 236, 243.
Hawley, Enos, 208, 212, 224.
Hawley, Ephraim, 236.
Hawley, Ichabod, 25.
Hawley, Isaac, 109, 112, 117.
Hawley, John, 243.
Hawley, Joseph, 37.
Hawley, Joseph C., 18, 89.
Hawley, Josiah, 141.
Hawley, Moses, 173.
Hawley, Nathan, 269.
Hawley, Nero, 53, 269.
Hawley, Samuel, 236.

Hawley, Siras, 84.
Hawley, Sirus, 215.
Hawley, Stephen, 37.
Hawley, William, 180.
Hawley, Wolcott, 212.
Hawley, Woolcutt, 181.
Hawley, Zadock, 35.
Hay, John, 247.
Hayden, N., 214.
Hayden, Samuel, 22.
Hayden, Seth, 39.
Haydon, Daniel, 220.
Haydon, Hezekiah, 27.
Haydon, Jacob, 178.
Hayes, John, 236.
Hayes, Titus, 89.
Hays, Abraham, 235.
Hays, Asa, 142.
Hays, Elijah, 67.
Hays, Ezekiel, 67.
Hays, Joel, 210, 221.
Hays, Jonathan, 200.
Hays, Juda, 203.
Hays, Samuel, 205, 210, 221.
Hays, Stephen, 233.
Hays, Zenas, 67.
Hayse, Benjamin, 57.
Hayse, Zenas, 138.
Hayt, Isee, 269.
Hayward, Nathaniel, 14.
Hazelton, Arnold, 212.
Hazelton, John, 233.
Hazen, Adrew, 126.
Hazen, Andrew, 106.
Hazen, Elijah, 208, 211, 225.
Hazen, Moses, 83.
Heacock, David, 89.
Heacock, William, 89, 278.
Head, Henry, 109.
Healy, George, 98.
Heard, Isaac, 204.
Heart, Elisha, 59.
Heart, James, 94.
Heart, Selah, 209.
Heart, Timothy, 59.
Heath, Basok, 65.
Heath, John, 245, 250.
Heath, Peleg, 46.
Heath, Phinihas, 35.
Heath, Simeon, 35.
Heath, William, 216.
Hebard, Asa, 74.
Hebard, Jededinh, 74.
Hebard, Jonathan, 248.
Hebard, Timothy, 74.
Hebbard, J., 172.
Hebbard, John, 171.
Hebbard, John, Jr., 171.

Hebbard, Rufus, 172.
Hebbard, Timothy, 255.
Hebbard, William, 171, 172.
Hebbard, William, Jr., 171.
Heberd, Ebenezer, 74.
Heberd, Uriah, 74.
Hebron, 56, 57, 58, 59, 60, 62, 65, 66, 80, 81, 82, 90, 91, 114, 118.
Hecock, Asher, 77.
Hedge, John, 259.
Hedges, Timothy, 29.
Heminway, Enos, 10.
Heminway, Jared, 10.
Heminway, Moses, 10.
Hempstead, John, 212.
Hempstead, Stephen, 269.
Hempsted, Nathaniel, Jr., 140.
Hempsted, Stephen, 28.
Hemstead, Stephen, 267.
Hendee, Caleb, 15, 222.
Henderson, John, 12, 41, 43.
Henderson, Joseph, 35.
Hendrick, Dodatey, 85.
Hendrick, Josiah, 110.
Hendrick, P., 180.
Hendrick, Richard, 260.
Hendricks, Abner, 260.
Hendricks, Samuel, 236.
Hendry, Daniel, 80.
Hendy, Eliphalet, 161.
Henerdricks, Adner, 243.
Henfield, Benjamin, 15.
Henman, Enoch, 192.
Henman, Samuel, 53.
Henry, John, 4, 161, 257.
Henry, Thomas, 51.
Henshaw, Benjamin, Jr., 9.
Henshaw, William, 48, 50.
Hepburne, Peter, 204, 212.
Herick, Andrew, 169.
Hering, Perley, 57.
Herington, Daniel, 172.
Herren, John, 267.
Herrick, Asahel, 185.
Herrick, Daniel, 172, 185.
Herrick, Elijah, 65.
Herrick, Ephraim, 174, 253.
Herrick, John, 110.
Herrick, Lebeus, 74.
Herrick, Lemuel, 24, 74.
Herrington, Samuel, 101.
Herrington, Stephen, 118.
Herrington, Timothy, 98.
Herris, Thomas, 172.
Herron, John, 267, 269.
Hethe, William, 186.
Hewett, Joshua, 251.
Hewit, Asa, 39.

Hewit, Benjamin, 35.
Hewit, Elkanah, 216.
Hewit, Epheram, 35.
Hewit, Henrey, 186.
Hewit, John, 35.
Hewit, Randol, 35.
Hewit, Stephen, 172.
Hewitt, Daniel, 269.
Hewitt, Nathaniel, 269.
Hewlet, Nabl, 169.
Heydon, Benajah, 139.
Hibbard, Jedediah, 114.
Hibberd, Andrew, 64.
Hickcox, James, 192.
Hickcox, Nathaniel, 192.
Hickock, Benjamin, 212.
Hickock, Daniel, 208.
Hickocks, Daniel, 224.
Hickok, Daniel, 199.
Hickoxs, J., 227.
Hickum, Elisha, 127.
Hicock, Nathan, 19.
Hicock, Samuel, 46.
Hicok, Silas, 173.
Hide, Andrew, 162.
Hide, Clark, 82.
Hide, Elijah, 227.
Hide, James, 54, 121.
Hide, Joel, 124.
Hide, Joshua, 37, 201.
Hide, Oliver, 5.
Hide, Rufus, 277.
Hide, Samuel, 190.
Higbe, Noah, 204.
Higbee, John, 17.
Higgans, Isaac, 102.
Higgins, Benjamin, 132.
Higgins, Cornelius, 48, 89.
Higgins, George, 199.
Higgins, Isaac, 109, 130, 269.
Higgins, Jesse, 229.
Higgins, John, 59.
Higgins, Lawdin, 241.
Higgins, Seth, 261.
Higgins, William, 47, 50, 59, 234, 250, 252, 256.
Higley, Carmi, 27.
Higley, Eber, 142.
Higley, Obed, 27, 142.
Higley, Seth, 7.
Hildreth, Luther, 238, 239.
Hill, 55, 114.
Hill, Abraham, 38.
Hill, Bela, 67.
Hill, David, 10.
Hill, Ebenezer, 180.
Hill, Eliphalot, 81.
Hill, Henry, 45.

Hill, Isaac, 115, 117.
Hill, James, 245, 249.
Hill, John, 63, 247, 251.
Hill, Jonathan, 58, 120, 263.
Hill, Philip, 103, 131.
Hill, Phinhas, 38.
Hill, Reuben, 79, 213.
Hill, Russell, 81.
Hill, Samuel, 113.
Hill, Seth, 39.
Hill, Squier, 14.
Hill, Squire, 14.
Hill, Thomas, 58.
Hillard, Azariah, 186.
Hillard, Daniel, 264.
Hilleyer, Theodore, 145.
Hilliard, Azariah, 253.
Hilliard, Benjamin, 174.
Hilliard, James, 253.
Hilliard, Thurston, 269.
Hilliard, William, 181, 219.
Hillman, George, 253.
Hillman, Peleg, 252.
Hills, 225.
Hills, Ebenezer, 48, 73.
Hills, Elisha, 157.
Hills, Ephrm, 163.
Hills, Erastus, 41, 43.
Hills, George, 145, 146, 147, 148.
Hills, Israel, 157.
Hills, J., 226.
Hills, Jabez, 223.
Hills, James, 148.
Hills, John, 25, 210.
Hills, Joseph, 157.
Hills, Libbius, 160.
Hills, Medad, 225.
Hills, Phillip, 125.
Hills, Samuel, 116.
Hills, Samuel, Jr., 137.
Hills, Seth, 37.
Hills, Squier, 183.
Hills, Thomas, 160.
Hillyard, Azeriah, 256.
Hillyard, Daniel, 257, 261.
Hillyer, Theodore, 147.
Hilyer, Asa, 203.
Hinckley, Ichabod, 46, 54.
Hinckley, Wiat, 267.
Hindman, Benjamin, 83.
Hine, Ambrose, 223.
Hine, Isaac, 200, 208.
Hine, Nathan, 208, 212, 224.
Hine, Noble, 206, 209, 225.
Hine, Titus, 109.
Hines, H., 214.
Hines, Patrick, 54.
Hinkley, Gershom, 134.

INDEX. 323

Hinkley, Thomas, 32.
Hinkley, Wait, 266.
Hinman, 12, 136.
Hinman, Agur, 213.
Hinman, Asa, 224.
Hinman, Benjamin, 16, 18, 19, 20. 21, 22, 23, 24, 25, 227.
Hinman, David, 208, 224, 225.
Hinman, E., 177, 206.
Hinman, Elijah, 85, 210, 224, 225.
Hinman, Enos, 213.
Hinman, Hugh, 71.
Hinman, Joel, 213, 269.
Hinman, Joseph, 52.
Hinman, Justus, 85.
Hinman, Lewis. 37.
Hinman, N., 213.
Hinman, Nathan, 98.
Hinman, Samuel, 122.
Hinman, Wait, 85.
Hinsdale, Abiel, 105.
Hinsdale, Jacob, 209, 225.
Hinsdale, Samuel, 139.
Hinsdale, William, 37.
Hird, Philow, 215.
Hiscox, Simeon, 212.
Hiscox, Thomas, 89.
Hitchcock, Abel, 109.
Hitchcock, Benjamin, Jr., 85.
Hitchcock, D., 207.
Hitchcock, Daniel, 194.
Hitchcock, David, 24, 71, 208, 212, 226.
Hitchcock, Jared, 109.
Hitchcock, Jonathan, 189.
Hitchcock, Lemuel, 89.
Hitchcock, Levi, 76.
Hitchcock, Samuel, 138.
Hoadley, 210.
Hoadley, Ralph, 252.
Hoadley, Samuel, 112, 179.
Hoadly, Ralph, 256.
Hoadly, Samuel, 10.
Hoadly, Timothy, 179.
Hobart, John, 76, 104, 129, 131.
Hobart, Mason, 10, 24.
Hobbard, Elisha, 197.
Hobbol, Ezra, 198.
Hobby, Thomas, 21.
Hodg, Gulielmas, 79.
Hodge, Asahel, 36, 75, 119.
Hodge, David, 70, 103, 109, 130.
Hodge, William. 266.
Hodges, Abel, 197.
Hodges, Abel, Jr., 106.
Hodges, Asahel, 49.
Hodges, Thomas, 86.
Hodgkiss, Ladwick, 59.

Hodnett, Richard, 12.
Hoit, Samuel, 85.
Holabird, Timothy, Jr., 37.
Holaday, Jonathan, 27.
Holaday, Simeon, 146.
Holbrook, Daniel, 210, 225.
Holbrook, Daniel, Jr., 189.
Holbrook, John, 163.
Holbrook, Pelatiah, 3.
Holbrook, Peletiah, 162.
Holbrook, Thomas, 246, 248, 255.
Holburton, William, 243.
Holcom, Jedidiah, 146.
Holcomb, Adonijah, 203.
Holcomb, Amos, 67.
Holcomb, Asahel, 221.
Holcomb, Benajah, 211.
Holcomb, Benjamin, 147.
Holcomb, Carmi, 142.
Holcomb, David, 203.
Holcomb, Dosa, 67.
Holcomb, Ebenezer, 146, 148.
Holcomb, Elijah, 146, 148.
Holcomb, Ephraim, 203.
Holcomb, Hezekiah, 203.
Holcomb, Increase, 117, 127.
Holcomb, Jachish, 95.
Holcomb, Jed, 147.
Holcomb, Jedediah, 147.
Holcomb, Jedidiah, 145, 146.
Holcomb, John, 199.
Holcomb, John G., 123.
Holcomb, Joseph, Jr., 142.
Holcomb, Joshua, 203.
Holcomb, Nathaniel, 142.
Holcomb, Peter, 146.
Holcomb, Peter, Jr., 148.
Holcomb, Phineas, 67, 146, 147.
Holcomb, Phinehas, 147.
Holcomb, Seth, 146.
Holcomb, Silas, 203.
Holcomb, Timothy, 21.
Holcomb, Zacheus, 67.
Holden, Amos. 94, 103, 131.
Holdrath, William, 157.
Holdridge, Hezekiah, 48.
Holdridge, Robert, 123.
Holdridge, Rufus, 113.
Holebrook, Peletiah, 2.
Holiday, Jacob, 57.
Holladay, Simeon, 67.
Holladay, Thomas, 245, 251.
Hollady, Simeon, 146.
Holland, Michael, 264.
Hollenbeak, John, 37.
Hollester, Giles, 245.
Holley, Abraham, 76.
Holley, Crandal, 186.

Holley, Joseph, 239.
Holley, Silas, 20.
Holliday, Simeon, 138.
Hollister, Aaron, 137.
Hollister, Appleton, 119.
Hollister, Charles, 77.
Hollister, David, 157.
Hollister, Elijah, 23.
Hollister, George, 157.
Hollister, Giles, 240.
Hollister, Ichabod, 157.
Hollister, Jared, 157.
Hollister, Josiah, 137.
Hollister, Nehimiah, 157.
Hollister, Thomas, 137.
Hollit, John, 204.
Holm, Thomas, 150.
Holman, Samuel, 256.
Holmes, Appleton, 157.
Holmes, Cudjo, 123.
Holmes, David, 49.
Holmes, Daniel, 81.
Holmes, Edward, 96, 185.
Holmes, Eliphalet, 45.
Holmes, Gershom, 85.
Holmes, John, 15, 29.
Holmes, John, 3d, 15.
Holmes, Samuel, 235, 274.
Holmes, Uriel, 206, 208.
Holmes, William, 253.
Holms, John, 231.
Holms, Samuel, 38, 150.
Holomback, John, 49.
Holt, Abiel, 143.
Holt, Daniel, 208.
Holt, Jacob, 184.
Holt, James, 140.
Holt, Jim, 124.
Holt, Josiah, 15.
Holt, Livenus, 62.
Holt, Nicholas, 30.
Holt, Peter, 124.
Holt, Samuel, 254.
Holt, Silas, 15, 47.
Holt, Uriah, 167.
Holton, Samuel, 145.
Hood, Richard, 188.
Hooker, 224.
Hooker, James, 76.
Hooker, Josiah, 38.
Hooker, N., 221, 224, 225, 266.
Hooker, Noadiah, 18, 21, 24, 25, 133, 207, 222, 223.
Hooks, William, 231.
Hooper, Reynold, 30.
Hopkins, 122.
Hopkins, Bazalileen, 186.
Hopkins, Daniel, 171.

Hopkins, George, 36.
Hopkins, Harris, 273.
Hopkins, James, 95, 229.
Hopkins, Josiah, 274.
Hopkins, Roderick, 36.
Hopkins, Thomas, 140.
Hopkins, William, 274.
Hopping, Henry, 29.
Harlehoy, John, 114.
Horseneck, 52, 54, 68, 201, 203, 207, 228, 278.
Horsewett, Jonas, 246.
Horsey, Thomas, 210.
Horsford, Aaron, 209.
Horsford, Isaac, 201.
Horsford, John, 269.
Horsford, Reuben, 276.
Horskins, John, 203.
Horswett, Jonas, 250.
Horton, 123.
Horton, Nathan, 32.
Hosford, Aaron, 211.
Hosford, O., 227.
Hosford, Obadiah, 159, 162.
Hosford, Obediah, 160, 161, 163.
Hoskins, Anthony, 34.
Hoskins, Asa, 34.
Hoskins, Benjamin, 16.
Hoskins, Daniel, 55.
Hoskins, Eli, 145, 146, 147.
Hoskins, Timothy, 114.
Hoskins, Zebulon, 68.
Hosmer, Ashbel, 269, 274.
Hosmer, David, 65, 184.
Hosmer, Elisha, 35.
Hosmer, John, 114.
Hosmer, Joseph, 235.
Hosmer, Prentice, 23.
Hosmer, Prentis, 46.
Hosmer, Robert, 15.
Hotchkis, Leveret, 189.
Hotchkiss, A., 84.
Hotchkiss, Ephraim, 235.
Hotchkiss, Jacob, 179.
Hotchkiss, Jared, 110, 116.
Hotchkiss, Joseph, 17.
Hotchkiss, L., 209.
Hotchkiss, Ladwick, 211.
Hotchkiss, Lemuel, 223.
Hotchkiss, Levi, 39, 49, 89.
Hotchkiss, Moses, 189.
Hotchkiss, Prince, 76.
Hotchkiss, Robert, 235, 276.
Hotchkiss, Samuel, 20, 182.
Hotchkiss, Samuel B., 118.
Houd, Joel, 184.
Hough, David, 210.
Hough, Joel, 194, 276.

# INDEX. 325

Hough, John, 18, 169, 193, 223, 276.
Hough, Lent, 194, 276.
Hough, Samuel, 16.
Hough, Simon, 113, 178, 237.
Houghton, Lebbeus, 29.
House, Abner, 157.
House, Alexander, 161.
House, Daniel, 157.
House, Eleazer, 27.
House, Elijah, 4.
House, Eliphalet, Jr., 259.
House, Israel, 157.
House, James, 161.
House, Lazarus, 157.
House, Rial M., 234.
House, Simon, 2, 3.
House, William, 157.
Hovey, Jonathan, 143.
Hovey, Joseph, 259.
Hovey, Nathan, 105, 120.
Hovey, S., 172.
Hovey, Samuel, 171, 172.
Hovey, Zacheus, 114, 116.
How, Elisha, 157.
How, James, 169.
How, Jazaniah, 269.
How, John, 137, 201.
How, Squier, 108.
How, Zachariah, 110, 116.
Howard, Benjamin, 137.
Howard, Charles, 261.
Howard, Elijah, 95.
Howard, Hiram W., 99.
Howard, John, 64, 140.
Howard, Richard, 74.
Howard, Solomon, 95.
Howard, William, 207, 211, 245, 249, 262.
Howd, Benjamin, 269.
Howd, Joel, 10.
Howe, Isaac, 207, 210, 225, 226.
Howe, Jaazmah, 68.
Howe, Joseph, 96.
Howell, Jason, 187.
Howell, Nicholas, 102, 108, 130.
Howes, Jos., 3.
Howes, Joseph, 3.
Howis, Zenas, 4.
Hoyt, Agur, 194.
Hoyt, Amos, 85, 104.
Hoyt, Benajah, 199.
Hoyt, Comfort, 198, 226.
Hoyt, Daniel, 194, 218.
Hoyt, David, 200.
Hoyt, Elijah, 269.
Hoyt, Enos, 108.
Hoyt, James, 199, 218.
Hoyt, Job, 218.
Hoyt, John, 200.
Hoyt, Jonathan, 195, 200, 218.
Hoyt, Justus, 200.
Hoyt, Nathan, 195.
Hoyt, Nathaniel, 198.
Hoyt, Noah, 200.
Hoyt, Samuel, 199.
Hoyt, Walter, 218.
Hozard, Samuel, 142.
Huatt, Alvin, 243.
Hubard, George, 53.
Hubbard, Aaron, 137.
Hubbard, Abner, 61.
Hubbard, Asa, 145.
Hubbard, Daniel, 98.
Hubbard, David, 127, 128, 137.
Hubbard, Elihu, 89.
Hubbard, Elijah, 137.
Hubbard, Eliz., 222.
Hubbard, Elizer, 137.
Hubbard, Elizur, 22, 208.
Hubbard, George, 208.
Hubbard, Hezekiah, 46, 61.
Hubbard, John, 49.
Hubbard, Jonathan, 107, 246.
Hubbard, Joseph, 256.
Hubbard, Matthew, 98.
Hubbard, Samuel, 56, 209.
Hubbart, John, 41.
Hubbart, Simon, 51.
Hubbel, Nathan, 77.
Hubbel, Salmon, 49, 77, 78.
Hubbel, William G., 224, 225.
Hubbell, Amos, 197.
Hubbell, David, 120, 269.
Hubbell, Egbon, 75.
Hubbell, Gideon, 196.
Hubbell, Isaac, 85.
Hubbell, Peter, 195.
Hubbell, Seth, 77.
Hubbell, Shadrack, 197.
Hubbell, William G., 199, 208.
Hubbert, Ephraim B., 215.
Hubbert, Gideon, 135.
Hubbert, John, 43.
Hubbil, Ebenezer, 181, 219.
Hubbil, John, 190.
Hubbil, John, Jr., 190.
Hubble, David, 106, 126.
Hubble, Enoch, 107.
Hubble, William G., 16, 17, 20, 21.
Hubburd, David, 157.
Hubburd, Joseph, 157.
Huble, Silas, 197.
Huchans, Ezra, 168.
Huchans, Shubl, 168.

Huchans, Silas, 167.
Hudson, B., 220.
Hudson, Eleazer, 269.
Hudson, George, 39.
Hudson, John, 89.
Hues, John, 141.
Huet, Elkanah, 184.
Huffman, Timothy, 255.
Hugg, Isaac, 37.
Hugh, John, 207.
Hughes, 211.
Hughs, John, 62.
Hugins, Samuel, 220.
Huit, Increse, 167.
Huit, Stephen, 167.
Hulbert, Lucius, 57.
Hulet, Aaron, 63.
Hulet, Elim, 168.
Hulet, Nehemiah, 65.
Hulett, Joseph, 135.
Hulett, Phineas, 95.
Hull, Aaron, 200.
Hull, Andrew, 19.
Hull, Asael, 95.
Hull, Asahel, 127, 184, 275.
Hull, Charles, 192, 194.
Hull, Daniel, 111.
Hull, David, 48, 61, 70, 110, 191.
Hull, David, 2d, 94.
Hull, Ebenezer, 194.
Hull, Eli, 97, 110.
Hull, Ephraim, 98.
Hull, Gordon, 192.
Hull, Henry, 21, 37, 102, 111.
Hull, Henery, 129.
Hull, James, 89.
Hull, Jehiel, 20.
Hull, John, 192.
Hull, Jonathan, 111.
Hull, Joseph, 32.
Hull, Miles, 134, 208, 211.
Hull, Mills, 226.
Hull, Robart, 97.
Hull, Samuel, 103, 131.
Hull, Stephen, 89, 269.
Hull, Sylvanus, 193.
Hull, Wakeman, 69.
Hultman, Jonas, 246.
Humiston, Thomas, 179.
Hummiston, David, 119.
Humphrevile, Lemuel, 179.
Humphrey, 147.
Humphrey, David, 36.
Humphrey, Elihu, 20.
Humphrey, Erastus, 27.
Humphrey, Joel, 27.
Humphrey, John, 27.
Humphrie, J., 177.
Humphry, Asher, 145, 146, 147, 148.
Humphry, Benoni, 146, 147, 148.
Humphry, Charles, 145, 147, 148
Humphry, David, 48.
Humphry, Elihu, 24.
Humphry, Elijah, 48.
Humphry, Giles, 146, 148.
Humphry, John, 223.
Humphry, Jonathan, 145, 146, 147, 148.
Humphry, Joseph, 7.
Humphry, Noah, 142, 202.
Humphry, Noah, Jr., 164.
Humphry, Richard, 164.
Humphry, Simeon, 202.
Humphy, Jonathan, 147.
Humphy, Martin, 145, 147.
Humphy, Solomon, 145.
Hungerford, David, 70.
Hungerford, Ezra, 199.
Hungerford, Isaiah, 199.
Hungerford, John, 139.
Hungerford, Josiah, 197.
Hungerford, Thomas, 182.
Hungerford, Uri, 114.
Hungerford, Z., 209.
Hunt, Edmon, 34.
Hunt, Eldad, 163.
Hunt, Elijah, 105, 186.
Hunt, Henry, 247, 251, 253, 255.
Hunt, John, 262.
Hunt, Richard, 89, 230, 232.
Hunt, Russell, 2d, 37.
Hunt, Simeon, 105.
Hunt, Walter, 260.
Hunt, Ziba, 210.
Hunter, Turtle, 253, 256.
Huntington, 265, 267.
Huntington, Andrew, 161.
Huntington, Christopher, 186.
Huntington, Ebenezer, 67, 122.
Huntington, Elijah, 185.
Huntington, Eliphlet, 186.
Huntington, Gamalel, 184.
Huntington, Jedediah, 16, 17, 18, 19, 22, 23, 24, 25, 27, 51, 267.
Huntington, Robert, 79.
Huntington, Simeon, 220.
Huntley, Amos, 1.
Huntley, Phineas, 132.
Huntly, Moses, 185.
Huntly, Zadock, 185.
Hurd, Abner, 136.
Hurd, Adam, 136.
Hurd, Asahel, 38.
Hurd, Curtis, 136.
Hurd, Daniel, 136.

Hurd, David, 54, 122, 269.
Hurd, Elijah, 120.
Hurd, Jacob, 118, 184.
Hurd, John, 38.
Hurd, Joshua, 38.
Hurd, Justice, 38.
Hurd, Lewis, 54, 121, 267.
Hurd, Lovewel, 136.
Hurd, Nathan, 208.
Hurd, Samuel, 136.
Hurd, Simeon, 136.
Hurd, Simeon, Jr., 136.
Hurd, Solomon, 173.
Hurd, Stephen, 136.
Hurd, Thomas, 135.
Hurd, W., 213.
Hurlbard, Gideon, 202.
Hurlbard, John, 202.
Hurlbat, Abraham, 218.
Hurlburt, Caleb, 21.
Hurlburt, Elijah, 34.
Hurlburt, James, 213.
Hurlburt, Jeremiah, 20.
Hurlburt, John, 81.
Hurlburt, Matthias, 36.
Hurlburt, Samuel, Jr., 38.
Hurlburt, Silas, 154, 156.
Hurlbut, Adam, 209, 225, 226.
Hurlbut, George, 28.
Hurlbut, Gideon, 68.
Hurlbut, Truman, 173.
Hurlbutt, John, 222.
Hussey, Ben, 246.
Hussey, Benjamin, 250, 253.
Hussy, Benjamin, 247.
Huston, John, 171.
Hutchenson, Josh, 182.
Hutchenson, Thomas, 233.
Hutchingson, Abijah, 246.
Hutchins, 214.
Hutchins, Amasa, 172.
Hutchins, B., 206, 214.
Hutchins, Benjamin, 221, 225.
Hutchins, Ezra, 172.
Hutchins, N., 211.
Hutchinson, Abijah, 248, 260.
Hutchinson, Amasa, 119.
Hutchinson, Ebenezer, 159.
Hutchinson, Eleazer, 161.
Hutchinson, Elisha, 4, 161.
Hutchinson, Isireal, 163.
Hutchinson, John, 265.
Hutchinson, Jonathan, 82.
Hutchinson, Jonothan, 163.
Hutchinson, Joseph, 163.
Huxford, Henry, 157.
Huxford, John, 160.
Hyatt, Isaac, 217.

Hyatt, Samuel, 217.
Hyatt, Stephen, 217.
Hyatt, Thomas, 217.
Hyde, Alexander, 132.
Hyde, Daniel, 149.
Hyde, Eliphalet, 5.
Hyde, Elijah, Jr., 5, 6.
Hyde, James, 47.
Hyde, Moses, 149, 183.
Hyde, Oliver, 3, 4.
Hyde, Rufus, 89.
Hyde, Samuel, 149.
Hyde, Thomas L., 160.
Hyde, Walter, 149.
Hyde, William, 34, 160.
Hyllyard, David, 17.
Hyllyer, Andrew, 212.

Ingersol, Brigs, 110.
Ingham, Amasa, 95.
Ingham, Daniel, 184.
Ingham, Samuel, 163.
Ingersoll, Richard, 143.
Ingorson, Brigs, 116.
Ingraham, Amaziah, 127.
Ingraham, Amos, 185.
Ingraham, Daniel, 160.
Ingraham, Edward, 234.
Ingraham, Hezekiah, 51.
Ingraham, Jacob, 160.
Ingraham, Jareth, 27.
Ingraham, John, 191.
Ingraham, Nathaniel, 191.
Ingraham, S., 85.
Ingraham, Samuel, 79.
Ingraham, William, 253.
Ingram, Henry, 34.
Ireland, 103.
Isham, Ebenezer, 57.
Isham, John, 211.
Isham, Jonathan, 57.
Isham, Joseph, 209.
Isham, Joshua, 57.
Isham, William, 57.
Ives, Abijah, 194.
Ives, Alling, 179.
Ives, Amos, 192, 224.
Ives, Asahel, 213.
Ives, Bazaliel, 223.
Ives, Bezaleel, 192.
Ives, Buller, 276.
Ives, Jesse, 36.
Ives, Joel, Jr., 265.
Ives, John, 105, 126, 192.
Ives, Joseph, 36.
Ives, Lazarus, 133, 134.
Ives, Lent, 266, 267, 270.
Ives, Levy, 19.

Ives, Noah, 211.
Ives, Samuel, 194.
Ives, Timothy, 192.
Ives, William, 235.

Jack, Andrew, 71.
Jacklin, Thaddeus, 110.
Jacklin, Thadeus, 116.
Jackson, Daniel, 106, 127, 243.
Jackson, David, 123.
Jackson, Elijah, 34.
Jackson, Ephraim, 32.
Jackson, Francis, 254.
Jackson, Garshum, 196.
Jackson, John, 69.
Jackson, John, Jr., 34.
Jackson, Nathan, 243.
Jackson, Nathan P., 89.
Jackson, Nathaniel, 49.
Jackson, Salah, 146, 147.
Jackson, Samuel, 78.
Jackson, William, 69, 99.
Jackways, William, 69.
Jacobs, John, 253.
Jacobs, M., 89.
Jacobs, Zebulon, 10.
Jacobson, George, 260.
Jacques, Launcelot, 49.
James, John, 174.
James, Robert A., 245, 250, 252.
Janes, Daniel, 192.
Janeways, Daniel, 35.
Jaquies, William, 138.
Jarvis, Francis, 260.
Jarvis, William, 243.
Jeffers, Peter, 240, 241.
Jeffery, James, 264.
Jeffords, George, 175.
Jelleff, James, 217.
Jellits, 138.
Jemson, John, 54.
Jenkins, Calvin, 68.
Jenkins, Samuel, 103.
Jennings, Charles, 38.
Jennings, D., 3d, 84.
Jennings, Elnathan, 89.
Jennings, Isban, 69.
Jennings, James, 232.
Jennings, Jonathan, 246, 249.
Jennings, Justin, 266.
Jennings, Lyman, 16.
Jennings, Michael, 236.
Jennings, Nathan, 23, 254.
Jennings, Nathan, Jr., 18.
Jennings, Nathaniel, 243, 254.
Jerison, Michael, 87.
Jermain, Charles, 19.
Jermain, Peter, 19.

Jerry, Ephraim, 74.
Jervis, Jonathan, 232.
Jervis, Nathaniel, 232.
Jesup, Eben, 180.
Jewell, Joshua, Jr., 37.
Jewett, Caleb, 270.
Jewett, Caleb, Jr., 34.
Jewett, Joseph, 22, 23.
Jewit, N., 209.
Jinings, David, 234.
Jinkens, Samuel, 130.
Jinnings, Jacob, 217.
Jinnings, Joseph, 74.
Johns, William, 119.
Johnson, 59, 146.
Johnson, Abraham, 109.
Johnson, Alpheus, 254.
Johnson, Amos, 189, 276.
Johnson, Artemas, 10, 24, 265.
Johnson, Asa, 32.
Johnson, Ashel, 189.
Johnson, Benoni, 202.
Johnson, Charles, 82, 276.
Johnson, D., 84.
Johnson, Daniel, 18, 23.
Johnson, David, 194.
Johnson, Ebenezer, 202.
Johnson, Eliakim, 58.
Johnson, Elias, 98.
Johnson, Elijah, 56.
Johnson, Gideon, Jr., 189.
Johnson, Grant, 267.
Johnson, Hamlin, 67.
Johnson, Henry, 112.
Johnson, Hezekiah, 189.
Johnson, Isaac, 135, 146, 147, 209.
Johnson, Israel, 58.
Johnson, J., 206.
Johnson, James, 141, 230.
Johnson, James A., 59.
Johnson, Joel, 113, 277.
Johnson, John, 71, 134, 147, 220, 238, 239, 240.
Johnson, John, Jr., 277.
Johnson, Jonathan, 47, 194.
Johnson, Joseph, 122, 146, 147.
Johnson, Joseph, Jr., 189.
Johnson, Justis, 183.
Johnson, Justus, 265, 270.
Johnson, Miles, 208, 222, 224, 275.
Johnson, Nathaniel, 53.
Johnson, Nathaniel, Jr., 189.
Johnson, O., 206.
Johnson, Obadiah, 221.
Johnson, Peter, 54, 211.
Johnson, Phinehas, 109.
Johnson, Prince, 114.
Johnson, Robert, 29, 31.

Johnson, Rufus, 139.
Johnson, Samuel, 34, 189, 192, 230, 258.
Johnson, Seth, 266.
Johnson, Shubael, 32, 110.
Johnson, Solomon, 126, 274.
Johnson, Stephen, 66, 276.
Johnson, Thomas, 39.
Johnson, Timothy, 109.
Johnson, Ward, 275.
Johnson, Wilford, 205.
Johnson, William, 66, 71, 107, 244, 247, 249, 270.
Johnson, Zachary, 201.
Johnsons, John, 191.
Johnston, Isaac, 80.
Johnston, James, 120.
Johnston, Robert, 89.
Johnston, Stephen, 184.
Johonnot, Andrew, 229.
Jone, John F., 125.
Jones, Aaron, 141.
Jones, Amos, 212, 220.
Jones, Asaph, 175.
Jones, Benajah, 160.
Jones, Benjamin, 141, 161, 256.
Jones, Benjamin, Jr., 260.
Jones, Charles, 270.
Jones, David, 109.
Jones, Eaton, 224.
Jones, Ebenezer, 200.
Jones, Elijah, 218.
Jones, George, 21.
Jones, Harris, 201.
Jones, Henry, 89.
Jones, Isahel, 161.
Jones, Isaiah, 69.
Jones, James, 57.
Jones, Jasper, 109.
Jones, Job, 85.
Jones, Joel, 159.
Jones, John, 22, 193.
Jones, Jonah, 99.
Jones, Joseph, 10, 17, 39, 89.
Jones, Luther, 74, 175, 228.
Jones, Nicholas, 194.
Jones, Pratt, 70, 112.
Jones, Robert, Jr., 37.
Jones, Robinson, 246, 251.
Jones, Samuel, 82, 159, 161, 201, 211.
Jones, Simeon, 186.
Jones, Simon, 2, 3.
Jones, Stephen, 99.
Jones, Thomas, 89, 140, 245, 249, 251, 254.
Jones, William, 32, 69, 119, 139, 259.

Jonson, Hamlin, 36.
Jonson, John, 74.
Jordan, John, 89, 110, 117.
Jordan, Stephen, 230.
Joy, John, 4, 163.
Joyce, John, 66.
Judd, Abner, 86, 198.
Judd, Alexander, 111.
Judd, Chandler, 103, 117, 127, 131.
Judd, Daniel, 59, 89, 173.
Judd, Ebenezer, 24, 199.
Judd, Elihu, 98, 109.
Judd, Ephraim, 59.
Judd, Jacob, 198.
Judd, Johuel, 270.
Judd, Reuben, 18, 235.
Judd, Ruben, 274.
Judd, Thomas, Jr., 198.
Judd, William, 46.
Jude, Brestor, 54.
Judson, Aaron, 181, 219.
Judson, Abel, 151.
Judson, Chapman, 173.
Judson, Curtis, 136.
Judson, D., 177.
Judson, David, 49, 76, 173.
Judson, Elihew, 181, 219.
Judson, Ira, 138.
Judson, James, 151, 173, 181, 219, 232.
Judson, Joel, 151, 181, 196, 219.
Judson, Lemuel, 215.
Judson, Nathaniel, 215.
Judson, Noah, 142.
Judson, Silas, 151.
Judson, Stephen, 201.
Judson, Stiles, 151, 211, 226.
Judson, Timothy, 208.
Judson, William, 181, 219.

Kane, Thomas, 12.
Kane, William, 102, 130.
Karsen, James, 173.
Kay, Timothy, 202.
Kaver, John, 231.
Kee, Uriah, 168.
Keeler, 195.
Keeler, Aaron, 77.
Keeler, Aron, 129.
Keeler, Benjimin, 195.
Keeler, David, 195.
Keeler, Henry, 68.
Keeler, Hezekiah, 77.
Keeler, Isaac, 46.
Keeler, Jacob, 86.
Keeler, Jeremiah, 69.
Keeler, John, 200.
Keeler, Mathew, 195.

330  REVOLUTION ROLLS AND LISTS.

Keeler, Thaddeus, 48.
Keeler, Thomas, 69.
Keeler, Timothy, 200.
Keeler, Timothy, 2d, 200.
Keeler, Uriah, 78, 103, 130.
Keelor, Aaron, 50.
Keelor, Ebenezer, 73.
Keelor, S., 212.
Keeney, Benjamin, 5.
Keeney, Ethel, 189.
Keeney, Isaac, 157.
Keeney, James, 58.
Keeney, Medad, 189.
Keeney, Theodore, 133.
Keenne, Joseph, 263.
Keith, Peter, 222.
Kelcey, Aaron, 210, 266.
Kelcey, Jeremiah, 178.
Kelcey, Samuel, 21.
Kelcy, Aaron, 206.
Kelcy, Daniel, 36.
Keley, Joel, 184.
Keley, Nathan, 202.
Keley, Ruben, 184.
Kelley, Ephraim, 212.
Kelley, John, 53.
Kellogg, Aaron, 94.
Kellogg, Alen, 203.
Kellogg, Asahel, 37.
Kellogg, Bradford, 67, 139.
Kellogg, Charles, 221, 223, 224.
Kellogg, David, 160.
Kellogg, Daniel, 200.
Kellogg, Eldad, 35.
Kellogg, Elijah, 200.
Kellogg, Enoch, 77.
Kellogg, Enos, 274.
Kellogg, Ezekil, 186.
Kellogg, George, 274.
Kellogg, Grove, 77.
Kellogg, Helmont, 105, 201.
Kellogg, John, 159, 218, 227.
Kellogg, Joseph, 36, 208.
Kellogg, Leveret, 36.
Kellogg, Martin, 36.
Kellogg, N., 188.
Kellogg, Nathan, 195.
Kellogg, Noah, 36, 211.
Kellogg, Oliver, 274.
Kellogg, Phinihas, 27.
Kellogg, Samuel, 22, 39.
Kellogg, Stephen, 154, 156.
Kellogg, Thomas, 86.
Kelly, John, 235, 267.
Kelsey, Elisha, 273.
Kelsey, John, 191.
Kelsey, Nathan, 71.
Kelscy, Noah, 106.

Kelsey, Presto, 113.
Kelsey, Preston, 116.
Kelsey, Samuel, 37.
Kelsey, Timothy, 273.
Kelsey, William, 191.
Kelsey, Zach, 274.
Kelsey, Zechariah, 133.
Kelsy, Noah, 69.
Kene, Thadeus, 189.
Kenedy, Andrew, 1.
Keney, Cyrus, 171.
Keney, Thomas, 254.
Kennedy, Henry, 247, 252.
Kennedy, James, 95.
Kennedy, Thomas, 1, 165.
Kenney, Benjamin, 235.
Kenney, Charles, 253.
Kenny, Benjamin, 118.
Kensington, 79.
Kent, Elihu, 209.
Kent, Samuel, 80.
Kent, Zenas, 63.
Kent, 73, 89, 90, 103.
Kesley, Noah, 126.
Ketcham, Ezra, 110.
Ketcham, Timothy, 198.
Kettell, Jonathan, 202.
Kettle, Thomas, 55.
Keyes, Marshall, 124.
Kibbe, Elisha, 165.
Kibbee, Elijah, 128.
Kibbee, Frederick, 120.
Kibbee, Phillip, 120.
Kibby, Samuel, 139.
Kilbey, Ebenezer, 154.
Kilborn, Charles, 23.
Kilborn, Jarey, 201.
Kilborne, Araunah, 93.
Kilborne, Jonathan, 209.
Kilby, Ebenezer, 133, 156.
Kilby, Elijah, 127.
Killam, Cyrus, 74.
Killey, John, 260.
Killingley, 6, 55, 57, 58, 59, 64, 65, 66, 78, 79, 82, 90, 103, 104, 267.
Killington, 67.
Killingworth, 53, 55, 56, 88, 89, 113.
Kimbal, Charles, 15.
Kimbal, Jesse, 64.
Kimbalin, William, 252.
Kimball, Jared, 124.
Kimball, Jedediah, 103, 121, 131.
Kimball, Jesse, 35.
Kimball, John, 124.
Kimball, Richard, 254.
Kimball, Samuel, 105.

# INDEX.

Kimball, Taman, 97.
Kimberley, 212.
Kimberley, John, 196.
Kimberly, Ephraim, 49, 77.
Kimberly, Fitch, 197.
Kimberly, George, 133.
Kimberly, Isaac S., 179.
Kimey, Stephen, 186.
Kindal, Ebenezer, 184.
King, David, 154, 156.
King, Ezekiel, 63.
King, George, 81.
King, Joseph, 63, 246, 250, 262.
King, Josiah, 209, 223.
King, Lemuel, 266, 270.
King, Peter, 274.
King, Samuel, 1.
Kingham, Elias, 74.
Kingman, Mitchell, 154, 156.
Kings Bridge, 149.
Kingsbery, Elijah H., 1.
Kingsbery, Joseph, 1.
Kingsbery, Phinehas, 41.
Kingsbery, Simon, Jr., 1.
Kingsbury, Elijah, 165.
Kingsbury, Ephraim, 105.
Kingsbury, Jacob, 121, 240.
Kingsbury, Joseph, 161.
Kingsbury, Phinehas, 43.
Kingsbury, Samuel, 82.
Kingsbury, Thomas, 28.
Kingsbury, Willard, 35.
Kingsley, 123.
Kingsley, Ebenezer, 185.
Kingsley, Jabez, 263.
Kingsley, James, 74.
Kingsley, Uriah, 143.
Kinman, Pain, 184.
Kinne, Benjamin, 160.
Kinne, Samuel, 171.
Kinnee, Ezra, 212.
Kinney, Ezra, 208.
Kinney, Jacob, 64.
Kinney, James, 165.
Kinney, William, 165.
Kinning, Thomas, 89.
Kinnion, Griffin, 201.
Kinyon, Arnold, 253.
Kirkam, Henery, 27.
Kirkam, Samuel, 27.
Kirkum, Benjamin, 121.
Kirkum, John, 100.
Kirkum, Pileman, 124.
Kirrit, John, 89.
Kirtland, 50, 140, 141.
Kirtland, Billious, 212.
Kirtland, Isaac, 275.
Kirtland, Jabez, 124.

Kirtland, James, 151.
Kirtland, John, 82.
Kirtland, M., 227.
Kirtland, Thomas, 89.
Kitchel, David, 12.
Kitchel, Joseph, 12.
Knap, Abram, 39.
Knap, Amos, 200.
Knap, Elnathan, 200.
Knap, Jared, 69.
Knap, John, 235.
Knap, Joseph, 39.
Knap, Moses, 197.
Knap, Nehemiah, 235.
Knap, Uzual, 53.
Knapen, Thomas, 85.
Knapp, Benjamin, 97.
Knapp, Cyrenus, 67.
Knapp, James, 65, 69.
Knapp, Jared, 270.
Knapp, John, 16.
Knapp, Jonas, 34.
Knapp, Silvanus, 226.
Knapp, Usell, 89.
Knapp, William, 94.
Kneeland, Joseph, 1.
Kneland, Hezekiah, 160.
Knickerbacor, Lawrance, 34.
Knight, Daniel, 106, 126.
Knight, Jonathan, 47.
Knight, Phinehas, 124.
Knolton, Joshua, 57.
Knowles, John, 261, 262.
Knowles, Seth, 59.
Knowlton, Frederick, 15.
Knowlton, Stephen, 15.
Knowlton, Steven, 15.
Knowlton, Thomas, 14, 24, 25, 254.
Knox, Micael, 263.
Korton, Alexander, 139.
Kough, Lent, 205.
[ ]kwood, Gol[ ], 85.
Kyes, Edward, 15.
Kyes, John, 14.
Kyes, Zachariah, 15.
Kyesby, Levy, 64.

Lacey, Bille, 84.
Lacey, Ebenezer, 136.
Lacey, Enoch, 236.
Lacey, Ezra, 136.
Lacey, Isaac, 82.
Lacey, Thaddeus, 85, 136.
Lacey, Thadeus, 136.
Lacy, David, 243.
Lacy, Josiah, 47.
Ladd, Amisa, 186.

Ladd, Jesse, 1.
Ladd, Oliver, 64.
Lade, John, 56.
La Fayette, Marquis de, 121.
Laflen, John, 15.
Laflin, Abraham, 15.
Lain, Allen, 55.
Lain, John, 57.
Lake, Phinehas, 270.
Lake Champlain, 18.
Lamb, Benjamin, 74.
Lamb, David, 175.
Lamb, George, 260.
Lamb, Isaac, 34.
Lamb, John, 258.
Lamb, Joseph, 19.
Lamb, Lemuel, 212.
Lamb, Rufus, 163.
Lamb, Silas, Jr., 216.
Lamb, Thomas, 229.
Lamb, William, 254, 260, 264.
Lambart, Samuel, 55.
Lamberton, Nathaniel, 27.
Lamberton, Obed, 138.
Lamberton, Obediah, 68.
Lament, William, 110.
Lamphear, Abel, 199.
Lamphear, Roswell, 257.
Lamphear, William, 38.
Lamphere, Roswell, 128.
Lamson, Elnathan, 203.
Lamson, Nathaniel, 190.
Lamson, Nathaniel, Jr., 190.
Landers, Samuel, 27.
Landon, David, 191, 210.
Landon, Hazia, 81.
Landon, James, 201.
Landon, Reuben, 201.
Landor, Gael, 91.
Lane, Allen, 82, 212.
Lane, Allin, 141.
Lane, Daniel, 81.
Lane, Isaac, 205.
Lane, Joel, 79.
Lane, John, 135.
Lane, William, 89.
Lanford, James, 73.
Langton, John, 210.
Langworthy, Rober, 175.
Lankton, Daniel, 210.
Lanphere, James, 246.
Lanphere, James, Jr., 249.
Lansing, Jacob J., 72.
Larence, Jonas, 205.
Larkam, Thomas, 264.
Larkim, Rodrick, 188.
Larkin, John, 79.
Larkings, Joseph, 190.

Larned, Daniel, 183.
Larrabee, Seth, 74.
Larrabee, Willet, 89.
Larrance, James, 147, 148.
Larrenc, James, 145, 146.
Lary, Luman, 154.
Lasseur, John, 239.
Latham, 124.
Latham, Amos, 175.
Latham, Cary, 175.
Latham, Christopher, Jr., 270.
Latham, Daniel, 175.
Latham, Jasper, 175.
Latham, Joseph, 2d, 175.
Latham, Joseph, 4th, 175.
Latham, Joseph, 5th, 175.
Latham, William, 174, 212.
Lathergo, John, 246, 251.
Lathrop, E., 212.
Lathrop, Ebenezer, 212.
Lathrop, Neal, 260.
Latimer, John, 145, 146, 147.
Latimer, Robert, 140, 174.
Lattimer, 267.
Lattimer, J., 220, 221, 266.
Lattimer, Samuel, 220.
Lattimer, Solomon, 154, 156.
Lattimore, John, 147.
Laughlane, James, 34.
Laurence, Nehemiah, 208.
Laurence, Rosamus, 253.
Law, James, 5.
Law, Nathan, 113, 127.
Lawrance, James, 27.
Lawrence, Aaron, 35.
Lawrence, Amos, 68.
Lawrence, James, 147.
Lawrence, John, 32.
Laws, Thomas, 162.
Lawson, Joseph, 123.
Lawson, Samuel, 154, 156.
Lawson, Thomas, 32.
Lay, Asa, 48, 50, 71.
Lay, John, 113.
Lay, Lee, 132, 183, 207, 270.
Lay, Simeon, 210.
Lay, William, 211.
Leach, Caleb, 20.
Leach, James, 172.
Leach, Jonas, 164.
Lench, Joseph, 169.
Leach, Joshua, 20.
Leach, Lewis, 65.
Leach, Thomas, 174.
Leach, William, 105, 270.
Leaming, Judah, 18.
Learned, Darias, 184.
Leatch, William, 66.

# INDEX.

Leathercoat, John, 74.
Leavensworth, D., 224, 266.
Leavensworth, David, 223.
Leavenworth, D., 207.
Leavenworth, David, 136.
Leavenworth, Edmond, 181.
Leavenworth, Eli, 71, 72.
Leavit, David, 173.
Lebanon, 2, 3, 4, 5, 6, 25, 55, 56, 65, 75, 78, 79, 80, 81, 82, 88, 89, 90, 91, 103, 104, 113, 114, 118, 149, 182.
Ledgyrd, John, 35.
Ledley, James, 12.
Ledyard, E., 212.
Ledyard, John, 270.
Ledyard, William, 212.
Lee, Dan, 160, 184.
Lee, Daniel, 80, 258.
Lee, Elias, 20, 35.
Lee, Elijah, 1.
Lee, Elisha, 63, 89, 270.
Lee, Ezra, 45, 132.
Lee, John, 114.
Lee, Levi, 89.
Lee, Levy, 277.
Lee, Martin, 132.
Lee, Nathan, 2, 3, 162.
Lee, Samuel, 77, 138, 277.
Lee, Seth, 200.
Lee, Squire, 5.
Lee, Stephen, 185, 230, 252.
Lee, Timothy, 277.
Leech, Alexander, 39.
Leech, Ebenezer, 13, 42, 43.
Leech, Jonas, 202.
Leech, Joseph, 149.
Leech, Richard, 164.
Leech, William, 39.
Leeds, Thomas, 51.
Leemon, George, 236.
Leet, Allen, 89.
Leet, Asahel, 274.
Leet, John, 277.
Leffingwell, Asa, 169.
Leffingwell, Benajah, 210.
Leffingwell, Christopher, 210.
Leffingwell, Daniel, 142.
Leffingwell, Samuel, 211.
Lenimey, Henry, 204.
Leonard, Ebenezer, 40.
Leonard, Silas, 98.
Lerow, John, 111.
Lerrow, John, 70.
Leseur, Johan, 240.
Leseur, John, 241.
Leskomb, Darias, 184.
Lessieur, John, 238.

Lester, Jesse, 262.
Lester, Phinehas, 170.
Lesure, John, 262.
Levans, Cal., 190.
Levensworth, Gideon, 190.
Levenworth, Eli, 48.
Lewardy, George, 27.
Lewes, Abel, 76.
Lewes, David, 233.
Lewes, Jabez, 35.
Lewis, 180.
Lewis, Abel, 253.
Lewis, Asa, 80.
Lewis, Augustus, 22, 141.
Lewis, Beach, Jr., 215.
Lewis, Benjamin, 2, 165.
Lewis, Charles, 106, 126.
Lewis, Christopher, 231.
Lewis, David, 24, 186, 240.
Lewis, Ebenezer, 89.
Lewis, Elijah, 182.
Lewis, Enoch, 180.
Lewis, Ezekiel, 173.
Lewis, George, 181, 219, 229.
Lewis, George R., 132.
Lewis, Hezekiah, 78.
Lewis, I., 206.
Lewis, Ichabod, 151.
Lewis, Jacob, 69.
Lewis, John, 113, 116, 194, 209, 220, 234, 275.
Lewis, Joseph, 82, 213.
Lewis, Judah, 20.
Lewis, Naboth, 270.
Lewis, Nathaniel, 182, 270.
Lewis, Nehemiah, 227.
Lewis, Peter, 54, 270.
Lewis, Philo, 254.
Lewis, Samuel, 89, 270.
Lewis, Shearman, 234.
Lewis, Shirman, 252.
Lewis, Stephen, 151.
Lewis, Thomas, 78.
Lewis, Valentine, 51.
Lewis, Wait, 130.
Lowis, Weight, 103.
Lewis, William, 201.
Lexington, 3, 5, 6, 227.
Leygoit, James, 66.
Libberty, James, 77.
Liberty, Cuff, 107.
Liberty, James, 103, 130.
Liberty, Pomp, 113.
Lilley, Abner, 114, 127.
Lilley, Chester, 114.
Lilley, Elijah, 64, 79, 185.
Lilley, Emanus, 94.
Lilley, John, 172.

Lilley, Richard, Jr., 142.
Lillie, Richard, 254.
Lilly, Chester, 116.
Lilly, Jarod, 64.
Linch, Patrick, 75.
Linchon, Samuel, 184.
Lincoln, Elijah, 265, 270.
Lincoln, James, 85, 98, 194.
Lindsey, 59.
Lindsey, David, 100.
Lindsley, James, 200, 210.
Lindsley, John, 200.
Lindsley, Joseph, 74.
Lindsley, Lemuel, 200.
Lindsley, Matthew, 200.
Lines, Benjamin, 65.
Lines, John, 89.
Lingdyon, Peter, 262.
Linkhorn, Nathan, 20.
Linkon, Elijah, 74.
Linley, Abiel, 75.
Linley, Simeon, 242.
Linly, Solomon, 201.
Linly, Timothy, 201.
Linn, William, 46.
Linsey, Timothy, 98.
Linsley, John, 72.
Linsley, Solomon, 273.
Linsley, Timothy, 273.
Linslie, John, 255.
Linsly, Simeon, 243.
Linston, John, 250.
Linstrum, John, 246.
Lion, Peter, 113.
Litchfield, Eleazer, 167.
Litchfield, 23, 53, 55, 67, 68, 69, 70, 80, 81, 82, 88, 90, 103, 111, 273.
Little, David, 222.
Little, George, 82, 172.
Little, Jack, 71, 108.
Little, Nathaniel, 23.
Little, Samuel, 201, 235.
Little, William, 51, 201.
Littlefield, Ebenezer, 79.
Loatwell, Ephraim, 68.
Lock, William, 32.
Lockwood, 139.
Lockwood, Eliphalet, 212.
Lockwood, Isaac, 195.
Lockwood, Jeremiah, 196.
Lockwood, John R., 243.
Lockwood, John, 3d, 84.
Lockwood, Samuel, 89.
Lockwood, Seth, 202.
Lockwood, Timothy, 210.
Loggan, Matthew, 173.
Lollard, Samuel, 256.

Lomis, Joseph, 160.
Lomis, Samuel, 59.
Lomiss, Eleazer, 161.
Lommis, Grove, 67.
London, Charles, 70, 112.
London, Eliel, 123.
London, Pomp, 76.
Long, Jesse, 78.
Long, Lumon, 156.
Long, Paul, 245, 250.
Long, Stephen, 105.
Long Island, 30, 61, 138, 139, 279.
Loomer, Samuel, 40.
Loomis, A., 206, 214.
Loomis, Abraham, 202.
Loomis, Amasa, 87, 222.
Loomis, Asa, 4, 5, 160.
Loomis, Benjamin, 119.
Loomis, Benoni, 163.
Loomis, Brigadore, 202.
Loomis, Dick, 60.
Loomis, Elijah, 27, 36.
Loomis, Epaphras, 202, 210.
Loomis, Ephraim, 202.
Loomis, Ezekiel, 162.
Loomis, Grove, 202.
Loomis, Jacob, 4.
Loomis, Joseph, 5.
Loomis, Isaiah, 160, 202.
Loomis, Isaih, 162.
Loomis, Jabez, 161.
Loomis, Jesse, 259.
Loomis, Jonathan, 143.
Loomis, Joseph, 202.
Loomis, Josiah, 137, 139.
Loomis, Lebbeus, 47.
Loomis, Moses, 89.
Loomis, Oliver, 202.
Loomis, Thomas, 5.
Loomis, Timothy, 273.
Loomis, William, 143.
Loomise, Asa, 3.
Loomise, Jacob, 3.
Loomiss, 164.
Loomiss, Benjamin, 105.
Loomiss, Grove, 98.
Lord, Abner, 103, 130.
Lord, Eliphalet, 1, 59.
Lord, Elisha, 51, 52.
Lord, Fradrick, 188.
Lord, George, 245, 249, 266.
Lord, Jabez, 109.
Lord, James, 45.
Lord, Joel, 274.
Lord, Richard, 53, 102, 129.
Lord, Soloman, 244, 245, 248.
Lord, William, 50, 187.
Lorde, Frederick, 187.

Lothrop, James, 160.
Lothrop, Samuel, 5, 40.
Loudon, Mass., 56.
Lounsberry, Richard, 109.
Lounsbury, David, 121.
Love, Thomas, 79.
Lovejoy, John, 79.
Loveland, Amos, 74.
Loveland, Ashbel, 189.
Loveland, Charles, 61.
Loveland, Daniel, 160.
Loveland, Elijah, 245, 251.
Loveland, Epafrus, 160.
Loveland, Jonathan, 107, 137, 139.
Loveland, Joseph, 179, 210.
Loveland, Levi, 58, 89, 154, 156, 157.
Loveland, Nathan, 74.
Loveland, Truman, 189.
Lovet, David, 1.
Lovet, James, 2.
Lovet, John, 2.
Lovet, Samuel, 2.
Lovett, James, 165.
Lovett, John, 165.
Lovland, Elizur, 157.
Lovland, Pelitiah, 157.
Low, Abraham, 259.
Lowell, Samuel, 32.
Lowry, Alexander, 263.
Lucas, George, 230.
Lucas, John, 230.
Lucas, Samuel, 89, 107, 133.
Lucas, William, 17, 193, 265.
Luce, Barzilla, 233.
Luce, Ebenezer, 185.
Luce, Ephraim, 87.
Luce, Jabez, 264.
Luce, Jonathan, 54, 124.
Luce, Nathaniel, 170.
Luddenton, Stephen, 127.
Ludeman, John, 69.
Ludinton, Eliphalet, 10.
Ludlow, Stephen, 54.
Ludonton, Samuel, 10.
Luis, Jams, 203.
Lumbard, Justin, 81.
Lumis, Josiah, 137.
Lummis, Samuel, 99.
Lung, Joseph, 61.
Lusey, James, 200.
Lusk, Elijah, 27.
Lusk, J., 214.
Lusk, James, 209.
Luther, Edward, 162.
Luther, Ellis, 163.
Luther, Theophilus, 123.

Lydleman, John, Jr., 40.
Lyman, Abiather, 161.
Lyman, Asa, 259.
Lyman, Daniel, 80, 106, 126, 177.
Lyman, Ezekiel, 114.
Lyman, Ezekiel, Jr., 116.
Lyman, Ichabod, 274.
Lyman, Jesse, 81.
Lyman, Phineas, 16.
Lyman, Phinehas, 193.
Lyman, Richard, 5, 162.
Lyman, Thomas, 193.
Lyme, 53, 56, 59, 60, 64, 69, 75, 82, 88, 89, 90, 91, 102, 103, 113, 118, 132, 207, 267.
Lynch, Timothy, 262.
Lynds, Samuel, 97.
Lynn, William, 104, 121, 129.
Lyon, Abel, 169.
Lyon, Asahel, 15.
Lyon, Daniel, 210.
Lyon, Enos, 35.
Lyon, Ephraim, 180.
Lyon, Ezekael, 246.
Lyon, Ezekiel, 250.
Lyon, Henry, 57.
Lyon, John, 236.
Lyon, Samuel, 101.
Lyon, Stephen, 210.
Lyons, Amariah, 15.

McCall, Eleazer, 143.
McCarty, John, 127.
McCauley, Robert, 13.
McClanning, Edward, 68.
McClarry, Andrew, 74.
McClean, Jacob, 37.
McClean, John, 37.
McClean, Neal, 277.
McClellan, S., 222.
McClellan, Samuel, 145, 146, 147, 183, 221.
McClellen, Samuel, 148.
McClentock, John, 98.
McCorne, William, 89.
McCoy, Alexander, 90.
McCoy, John, 83.
McCracken, 12, 13.
McCray, David, 2, 165.
McCray, Reuben, 2.
McCray, William, 165.
McCray, William, Jr., 2.
McCune, Abijah, 190.
McCune, Ephraim, 141.
McCune, John, 141.
McCune, Nathan, 141.
McCurthy, Nathan, 165.
McDaniel, Charles, 21.

McDavid, James, 230.
McDonald, John, 89.
McDowal, 89.
McDowel, Alexander, 47.
McDowell, Alexander, 58.
McFall, William, 56.
McFee, Angus, 22, 25.
McGeer, Gilbert, 126.
McGoon, John, 35.
McGraw, John, 181, 219.
McGregier, John, 63.
McGreigur, John, 47.
McGuire, Peleg, 254.
McHood, Joseph, 60.
McIngtosh, David, 245.
Macintire, Benjamin, 34.
Mack, 50.
Mack, Abner, 60.
Mack, Benjamin, 24.
Mack, Joel, 96.
Mack, John, 278, 279.
Mack, Josiah, 163.
Mack, Orlando, 90.
Mackarel, James, 160.
Mackaul, Jacob, 160.
McKee, Michael, 34.
McKenney, Andrew, 2.
McKenney, Wiliam, 2.
McKensey, James, 90.
McKenstry, Ezekiel, 2.
Mackentash, Samuel, 257.
Mackentosh, David, 252.
Mackhall, William, 89.
Mackinborough, Jedediah, 90.
Mackingtosh, David, 249.
McKinney, James, Jr., 1.
McKinney, James, 3d, 2.
McKinsey, John, 75.
Mackintosh, David, 244, 247.
McKilliss, Abraham, 12.
Macknel, Alexander, 15.
McKnight, Thomas, 2, 18, 55, 165.
Macksun, Robert, 39.
Mackswell, John, 149.
McLain, Alexander, 260.
McLean, Henry, 113.
McLean, Jacob, 110.
McLean, John, 21, 110.
McMann, John, 1st, 67.
McMann, John, 2d, 67.
McMannes, Hugh, 260.
McMullin, John, 62.
McNaal, James, 147.
McNall, James, 145, 146, 148.
McNally, John, 53.
McNe[ ], Mical, 61.
McNeal, A., 211.
McNeal, Arch., 209.

McNeal, Neal, 127, 128.
McNeil, Alexander, 201.
McNeil, Neil, 13.
McNiel, Niel, 37.
McPerson, Cornelius, 246, 249.
McPharson, Erie, 79.
McQuavy, Nathan, 165.
McQueen, William, 242, 243.
McRowe, Daniel, 78.
McRowe, John, 78.
McVey, James, 253.
McWavy, Ephrim, 2.
McWavy, Nathan, 2.
Maden, James, 234.
Maggott, Zebulon, 156.
Mahan, Phillip, 230.
Main, Amos, 211.
Main, Ezekiel, 80.
Main, Henrey, 186.
Main, Jerimiah, 186.
Main, John, Jr., 90.
Main, Stephen, 150.
Malbone, Jonah, 263.
Malbury, 60.
Malcolm, Daniel, 260.
Mallery, Abner, 208, 224.
Mallery, Amos, 108.
Mallery, Daniel, 242, 243.
Mallery, David, 10, 17.
Mallery, John, 10.
Mallery, John, Jr., 136.
Mallery, Jonah, 75.
Mallery, Levi, 16.
Mallery, Levy, 242, 262.
Mallery, Nathan, 123.
Mallery, Walker, 173.
Mallett, Lewis, 210, 211.
Malley, Abner, 225.
Malone, William, 264.
Maloney, Michael, 107, 116.
Malsby, John, 164.
Maltbie, Zaccheus, 10.
Man, Andrew, 162.
Man, Zadock, 163.
Manard, Cyrus, 171.
Mandwill, Ira, 79.
Maney, John, 116.
Manfeld, Phineus, 247.
Manley, Abner, 42, 43.
Manley, John, 42.
Manly, John, 43.
Mann, Elijah, 59.
Manning, 50.
Manning, Benjamin, 185.
Manning, David, Jr., 34.
Manning, Eleazer, 161.
Manning, Elijah, 64.
Manning, Joel, 64.

Manning, Philip, 120.
Manning, Roswell, 185.
Manning, Samuel, 54, 122.
Manning, William, 22, 90, 175.
Manord, Sirs, 172.
Mans, Charles, 232.
Mansfield, Amos, 64.
Mansfield, Charles, 108.
Mansfield, Dan, 270.
Mansfield, David, 202.
Mansfield, John, 48.
Mansfield, Joseph, 48.
Mansfield, Richard, 189.
Mansfield, Timothy, 108.
Mansfield, 55, 56, 57, 65, 87.
Manson, Samuel, 79.
Manson, Theophilus, 49.
Manton, Royal, 106.
Manuel, Anthony, 231.
Manuel, John, 253.
Manwaring, John, 185.
Maranday, Peter, 96.
Marbell, William, 252.
Marble, Sampson, 42, 43.
Marble, Thomas, 94, 127, 128.
Marcy, Adin, 15.
Mark, Abner, 58.
Markham, Jeremiah, 266, 270.
Markham, Samuel, 17.
Marks, Comfort, 90, 141.
Marks, Hezekiah, 57.
Marks, Robert, 254.
Maroneck, 227.
Marr, John, 36.
Marsh, Allyn, 270.
Marsh, Elijah, 37.
Marsh, Job, 36.
Marsh, John, 105.
Marsh, Nathaniel, 169.
Marsh, Pelatiah, 5, 6.
Marsh, Robert, 108.
Marsh, Stephen, 19.
Marsh, Thomas, 21.
Marsh, William, 247, 249, 254.
Marshal, Reuban, 170.
Marshall, Elisha, 95, 117, 127.
Marshall, Job, 19, 21.
Marshall, S., 212.
Marshall, Silvanus, 226.
Marshel, Roswel, 202.
Martin, Benjami, 198.
Martin, Charles O., 61.
Martin, Gideon, 173.
Martin, John, 29, 30, 96, 235.
Martin, Joseph, 76, 163.
Martin, Joshua, 95.
Martin, Laurance, 233.
Martin, Lemuell, 205.

Martin, Lewis, 90, 108.
Martin, Luther, 29.
Martin, Nathan, 65.
Martin, Robert, 208, 226.
Martin, Samuel, 95.
Martin, Solomon, 19, 24, 208.
Martin, Stephen, 65.
Marvell, Thomas, 82.
Marvin, Nathaniel, 17.
Marvin, O., 212.
Marvin, Ozias, 217, 226.
Marvin, Ozias, Jr., 217.
Marvin, Stephen, 217.
Marwin, 195.
Marwin, Matthew, 77.
Mash, John, 278, 279.
Masher, Joel, 54.
Mashier, Joel, 122.
Maskel, Peres, 164.
Mason, Asbel, 68.
Mason, Hubbard, 186.
Mason, Isaac, 1.
Mason, J., 207.
Mason, Jeremiah, 134, 159, 160, 162, 163, 182.
Mason, John, 69.
Mason, Luther, 201.
Mason, Samuel, 140.
Massachusetts, 12, 13, 58, 59, 188.
Masters, John, 240.
Masunall, Christopher, 184.
Mateson, Peleg, 170.
Mather, 141.
Mather, Cotton, 273.
Mather, Elias, 48, 132.
Mather, Elihu, 57, 114.
Mather, Increas, 27.
Mather, Joseph, 236.
Mather, Timothy, 49.
Mather, William, 132.
Mathews, Hugh, 245, 249.
Mathews, James, 245, 259.
Mathews, Jesse, 78.
Mathews, John, 251.
Mathews, Thomas, 259.
Mathews, William, 61.
Matson, Joseph, 265.
Matson, William, 22.
Matterson, David, 125, 131.
Mattesson, David, 103.
Matthews, John, 36.
Matthews, Obadiah, 34.
Matthews, Thomas, 273.
Matthews, William, 59.
Mattison, Joseph, 265.
Mattison, William, 105.
Mattocks, Samuel, 49, 90.
Mattoon, Samuel, 275.

Mawwee, Elihu, 136.
Maxum, Jacob, 34.
May, Ebinezar, 232.
May, John, 232.
May, Joseph, 153, 155.
Maynard, Jabez, 29.
Maynard, Lemuel, 28.
Maynard, Samuel, 29, 30.
Mazuzen, Mark, 9.
Meach, Hezekiah, 263.
Meach, Jacob, 74, 184, 228, 270.
Meacham, Barnabus, 203.
Meacham, Seth, 36, 202.
Mead, 207.
Mead, Andrew, 266, 270.
Mead, Caleb, 209.
Mead, Ezra, 195.
Mead, Isaac, 98.
Mead, J., 177, 223.
Mead, Jasper, 48.
Mead, Jeremiah, 199.
Mead, John, 210, 214, 225, 226, 227, 266.
Mead, Joseph, 98.
Mead, M., 266.
Mead, Matthew, 23, 212, 267.
Mead, N., 226.
Mead, Nathaniel, 209.
Mead, Reuben, 85.
Mead, Reuben, Jr., 85.
Mead, Samuel, 69.
Mead, Silvanus, 226.
Mead, Theophilus, 77, 267.
Mead, Uriah, 77.
Meaker, David, 233.
Meaker, Ebenezer, 69.
Meaker, Hezekiah, 69.
Meakor, John, 243.
Meason, Elias, 123.
Mebbins, John, 274.
Meech, Elijah, 186.
Meech, Elkanah, 29.
Meech, Elkenah, 31.
Meech, Jacob, 175.
Meech, Joshua, 175.
Meeker, Daniel, 193.
Meeker, J., 84.
Meeker, John, 71, 107.
Meeker, Stephen, 54, 89, 121.
Meeks, Levi, 66.
Megraugh, John, 136.
Meigs, 97, 265.
Meigs, Phineas, 71.
Meigs, Return J., 17, 48, 70, 71.
Meigs, Simeon, 111.
Meigs, Stephen, 104, 113, 130.
Mekye, Daniel, 193.
Mekye, Wyllys, 193.

Melony, Matthew, 29.
Menter, Thomas, 231.
Meranda, Peter, 127.
Merchant, Thomas, 17.
Mercy, Thomas, 89.
Meriden, 68.
Merifield, Abraham, 149.
Meriman, Enoch, 53.
Merrel, Titus, 35.
Merrell, Cyperan, 20.
Merrell, Isaac, 27.
Merrells, Elias, 36.
Merrells, Nehemiah, 36.
Merrett, William, 66.
Merrey, Frances, 27.
Merriam, Amasa, 193.
Merriam, Benjamin, 192.
Merriam, Edmund, 111.
Merriam, Ephraim, 111.
Merriam, Ichabod, 16.
Merriam, Jesse, 192.
Merriam, John, 192.
Merriam, Joseph, 192.
Merriam, Marshal, 193.
Merriam, Nathaniel, 193.
Merriam, Samuel, 193.
Merriam, Titus, 192.
Merriam, William, 192.
Merrill, Elizer, 274.
Merrill, Gideon, 274.
Merrill, Samuel, 274.
Merrills, Cyprian, 89.
Merrills, Joseph, 251.
Merrills, Medad, 111.
Merrills, Nathaniel, 59.
Merrills, Noah, 124.
Merrils, Joseph, 247.
Merrils, Meade, 71.
Merriman, Amos, 276.
Merriman, Cabb, 276.
Merriman, Caleb, 192, 193, 194.
Merriman, Charles, 112.
Merriman, Elisha, 193.
Merriman, Israel, 202.
Merriman, Jesse, 193.
Merrit, Thomas, 29, 31.
Merritt, Ebenezer, 79.
Merrow, Elisha, 132.
Merrow, John, 245, 249.
Merry, Ebenezer, 235, 274.
Merwin, Daniel, 276.
Messenger, David, 145, 146, 147.
Messenger, Elisha, 27.
Messenger, Lemuel, 67.
Metcalf, Andrew, 149.
Metcalf, Dan, 149.
Metcalf, David, 162.
Metcalf, Ebenezer, 149.

## INDEX.

Metcalf, John, 201.
Metcalf, Theodore, 6.
Mezen, Joseph, 74.
Michal, George, 63.
Michel, George, 127.
Middlebrook, Stephen, 278.
Middletown, 18, 55, 58, 59, 60, 61, 62, 66, 68, 69, 70, 71, 80, 81, 82, 88, 89, 90, 107, 204.
Midelbrooks, Oliver, 232.
Miel, 266.
Miel, Charles, 49.
Mildren, Mark, 69.
Miles, Charles, 22.
Miles, Daniel, 242, 243.
Miles, David, 204.
Miles, Isaac, 23.
Miles, Jesse, 172.
Miles, John, 192.
Miles, Joshua, 172.
Miles, William, 229.
Milford, 58, 60, 64, 66, 70, 75, 76, 88, 90, 103, 109, 204.
Millally, Michail, 249.
Millar, Hosea, 154.
Millenor, Charles, 262.
Miller, 210.
Miller, Augustus, 27.
Miller, Charles, 46, 58, 60.
Miller, David, 159, 160, 221.
Miller, Edward, 107.
Miller, Elijah, 143.
Miller, Enoch, 89.
Miller, Ezekiel, 238.
Miller, Ezekle, 239.
Miller, Giles, 135, 207.
Miller, Hosea, 156.
Miller, Ichabod, 210.
Miller, Jacob, 81.
Miller, Joel, 39.
Miller, John, 27, 120, 203, 235, 277.
Miller, Jonathan, 121, 203, 273.
Miller, Joseph, 257.
Miller, Nathaniel, 17, 60.
Miller, Samuel, 148.
Millington, 79.
Mills, A., 84.
Mills, Aaron, 21.
Mills, Alexander, 78.
Mills, Amasa, 209.
Mills, Benjamin, 202, 209.
Mills, Daniel, 85.
Mills, Jeddn, 180.
Mills, John, 55, 123.
Mills, Lewis, 210.
Mills, M., 214.
Mills, Peter, 2, 210, 225, 226.

Mills, Sally S., 275.
Mills, Samuel, Jr., 39, 267, 270.
Mills, Samuel F., 215.
Mills, Simeon, 39, 265.
Miner, 150.
Miner, Amos, 3, 4, 5, 150.
Miner, Charles, 128.
Miner, Clement, 264.
Miner, David, 150.
Miner, Israel, 136.
Miner, James, 124.
Miner, John, 156.
Miner, Jonathan, 140, 245.
Miner, Reuben, 85.
Miner, Stephen, 270.
"Minerva," 229, 230.
Minor, Aaron, 22.
Minor, Abel, 248.
Minor, Abele, 246.
Minor, Andrew, 24, 89.
Minor, Charles, 127.
Minor, James, 89.
Minor, John, 154.
Minor, Jonathan, 251.
Minor, Joseph, 232.
Minor, Richardson, 232.
Minor, Sylvester, 89.
Minor, Titus, 75.
Mitchel, Ephraim, 190.
Mitchel, George, 89, 128.
Mitchel, Hezekiah, 109.
Mitchel, John, 54, 185.
Mitchel, Joseph, 213.
Mitchel, Seth, 136.
Mitchel, Simeon, 173.
Mitchel, William, 127.
Mitchel, Zechariah, 117.
Mitchell, David, 23.
Mitchell, Samuel, 270.
Mitchell, William, 128.
Mitts, John, 231.
Mix, 97.
Mix, Amos, 23, 111, 266.
Mix, Caleb, 210, 224.
Mix, Elisha, 37, 274.
Mix, Enos, 118.
Mix, Isaac, 27.
Mix, John, 46, 104, 211.
Mix, Joseph, 266.
Mix, Josiah, 138, 276.
Mix, Peter, 104, 113, 130.
Mix, Thomas, 235.
Mix, Timothy, 270.
Mix, Zebediah, 230.
Mix, Zenas, 112.
Mix, Zenos, 70.
Moan, John, 264.
Mobbs, Samuel, 79.

Moffat, John, 184.
Moffitt, Andrew, 168.
Moffitt, John, 168.
Moger, Joseph, 69.
Molatto, Dick, 60.
Molbone, Peter, 260.
Molthrop, Acher, 242.
Molthrop, Jacob, 242.
Molton, Benjamin, 143.
Molton, Gurdon, 127.
Moltrop, John, 29.
Moltroup, Eli, 10.
Moltroup, Elihu, 10.
Moltroup, Joseph, 10.
Monroe, Joshua, 141.
Monson, Theophilus, 78.
Montague, Richard, 154.
Montigou, Bryon, 121.
Montigue, Richard, 156.
Moodus, 81.
Moody, Ebenezer, 85.
Moody, John, 42, 43.
Moody, Pero, 175.
Moody, Pichol, 19.
Moody, Tubal, 186.
Mookler, James, 188.
Moon, Isaac, 12.
Moor, Andrew, 39.
Moor, Ebenezer, 188.
Moor, Eber, 142.
Moor, Isaac, 203.
Moor, James, 233.
Moore, B., 170.
Moore, Eli, 278.
Moore, Michael, 254.
Moore, Obediah, 203.
Moore, Retrieve, 264.
Moore, Return, 238, 239.
Moore, Roger, 209.
Moore, William, 123.
Moorhouse, Ephraim, 119.
Moory, 55.
Morando, Peter, 117.
Morce, William, 15, 24.
Mordock, William, 161.
More, Caleb, 2.
More, William, 15.
Moredock, Daniel, 169.
Morehouse, David, 69, 152.
Morehouse, Ebenezer, 211.
Morehouse, James, 136.
Morehouse, Jesse, 152.
Morehouse, N., 84.
Morehouse, S., 177.
Morehouse, Solomon, 212.
Moretrup, David, 21.
Morey, Asa, 201.
Morey, Joseph, 64.

Morey, Reuben, 97.
Morgain, James, 60.
Morgan, Amos, 150.
Morgan, Asher, 185.
Morgan, Bemnir, 94.
Morgan, Christopher, 216.
Morgan, Daniel, 61.
Morgan, David, 276.
Morgan, Ephraim, 175.
Morgan, Isaac, 29, 216.
Morgan, Jacob, 205.
Morgan, James, 93, 208.
Morgan, James, Jr., 270.
Morgan, Jedediah, 216.
Morgan, Jesse, 82.
Morgan, John, 193, 216.
Morgan, John, 3d, 270.
Morgan, Jonathan, 150.
Morgan, Joseph, 95.
Morgan, Nathan, 74.
Morgan, Stephen, 216.
Morgan, Thomas, 216.
Morgan, William, 216.
Morgin, Peter, 171.
Morgin, Seth, 171.
Moriner, Henry, 81.
Morley, John, 137.
Morley, Thomas, 137.
Morrel, John, 85.
Morrill, Benjamin, 243.
Morris, Andrew, 252, 256, 262.
Morris, David, 19, 242.
Morris, Edmond, 257.
Morris, Edmund, 255.
Morris, Hial, 105.
Morris, Henry, 66.
Morris, James, 47, 50, 253.
Morris, John, 64, 200.
Morris, Thomas, 231.
Morris, William, 142.
Morrison, John, 245, 251.
Morrison, Norman, 262.
Morriss, Edmond, 262.
Morriss, Nathaniel, 52.
Morriss, William, 183.
Morse, Benjamin, 172.
Morse, James, 96.
Morse, Jesse, 134.
Morse, John, 227.
Morse, Joshua, Jr., 20.
Morse, Solomon, 139.
Morten, Jabez, 122.
Mortimer, John, 254.
Mortimore, Benjamin, 238, 239, 240.
Morton, Jedediah, 264.
Morwin, Samuel, 235.
Moseley, 214.

# INDEX. 341

Moseley, Abner, 208.
Moseley, E., 206.
Moseley, Ebenezer, 24.
Moseley, Increase, 212, 213, 223, 224, 225, 226, 227, 267.
Moseley, J., 177, 225, 226.
Moseley, Samuel, 14.
Moseley, William, 245, 248.
Mosely, Ebenezer, 23.
Mosely, Increase, 85, 222.
Moses, Abel, 13.
Moses, Abner, 98.
Moses, Daniel, 27.
Moses, Seba, 146, 147, 148.
Mosher, Joel, 103, 130.
Mosher, Naman, 185.
Mosher, Stephen, 127.
Moshier, Stephen, 117.
Mosley, Abner, 208.
Mosley, Daniel, 101.
Mosley, William, 244.
Moss, Benoni, 54.
Moss, Daniel, 108.
Moss, Ebenezer, 194.
Moss, Isiah, 78.
Moss, Jesse, 223.
Moss, John, 90.
Moss, Linus, 78.
Moss, Reuben, 111.
Moss, Solomon, 202.
Mossett, Thomas, 140.
Mott, Adam, 39.
Mott, Edward, 16, 17, 18, 19, 22, 23, 24, 174, 221.
Mott, Elihue, 62.
Mott, Lyman, 79.
Mott, Samuel, 211, 221.
Mott, William, 217.
Moucher, Stephen, 95.
Moulthrop, Joseph, 90.
Moulton, 114.
Moulton, Eli, 16.
Mourhouse, Thaddeus, 200.
Mouterdier, John, 255.
Moxley, Joseph, 270.
Moyer, George, 232.
Mullally, Micael, 245.
Munger, Bille, 111.
Munger, Billy, Jr., 37.
Munger, Daniel, 90.
Munger, Jonathan, 39.
Munger, Jehiel, 113, 116.
Munger, Timothy, 210.
Munn, Joseph, 66.
Munn, Oliver, 107.
Munn, Thomas, 38.
Munroe, John, 211.
Munroe, Noah, 98.

Munrow, Josiah, 169.
Munsell, Alpheus, 27.
Munsell, Daniel, 27.
Munsell, Pheneus, 249.
Munsill, John, 124.
Munsill, Levi, 124.
Munson, Hine, 275.
Munson, Ithael, 184.
Munson, Joseph, 190.
Munson, Lent, 112.
Munson, Levi, 9, 48.
Munson, Moses, 201.
Munson, Nathan, 201.
Munson, Orange, 112.
Munson, Thomas, 37.
Munson, Timothy, 21, 22.
Munson, William, 83, 90.
Murfey, Frederick, 247.
Murfey, Patrick, 58.
Murfy, James, 156.
Murooy, Benjamin, 39.
Murphey, Timothy, 251.
Murphy, Timothy, 253.
Murpy, James, 154.
Murrain, Jesse, 202.
Murray, James, 254.
Murray, John, 110, 116.
Murray, Noah, 89.
Murray, Warren, 71, 107.
Murrey, Abraham, 103.
Murrwin, Levi, 196.
Murry, Abraham, 54, 130.
Murry, Asael, 277.
Murry, Reuben, 33.
Murry, William, 231.
Musson, John, 37.
Myggott, Zebulon, 154.

N. Fairfield, 56, 57, 65.
N. Stratford, 53.
N. Winsor, 130.
Nails, Archibald, 238, 239.
Nails, John, 238.
Nales, John, 108.
Nash, Abram, 200.
Nash, Ezra, 195.
Nash, Jacob, 195.
Nash, Jedediah, 85.
Nash, John, 274.
Nash, Jonathan, 195.
Nash, Moses, 36.
Nash, Nathaniel, 66.
Nash, Noah, 217.
Nash, Thomas, 180.
Neal, Jeremiah, 79.
Neal, Thomas, 85.
Nearen, Loam, 7.
Nearin, 195.

Nearin, Joseph, 195.
Nearing, John, 36, 145, 146, 147, 148.
Nearing, Loammi, 27.
Neason, James, 123.
Neason, Robin, 123.
Neff, Daniel, 114, 116.
Neff, Salathiel, 114, 116.
Negro, Brestor, 131.
Negro, Briston, 90.
Negro, Cato, 104, 131.
Negro, Cuff, 90.
Negro, George, 232.
Negro, Jack, 35.
Negro, Newport, 61.
Negro, Peter, 237.
Negro, Phillip, 68, 71.
Negro, Plymouth, 68.
Negro, Prince, 54.
Negro, Roman, 213.
Negro, Sippo, 35.
Negro, Syfax, 61.
Negro, Titus, 18.
Negus, John, 10, 252.
Neil, Simon, 30, 31.
Neile, Edward, 235.
Nellson, Isaac, 123.
New Britain, 75.
New Fairfield, 88, 89, 118, 196, 197, 199.
New Hampshire, 12, 13, 59, 103.
New Hartford, 68, 89, 90, 99.
New Haven, 53, 54, 55, 58, 60, 61, 64, 65, 66, 69, 70, 76, 78, 81, 83, 88, 89, 90, 91, 102, 103, 104, 108, 109, 171, 178, 179, 189, 190, 191, 192, 193, 194, 207, 274, 279.
New London, 4, 30, 31, 54, 55, 56, 58, 60, 88, 89, 90, 91, 103, 141, 171, 183, 207, 216, 266, 267.
New Milford, 21, 23, 24, 52, 67, 68, 82, 83, 88, 89, 91, 102, 103, 104, 110, 202, 267.
New York, 12, 13, 31, 42, 59, 103, 136, 138, 139, 149, 150, 151, 155, 157, 164, 165, 167, 168, 170, 173, 196, 222, 226, 264, 274, 279.
Newberry, Roger, 207, 223, 274.
Newbury, 207.
Newbury, John, 27.
Newbury, R., 206.
Newbury, Roger, 223, 227.
Newbury, 195.
Newcomb, Bethewell, 163.
Newcomb, George, 234.
Newcomb, Joseph, 56.
Newcomb, Thomas, 98.

Newel, Asahel, 138.
Newel, Mark, 138.
Newel, Medad, 35.
Newel, Simean, 182.
Newell, Hanford, 110.
Newell, Isaac, Jr., 133.
Newell, Nathan, 19, 20.
Newell, Robert, 113.
Newhall, Daniel, 2.
Newhall, Jacob, 2.
Newhall, John, 2, 165.
Newman, Jonathan, 110.
Newport, 31.
Newson, Robert, 245, 249.
Newton, Abel, 216.
Newton, Asahel, 60.
Newton, Burwell, 193.
Newton, Daniel, 113, 116.
Newton, Enoch, 179.
Newton, Ezekiel, 110, 116.
Newton, George, Jr., 136.
Newton, Isaac, 2, 165.
Newton, John, 193.
Newton, Joseph, 134.
Newton, Matthew, 171.
Newton, Samuel, 186.
Newtown, 22, 52, 77, 78, 103, 195, 278.
Nichalson, Frances, 137.
Nichalson, Nathan, 137.
Nicholds, Thomas, 250.
Nichols, Asaph, 37.
Nichols, Benjamin, 225.
Nichols, Caleb, 38.
Nichols, Ebenezer, 198.
Nichols, Elnathan, 211, 265, 267.
Nichols, Gideon, 38.
Nichols, Hanford, 116.
Nichols, James, 184.
Nichols, Lemuel, 212.
Nichols, Noah, 37.
Nichols, Samuel, 77, 110, 116, 127.
Nicholson, Ebenezer, 234.
Nickalds, John, 60.
Nickerson, Baruck, 69.
Nickerson, Daniel, 216.
Nickerson, Eliphalet, 99.
Nickerson, Urane, 90.
Nickinson, Fransis, 139.
Nickolas. 230.
Nicols, Robart, 73.
Nicols, William, 196.
Nigh, David, 137.
Niles, Ceaser, 246, 250.
Niles, Frederick, 264.
Niles, Robert, 238, 239, 240, 241.
Niles, Robert, Jr., 262.

# INDEX. 343

Nivens, Robert, 188.
Nobels, Gideon, 54.
Noble, 12.
Noble, Elisha, 213.
Noble, Gideon, Jr., 18.
Noble, Mark, 270.
Noble, Morgan, 20, 23, 225.
Noble, Nathan, 209.
Noble, Roswell, 146, 148.
Noiles, David, 64.
Norfolk, 55, 90, 103, 267.
Norket, Silvenus, 160.
Norris, B., 84.
Norris, Jonathan, 38.
Norris, Samuel, 233.
North, Abijah, 39, 87.
North, Remembrance, 202.
North, Samuel, 191.
North, Seth, 39.
North, Simeon, 274.
North, Stephen, 39.
North Castle, 150, 170, 172.
North Fairfield, 278.
North River, 71, 138, 139.
North Stratford, 53, 69.
Northover, Richard, 12.
Northrop, Elijah, 94, 127.
Northrop, Josiah, 195.
Northrup, Aaron, 200.
Northrup, Andrew, 196.
Northrup, Elijah, 38, 117.
Northrup, Isaac, 109.
Northrup, Joshua, 195, 196.
Northward, 220.
Northway, George, 142.
Norton, 139, 222.
Norton, Abel, 39.
Norton, Abraham, 71, 113.
Norton, Andrew, 134.
Norton, Benjamin, 10.
Norton, Bethuel, 18, 95.
Norton, C., 214.
Norton, Charles, 193, 207, 223, 275.
Norton, Daniel, 191.
Norton, David, 163, 232, 252.
Norton, Eber, 202.
Norton, Eleazer, 34.
Norton, Elijah, 114, 116.
Norton, Elisha, 202.
Norton, Elnathan, 193, 270.
Norton, Henry, 23.
Norton, Ichabod, 211, 221.
Norton, J., 224.
Norton, Jacob, 13, 95, 117, 127.
Norton, Jera, 32.
Norton, Jerediah, 229.
Norton, Joel, 24.

Norton, John, 192, 193.
Norton, John A., 136.
Norton, Joseph, 68.
Norton, Levi, 139.
Norton, Nathan, 37.
Norton, Noah, 106, 126, 193.
Norton, Noah U., 105.
Norton, Samuel, 78.
Norton, Stephen, 193.
Norton, Thomas, 141.
Norton, William, 38, 126, 136.
Norwalk, 53, 54, 55, 56, 66, 68, 69, 77, 78, 102, 103, 104, 109, 194, 195, 196, 197, 198, 199, 200, 201, 202, 205, 217.
Norwich, 54, 55, 56, 59, 64, 66, 74, 80, 81, 82, 88, 89, 90, 91, 102, 103, 118, 267.
Nostrand, Peter, 242.
Nott, Hezakiah, 154.
Nott, Hezekiah, 100, 156.
Nott, John, 274.
Nott, William, 242.
Nowlan, Richard, 261.
Nuchcold, Thomas, 246.
Nugen, John, 113.
Nuton, Henry, 171.
Nyack, N. Y., 100.
Nye, Melitiah, 157.
Nye, Samuel, 97.
Nye, Silas, 149.

Oakes, Isaac, 188.
Oakley, John, 61.
Obey, Sampson, 19.
OBriant, John, 108.
Ocain, Oliver, 61.
Odell, Isaac, 69.
Odell, William, 253.
Odle, Nathan, 67.
Oen, Ebeneze, 186.
Ogden, Nathan, 152.
Oharra, Timothy, 90.
Olcott, 22.
Olcott, Hezekiah, 36.
Olcott, J. E., 84.
Olcott, James, 17.
Olcott, Jedediah, 133, 142.
Olcott, John E., 181, 219, 254.
Olcott, Jonathan, 187, 188.
Olcutt, Giles, 68.
Olcutt, Isaac, 126.
Olds, Aaron, 77, 136.
Olds, Daniel, 186.
Oliv, William, 63.
Oliver, Isaac, 140.
Oliver, Nathaniel, 259.

"Oliver Cromwell," 244, 245, 247, 248, 249, 252, 256, 261, 262, 263, 264.
Ollin, William, 90.
Olmstead, Ashbel, 97.
Olmstead, D., 206.
Olmstead, David, 224, 226.
Olmstead, Matthew, 85.
Olmsted, Abijah, 68.
Olmsted, Daniel, 27, 200.
Olmsted, Daniel, Jr., 142.
Olmsted, David, 195, 208.
Olmsted, David, 2d, 200.
Olmsted, Elihu, 274.
Olmsted, James, 49, 76.
Olmsted, Jered, 195.
Olmsted, Jesse, 123.
Olmsted, John, 181.
Olmsted, Joshua, 106, 126.
Olmsted, Mathew, 195.
Olmsted, Moses, 278.
Olmsted, Richard, 22.
Olmsted, Ruben, 218.
Olmsted, Samuel, 200.
Olmsted, Thomas, 23, 274.
Olvord, Huit, 80.
Orcutt, Caleb, 18, 23, 54.
Orcutt, Darius, 100.
Orcutt, David, 270.
Orms, Jonathan, 63.
Ormsby, Amos, 23.
Ormsby, Elijah, 247, 252.
Ormsby, Eliphalet, 185.
Ormsby, John, 143.
Ormsby, Stephen, 143.
Orton, Darius, 201.
Orton, Eliada, 201.
Orton, Samuel, 201.
Orvis, Roger, 39.
Orsborn, Samuel, 16.
Osborn, 164.
Osborn, Asahel, 120.
Osborn, Benjamin, 235.
Osborn, Isaac, 201.
Osborn, Israel, 57.
Osborn, Jeremiah, 201.
Osborn, John, 201, 224.
Osborn, Josiah, 29.
Osborn, Nathan, 181, 219.
Osborn, Samuel, 181, 208, 219
Osborn, William, 57, 141.
Osborne, Samuel, 211.
Osborne, William, 266.
Oshourn, Josiah, 105.
Osburn, Thaddeus, 119.
Oswald, Colonel, 90.
Otis, Joseph, 113, 270.
Otis, Levi, 58.
Otis, Richard, 175.
Otis, William, 264.
Ouer, Daniel, 213.
Overton, Aron, 81.
Oviat, Ebenezer, 204.
Ovit, Samuel, 263.
Ovitt, William, 109.
Owen, Alvan, 68.
Owen, Asa, 111.
Owen, Isaac, 82.
Owens, Daniel, 15.

Packerr, James, 127.
Page, Abel, 199, 201.
Page, Asa, 201.
Page, Daniel, 201.
Page, Ephraim, 65.
Page, Gad, 96.
Page, Jacob, 10, 16.
Page, Jeremiah, 55.
Page, John, 197.
Page, Luther, 10, 23, 71, 112.
Page, Rayner, 79.
Page, Reuben, 201.
Page, William, 38.
Page, Zera, 5.
Pain, Edward, 2.
Paine, Edward, 165.
Paine, John, 79.
Paine, Rufus, 35.
Palingtine, Cash, 75.
Palley, Daniel, 63.
Palmer, 112.
Palmer, Barnabas, 10.
Palmer, Benjamin, 171, 273.
Palmer, Bristow, 264.
Palmer, Chiliab, 73.
Palmer, Daniel, 64.
Palmer, E., 84.
Palmer, Edward, 47.
Palmer, Elias, 222.
Palmer, Elijah, 40, 149, 212.
Palmer, Ichabod, 210.
Palmer, Ichabud, 186.
Palmer, Jabez, 259.
Palmer, Jarius, 171.
Palmer, John, 10.
Palmer, Jonah, 74.
Palmer, Jonathan, 171.
Palmer, Joseph, 171.
Palmer, Joshua, 262.
Palmer, Nathan, 71.
Palmer, Stephen, 210.
Palmer, Thadeus, 170.
Palmer, Thomas, 104, 131.
Palmer, Vaniah, 143, 184.
Palmer, William, 245, 251, 262.
Palmeter, Amaziah, 35.

INDEX. 345

Palmetur, Silvenus, 199.
Palmister, William, 66.
Palms, Guy, 264.
Pangbourn, Adonijah, 34.
Parce, David, 188.
Pardee, Isaac, 10, 34, 41, 43.
Pardee, Jacob, 10.
Pardee, Jonathan, 90.
Pardee, Lemuel, 196.
Pardee, Nathaniel, 78.
Pardee, Stephen, 197, 208.
Pardie, Chandler, 270.
Pardy, Eli, 138.
Parish, Oliver, 114, 185.
Parish, Roswell, 170, 185, 267.
Parish, Samuel, 171.
Parish, William, 29, 185.
Park, Ezekiel, 170.
Park, J., 170.
Park, John, 138.
Park, Jonas, 258.
Park, Levi, 175.
Park, Levy, 258.
Park, Moses, 175.
Park, Rufus, 175.
Park, Stephen, 216.
Parke, Amaziah, 170.
Parke, Elijah, 172.
Parke, Robart, 170.
Parke, Robert, 170.
Parke, Simeon, 169.
Parker, Abraham, 111.
Parker, Amasa, 39.
Parker, Charles, 194.
Parker, Daniel, 194.
Parker, Eliab, 90.
Parker, Eliada, 235.
Parker, Eliakim, 194, 235.
Parker, Elijah, 73.
Parker, Ephrim, Jr., 2.
Parker, Gamaliel, 69.
Parker, Isaac, 111.
Parker, John, 58, 69, 70, 111, 165.
Parker, Jonathan, 18, 23.
Parker, Joshua, 194, 235.
Parker, Leve, 235.
Parker, Levi, 95, 194.
Parker, Matthew, 38.
Parker, Nathaniel, 126.
Parker, Peter, 261.
Parker, Phinehas, 111, 116.
Parker, Samuel, 178.
Parker, Seth, 2.
Parker, Timothy, 111, 238, 239, 252, 256, 261, 262, 263.
Parker, William, 64, 71.
Parker, Zechariah, 183.
Parkhurst, Duthan, 63.
Parkhurst, Joseph, 2.
Parkhurst, Lemuel, 63.
Parkiton, Denis, 69.
Parks, Aaron, 125, 130.
Parks, Aron, 104.
Parks, Daniel, 61, 135.
Parks, John, 61.
Parks, Nehemiah, 171.
Parks, Rufus, 184.
Parks, Samuel, 106, 126.
Parlms, Samuel, 56.
Parmalee, 42.
Parmele, Charles, 102.
Parmele, Isaac, 277.
Parmele, Joel, 192, 277.
Parmele, Phinehas, 193.
Parmelee, Jeremiah, 90.
Parmelee, Oliver, 38.
Parmeley, Amos, 201.
Parmelie, Thomas, 270.
Parmerle, Charles, 17.
Parmile, Thomas, 173.
Parret, David, 233.
Parrish, Oliver, 116.
Parrot, John, 109.
Parry, Henry, 252.
Parseval, Thomas, 247.
Parsivel, James, 2.
Parson, 124.
Parson, Amos, 189.
Parson, Joseph, 189.
Parsons, 279.
Parsons, Benjamin, 36.
Parsons, Chattwil, 145, 147.
Parsons, Daniel, 34.
Parsons, David, 46, 53, 78, 191.
Parsons, Hezekiah, 18, 23, 188.
Parsons, Jahez, 46.
Parsons, John, 240, 254, 259.
Parsons, Jonathan, 54.
Parsons, Joseph, 101.
Parsons, Marshfield, 211.
Parsons, Moses, 79.
Parsons, Osburn, 68.
Parsons, Samuel H., 17, 18, 19, 21, 22, 23, 24, 25, 71.
Parsons, Simeon, 134, 191.
Parsons, Thomas, 57.
Pasco, Jonathan, 105.
Pason, Jacob, 68.
Patague, George, 251.
Patchen, Azor, 68.
Patchen, Azur, 77.
Patchen, Elijah, 69.
Patchen, Jacob, 110.
Patchen, Joseph, 85.
Patchen, William, 85.
Patchen, Woolcot, 69.

Patchers, Samuel, 126.
Patchin, David, 233.
Patchin, James, 128.
Patchin, Jared, 198.
Patchin, Martin, 232.
Pater, Shelden, 53.
Paterson, John, 241.
Paterson, William, 37.
Patten, Israel, 90.
Patterson, Andrew, 90, 236.
Patterson, Ansel, 114.
Patterson, James, 244, 247, 248.
Patterson, John, 23.
Patterson, Matthew, 35.
Patterson, Robert, 15.
Patterson, Samuel, 141, 181, 190, 219.
Patterson, William, 13.
Pauridge, Ananias, 35.
Paylon, Andrew, 141.
Payn, Benjamin, Jr., 6.
Payn, Dan, 6.
Payn, Nehemiah, 6.
Payn, Nehimiah, 182.
Payn, Stephen, 6, 259.
Payn, Stephen, Jr., 6.
Payne, Barnabas, 41.
Payne, Barnebas, 43.
Payne, Edward, 207.
Payne, Eleazer, 105.
Payne, Nehemiah, 149.
Payne, Rufus, 87.
Payne, Stephen, 149.
Payson, James, 207.
Peak, Samuel, 2.
Peake, Thomas, 184.
Pearce, Benjamin, 17.
Pearce, John, 16.
Pearle, John, 122.
Pearson, Daniel, 2.
Pearson, Ephrim, Jr., 2.
Pearson, Samuel, Jr., 2.
Peas, 133.
Peas, Pelatiah, 231.
Peas, Peter, 90.
Peas, Stephen, 231.
Pease, Abiel, 208.
Pease, Alpheus, 55.
Pease, Asaph, 255.
Pease, Benjamin, 32.
Pease, Daniel, 94.
Pease, David, 17, 94.
Pease, Eli, 23.
Pease, John, 2, 32, 250.
Pease, Joseph, 101.
Pease, Nathaniel, 159.
Pease, Silas, 57, 58, 60.
Pease, Sylvanus, 96.

Peat, James, 139.
Peat, William, 247.
Peck, Aaron, 17, 271.
Peck, Augustus, 108.
Peck, Benjamin, 98, 185, 211.
Peck, Dan, 275.
Peck, Daniel, 127.
Peck, Darius, 45, 90.
Peck, David, 101.
Peck, Eliphalet, 85, 109.
Peck, George, 212, 226.
Peck, Gideon, 202.
Peck, James, 18, 19, 151, 275.
Peck, Jesse, 95, 114, 116.
Peck, John, 71, 109, 181, 195, 219.
Peck, Josiah, 181, 219.
Peck, Judson, 181, 219.
Peck, Levy, 266.
Peck, Moses, 201.
Peck, Peter, 275.
Peck, Phinehas, 183.
Peck, Samuel, 25, 32, 127, 128, 209, 210.
Peck, Samuel, Jr., 16, 17, 19, 22, 24.
Peck, Silas, Jr., 90.
Peck, Stephen, 194.
Peck, Thomas, 93.
Peck, Ward, 108.
Peck, Zebulon, 90.
Peeck, Benjamin, 199.
Peek, Job, 151.
Peek, Josiah, 151.
Peek, Judson, 151.
Peekskill, 222.
Peepoon, Timothy, 5.
Peet, Benjamin, 38.
Peet, Daniel, 117.
Peet, Gideon, 135.
Peet, Samuel, 38.
Peet, William, 252.
Peirce, David, 187, 198.
Peirce, Deleno, 167.
Peirce, John, 168.
Peirce, Seth, 209.
Peirce, Silas, 198.
Peirson, Abel, 189.
Peirson, Abraham, 189.
Pelton, Daniel, 118.
Pelton, David, 90.
Pelton, George, 230.
Pelton, Jonathan, 135.
Pelton, Joseph, 134.
Pelton, Moses, 230.
Pember, Andrew, 2.
Pember, John, 40.
Pember, Samuel, 2.
Pember, Thomas, 2.

INDEX. 347

Pendleton, Daniel, 90.
Pendleton, David, 75.
Pembleton, Jabez, 267.
Pembleton, John, 264.
Pembleton, Simon, 264.
Penfield, Jesse, 135.
Penfield, John, 199, 208.
Penfield, Peter, 196, 208, 224.
Penfield, Simeon, 135.
Penneoyr, Thomas, 217.
Pennoyer, J., 84.
Pennoyer, John, 210.
Penoyer, Samuel, 85.
Pepoon, Benjamin, 159.
Pepoon, Joseph, 159.
Pepper, Michael, 240, 241.
Perce, Eli, 66.
Percival, Francis, 20.
Percival, John, 211.
Percival, Timothy, 221.
Perigo, John, 185.
Pering, Elisha, 146, 147.
Perit, Peter, 212.
Perkins, Abner, 202.
Perkins, Daniel, 93, 123.
Perkins, Daniel, Jr., 90.
Perkins, Ebenezer, 45.
Perkins, Elisha, 82, 174.
Perkins, Jabez, 210.
Perkins, Jabez, 3d, 256, 262.
Perkins, Jacob, 216.
Perkins, Jason, 17.
Perkins, John, 210.
Perkins, Obadiah, 270.
Perkins, Peter, 211.
Perkins, Philip, 94.
Perkins, Phineas, 277.
Perkins, Samuel, 25, 161.
Perkins, Simeon, 193, 276.
Perkins, Stephen, 192.
Perkins, William, 19.
Perpener, Solomon, 246.
Perren, John, 163.
Perren, Zachariah, 163.
Perrey, Abijah, 54.
Perries, John, 128.
Perrit, Peter, 32.
Perritt, Samuel, 24.
Perry, Aaron, 199.
Perry, Benjamin, 66.
Perry, Bennet, 86.
Perry, Ebenezer, 90.
Perry, Ezekiel, 21.
Perry, Isaac, 25.
Perry, Obadiah, 14.
Perry, Samuel, 66.
Perry, Sylvanus, 46, 90.
Perry, Thomas, 24.

Persevall, Thomas, 248.
Person, Daniel, 166.
Persons, Isaac, 34.
Persons, Jabez, 163.
Persons, Levi, 75.
Persons, Simeon, 75.
Peter, 230.
Peter, Galloway, 54.
Peters, Andrew, 114.
Peters, Joseph, 163.
Peters, Samuel, 123, 163.
Petott, Enos, 270.
Pettengall, Asaph, 123.
Pettibon, Elijah, 39.
Pettibone, A., 214.
Pettibone, Abel, 20, 142, 164.
Pettibone, Abraham, 182.
Pettibone, Ahijah, 164.
Pettibone, Dudly, 164.
Pettibone, Giles, 222.
Pettibone, Jacob, 7.
Pettibone, John, 212.
Pettibone, Jonathan, 164, 227.
Pettibone, Ozias, 188.
Pettingall, Jacob, 123.
Pettit, Enos, 34, 68.
Petty, William, 261.
Pharnum, Elijah, 185.
Phelps, 22, 202, 209.
Phelps, Aaron, 162.
Phelps, Abijah, 203.
Phelps, Alexander, 159, 270.
Phelps, Amos, 20, 39.
Phelps, Amos, Jr., 162.
Phelps, Beniah, 162.
Phelps, D., 177.
Phelps, Daniel, 162.
Phelps, David, 138, 148, 164, 207, 211, 212.
Phelps, David, Jr., 145.
Phelps, Eli, 163.
Phelps, Elijah, 69, 149, 203.
Phelps, Elisha, 6, 7, 163.
Phelps, Elkanah, 39.
Phelps, Ephraim, 162.
Phelps, Ezekiel, Jr., 203.
Phelps, Hezekiah, 118.
Phelps, Homer, 58.
Phelps, Ira, 203.
Phelps, Jeddiah, 2.
Phelps, Jedediah, 3.
Phelps, John, 139.
Phelps, Joseph, 39, 149, 197.
Phelps, Joshua, 159, 162.
Phelps, Joshua, Jr., 162.
Phelps, Josiah, 202, 207.
Phelps, Noah, 188, 203, 209, 221.
Phelps, Obediah, 162.

Phelps, Oliver, 20.
Phelps, Ozias, 205.
Phelps, Ozios, 164.
Phelps, Reuben, 51, 52, 139.
Phelps, Roger, 134, 162.
Phelps, Roswell, 162.
Phelps, Samuel, 162, 203.
Phelps, Seth, 47.
Phelps, Silas, 53, 121.
Phelps, Solomon, 160.
Phelps, Thomas, 59, 208.
Phelps, Thomas, Jr., 7.
Phelps, Timothy, Jr., 162.
Phelps, William, 67, 199.
Pheney, Joseph, 131.
Philemor, Henry, 274.
Philips, Eliphilet, 75.
Philips, Gideon, 273.
Philips, James, 51.
Phillips, G., 213.
Phillips, George, 208.
Phillips, Giddeon, 80.
Phillips, James, 29.
Phillips, Thomas, 110.
Phillips, Thompson, 229.
Phinney, Joseph, 104, 125.
Pick, Daniel, 95.
Picket, Benjamin, 197.
Picket, David, 200.
Picket, Ezra, 218.
Picket, Joseph, 189.
Picket, Ozias, 191.
Picket, Stephen, 218.
Picket, Thomas, 90, 270.
Pickett, Benjamin, 193.
Pickle, Hendrick, 254.
Picksley, Elijah, 76.
Pieno, Zenus, 81.
Pierce, Daniel, 93.
Pierce, Delino, 172.
Pierce, Henry, 254.
Pierce, John, 126, 127.
Pierce, Samuel, 35, 61, 133.
Pierce, Seth, 210.
Pierce, William, 13.
Pierpoint, John, 179.
Pierpoint, Thomas, 11.
Pierpont, Thomas, 10.
Pierson, Ephraim, 106.
Pierson, Samuel, Jr., 165.
Pike, James, 36.
Pike, Jonathan, 167.
Pike, Samuel, 36.
Pilgrim, Thomas, 61.
Pillias, A., 84.
Pimber, Andrew, 165.
Pineo, James, 159, 163.
Pineo, Jeams, Jr., 5.

Pinkham, Selvenus, 245, 249.
Pinnoo, James, 4.
Pinneo, Jeams, Jr., 6.
Pinney, Ebenezer, 165.
Pinney, Elezer, 2.
Pinney, John, 2.
Pinney, Joseph, Jr., 2.
Pinney, Lemuel, 1, 166.
Pitcher, Ebenezer, Jr., 22.
Pitkin, George, 18, 165, 227.
Pitkin, Richard, 221.
Pitts, Benjamin, 15.
Pitts, Richard, 110.
Placey, William, 74.
Plainfield, 65, 66, 74, 79, 82, 118.
Plank, Isaih, 79.
Plant, Ethiel, 140.
Plant, Solomon, 190.
Plant, Stephen, 164, 201.
Plats, Nathan, 196.
Platt, Dan, 178.
Platt, Daniel, 199, 211.
Platt, Ebenezer, 104, 131.
Platt, James, 85, 199.
Platt, Jonas, 84.
Platt, Jonathan, 85.
Platt, Joseph, 84.
Platt, Phineas, 277.
Platts, John, 178.
Platts, Noah, 178.
Platts, Radireck, 184.
Plum, Charles, 258.
Plum, Justis, 233.
Plumb, Amariah, 25.
Plumb, Jesse, 135.
Plumbe, Daniel, 29.
Plumley, Joseph, 21.
Pluymert, William, 229.
Poghcegh, Thomas, 125.
Pollard, Isaac, 76.
Polley, Alpheus, 90.
Polley, Amasa, 87.
Pomeroy, Benjamin, 90.
Pomeroy, Isaac, 188.
Pomeroy, Medad, 63.
Pomeroy, Ralph, 46.
Pomfret, 58, 66, 69, 79, 90, 101, 104, 118.
Pomp, Jacob, 90.
Pomroy, Peletiah, 57.
Pond, Bartholomew, 209.
Pond, Peter, 242, 243.
Pond, Timothy, 22.
Pond, Wiram, 69.
Ponds, Henry, 122.
Pool, Chester, 185.
Pool, David, 252, 270.
Poole, John, 55.

INDEX. 349

Pooley, Henery, 87.
Poor, Jonathan, 232.
Pope, Roberd, 189.
Popenah, Solomon, 251.
Pornett, Joseph, 246.
Porrage, Ananias, 130.
Porrutt, Joshua, 250.
Porter, A., 212.
Porter, Aaron, 27, 191, 200.
Porter, Abijah, 101.
Porter, Alexander, 59.
Porter, Amos, 162.
Porter, Ashbel, 20.
Porter, Benjamin, 79, 82.
Porter, Daniel, 2, 68, 165.
Porter, David, 244, 247, 248.
Porter, Elijah, 119, 133.
Porter, Eliot, 163.
Porter, Gideon, 138.
Porter, Increas, 162.
Porter, James, 209.
Porter, Joel, 162.
Porter, John, 2, 67, 80, 182, 207.
Porter, Jonathan, 160.
Porter, Jonathan, Jr., 2.
Porter, Joseph, 54, 133.
Porter, Joshua, 221.
Porter, Moses, 244.
Porter, Nathaniel, 0, 110.
Porter, Noah, 210.
Porter, Phineas, 17, 19, 22, 24, 25, 212.
Porter, Stephen, 100.
Porter, T., 84.
Porter, William, 105.
Porter, Zachariah, 35.
Post, Abraham, 136.
Post, David, 163.
Post, John, 163.
Post, Josiah, 178.
Post, Simeon, 259.
Post, Stephen, 55.
Poston, Samuel, 251.
Potague, George, 246.
Pottage, Jabez, 74.
Potter, 50, 112.
Potter, Amos, 235.
Potter, Benjamin, 71.
Potter, Daniel, 54, 138.
Potter, David, 162.
Potter, Edward, 137.
Potter, Joel, 70, 112, 182.
Potter, John, 15, 85.
Potter, Lemuel, 61.
Potter, Levi, 11.
Potter, Medad, 108.
Potter, Moses, 108.
Potter, Nathan, 106.

Potter, Shéldon, 121.
Potter, Stephen, 48, 70.
Poughkeepsie, 23.
Powel, Daniel, 59.
Powel, John, 170.
Powell, William, 244, 247, 248.
Powers, Asa, 85.
Powers, Cyrus, 66.
Powers, Gregory, 229.
Powers, James, 27, 79, 115.
Powers, James, Jr., 116.
Powers, Lawrence, 150.
Powers, Thomas, 138, 200.
Prat, Cary, 5.
Pratt, Abijah, 59.
Pratt, Abraham, 178.
Pratt, Abraham, Jr., 178.
Pratt, Asa, 178.
Pratt, Benjamin, 11.
Pratt, Daniel, 178.
Pratt, David, 96, 100.
Pratt, David B., 178.
Pratt, Edmond, 178.
Pratt, Et[ ], 178.
Pratt, Ezra, 67, 178.
Pratt, George, 187.
Pratt, Gideon, 178.
Pratt, Isaiah, 123.
Pratt, James, 81, 162.
Pratt, Jasper, 61.
Pratt, Jesse, 178.
Pratt, Jesse, 2d, 178.
Pratt, John, 178.
Pratt, Jonathan, 178.
Pratt, Joseph, 93, 188.
Pratt, Peter, 138.
Pratt, Phinis, 178.
Pratt, Ruben, 178.
Pratt, Russell, 105.
Pratt, Samuel, 63, 178.
Pratt, Taber, 178.
Pratt, William, 187.
Pratt, Zephemiah, 178.
Prechard, Jabez, 179.
Prentice, John, 245, 248.
Prentice, Jonas, 20, 48, 90.
Prentice, Samuel, 17.
Prescott, Titus, 57.
Presson, Joseph, 142.
Presson, Shubal, 186.
Preston, Benjamin, 194.
Preston, Charles, 276.
Preston, Daniel, 270.
Preston, David, 35.
Preston, Jacob, 143.
Preston, John, 139.
Preston, Jonathan, 76.
Preston, Joseph, 39, 101.

Preston, Noah, 202.
Preston, Zera, 15.
Preston, 22, 24, 52, 55, 58, 60, 66, 74, 88, 89, 90, 103, 104.
Prevett, John, 37.
Pribble, Samuel, 278.
Price, Ebenezer, 200.
Price, Joseph, 186.
Price, Levi, 90.
Price, Nathaniel, 101.
Price, Paul, 69.
Price, Rufus, 90.
Price, Samuel, 65.
Pride, Absolom, 279.
Pride, Reuben, 46.
Primas, Japhura, 75.
Prince, Christopher, 245, 249.
Prince, Joseph, 190.
Prince, Zeckry, 59.
Prindle, Abiel, 86.
Prindle, Abijah, 77.
Prindle, Ezra, 16.
Prindle, Zalmon, 77.
Prior, Abner, 47, 133.
Prior, Allen, 114.
Prior, Ebenezer, 23.
Prior, Jesse, 135.
Prior, Josiah, 81.
Prissnear, Asa, 55.
Pritchard, Benjamin, 109.
Pritchard, Ebenezer, Jr., 22.
Prout, James, 194.
Prout, William, 111.
Providence, R. I., 55, 103, 118.
Provost, Daniel, 76.
Provost, Richard, 243.
Prudden, John, 142.
Prunwugh, Joseph, 141.
Pryor, Rozll, 139.
Puffer, Daniel, 114, 116.
Puffer, George, 237.
Puffer, Lazarus, 90.
Puffer, Simeon, 160.
Pulford, Edmund, 215, 236.
Pulford, Elisha, 76.
Pulford, Samuel, 122.
Pullman, John, 255.
Pulman, John, 52.
Pumham, Ephraim, 262.
Punderson, Ahimz, 108.
Purkines, Charles, 70.
Purple, Elias, 82.
Putnam, 16, 18.
Putnam, Israel, 14, 16, 17, 20, 22, 23, 24, 25.
Putnam, Israel, Jr., 20.
Putnam, William, 29.
Putney, Jonathan, 64.

Quakenbush, Abraham, 99.
Quebec, 40.
Quecheats, Peter, 17.
Quin, Felix, 253.
Quinley, Thomas, 140.
Quintard, Evert, 218.
Quinturd, Peter, Jr., 218.
Quirk, William, 53.
Quochecks, Peter, 18.
Quy, Lebbeus, 231.

R[    ]l, Joshua, 66.
Racke, William, 118.
Rainsford, Joseph, 170.
Rambow, William, 238.
Ramond, Joshua, 171.
Ramsdale, Ezra, 19.
Randal, Christopher, 171.
Randal, Nicholas, 171.
Randall, David, 34.
Randall, Jedediah, 150.
Randall, Joseph, 171.
Randall, Pelik, 171.
Randol, Amos, 184.
Randol, Douty, 257.
Randol, John, 250.
Randolp, John, 246.
Ranney, Amos, 82.
Ranney, Comfort, 58, 61.
Ranney, David, 270.
Ranney, Solomon, 128.
Ranney, Stephen, 61, 77.
Ranny, Amos, 256.
Ranny, Comfort, 141.
Ranny, Nathaniel, Jr., 141.
Ranny, S., 84.
Ranny, Simo, 141.
Ranny, Solomon, 127.
Ransom, Abner, 251.
Ransom, Elijah, 46.
Ransom, Joseph, 185.
Ransome, Ebenezer, 170.
Rathbone, Theodore, 185.
Rathburn, Ashley, 105.
Rawland, Sherman, 68.
Rawles, Aaron, 107.
Rawlinson, Bartholomew, 113.
Rawlinson, Reuben, 113.
Ray, Daniel, 184.
Ray, Stevene, 171.
Raymond, Abraham, 85.
Raymond, Amaziah, 79.
Raymond, C., 177, 210.
Raymond, Clap, 226.
Raymond, D., 84.
Raymond, David, 152, 242.
Raymond, Elijah, 84.
Raymond, Hezekiah, 218.

## INDEX.

Raymond, Isaac, 218.
Raymond, James, 104, 131.
Raymond, Jesse, 212.
Raymond, John, 218.
Raymond, Moses, 265, 270.
Raymond, Nathaniel, 218.
Raymond, Nathaniel, Jr., 218.
Raymond, Samuel, 90.
Raymond, Seth, 35.
Raymond, Uriah, 85, 212, 218, 226.
Raymond, William, 85, 261.
Raymong, Samuel, 233.
Raymont, William, 16.
Raynsford, J., 209.
Raynsford, Joseph, 169.
Read, Jonathan, 85.
Read, Philip, 2.
Read, Richard, 32.
Read, Silas, 2.
Read, Zalmon, 19, 22, 23, 24, 25.
Reading, 110.
Redding, 54, 69, 80, 89, 90.
Redfield, Nathan, 277.
Redfield, Samuel, 135.
Redfield, William, 73.
Reed, 114.
Reed, Amas, 55.
Reed, Curtis, 233, 252, 256, 262.
Reed, Enoch, 45, 51.
Reed, Jonathan, 63, 135.
Reed, Joseph, 74.
Reed, Reuben, 90.
Reed, Silas, 165.
Reed, Stephen, 85.
Reed, Thomas, 69, 99, 232, 240.
Reed, William, 95, 117, 127.
Reed, Zalmon, 180.
Reen, John, 34.
Rees, John, 247, 253.
Remington, Josiah, 23.
Renner, Samuel, 164.
Resseguie, Alexander, 195.
Resseguie, James, 200.
Revers, Thomas, 259.
Reves, Elishua, 191.
Rexford, Isaac, 117, 127.
Reymond, Aaron, 53.
Reymond, Abraham, 54.
Reymond, Benjamin, 85.
Reymond, Isaac, 85.
Reymond, John, 85.
Reymond, William, 54.
Reynalds, Justice, 78.
Reynold, Samuel, 85.
Reynolds, David, 77.
Reynolds, Hezekiah, 136.
Reynolds, James, 136.
Reynolds, James B., 136.

Reynolds, John, 188.
Reynolds, Jonathan, 21.
Reynolds, Joshua, 124.
Reynolds, Matthew, 213.
Reynolds, Solomon, 270.
Rhode Island, 16, 31, 59, 64, 65, 66, 143, 221, 275.
Rice, Abner, 194.
Rice, Archibald, 19.
Rice, Asa, 34.
Rice, Charles, 94, 117, 127.
Rice, David, 18, 42, 43, 90.
Rice, Ezra, 192.
Rice, Jehiel, Jr., 194.
Rice, Jesse, 275.
Rice, Joel, 194.
Rice, John, 82.
Rice, Jonathan, 186.
Rice, Jotham, 111.
Rice, Nehemiah, 49, 76.
Rice, Samuel, 193, 276.
Rice, Thomas, 239, 252.
Rice, William, 186.
Rich, Amos, 96, 117, 127.
Rich, Lemuel, 267, 270.
Richards, 133.
Richards, B., 84, 214.
Richards, Benjamin, 133, 134, 175, 209, 210, 212, 225.
Richards, Isaac, 266.
Richards, J., 214.
Richards, Jacob, 85.
Richards, John, 263.
Richards, Nathaniel, 38, 69.
Richards, R., 212.
Richards, Samuel, 46, 47.
Richards, William, 45.
Richardson, Andrew, 3.
Richardson, Ephraim, 87.
Richardson, Roswell, 163.
Richardson, Samuel, 199.
Richenson, Stephen, 185.
Richmernd, Edward, 34.
Richmond, Abner, 105.
Richmond, Jonathan, 37.
Richmond, Oziel, 126.
Richmond, Samuel, 37.
Ridgefield, 67, 68, 69, 83, 90, 110, 200.
Ridgway, Thomas, 258.
Riggs, Jeremiah, 201.
Riggs, John, 211.
Riggs, Joseph, Jr., 189.
Riggs, Laban, 90.
Riley, 124.
Riley, Ashbell, 156.
Riley, Ashbil, 163.
Riley, Charles, 74.

Riley, Jonathan, 19.
Riley, Nathaniel, 257.
Riley, Roger, 207.
Rily, John, 39.
Rindge, Thomas, 95.
Rindge, William, 143.
Ringe, Daniel, 185.
Ripley, Charles, 74, 114.
Ripley, Gamaliel, 183.
Ripley, John, 20, 24, 25.
Ripley, Pirum, 258.
Ripton, 115.
Risley, James, 261.
Risley, Levi, 244, 247, 248.
Risley, Richard, 133, 244, 247, 248.
Risley, Ruben, 157.
Risley, Samuel, 157.
Ritch, John, 243.
Rix, Nathan, 175.
Rix, Rufus, 175.
Roach, John, 90.
Roads, Joseph, 156.
Roads, William, 156.
Robards, Aaron, 204.
Robarts, [ ], Jr., 244.
Robarts, Aaron, 244.
Robarts, Eliphalet, 244.
Robarts, Nathaniel, 82.
Robarts, William, 244.
Robartson, William, 37.
Robbarts, David, 122.
Robberds, Daniel, 141.
Robberds, Ebenezer, 141.
Robberds, Stephen, 141.
Robberts, Isaac, 70.
Robbin, Michael, 38.
Robbins, Ammi R., 33.
Robbins, Benoni, 106, 126.
Robbins, Daniel, 262.
Robbins, Frederick, 153, 155.
Robbins, Jacob, 124.
Robbins, John, 135, 222.
Robbins, Joseph, 74.
Robbins, Richard, 80.
Robbins, Samuel, 80.
Robbinson, Samuel, 160.
Roberds, Luke, 108.
Roberds, Noah, 103.
Roberson, Reuben, 101.
Roberts, Abial, 90.
Roberts, Amos, 17.
Roberts, Aron, 247, 252.
Roberts, Charles, 273.
Roberts, Clark, 60.
Roberts, Elefolett, 245.
Roberts, Elifelet, Jr., 247.
Roberts, Elifelett, 248.

Roberts, Elifelett, Jr., 248.
Roberts, Eliphalet, Jr., 257.
Roberts, Gideon, 55.
Roberts, Hiram, 87.
Roberts, Isaac, 107.
Roberts, John, 57, 167.
Roberts, Lemuel, 188, 208.
Roberts, Nathan, 57.
Roberts, Philemon, 230, 258, 261.
Roberts, Rosel, 34.
Roberts, Samuel, 101.
Roberts, Stephen, 208.
Roberts, Thomas, 245.
Roberts, William, 146, 147, 148, 246, 249.
Robertson, 31, 50.
Robertson, Arthur, 29.
Robertson, Eleazer, 74.
Robertson, Jared, 179.
Robertson, John, 123, 240.
Robertson, Peter, 28, 46.
Robertson, Samuel, Jr., 277.
Robertson, Simeon, 66.
Robins, Brintnell, 171.
Robins, Ebenezer, 185.
Robins, Enos, 114.
Robins, John, 245, 247, 249.
Robins, Solomon, 143, 184.
Robins, Thomas, 247.
Robinson, 71.
Robinson, Abner, 143, 183.
Robinson, Cato, 113.
Robinson, Chandler, 11.
Robinson, Charles, 13.
Robinson, Ebenezer, 264.
Robinson, Eber, 143.
Robinson, Ebor, 185.
Robinson, Eleazer, 114.
Robinson, Elias, 47, 50.
Robinson, Elijah, 18.
Robinson, Eliphalet, 30.
Robinson, J., 207.
Robinson, James, 143, 191, 223, 227.
Robinson, Jared, 9, 90.
Robinson, John, 90, 95, 117, 127, 193, 244, 246.
Robinson, Jonathan, 185.
Robinson, Joseph, 162, 168.
Robinson, Levi, 112.
Robinson, Ms, 71.
Robinson, Moses, 65, 66.
Robinson, Nathan, 143.
Robinson, Reuben, 143.
Robinson, Richard, 65, 185.
Robinson, Samuel, 90, 246, 248.
Robinson, Simeon, Jr., 90.
Robinson, Solomon, 173.

INDEX.

Robinson, William, 173.
Robinson, Ziba, 112, 117.
Robison, John, 61.
Rochester, Mass., 103.
Rockester, Valentine, 262.
Rockwell, Benjamin, 85, 231, 253.
Rockwell, Benjamin S., 194.
Rockwell, Daniel, 5, 85, 149, 260, 261.
Rockwell, Eanos, 85.
Rockwell, Ebenezer, 105.
Rockwell, Grove, 68.
Rockwell, Jabez, 74.
Rockwell, James, 200.
Rockwell, John, 68.
Rockwell, Joseph, 85, 117, 127.
Rockwell, Oswell, 154, 156.
Rockwell, Samuel, 154, 156, 209.
Rockwill, Theodore, 200.
Rockwood, Josiah, 96.
Rocky Hill, 104.
Rods, Benjamin, 171.
Roe, Daniel, 142.
Roes, Peter, 213.
Rogers, Chace, 257.
Rogers, Chester, 57.
Rogers, David, 112, 240.
Rogers, Edward, 138.
Rogers, Ephraim, 10.
Rogers, George, 140.
Rogers, Gideon, 185.
Rogers, Heman, 113.
Rogers, Hezekiah, 48, 102, 104, 129.
Rogers, Isaac, 244.
Rogers, Isaiah, 244, 246.
Rogers, Isaih, 248.
Rogers, Jacob, 11.
Rogers, James, 37.
Rogers, John, 109, 245, 251.
Rogers, John, Jr., 258.
Rogers, John, 5th, 257.
Rogers, Joseph, 105.
Rogers, Lemuel, 132.
Rogers, Levi, 11.
Rogers, Oliver, 270.
Rogers, Philemon, 11.
Rogers, Richard, 185.
Rogers, Rufus, 11.
Rogers, Sharp, 109.
Rogers, Thomas, 255.
Rogers, Timothy, 135, 252.
Rogerson, David, 254.
Roggers, David, 70.
Rohds, Thomas, 61.
Rologg, Aaron, 65.
Rood, David, 42.
Rood, Elijah, 126.

Rood, Ezekiah, 74.
Rood, Ezekiel, 228.
Rood, Isaac, 65.
Rood, Jason, 172.
Rood, John, 265, 267, 270.
Rood, Joseph, 154.
Rood, Jesse, 227.
Rood, Robert, 202.
Rood, Simeon, 54.
Rood, William, 154.
Root, 41, 226.
Root, Caleb, 159.
Root, Daniel, 119, 127, 128, 163.
Root, Ezekiel, 163.
Root, Ezra, 183.
Root, Jesse, 227.
Root, John, 38.
Root, Jonah, 160.
Root, Joseph, 80.
Root, Joshua, 163.
Root, Nathan, 90.
Root, Nathaniel, 55.
Root, Nethaniel, 37.
Rose, Adonijah, 123.
Rose, Herman, 112.
Rose, John, 37.
Rose, Levi, 11.
Rose, Peter, 243.
Rose, Reuben, 209.
Rose, Richard, 257.
Rosel, Jeremiah, 110.
Ross, Joseph, 99.
Ross, Simeon, 273.
Rossetter, Bryant, 107.
Rossetter, Samuel, 111, 270.
Rossiter, Stephen, 273.
Rosson, John, 254.
Roswell, Jeremiah, 90.
Roundey, John, 27.
Roundy, Uriah, 143.
Rouse, Jabez, 74.
Rouse, Joseph, 58, 60.
Rouse, Oliver, 51.
Rouse, Simeon, 90.
Row, Stephen, 242.
Rowe, Amos, 90.
Rowel, Daniel, 145, 146, 147.
Rowel, Jacob, 117.
Rowell, Caleb, 120.
Rowell, Jacob, 115.
Rowely, Stephen, 145, 147.
Rowlandson, Wilson, 258.
Rowlee, Abijah, 23.
Rowlee, Chauncey, 133.
Rowleson, Reuben, 16.
Rowley, John, 114.
Rowley, Joseph L., 233.
Rowley, Nathaniel, 251.
Rowlinson, Reubin, 24.

Rowlison, Reuben, 20.
Roxbury, 18, 130.
Roy, John, Jr., 175.
Royce, Asa, 143.
Royce, Clark, 201.
Royce, Elijah, 61, 270.
Royce, John, 213.
Roys, Clark, 225.
Rucket, Samuel, 97.
Rudd, Jonathan, 240.
Rude, Ezekiel, 175.
Rude, Rufus, Jr., 3, 4.
Rude, Simeon, 138.
Rude, Stephen, 168.
Ruff, Daniel, 186.
Ruggles, Ashbel, 196.
Ruggles, Benjamin, 110, 116.
Ruggles, Benjamin A., 195.
Ruggles, Bostwick, 195.
Ruggles, Comfor, 195.
Ruggles, Joseph, 24.
Ruggles, Lazarus, 209.
Ruggles, Nathaniel, 191.
Ruggles, Samuel, 196.
Rull, John, 217.
Rumbow, William, 239.
Rumsey, David, 85, 136.
Rumsey, Jeremiah, 126.
Rumsy, David, 139.
Rundalls, Timothy, 98.
Runey, George, 258.
Runnell, David, 38.
Runnels, Edward, 68.
Runo, Simeon, 34.
Rus, Benjamin, 15.
Rusco, David, 34.
Russ, Daniel, 13.
Russ, James, 21.
Russ, Jonathan, 21, 68.
Russel, Alpheus, 120.
Russel, Benjamin, 14.
Russel, Cornelius, 48.
Russel, Edward, 189.
Russel, Giles, 49.
Russel, Josiah, 36.
Russel, William, 76.
Russel, William, Jr., 23.
Russell, 214.
Russell, Benjamin, Jr., 14.
Russell, Cornelius, 27.
Russell, E., 177, 214.
Russell, Edward, 211.
Russell, Flezer, 57.
Russell, Gideon, 127, 128.
Russell, Hezekiah, 2, 166.
Russell, James, 66.
Russell, John, 154, 156, 201, 229.

Russell, Jonathan, 63.
Russell, Joseph, 184.
Russell, Nathan, Jr., 2.
Russell, Stephen, 1.
Russell, Thomas, 186.
Russell, William, 18, 254.
Rust, Amaziah, 211.
Ruston, William, 42, 43.
Ryan, Jeremiah, 270.
Rymond, David, 54.
Rynes, T., 84.
Ryon, John, 60.

Sabin, Elihu, 271.
Sabin, Elisha, 184.
Sabin, Hezekiah, 210.
Sabin, Samuel, 175.
Sabins, Nathaniel, 93.
Sachel, Jonathan, 240.
Sachem's Head, 277.
Safford, Joseph, 169.
Sage, 214.
Sage, Comfort, 208, 223, 224.
Sage, Francis, 28.
Sage, Michael, 135.
Sage, Solomon, 207.
St. John, Aaron, 53.
St. John, C., 212.
St. John, Caleb, 212, 226.
St. John, Daniel, 123.
St. John, David, 200.
St. John, James, 265.
St. John, Jesse, 54, 102, 130.
St. John, John, 47.
St. John, Justin, 53, 103, 122, 130.
St. John, Mathew, 13.
St. John, Stephen, 220, 266.
St. Johns, 17, 22, 25.
Salem, 54.
Sales, James, 108.
Salisbury, 21, 52, 55, 83, 88, 89, 102, 110, 111, 267.
Sally, James, 90.
Salmas, William, 218.
Salmon, Asahel, 108.
Salter, Francsis, 145.
Saltonstal, Nathaniel, 141.
Saltonstall, Gurdon F., 140.
Saltonstall, Nathaniel, 140.
Sandeforth, Daniel, 257.
Sanders, Amos, 77.
Sanders, William, 32.
Sandford, Ezekiel, 90.
Sandy Cruse, 102.
Sanford, Daniel, 180.
Sanford, Eli, 194.
Sanford, Elihu, 76.

Sanford, Ezekiel, 25.
Sanford, Joseph, 201, 211, 224, 225.
Sanford, Peleg, 203.
Sanford, Samuel, 49, 75.
Sanford, Strong, 76.
Sanford, Thomas, 72, 108.
Sapposorn, Abel, 251.
Satterlee, James, 51.
Satterlee, William, 263.
Saunders, Abel, 201.
Saunderson, Reuben, 45.
Savage, Cornelius, 241.
Savage, Ebenezer, 230.
Savage, Jacob, 184.
Savage, Samuel, 18, 20.
Savary, Jonathan, 161.
Savary, Joseph, 161.
Saveroy, Thomas, 3.
Savory, Joseph, 4.
Savory, Thomas, 4.
Sawer, Jacob, 246.
Sawyer, Amhel, 126.
Sawyer, Jacob, 248.
Sawyer, John, 38.
Sawyer, London, 72.
Sawyer, Samuel, 271.
Saxon, Simeon, 126.
Saybrook, 53, 54, 61, 64, 74, 79, 81, 88, 89, 90, 102, 113.
Sayer, Jacob, 21.
Sayers, Ezekiel, 239.
Sayers, Ezekle, 238, 239.
Saymour, Jonathan, 243.
Scarbrough, Stephen, 15.
Scheeswick, William, 122.
Schuyler, Philip, 42.
Scituate, 56, 74.
Scofel, Matthew, 184.
Scofeld, Abijah, 67.
Scoffield, Selah, 53, 270.
Scofield, Bouton J., 226.
Scofield, Hait, 56.
Scofield, Henry, 17.
Scofield, Jacob, 23.
Scofield, Jonah, 221.
Scofield, Joseph, 55.
Scofield, Peltet, 23.
Scofield, Reuben, 210, 212.
Scofield, Selah, 207.
Scofield, Sylvanus, 69.
Scofield, Thadeous, 53.
Scofield, Timothy, 56.
Scott, Amasa, 36.
Scott, Caleb, 213.
Scott, David, 200.
Scott, Elijah, 36.
Scott, Elisha, 182, 209.

Scott, Enos, 20, 36.
Scott, Ethiel, 76, 104, 130.
Scott, Ezekiel, 20.
Scott, Gideon, 200.
Scott, Ira, 85.
Scott, James, 195.
Scott, Moses, 69, 74.
Scott, Stephen, 221.
Scott, Thomas, 203.
Scott, Timothy, 17.
Scott, Zebadiah, 185.
Scouval, Timothy, 278.
Scovel, Elijah, 178.
Scovel, Noah, Jr., 178.
Scovil, David, 193.
Scovil, Ebenezer, 139.
Scovil, Elijah, 193.
Scovil, Elisha, 192.
Scovil, Nathan, 57.
Scovil, S., 84.
Scovil, Stephen, 139, 194.
Scovill, John, 101.
Scovill, John, Jr., 23.
Scovill, Levi, 110.
Scovill, Stephen, 90.
Scrantom, Ichabod, 192.
Scranton, Abraham, 192.
Scranton, David, 142.
Scranton, Joab, 253.
Scranton, Timothy, 113.
Scranton, Torrey, 23.
Scranton, Torry, 113.
Scranton, Tory, 72.
Scrborough, Steven, 15.
Scribner, Enoch, 208.
Scribner, Job, 21.
Scribner, Nathaniel, 23.
Scripture, Eleazer, 227.
Seabury, Benjamin, Jr., 6.
Seabury, Elisha, 149.
Searl, Constant, 90.
Sears, David, 146, 147, 184.
Sears, Knowles, 208, 212, 226.
Sears, Obadiah, 90, 254.
Sears, Rementon, 184.
Seartes, Gideon, 74.
Seaward, Brotherton, 39.
Second River, 60.
Sedgwick, Ebnezear, 35.
Sedgwick, John, 16, 18, 20, 21, 22, 23, 24, 33.
Sedgwick, Joseph, 27.
Seeley, Benjamin, 225.
Seeley, Eliphalet, 210.
Seeley, Ephraim, 58.
Seeley, George, 124.
Seeley, James, 208.
Seeley, N., 177.

Seeley, Nehemiah, 106, 126.
Seely, Benjamin, 271.
Seely, John, 68.
Seelye, James, 198.
Seelye, Nathan, 180, 181.
Seelye, Nehemiah, 197.
Seelye, Samuel, 180.
Seelye, Seth, 180.
Seelye, Zadok, 201.
Seelyes, James, 198.
Seep, Ammon, 248.
Selden, Ezra, 45.
Selleck, 56.
Selleck, David, 23.
Sellick, James, 56.
Sempson, 48.
Sergants, Jacob, 87.
Setchel, John, 259, 262.
Setchel, Jonathan, 262.
Setchele, Thomas, 245.
Setchell, John, 254.
Setchell, Jonathan, 247, 249, 252.
Severoy, Joseph, 3.
Seward, Asher, 191.
Seward, Daniel, 24, 90.
Seward, Eliakim, 124.
Seward, Samuel, 71.
Seward, Silas, 39.
Seward, William, 19, 90.
Sexton, Elijah, 55.
Sexton, Jonathan, 2.
Seyley, E., 213.
Seymor, Haz., 187, 188.
Seymor, Whiting, 187.
Seymour, Aaron, 274.
Seymour, Abijah, 195.
Seymour, Abraham, 85.
Seymour, Asa, 77.
Seymour, Charles, 274, 275.
Seymour, Daniel, 217.
Seymour, David, 218.
Seymour, Ebenezer, 274.
Seymour, Elias, 90.
Seymour, Elijah, 212.
Seymour, Freeman, 188.
Seymour, Israel, 211.
Seymour, James, 218.
Seymour, Jesse, 105.
Seymour, John, 218.
Seymour, John, Jr., 218.
Seymour, Moses, 212, 221.
Seymour, Samuel, 217.
Seymour, Seth, 227.
Seymour, Stephen, 208, 224.
Seymour, William, 36, 271.
Seymour, Zachariah, 154.
Seymour, Zachariah, Jr., 154.
Seymour, Zachariah, 156.

Seymour, Zacheriah, Jr., 156.
Shadin, Conklin, 264.
Shaford, Elijah, 240.
Shaftsbury, 21.
Shaldon, Danniel, 188.
Shaler, Joseph, 48.
Shapley, 140.
Shapley, Adam, 212.
Sharon, 52, 67, 68, 69, 89.
Sharp, 31, 123.
Sharp, James, 114.
Sharp, Josep, 90.
Sharp, Joseph, 140.
Sharp, Pharaoh, 29.
Sharp, Thomas, 278.
Sharpe, Isaac, 253.
Sharper, Pharaoh, 29, 264.
Shattock, David, 185.
Shattuck, Philip, 38.
Shattuck, Stephen, 108.
Shaw, Benjamin, 90.
Shaw, David, 23.
Shaw, Ebenezer, 123.
Shaw, Elias, '54.
Shaw, James, 81, 178.
Shaw, Jorge, 178.
Shaw, William, 90.
Shaylor, Joseph, 20.
Shearman, James, 151.
Sheffield, Ickebert, 250.
Sheffields, Achors, 212.
Shelden, Benjamin, 263.
Sheldon, Alm, 266.
Sheldon, Daniel, 187.
Sheldon, E., 266.
Sheldon, Elijah, 271.
Sheldon, Elisha, 173.
Sheldon, Epaphras, 164, 202, 203, 210, 221.
Sheldon, J., 266.
Sheldon, S., 265.
Sheldon, Simeon, 208.
Sheldon, William, 184, 231.
Shelley, John, 90.
Shelley, Reuben, 277.
Shelley, Samuel, 51.
Shelley, Timothy, 113.
Shelly, Ebenezer, 78.
Shelly, Edmund, 122.
Shelly, Medad, 277.
Shelly, Reuben, 277.
Shelly, Timothy, 116.
Shepard, 133.
Shepard, Amos, 35.
Shepard, Ashbel, 274.
Shepard, Cudgoe, 93.
Shepard, Daniel, 279.
Shepard, David, 279.

INDEX. 357

Shepard, Ebenezer, 21.
Shepard, James, 15.
Shepard, Jared, 134, 223.
Shepard, John, 11, 135.
Shepard, Moses, 36.
Shepard, Phinehas, 36.
Shepard, Thomas, 66, 134, 208, 210, 276.
Shepard, William, 27, 203.
Sheperd, Jonathan, 127.
Shepherd, Nathaniel, 138.
Shepherd, Thomas, 271.
Shepperd, Jared, 207.
Sherman, Daniel, 173.
Sherman, Enoch, 119.
Sherman, Ezra, 106.
Sherman, Isaac, 46, 75, 78, 119.
Sherman, James, 181, 219.
Sherman, John, 48, 117, 126, 127, 128, 181, 219.
Sherman, Nathaniel, 215
Sherman, Phineas, 180, 211.
Sherman, William, 90.
Sherwood, Albert. 180.
Sherwood, Asa, 109.
Sherwood, Benjamin, 200.
Sherwood, Daniel, 53.
Sherwood, E., 84, 213.
Sherwood, Levi, 85, 218.
Sherwood, Nehemiah, 69.
Sherwood, Phinehas, 24.
Sherwood, Stephen, 199.
Shetten, Benjamin, 259.
Shiffield, Ichabob, 245.
Shipman, Benoni, 46.
Shipman, Edward, 18, 210, 221.
Shipman, John, 90, 142, 212.
Shipman, John, 2d, 142.
Shipman, Samuel, 90, 126.
Shippard, Uriah, 188.
Shirtleff, Lothrop, 166.
Shiverick, Thomas, 246, 251.
Shoals, Jabez, 74.
Shoart, John, 244.
Shop, James, 54.
Short, Ben, 245.
Short, Benjamin, 249.
Short, John, 246, 251.
Short, Seth, 168.
Short, William, 104, 125, 131.
Shortman, William, 90.
Shumway, John, 45.
Shurtliff, Asael, 2.
Shurtliff, John, 2.
Shurtliff, Lothrup, 2.
Shurtliff, William, 2.
Shute, Richard, 198, 208, 211.
Shutes, Richard, 224.

Sidgwick, Jonathan, 274.
Sikes, Reuben, 208.
Siles, Solomon, 261.
Sill, Bennet, 199.
Sill, David F., 45.
Sill, Jeffy, 109.
Sill, Jesse, 109.
Sill, Richard, 49, 50, 75.
Sillick, 97.
Sillick, Charles, 218.
Sillik, Hezekiha, 218.
Silliman, 267.
Silliman, Daniel, 19.
Silliman, Gold S., 136, 180, 181, 219, 265.
Silliman, Isaac, 19.
Silliman, Samuel, 252.
Silsby, Jonathan, 234.
Simans, Adrial, 244.
Simans, Arad, 244.
Simbo, Prince, 73.
Simes, Selvenus, 246.
Simmonds, Ruben, 15.
Simmons, Chapman, 257.
Simmons, James, 90.
Simmons, Joshua, 97.
Simmons, Reuben, 15.
Simmons, Samuel, 35, 61.
Simmons, Stephen, 94.
Simms, John, 169.
Simms, Selvenus, 251.
Simonds, Adrial, 246, 248.
Simonds, Arad, 246, 248.
Simons, Adariah, 74.
Simons, Comma, 53.
Simons, David, 138.
Simons, Ebenezer, 172.
Simons, Elijah, 143.
Simons, Ephram, 35.
Simons, Jonathan, 122.
Simons, Monmoth, 52.
Simons, Pely, 127.
Simons, Stephen, 119.
Simons, Thomas, 65.
Simsbury, 6, 52, 53, 55, 56, 57, 58, 59, 60, 65, 66, 67, 68, 89. 103, 104, 114, 118, 145, 146, 147, 148, 164, 203.
Sinemon, Benjamin, 247.
Sinemon, Thomas, 246.
Sisco, Peter, 242.
Siseoll, Samuel, 243.
Sissen, William, 213.
Sizer, Abel, 204.
Sizer, Anthony, 98.
Sizer, Daniel, 100.
Sizer, Jonah, 90.
Skeel, Amos, 271.

Skeel, John, 85.
Skiff, Vallintine, 231.
Skiner, Adenijah, 103.
Skiner, Isarel, 163.
Skiner, Stephen, 274.
Skiner, Thomas, 202.
Skinner, Abraham, 3d, 160.
Skinner, Abram, 63.
Skinner, David, 159.
Skinner, Eleazer, 63.
Skinner, Enos, 18.
Skinner, Ezekiel, 158.
Skinner, John, 120, 134, 226.
Skinner, Richard, 98.
Skinner, Thomas, 78, 273.
Skinner, William, 239.
Skinner, Zamri, 36.
Slack, Comfort, 170.
Slade, Aaron, 2.
Slade, Abner, 2, 139.
Slade, Daniel, 2.
Slafter, Moses, 2.
Slarter, Amos, 142.
Slarter, James, 142.
Slate, Ezekal, 38.
Slater, Joel, 145, 146, 147, 148.
Slater, John, 24.
Slattury, John, 258.
Slitwell, Thomas, 34.
Sloan, Thomas, 187, 188.
Slooman, Thomas, 149.
Sloper, 222.
Sloper, A., 84.
Sloper, Ambris, 182.
Sloper, Ambrose, 209, 210.
Sloper, Ambrus, 138.
Sloson, Nathan, 210, 223.
Smalley, Daniel, 149.
Smedley, T., 180.
Smedly, Samuel, 233.
Smith, 19, 84, 212, 222.
Smith, Aaron, 197, 271.
Smith, Abijah, 15, 57, 124, 186.
Smith, Abner, 132.
Smith, Abraham, 179.
Smith, Alen, 213.
Smith, Allen, 210.
Smith, Ambrose, 108.
Smith, Amos, 184, 210, 279.
Smith, Asa, 138.
Smith, Asahel, 240.
Smith, Asail, 234.
Smith, Asher, 37.
Smith, Benajah, 55, 204.
Smith, Benjamin, 20, 200, 252.
Smith, Benoni, 200, 211.
Smith, Caleb, 11, 25, 257.
Smith, Chancy, 258.
Smith, Charles, 206, 207, 210.
Smith, Chauncey, 16.
Smith, Cuff, 97.
Smith, Dan, 19, 34.
Smith, Daniel, 15, 22, 51, 56, 197, 200.
Smith, David, 18, 23, 49, 76, 133, 185, 196, 202.
Smith, David, 2d, 134.
Smith, Ebenezer, 170, 202, 211, 224, 225, 254.
Smith, Edmund, 271.
Smith, Elezer, 57.
Smith, Eli, 195.
Smith, Eliakim, 212.
Smith, Eliakim, Jr., 85.
Smith, Elihu, 137.
Smith, Elijah, 63.
Smith, Elisha, 81.
Smith, Elkanah, 111, 117.
Smith, Elm, 226.
Smith, Epaphras, 252.
Smith, Ephraim, 119.
Smith, Ezra, 29, 31, 47.
Smith, Francis, 185, 274.
Smith, Fred, 94.
Smith, George, 90.
Smith, George C., 25.
Smith, Graves, 2.
Smith, Heber, 75, 271.
Smith, Heman, 22.
Smith, Henry, 65, 68.
Smith, Huttun, 217.
Smith, Isaac, 37, 77, 85.
Smith, Isaiah, 122.
Smith, Israel, 203, 261.
Smith, Ithamer, 63.
Smith, Jacob, 2d, 200.
Smith, James, 38, 90, 154, 156, 185, 212.
Smith, James G., 70.
Smith, Jared, 117, 127.
Smith, Jasper, 262.
Smith, Jeddidiah, 35.
Smith, Jedediah, 57.
Smith, Jehiel, 34, 86, 112.
Smith, Jeial, 106.
Smith, Jeremiah, 22.
Smith, Jesse, 99, 108, 202.
Smith, Joathan, 184.
Smith, Job, 48, 90, 142, 195.
Smith, John, 27, 57, 81, 99, 101, 179, 197, 209, 226, 245, 247, 249, 252, 262, 271.
Smith, Jordan, 71, 112.
Smith, Joseph, 10, 21, 22, 23, 24, 84, 122, 193, 196, 207, 208, 226, 257.

Smith, Josiah, 15, 20, 138, 220, 206, 270.
Smith, Jurden, 257.
Smith, Justus, 152.
Smith, Landon, 32.
Smith, Lemuel, 175.
Smith, M., 209.
Smith, Matthew, 210.
Smith, Micahel, 184.
Smith, Moses, Jr., 2.
Smith, N., 206, 214.
Smith, Nathan, 189, 195, 221, 265.
Smith, Nehemiah, 138, 183.
Smith, Noah, Jr., 213.
Smith, O., 222.
Smith, Oliver, 185, 210, 216, 221.
Smith, Peter, 57, 271.
Smith, Phineas, 98.
Smith, Reuben, 21, 38, 250.
Smith, Reubin, 125.
Smith, Richard, 15, 137, 195, 208, 224.
Smith, Ruben, 246.
Smith, S., 84.
Smith, Sam B., 204.
Smith, Samuel, 62, 90, 158, 179, 200.
Smith, Samuel R., 240.
Smith, Selevenus, 250.
Smith, Seth, 188, 210, 221.
Smith, Shermon, 195.
Smith, Silvanus, 211.
Smith, Silvenus, 246.
Smith, Stephen, 38, 211, 253, 273.
Smith, Tabor, 278.
Smith, Theophilus, 204.
Smith, Thomas, 9, 245, 250, 256, 261.
Smith, William, 19, 48, 69, 110, 115, 167, 218.
Smith, William G., 239.
Smith, William H., 227.
Smith, Zebadiah, 238, 239, 240, 262.
Smith, Zebina, 67.
Smithers, William, 90.
Snow, Edmond, 178.
Snow, Isaac, 94, 105.
Snow, Ivory, 254.
Snow, Joseph, 14.
Snow, Joseph, Jr., 14.
Snow, Levi, 186.
Snow, Patrick, 278.
Snow, Salvanus, 15.
Snow, Shubal, 95.
Snow, Silvanus, 16, 24.
Snow, Silas, 186.
Solland, Joseph, 163.

Solomon, Amos, 150.
Somers, 17, 53, 55, 56, 69, 87, 118.
Soppoosor, Abele, 246.
Southard, Nathan, 178.
Southard, William, 178.
Southington, 115.
Southward, Thomas, 15.
Southworth, Joseph, 193.
Southworth, Lemuel, 87.
Southworth, Samuel, 34.
Southworth, Thomas, 15.
Southworth, William, 181, 219.
Soutice, Solomon, 109.
Sowers, William, 109.
Spafford, Elijah, 118.
Spalding, Daniel, 109.
Spalding, Derias, 221.
Spalding, Ephraim, 82.
Spalding, Ezra, 168.
Spalding, Silas, 168.
Sparford, Elijah, 248.
Sparks, Henry, 108.
Sparks, Icahd, 168.
Sparks, John, 168.
Sparks, Ruben, 157.
Spary, Stephen, 38.
Spaulding, John, 35.
Spaulding, Joseph, 168.
Spaulding, Nat, 167.
Spaulding, William, 168.
Spear, Elihue, 54.
Spear, Elijah, 54.
Spear, William, Jr., 2, 166.
Spears, John, 74, 90.
Spears, Nathaniel, 12.
Spears, States, 90.
Spelman, Richard, 133, 191.
Spencer, 50.
Spencer, Abner, 35.
Spencer, David, 90, 122.
Spencer, Elijah, 185, 254.
Spencer, Emmon, 185.
Spencer, Ezra, 36.
Spencer, George, 230.
Spencer, Ichabod, 45, 51.
Spencer, Israel, 209.
Spencer, James, 36, 184.
Spencer, Joel, 97.
Spencer, John, 94, 244, 245, 246, 248, 274.
Spencer, Joseph, 17, 18, 19, 20, 21, 22, 23, 24, 25.
Spencer, Noah, 95, 117, 127.
Spencer, Obadiah, 90.
Spencer, Samuel, 41, 43.
Spencer, Seth, 36.
Spencer, Simeon, 233.
Spencer, Steven, 192.

Spencer, Thomas, 76, 193.
Sperry, Chauncey, 90.
Sperry, Enoch, 69, 273.
Sperry, Jabez, 32.
Sperry, Silas, 12.
Spicer, Abbe, 231.
Spicer, Abel, 82.
Spicer, Nathan, 140.
Spicer, O., 206.
Spicer, Oliver, 211.
Spicer, Samuel, 90.
Spink, Asa, 28.
Spooner, Judah P., 246, 247, 250, 252.
Spooner, Walter, 230.
Sprage, John, 4.
Sprague, 50.
Sprague, Benjamin, 161.
Sprague, Beriah, 3, 5, 162.
Sprague, Elisha, 161.
Sprague, James, 90.
Sprigs, Thomas, 264.
Sprigs, William, 238.
Spring, Thomas, 203.
Springer, John, 99.
Springfield, 115.
Springger, Whala, 97.
Spurr, William, 77.
"Spy," 238, 239, 240, 241.
Squib, Joseph, 263.
Squier, Daniel, 14, 85.
Squier, David, 266.
Squier, John, 35.
Squier, Justus, 39.
Squier, Samuel S., 90.
Squire, Abiather, 72.
Squire, Asa, 100.
Squire, Asher, 107.
Squire, Daniel, 14.
Squire, Dudley, 107.
Squire, Elijah, 186.
Squire, Ephraim, 15.
Squire, J., 84.
Squire, Jonah, 152.
Squire, Jonathan, 180.
Squire, Joseph, 232.
Squire, Nathan, 233.
Squire, Nathaniel, 199.
Squire, Phillip, 186.
Squire, Phineas, 19.
Squire, Samuel, 193.
Squire, Sorel, 106.
Squire, Stephen, 238, 239.
Squires, Charles, 126.
Squires, Ebenezer, 237.
Squires, Isaac, 16, 99, 233.
Squires, Phinehas, 70, 107.
Squires, Sarel, 126.

Squires, Sariel,- 104.
Stacey, Nathaniel, 235.
Stafford, 53, 54, 56, 114.
Stalker, Levi, 198.
Stalker, Peter, 102, 129.
Stamford, 53, 54, 55, 56, 68, 69, 70, 76, 77, 78, 79, 83, 89, 103, 104, 197, 199, 205, 267, 278.
Stanard, Seth, 39.
Stanbrough, Lemuel, 107.
Stanhrough, Silas, 107.
Stanclift, John, 36.
Stanclift, Lemuel, 122.
Standley, Fradrick, 188.
Standley, Fredrick, 235.
Standley, Lewis, 27.
Standly, Frederick, 187.
Stanley, Abraham, 194, 208, 210, 276.
Stanley, Abraham, Jr., 194.
Stanley, Gad, 203, 210.
Stanley, Oliver, 208, 210, 212, 222, 224, 275.
Stanley, Salmon, 22.
Stanley, Thomas, 100.
Stanley, Timothy, 225.
Stanliff, Samuel, 97.
Stanly, Gad, 138, 203, 222.
Stanly, Salmon, 20.
Stanly, Samuel, 274.
Stannard, Eliakim, 183.
Stannard, Jasper, 90.
Stannard, Limbo, 72.
Stannard, Peter, 140.
Stannard, Samuel, 69, 139.
Stannard, Seth, 122.
Stanton, 12, 13.
Stanton, Asa, 175.
Stanton, Daniel, 2d, 263.
Stanton, Daniel, 3d, 263.
Stanton, David, 175.
Stanton, Edward, 270.
Stanton, I., 212.
Stanton, James, 69.
Stanton, Nathaniel, 262.
Stanton, Solomon, 205.
Stanton, Thomas, 263.
Stanton, William, 210.
Staples, Ebenezer, 185.
Staples, Jacob, 172.
Stark, Diah, 159.
Stark, Solomon, 267.
Stark, Stephen, 90.
Stark, Timothy, 90.
Starkey, Stephen, 178.
Starkey, Timothy, 178, 210.
Starkweather, Amos, 96.
Starkweather, Asa, 90.

INDEX. 361

Starkweather, Ephraim, 175.
Starkweather, James, 258, 261.
Starkweather, Jesse, 212.
Starkweather, Joseph, 58, 258, 261.
Starkweather, Simeon, 264.
Starkweather, Woodbury, 184.
Starling, John, 185.
Starling, Silvanus, 278.
Starr, 195, 265.
Starr, Abijah, 198.
Starr, Amos, 199.
Starr, Daniel, 134, 140, 258.
Starr, David, 48.
Starr, Eleazer, 198.
Starr, Eli, 52.
Starr, Eliakim, 198.
Starr, Ezra, 212.
Starr, John, 200, 267, 270, 277.
Starr, Jonathan, 198.
Starr, Joshua, 198.
Starr, Josiah, 18, 20, 22, 24, 25, 45, 51.
Starr, Mathew, 199.
Starr, Nathan, 194.
Starr, Nathaniel, 185.
Starr, Noah, 200.
Starr, Peter, 198.
Starr, Samuel, 199.
Starr, Thomas, 49.
Starr, William, 49, 271.
Staten, 139.
States, George, 99.
Stawson, Jonathan, 78.
Stawston, Augustus, 78.
Steal, Josiah, 61.
Steavens, Samuel, 178.
Stebbens, Clemment, 185.
Stebbins, Jacob, 200.
Steckland, Jonah, 126.
Stedman, Benjamin, 216.
Stedman, John, 172.
Stedman, Jon, 168.
Stedman, Philamon, 77.
Stedman, Selah, 72.
Steel, Allyn, 25.
Steel, Bradford, 211.
Steel, Eliphas, 35.
Steel, John, 36.
Steel, Moses, 21.
Steel, Samuel, 35.
Steel, William, 36.
Stely, John, 139.
Stephens, Aaron, 48, 271.
Stephens, Lemuel, 170, 185.
Stephens, Peter, 53.
Stephens, Phineas, 35, 64.
Stephens, Robert, 170.

Stephens, Ruben, 55.
Steuart, John, 244.
Stevens, Ager, 196.
Stevens, Benjamin, 35, 137, 197.
Stevens, Caleb, 196.
Stevens, Daniel, 77.
Stevens, Eli, 25, 197.
Stevens, Elnathan, 191.
Stevens, Ezra, 200.
Stevens, Forod, 198.
Stevens, Fraderick, 37.
Stevens, Henry, 99.
Stevens, John, 24, 35, 167, 172.
Stevens, Josiah, 137.
Stevens, Moses, 212, 221.
Stevens, Noah, 255.
Stevens, Olover, 35.
Stevens, Peter, 137.
Stevens, Peter, Jr., 90.
Stevens, Reuben, 97.
Stevens, Roswel, 90.
Stevens, Samuel, 198.
Stevens, Timothy, 23, 113, 137.
Stevens, William, 140.
Stevens, Zebulon, 35.
Steward, James, 12.
Steward, John, 234, 247, 251.
Steward, Joseph, 185.
Steward, William, 243.
Stewart, 50.
Stewart, Alexander, 197.
Stewart, D., 84.
Stewart, Daniel, 208.
Stewart, John, 109.
Stewart, Richard, 239, 240.
Stewart, Robert, 11.
Stewart, Samuel, 199.
Stewart, Stephen, 199.
Stewart, Thomas, 171.
Stiles, Benoni, 119.
Stiles, Beriah, 135.
Stiles, John, 2.
Stiles, Martin, 63.
Stilken, George, 254.
Still, John, 233.
Still, Samuel, 48.
Stillman, 152.
Stillman, David, 80.
Stillman, Samuel, 271.
Stillwater, 17, 18, 19.
Stilson, Daniel, 38.
Stilwel, Elias, 46.
Stilwell, John, 61.
Stimpson, Simeon, 106.
Stimson, Abel, 123.
Stimson, Simeon, 127.
Stish, Phillip H., 114.
Stocking, Amasa, 82.

Stocking, Eber, 69, 135.
Stocking, Jonathan, 61.
Stocking, Marshall, 135.
Stockwell. Abel, 108.
Stodard, Cyrenus, 38.
Stodard, Eli, 76.
Stodard, Samuel, 244.
Stoddard, Abijah, 38.
Stoddard, Anthony, 75.
Stoddard, B., 209.
Stoddard, Briant, 212.
Stoddard, Bryan, 210.
Stoddard, Daniel, 82.
Stoddard, David, 6, 201.
Stoddard, Elisha, 74.
Stoddard, Enoch, 154, 156.
Stoddard, Ichabod, 173.
Stoddard, J., 225.
Stoddard, James, 207, 221, 222, 224, 278.
Stoddard, Jesse, 201.
Stoddard, John, 154, 156.
Stoddard, Jonathan, 153, 155.
Stoddard, Luther, 37.
Stoddard, Nathan, 38.
Stoddard, Samuel, 154, 156, 246.
Stoddard, Simeon C., 119.
Stoddard, Solomon, 212.
Stoddard, Thaddeus, 38.
Stoddart. Samuel, 248.
Stokes, Richard, 113, 117.
Ston, William, 278.
Stone, Aaron, 194.
Stone, Ambermarle, 185.
Stone, Bela, 242, 243.
Stone, Benjamin, 209, 212, 273.
Stone, Daniel, 194.
Stone, David, 90.
Stone, Joel, 194.
Stone, John. 277.
Stone, Joseph, 135.
Stone, Josiah, 90, 164.
Stone, Reuben, 209, 225.
Stone, Russel. 277.
Stone, Samuel, 111.
Stone, William, 194.
Stones, Benjamin, 225.
Stonington. 31, 56, 60, 64, 65, 68, 74, 88, 89, 90, 91, 113, 118, 267.
Store, 17.
Storrs, Amaziah, 143.
Storrs, E., 210, 222, 227.
Storrs, Experience, 22, 24.
Story, John, 135.
Story, Solomon, 33, 40.
Stoughton, E., 220.
Stoughton, James, 89.
Stow, George, 230.

Stow, Jene, 204.
Stow, Samuel, 256.
Stow, William, 141.
Stow, Zacheus, 107.
Stowe, Samuel, 202.
Stowe, William, 278.
Stowel, Abel, 101.
Stowel, Elisha, 90.
Stowel, Nathaniel, 101.
Stowel, Samuel, 101.
Stowell, Nathan, 63.
Stratford, 53, 54, 58, 69, 75, 76, 77, 78, 82, 88, 89, 102, 103, 104, 109, 135, 136, 141, 171, 180, 190, 267, 278.
Stratton, Lemuel, 158.
Stratton, Samuel, 244, 245, 251.
Stratton, Thomas, 181, 219.
Strickland, Stephen, 135.
Stricklin, Jonah, 80.
Stricland, Jonathan, 32.
Stromthorn, James, 169.
Strong, 223.
Strong, Adonijah, 33, 160.
Strong, Asahel, 9.
Strong, Benajah, 90.
Strong, Benjamin, 66.
Strong, David, 34, 47, 50, 160, 162.
Strong, Eliakim, 71.
Strong, Israel, 46.
Strong, Jacob. 122.
Strong, Jedediah, 50.
Strong, John, 49, 58, 60, 75, 202, 224, 225.
Strong, Josiah, 270.
Strong, Olliver, 160.
Strong, Phinehas, 111, 162.
Strong, Roger, 5.
Strong, Samuel, 105.
Strong, Selah, 192.
Strong, Seth, 71.
Strong, Simeon, 227.
Strong, Thomas, 192, 193.
Stronge, Josiah, 34.
Stuard, Daniel, 34.
Stuard, William, 171.
Stuart, Alexander, 198.
Stuart, William, 69, 242.
Stubbs, Maning, 251.
Stubbs, Samuel, 23, 24, 74.
Sturdavant, John, 199.
Sturdevant, Nathaniel, 90.
Sturdivant, Samuel, 99.
Sturges, Elias, 84.
Sturgis, Abraham, 232.
Sturgis, Aquilla, 77.
Sturgis, David, 16.
Sturgis, Thadeus, 200.

INDEX. 363

Stwart, Charles, 54.
Suffield, 53, 54, 57, 58, 59, 60, 75, 78, 80, 81, 82, 87, 89, 267.
Sugden, Abraham, 108.
Sugdon, Abraham, 235.
Summer, Benjamin, 211.
Summers, Benjamin, 212.
Summit, Prince, 90.
Sumner, E., 225.
Sumner, John, 47.
Sumner, Joshua, 63.
Sumner, Luke, 100.
Sumner, Robert, 06, 278.
Suncheman, Nathaniel, 90.
Sunderlin, Pheleg, 135.
Suntsimons, Aaron, 90.
Sup, Hammond, 247.
Surdan, Peter, 99.
Sutliff, Jannah, 98.
Sutton, Edward, 33.
Swain, Boston, 254, 259.
Swain, Peter, 251.
Swan, Aden, 186.
Swan, Christopher, 78.
Swan, John, 206.
Swan, Nathaniel, 240, 254.
Swan, William, 238, 239, 240, 259.
Swasey, Anthony, 253.
Swazey, Manuel, 238.
Sweet, Benjamin, 79.
Sweet, Isaac, 64.
Sweet, John, 36, 79.
Sweet, Jonathan, 37.
Sweet, Josiah, 38.
Sweetland, Ebenezer, 161.
Swetland, Aaron, 161.
Swift, 265.
Swift, Charles, 161.
Swift, Heman, 48, 73, 74, 97, 99, 135, 267.
Swift, Isaac, 33.
Swift, Jeriah, 33.
Swift, Robert, 90.
Swift, Seth, 251.
Swift, William, 3d, 4.
Swords, Francis, 231.
Sydleman, John, 90.
Syzer, Jabez, 22.

Taaffe, Nicholas, 254.
Tack, Andrew, 108.
Taft, Silas, 65.
Taintor, Michael, 205.
Talbat, Job, 170.
Talbott, Jonathan, 98.
Talcot, Matthew, 227.
Talcott, Elizur, 227.
Tallcot, Isaac, 157.

Tallcott, Abraham, 137.
Tallcott, Gad, 163.
Tallcott, George, 137.
Tallcott, William, 163.
Tallmadge, Jeremiah, 29, 30, 31.
Talmadge, Josiah, Jr., 276.
Talmage, Ichabod, 79.
Talmage, Solomon, 11.
Talman, Moses, 246, 251.
Talor, Ruben, 106.
Tankerd, George, 68.
Tanner, Joseph A., 35.
Tanner, Trial, 12, 41, 49.
Tanner, Tyral, 21, 49.
Tapping, Zephaniah, 238, 239.
Tarball, William, 265, 271.
Tarbox, 227.
Tarbox, Benjamin, 60, 99.
Tarbox, David, 159.
Tarbox, Jonathan, 162.
Tarbox, Solomon, 134, 159.
Tarbox, Zenas, 159.
Tarry, 111.
Tawsin, Dominique, 260.
Tawzin, Dominioque, 264.
Tawzin, Dominique, 262.
Tayler, Henry, 243.
Tayler, Jonathan, 107.
Taylor, 22.
Taylor, A., 228.
Taylor, Augustine, 49.
Taylor, Azariah, 74.
Taylor, Baruck, 69.
Taylor, Daniel, 38, 80.
Taylor, David, 123.
Taylor, E., 142.
Taylor, Eleazer, 198.
Taylor, Elijah, 77.
Taylor, Eliud, 199.
Taylor, Elizer, 86.
Taylor, Gad, 73.
Taylor, Gamaliel, 212.
Taylor, Harry, 242.
Taylor, Henry, 234, 252.
Taylor, James, 73, 235.
Taylor, Jesse, 85, 217.
Taylor, Joel, 273.
Taylor, John, 2, 56, 68, 74, 90, 99, 150, 199, 254.
Taylor, John, Jr., 2.
Taylor, Jonathan, 194.
Taylor, Josiah, 77.
Taylor, Justus, 110.
Taylor, Levi, 217.
Taylor, Major, 198.
Taylor, Medad, 202.
Taylor, Micha, 65.
Taylor, Nathaniel, 16.

Taylor, Phineas, 98.
Taylor, Reuben, 74, 195, 228.
Taylor, Salmond, 19.
Taylor, Samuel, 109, 233.
Taylor, Silas, 198.
Taylor, Simeon, 38, 76.
Taylor, Theodore, 74.
Taylor, Timothy, 46.
Taylor, William, 36, 53.
Taylor, Zeb, 209.
Teacomwaus, Isaac, 17.
Teal, Timothy, 253.
Teal, Titus, 140.
Teale, Samuel, 72.
Teall, Nathan, 97.
Tease, John, 245.
Tee, Joseph, 261.
Teleder, William, 253.
Temple, Amos, 75, 104, 130.
Ten Eyck, Henry, 46, 54.
Terrell, Hezekiah, 106.
Terrey, Dan, 149.
Terril, Thomas, 161.
Terrill, Caleb, 119.
Terrill, George, 207.
Terrill, Josiah, 209.
Terry, Jesse, 127.
Terry, Josiah, 93.
Terry, N., 224.
Terry, Nathaniel, 165, 222, 223.
Teuky, Jared, 58.
Thaires, Asa, 78.
Tharp, Aaron, 54.
Tharp, Abner, 11, 205.
Tharp, Amasa, 70.
Tharp, Amos, 70.
Tharp, Elias, 79.
Tharp, Jeremiah, 98.
Tharp, Nathaniel, 55, 140.
Tharp, Samuel, 235.
Thatcher, Joseph, 246, 251.
Thatcher, Stephen G., 235.
Thayer, David, 167.
Theaf, John, 230.
Thomas, 59.
Thomas, Absalom, 90.
Thomas, Caleb, 120.
Thomas, Daniel, 55.
Thomas, David, 145, 146, 147, 148.
Thomas, Ebenezer, 209.
Thomas, Ebenezer, Jr., 136.
Thomas, Elihu, 160.
Thomas, Enoch, 77.
Thomas, Ephraim, 108.
Thomas, Gregory, 69.
Thomas, Isaac, 136.
Thomas, James, 90.
Thomas, Jesse, 127, 128.

Thomas, John, 11, 85, 133, 136.
Thomas, Jonah, 82.
Thomas, Joseph, 85, 234.
Thomas, Josiah, 163.
Thomas, Malachi, 5.
Thomas, Malicha, 162.
Thomas, Samuel, 108.
Thomas, Sarrid, 164.
Thomas, William, 229.
Thomblenson, Joseph, 196.
Thompson, Abraham, 190.
Thompson, Absalom, 175.
Thompson, David, 113, 123, 151, 181, 219.
Thompson, Jabez, 17.
Thompson, James, 2, 123.
Thompson, John, 139.
Thompson, Joseph, 69, 179.
Thompson, Lins, 190.
Thompson, Nathan, 215.
Thompson, Nathaniel, 75.
Thompson, Nehemiah, 151.
Thompson, Samuel, 118.
Thompson, Stephen, 78, 104.
Thompson, Thomas, 173.
Thompson, William, 169.
Thomson, 177.
Thomson, Alexander, 27.
Thomson, Ebenezer, 20.
Thomson, Edward, 55.
Thomson, Elihu, 21.
Thomson, Isaac, 201.
Thomson, J., 177.
Thomson, James, 20.
Thomson, John, Jr., 37.
Thomson, Joseph, 17, 216, 222.
Thomson, Joshua, 36.
Thomson, Justus, 18, 23.
Thomson, Samuel, 222, 227.
Thomson, Stephen, 130, 203.
Thomson, William, 180.
Thorp, Aaron, 160.
Thorp, Amasa, 112.
Thorp, Amos, 112.
Thorp, Andrew, 234.
Thorp, Asher, 201.
Thorp, E., 212.
Thorp, Eliphalet, 181.
Thorp, Esra, 152.
Thorp, James, 117.
Thorp, Jeremiah, 257.
Thorp, John, 138.
Thorp, Joseph, 19, 25.
Thorp, Nehemiah, 16.
Thorp, Peter, 234.
Thorp, Steph, 180.
Thorp, Stephen, 180.
Thrall, John, 209.

INDEX. 365

Thrall, Joshua, 170.
Thrall, Rufus, 39.
Thrasher, Samuel, 262.
Thresher, James, 56.
Throop, Benjamin, 47, 120, 149, 201.
Throop, Dan, 5.
Throop, Dyer, 211, 227.
Throop, Joseph, 149.
Throope, Benjamin, 40.
Thulford, Edmond, 190.
Tibbals, Abel, 193.
Tibbals, Ebenezer, 191.
Tibbals, Joseph, 191.
Tibbals, Samuel, 98.
Tibbals, Thomas, 13, 42, 43.
Tibbles, Nathaniel, 80.
Tibits, Obadiah, 199.
Ticknor, Elisha, 34.
Tickour, James, 162.
Ticonderoga, 18.
Tiel, John, 188.
Tiff, Johnson, 104, 125, 131.
Tiffany, John, 45.
Tiffany, John, Jr., 40.
Tiffany, Josiah, 45, 50.
Tiffany, Philimon, 118.
Tiffany, Timothy, 20.
Tiffeny, Asa, 162.
Tiffeny, Isaih, 162.
Tift, John, 186.
Tilden, Benjamin, 162.
Tilden, Charles, 13.
Tilden, Daniel, 2, 3, 4, 183, 212.
Tiler, Oliver, 172.
Tiley, James, 81.
Tillinghast, John, 256.
Tillinghast, Thomas, 256.
Tinker, Amos, 108.
Tinker, Harris, 240.
Tinker, Jesse, 56.
Tinker, Jonathan, 229.
Tinker, Nehemiah, 208, 212.
Tirrel, Thomas, 2.
Tisaker, John, 238.
Tisdale, 3.
Tisdale, William, 98.
Tobias, Daniel, 69.
Tobias, James, 99.
Tobias, Jonathan, 68.
Toby, Elisha, 211.
Toby, Ephram, 34.
Tocomuaus, Jacob, 18.
Tod, Jehial, 184.
Todd, Thadeus, 112.
Tolcut, Ebenezer, 258.
Tolland, 18, 53, 54, 55, 56, 57, 89, 90.

Tolles, Elnathan, 108.
Tomkins, Abraham, 95, 127.
Tomlinson, Beach, 180.
Tomlinson, David, 90.
Tomlinson, Jabez, 271.
Tomlinson, John, 225.
Tomlinson, Joseph, 110.
Tomlinson, Levi, 179.
Tomlinson, William, 181, 219.
Tommas, Tom, 80.
Tompson, 58.
Tompson, Alexander, 58.
Tomson, Thomas, 161.
Tone, John F., 104, 131.
Toney, Jesse, 128.
Toney, Jethro, 75, 104, 131.
Tongue, Jonathan, 181.
Tongue, Jono, 219.
Toomy, Daniel, 238.
Toping, Josiah, 203.
Toppand, Ezekiel, 109.
Topping, Paul, 62.
Torrance, William, 136, 142.
Torrell, Hezekiah, 126.
Torrence, Joseph, 136.
Torrence, Samuel, Jr., 136.
Torrence, Thomas, 136.
Torrence, William, 38.
Torrey, Asa, 79.
Torrey, Dennis, 69.
Torrey, William, Jr., 6.
Torringsford, 75.
Torrington, 20, 67, 273.
Torry, John, 163.
Torry, Samuel, 230.
Tossell, John, 79.
Tousley, Sylvenus, 37.
Tower, Gideon, 170.
Towers, John, 62.
Towner, Dan, 85.
Towner, Jacob, 72.
Townsand, Solomon, 61.
Townsen, David, 161.
Townsen, Jonathan, 161.
Townsend, Solomon, 271.
Townshand, Benjaman, 188.
Towsley, Micah, 58, 59.
Towstey, Micah, 60.
Tozen, Jared, 56.
Tracey, Benajah, 55.
Tracey, Dudley, 81.
Tracey, Elias, 95.
Tracey, Silas, 82.
Tracey, Solomon, 246, 248.
Tracy, 50.
Tracy, Bela, 175.
Tracy, Cyrus, 175.
Tracy, Elias, 66.

Tracy, Gilbart, 186.
Tracy, Giles, 258.
Tracy, Hezekiah, 91.
Tracy, Levi, 174.
Tracy, Moses, 64, 271.
Tracy, Peris, 174.
Tracy, Phineas L., 278.
Tracy, Richmond, 175.
Tracy, S., 213.
Tracy, Solomon, 6.
Tracy, William, 45.
Treadway, David, 4, 163.
Treadway, John, 134.
Treadwell, Benjamin, 109.
Treat, Bethuel, 211, 225.
Treat, Charles, 154, 156.
Treat, Gershom, 74, 228.
Treat, John, 90.
Treat, Joseph, 101.
Treat, Oliver, 153, 155.
Treat, Salmon, 74, 186, 228.
Tredaway, John, 141.
Treet, James, 241.
Treet, Jonathan, 158.
Treet, Mingo, 73.
Trickey, Jered, 61.
Tripp, Isaac, 199.
Trobridg, Seth, 197.
Trobridge, Oliver, 196.
Trowbridg, Eli, 196.
Trowbridge, 22.
Trowbridge, Abel, 196.
Trowbridge, B., 142.
Trowbridge, Caleb, 17, 24.
Trowbridge, Isaac, 37, 206.
Trowbridge, John, 17, 48.
Trowbridge, Stephen, 199.
Trowbridge, William, 67.
Trueman, David, 240.
Truesdel, Ebenezer, 170.
Truesdil, Darius, 131.
Trumble, Jonathan, Jr., 42.
Trumbul, Ezekiel, 201.
Trumbul, Grig, 73.
Trumbull, David, 221.
Trumbull, Ezekiel, 19.
Trumbull, George, 228.
"Trumbull," 237.
Trusdale, Darius, 125.
Trusdell, Darius, 104.
Trusdell, Ebenezer, 9.
Tryon, Edward, 230.
Tryon, Eli, 153, 156.
Tryon, Ezra, 122.
Tryon, Ezry, 61.
Tryon, Josiah, 80.
Tryon, William, 60, 189.
Tubbs, Eleazer, 185.

Tubbs, Elemuel, 137.
Tubbs, Isaac, 158.
Tubbs, Lemuel, 137, 139.
Tubbs, Martin, 111.
Tubbs, Nathan, 30, 124.
Tucker, Daniel, 38, 76.
Tucker, Daniel, Jr., 38.
Tucker, Elisha, 78.
Tucker, Isaac, 212.
Tucker, John, 110, 238, 239.
Tucker, Timothy, 64.
Tucker, Zepheniah, 189.
Tuder, Thomas, 278.
Tudor, Daniel, 278.
Tuels, Samuel, 134.
Tullar, Eli, 125.
Tullar, Israel, 142.
Tuller, Ehud, 164.
Tuller, Eli, 104.
Tuller, Elijah, 164.
Tuller, Joel, 164.
Tuller, John, 184.
Tully, Christopher, 53.
Tupper, Ezra, 95.
Tupper, Mahu, 32.
Tupper, Nathan, 231.
Tupper, William, 111.
Turkens, Tiras, 54.
Turner, 97.
Turner, Charles, 240.
Turner, Enoch, Jr., 271.
Turner, Joseph, 184.
Turner, Moses, 39.
Turner, Thomas, 119.
Turner, William, 127.
Turney, Jana, 54.
Turrel, Daniel, 195.
Turrell, Noah, 38.
Turtle Bay, 137.
Tuthill, Daniel, 101.
Tuttle, Aaron, 83, 271.
Tuttle, Beri, 276.
Tuttle, Charles, 24.
Tuttle, Clement, 16, 235.
Tuttle, Edmond, 217.
Tuttle, Eli, 17, 20.
Tuttle, Enos, 72, 104, 109, 130.
Tuttle, Ezekiel, 90.
Tuttle, Hezekiah, 91.
Tuttle, Ichabod, 39.
Tuttle, Jasphat, 19.
Tuttle, Japhat, 24.
Tuttle, Joel, 37.
Tuttle, Jonathan, Jr., 133.
Tuttle, Josiah, 275.
Tuttle, Levi, 271.
Tuttle, Lucius, 223.
Tuttle, Nathaniel, 20, 29, 31.

## INDEX. 367

Tuttle, Peter, 217.
Tuttle, Solomon, 13.
Tuttle, Timothy, 90.
Tyack, William, 203.
Tylar, Nathaniel, 69.
Tyler, 17, 207, 222, 225.
Tyler, A., 206.
Tyler, Abel, 30.
Tyler, Abraham, 16, 223, 278.
Tyler, Asa, 266.
Tyler, Daniel, 212, 222.
Tyler, Jacob, 202.
Tyler, Nathaniel, 34.
Tyler, Oliver, 170.
Tyler, Rufus, 186.
Tyler, Samuel, 102 203.
Tyng, Cato, 260.
Tyrrel, Thomas, 3.

Uffoot, Benjamin, 141.
Uffoot, John, 141.
Uffoot, Samuel, 141.
Ufford, Eliakim, 135.
Uffott, Job, 77.
Uffott, Samuel, 211.
Umsted, Roger, 22.
Uncas, Bimeleck, 263.
Unchous, Benjamin, 263.
Union, 58, 61, 89, 90, 103.
Upham, Chester, 122.
Upson, Ashbel, 119.
Upson, Samuel, 182, 209.
Upton, Elias, 114, 116.
Usher, Robert, 133.
Utley, John, 150.
Utter, Isaac, 82.
Utter, James, 178, 184.

Vail, Moses, 190.
Vallants, John, 203.
Vallet, Samuel, 122.
Van Dosen, Thomas, 242.
Van Duson, Thomas, 246, 250.
Van Dyke, Peter, 24.
Vaughan, John, 140, 182.
Vaughn, Benjamin, 37.
Vaughn, John, 127, 128, 149.
Vaughn, William, 170.
Veale, Guillam, 232.
Verguson, John, 112.
Verrey, Jonathan, 61.
Vial, Peter, 222.
Viall, Joseph, 224.
Viets, Seth, 203.
Violet, Dick, 113.
Virginia, 110, 120, 188.
Voas, Adam, 32.
Voigson, John, 72.

Voluntown, 57, 64, 65, 66, 79, 81, 82, 89, 90, 102, 104, 171.
Vose, Jesse, 112.

Wacker, Rodolphus, 102.
Waddams, Caleb, 13.
Wade, Martin, 91.
Wade, Stephen, 72.
Wadsworth, 114.
Wadsworth, George, 187.
Wadsworth, Ichabod, 1, 165.
Wadsworth, Isrcl, 187.
Wadsworth, James, 133, 134, 223, 225, 274.
Wadsworth, John N., 192.
Wadsworth, Luke, 59.
Wadsworth, Nathen, 187.
Wadsworth, Roger, 47.
Wadsworth, Theodore, 48.
Wadsworth, William, 192.
Waggs, Daniel, 246, 250.
Wahlee, Mel, 230.
Waid, Ebenezer, 184.
Wailes, William, 185.
Wailey, Aron, 69.
Wainwright, Thomas, 38.
Wait, Daniel, 47.
Wait, Richard, 211.
Wait, Samuel, 79.
Wakeley, Abiel, 76.
Wakeley, Benjamin, 122.
Wakeley, Henry, 136.
Wakeley, John J., 76.
Wakely, Joseph, 109.
Wakely, Thomas, 119.
Wakeman, Jabez, 86.
Wakeman, Squier, 197.
Wakeman, Stephen, 181.
Wakins, John, 57.
Waklee, Benjamin, 54.
Waklee, John, 271.
Walace, Abram, Jr., 2.
Walan, Ezekiel, 108.
Walbridge, Ames, 46.
Walbridge, Amos, 53.
Walden, Ichabod, 109.
Walding, David, 65.
Waldo, Albegence, 240.
Waldo, Albigence, 91.
Waldo, Allegence, 245.
Waldo, Henry, 94, 120.
Waldo, Joseph, 143.
Waldo, Zacheriah, 109.
Waldo, Zacheus, 64.
Waldon, Henry, 120.
Walds, Albigence, 45.
Wales, Aron, 15.
Wales, Ebenezer, 15, 47.

Wales, Eleazer, 32.
Wales, Elieazr, 15.
Wales, Nathaniel, 223.
Walker, 122, 130.
Walker, Abel, 151.
Walker, David, 79.
Walker, Elisha, 76.
Walker, Henry, 238.
Walker, James, 15, 58.
Walker, John, 140.
Walker, Joseph, 263.
Walker, Josiah, 181, 219, 232, 253.
Walker, Nathan, 76, 104, 131.
Walker, Peter, 173.
Walker, Samuel, 15.
Wall, James, 253.
Wallace, James, 2, 166.
Wallace, John, 2, 166.
Wallace, Joseph, 69.
Wallace, William, 2, 166.
Waller, Ashbel, 56.
Waller, Daniel, 27.
Waller, Levi, 42, 43.
Walles, Charles, 32.
Wallingford, 18, 19, 22, 24, 53, 54, 58, 61, 70, 71, 76, 78, 81, 82, 88, 89, 90, 111, 112, 118, 194, 276.
Wallis, Charles, 62.
Wallor, Nathan, 190.
Walsore, Moses, 55.
Walter, Charles, 39.
Walter, John, 39.
Walter, William, 91.
Walters, Charles, 124.
Walton, Henry, 175, 254.
Walton, John, 254, 264.
Wampey, Charles, 59.
Waples, Thomas, 257.
Ward, 223.
Ward, A., 206.
Ward, Aaron, 58, 59, 60.
Ward, Allin, 141.
Ward, Andrew, 133, 210, 265, 278.
Ward, Andrew, Jr., 16, 21, 22, 23, 24, 25.
Ward, Benjamin, 95.
Ward, Cruttenden, 257.
Ward, Cruttendon, 263.
Ward, Daniel, 15.
Ward, David, 80, 193.
Ward, Eber, 205.
Ward, Elisha, 230.
Ward, James, 29, 31.
Ward, Jeremiah, 257.
Ward, Nathan, 15.
Ward, Samuel, 181, 190, 219.
Ward, Simon R., 264.
Ward, Stephen, 244, 245, 246, 248, 251, 258.
Ward, Stephen, Jr., 258.
Ward, Thelus, Jr., 277.
Ward, William, 91, 213.
Wardell, Samuel, 112.
Warden, Thomas, 123.
Warden, Walter, 91.
Wardon, Henry, 29.
Wardwell, Jacob, 53.
Ware, Josiah, 246, 250.
Wareing, Enoch, 218.
Wares, Elias, 58, 60.
Wares, Joseph, 158.
Waring, Abraham, 194.
Waring, James, 217.
Waring, Joseph, 217.
Waring, Jesse, 218.
Waring, Jonathan, 226.
Waring, Samuel, Jr., 85.
Warner, 13, 265, 267.
Warner, Abner, 27.
Warner, Abraham, 185.
Warner, Amasa, 34, 97.
Warner, Amos, 108.
Warner, Andrew, 74.
Warner, Charles, 78, 105.
Warner, Daniel, 1, 38, 154, 156, 165.
Warner, David, 237.
Warner, Elisha, 163.
Warner, Josiah, 278.
Warner, Justice, 278.
Warner, Mark, 278.
Warner, Marles, 196.
Warner, Moses, 23, 24.
Warner, Robert, 38, 46, 61, 62, 153, 155.
Warner, Roswell, 27.
Warner, Seth, 237.
Warner, Solomon, 110, 116.
Warner, Stephen, 1.
Warner, William, 229.
Warnor, Amos, 70.
Warren, Ahijah, 201.
Warren, Edward, 110.
Warren, Ezra, 169.
Warren, James, 42, 43.
Warren, John, 57, 58, 60.
Warren, Lemuel, 169.
Warren, Reuben, 36.
Warrin, John, 97.
Warring, Jonathan, 210.
Warron, Doris, 188.
Warron, Dorus, 187.
Warsan, John, 233.
Washbon, Edward, 66.

INDEX. 369

Washborn, Levy, 159.
Washington, George, 84, 138, 160, 161, 162, 163.
Washington, 52, 80, 82, 88, 89, 91, 110, 268, 279.
Wasson, James, 121.
Waterbury, 24, 267.
Waterbury, David, 17, 18, 19, 21, 22, 23, 24, 25.
Waterbury, John, 201.
Waterbury, William, 104, 131.
Waterbury, 17, 24, 52, 53, 54, 55, 58, 60, 66, 75, 76, 77, 78, 79, 81, 82, 88, 89, 90, 91, 104, 111, 220.
Waterhouse, Isaac, 32.
Waterhouse, John, 35, 211.
Waterhouse, Jonathan, 257.
Waterhouse, Samuel, 37.
Waterman, A., 200.
Waterman, Amasa, 258.
Waterman, Andrew, 5, 134, 159, 160.
Waterman, Chester, 123.
Waterman, Derias, 259.
Waterman, Ezekiel, 185.
Waterman, Gladden, 260.
Waterman, Joseph, 267, 271.
Waterman, N., 207, 209.
Waterman, Nehemiah, 209.
Waterman, Robert, 187.
Waterman, William, 259, 262.
Waters, Benjamin, 55.
Waters, Bigelow, 80.
Waters, Daniel, 159.
Waters, Gideon, 63, 160.
Waters, Joseph, 159.
Waters, Timothy, 163.
Waters, William, 57.
Watertown, 102, 111.
Watkins, John, 244, 247, 248.
Watkins, Nathan, 15.
Watkins, Robart, 97.
Watkins, Thomas, 13, 42, 43.
Watkins, William, 15.
Watrous, Benjamin, 113.
Watrous, Elisha, 160.
Watrous, John R., 47.
Watrous, Richard, 91, 266, 271.
Watrous, Thomas, 61.
Watrous, William, 15.
Watson, Asa, 185.
Watson, Heman, 39.
Watson, John, 20, 22, 23, 227.
Watson, John, Jr., 16, 17, 19, 21.
Watson, Nathaniel, 18, 24.
Watson, Thomas, 95, 117, 127.
Watson, Titus, 39, 48.
Watson, William, 187.

24

Watterman, Robert, 188.
Watteson, William, 188.
Wattles, Chandlor, 259.
Wattles, Samuel, 260.
Wattles, Samuel, Jr., 5, 160.
Wattles, Thomas, 6.
Wattles, William H., 259.
Watton, Henry, 118.
Waugh, Alexander, 201, 209.
Waugh, Samuel, 69.
Waugh, Thadeus, 69.
Way, 19.
Way, Abner, 193, 276.
Way, Elisha, 132.
Way, Hammon, 91.
Way, John, 273.
Way, Moses, 193.
Way, Seely, 201.
Wayland, James, 271.
Wayland, John, 181, 219.
Wayley, Aaron, 106, 126.
Waymend, Increase, 55.
Wealer, William, 35.
Weathers, Thomas, 135.
Weaver, Francis, 80.
Weaver, Samuel, 63, 87.
Webb, 227, 267.
Webb, Abner, 143.
Webb, Abnor, 185.
Webb, Charles, 16, 17, 20, 21, 22, 23, 28, 29, 30, 265, 267.
Webb, Constant, 266, 271.
Webb, David, 53.
Webb, Isaac, 178.
Webb, John, 262.
Webb, Jonah, 94, 111, 116, 117, 127.
Webb, Jonas, 36.
Webb, Jonathan, 63, 91.
Webb, Jooseph, 240.
Webb, Joseph, 241.
Webb, Nathaniel, 47, 63.
Webb, Samuel B., 80, 100, 104, 129, 265, 267.
Webster, Aaron, 145, 147.
Webster, Abraham, 35.
Webster, Amos, 202.
Webster, Ashbel, 128, 145.
Webster, Ashbil, 137.
Webster, Benjamin, 127, 128, 201.
Webster, David, 6.
Webster, Elijah, 201.
Webster, Elisha, 154, 156.
Webster, George, 6.
Webster, Guida, 6.
Webster, Isaac, 274.
Webster, James, 6, 163.
Webster, Jonathan, Jr., 6.

## REVOLUTION ROLLS AND LISTS.

Webster, Joshua, 91.
Webster, Noah, 223.
Webster, Oliver, 66.
Webster, Reuben, 201.
Webster, Samuel, 254.
Webster, William, 163.
Wedge, Joshua, 55, 91.
Wedge, Stephen, 56.
Wedge, Thomas, 17.
Weeb, Benjamin, 205.
Weed, Benjamin, 53.
Weed, Benjamin, Jr., 271.
Weed, Eleazer, 198.
Weed, Gideon, 85.
Weed, Nathaniel, 226.
Weed, Samuel, 200.
Weed, Seth, 271.
Weed, Thaddeus, 47.
Weed, Thadeus, 50.
Weedg, Elijah, 200.
Weeks, Joseph, 30, 31, 91.
Weeks, Micajah, 69.
Weeks, Timothy, 246, 251.
Weight, Jacob, 1st, 122.
Weight, Jacob, 2d, 122.
Welch, Christopher, 68.
Welch, David, 18, 19, 21, 23, 82.
Welch, Ebenezer, 59.
Welch, Eleazer, 246, 248.
Welch, John, 13, 81, 184.
Welch, Michael, 83, 91.
Welden, Isaac, 69.
Welden, Peleg, 158.
Welding, Jonathan, 250.
Weller, Amos, 38.
Weller, Asahel, 38.
Weller, William G., 34.
Welles, G., 84.
Welles, Hezekiah, 133.
Welles, John, 158.
Welles, Jonathan, 133.
Welles, Roger, 121.
Welles, Samuel, 137.
Wellman, John, 115, 116, 264.
Wellman, Paul, 24.
Wellman, William, 113.
Welman, John, 257.
Wells, 214, 266.
Wells, Abijah, 190.
Wells, Ashbel, 274.
Wells, Austen, 42.
Wells, Austin, 43.
Wells, Bayze, 35.
Wells, Benjamin, 181, 210.
Wells, C., 207.
Wells, Chester, 153, 155, 188, 209.
Wells, David, 73.
Wells, Ebenezer, 154, 156.
Wells, Elias, 151.
Wells, Elihu, 163.
Wells, Elisha, 154, 156.
Wells, Gideon, 232.
Wells, Hezekiah, 209.
Wells, J., 214.
Wells, James, 22, 151.
Wells, Jedediah F., 22.
Wells, Jehiel, 146.
Wells, John, 159, 181, 219.
Wells, John, Jr., 274.
Wells, John H., 163.
Wells, Jonah, 263.
Wells, Jonathan, 188, 192, 211.
Wells, Joshua, 154, 155.
Wells, Levi, 18, 23, 212.
Wells, Noah, 212.
Wells, Robert, 211.
Wells, Samuel, 139, 190, 209, 211.
Wells, Solomon, 23.
Wells, Thomas, 76, 102, 129, 175.
Wells, Wate, 175.
Weltch, David, 66.
Welton, Benjamin, 61, 113.
Welton, Stephen, Jr., 91.
Wentworth, Gibbens, 39.
Wentworth, Gibbon, 20.
Wentworth, Shuble, 39.
Wentworth, Sion, 154.
Wert, Joseph, 117.
Wesson, Samuel, 21.
West, Aaron, 82.
West, David, 61.
West, Ichabod, 124.
West, Jabez, 18.
West, John, 51.
West, Jonathan, 82.
West, Joseph, 91, 94, 127.
West, Jude, 6.
West, Lemuel, 166.
West, N., 142.
West, Samuel, 4, 163.
West Point, 59, 214.
Westchester, 61, 159, 163, 171, 226.
Westcoat, Eleazer, 74.
Western, Benjamin, 91.
Westland, Amos, 93, 128.
Westland, Joseph, 51.
Westmoreland, 227.
Weston, John, 203.
Weston, Robert, 68.
Weston, Samuel, 203.
Wetherbee, Hezekiah, 85.
Wetherlegs, George, 250.
Wethersfield, 58, 59, 60, 61, 62, 80, 81, 82, 87, 89, 91, 222.
Wetherty, David, 81.
Wethey, Elijah, 175.

# INDEX. 371

Wethey, Ephraim, 175.
Wethey, Henry, 175.
Wetmore, Amos, 208.
Wetmore, David, 201.
Wetmore, Jacob, 134.
Wetmore, John, 208.
Wetmore, Josiah, 135.
Whaley, Jonathan, 271.
Whaley, Theophilus, 253.
Whaling, Walter, 35.
Whealer, Caleb, 38.
Whealor, Joseph, 155.
Wheat, Samuel, 209.
Wheaten, Jonathan, 30.
Wheaton, Jeremiah, 99.
Wheaton, Joseph, 242.
Whedon, Roswell, 70. 112.
Whedon, Rufus, 112.
Whedon, Samuel, 9.
Wheedon, Rufus, 72.
Wheeler, A., 84.
Wheeler, Benjamin, 76.
Wheeler, Daniel, 57, 58. 60.
Wheeler, David, 180.
Wheeler, Elizur, 213.
Wheeler, Elnathan, 181. 219.
Wheeler, Ephraim, 68.
Wheeler, Hezekiah, 101.
Wheeler, J., 213.
Wheeler, Jabez, 180.
Wheeler, Jacob, 35.
Wheeler, Job, 237.
Wheeler, John, 56, 124.
Wheeler, Johnson, 213.
Wheeler, Joseph, 154.
Wheeler, Joshua, 53, 122.
Wheeler, M., 190.
Wheeler, N., 177.
Wheeler, Nathaniel, 151.
Wheeler, Samuel, 151.
Wheeler, Stephen, 68.
Wheeler, Thomas, 72, 113, 211.
Wheelock, Thaddeus, 67.
Wheetor, Aaron, 169.
Whelden, Thomas, 252.
Whelding, Jonathan, 246.
Wheler, 150.
Wheler, Abel, 189.
Wheler, Amos, 150.
Wheler, Jeremiah, 150.
Wheler, John, 189.
Wheler, Joseph, 150.
Wheler, Moses, 189.
Wheler, Nathan, 189.
Whelor, Ely, 195.
Whippell, Joseph, 68.
Whipple, Eleazer, 66.
Whipple, Frederick, 102, 124, 130.
Whipple, Jonathan, 82.
Whipple, William, 32.
Whitcomb, John, 94.
Whitcomb, Robert, 37.
Whitcomb, Simon, 34.
White, 56.
White, Aaron, 229.
White, Adonijah, 2, 3, 161.
White, Alexsander, 163.
White, Asa, 162.
White, Charles, 263.
White, Daniel, 115, 161.
White, David, 20.
White, Eli, 56.
White, Fadrick, 163.
White, George, 138.
White, Gideon, 32.
White, John, 27, 120, 138.
White, Jonathan, 100.
White, Joseph, 110.
White, Lemuel, 79.
White, Nathan, 69.
White, Obediah, 162.
White, Oliver, 113.
White, Thomas, 274.
White, William, 95, 111, 117, 127, 135, 163, 184.
White Plains, 139.
Whitehead, Christopher, 141.
Whitehead, Nathaniel, 16.
Whitely, William, 91.
Whitemore, Joseph, 232.
Whiting, 190.
Whiting, Daniel, 58.
Whiting, Frederick J., 143.
Whiting, Henry, 91.
Whiting, Hervy, 105, 202.
Whiting, John, 27, 151, 181, 219, 225.
Whiting, Jonathan, 227.
Whiting, Joseph, 204.
Whiting, Nathan H., 50, 104, 122.
Whiting, Nehemiah, 232.
Whiting, S., 177, 224.
Whiting, Samuel, 18, 22, 23, 24, 143, 151, 152, 177, 180, 212, 222, 225, 226, 227, 265.
Whiting, William, 16, 21, 274.
Whitlock, Justus, 213.
Whitlock, Thaddeus, 85.
Whitman, Jesse, 78.
Whitman, John, 160.
Whitman, Samuel, 21.
Whitmore, Joseph, 211.
Whitnay, John, 138.
Whitney, 111.
Whitney, Cornas, 168.
Whitney, Daniel, 61.

Whitney, Ebenezer, 212.
Whitney, Ezekiel, 69.
Whitney, Gilbert, 118.
Whitney, Henry, 225.
Whitney, Hezekiah, 213.
Whitney, Jedediah, 174.
Whitney, John, 175.
Whitney, Joseph, 168.
Whitney, Joshua, 49, 50, 76.
Whitney, Josiah, 21, 39, 68.
Whitney, Mathias, 168.
Whitney, Peter, 101.
Whitney, Rufus, 37.
Whitney, Samuel, 53, 99, 121.
Whitney, Tarbal, 221.
Whitney, William, 174, 183, 211, 222.
Whiton, Ebenezer, 186.
Whiton, Elijah, 133.
Whiton, James, 133.
Whiton, Thomas, 146, 147.
Whittlecey, Dave, 230.
Whittlesey, John, 261, 264.
Whittlesey, Joseph, 113.
Wiar, Thomas, 39, 91.
Wick, John, 277.
Wickham, Hezekiah, 137.
Wickham, John, 158.
Wickham, William, 61.
Wickwire, Grant, 51.
Widger, John, 53.
Wiggins, Cocher, 99.
Wiggins, Coker, 68.
Wilborn, Cato, 104.
Wilbrow, Cato, 108, 131.
Wilbur, Adin, 175.
Wilbur, Stephen, 65.
Wilcockson, Nathan, 184.
Wilcockson, Elnathan, 151.
Wilcockson, Ephraim, 219.
Wilcott, John, 235.
Wilcox, Comfort, 135.
Wilcox, Daniel, 6, 37, 162.
Wilcox, Ephraim, 163.
Wilcox, Ezra, 271.
Wilcox, Francis, 194.
Wilcox, Janna, 126.
Wilcox, Jehial, 163.
Wilcox, Jehiel, 113.
Wilcox, John, 202.
Wilcox, Joseph, 49.
Wilcox, Joshua, 150.
Wilcox, Lemuel, 107.
Wilcox, Martin, 36.
Wilcox, Moses, 202.
Wilcox, Moses, 2d, 202.
Wilcox, Oliver, 203.
Wilcox, Philemon, 273.

Wilcox, Sammuel, 43.
Wilcox, Samuel, 37.
Wilcox, Stephen, 34.
Wilcoxon, John, 93.
Wild, Jehiel, 146.
Wilder, Aaron, 267.
Wilder, Thomas, 146, 147, 148.
Wildman, Comfort, 108.
Wildman, Daniel, 198, 208.
Wildman, David, Jr., 198.
Wildman, Isaac, 200.
Wildman, Obed, 198.
Wildman, Samuel, Jr., 198.
Wildor, Thomas, 145.
Wiley, John, 142.
Wiliams, Samuel, 182.
Wilkee, Matthew, 200.
Wilkinson, Ichabod, 73.
Wilkinson, Reuben, 39.
Willard, Daniell, 205.
Willard, John, 253.
Willcocks, Aaron, 164.
Willcocks, Charles, 145, 147, 148.
Willcocks, Isaac, 164.
Willcocks, Jehel, 146.
Willcocks, Jehial, 148.
Willcocks, Samuel, 42.
Willcocks, William, 145, 148.
Willcockson, Ephraim, 181.
Willcok, Elisha, 164.
Willcoks, Aaron, 148.
Willcoks, Jehiall, 147.
Willcoks, Sedose, 164.
Willcon, Joel, 97.
Willcox, Ezra, 266.
Willcox, Isaac, 23.
Willcox, Janna, 106.
Willcox, Jeremiah, 142.
Willcox, John, 135.
Willes, John, 20.
Willes, Solomon, 18, 24, 25, 133.
Willey, John, 133, 134, 210.
Willey, Josiah, 231.
William, Simeon, 175.
Williams, 124.
Williams, Absalom, 212.
Williams, Andrew, 5.
Williams, Asahel, 3, 4.
Williams, Asher, 64.
Williams, Benjamin, 65, 186.
Williams, Benjamin, Jr., 178.
Williams, Billy, 5.
Williams, Charles, 5, 162.
Williams, Daniel, 24, 119.
Williams, David, 122, 178, 180, 265.
Williams, Davidson, 29, 31.
Williams, Ebenezar, 178.

Williams, Ebenezer, 227.
Williams, Ezra, 30, 31.
Williams, Harry, 110.
Williams, Hector, 109.
Williams, Henry, 246, 248.
Williams, Isaac, 39, 150, 216.
Williams, Isaac, 2nd, 150.
Williams, Israel, 162.
Williams, Jabez, 69.
Williams, Jacob, 39, 271.
Williams, Jehiel, 5.
Williams, Jeremiah, 218.
Williams, Johiel, 162.
Williams, John, 6. 77, 162. 178, 207, 208, 210, 240, 244, 246, 248, 250, 267.
Williams, John, 2d, 178.
Williams, Joseph, 216.
Williams, Nat, 150.
Williams, Othniel, 208, 211.
Williams, Peter, 175.
Williams, Prince, 114, 116.
Williams, Ralph, 216.
Williams, Rufus, 216.
Williams, Samuel, 21, 37, 210, 259.
Williams, Samuel, 4th, 216.
Williams, Seth, 216.
Williams, Thomas, 245, 247, 249, 260, 271.
Williams, Vetch, 5, 6.
Williams, Vetch, Jr., 6, 160.
Williams, Warren, 172.
Williams, William, 5, 6, 15, 25, 34, 170, 216, 233.
Williamson, Zelophehad, 69.
Willington, 23, 54, 55, 89, 90, 102, 133.
Willis, John, 23.
Willis, Jonathan, 160.
Willis, Joseph, 107.
Willis, Reuben, 34.
Willmot, Samuel, 20, 21, 22.
Willocks, Hose, Jr., 39.
Willoughbey, Bliss, 105.
Willoughbey, Christopher, 105.
Wills, Jonathan, 6.
Willson, Abiel, 20.
Willson, Abner, 20.
Willson, James, 138.
Willson, John, 17, 22, 24.
Willson, Joseph, 101.
Willson, Moses, 220.
Willson, Stephen, 235.
Willson, William, 28, 208.
Wilmot, Elisha, 276.
Wilson, Amos, 139.
Wilson, Calvin, 114.
Wilson, David, Jr., 190.
Wilson, Eli, 202.
Wilson, Ezekiel, 200.
Wilson, Jacob, 63.
Wilson, James, 82.
Wilson, John, 27, 109, 235, 244. 247, 248.
Wilson, Nathaniel, 245, 249.
Wilson, Robert, 85, 195.
Wilson, Thomas, 54, 68, 254.
Wilson, William, 271.
Wilton, Solomon, 64.
Wilton, 78, 202, 205.
Wimberly, James, 254.
Winban, Prince, 204.
Winchel, Daniel, 22, 53.
Winchel, John. 67, 202.
Winchell, Daniel, 121, 273.
Winchester, 66, 67, 78.
Winchil, Nath, 203.
Windham, 23, 24, 58, 65, 66, 74. 75, 78, 79, 88, 89, 90, 91, 103. 114, 118.
Windsor, 24, 57, 58, 59, 60, 62. 67, 68, 69, 76, 78, 80, 91. 114.
Winfield, Daniel, 264.
Winifred, Daniel, 236.
Winkley, Henry, 152.
Winship, John, 118.
Winston, Thomas, 245, 246, 250.
Winter, Timothy, 185.
Winthrop, Frederick, 17.
Winton, Nathan, 69.
Winton, Peter, 84.
Wintworth, Zion, 156.
Winwright, William, 135.
Wire, John, 157.
Wire, Nehimiah, 158.
Wire, Samuel, 42, 43.
Wires, Elias, 61.
Wiry, Samuel, 13.
Wiscutt, Zebulon, 243.
Wise, Joseph, 235.
Wise, Samuel, 184.
Wise, Uriah, 91.
Witherill, Samuel, 68.
Withey, Lemuel, 174.
Witmore, Jacob, 208.
Witmore, Nathaniel, 230.
Witt, Edward J., 74.
Witter, Ebenezer, 186.
Witters, Ebenezer, 210.
Wittlesey, John, 257.
Wodard, Lee, 171.
Wolcott, 221.
Wolcott, Elisha, 154.

Wolcott, Elizur, 154.
Wolcott, Erastus, 46, 54, 133, 149. 211.
Wolcott, Josiah, 255.
Wolcott, O., 221, 225.
Wolcott, Oliver, 210.
Wolcott, Samuel, 39.
Wolcott, William, 154, 242.
Wolcut, Benajah, 108.
Wolcut, Elijah, 108.
Wolf, Aaron D., 228.
Wolf, Anthony, 240.
Woobrig, Timothy, 146.
Woobury, John, 246, 250.
Wood, Alexander, 255.
Wood, Benjamin, 93, 194.
Wood, Daniel, 198.
Wood, David, 209, 226.
Wood, Eli, 25.
Wood, Elijah, 194.
Wood, Henry, 212.
Wood, Israel, 79.
Wood, Jacob, 61.
Wood, Jacob, Jr., 61.
Wood, James, 56.
Wood, Joel, 135.
Wood, John, 32, 211, 260.
Wood, John, Jr., 175.
Wood, Joseph, 194.
Wood, Lemuel, Jr., 198.
Wood, Samuel, 72, 146, 147.
Wood, Stephen, 218.
Wood, Thomas, 54, 240.
Wood, Timothy, 137.
Woodard, Amos, 14.
Woodard, John, 15.
Woodard, Lee, 172.
Woodard, Samuel, 149.
Woodard, Ward, 167.
Woodbridg, Timothy, 145.
Woodbridge, 146.
Woodbridge, Christopher, 28, 31.
Woodbridge, Hoel, 227.
Woodbridge, Howel, 208.
Woodbridge, Theodore, 12, 41, 42, 43, 48.
Woodbridge, Theophilus, 7, 46, 58, 60.
Woodbridge, Timothy, 146, 147, 148, 261.
Woodburn, Francoes, 233.
Woodbury, 20, 22, 23, 24, 53, 54, 55, 66, 67, 75, 76, 77, 78, 79, 80, 83, 88, 89, 102, 103, 104, 110, 267.
Woodcock, Samuel, 69, 271.
Wooden, Joseph, 202.
Woodfood, Joseph, 79.
Woodford, Joseph, 182, 211.
Woodford, Timothy, 37.
Woodhoop, Lemuel, 153.
Woodhouse, John, 154, 156.
Woodhouse, Lemuel, 155.
Woodhouse, Samuel, 154, 156.
Wooding, Calvin, 187.
Wooding, Jer., 109.
Woodman, Samuel, 173.
Woodmansee, Joseph, 271.
Woodroof, Asa, 52.
Woodrose, David, 179.
Woodruff, 223.
Woodruff, Andrew, 201.
Woodruff, Benjamin, 258.
Woodruff, Enoch, 205, 211.
Woodruff, John, 201, 209, 273.
Woodruff, Judah, 182, 207, 223, 224.
Woodruff, Martin, 21.
Woodruff, Philo, 273.
Woodruff, Samuel, 201.
Woodruff, Solomon, 201, 273.
Woodruff, William, 75, 271.
Woodruff, Zebulon, 59.
Woodstock, 53, 54, 64, 65, 66, 68, 88, 89, 90, 103, 104.
Woodward, Ambrous, 82.
Woodward, Amos, 14, 74, 185, 206, 222.
Woodward, Benjamin, 2.
Woodward, Daniel, 114, 120.
Woodward, Fredrick, 82.
Woodward, John, 15, 140.
Woodward, Lee, 172.
Woodward, Noah, Jr., 136.
Woodward, Oliver, 91.
Woodwarth, Benjamin, 3.
Woodworth, Abel, 246, 247, 248, 253, 256.
Woodworth, Able, 262.
Woodworth, Azel, 271.
Woodworth, Benjamin, 4.
Woodworth, Heman, 116.
Woodworth, James, 163.
Woodworth, Jedediah, 80.
Woodworth, Jonathan, 252.
Woodworth, Joshua, 163.
Woodworth, Josiah, 260, 261.
Woodworth, Recompense, 118.
Woodworth, Reuben, 4.
Woodworth, Ruel, 185.
Woolcot, Erastus, 149.
Woolcott, Elisha, 156.
Woolcott, Elizur, 156.
Woolcott, Simeon, 139.
Woolcott, William, 156.
Woolcut, Bennajor, 70.

# INDEX. 375

Woolcut, Samuel, 82.
Woolf, Anthony, 257.
Woolf, John, 245, 249.
Woolf, Stephen D., 245.
Woolworth, Ebenezer, 68.
Wooster, 190, 221, 265.
Wooster, David, 9, 12, 16, 17, 18, 19, 20, 21, 22, 23, 24, 25, 43.
Wooster, Ephraim, 190.
Wooster, Henman, 78.
Wooster, Thomas. 91.
Worden, Arnold, 95.
Worden, Henry, 31, 51.
Worden, Ichabud. 186.
Worden, Wait, 51.
Wording, Ichabod, 124.
Wordwell, Nathan, 55.
Worner, Eliphaz. 136.
Worthington, 222.
Worthington, E., 210.
Worthington, William, 178, 191, 200, 210, 211, 221, 223, 277.
Worthington, Mass., 103.
Worthylake, George. 246, 247, 253.
Wright, 4, 6, 209.
Wright, Amaziah, 227.
Wright, Asher, 29, 31, 192.
Wright, Beriah, 56.
Wright, Charles, 21, 39, 209.
Wright, Daniel. 59, 65, 116, 185.
Wright, David, 21, 39.
Wright, Ebenezer, 153, 155.
Wright, Ezekiel, 91.
Wright, Frances, 61.
Wright, Isaiah, 91.
Wright, J., 69, 206.
Wright, Jabez, 209, 210, 225.
Wright, James, 68.
Wright, Jeriah. 149.
Wright, Jesse, 163.
Wright, Job, 210.
Wright, John, 58, 61, 97, 230.
Wright, Jonathan. 105.
Wright, Joseph. 154, 156, 192.
Wright, Joseph A., 47.
Wright, Moses, 105.
Wright, Samuel, 25, 34, 64, 211.
Wright, Sim., 18.

Wright, Solomon, 149.
Wright, Timothy, 185.
Write, Abel, 163.
Write, Ezekiel, 163.
Wyard, Lemuel, 138.
Wyett, Benjamin, 259.
Wylder, Moses, 185.
Wylie, John, 171.
Wylie, Robart, 171.
Wyllys, H., 206, 207.
Wyllys, Hezekiah, 84, 207, 222.
Wyllys, J., 206.
Wyllys, John P., 82, 121.
Wyllys, Samuel, 23, 24, 25, 46, 57, 58, 60.
Wyoming, 115.
Wyyaung, Guardin, 264.

Yale, Ameton, 193.
Yale, Asa, 209.
Yale, Asahel, 276.
Yale, Daniel, 193.
Yale, Elihu, 194.
Yale, John, 193.
Yale, Jonathan, 193.
Yale, Nash, 112.
Yale, Nathaniel, 193.
Yale, Noah, 276.
Yarrington, Ezekiel, 175.
Yates, Paul, 223, 225.
Yates, William, 111.
Yatman, James, 32.
Yeates, John, 212.
Yellis, Abram, 77.
Yeomans, Elijah, 193.
Yeomans, Ovorus, 63.
Yerrington, David, 74.
Yeumons, Andrew, 32.
York, Elisha, 175.
York Island, 138, 139.
Yorkshire, Eng., 22.
Young, Alexander, 2, 262.
Young, David, 74, 247, 252.
Young, James, 231, 234.
Young, Levi, 245, 249.
Young, William, 143, 264.
Youngs, Benjamin, 34.
Youngs, Eliphalet, 163.

www.ingramcontent.com/pod-product-compliance
Lightning Source LLC
Chambersburg PA
CBHW031702230426
43668CB00006B/83